Preface

This book is designed primarily to supplement standard texts in elementary machine design, based on the belief that numerous solved problems constitute one of the best means for clarifying and fixing in mind basic principles. Moreover, the statements of theory and principle are sufficiently complete that, with suitable handling of lecture-recitation time, the book could be used as a text by itself.

Each chapter begins with statements of pertinent definitions, principles and theorems together with illustrative and descriptive material. This is followed by graded sets of solved and supplementary problems. The solved problems serve to illustrate and amplify the theory and bring into sharp focus those fine points without which the student continually feels himself on unsafe ground. Numerous proofs of theorems and derivations of formulas are included among the solved problems. The supplementary problems serve as a review of the material of each chapter.

Chapter topics correspond to material usually covered in standard machine design courses. It is felt that these are representative topics for illustrating the general approach to design problems. Where more than one accepted procedure for handling a problem exists, the authors have in some cases adopted what they feel to be the best; in other cases, alternative procedures are shown; and in a few situations there is some innovation in treatment. As a result, while this book will not mesh precisely with any one text, the authors feel that it can be a very valuable adjunct to all.

The following are some of the special features of this book. It contains a wide range of applied mechanics review problems. Solved problems are used to review Strength of Materials and to demonstrate the application of many previous courses to design situations. Step functions and the theorem of Castigliano are introduced as tools for determining deflections in machine members. An introduction to Vibration Studies is presented. The latest techniques as developed by Boyd and Raimondi for solving lubrication problems are included. Excerpts from the latest AFBMA Standards are given for evaluating static and dynamic load ratings of radial ball bearings. Gear forces are covered in much more detail than in standard texts. A careful treatment of critical speeds of shafting is presented. An exhaustive treatment is given for determining the rigidity as well as the strength of machine members. Thirty-six design projects are presented, including flow control, automatic electrical control, quality control, and creative design problems.

It is realized that competence in design rests on many factors other than scientific training — ingenuity, judgment, familiarity with empirical data, knowledge of design codes and standards, to name a few. Many of these can be fully developed only over a number of years of actual experience in industry. However, the student can be provided with what is basic, namely a good training in the logical application of theory to the design of machine elements plus some feeling for the accompanying assumptions and approximations. It is to this end that this book is directed.

The authors are deeply indebted to many people. Published texts in machine design, strength of materials and dynamics of machinery have been studied and compared; all have contributed to the authors' thinking. Members of the machine design staff at Purdue University have served to sharpen and refine the treatment of many topics. The authors are extremely grateful to them for constructive criticisms and suggestions.

Special appreciation is expressed to E. S. Ault, Professor of Machine Design at Purdue University. In addition to general encouragement of the authors' efforts, Professor Ault is to be credited with the procedure presented in the chapters on Toothed Gearing for handling the Lewis formula in design calculations.

Particular thanks are extended to Mr. Henry Hayden for typographical layout and art work for the figures. The realism of these figures adds greatly to the effectiveness of presentation in a subject where spatial visualization plays such an important role.

We would also like to thank the following for permission to publish copyrighted material: The Lincoln Electric Company, The Anti-Friction Bearing Manufacturers Association, and Mr. A. A. Raimondi and Mr. John Boyd of the Westinghouse Electric Company.

A. S. Hall, Jr.
A. R. Holowenko
H. G. Laughlin

Purdue University
June, 1961

THEORY AND PROBLEMS

of

MACHINE DESIGN

•

BY

ALLEN S. HALL, JR., M.S.M.E., Ph.D.
Professor of Mechanical Engineering, Purdue University

ALFRED R. HOLOWENKO, M.S.
Professor of Mechanical Engineering, Purdue University

HERMAN G. LAUGHLIN, M.S.M.E.
Associate Professor of Mechanical Engineering, Purdue University

SCHAUM'S OUTLINE SERIES

McGRAW-HILL

New York San Francisco Washington, D.C. Auckland Bogotá
Caracas Lisbon London Madrid Mexico City Milan
Montreal New Delhi San Juan Singapore
Sydney Tokyo Toronto

McGraw-Hill

*A Division of The **McGraw-Hill** Companies*

ISBN 07-025595-4

28 29 30 VHG 06 05 04 03 02 01

Contents

Chapter 1

Introduction

ENGINEERING DESIGN is the creation of plans for machines, structures, systems, or processes to perform desired functions.

THE DESIGN PROCESS includes the following.

(1) The recognition of a **need** and a statement of this need in general terms. This defines the **problem.**

(2) The consideration of different schemes for solving the problem and the selection of one to be investigated in more detail. **Feasibility studies**, backed up by **special research** if necessary, are a feature of this stage in the process.

(3) A **preliminary design** of the machine, structure, system, or process selected. This establishes broad overall features and makes it possible to write **specifications** for major components.

(4) Design of all components and preparation of all necessary drawings and detail specifications.

In the early stages of the design process the designer is a **creator**. Here his ingenuity and power of imaginative thinking should be given full play.

The drawings and detail specifications for a completed design are a record of a multitude of decisions, some large and some small. The designer, in the later stages of the design process, is basically a **decision maker**. He must work from a sound basis of scientific principles supplemented by empirical data. However, it must be understood that science can only establish limits within which a decision must be made, or give a statistical picture of the effects of a particular decision. The decision itself is made by the designer. Hence **judgment** in making decisions is one of the outstanding characteristics of a good designer.

THE DESIGN OF A MACHINE must follow a plan somewhat as shown in the adjacent figure.

After the general specifications have been set, the kinematic arrangement, or **skeleton**, of the machine must be established. This is followed by a force analysis (incomplete because masses of moving parts are not yet known in designs where dynamics is of importance). With this information the components can be designed (tentatively, because forces are not known exactly). Then a more exact force analysis can be made and the design re-

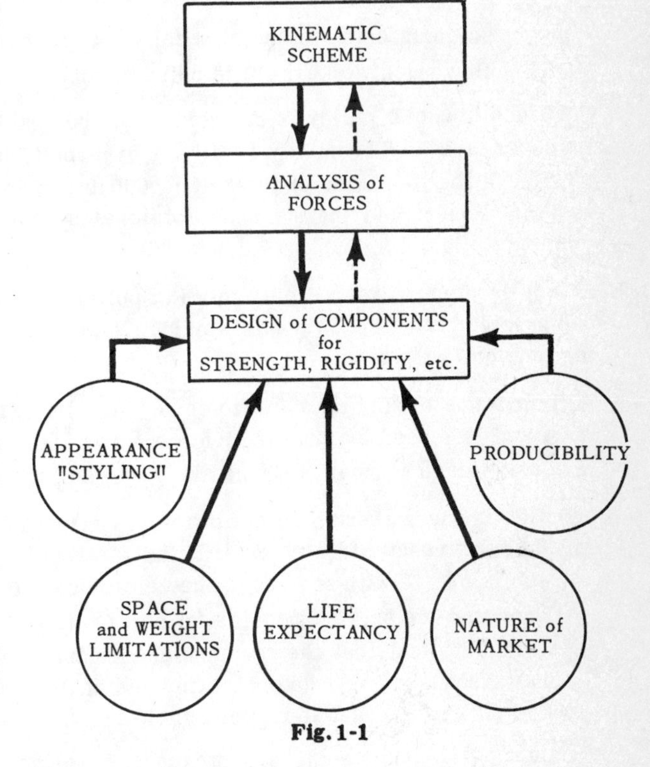

Fig. 1-1

fined. Final decisions are affected and modified by many factors other than strength and rigidity – appearance, weight and space limitations, availability of materials and fabrication techniques, etc.

This is an over-simplification of the problem, but nevertheless a useful outline to keep in mind. None of the steps mentioned are independent of the others. There is continual feedback as suggested by the broken arrows in the diagram. For example, after the first tentative design of parts, a dynamic analysis may show undesirably high inertia effects and dictate a change in the kinematic scheme of the machine.

THE SCIENCES UNDERLYING MACHINE DESIGN are Mathematics and Physics, with emphasis on Kinematics, Statics, Dynamics, and Strength of Materials. However, it would be difficult to pick out any of the technical or scientific courses in an engineering curriculum which do not make important contributions to the designer's equipment. Among those of importance are Graphics, Economics, Metallurgy, Thermodynamics and Heat Transfer, Fluid Mechanics, and Electric Circuit Theory. The student beginning the study of Machine Design should have some preparation in all these areas.

The following list of review questions and problems, primarily from Mechanics, will enable the reader to quiz himself on some of this basic material. Without the use of references he should answer correctly at least 90% of these. Otherwise the indication is that some review of Mechanics is in order.

MECHANICS REVIEW QUIZ

(*Reasonable working time, 3 hours. Answers are given at the end of this chapter.*)

Make free use of sketches. Give correct units for answers.

1. What hp is required to move a car along a level road at 60 mph against a horizontal resisting force of 500 lb along the line of motion if the overall mechanical efficiency is 85%?

2. A power screw is being turned at a constant rpm by the application of a steady torque of 150 inch-pounds. How much work (in-lb) is being expended per revolution?

3. A 10 inch diameter pulley is mounted on a shaft midway between two supporting bearings that are 30 inches apart. The pulley is driven by a belt, both strands pulling vertically upward. If the tension in the tight side of the belt is 600 lb and in the slack side is 200 lb, what is the maximum bending moment and the maximum torsional moment if power is taken from one end of the shaft through a flexible coupling?

4. A rope is draped over a freely rotating pulley. On one end of the rope is a 200 pound weight and on the other end is a 50 pound weight. Neglecting the mass of the pulley and friction, determine the tension in the rope.

5. A rigid frame resting on a frictionless plane is made of three straight members pin-joined to form an A and is loaded by applying a force F vertically downward on the vertex pin. Draw a free body diagram of each member, showing all forces acting in their proper locations and directions.

6. (*a*) What is the mathematical definition of moment of inertia of an area?

   (*b*) Show by means of calculus that the rectangular moment of inertia of a rectangular cross section is $bd^3/12$ with respect to the centroidal axis parallel to the base.

   (*c*) Show that the section modulus for part (*b*) is $bd^2/6$.

   (*d*) Using the fact that the rectangular moment of inertia of a circular section with respect to a diameter is $\pi d^4/64$, determine the rectangular moment of inertia of a hollow shaft having an o.d. of 4 inches and an i.d. of 2 inches.

   (*e*) Demonstrate how a close approximation to the rectangular moment of inertia of a very irregular area could be determined with a high degree of accuracy.

7. The rotor of an electric motor weighs 10 pounds and is 4 inches in diameter. What is the length of time required for the motor speed to increase from 0 to 1800 rpm, assuming a constant electrical torque of 20 in-lb and zero external load during this period? Assume that the rotor is a homogeneous cylinder.

8. Define bending moment. What arbitrary convention is ordinarily used to determine the sign of a bending moment? Demonstrate the above by means of free bodies consisting of short sections taken from the ends of a freely supported beam, loaded in such a manner that a positive bending moment exists in the vicinity of the left end and a negative moment exists in the vicinity of the right end.

9. If a spring deflects 2" under a 500 lb load, what energy does the spring absorb in one gradual application of this load?

10. Define one horsepower and show that horsepower may be expressed by:

$$\text{hp} = \frac{F(\text{lb}) \times V(\text{fpm})}{33{,}000} \quad \text{and} \quad \text{hp} = \frac{T(\text{in-lb}) \times N(\text{rpm})}{63{,}000}$$

11. Illustrate graphically the distribution of stress over the cross section perpendicular to the axis of a beam for the following cases.
(*a*) Bending stress, Mc/I, in a simple beam which is (*1*) symmetrical with respect to the neutral axis of the cross section, and (*2*) unsymmetrical with respect to the neutral axis of the cross section.
(*b*) Tensile or compressive stress, P/A, due to an axial load in a member of any cross section.
(*c*) Torsional stress, Tr/J, due to an applied torque on a member of circular cross section.
(*d*) Transverse shear, VQ/Ib, in a simple beam of (*1*) rectangular cross section, (*2*) circular cross section, and (*3*) a symmetrical I-section.

12. (*a*) If a machine member is loaded in such a way that the three principal stresses at a point are 600 psi tension, 800 psi tension, and zero, what is the maximum shear stress at the point?
(*b*) Same as above except the three principal stresses are 600 psi compression, 800 psi tension, and zero.

13. (*a*) If a man ties one end of a rope to a tree and pulls on the other end with a force of 100 pounds, what is the tensile force set up in the rope?
(*b*) What tension would exist in the rope if one man on each end of the rope pulled with a force of 100 pounds?

14. A truck with tires of 3 ft outside diameter moves at 60 fps. What is the velocity relative to the ground of that point on the tire tread farthest from the ground at a given instant? What is the angular velocity (rpm) of the wheels under these conditions? What is the acceleration of the point on the tread in contact with the ground?

15. A bevel gear having a 7" mean diameter is mounted on the overhung end of a shaft 14 inches from the nearer bearing. The load on the bevel gear has components as follows: tangential, $F_t = 1200$ lb; radial, $F_r = 700$ lb; axial, $F_a = 500$ lb.
(*a*) Calculate the shaft torque due to each force.
(*b*) Calculate the bending moment on the shaft at the nearer bearing due to each force.
(*c*) Calculate the total or resultant bending moment on the shaft at the nearer bearing.

16. A speed reducer having a speed ratio of 10 to 1 when tested at an input speed of 1000 rpm with an output torque of 50 in-lb was found to require an input torque of 6 in-lb. What was the efficiency of the speed reducer?

17. Sand drops from the bottom of a hopper onto a horizontally moving belt conveyor. If the conveyor is traveling at 2000 fpm and the sand is fed at the rate of 15,000 lb/min, what force is necessary to drive the conveyor? Neglect friction within the conveyor drive mechanism.

18. A simply supported steel beam when loaded with a force of 200 lb at A is found to deflect 0.4 in. at B. What force at B would cause a deflection of 0.1 in. at A?

19. A planet gear in a planetary gear system moves such that the velocity of the center of the gear is 40 fps and the gear has an angular velocity of 20 rad/sec. What is its kinetic energy? Consider the gear as a solid cylinder weighing 10 lb and having diameter 6″

20. The differential equation of motion for a certain single degree of freedom mass-spring damped system is $8\ddot{x} + 5\dot{x} + 12x = 0$. What is the natural frequency of vibration? (Units used are lb, in., and sec.)

21. A connecting rod is moving such that the acceleration of one end relative to the other end is 200 fps^2 at an angle of 30° with respect to the line joining the two points which are 8 in. apart. What are the magnitudes of the angular velocity and angular acceleration?

22. A steel cable is wrapped twice around a post. A force P is applied to one end of the cable and a force of 3000 lb is applied to the other end of the cable. For a coefficient of friction of 0.15 determine (*a*) the force P necessary to cause the cable to move in the direction of the force P, (*b*) the force P' necessary to prevent the cable from moving in the direction of the 3000 lb force.

23. A block weighing 100 lb rests on a horizontal surface. If the coefficient of friction is 0.3 (both static and kinetic), what frictional force is developed if the force applied to the block in the direction parallel to the horizontal surface is (*a*) 10 lb, (*b*) 20 lb, (*c*) 30 lb, (*d*) 40 lb?

24. The rigid steel bar shown in Fig. 1-2 is 20 inches long, 1 inch wide, and 1 inch thick. The bar is at rest on a horizontal frictionless surface when a force P = 200 lb is applied suddenly. Determine (*a*) the magnitude of the maximum bending moment, (*b*) the maximum bending stress.

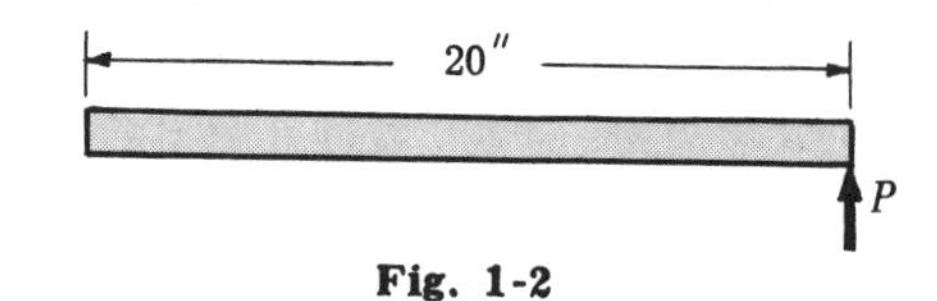

Fig. 1-2

25. A constant electrical torque is applied to the motor rotor (Fig. 1-3), which has a moment of inertia = I_M. The pinion drives two gears, one of which is connected to a mass which has a moment of inertia = I_M and the other is connected to a mass which has a moment of inertia = $2I_M$. The gear ratio $R_1 = D_3/D_2$ is fixed and is equal to 3. What should the gear ratio $R_2 = D_4/D_2$ be to give the maximum angular acceleration of gear 4? Neglect the mass of the gears.

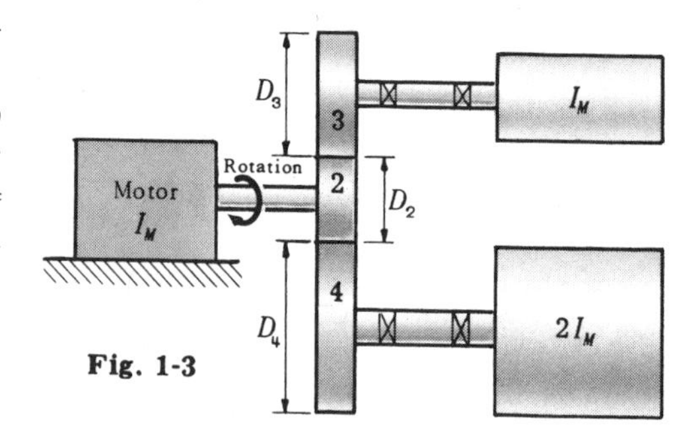

Fig. 1-3

26. The steel bar shown in Fig. 1-4 is 30 inches long, 1 inch wide, and 1 inch thick. The bar is at rest on a horizontal surface, with negligible friction. Two equal and opposite forces of 200 lb each are applied suddenly. Considering the bar as rigid, determine (*a*) the maximum bending moment, (*b*) the maximum bending stress.

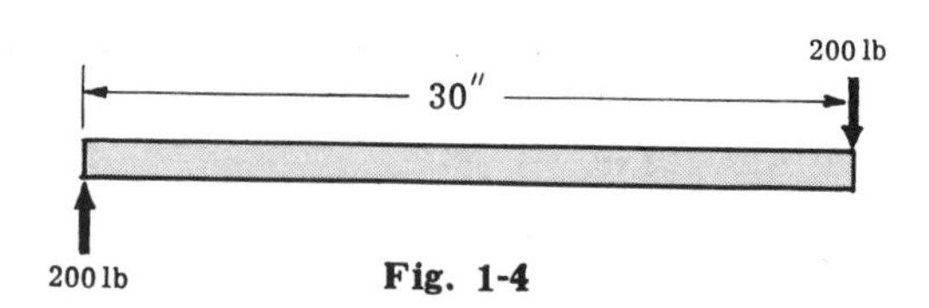

Fig. 1-4

COMPETENCE IN APPLYING THE PRINCIPLES OF MECHANICS to the rational analysis and design of machine components, as with any other activity, is developed through practice. The following chapters, through the problem approach, are designed to provide that practice.

The student is urged to use the following plan of study for each chapter.

(1) Read the statements of theory and principle.

(2) Follow through the solved problems. Use paper and pencil. Develop all details yourself following the leads given. (Some of the solved problems are highly detailed. Others have some steps omitted.)

(3) Work the supplementary problems. After reading a problem statement ask yourself what principles apply. Refer back to a similar solved problem only if you find this assistance absolutely necessary.

Preserve your work in good form for future reference. In studying a later chapter you may find some assistance in work you have previously done.

(4) Re-study the statements of theory until you have them well fixed in mind.

Answers to Review Questions – Chapter 1

1. 94.2 hp

2. 942 in-lb

3. M_b = 6000 in-lb, T = 2000 in-lb

4. 80 lb

5. Sides are three force members.

6. Refer to any standard text on Mechanics.

7. 0.49 sec

8. Refer to any standard text on Mechanics of Materials.

9. 500 in-lb

10. $\text{hp} = \dfrac{2\pi TN}{(12)(33{,}000)} = \dfrac{TN}{63{,}000}$

11. Refer to any standard text on Mechanics of Materials.

12. (*a*) 400 psi, (*b*) 700 psi

13. (*a*) 100 lb, (*b*) 100 lb

14. 382 rpm, 2400 fps^2

15. (*a*) Torque due to 500 lb = 0, to 700 lb = 0, to 1200 lb = 4200 in-lb.

(*b*) Bending moment due to 500 lb = 1750 in-lb, to 700 lb = 9800 in-lb, to 1200 lb = 16,800 in-lb.

(*c*) 18,600 in-lb

16. 83.4%

17. 258 lb

18. 50 lb

19. 250.93 ft-lb

20. 1.225 rad/sec

21. 16.15 rad/sec, 150 rad/sec^2

22. P = 19,770 lb, P' = 455 lb

23. (*a*) 10 lb, (*b*) 20 lb, (*c*) 30 lb, (*d*) 30 lb

24. 592 in-lb, 3550 psi

25. $R_2 = \sqrt{1.8} = 1.34$

26. 575 in-lb, 3450 psi

Chapter 2

Stresses in Simple Machine Members

MACHINE DESIGN involves, among other considerations, the proper sizing of a machine member to safely withstand the maximum stress which is induced within the member when it is subjected separately or to any combination of bending, torsional, axial, or transverse loads. In general, ductile materials, such as the soft steels, are weaker in shear and are designed on the basis of the maximum shear stress; while brittle materials, such as cast iron and certain hard steels, are usually designed on the basis of the maximum normal stress in either tension or compression.

THE MAXIMUM AND MINIMUM NORMAL STRESSES, $s_n(\text{max})$ or $s_n(\text{min})$, which are tensile or compressive stresses, can be determined for the general case of two-dimensional loading on a particle by

$$(1) \qquad s_n(\text{max}) = \frac{s_x + s_y}{2} + \sqrt{\left(\frac{s_x - s_y}{2}\right)^2 + \tau_{xy}^2}$$

$$(2) \qquad s_n(\text{min}) = \frac{s_x + s_y}{2} - \sqrt{\left(\frac{s_x - s_y}{2}\right)^2 + \tau_{xy}^2}$$

Equations (*1*) and (*2*) give algebraic maximum and minimum values, where

s_x is a stress at a critical point in tension or compression normal to the cross section under consideration, and may be due to either bending or axial loads, or to a combination of the two. When s_x is in tension it must be preceded by a plus (+) sign, and when it is compression it must be preceded by a minus (−) sign.

s_y is a stress at the same critical point and in a direction normal to the s_x stress. Again, this stress must be preceded by the proper algebraic sign.

τ_{xy} is the **shear stress** at the same critical point acting in the plane normal to the y axis (which is the xz plane) and in the plane normal to the x axis (which is the yz plane). This shear stress may be due to a torsional moment, a transverse load, or to a combination of the two. The manner in which these stresses are oriented with respect to each other is shown in Fig. 2-1 below.

$s_n(\text{max})$ and $s_n(\text{min})$ are called **principal stresses** and occur on planes that are at 90° to each other, called **principal planes**. These are also planes of zero shear. For two-dimensional loading, the third principal stress is zero. The manner in which the principal stresses are oriented with respect to each other is shown in Fig. 2-2 below.

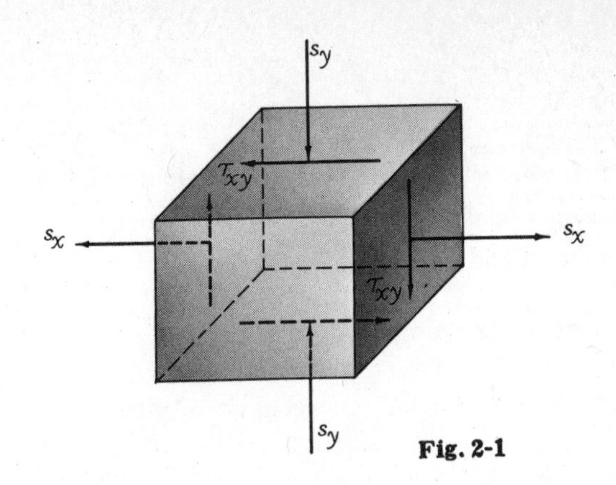

Fig. 2-1

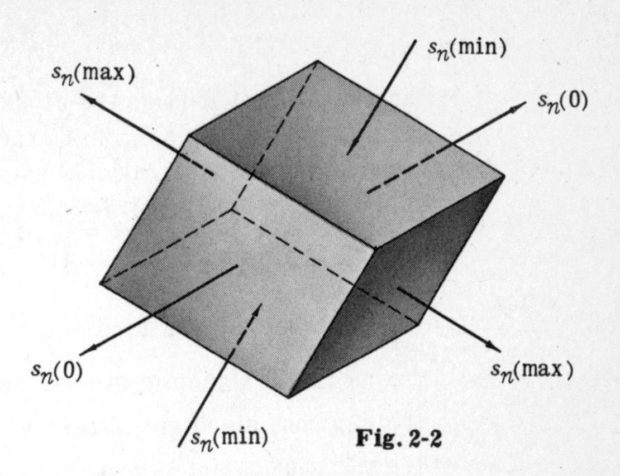

Fig. 2-2

THE MAXIMUM SHEAR STRESS, τ(max), at the critical point being investigated is equal to half of the greatest difference of any two of the three principal stresses (do not overlook any of the principal stresses which are zero). Hence, for the case of two-dimensional loading on a particle causing a two-dimensional stress,

$$\tau(\text{max}) = \frac{s_n(\text{max}) - s_n(\text{min})}{2} \quad \text{or} \quad \frac{s_n(\text{max}) - 0}{2} \quad \text{or} \quad \frac{s_n(\text{min}) - 0}{2}$$

depending upon which results in the greatest numerical value. The planes of maximum shear are inclined at 45° with the principal planes as shown in Fig. 2-3 below.

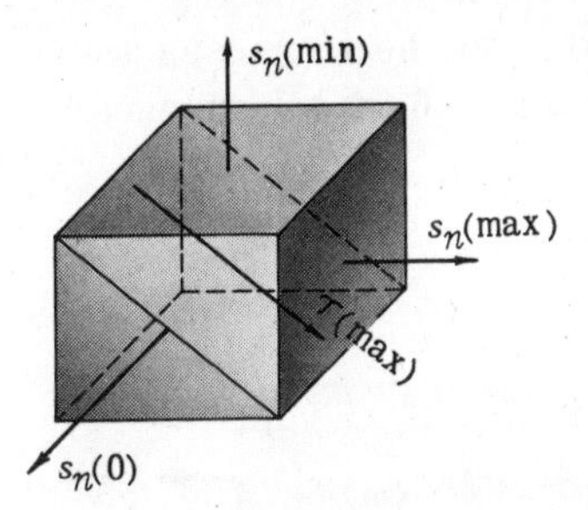

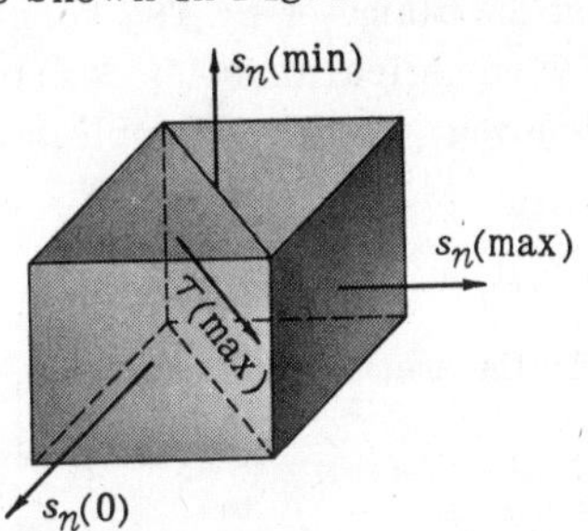

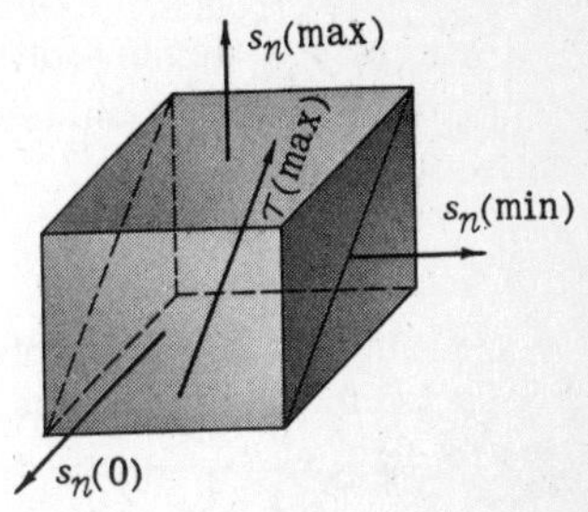

Fig. 2-3

THE APPLICATION of equations (*1*) and (*2*) requires the determination of s_x, s_y, and τ_{xy} at the critical point in the machine member. The critical point is the point at which the applied loads produce the maximum combined stress effects. In a beam, the following are representative stresses that can occur, to be included in equations (*1*) and (*2*) if they act at the same point.

s_x and s_y $= \pm \dfrac{Mc}{I} \pm \dfrac{P}{A}$, remembering that these stresses may be either plus or minus depending upon whether they are tension or compression.

$\tau_{xy} = \dfrac{Tr}{J} + s_v$ for a circular cross section (when these stresses are parallel).

M = bending moment, in-lb
c = distance from neutral axis to outer surface, in.
r = radius of circular cross section, in.
I = rectangular moment of inertia of cross section, in^4
P = axial load, lb
A = area of cross section, in^2
T = torsional moment, in-lb
J = polar moment of inertia of cross section, in^4
s_v = transverse shear, psi.

$s_v = \dfrac{VQ}{Ib}$ where

V = transverse shear load on the cross section, lb

b = width of the section containing the critical point, in.

Q = moment of the cross-sectional area of the member, above or below the critical point, with respect to the neutral axis, in^3.

$s_v(\max) = \dfrac{4V}{3A}$ for a circular cross section, and occurs at the neutral axis.

$s_v(\max) = \dfrac{3V}{2A}$ for a rectangular cross section, and occurs at the neutral axis.

$s_n(\max)$ = the maximum algebraic stress, psi.

$s_n(\min)$ = the minimum algebraic stress, psi.

$\tau(\max)$ = the maximum shear stress, psi.

SOLVED PROBLEMS

1. A hypothetical machine member 2" diameter by 10" long and supported at one end as a cantilever will be used to demonstrate how numerical tensile, compressive, and shear stresses are determined for various types of uniaxial loading. In this example note that $s_y = 0$ for all arrangements, at the critical points.

(a) **Axial load only.**

In this case all points in the member are subjected to the same stress.

$A = \pi$ in^2

$s_x = +\dfrac{P}{A} = +\dfrac{3000}{\pi} = +954$ psi

$\tau_{xy} = 0$

$s_n(\max) = s_x = +954$ psi (tension)

$\tau(\max) = \frac{1}{2}(954) = 477$ psi (shear)

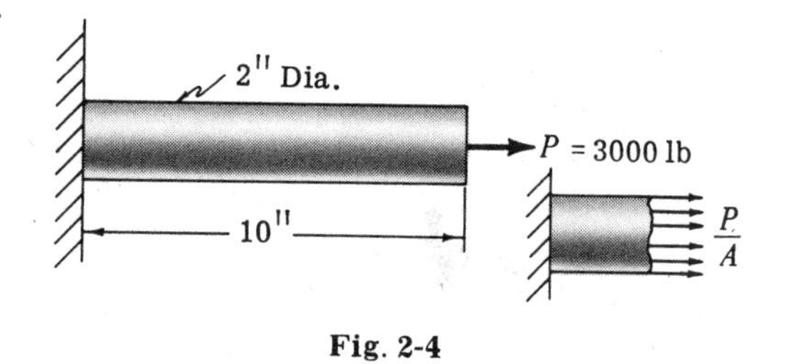

Fig. 2-4

(b) **Bending only.**

Points A and B are critical.

$\tau_{xy} = 0$ at points A and B (no transverse shear).

$s_x = +\dfrac{Mc}{I} = +\dfrac{(600)(10)(1)(64)}{\pi 2^4} = +7650$ psi at point A

$s_x = -\dfrac{Mc}{I} = -7650$ psi at point B

$s_n(\max) = +7650$ psi (tension at point A)

$s_n(\min) = 0$ at point A

$s_n(\max) = 0$ at point B

$s_n(\min) = -7650$ psi (compression at point B)

$\tau(\max) = \frac{1}{2}(7650)$

$= 3825$ psi (shear at points A and B)

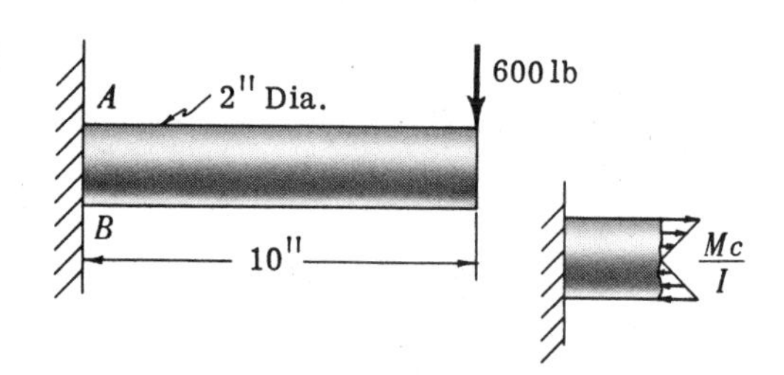

Fig. 2-5

(*c*) **Torsion only.**

In this case the critical points occur all along the outer surface of the member.

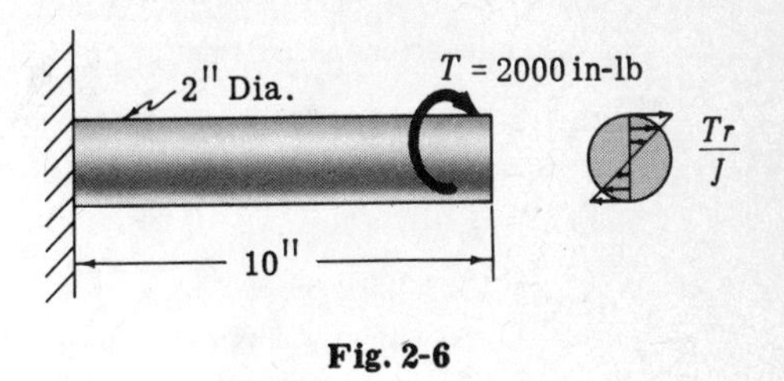

Fig. 2-6

$s_x = 0$

$\tau_{xy} = \frac{Tr}{J} = \frac{(2000)(1)(32)}{\pi 2^4} = 1272$ psi

$s_n(\max) = +1272$ psi (tension)

$s_n(\min) = -1272$ psi (compression)

$\tau(\max) = 1272$ psi (shear)

(*d*) **Bending and torsion.**

Points *A* and *B* are critical.

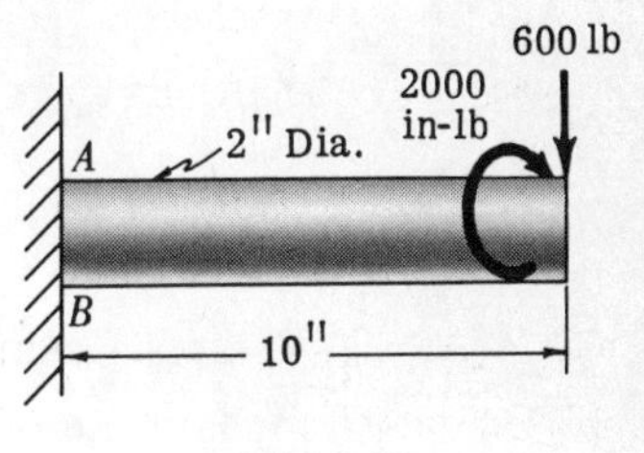

Fig. 2-7

$s_x = +Mc/I = +7650$ psi at point *A*

$s_x = -7650$ psi at point *B*

$\tau_{xy} = Tr/J = 1272$ psi at points *A* and *B*

$s_n(\max) = +7650/2 + \sqrt{(7650/2)^2 + (1272)^2}$

$= +3825 + 4030 = +7855$ psi (tension at point *A*)

$s_n(\min) = +3825 - 4030 = -205$ psi (compression at point *A*)

$s_n(\max) = -3825 + 4030 = +205$ psi (tension at point *B*)

$s_n(\min) = -3825 - 4030 = -7855$ psi (compression at point *B*)

$\tau(\max) = \frac{+7855 - (-205)}{2} = +4030$ psi (shear at point *A*)

$\tau(\max) = \frac{-7855 - 205}{2} = -4030$ psi (shear at point *B*)

Note that the magnitudes of the stresses at points *A* and *B* are the same. The signs of the maximum normal stresses indicate tension or compression, while the sign of the maximum shear stress is of no consequence since design is based on the magnitude.

(*e*) **Bending and axial load.**

$\tau_{xy} = 0$ at the critical points *A* and *B*.

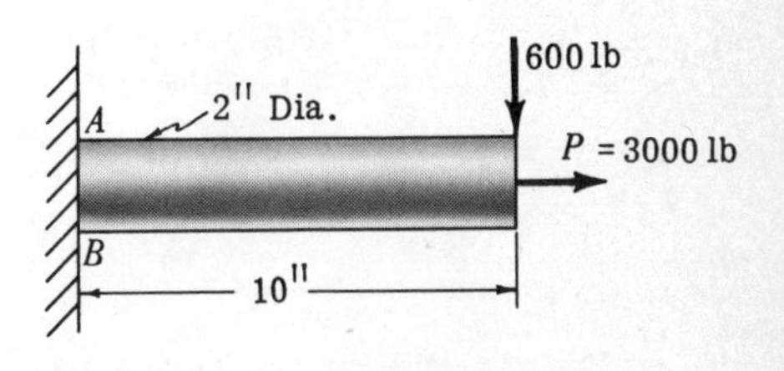

Fig. 2-8

At point *A*:

$s_x = +P/A + Mc/I = +954 + 7650 = +8604$ psi (tension)

$s_n(\max) = s_x = +8604$ psi (tension)

$s_n(\min) = 0$

$\tau(\max) = \frac{1}{2}(8604) = 4302$ psi (shear)

At point *B*:

$s_x = +P/A - Mc/I = +954 - 7650 = -6696$ psi (compression)

$s_n(\max) = 0$

$s_n(\min) = -6696$ psi (compression)

$\tau(\max) = \frac{1}{2}(6696) = 3348$ psi (shear)

(*f*) **Torsion and axial load.**

The critical points are the points on the outer surface of the member.

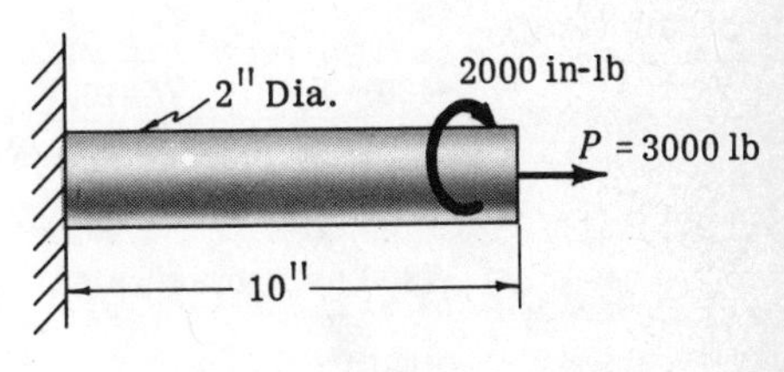

Fig. 2-9

$s_x = +P/A = +954$ psi

$\tau_{xy} = Tr/J = 1272$ psi

$s_n(\max) = +954/2 + \sqrt{(954/2)^2 + (1272)^2}$

$= +477 + 1360 = +1837$ psi (tension)

$s_n(\min) = +477 - 1360 = -883$ psi (compression)

$\tau(\max) = 1360$ psi (shear)

(*g*) **Bending, axial load, and torsion.**

Maximum stresses will occur at points *A* and *B*.

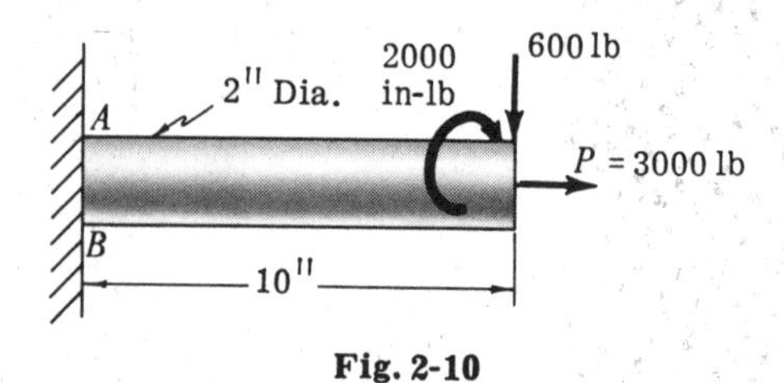

Fig. 2-10

At point *A* :

$s_x = +Mc/I + P/A = +7650 + 954 = +8604$ psi

$\tau_{xy} = Tr/J = 1272$ psi

$s_n(\text{max}) = +8604/2 + \sqrt{(8604/2)^2 + (1272)^2}$
$= +4302 + 4480 = +8782$ psi (tension)

$s_n(\text{min}) = +4302 - 4480 = -178$ psi (compression)

$\tau(\text{max}) = 4480$ psi (shear)

At point *B* :

$s_x = -7650 + 954 = -6696$ psi

$\tau_{xy} = 1272$ psi

$s_n(\text{max}) = -6696/2 + \sqrt{(6696/2)^2 + (1272)^2} = -3348 + 3581 = +233$ psi (tension)

$s_n(\text{min}) = -3348 - 3581 = -6929$ psi (compression)

$\tau(\text{max}) = 3581$ psi (shear)

2. A cantilever member 4" long having a rectangular cross section of 2"×10" supports a load of 6000 lb. What is the maximum shear stress and where does it occur?

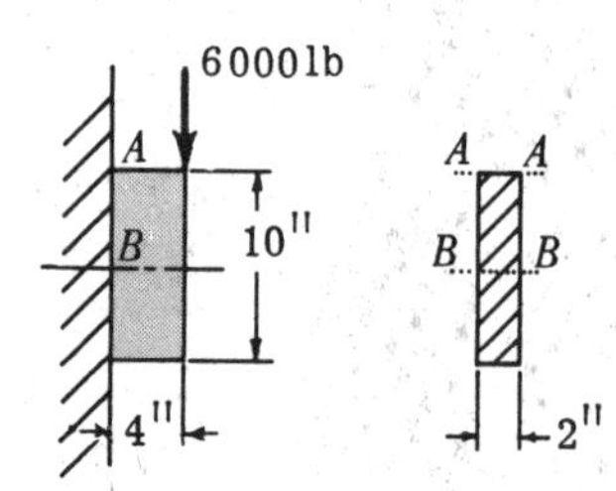

Fig. 2-11

Solution:

The maximum shear stress may occur at points along A-A due to the bending moment, or it may occur at points along B-B due to the transverse shear load.

At points along A-A,

$$\tau(\text{max}) = \frac{1}{2}\frac{Mc}{I} = \frac{(6000)(4)(5)(12)}{(2)(2)(10^3)} = 360 \text{ psi (shear)}$$

At points along B-B,

$$\tau(\text{max}) = \frac{3}{2}\frac{V}{A} = \frac{(3)(6000)}{(2)(20)} = 450 \text{ psi (shear)}$$

Therefore the maximum shear stress is due to the transverse shear load and it occurs along the neutral axis at B-B.

3. A critical point in a machine member is subjected to biaxial loading which produces s_x, s_y, and τ_{xy} stresses as shown. Determine the maximum and minimum normal stresses and the maximum shear stress.

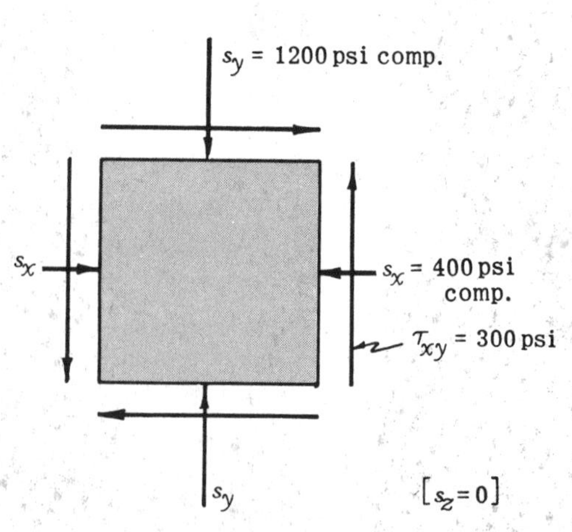

Fig. 2-12

Solution:

$$s_n(\text{max}) = \frac{-400-1200}{2} + \sqrt{\left(\frac{-400-(-1200)}{2}\right)^2 + (300)^2}$$
$$= -300 \text{ psi (compression)}$$

$$s_n(\text{min}) = -1300 \text{ psi (compression)}$$

$$\tau(\text{max}) = \frac{s_n(\text{min}) - 0}{2} = -650 \text{ psi,}$$

since the third principal stress = 0.

4. Draw bending moment diagrams for the machine members as shown.

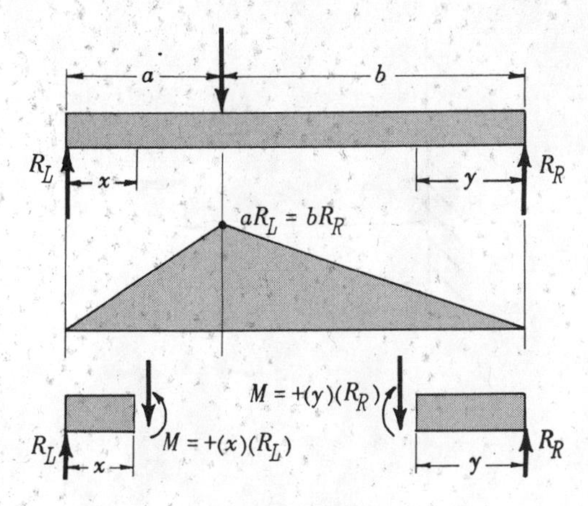

Fig. 2-13

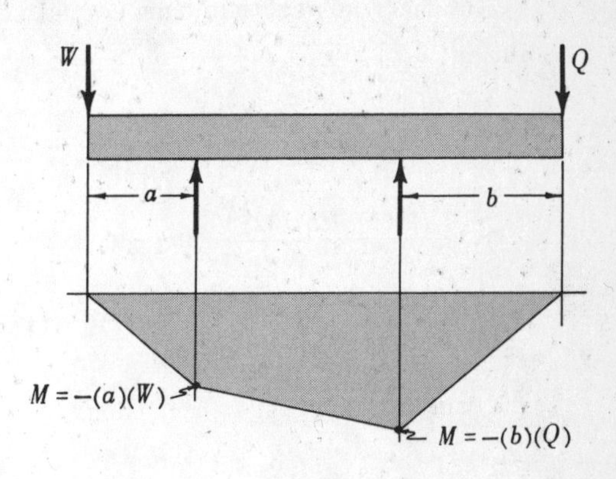

Fig. 2-14

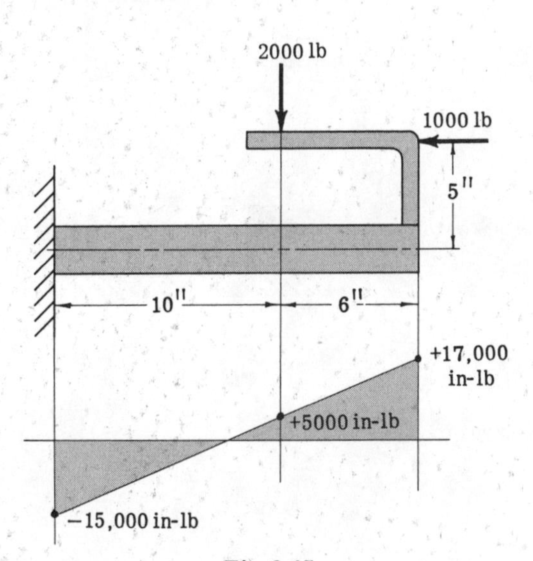

Fig. 2-15

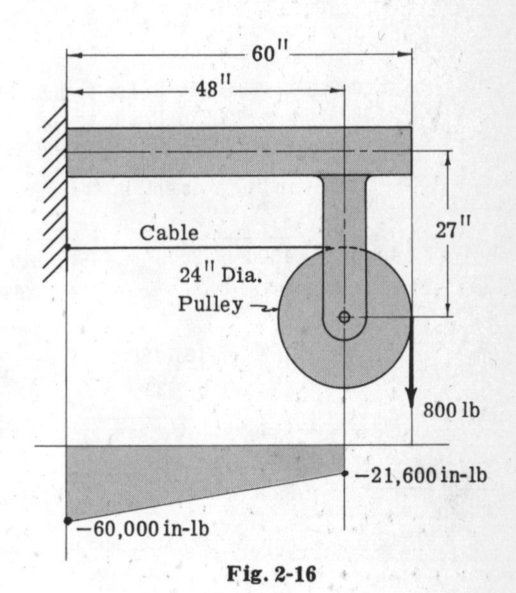

Fig. 2-16

5. A 2 in. diameter steel rod supports a 2000 lb load and in addition is subjected to a torsional moment of 1000 in-lb as shown in Fig. 2-17. Determine the maximum tensile and the maximum shear stresses.

Solution: The critical stress is at point A.

$$s_y = 0$$

$$I = \pi d^4/64 = \pi 2^4/64 = 0.785 \text{ in}^4$$

$$J = \pi d^4/32 = \pi 2^4/32 = 1.57 \text{ in}^4$$

$$s_x = +\frac{P}{A} + \frac{Mc}{I} = +\frac{2000}{\pi} + \frac{(2000\times 1)(1)}{0.785} = +3180 \text{ psi}$$

$$\tau_{xy} = \frac{Tr}{J} = \frac{(1000)(1)}{1.57} = 637 \text{ psi}$$

$$s_n(\text{max}) = +3180/2 + \sqrt{(3180/2)^2 + (637)^2} = +3305 \text{ psi (tension)}$$

$$\tau(\text{max}) = \sqrt{(3180/2)^2 + (637)^2} = 1715 \text{ psi (shear)}$$

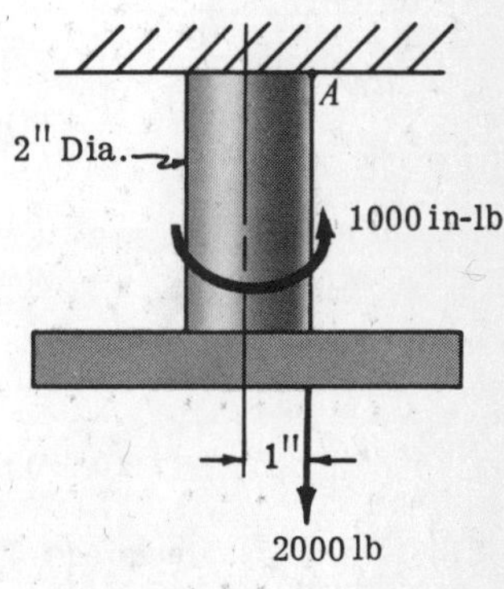

Fig. 2-17

6. A 3 inch diameter cast iron rod is subjected to an axial compressive load of 12,000 lb plus a torsional moment of 2500 in-lb as shown in Fig. 2-18. Determine the maximum and minimum normal stresses.

Solution:

$$s_y = 0$$

$$s_x = -\frac{(12{,}000)(4)}{\pi 3^2} = -1700 \text{ psi}$$

$$\tau_{xy} = \frac{(2500)(1.5)(32)}{\pi 3^4} = 472 \text{ psi}$$

$$s_n(\max) = -1700/2 + \sqrt{(1700/2)^2 + (472)^2} = +122 \text{ psi (tension)}$$

$$s_n(\min) = -1822 \text{ psi (compression)}$$

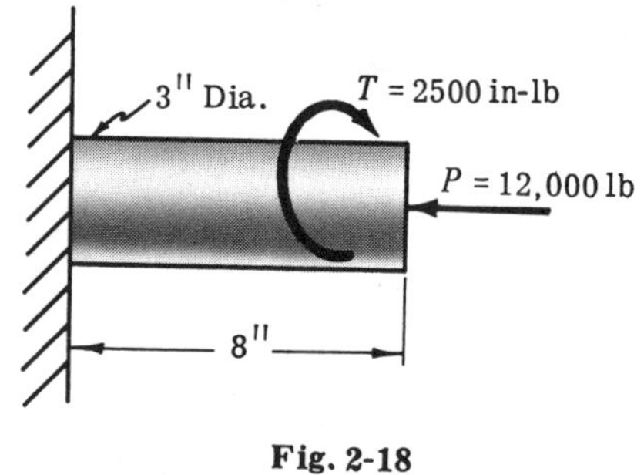

Fig. 2-18

7. Calculate the maximum numerical normal stress and the maximum shear stress at section A-A in the member loaded as shown in Fig. 2-19.

Solution:

T = (200)(8) = 1600 in-lb due to the 200 lb load
M = (500)(8) = 4000 in-lb due to the 500 lb load
M = (200)(10) = 2000 in-lb due to the 200 lb load

The total bending moment is the vector sum of the two bending moments.

$$M(\text{total}) = \sqrt{4000^2 + 2000^2} = 4470 \text{ in-lb}$$

$$s_x = -\frac{P}{A} - \frac{Mc}{I} = -\frac{500}{\pi} - \frac{(4470)(1)(64)}{\pi 2^4} = -5849 \text{ psi}$$

$$\tau_{xy} = \frac{Tr}{J} = \frac{16T}{\pi d^3} = \frac{(16)(1600)}{\pi 2^3} = 1020 \text{ psi}$$

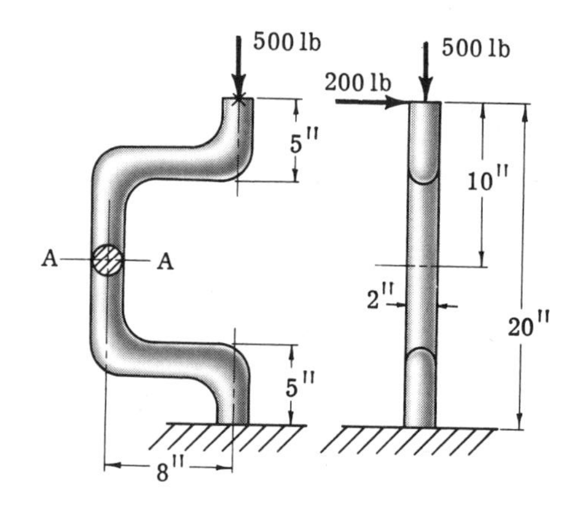

Fig. 2-19

$$s_n(\min) = -5849/2 - \sqrt{(5849/2)^2 + (1020)^2} = -6025 \text{ psi (compression)}$$

$$\tau(\max) = \sqrt{(5849/2)^2 + (1020)^2} = 3100 \text{ psi (shear)}$$

Note that $s_n(\min)$ is the maximum numerical normal stress.

8. Determine the required thickness of the steel bracket at section A-A, when loaded as shown in Fig. 2-20, in order to limit the tensile stress to 10,000 psi.

Solution:

$$M = (1000)(2) = 2000 \text{ in-lb at section A-A}$$

$$\frac{P}{A} = \frac{1000}{2b}$$

$$s_n(\max) = s_x = \frac{P}{A} + \frac{Mc}{I} = \frac{1000}{2b} + \frac{(2000)(1)(12)}{2^3 b} = 10{,}000 \text{ psi}$$

b = 0.35 in. required to limit the stress to 10,000 psi.

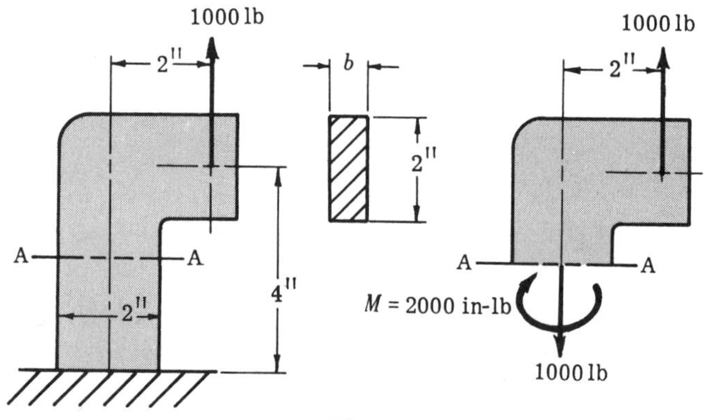

Fig. 2-20

9. The parallel side rod of a locomotive weighs 60 lb per ft. The crank length OP is 15 inches and the radius of the driver is 3 feet. If the speed of the engine is 60 mph and the tractive effort per wheel is 10,000 lb, find the maximum normal and the maximum shear stresses in the side rod due to inertia and axial loading for the position shown in Fig. 2-21. Take into account the weight of the rod. The cross section of the side rod is 3" × 6".

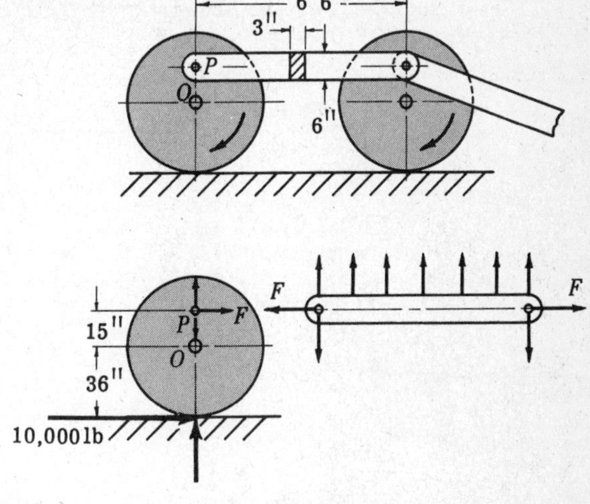

Fig. 2-21

Solution:

At 60 mph the wheels are making 4.67 rps.

All points on the side rod have a downward acceleration, a_p.

$a_p = a_o \leftrightarrow a_{po} = a_{po}$, since $a_o = 0$.

$a_{po} = r\omega^2 = (15/12)(2\pi \times 4.67)^2 = 1080 \text{ fps}^2$

Total weight of side rod = (60)(6.5) = 390 lb.

Inertia force acting upward on rod = (390/32.2)(1080) = 13,100 lb.

Net upward force on rod = 13,100 − 390 = 12,710 lb.

The axial force F can be determined by using the rear wheel and the rod as free bodies and taking the summation of moments about the center of the wheel, O.

$15F = (10{,}000)(36)$, $F = 24{,}000$ lb axial load

The maximum bending moment for a simple beam carrying a uniformly distributed load is

$$WL/8 = (12{,}710)(78)/8 = 124{,}000 \text{ in-lb}$$

$$s_x = \frac{P}{A} + \frac{Mc}{I} = \frac{24{,}000}{18} + \frac{(124{,}000)(3)(12)}{(3)(6)^3} = 8230 \text{ psi}$$

$s_n(\max) = s_x = 8230$ psi (tension)

$\tau(\max) = 8230/2 = 4115$ psi (shear)

10. A Z-bracket is supported and loaded as shown in Fig. 2-22. Compute the maximum shear stress at section A-A and at section B-B.

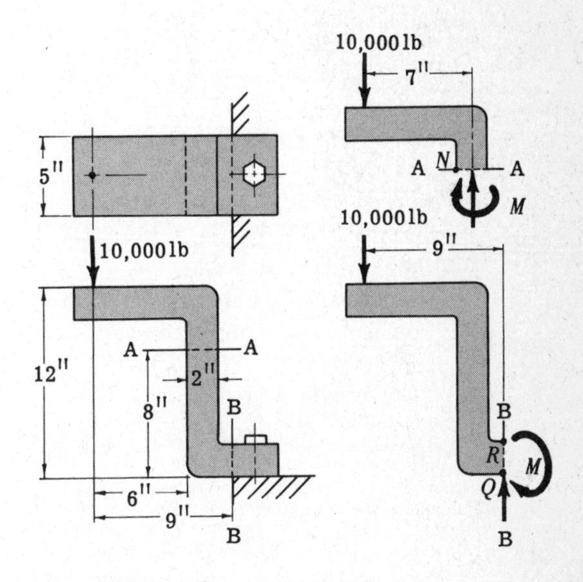

Fig. 2-22

Solution:

Using the portion of the bracket above section A-A as a free body: at point N, $s_y = 0$ and $\tau_{xy} = 0$.

$$s_x = \frac{P}{A} + \frac{Mc}{I} = -\frac{10{,}000}{10} - \frac{(10{,}000)(7)(1)(12)}{(5)(2)^3}$$

$$= -22{,}000 \text{ psi (compression)}$$

$\tau(\max) = 22{,}000/2 = 11{,}000$ psi (shear)

Using the portion of the bracket to the left of section B-B as a free body: at points Q and R, $s_y = 0$ and $\tau_{xy} = 0$.

$$s_x = \frac{Mc}{I} = \frac{(10{,}000)(9)(1)(12)}{(5)(2)^3}$$

= 27,000 psi (tension at point R and compression at point Q)

$\tau(\max) = 27{,}000/2 = 13{,}500$ psi (shear at section B-B).

11. A steel latch is $\frac{1}{4}$'' thick. A force P of 600 pounds is uniformly distributed as shown in Fig. 2-23. Determine the maximum shear, tensile, and compressive stresses at section A-A and at point B.

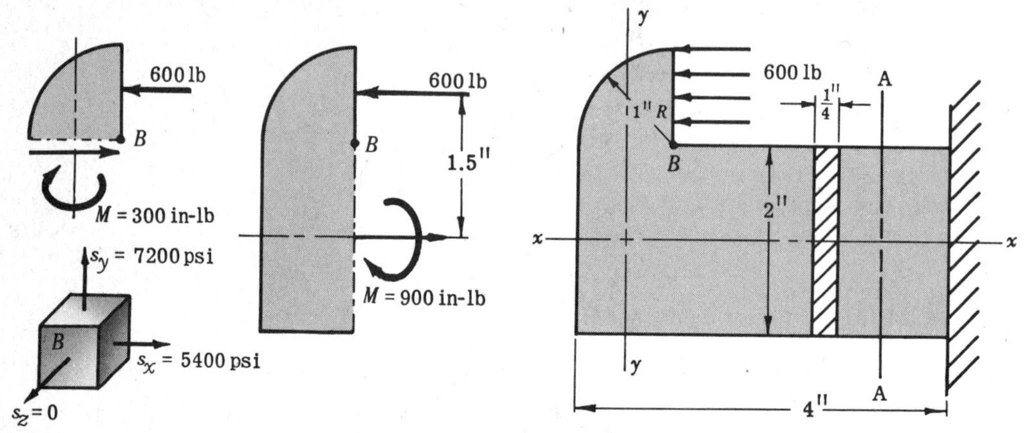

Fig. 2-23

Solution:

At section A-A:

The critical point is at the top fibers.

$$s_x = \frac{Mc}{I} + \frac{P}{A} = \frac{(600 \times 1.5)(1)(12)}{(0.25)(2)^3} + \frac{600}{(0.25)(2)} = 6600 \text{ psi}$$

$s_n(\max) = s_x = 6600$ psi (tension) at top fibers of section A-A.

$s_n(\min) = -4200$ psi (compression) at bottom fibers of section A-A.

$\tau(\max) = 6600/2 = 3300$ psi (shear) at top fibers of section A-A.

At point B (neglecting stress concentration):

$$s_x = \frac{Mc}{I} + \frac{P}{A} = \frac{(900)(1)(12)}{(0.25)(2)^3} + \frac{600}{(0.25)(2)} = 6600 \text{ psi (tension)}$$

$$s_y = \frac{Mc}{I} = \frac{(300)(0.5)(12)}{(0.25)(1)^3} = 7200 \text{ psi (tension)}$$

$s_z = 0, \quad \tau_{xy} = 0$

$$s_n(\max) = \frac{6600+7200}{2} + \sqrt{\left(\frac{6600-7200}{2}\right)^2 - 0} = 7200 \text{ psi (tension)}$$

$$s_n(\min) = \frac{6600+7200}{2} - \sqrt{\left(\frac{6600-7200}{2}\right)^2 - 0} = 6600 \text{ psi (tension)}$$

$$\tau(\max) = \frac{s_n(\max) - 0}{2} = 3600 \text{ psi (shear)}$$

12. Determine the maximum normal stress and the maximum shear stress at section A-A for the crank shown in Fig. 2-24 when a load of 2000 lb is assumed to be concentrated at the center of the crank pin.

Solution:

The critical points are at the front and back fibers of the section.

$M = (2000)(3.5) = 7000$ in-lb

$T = (2000)(5) = 10{,}000$ in-lb

$$s_x = \frac{Mc}{I} = \frac{(7000)(1.5)(64)}{\pi(3^4)} = 2640 \text{ psi}$$

$$\tau_{xy} = \frac{Tr}{J} = \frac{(10{,}000)(1.5)(32)}{\pi(3^4)} = 1885 \text{ psi}$$

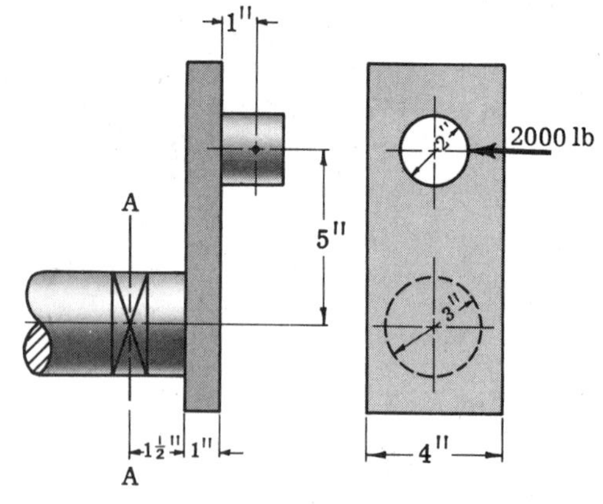

Fig. 2-24

$s_n(\max) = 2640/2 + \sqrt{(2640/2)^2 + (1885)^2} = 3620$ psi (tension)

$\tau(\max) = \sqrt{(2640/2)^2 + (1885)^2} = 2300$ psi (shear)

13. In a gas turbine rotor, a radial stress of +3000 psi and a tangential stress of +7000 psi have been found at a point as shown in Fig. 2-25. What is the maximum shear stress at this point?

Solution:

$s_x = +3000$ psi

$s_y = +7000$ psi

$s_n(\text{max}) = s_y = 7000$ psi (tension)

$\tau(\text{max}) = \dfrac{7000 - 0}{2} = 3500$ psi (shear)

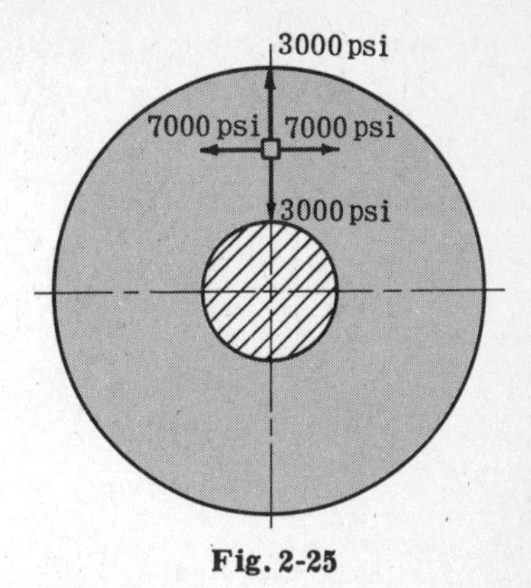

Fig. 2-25

SUPPLEMENTARY PROBLEMS

14. A cantilever beam of circular cross section is loaded as shown in Fig. 2-26. In terms of T, F, L, d, and P, write an expression for
(a) maximum tensile stress at point A,
(b) maximum compressive stress at point A,
(c) maximum tensile stress at point B,
(d) maximum compressive stress at point B,
(e) maximum shear stress at both points A and B.
Ans. See Solved Problem 1.

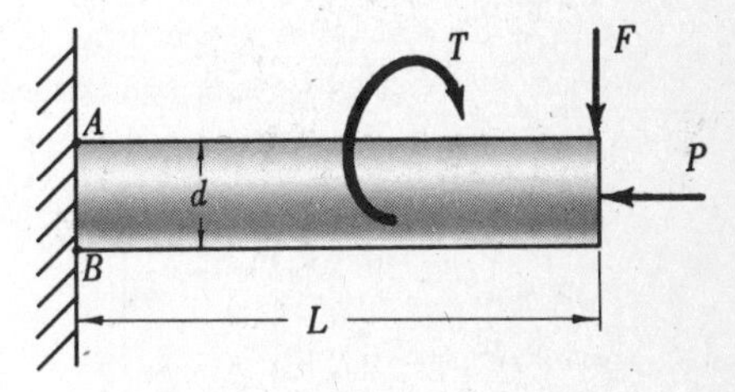

Fig. 2-26

15. A steel member has a torque of 1000 in-lb and an axial load of 2000 lb applied as shown in Fig. 2-27 below. What is the magnitude of (a) the maximum shear stress, (b) the maximum normal stress, (c) the minimum normal stress? *Ans.* (a) 1740 psi, (b) 3330 psi, (c) −2100 psi (compression)

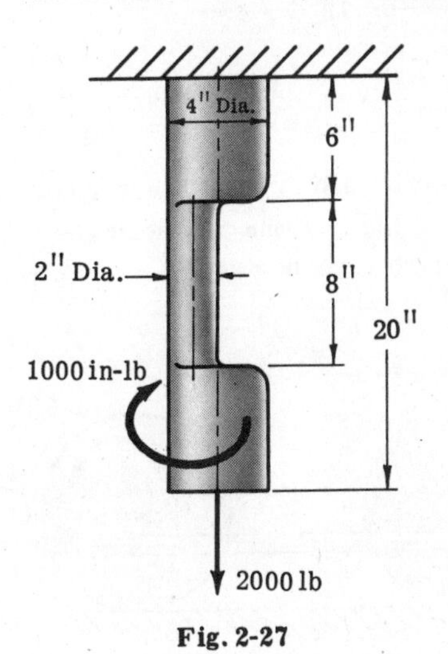

Fig. 2-27

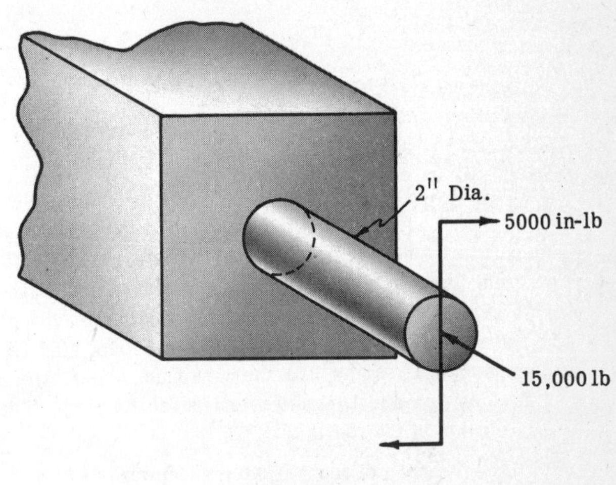

Fig. 2-28

16. A short circular bar 2 inches in diameter has a couple of 5000 in-lb and a compressive load of 15,000 lb applied as shown in Fig. 2-28 above. Determine (a) the maximum shear stress in the bar, (b) the maximum tensile stress in the bar, (c) the maximum compressive stress in the bar.
Ans. (a) 3980 psi, (b) 1590 psi, (c) −6370 psi (compression)

17. Determine the maximum shear stress in the member loaded as shown in Fig. 2-29 below.
Ans. 1785 psi (shear)

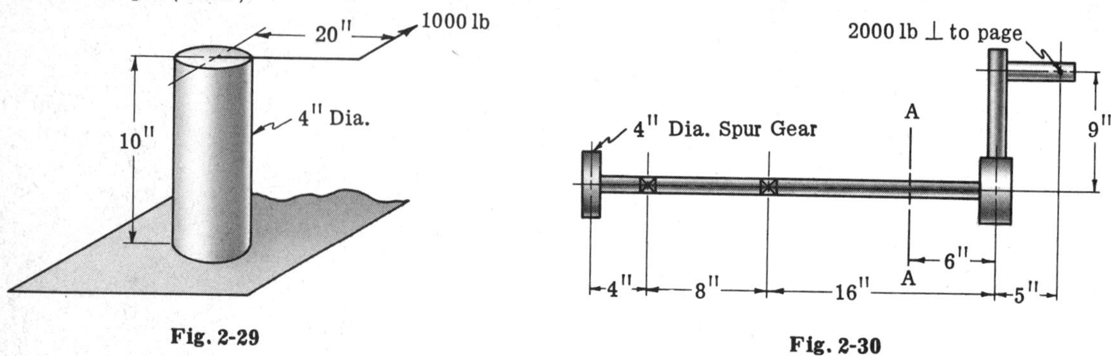

Fig. 2-29

Fig. 2-30

18. An overhung crank has a load of 2000 lb applied as shown in Fig. 2-30 above. Determine the maximum shear stress at section A-A where the diameter is 2 inches.
Ans. (s_x = 28,000 psi, τ_{xy} = 11,450 psi), τ(max) = 18,100 psi

19. The three components of the total force acting on the bevel gear are mutually perpendicular, with the 1000 lb force being perpendicular to the paper and acting at the mean radius of the gear as shown in Fig. 2-31 below. Determine the bending moment and the maximum shear stress at section A-A.
Ans. M = 8150 in-lb, τ(max) = 6120 psi

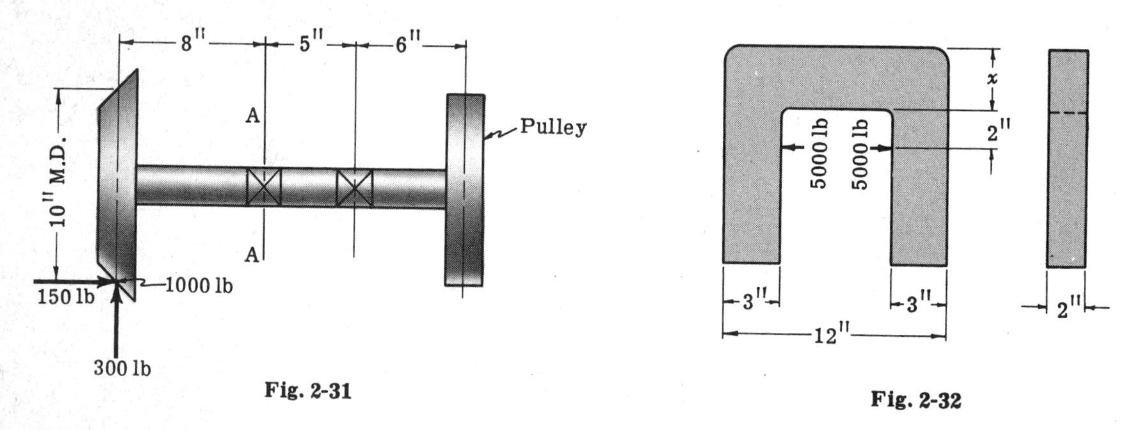

Fig. 2-31

Fig. 2-32

20. A steel bracket of the dimensions shown in Fig. 2-32 is loaded with two 5000 lb forces. The weight of the bracket as well as any stress concentration present is to be neglected. If the maximum tensile stress in the bracket is not to exceed 5000 psi, what is the minimum value that the length x can be made? *Ans.* 4.29 in.

21. The parallel side rod of a locomotive weighs 60 lb/ft. The crank length OP is 16 inches and the radius of the driver is 3 feet. If the speed of the engine is 75 mph and the tractive effort per wheel is 10,000 lb, find the maximum normal stress and the maximum shear stress in the side rod due to inertia and axial loading. The cross section of the rod is 3" × 6".

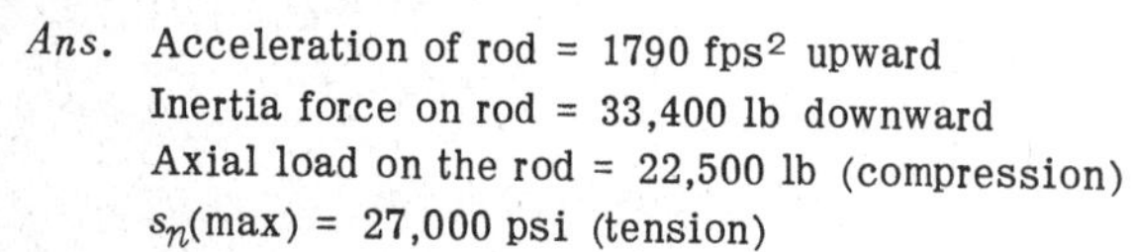

Ans. Acceleration of rod = 1790 fps² upward
Inertia force on rod = 33,400 lb downward
Axial load on the rod = 22,500 lb (compression)
s_n(max) = 27,000 psi (tension)
s_n(min) = −29,500 psi (compression)
τ(max) = 15,750 psi (shear)

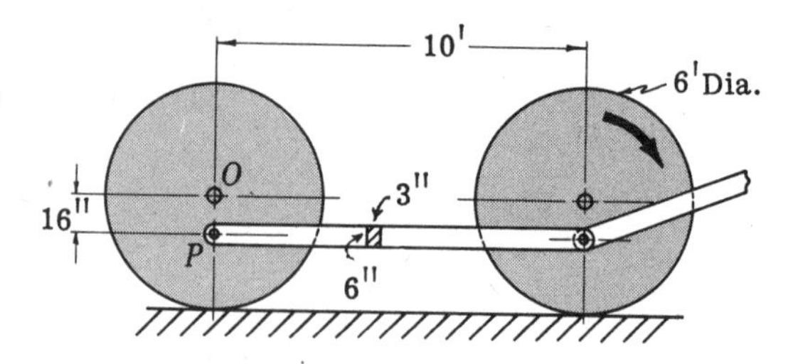

Fig. 2-33

22. Stresses in a hollow shaft due to a press fit are found to be 5000 psi and 9000 psi tension at a point as shown in Fig. 2-34 below. What is the maximum shear stress at the point? *Ans.* 4500 psi (shear)

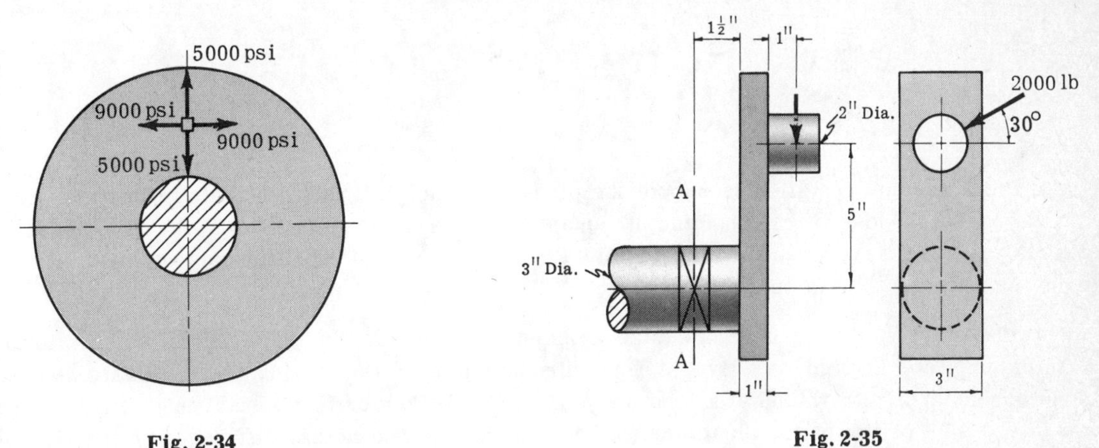

Fig. 2-34 **Fig. 2-35**

23. Determine the maximum normal and maximum shear stress at section A-A for the crank shown in Fig. 2-35 above, when a load of 2000 lb, assumed concentrated, is applied at the center of the crank pin. Neglect the effect of transverse shear in this problem.
Ans. s_x = 2640 psi, τ_{xy} = 1630 psi, τ(max) = 2100 psi (shear), s_n(max) = 3420 psi

24. Ladder rungs one inch in diameter are welded to the flange of an I-beam, as shown in Fig. 2-36 below. The rung is bent outward 3 inches in a horizontal plane to provide toe room. Assuming the flanges provide rigid end supports, compute the maximum shear stresses induced in the rung by a 180 lb man with his foot at the center of the span. Neglect the curvature of the rung in the calculation of maximum stress.
Ans. τ(max) = 2200 psi

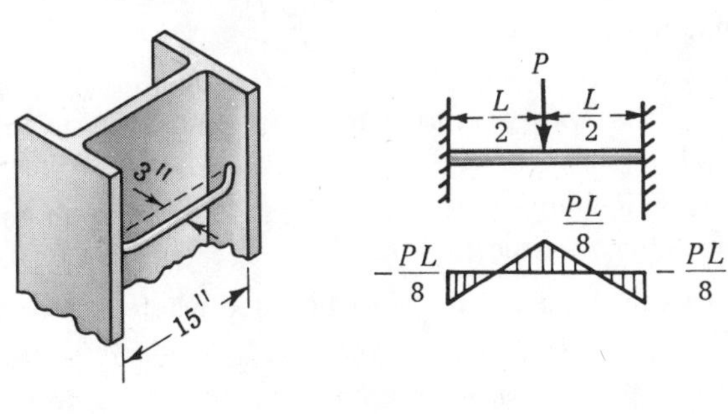

Fig. 2-36

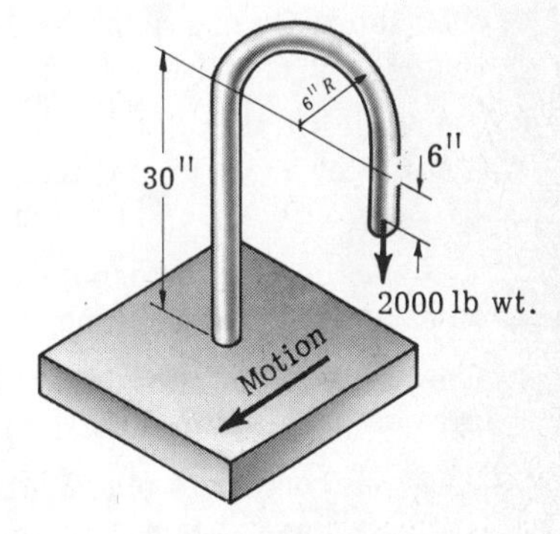

Fig. 2-37

25. A weight of 2000 lb is suspended from a bent supporting member as shown in Fig. 2-37 above. This is being carried on a moving platform which is accelerated at the rate of 8 fps^2. Find the diameter of bar necessary such that the maximum shear stress at the base of the rod does not exceed 10,000 psi. *Ans.* 2.41 in.

26. A crank built up from cylindrical sections by welding required a loading of 250 lb to overcome the resistance when in the position shown.

(*a*) Compute the maximum normal and shear stresses induced in the section A-A.

(*b*) Determine the maximum shear stresses induced in parts I, II, and III.

Ans. (*a*) s_n(max) = 29,000 psi, τ(max) = 15,000 psi
(*b*) 10,550 psi for part I, 6880 psi for II, 15,000 psi for III

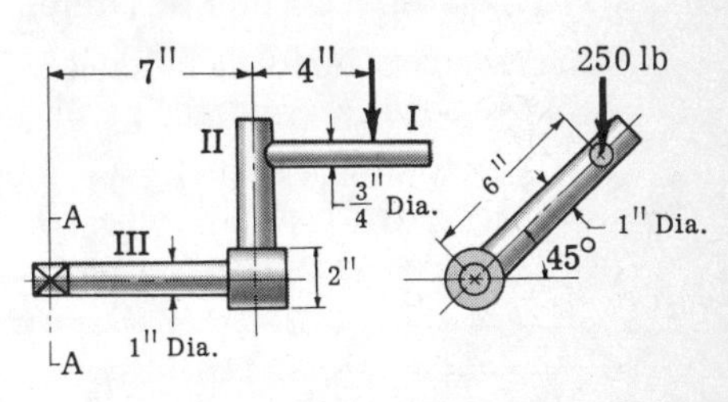

Fig. 2-38

Chapter 3

Metal Fits and Tolerances

METAL FITS must be specified to ensure the proper assembly of mating machine members. Since it is impossible to manufacture quantities of machine parts with exactly the same dimensions, systems have been devised to tolerate small dimensional variations of the mating parts without sacrificing their proper functioning.

Nominal size* is the approximate size decided upon by the designer and to which allowances and tolerances are applied to arrive at final dimensioning of the mating parts. **Basic dimensions** are the dimensions from which variations are permitted. **Tolerance** is the maximum permissible variation in the size of the part. **Clearance** (or interference) is the actual difference in the size of the mating parts. **Allowance** is the difference between basic dimensions of the mating parts. The tolerance may be **bilateral,** in which case the size of the part is permitted to vary above and below basic size, such as 2.500 ± 0.003; or the tolerance may be **unilateral**, in which case the part may be either larger or smaller than the basic size, but not both, such as $2.500\ {}^{+0.000}_{-0.003}$. The basic hole standard having unilateral tolerances has been recommended by the American Standards Association. In the basic hole system the minimum hole diameter is the nominal dimension.

BASIC HOLE standard provided for eight classes of fits ranging from loose to heavy force or shrink fits.

1. The loose fit has a large allowance and is intended for use where accuracy is not essential, such as in some agricultural, road-building, and mining equipment.
2. The free fit is suitable for use on rotating journals where the speeds are 600 rpm or greater. The allowance is sufficient for providing satisfactory lubrication, for such equipment as dynamos, engines, and some automotive parts.
3. The medium fit is for use with running fits under 600 rpm and for sliding fits, in such equipment as accurate machine tools and precise automotive parts.
4. The snug fit is the closest fit that can be assembled by hand, to be used where very small play is permissible and where moving parts are not intended to move freely under load.
5. The wringing fit is practically a metal-to-metal fit and is not interchangeable, but is selective in assembly. Light tapping with a hammer is necessary to assemble the parts.
6. The tight fit has a metal interference and is used for semi-permanent assembly suitable for drive or shrink fits on light sections.
7. The medium force fit requires considerable pressure to assemble and is used for shrink fits on medium sections or long shafts and is the tightest fit that is safe to use with cast iron external members. This fit is suitable for press fits on locomotive wheels, car wheels, generator and motor armatures.
8. The heavy force fit is used as a force or shrink fit for steel external members where considerable bond is required, as on locomotive wheel tires and heavy crank disks of large engines.

*In other contexts "nominal" size can mean a "name" dimension which bears no specific relation to actual dimensions, such as nominal pipe sizes.

RECOMMENDED ALLOWANCES AND TOLERANCES

Class of Fit	Method of Assembly	Allowance	Average Interference (negative allowance)	Hole Tolerance	Shaft Tolerance
1. Loose	Interchangeable	$0.0025\,d^{\frac{2}{3}}$	--------	$0.0025\,d^{\frac{1}{3}}$	$0.0025\,d^{\frac{1}{3}}$
2. Free	"	$0.0014\,d^{\frac{2}{3}}$	--------	$0.0013\,d^{\frac{1}{3}}$	$0.0013\,d^{\frac{1}{3}}$
3. Medium	"	$0.0009\,d^{\frac{2}{3}}$	--------	$0.0008\,d^{\frac{1}{3}}$	$0.0008\,d^{\frac{1}{3}}$
4. Snug	"	0.0000	--------	$0.0006\,d^{\frac{1}{3}}$	$0.0004\,d^{\frac{1}{3}}$
5. Wringing	Selective	--------	0.0000	$0.0006\,d^{\frac{1}{3}}$	$0.0004\,d^{\frac{1}{3}}$
6. Tight	"	--------	$0.00025\,d$	$0.0006\,d^{\frac{1}{3}}$	$0.0006\,d^{\frac{1}{3}}$
7. Medium Force	"	--------	$0.0005\,d$	$0.0006\,d^{\frac{1}{3}}$	$0.0006\,d^{\frac{1}{3}}$
8. Heavy Force or shrink	"	--------	$0.0010\,d$	$0.0006\,d^{\frac{1}{3}}$	$0.0006\,d^{\frac{1}{3}}$

ALLOWANCES AND TOLERANCES as applied to the basic hole standard are shown in Fig.3-1. Note that the hole dimensions are the same for both running and tight fits.

d = nominal dimension

t_h = hole tolerance

t_s = shaft tolerance

a = allowance

i = selected average interference (also called negative allowance in interference fits)

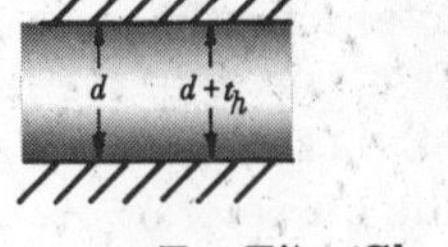

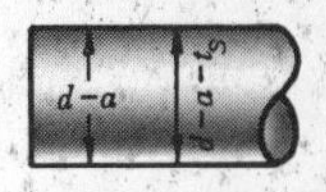

For Fits (Class 1-4)

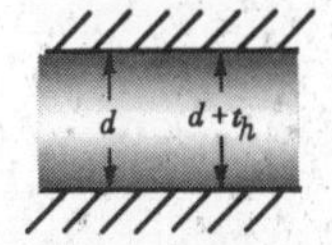

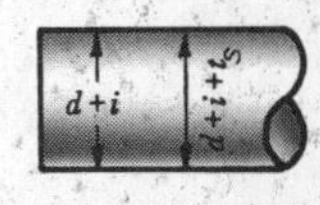

For Fits (Class 5-8)

Fig. 3-1

SELECTIVE ASSEMBLY is the practice of sorting parts into different size groups and then assembling the parts in corresponding groups, to obtain closer fits than would otherwise be economically feasible. For example, suppose 1 inch shafts are to be manufactured in accordance with a class 2 fit, with dimensions ranging from 0.9986 in. to 0.9973 in. The corresponding bearings are manufactured with dimensions ranging from 1.0000 in. to 1.0013 in. If fully interchangeable assembly is practiced, clearance would range from 0.0014 in. to 0.0040 in.

However, if it is desired to hold the clearance range from 0.0020 in. to 0.0034 in., perhaps for lubrication reasons, we might sort the shafts and bearings into two groups as follows:

Group A	**Bearings**	1.0000 in.	to	1.0007 in.
	Shafts	0.9973 in.	to	0.9980 in.
Group B	**Bearings**	1.0007 in.	to	1.0013 in.
	Shafts	0.9980 in.	to	0.9986 in.

With complete interchangeability within **Group A**, the range of clearances obtained will be 0.0020 in. to 0.0034 in.; and with complete interchangeability within **Group B**, from 0.0021 in. to 0.0033 in. Effectively what has been done was to obtain the benefits of smaller tolerances than those to which the parts were machined. This has been done at the expense of some interchangeability.

If the parts were sorted into more groups, then the range of clearance would be further reduced.

The same procedure of using selective assembly is followed for interference fits. Here the reason is to keep maximum stresses within suitable limits.

In the table for Recommended Allowances and Tolerances, under Method of Assembly, the classes 1 through 4 are described as interchangeable, where interchangeable means simply that all parts within a class will fit freely; similarly, with classes 5 through 8, Selective Assembly means that parts have to be grouped to permit the method of assembly with proper tightness as described.

STRESSES DUE TO INTERFERENCE FITS may be calculated by considering the fitted parts as thick-walled cylinders, as shown in Fig. 3-2, by the following equations:

$$p_c = \frac{\delta}{d_c\left[\dfrac{d_c^2+d_i^2}{E_i(d_c^2-d_i^2)} + \dfrac{d_o^2+d_c^2}{E_o(d_o^2-d_c^2)} - \dfrac{\mu_i}{E_i} + \dfrac{\mu_o}{E_o}\right]}$$

where

p_c = pressure at the contact surface, psi
δ = the total interference, in.
d_i = inside diameter of the inner member, in.
d_c = diameter of the contact surface, in.
d_o = outside diameter of outer member, in.
μ_o = Poisson's ratio for outer member
μ_i = Poisson's ratio for inner member
E_o = modulus of elasticity of outer member, psi
E_i = modulus of elasticity of inner member, psi

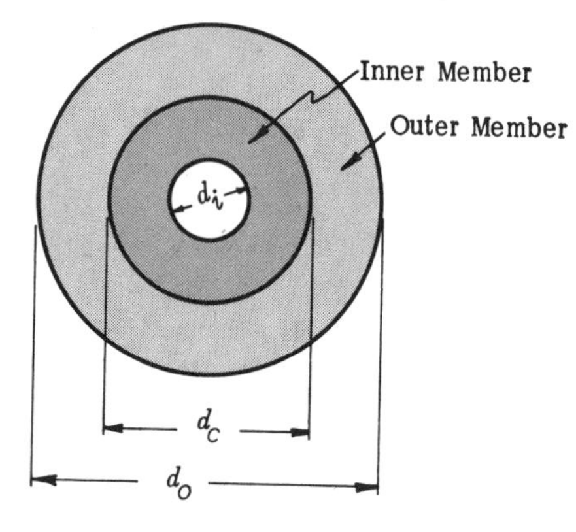

Fig. 3-2

If the outer and inner members are of the same material, the above equation reduces to

$$p_c = \frac{\delta}{\dfrac{2d_c^3(d_o^2-d_i^2)}{E(d_c^2-d_i^2)(d_o^2-d_c^2)}}$$

After p_c has been determined, then the actual tangential stresses at the various surfaces, in accordance with Lame''s equation, for use in conjunction with the maximum shear theory of failure, may be determined by:

On the surface at d_o, $\quad s_{to} = \dfrac{2p_c d_c^2}{d_o^2 - d_c^2}$

On the surface at d_c for the outer member, $\quad s_{tco} = p_c\left(\dfrac{d_o^2+d_c^2}{d_o^2-d_c^2}\right)$

On the surface at d_c for the inner member, $\quad s_{tci} = -p_c\left(\dfrac{d_c^2+d_i^2}{d_c^2-d_i^2}\right)$

On the surface at d_i, $\quad s_{ti} = \dfrac{-2p_c d_c^2}{d_c^2 - d_i^2}$

The equivalent tangential stresses at the various surfaces, in accordance with Birnie's equation, for use in conjunction with the maximum-strain theory of failure may be determined by:

On the surface at d_o for the outer member, $s'_{to} = \dfrac{2p_c d_c^2}{d_o^2 - d_c^2}$

On the surface at d_c for the outer member, $s'_{tco} = p_c\left(\dfrac{d_o^2 + d_c^2}{d_o^2 - d_c^2} + \mu_o\right)$

On the surface at d_c for the inner member, $s'_{tci} = -p_c\left(\dfrac{d_c^2 + d_i^2}{d_c^2 - d_i^2} - \mu_i\right)$

On the surface at d_i, $s'_{ti} = \dfrac{-2p_c d_c^2}{d_c^2 - d_i^2}$

FORCES AND TORQUES. The maximum axial force F_a required to assemble a force fit varies directly as the thickness of the outer member, the length of the outer member, the difference in diameters of the mating members, and the coefficient of friction. This force in pounds may be approximated by

$$F_a = f\pi d L p_c$$

The torque that can be transmitted by an interference fit without slipping between the hub and shaft can be estimated by

$$T = \frac{f p_c \pi d^2 L}{2}$$

where

F_a = axial load, lb
T = torque transmitted, in-lb
d = nominal shaft diameter, in.
f = coefficient of friction
L = length of external member, in.
p_c = contact pressure between the two members, psi

ASSEMBLY OF SHRINK FITS is often facilitated by heating the hub until it has expanded by an amount at least as much as the interference. The temperature change ΔT required to effect an increase δ in the inside diameter of the hub may be determined by

$$\Delta T = \frac{\delta}{\alpha d_i}$$

where

δ = diametral interference, in.
α = coefficient of linear expansion, per °F
ΔT = change in temperature, °F
d_i = initial diameter of the hole before expansion, in.

An alternate to heating the hub is to cool the shaft by means of a coolant such as dry ice.

SOLVED PROBLEMS

1. What are the values of allowance, hole tolerance, and shaft tolerance for the following dimensions of mated parts according to the basic hole system?

Hole	1.5000"	**Shaft**	1.4988"
	1.5009"		1.4978"

Solution:

Hole 1.5000" to $1.5'' + t_h$ $t_h = 0.0009''$

Shaft $1.5'' - a$ $a = 0.0012''$ to $1.5'' - a - t_s$ $t_s = 0.0010''$

2. A 3" shaft rotates in a bearing. The tolerance for both shaft and bearing is 0.003" and the required allowance is 0.004." Dimension both the shaft and bearing bore in accordance with the basic hole standard.

Solution:

Hole $d = 3.000''$, $d + t_h = 3.003''$

Shaft $d - a = 2.996''$, $d - a - t_s = 2.993''$

3. A medium force fit on a 3 inch shaft requires a hole tolerance of 0.009 in., a shaft tolerance of 0.009 in., and an average interference of 0.0015 in. Give the proper hole and shaft dimensions in accordance with the basic hole standard.

Solution:

Hole $d = 3.0000''$, $d + t_h = 3.0009''$

Shaft $d + i = 3.0015''$, $d + i + t_s = 3.0024''$

4. (*a*) What is the difference in the type of assembly generally used in running fits and interference fits?
(*b*) If a medium force fit (0.0015 in. interference) is desired, which axle should be fitted to each car wheel in the following group?

Wheel	**A**	**B**	**C**
Hole Diameter	3.0009"	3.0005"	3.0000"
Axle	**A′**	**B′**	**C′**
Diameter	3.0015"	3.0020"	3.0024"

Solution:

(*a*) Running fits are strictly interchangeable while interference fits require selective assembly.
(*b*) For selective assembly **A′** should be mated with **C**, **B′** with **B**, and **C′** with **A**.

5. Give the dimensions for the hole and shaft for the following: (*a*) a $\frac{1}{2}$ inch electric motor sleeve bearing, (*b*) a medium force fit on an 8 inch shaft, (*c*) a 2 inch sleeve bearing on the elevating mechanism of a road grader.

Solution:

(*a*) A class 2, free fit, would be suitable for an electric motor sleeve bearing.
Allowance = $0.0014 \times 0.5^{2/3} = 0.0009$ in.   Tolerance (shaft and hole) = $0.0013 \times 0.5^{1/3} = 0.0010$ in.
Hole dimen. = d to $d + t_h$ = 0.5000 to 0.5010 in.   Shaft dimen. = $d - a$ to $d - a - t_s$ = 0.4991 to 0.4981 in.

(*b*) Interference = $0.0005 \times 8 = 0.0040$ in.   Tolerance (shaft and hole) = $0.0006 \times 8^{1/3} = 0.0012$ in.
Hole dimen. = d to $d + t_h$ = 8.0000 to 8.0012 in.   Shaft dimen. = $d + i$ to $d + i + t_s$ = 8.0040 to 8.0052 in.

(*c*) A class 1, loose fit, would be suitable.
Allowance = $.0025 \times 2^{2/3} = 0.004$ in.   Tolerance (shaft and hole) = $.0025 \times 2^{1/3} = 0.003$ in.
Hole dimensions = 2.000 to 2.003 in.   Shaft dimensions = 1.996 to 1.993 in.

6. It is usual practice to design a hub such that its outside diameter is about twice the bore diameter. It is also known that a selective assembly should be used when shrinking a hub on a shaft. The purpose of this problem is to determine how small and how large stresses can be with a shrink fit (class 8 fit) if a selective assembly is **not** used. Determine for a 1" diameter solid shaft, the actual maximum and minimum **tangential** stresses that will result if the maximum and minimum interferences should be used for a hub with a 2" outside diameter. The shaft and hub are both made of steel. Poisson's ratio may be taken as equal to 0.3.

Solution:

$d_i = 0,\ d_c = 1'',\ d_o = 2''$

First determine the radial pressure on the contact surface, p_c. Since both hub and shaft are made of the same material,

$$p_c = \frac{\delta E(d_c^2 - d_i^2)(d_o^2 - d_c^2)}{2d_c^3(d_o^2 - d_i^2)} = \frac{\delta(30)(10^6)(1^2 - 0)(2^2 - 1^2)}{(2)(1^3)(2^2 - 0)} = \delta(11.25)(10^6)$$

Then, using Lamé's equation, determine the tangential stress at the contact surface of the outer member.

$$s_{tco} = p_c \frac{d_o^2 + d_c^2}{d_o^2 - d_c^2} = \delta(11.25)(10^6)\frac{2^2 + 1^2}{2^2 - 1^2} = \delta(18.75)(10^6)$$

For a class 8 fit, hole dimension may vary from 1.0000" to 1.0006" and shaft dimension may vary from 1.0010" to 1.0016"; then $\delta(\max) = 0.0016''$, $\delta(\min) = 0.0004''$, and

$$s_{tco}(\max) = (0.0016)(18.75)(10^6) = 30{,}000 \text{ psi}$$
$$s_{tco}(\min) = (0.0004)(18.75)(10^6) = 7{,}500 \text{ psi}$$

7. A 6 in. diameter steel shaft is to have a press fit with a 12 in. o.d. by 10 in. long hub of cast iron. The maximum tangential stress is to be 5000 psi. $E = 30 \times 10^6$ psi for steel and 15×10^6 psi for cast iron; $\mu = 0.3$ assumed for both steel and cast iron; $f = 0.12$.
(*a*) Determine the maximum diametral interference.
(*b*) What axial force F_a will be required to press the hub on the shaft?
(*c*) What torque may be transmitted with this fit?

Solution:

(*a*) The tangential maximum stress occurs on the surface d_c for the outer member:

$$s_{tco} = p_c\left(\frac{d_o^2 - d_c^2}{d_o^2 + d_c^2}\right), \quad 5000 = p_c\left(\frac{12^2 + 6^2}{12^2 - 6^2}\right), \quad p_c = 3000 \text{ psi}$$

Using

$$p_c = \frac{\delta}{d_c\left[\dfrac{d_c^2 + d_i^2}{E_i(d_c^2 - d_i^2)} + \dfrac{d_o^2 + d_c^2}{E_o(d_o^2 - d_c^2)} - \dfrac{\mu_i}{E_i} + \dfrac{\mu_o}{E_o}\right]}$$

$$3000 = \frac{\delta}{6\left[\dfrac{6^2 + 0}{(30)(10^6)(6^2 - 0)} + \dfrac{12^2 + 6^2}{(15)(10^6)(12^2 - 6^2)} - \dfrac{0.3}{(30)(10^6)} + \dfrac{0.3}{(15)(10^6)}\right]}$$

from which $\delta = 0.00278$ in. (maximum permissible diametral interference).

(*b*) $F_a = f\pi d L p_c = 0.12\pi(6)(10)(3000) = 67{,}800$ lb

(*c*) $T = fp_c \pi d^2 L/2 = F_a(d/2) = 67{,}800(6/2) = 203{,}400$ in-lb

8. A cast steel hub having a minimum diameter of 4.000 in. is to be shrunk on a shaft which has a maximum diameter of 4.006 in. Assuming a room temperature of 70°F, a coefficient of linear expansion for steel of 0.0000063 per degree Fahrenheit, and a desired diametral clearance of 0.002 in., to what minimum temperature should the hub be heated in order to permit assembly without interference?

Solution:

The hub diameter is to be expanded to 4.008 in. $\Delta T = \dfrac{0.008}{0.0000063 \times 4.0000} = 317^\circ$.

The hub should then be heated to a minimum temperature of: $70^\circ + 317^\circ = 387^\circ$F.

SUPPLEMENTARY PROBLEMS

9. What are the values of allowance, hole tolerance, and shaft tolerance for the following dimensions of mated parts according to the basic hole system?

Hole 1.7500 **Shaft** 1.7490
1.7506 1.7483 *Ans.* t_h 0.0006, $a = 0.0010$, $t_s = 0.0007$

10. What are the correct dimensions for mating a 6 inch diameter shaft with a hub to give a class 8 fit?
Ans. **Hole** 6.0000 **Shaft** 6.0060
6.0011 6.0071

11. A medium force fit on a 3 inch diameter shaft requires a hole tolerance of 0.0009 in., a shaft tolerance of 0.0009 in., and an average interference of 0.0015 in. Determine the proper dimensions for the hole and shaft.

Ans. $\dfrac{3.0000}{3.0009}$ and $\dfrac{3.0015}{3.0024}$

12. A $17\frac{1}{2}$ inch o.d. × 10 inch i.d. steel hub is to have a shrink fit on a 10 inch diameter steel shaft. The tangential stress at the contact surface is to be 15,000 psi. The length of the hub is 12 inches. (*a*) What is the radial stress at the contact surface? (*b*) How much torque may be transmitted assuming a coefficient of friction of 0.18? *Ans.* $p_c = 7600$ psi, $T = 215{,}000$ ft-lb

13. A 2" o.d. × 1" i.d. steel hub is to be assembled on a 1" diameter steel shaft with a class 8 fit, not using a selective assembly.

(*a*) Determine the tolerance, interference, and dimensions of the mating parts.

(*b*) What will be the maximum radial contact stress?

(*c*) What will be the actual maximum and minimum tangential stresses at the contact surface? (Use the Lamé equation.)

(*d*) What will be the equivalent maximum and minimum tangential stresses, based on the maximum-strain theory, at the contact surface? (Use Birnie's equation.)

(*e*) What is the maximum axial force F_a required for assembly of the mating parts, assuming a hub length of 3 in. and $f = 0.12$?

(*f*) What is the maximum torque that may be transmitted with this assembly? (Base solution on maximum interference.)

Ans. (*a*) **Tolerance** 0.0006 in. **Maximum interference** 0.0016 in. **Hole** 1.0000 in. **Shaft** 1.0010 in.
Minimum interference 0.0004 in. 1.0006 in. 1.0016 in.

(*b*) $p_c(\text{max}) = 18{,}000$ psi (*c*) $s_t(\text{max}) = 30{,}000$ psi, $s_t(\text{min}) = 7{,}500$ psi (*d*) $s'_t(\text{max}) = 35{,}400$ psi, $s'_t(\text{min}) = 8{,}850$ psi (*e*) $F_a = 20{,}400$ lb (*f*) $T = 10{,}200$ in-lb

14. A steel hub of 1" i.d. is to be assembled on a shaft having a diameter of 1.001. To what temperature should the shaft be cooled to permit a slip fit, assuming a room temperature of 70°F and a coefficient of linear expansion of 0.0000063 per degree Fahrenheit? *Ans.* −88.5°F

15. It is desired to assemble two steel cylinders having nominal diameters of 1" i.d. × 2" o.d. and 2" i.d. × 3" o.d. with the tangential stress at the inner surface of the outer member limited to 12,000 psi. Determine the required interference and the tangential stresses at the inner and outer surfaces of the two members, in accordance with Birnie's equation.

Ans. p_c = 4,130 psi, δ = 0.001178" interference

s'_{ti} = −11,020 psi
s'_{tci} = − 5,650 psi
s'_{tco} = 12,000 psi
s'_{to} = 6,608 psi

16. A centering fit for a flange coupling is to locate the two halves of the coupling. If a class 4 fit is used to provide for a close fit, the allowance is proper but the tolerances are small. Determine the necessary dimensions of the centering fit for a nominal dimension of 6 in., if a compromise is made by using the allowance of a class 4 fit with the tolerances of a class 3 fit. Note that some of the benefit of a class 4 fit is obtained with the economy of a class 3 fit.

Ans. $\dfrac{6.0015}{6.0000}$ and $\dfrac{6.0000}{5.9985}$

17. A class 8 fit is used for a hub shrunk on a 2 in. shaft. How many groups of the parts are necessary for selective interchangeable assembly to yield a maximum interference of 0.0022 in. and minimum interference of 0.0018 in.?

Ans. 4 groups separated as follows:

Group	A	B	C	D
Hole	2.0002 / 2.0000	2.0004 / 2.0002	2.0006 / 2.0004	2.0008 / 2.0006
Shaft	2.0022 / 2.0020	2.0024 / 2.0022	2.0026 / 2.0024	2.0028 / 2.0026

Chapter 4

Curved Beams

BENDING STRESSES IN CURVED BEAMS do not follow the same linear variation as straight beams, because of the variation in arc length. Even though the same assumptions are used for both types, i.e. that plane sections perpendicular to the axis of the beam remain plane after bending and that stress is proportional to strain, the distribution of stress is quite different. Fig. 4-1 shows the linear stress variation in a straight beam and the hyperbolic stress distribution in a curved beam. Note that the bending stress in the curved beam is zero at a point other than at the center of gravity axis. Also, note that the neutral axis is located between the gravity axis and the center of curvature; this always occurs in curved beams.

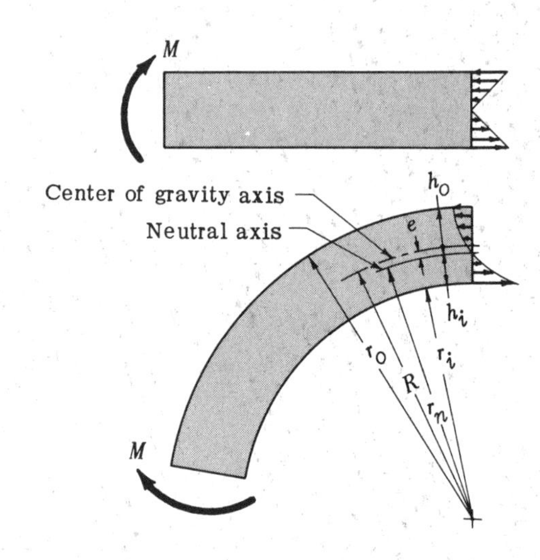

Fig. 4-1

STRESS DISTRIBUTION due to bending is given by $s = \dfrac{My}{Ae(r_n - y)}$

where s is the bending stress, psi

M is the bending moment with respect to the centroidal axis, in-lb

y is the distance from the neutral axis to the point in question, inches (positive for distances toward the center of curvature, negative for distances away from the center of curvature)

A is the area of the section, sq in.

e is the distance from the center of gravity axis to the neutral axis, inches

r_n is the radius of curvature of the neutral axis, inches.

BENDING STRESS AT THE INSIDE FIBER is given by $s = \dfrac{Mh_i}{Aer_i}$

where h_i is the distance from the neutral axis to the inside fiber, inches ($h_i = r_n - r_i$)

r_i is the radius of curvature of the inside fiber, inches.

BENDING STRESS AT THE OUTSIDE FIBER is given by $s = \dfrac{Mh_o}{Aer_i}$

where h_o is the distance from the neutral axis to the outside fiber, inches ($h_o = r_o - r_n$)

r_o is the radius of curvature of the outside fiber, inches.

If the section is a **symmetrical** one (as a circle, rectangle, I-beam with equal flanges) the maximum bending stress will **always** occur at the inside fiber. If the section is unsymmetrical, the maximum bending stress may occur at either the inside or outside fiber.

If the section has an axial load in addition to bending, the axial stress must be added algebraically to the bending stress.

Considerable care must be taken in the arithmetic. The distance "e" from the center of gravity axis to the neutral axis is usually small. A numerical variation in the calculation of "e" can cause a large percentage change in the final results.

Table I below gives the location to the neutral axis, the distance from the centroidal axis to the neutral axis, and the distance to the centroidal axis from the center of curvature for various commonly encountered shapes.

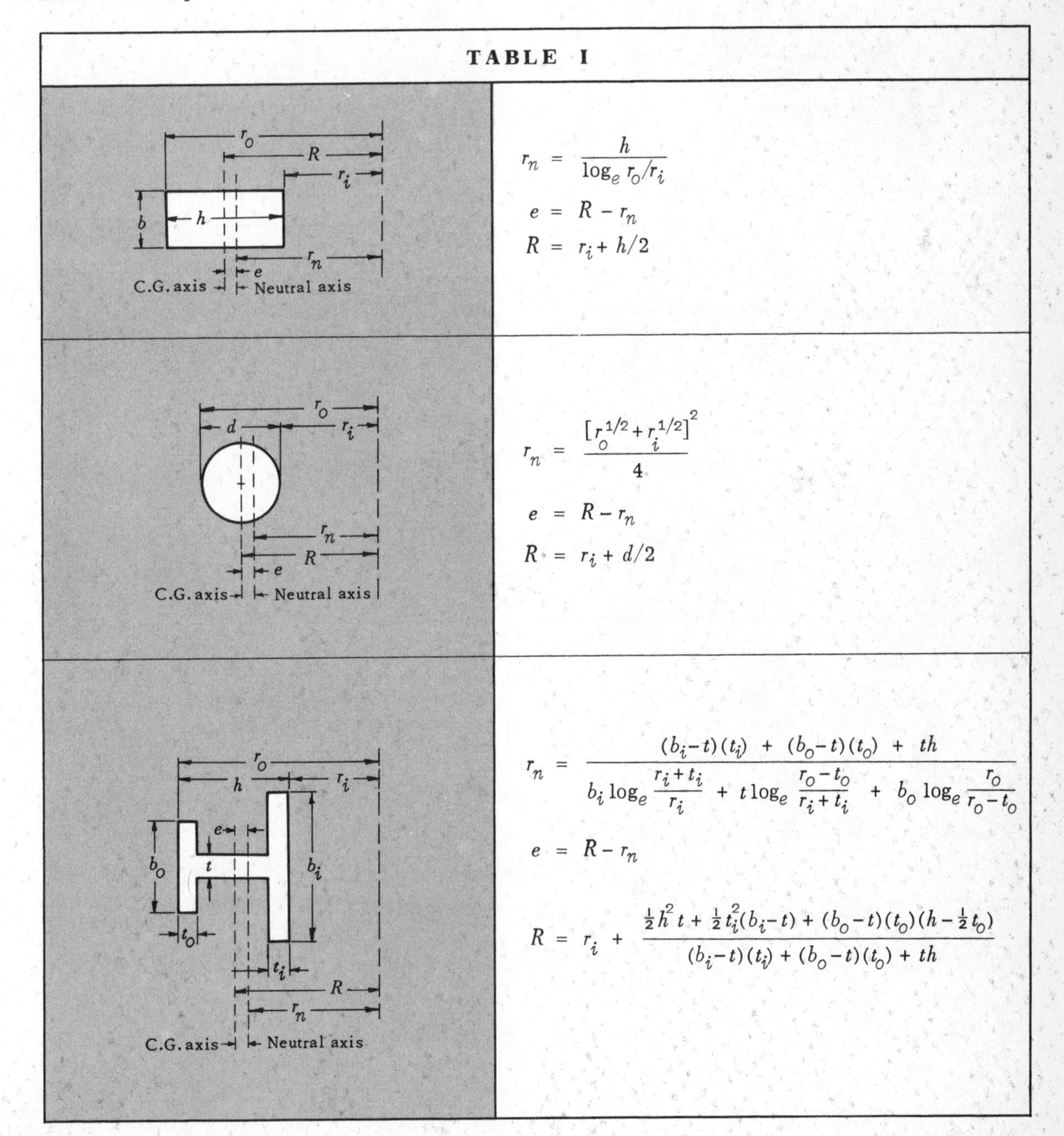

TABLE I

Section	Formulas
Rectangle	$r_n = \frac{h}{\log_e r_o/r_i}$ $e = R - r_n$ $R = r_i + h/2$
Circle	$r_n = \frac{[r_o^{1/2} + r_i^{1/2}]^2}{4}$ $e = R - r_n$ $R = r_i + d/2$
I-section (unequal flanges)	$r_n = \frac{(b_i - t)(t_i) + (b_o - t)(t_o) + th}{b_i \log_e \frac{r_i + t_i}{r_i} + t \log_e \frac{r_o - t_o}{r_i + t_i} + b_o \log_e \frac{r_o}{r_o - t_o}}$ $e = R - r_n$ $R = r_i + \frac{\frac{1}{2}h^2 t + \frac{1}{2}t_i^2(b_i - t) + (b_o - t)(t_o)(h - \frac{1}{2}t_o)}{(b_i - t)(t_i) + (b_o - t)(t_o) + th}$

TABLE I (continued)

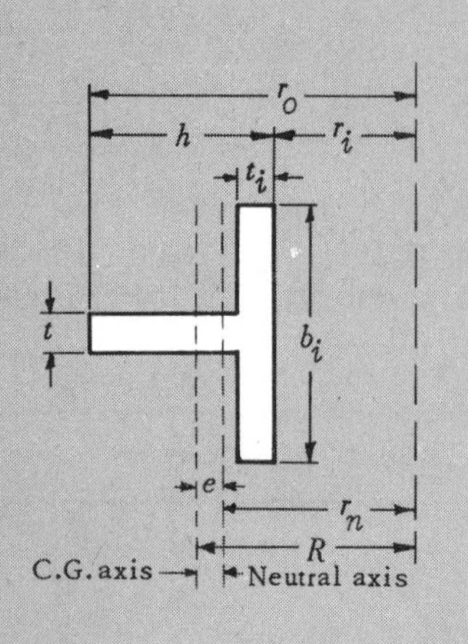

$$r_n = \frac{(b_i - t)(t_i) + th}{(b_i - t)\log_e \dfrac{r_i + t_i}{r_i} + t\log_e \dfrac{r_o}{r_i}}$$

$$e = R - r_n$$

$$R = r_i + \frac{\frac{1}{2}h^2 t + \frac{1}{2}t_i^2 (b_i - t)}{ht + (b_i - t)t_i}$$

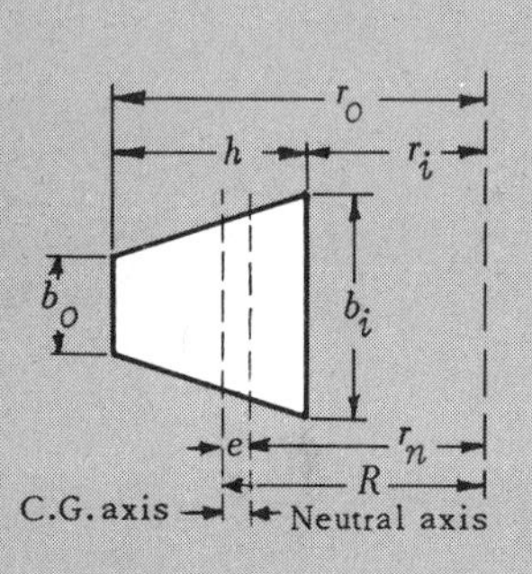

$$r_n = \frac{\left(\dfrac{b_i + b_o}{2}\right)h}{\left(\dfrac{b_i r_o - b_o r_i}{h}\right)\log_e\left(\dfrac{r_o}{r_i}\right) - (b_i - b_o)}$$

$$e = R - r_n$$

$$R = r_i + \frac{h(b_i + 2b_o)}{3(b_i + b_o)}$$

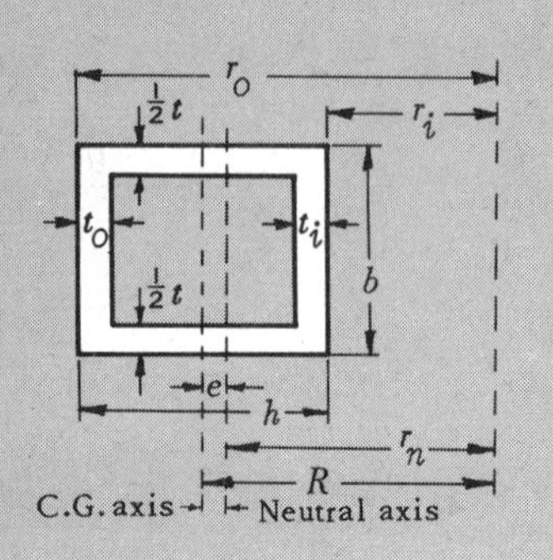

$$r_n = \frac{(b - t)(t_i + t_o) + th}{b\left[\log_e \dfrac{r_i + t_i}{r_i} + \log_e \dfrac{r_o}{r_o - t_o}\right] + t\log_e \dfrac{r_o - t_o}{r_i + t_i}}$$

$$e = R - r_n$$

$$R = r_i + \frac{\frac{1}{2}h^2 t + \frac{1}{2}t_i^2(b - t) + (b - t)(t_o)(h - \frac{1}{2}t_o)}{ht + (b - t)(t_i + t_o)}$$

SOLVED PROBLEMS

1. The offset bar has forces applied as shown. The bar is $1'' \times 2''$. The effect of the two applied forces is a pure couple which causes the same bending moment at every section of the beam. Determine the maximum tension, compression and shear stresses, and state where each occurs.

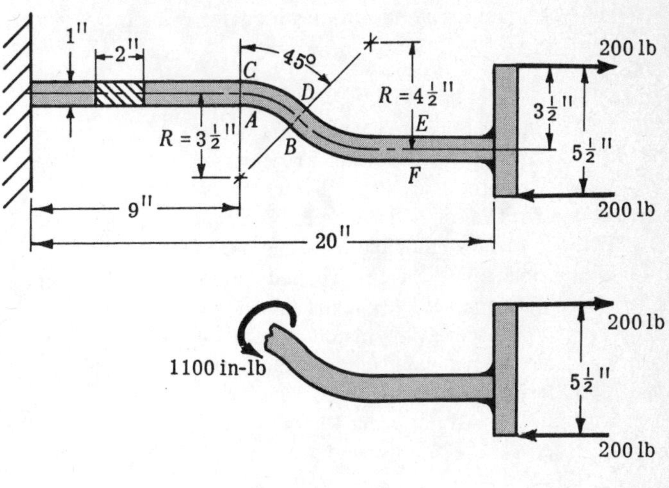

Fig. 4-2

Solution:

(a) The bending moment at every section is

$$200(5\tfrac{1}{2}) = 1100 \text{ in-lb}$$

(b) Since the couple for equilibrium is as shown, tension occurs in the upper fiber *CDE* and compression occurs in the lower fiber *ABF*. Because the beam is symmetrical, the maximum normal stress occurs at the inner fiber of the portion with the smaller radius of curvature, with $R = 3\tfrac{1}{2}''$, $r_i = 3''$, $r_o = 4''$; the maximum stress at the inner fiber is compression. However, the location of the maximum tensile stress is not evident. The sections with $R = 3\tfrac{1}{2}''$ and $R = 4\tfrac{1}{2}''$ should be checked.

(c) To determine e:

$$r_n = \frac{h}{\log_e r_o/r_i} = \frac{1}{\log_e \frac{4}{3}} = 3.485'', \qquad e = R - r_n = 3.5 - 3.485 = .015''$$

(d) For the section with $R = 3\tfrac{1}{2}''$ the stress at the inner fiber is

$$s_i = \frac{Mh_i}{Aer_i} = \frac{1100(.485)}{2(.015)(3)} = 5930 \text{ psi compression}$$

The stress at the outer fiber is

$$s_o = \frac{Mh_o}{Aer_o} = \frac{1100(.515)}{2(.015)(4)} = 4720 \text{ psi tension}$$

(e) For the section with $R = 4\tfrac{1}{2}''$, $r_n = \dfrac{h}{\log_e r_o/r_i} = \dfrac{1}{\log_e \frac{5}{4}} = 4.480''$ or $e = R - r_n = 4.5 - 4.480 = 0.020''$.

The stress at the inner fiber is $s_i = \dfrac{Mh_i}{Aer_i} = \dfrac{1100(.480)}{2(.02)(4)} = 3300$ psi tension.

The stress at the outer fiber is $s_o = \dfrac{Mh_o}{Aer_o} = \dfrac{1100(.520)}{2(.02)(5)} = 2860$ psi compression.

(f) Hence, the maximum tension occurs at the outside fiber of the section with $R = 3\tfrac{1}{2}''$.

The maximum compression occurs at the inside fibers of the section with $R = 3\tfrac{1}{2}''$. The maximum shear stress is half of the greatest difference of any two of the three principal stresses. Since only bending stresses are present at the outer fiber, the maximum shear is $\tfrac{1}{2}(-5930 - 0) = 2965$ psi.

(For comparison, the maximum stress in the straight beam is

$$s = \frac{Mc}{I} = \frac{1100(\frac{1}{2})}{2(1^3)/12} = 3300 \text{ psi tension and compression.)}$$

2. A spring clip, made from a 1" diameter rod, is shown in Fig. 4-3. Determine the maximum shear stress and specify its location or locations.

Solution:

(*a*) The location of the maximum normal stress can be found from inspection and comparison. Any free body of the bar which includes the two applied forces of the upper or lower parts would have the same bending moment since the two applied forces give a pure couple. The maximum bending stress will occur at the inside fiber of the sections with the inside radius of curvature $r_i = 3''$ (from A to B and C to D). The maximum stress will not occur where $r_i = 4''$.

(*b*) $r_n = \dfrac{[r_o^{1/2} + r_i^{1/2}]^2}{4} = \dfrac{[4^{1/2} + 3^{1/2}]^2}{4} = 3.482''$

(*c*) $e = R - r_n = 3.5 - 3.482 = .018''$

$h_i = .50 - .018 = .482$

(*d*) $s_i = \dfrac{Mh_i}{Aer_i} = \dfrac{500(.482)}{\frac{1}{4}\pi(1)^2(.018)(3)} = 5680 \text{ psi}$

(*e*) The stress from A to B is tension and from C to D is compression.

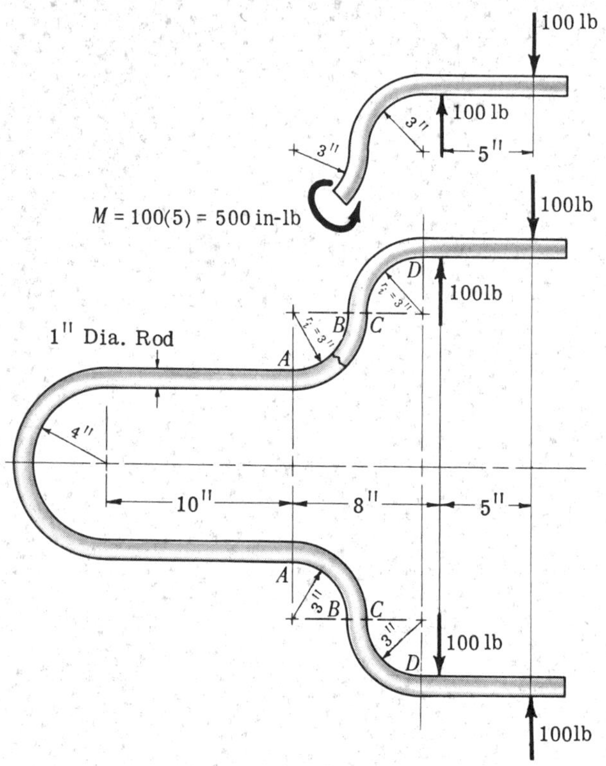

Fig. 4-3

(*f*) The maximum shear stress is $\frac{1}{2}(5680) = 2840$ psi and occurs at every point from A to B and from C to D.

(*g*) Since the section is symmetrical, the maximum stress at the outer fibers need not be checked.

3. An open S link is made from a 1" diameter rod. Determine the maximum tensile stress and maximum shear stress.

Solution:

(*a*) A comparison of section A-A and B-B, in Fig. 4-4, shows that the bending moment at A-A is less than at section B-B, but the radius of curvature is less at A-A than B-B. It will be necessary to investigate both sections.

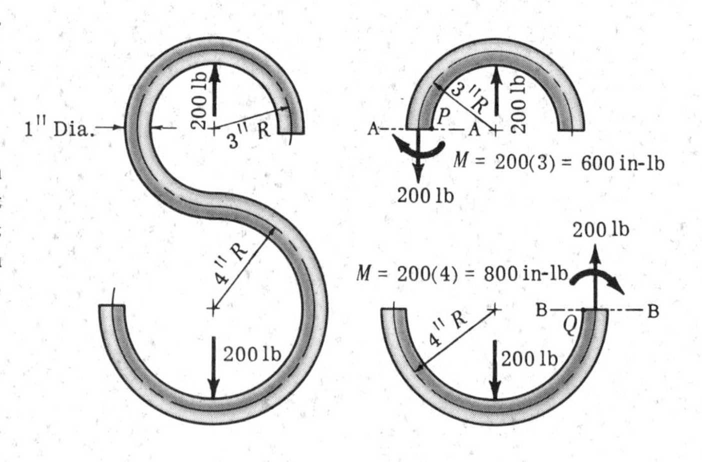

Fig. 4-4

At Section A-A, point P:

(*b*) $M = 600$ in-lb

(*c*) $r_n = \dfrac{[r_o^{1/2} + r_i^{1/2}]^2}{4} = \dfrac{[(3\frac{1}{2})^{1/2} + (2\frac{1}{2})^{1/2}]^2}{4} = 2.979''$

$e = R - r_n = 3.0 - 2.979 = .021''$, $\quad h_i = .5 - .021 = .479''$

Bending stress + direct tension $= \dfrac{Mh_i}{Aer_i} + \dfrac{P}{A} = \dfrac{600(.479)}{\frac{1}{4}\pi(1)^2(.021)(2.5)} + \dfrac{200}{\frac{1}{4}\pi(1)^2} = 6960 + 260 = 7220$ psi tension

At Section B-B, point Q:

(*d*) M = 800 in-lb

$$r_n = \frac{[r_o^{1/2} + r_i^{1/2}]^2}{4} = \frac{[(4.5)^{1/2} + (3.5)^{1/2}]^2}{4} = 3.984''$$

$$e = 4.0 - 3.984 = .016'', \qquad h_i = .5 - .016 = .484''$$

(*e*) Bending stress + direct tension $= \dfrac{Mh_i}{Aer_i} + \dfrac{P}{A} = \dfrac{800(.484)}{\frac{1}{4}\pi(1)^2(.016)(3.5)} + \dfrac{200}{\frac{1}{4}\pi(1)^2}$

$$= 8800 + 260 = 9060 \text{ psi tension}$$

(*f*) Maximum shear $= \frac{1}{2}(9060) = 4530$ psi at point Q.

4. An offset bar is loaded as shown in Fig. 4-5. The weight of the bar can be neglected. What is the maximum offset (dimension X) if the allowable stress in tension is limited to 10,000 psi? Where will the maximum tensile shear stress occur?

Solution:

(*a*) Since the bar is symmetrical, bending causes the greatest stress at the inside fiber. Point P on section A-A will be stressed the greatest.

(*b*) M for section A-A = 2000(X) in-lb.

$$r_n = \frac{[r_o^{1/2} + r_i^{1/2}]^2}{4} = \frac{[(6.0)^{1/2} + (2.0)^{1/2}]^2}{4} = 3.732''$$

$$e = R - r_n = 4 - 3.732 = .268''$$
$$h_i = 2 - .268 = 1.732''$$
$$A = \tfrac{1}{4}\pi(4)^2 = 12.56 \text{ in}^2$$

(*c*) The allowable tensile stress is 10,000 psi.

Bending tensile stress + direct tensile stress $= \dfrac{Mh_i}{Aer_i} + \dfrac{P}{A}$

or
$$10{,}000 = \frac{2000(X)(1.732)}{12.56(.268)(2)} + \frac{2000}{12.56}$$

from which $X = 19''$, the maximum offset.

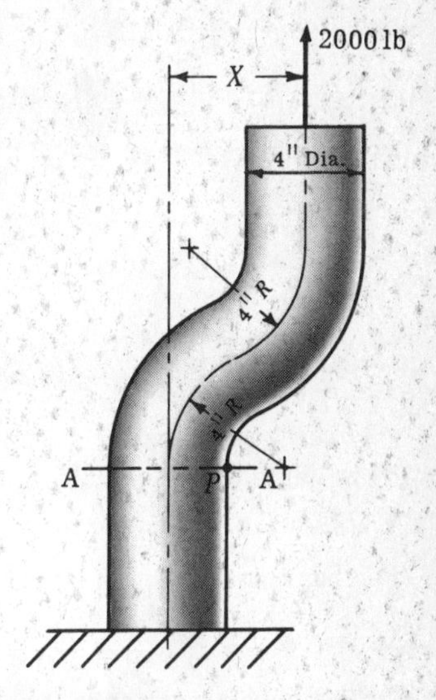

Fig. 4-5

5. Set up the basic relations necessary to obtain the stress distribution in a curved beam due to bending alone and derive the equation to give the bending stress distribution. See Fig. 4-6.

Solution:

(*a*) Consider a differential element of the beam subtending an angle $d\theta$.

(*b*) As a result of bending, and *plane sections remaining plane*, an arbitrary section p-q rotates to p'-q', with tension on the inner fiber and compression on the outer fiber. The rotation occurs with a point on the neutral axis remaining fixed.

(*c*) The elongation of the fiber a distance y from the neutral surface is $y\,d\phi$.

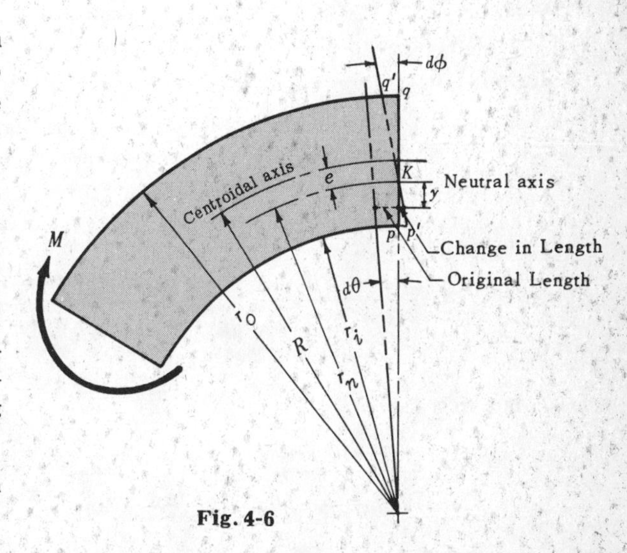

Fig. 4-6

(*d*) The original length of the differential fiber is $(r_n - y)\,d\theta$.

(*e*) Since stress is proportional to strain,

$$s = \epsilon E = \frac{\Delta l}{l}E \quad \text{or} \quad s = \frac{y\,d\phi}{(r_n - y)\,d\theta}E, \qquad \text{where } s \text{ is the bending stress.}$$

(*f*) The summation of all differential forces must be zero for equilibrium; hence

$$\int s\,dA = 0 \quad \text{or} \quad \int \frac{y\,d\phi\,E\,dA}{(r_n - y)\,d\theta} = 0 \quad \text{or} \quad \frac{d\phi}{d\theta}E\int \frac{y\,dA}{r_n - y} = 0$$

(*g*) Also, the moment of the differential forces about any point should be equal to the applied couple M. Take the point K as a convenient center of moments.

$$\int s\,y\,dA = M \quad \text{or} \quad \int \left[\frac{y\,d\phi}{(r_n - y)\,d\theta}E\right] y\,dA = M \quad \text{or} \quad \frac{d\phi}{d\theta}E\int \frac{y^2}{r_n - y}\,dA = M$$

(*h*) Manipulation of $\int \frac{y^2}{r_n - y}\,dA = M$, by dividing $(r_n - y)$ into y^2, gives

$$r_n \int \frac{y}{r_n - y}\,dA - \int y\,dA = M$$

(*i*) But from (*f*), $\int \frac{y}{r_n - y}\,dA = 0$ and $\int y\,dA$ represents the moment about the neutral axis of the differential areas comprising the section. Hence $\int y\,dA$ can be written as Ae, where e is the distance from the neutral axis to the centroidal axis.

(*j*) Thus the equation in (*g*) can be written $\dfrac{d\phi}{d\theta}E\displaystyle\int \frac{y^2}{r_n - y}\,dA = M = \frac{d\phi}{d\theta}E\,[Ae]$ or $\dfrac{d\phi}{d\theta}E = \dfrac{M}{Ae}$.

(*k*) The stress equation in (*e*) can be written $s = \dfrac{y\,d\phi}{(r_n - y)\,d\theta}E = \dfrac{M}{Ae}\,\dfrac{y}{r_n - y}$ which gives the stress variation.

6. A section of a C-clamp is shown in Fig. 4-7. What force F can be exerted by the screw if the maximum tensile stress in the clamp is limited to 20,000 psi?

Solution:

(*a*) The maximum tensile stress will occur at point P at section A-A, on which section the bending is maximum, curvature exists, and a direct tensile stress acts.

(*b*) The distance from the center of curvature to the C.G. axis is, from Table I,

$$R = r_i + \frac{\frac{1}{2}h^2 t + \frac{1}{2}t_i^2(b_i - t)}{ht + (b_i - t)t_i} = 1 + \frac{\frac{1}{2}(1)^2(\frac{1}{8}) + \frac{1}{2}(\frac{1}{8})^2(\frac{3}{4} - \frac{1}{8})}{(1)(\frac{1}{8}) + (\frac{3}{4} - \frac{1}{8})(\frac{1}{8})} = 1.332''$$

(*c*) Also, from Table I,

$$r_n = \frac{(b_i - t)(t_i) + th}{(b_i - t)\log_e \frac{r_i + t_i}{r_i} + t\log_e \frac{r_o}{r_i}} = \frac{(\frac{3}{4} - \frac{1}{8})(\frac{1}{8}) + (\frac{1}{8})(1)}{(\frac{3}{4} - \frac{1}{8})\log_e \frac{1 + \frac{1}{8}}{1} + \frac{1}{8}\log_e \frac{2}{1}} = 1.267''$$

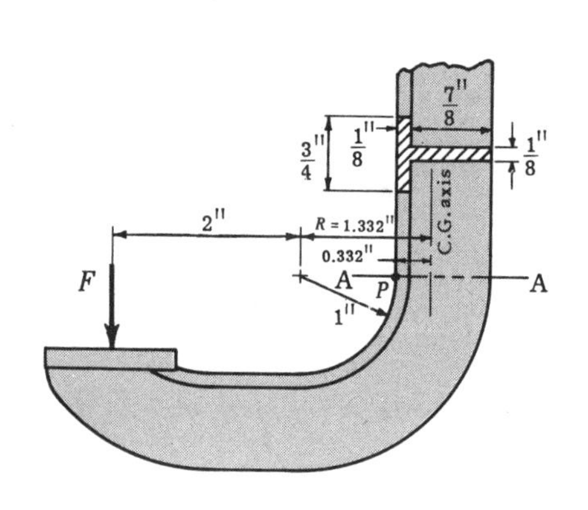

Fig. 4-7

(*d*) $e = R - r_n = 1.332 - 1.267 = 0.065''$. $h_i = r_n - r_i = 1.267 - 1.0 = 0.267''$.

(*e*) Area $= \frac{1}{8}(\frac{3}{4}) + \frac{7}{8}(\frac{1}{8}) = 0.203$ sq in.

(*f*) Bending moment (about C.G.) $= F(2 + 1.332) = 3.332F$

(*g*) Bending stress + direct stress $= \dfrac{Mh_i}{Aer_i} + \dfrac{F}{A}$

$$20{,}000 = \frac{3.332F(0.267)}{(0.203)(0.065)(1)} + \frac{F}{0.203}, \quad \text{and} \quad F\,(\text{maximum}) = 276\text{ lb}$$

(*h*) Note that the stress at the outer fiber may be larger in this case than at the inner fiber, but this stress at the outer fiber is compression.

7. A trough 1" thick by 8" long is subjected to a concentrated load of 400 lb. Determine the magnitude and location of the maximum tension, compression, and shear stresses.

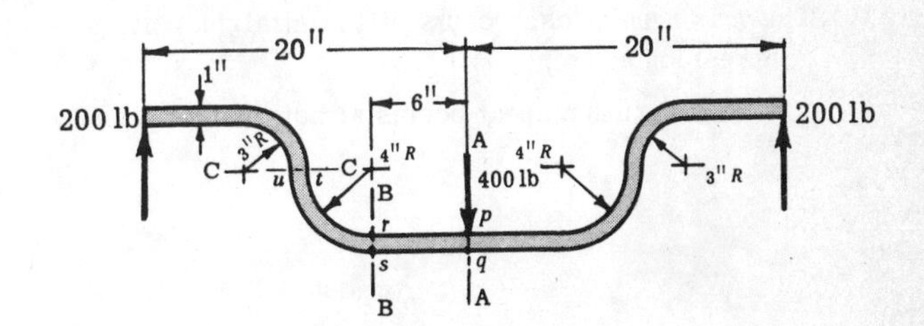

Fig. 4-8

Solution:

(*a*) The location of the maximum bending stress can be reduced, by inspection, to three different locations:

1) **Section A-A**
2) **Section B-B**
3) **Section C-C**

At section A-A, the bending moment is maximum but the beam is straight.

At section B-B, the bending moment is less than at A-A but the beam has curvature.

At section C-C, the bending moment is less than at A-A and B-B but the beam has a smaller radius of curvature. Also, at C-C a direct tensile stress is applied, which is not present at the other two sections.

Hence the stress will be computed at the three different sections and compared. (The stresses need be computed on only one side of the centerline since the beam is symmetrical.)

(*b*) **Section A-A**

$$s = \frac{Mc}{I} = \frac{Mc}{bh^3/12} = \frac{(200\times 20)\frac{1}{2}}{8(1^3)/12} = 3000 \text{ psi (tension at point } q\text{, compression at point } p)$$

Note. Transverse shear stress is zero at points p and q.

(*c*) **Section B-B**

Point r:
$$s_i = \frac{Mh_i}{Aer_i} = \frac{(200\times 14)(0.5-0.019)}{8(0.019)(4)} = 2215 \text{ psi (compression)}$$

where $r_n = \dfrac{h}{\log_e r_o/r_i} = \dfrac{1}{\log_e 5/4} = 4.481''$, $e = R - r_n = 4.5 - 4.481 = 0.019''$

Point s:
$$s_o = \frac{Mh_o}{Aer_o} = \frac{(200\times 14)(0.5+0.019)}{8(0.019)(5)} = 1910 \text{ psi (tension)}$$

(*d*) **Section C-C**

Point t: At point t the stress due to bending is compression and the direct stress is tension. Hence the stresses subtract from each other. The bending stress at point t is

$$s_o = \frac{Mh_o}{Aer_o} = \frac{(200\times 9.5)(0.5+0.024)}{8(0.024)(4)} = 1300 \text{ psi (compression)}$$

where $r_n = \dfrac{h}{\log_e r_o/r_i} = \dfrac{1}{\log_e 4/3} = 3.476''$, $\quad e = R - r_n = 3.5 - 3.476 = 0.024''$

$P/A = 200/8 = 25$ psi

Net stress = 1300 − 25 = 1275 psi (compression)

Point u:

$$s_i = \frac{Mh_i}{Aer_i} = \frac{(200\times 9.5)(0.5-0.024)}{8(0.024)(3)} = 1570 \text{ psi (tension)}$$

$P/A = 200/8 = 25$ psi

Total stress = 1570 + 25 = 1595 psi (tension)

(e) The maximum stress occurs at the straight portion, section A-A, and is 3000 psi (tension at point q and compression at point p).

The maximum shear occurs at both points p and q and is $\frac{1}{2}(3000) = 1500$ psi.

SUPPLEMENTARY PROBLEMS

8. Interference of machine parts necessitated the use of a steel member as shown in Fig. 4-9 below. If a load of 175 lb is applied, determine the maximum tensile stress and maximum shear stress and indicate the location. *Ans.* 2670 psi, 1335 psi; both occur at point A

9. A portable hydraulic riveter has a maximum riveting force of 15,000 lb. The U frame is made of cast steel with an ultimate tensile stress of 70,000 psi and a yield point in tension of 35,000 psi. Referring to Fig. 4-10 below, consider only the section A-A and determine the following:
   (a) bending moment
   (b) distance from centroidal axis to neutral axis
   (c) direct tensile force
   (d) maximum tensile stress and location
   (e) maximum shear stress and location

   Ans. (a) 159,000 in-lb
   (b) 0.334″
   (c) 10,600 lb
   (d) 17,860 psi at point P
   (e) 8930 psi at point P

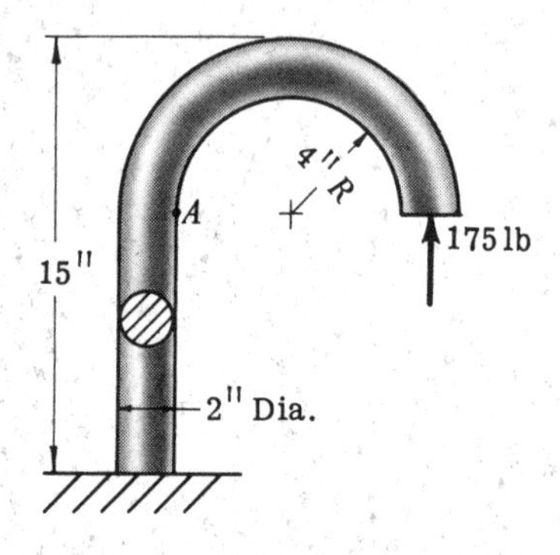

Fig. 4-9

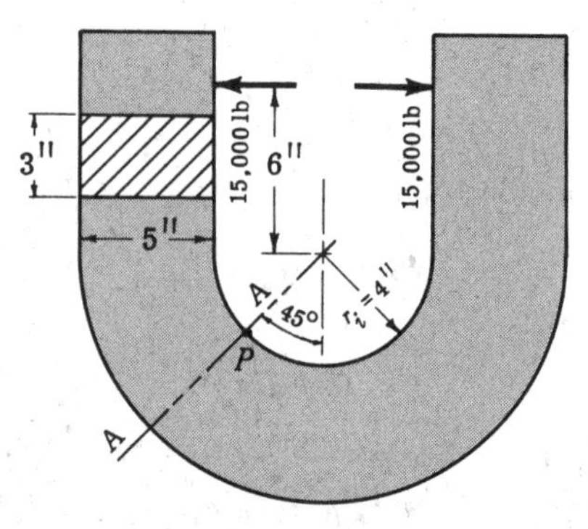

Fig. 4-10

10. A ring is made from a 3 inch diameter bar. The inside diameter of the ring is 4 inches. For the load shown in Fig. 4-11 below, calculate the maximum shear stress in the bar, and specify its location.
Ans. 4210 psi at point A

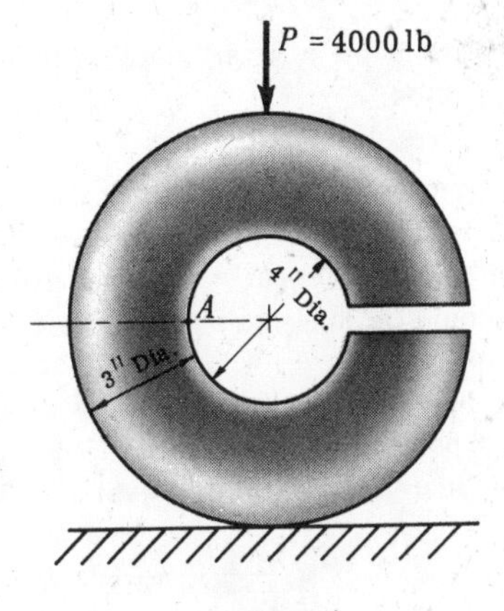

Fig. 4-11

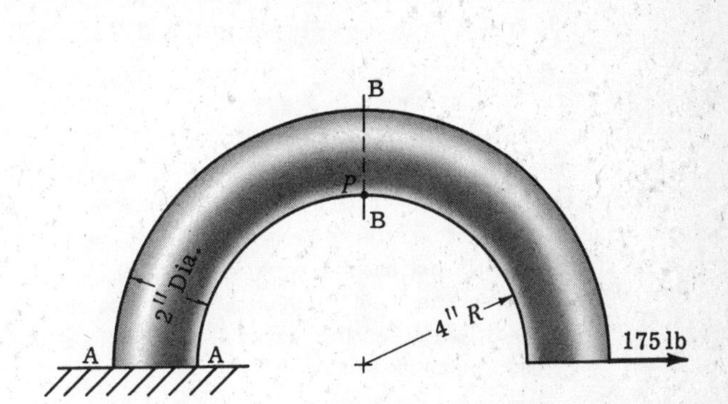

Fig. 4-12

11. Determine the magnitude and location of the maximum tensile stress of the machine part loaded as shown in Fig. 4-12 above. *Ans.* 1360 psi at point P

12. Consider a crane hook made from a two-inch diameter bar and loaded as shown in Fig. 4-13 below. Determine the maximum tensile stress and specify its location. *Ans.* 5680 psi at point A

13. A machine member is made from a one-inch diameter rod and is loaded as shown in Fig. 4-14 below.

(*a*) Where does the maximum tensile stress occur?	*Ans.* (*a*) point P on section A-A
(*b*) What is the bending moment at the worst stressed section?	(*b*) 210 in-lb
(*c*) What is the direct load at the worst stressed section?	(*c*) 20 lb
(*d*) What is the maximum tensile stress?	(*d*) 2430 psi

14. The supporting structure of a movable 1 ton crane has the dimensions as shown in Fig. 4-15. Determine the following: (*a*) location of the maximum compressive stress, (*b*) location of the maximum shear stress, (*c*) bending moment at section A-A, (*d*) direct compressive load at section A-A, (*e*) maximum compressive stress, *f*) maximum shear stress. *Ans.* (*a*) point P on section A-A, (*b*) point P on section A-A, (*c*) 71,000 in-lb, (*d*) 2000 lb, (*e*) 4800 psi, (*f*) 2400 psi

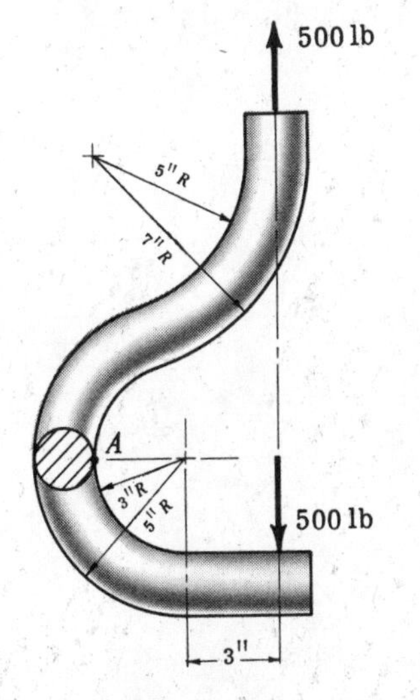

Fig. 4-13

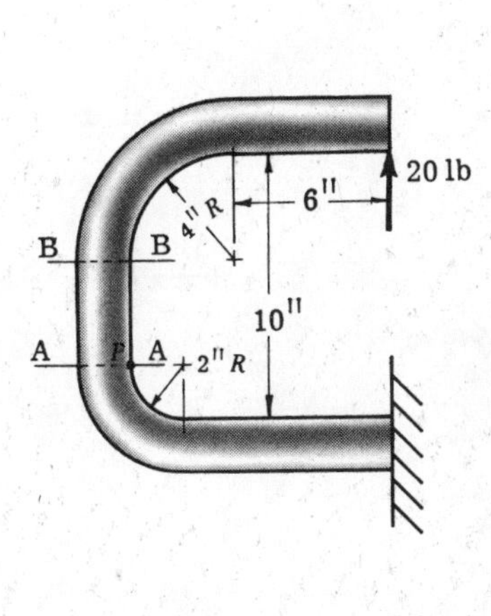

Fig. 4-14

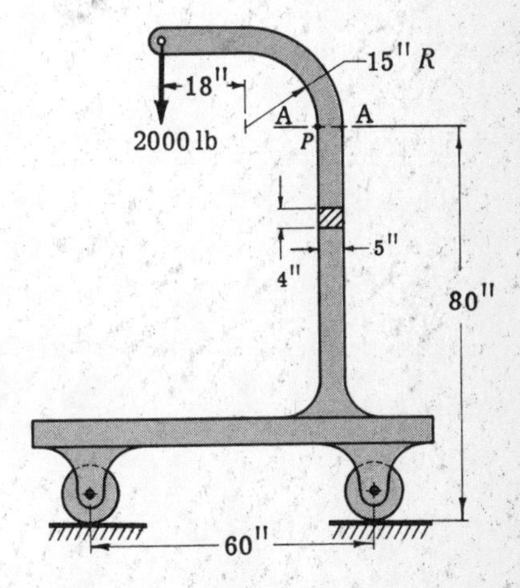

Fig. 4-15

15. The *centerline* of the supporting beam of the undercarriage of a crane is as shown in Fig. 4-16 below. The beam is supported in bearings at C and D. Consider the beam as made from a 2-inch diameter bar. (*a*) What are the reactions at C and D? (*b*) How does the bending moment at sections perpendicular to the axis of the beam vary between A and B? (*c*) Determine the worst stressed section or sections. (*d*) What is the maximum stress?

Ans. (*a*) Reaction at C = 1000 lb, at D = 1000 lb. (*b*) Bending moment is the same at every section from A to B, 10,000 in-lb. (*c*) From A to E and F to B. (*d*) 15,700 psi tension.

16. In the small C-clamp shown in Fig. 4-17 below, a force W = 1000 lb is exerted between the C-clamp and screw. (*a*) If the maximum allowable shear stress is 7,500 psi, the maximum allowable tensile stress is 15,000 psi and the maximum allowable compressive stress is 15,000 psi, is the C-clamp properly designed from the standpoint of strength? (*b*) If the design is not proper, what changes could be made to improve the design? Assume that the analysis is to be made after the screw has been tightened.

Ans. (*a*) Design is not satisfactory, since the maximum tensile stress is 45,300 psi and the allowable tensile stress is 15,000 psi (or the maximum shear stress is 22,700 psi and the allowable is 7,500 psi).
(*b*) *1.* A different section, as an I or T section might be used. *2.* Increase radius of curvature. *3.* Increase diameter of C-clamp.

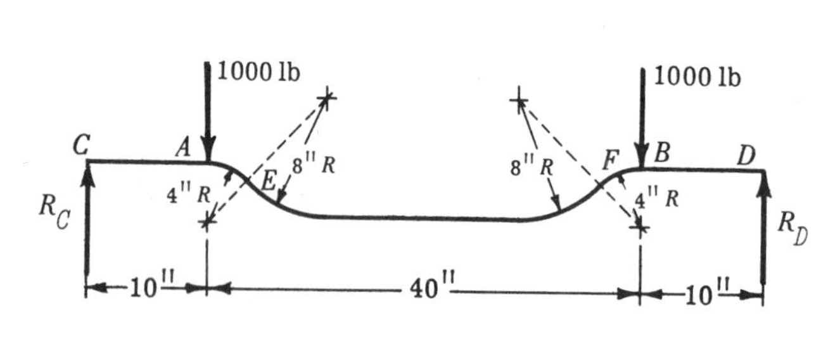

Fig. 4-16

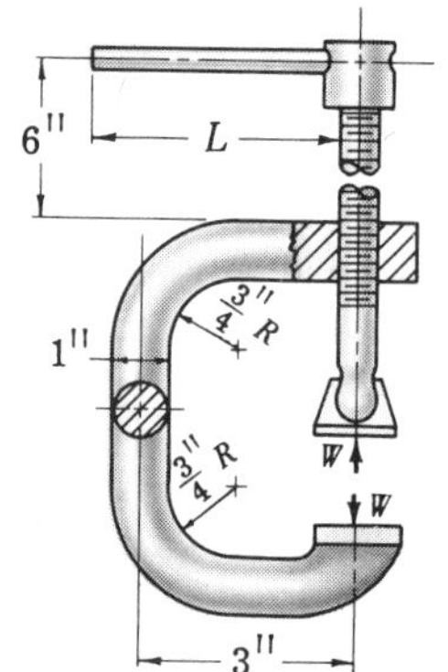

Fig. 4-17

17. A crane hook has a section which, for purposes of analysis, is considered trapezoidal. The maximum tension (and shear) stress occur at point P, as shown in Fig. 4-18 below. Determine the (*a*) distance R from the center of curvature to the centroidal axis, (*b*) bending moment for section A-A, (*c*) distance from the center of curvature to the neutral axis, (*d*) area, (*e*) maximum tensile stress (point P), (*f*) maximum stress at point Q.
Ans. (*a*) 4.33'', (*b*) 86,600 in-lb, (*c*) 4.0'', (*d*) $10\frac{1}{8}$ sq in., (*e*) 17,500 psi, (*f*) 9130 psi (compression)

18. A link is offset, as shown in Fig. 4-19 below, to provide clearance for adjacent parts. Determine the maximum shear stress and specify its location (or locations). *Ans.* 1970 psi; points A and B

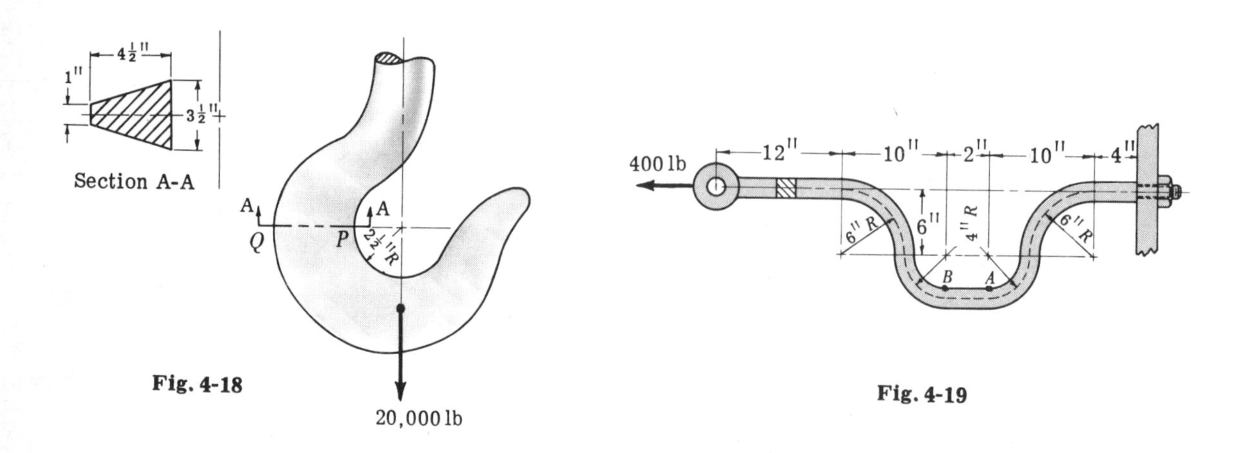

Fig. 4-18

Fig. 4-19

Chapter 5

Deflection and Buckling of Machine Members

RIGIDITY may in some cases determine the design of a machine member. The member may be strong enough to prevent a stress failure, but may not be sufficiently rigid for satisfactory operation. The following topics will discuss rigidity from the standpoint of axial deflection, torsional deflection, deflection due to bending, deflection due to shear, and buckling due to column effect.

AXIAL DEFLECTION δ due to an axial load F is based on Hooke's Law,

$$s = \left(\frac{\delta}{L}\right)(E) = \frac{F}{A}$$

from which

$$\delta = \frac{FL}{AE}$$

where

δ = axial deflection, inches

L = axial length of member before application of the axial load, inches

A = cross sectional area, in^2

E = modulus of elasticity, psi

TORSIONAL DEFLECTION $\theta°$ due to a torsional load on a solid circular section is

$$\theta° = \frac{584\,TL}{GD^4}$$

For a hollow member of circular cross section, the angular deflection is

$$\theta° = \frac{584\,TL}{G(D_o^4 - D_i^4)}$$

where

$\theta°$ = torsional deflection, degrees

T = torque, in-lb

D = diameter of solid member, inches

D_o = outside diameter of hollow member, inches

D_i = inside diameter of hollow member, inches

L = axial length of member between the applied and resisting torques, inches

G = modulus of rigidity, psi

For a solid rectangular member the torsional deflection is

$$\theta^\circ = \frac{57.3\,TL}{abc^3 G}$$

where

b = long side of rectangle, in.
c = short side of rectangle, in.
a = a factor depending upon the ratio of b/c as follows:

b/c =	1.000	1.500	1.750	2.000	2.500	3.000	4.000	6.000	8.000	10.000	∞
a =	0.141	0.196	0.214	0.229	0.249	0.263	0.281	0.299	0.307	0.313	0.333

G = modulus of rigidity, psi.
L = length of member, in.

LATERAL DEFLECTION due to bending only may be determined by solving the differential equation of the elastic curve of the neutral axis,

$$\frac{d^2y}{dx^2} = \frac{M}{EI}$$

where

M = the bending moment, in-lb
I = the rectangular moment of inertia, in^4
E = modulus of elasticity, psi
y = deflection, in.
x = distance from end of member to the section where the deflection is to be determined, in.

A straight analytical solution of this equation by double integration is quite tedious for multiple loads and for beams that have changes in cross section. Easier solutions may usually be obtained by resorting to other methods such as: area moment method, conjugate beam method, the use of step functions, application of the theorem of Castigliano, or by graphical integration.

THE AREA MOMENT method for determining the deflection of a beam due to bending is based on the proposition that the vertical distance of any point A on the elastic curve of a beam from the tangent at any other point B on the elastic curve is equal to the moment with respect to the ordinate at A of the area of the M/EI diagram between the points A and B. (See Fig. 5-1.)

$$\Delta = A_1\bar{x}_1 + A_2\bar{x}_2 + \ldots.$$

where

A_1 = area of portion I of the M/EI diagram
$\bar{x}_1$ = distance from the ordinate at point A to the center of gravity of A_1
A_2 = area of portion II of the M/EI diagram
$\bar{x}_2$ = distance from the ordinate at point A to the center of gravity of A_2.

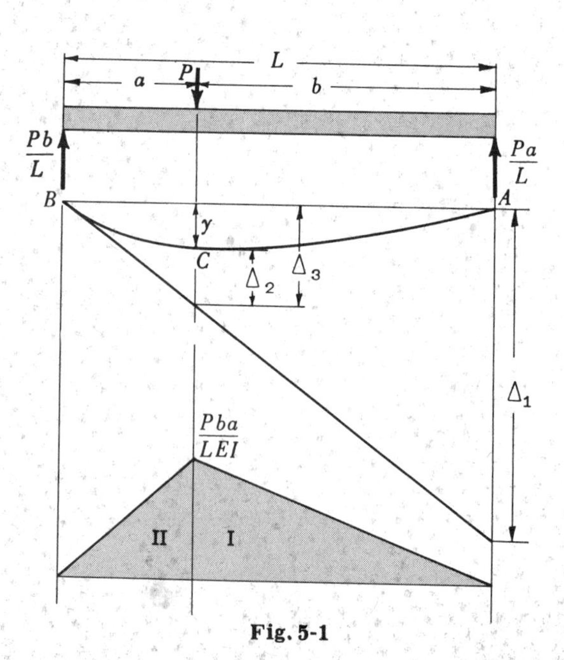

Fig. 5-1

A simple beam of length L having a concentrated load P located at a distance a from the left support and at a distance b from the right support may be used to illustrate the above procedure. Referring to Fig. 5-1, in order to determine the deflection y under the load P complete the following steps:

1. Sketch the elastic curve.
2. Sketch a tangent to the elastic curve at point B located at the left reaction.
3. Sketch the M/EI diagram.
4. Determine Δ_1 by summing the moments of the areas of section I and section II with respect to the right support:

$$\Delta_1 = \left(\frac{Pb^2a}{2LEI}\right)\left(\frac{2b}{3}\right) + \left(\frac{Pba^2}{2LEI}\right)\left(b + \frac{a}{3}\right) = \frac{Pb^3a}{3LEI} + \frac{Pb^2a^2}{2LEI} + \frac{Pba^3}{6LEI}$$

5. Determine Δ_2 which is equal to the moment of section II with respect to a vertical axis through point C:

$$\Delta_2 = \left(\frac{Pba^2}{2LEI}\right)\left(\frac{a}{3}\right) = \frac{Pba^3}{6LEI}$$

6. Determine Δ_3 by proportion:

$$\Delta_3 = \frac{a\,\Delta_1}{L} = \frac{Pb^3a^2}{3L^2EI} + \frac{Pb^2a^3}{2L^2EI} + \frac{Pba^4}{6L^2EI}$$

7. Then $y = \Delta_3 - \Delta_2 = \dfrac{Pb^3a^2}{3L^2EI} + \dfrac{Pb^2a^3}{2L^2EI} + \dfrac{Pba^4}{6L^2EI} - \dfrac{Pba^3}{6LEI}$.

It should be noted that in the above illustration the areas of both section I and section II are positive. If any part of the M/EI diagram is negative, then the moment of that part of the M/EI diagram must be taken as negative.

THE CONJUGATE BEAM method for determining the lateral deflection due to bending of a beam is based on the mathematical similarity of the loading, shear, and bending moment diagrams to the M/EI loading, slope, and deflection diagrams:

$$f(x) = w = \frac{dV}{dx} = \frac{d^2M}{dx^2}, \qquad f(x) = \frac{M}{EI} = \frac{d\alpha}{dx} = \frac{d^2y}{dx^2}$$

Due to the similarity of the above equations, the following statements are the basis of the solution:

1. The "shear" force of the conjugate beam is equivalent to the slope of the actual beam.
2. The "bending moment" of the conjugate beam is equivalent to the deflection of the actual beam.

It is necessary, however, to first set up the conjugate beam such that boundary conditions are satisfied. Where the slope of the original beam is not zero, a "shearing" force on the conjugate beam must exist. If the loading is such that no "shear" is present, a "shear" force must be inserted in the conjugate beam loading. Similarly with the deflection – if the deflection is not zero, a "moment" must exist. If the loading is such that no "moment" is present, a "moment" must be inserted in the conjugate beam loading.

In order to demonstrate the above procedure, consider a cantilever beam having a constant cross section and a concentrated load P at the end as shown in Fig. 5-2 below. The following steps will determine the deflection at the end of the beam:

a. Sketch the bending moment diagram.

b. Load the conjugate beam so that the intensity of load at any section is equal to the ordinate of M/EI.

c. In order to satisfy the boundary conditions, there must be a value of slope, or "shear", at the section of the conjugate beam under the load P represented by the reaction "R". In order for a deflection, or "moment", to exist at the reaction, there must be a "moment"("M") applied at the right end of the beam.

d. The triangular distributed "load" on the conjugate beam may then be considered as equivalent to the area of this triangle, $PL^2/2EI$, concentrated at the centroid of the triangle.

e. By summation of vertical "forces", the "reaction" at the right end of the beam is $PL^2/2EI$.

f. Taking moments at the right end of the conjugate beam, we have

$$-\frac{PL^2}{2EI}\left(\frac{2L}{3}\right) + "M" = 0$$

or "M" $= PL^3/3EI$ which is the deflection at the right end of the beam.

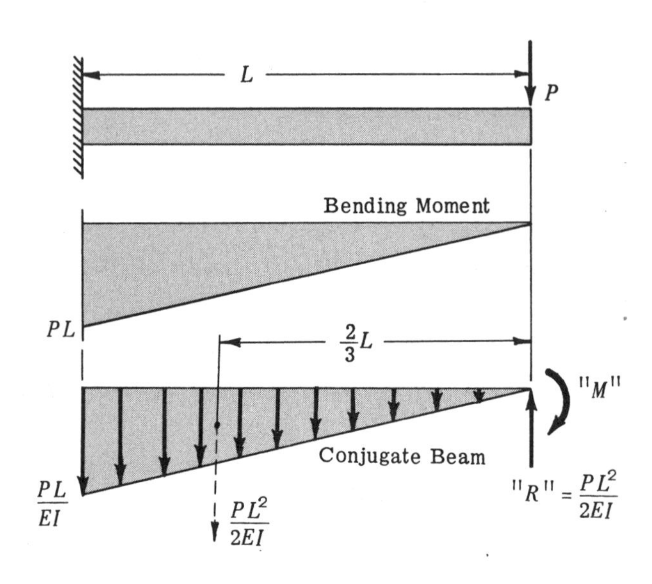

Fig. 5-2

APPLICATION OF STEP FUNCTIONS for determining the deflection of a beam due to bending requires the evaluation of only two constants of integration for a beam subjected to any number of loads and changes of section. In applying the usual double integration method of writing the M/EI equation in each section of a beam, one must evaluate two constants of integration for each section.

The use of step functions provides a means of writing mathematically a single expression for M/EI that is valid for any section of the beam, which, after double integration, results in a single expression for deflection valid for any section of the beam.

A step function, as used later, is defined by the following notation:

H_a is a step function where $H_a = 0$ if $x < a$
$H_a = 1$ if $x \geqq a$

H_b is a step function where $H_b = 0$ if $x < b$
$H_b = 1$ if $x \geqq b$

The product of the two step functions then is, for $b>a$,

$$H_aH_b = 0 \text{ if } x < b$$
$$H_aH_b = 1 \text{ if } x \geqq b$$

A plot of the above step functions is shown in Fig. 5-3.

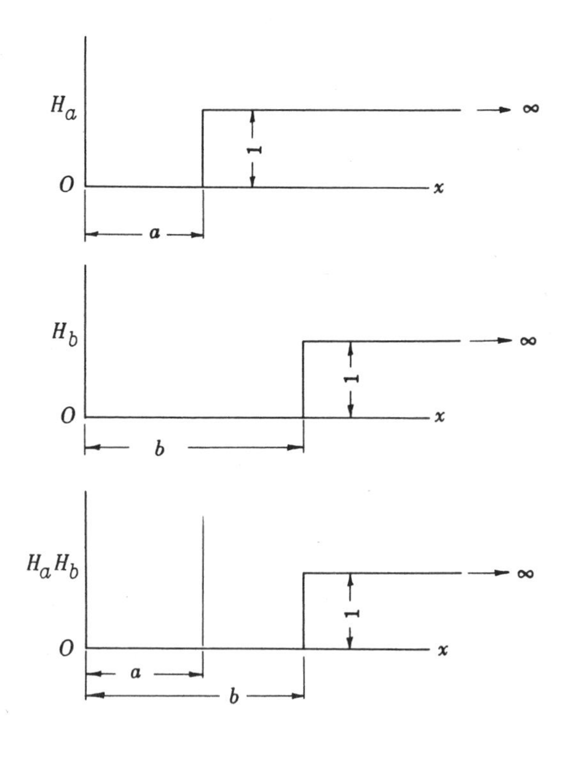

Fig. 5-3

The mathematical procedure for integrating a step function multiplied by a function $f(x)$ is

$$\int_0^x H_a f(x)\,dx = H_a \int_a^x f(x)\,dx$$

Example 1. Let $f(x) = x^2$.

$$\int_0^x H_a x^2\,dx = H_a \int_a^x x^2\,dx = \left[H_a \frac{x^3}{3}\right]_a^x + C = H_a \frac{x^3 - a^3}{3} + C$$

where C = constant of integration.

Example 2. When $b > a$,

$$\int_0^x H_b H_a (x-a)\,dx = H_b \int_b^x (x-a)\,dx$$

$$= H_b \left[\frac{(x-a)^2}{2}\right]_b^x + C = H_b \frac{(x-a)^2 - (b-a)^2}{2} + C$$

Example 3. The method of handling changes of section by means of step functions is demonstrated as follows: Fig. 5-4 shows a beam having three sections of different moments of inertia. F_1 and F_2 are overhung loads and there are fixed bearings at R_L and R_R. The moment equation valid for any section is

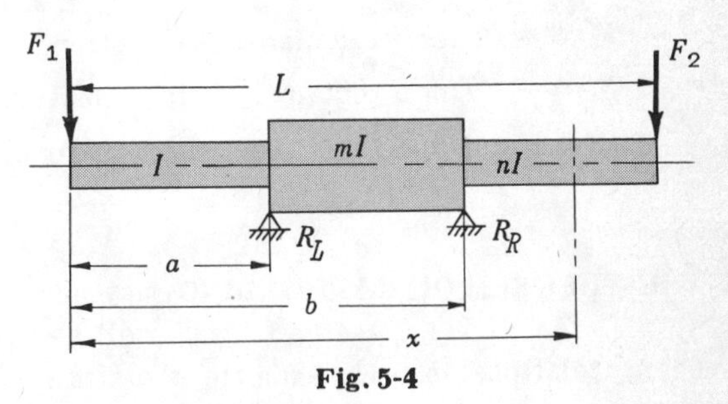

Fig. 5-4

$$M = -F_1 x + R_L (x-a) H_a + R_R (x-b) H_b$$

Now $1/I_x$, the reciprocal of the moment of inertia at any section, may be written

$$\frac{1}{I_x} = \frac{1}{I}\left[1 - H_a + \frac{H_a}{m} - \frac{H_b}{m} + \frac{H_b}{n}\right]$$

from which

$$IE\frac{d^2y}{dx^2} = \left[-F_1 x + R_L(x-a)H_a + R_R(x-b)H_b\right]\left[1 + H_a(\frac{1}{m} - 1) + H_b(-\frac{1}{m} + \frac{1}{n})\right]$$

$$= -F_1 x + R_L(x-a)H_a + R_R(x-b)H_b - F_1 x H_a(\frac{1}{m} - 1)$$

$$+ R_L(x-a)H_a H_a(\frac{1}{m} - 1) + R_R(x-b)H_b H_a(\frac{1}{m} - 1)$$

$$-F_1 x H_b(-\frac{1}{m} + \frac{1}{n}) + R_L(x-a)H_a H_b(-\frac{1}{m} + \frac{1}{n})$$

$$+ R_R(x-b)H_b H_b(-\frac{1}{m} + \frac{1}{n})$$

Double integration may be completed as explained above, noting that $H_a H_a = H_a$ and $H_a H_b = H_b$.

DEFLECTION DUE TO SHEAR may be significant, for example, in machine members which are short in comparison to their depth, or for large diameter hollow members. In such cases the deflection due to shear should be added to the deflection due to bending. This could be of considerable importance when calculating deflections for determining critical speeds of rotating members. An expression for the deflection y_1 due to shear may be determined by considering a differential element taken at the centroidal axis of a member subjected to a transverse load as shown in Fig. 5-5.

$$\frac{dy_1}{dx} = \frac{s_s \text{ (at neutral axis)}}{G} + C_1 = \frac{VQ_{max}}{IbG} + C_1$$

(See Chapter 2 for discussion of $\frac{VQ}{Ib}$.)

where C_1 is a constant which accounts for the angle of rotation of the cross sections with respect to the zero deflection line. (All cross sections rotate through the same angle.) Integrating,

$$y_1 = \frac{KVx}{AG} + C_1 x + C_2 \qquad \text{where } K = \frac{QA}{Ib}$$

$K = 4/3$ for a circular cross section,

$K = 3/2$ for a rectangular cross section.

(For Fig. 5-5, $C_1 = 0$. See Fig. 5-19 for illustration of C_1.)

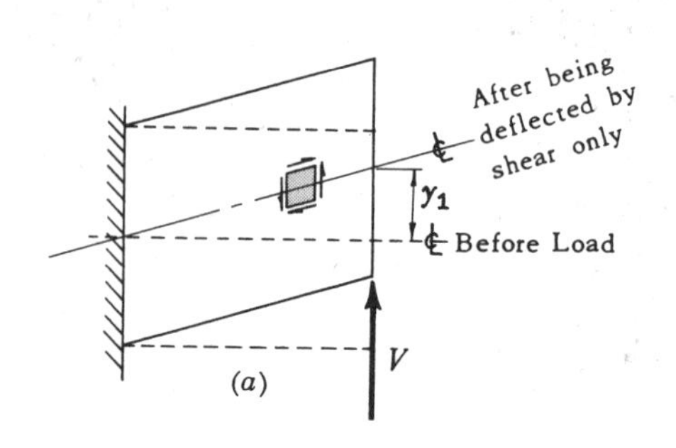

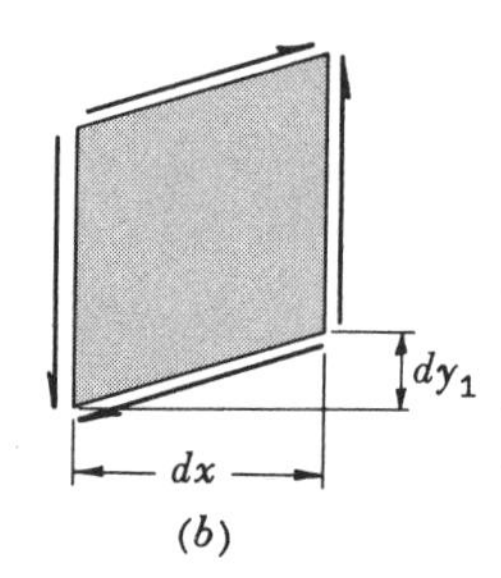

Fig. 5-5

THE THEOREM OF CASTIGLIANO may be used for determining the deflection of simple members as well as more complex structures. This theorem is based on strain energy relationships. For example, the strain energy U for a member of length L under simple tension is

$$U = \frac{F^2 L}{2AE}$$

and by taking the partial derivative of this expression with respect to F, we determine the axial deflection δ for the member in the direction of the applied force F:

$$\frac{\partial U}{\partial F} = \frac{FL}{AE} = \delta$$

Also, by taking the partial derivative of the torsional strain energy, we may determine the angle of twist for a member having a circular cross section when subjected to a torque T:

$$U = \frac{T^2 L}{2GJ} \quad \text{and} \quad \frac{\partial U}{\partial T} = \frac{TL}{GJ} = \theta \text{ (radians)}$$

In the above as well as in the following expressions, it is assumed that the material of the system follows Hooke's Law. The strain energy in a straight beam subjected to a bending moment M is

$$U = \int \frac{M^2\,dx}{2EI}$$

The strain energy in a curved beam subjected to a bending moment M is

$$U = \int \frac{M^2\,d\phi}{2AeE}$$

The strain energy in a straight member subjected to a transverse shearing force V is

$$U = \int \frac{KV^2\,dx}{2AG}$$

The strain energy in a curved beam subjected to a transverse shearing force V is

$$U = \int \frac{KV^2\,ds}{2AG} = \int \frac{KV^2 R\,d\phi}{2AG}$$

Referring to Fig. 5-6 below, the differential energy stored in the differential section due to the bending moment M, the normal force P, and the shearing force V, may be written

$$dU = \frac{M^2\,d\phi}{2AeE} + \left(\frac{P^2R\,d\phi}{2AE} - \frac{MP\,d\phi}{AE}\right) + \frac{KV^2R\,d\phi}{2AG}$$

where

$\dfrac{M^2\,d\phi}{2AeE}$ = the strain energy due to the bending moment M acting alone.

$\dfrac{P^2R\,d\phi}{2AE}$ = the strain energy due to the normal force P acting alone.

$-\dfrac{MP\,d\phi}{AE}$ = the strain energy resulting from the fact that P tends to rotate the faces of the element against the resisting couples M.

Note that in the case of Fig. 5-6, this term is negative since the force P tends to increase the angle between the two faces, while the couples M tend to decrease the angle between the two faces of the section. If the sense of P were reversed, then both P and the couples M would tend to decrease the angle between the two faces.

$\dfrac{KV^2R\,d\phi}{2AG}$ = the strain energy due to the shearing force V.

Application of the above expressions will solve deflection problems based on the theorem of Castigliano which states that the partial derivative of strain energy with respect to any force (or couple) gives the displacement (or angle of twist) corresponding to the force (or couple). In other words, if the total strain energy of a system is written as a function of one or more forces, then the deflection in the direction of any selected force may be determined by taking the partial derivative of the total strain energy with respect to the particular force selected. Also, if the total strain energy is a function of a couple as well as one or more forces, then the partial derivative of the total strain energy with respect to the couple will give the angle of rotation of the section on which the couple acts. The theorem of Castigliano may also be used to find the deflection at a point, where no load exists in the direction of the desired deflection, by adding a load Q at the selected point and in the direction in which the deflection is required. Then the partial derivative $\partial U/\partial Q$ will give the desired deflection when Q is made equal to zero.

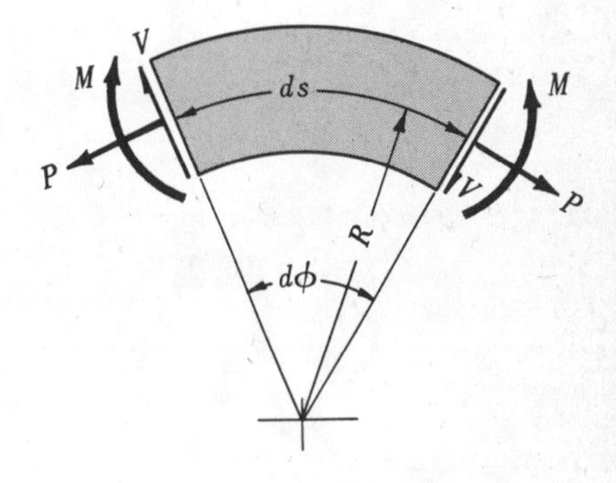

Fig. 5-6

GRAPHICAL INTEGRATION is another method to obtain a deflection curve for a shaft subjected to bending loads. The method is illustrated by the following simplified example with the following steps. Refer to Fig. 5-7.

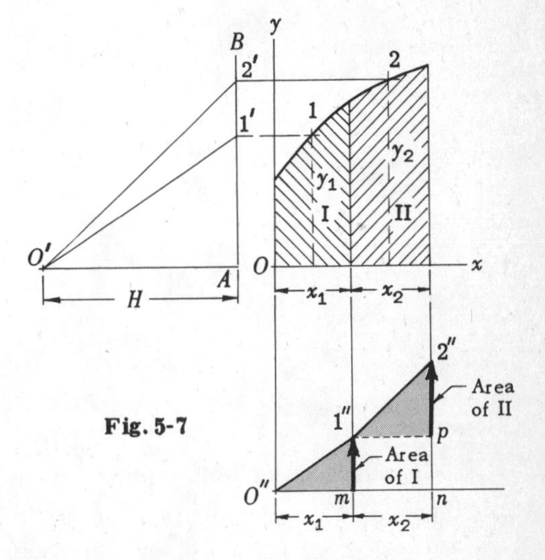

Fig. 5-7

1. Divide the area into sections, with ordinates y_1, y_2, etc., at the midpoints of x_1, x_2, etc., to locate points 1, 2, etc. (x_1 need not be equal to x_2, although these are usually taken equal for simplification in drafting).
2. Project from points 1, 2, etc., to locate points 1′, 2′, etc., on any vertical line AB. From any point O' on the horizontal axis (thus determining distance H), draw rays O'-1′, O'-2′, etc.

3. Draw line O''-1$''$ parallel to line O'-1$'$ and line 1$''$- 2$''$ parallel to O'- 2$'$. Line m-1$''$ is proportional to area I and line p-2$''$ is proportional to area II, or, line n-2$''$ is proportional to the sum of the areas I and II.

4. The proof is obtained from the property of similar triangles. Consider triangles O'-A-1$'$ and O''-m-1$''$:

$$\frac{A-1'}{O'-A} = \frac{m-1''}{O''-m} \quad \text{or} \quad \frac{y_1}{H} = \frac{m-1''}{x_1} \quad \text{or} \quad m-1'' = \frac{x_1 y_1}{H}$$

or the area $x_1 y_1 = H(m-1'')$. Thus the vertical distance $m-1''$ is proportional to the area of I, which is approximated by $(x_1 y_1)$. If the distance x_1 *is* small, the approximation is very close to the true area. Thus the smaller the divisions, the closer the approximation is to the true area.

5. In a similar manner,

$$p-2'' = \frac{x_2 y_2}{H}$$

or the area $x_2 y_2 = H(p-2'')$. Then the total intercept $n-2''$ is the sum of the two areas shown.

6. The above procedure is illustrated for two cases:
   - (*a*) Beam supported at the ends, Fig. 5-8(*a*) below, diameters given.
   - (*b*) Beam with an overhung load, Fig. 5-8(*b*) below, diameters not given.

Example (*a*). Determine the deflection at each load. Use double integration, graphically.

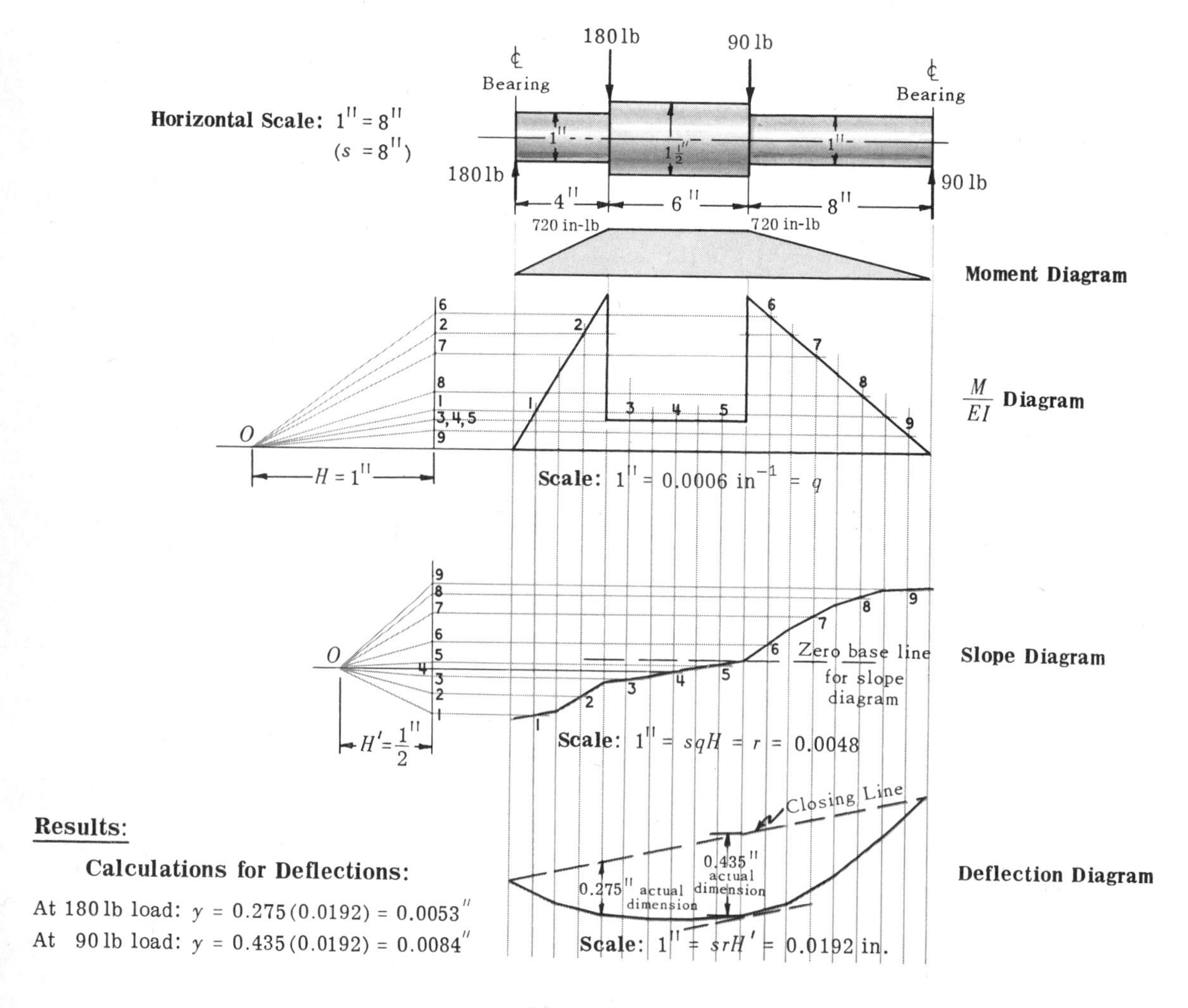

Fig. 5-8(*a*)

Example (*b*). Determine diameter D to limit the deflection at the 90 lb load to 0.001''. Use double integration, graphically. The moment of inertia of the sections of diameter D is I.

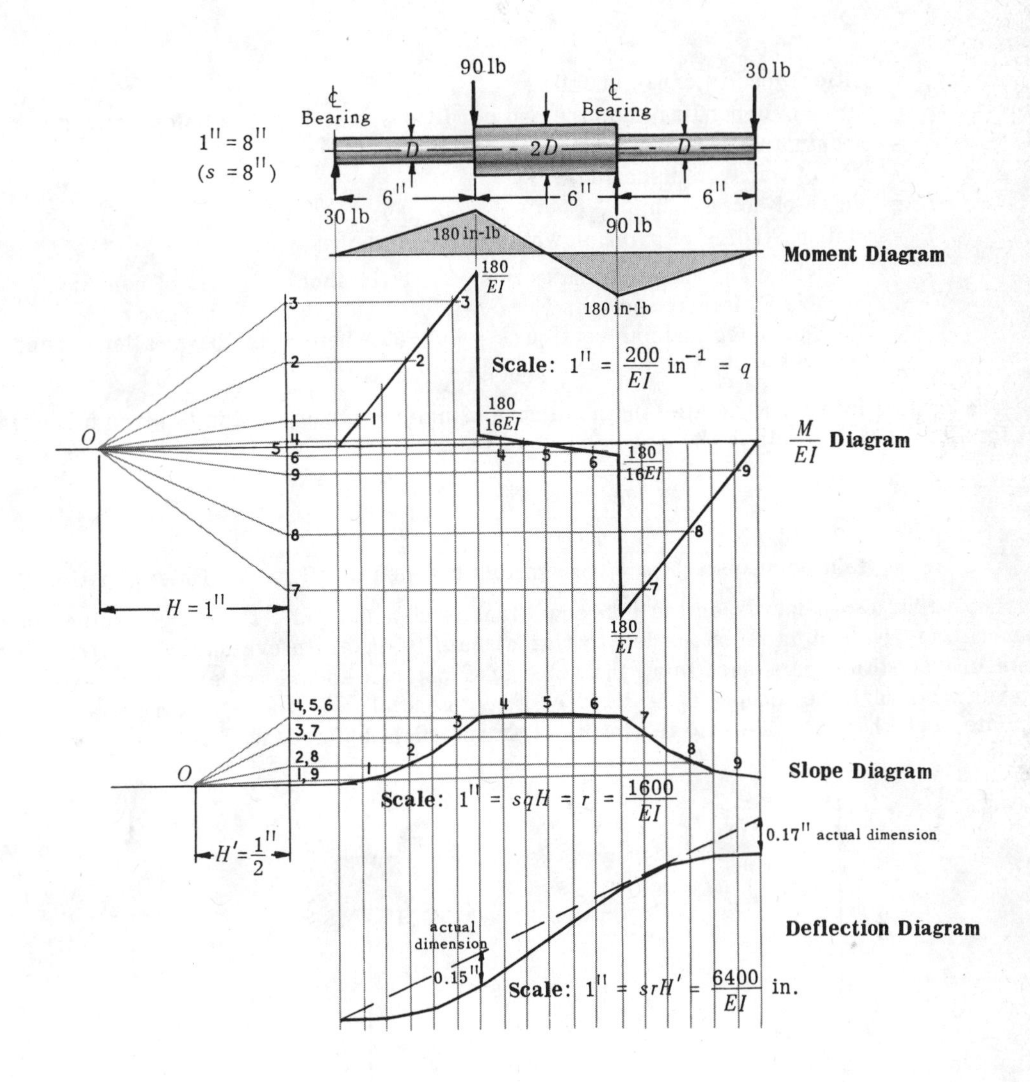

Result:

Deflection at 90 lb load is $y = (0.15)(\frac{6400}{EI})$.

If the deflection at the 90 lb load is limited to 0.001'',
$I = 0.032\text{ in}^4$ for $E = 30 \times 10^6$ psi, or $D = 0.90''$.

Fig. 5-8 (*b*)

COLUMN ACTION due to axial loading of machine parts occurs very frequently. If the axial load is a tensile load, then the application of $S = P/A$ is in order. If the axial load is a compressive load, then an appropriate column equation should be used.

The Euler equation for the critical load for slender columns of uniform cross section is

$$F_{cr} = \frac{C\pi^2 EA}{(L/k)^2}$$

where

F_{cr} = critical load to cause buckling.
C = constant depending upon the end conditions (see Fig. 5-9 below for values).
E = modulus of elasticity, psi.
A = area of transverse section, in.^{2}
L = length of column, in.
k = minimum radius of gyration which is $\sqrt{I/A}$ inches,
where I is the minimum moment of inertia about the axis of bending.
For a circular section, $k = D/4$.
For a rectangular section $k = h\sqrt{3}/6$, where h is the smaller dimension of the rectangle.

The critical load for moderate length columns of uniform cross section is given by several empirical formulas, one of which is the J. B. Johnson formula:

$$F_{cr} = s_y A\left(1 - \frac{s_y (L/k)^2}{4C\pi^2 E}\right)$$

where

s_y = yield point, psi. The other symbols are as defined for the Euler equation.

The value of C depends on the end conditions, Fig. 5-9. While theoretical values of C greater than one are given, it is recommended that great care be taken in evaluating the fixity of the ends. Where end conditions are uncertain, the value of C perhaps should not exceed a value of around 2, for even what might be thought of as fixed ends. In general, $C = 1$ as a maximum value might be appropriate, and where considerable flexibility of an end might be present, a value of $C = \frac{1}{4}$ might be desirable.

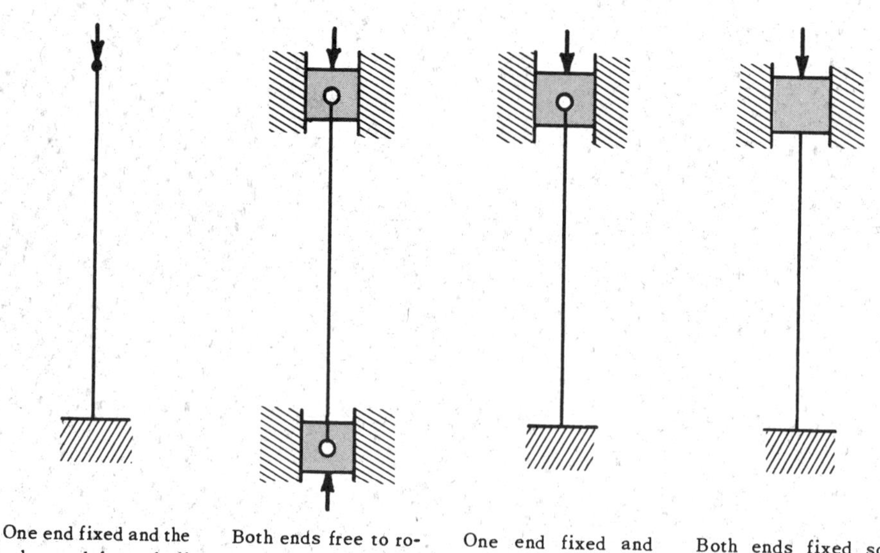

One end fixed and the other end free of all restraint $C = \frac{1}{4}$

Both ends free to rotate, but not free to move laterally (so-called round, or pivot, or hinged end columns) $C = 1$

One end fixed and one end free to rotate, but not free to move laterally $C = 2$

Both ends fixed so that the tangent to the elastic curve at each end is parallel to the original axis of the column $C = 4$

Fig. 5-9

The safe load is obtained by dividing the critical load by a factor of safety N:

$$\text{Safe load } F\text{, Euler equation:} \qquad F = \frac{F_{cr}}{N} = \frac{C\pi^2 EA}{N(L/k)^2}$$

$$\text{Safe load } F\text{, J. B. Johnson equation:} \qquad F = \frac{s_y A}{N}\left(1 - \frac{s_y (L/k)^2}{4C\pi^2 E}\right)$$

The value of L/k which determines whether the Euler equation or J. B. Johnson equation should be used is found by equating the critical load from the Euler equation to the critical load from the J. B. Johnson formula:

$$\frac{C\pi^2 EA}{(L/k)^2} = s_y A\left(1 - \frac{s_y (L/k)^2}{4C\pi^2 E}\right) \qquad \text{from which} \qquad L/k = \sqrt{\frac{2C\pi^2 E}{s_y}}$$

The value of L/k above which the Euler equation should be used and below which the J. B. Johnson formula should be used, for different representative data are:

C	E	s_y	$(L/k)^2$	(L/k)
$\frac{1}{4}$	30×10^6 psi	80,000 psi	1,849	43
		70,000	2,113	46
		60,000	2,465	50
		50,000	2,958	54
		40,000	3,697	61
1	30×10^6 psi	80,000 psi	7,394	86
		70,000	8,451	92
		60,000	9,860	99
		50,000	11,832	109
		40,000	14,789	121
2	30×10^6 psi	80,000 psi	14,789	121
		70,000	16,902	130
		60,000	19,719	140
		50,000	23,663	154
		40,000	29,579	172

If L/k is below that given by $\sqrt{2C\pi^2 E/s_y}$, use the J. B. Johnson formula, which is valid down to $L/k = 0$.

Equivalent Column Stresses are used where column action is to be combined with other effects as torsion and bending. The equivalent stress is a fictitious stress related to the yield point stress in the same way as the actual load is related to the critical load. The equivalent column stress for an actual load F, derived from Euler's equation, is

$$s_{eq} = \frac{F}{A}\left(\frac{s_y (L/k)^2}{C\pi^2 E}\right) = \frac{F}{A}\alpha \qquad \text{where } \alpha = \frac{s_y (L/k)^2}{C\pi^2 E}$$

Note that the equivalent stress depends upon the yield point stress, whereas the critical load is independent of the yield point. If a column is of given proportions and length, changing materials does not change the critical load, whereas the equivalent stress changes. The ratio of the actual load to the critical load is the same, however, as the ratio of the equivalent stress to the yield point stress.

The equivalent column stress for an actual load F, derived from J. B. Johnson's equation, is

$$s_{eq} = \frac{F}{A}\left(\frac{1}{1 - \frac{s_y (L/k)^2}{4C\pi^2 E}}\right) = \frac{F}{A}\alpha \qquad \text{where } \alpha = \frac{1}{1 - \frac{s_y (L/k)^2}{4C\pi^2 E}}$$

In the equivalent stress equations, the following relations hold, with the symbols as defined above:

$$\frac{F_{cr}}{F} = \frac{s_y}{s_{eq}} = N$$

SOLVED PROBLEMS

1. Derive an expression for the elastic strain energy of bending in a straight beam.

Solution:

The change of angle $d\alpha$ between two transverse planes at a distance dx apart in a straight beam subjected to a bending moment M is $d\alpha = M\,dx/EI$. The strain energy in the section of the beam of length dx is

$$dU = \frac{M\,d\alpha}{2} = \frac{M^2\,dx}{2EI} \qquad \text{or} \qquad U = \int \frac{M^2\,dx}{2EI}$$

2. Derive an expression for the elastic strain energy of bending in a curved beam.

Solution:

The change of angle $d\alpha$ between two transverse planes separated by an angle $d\phi$ in a curved beam subjected to a bending moment M is $d\alpha = M\,d\phi/AeE$, where e is the distance from the centroidal axis to the neutral axis, always measured from the centroidal axis toward the center of curvature. The strain energy in the section between the two planes is

$$dU = \frac{M\,d\alpha}{2} = \frac{M^2\,d\phi}{2AeE} \qquad \text{or} \qquad U = \int \frac{M^2\,d\phi}{2AeE}$$

3. Determine that the deflection due to bending at the load P located at the end of a cantilever beam of length L is $PL^3/3EI$ by using
(*a*) double integration, (*b*) area moment method, (*c*) the theorem of Castigliano.

Solution:

(*a*) **Using double integration.**

The equation of the elastic curve is

$$EI\frac{d^2y}{dx^2} = M = -Px$$

where x is measured from the load toward the support. Integrating once, we have

$$EI\frac{dy}{dx} = \frac{-Px^2}{2} + C_1$$

Since the slope is zero at $x = L$, $C_1 = PL^2/2$ and

$$EI\frac{dy}{dx} = \frac{-Px^2}{2} + \frac{PL^2}{2}$$

The second integration gives

$$EIy = \frac{-Px^3}{6} + \frac{PL^2x}{2} + C_2$$

Since $y = 0$ at $x = L$, $C_2 = -PL^3/3$ and

$$EIy = \frac{-Px^3}{6} + \frac{PL^2x}{2} - \frac{PL^3}{3}$$

and for $x = 0$,

$$y = \frac{-PL^3}{3EI}$$

(*b*) **Using area moment method, Fig. 5-10.**

(*1*) Sketch the beam showing load P.

(*2*) Sketch the elastic curve and draw a tangent to the curve at point B.

(*3*) Sketch the M/EI diagram.

(*4*) The deflection y is then obtained by taking the moment of the area of the M/EI between points A and B with respect to point A. The moment arm of this area is $2L/3$. The area is $-PL^2/2EI$. Then

$$y = \left(\frac{2L}{3}\right)\left(\frac{-PL^2}{2EI}\right) = \frac{-PL^3}{3EI}$$

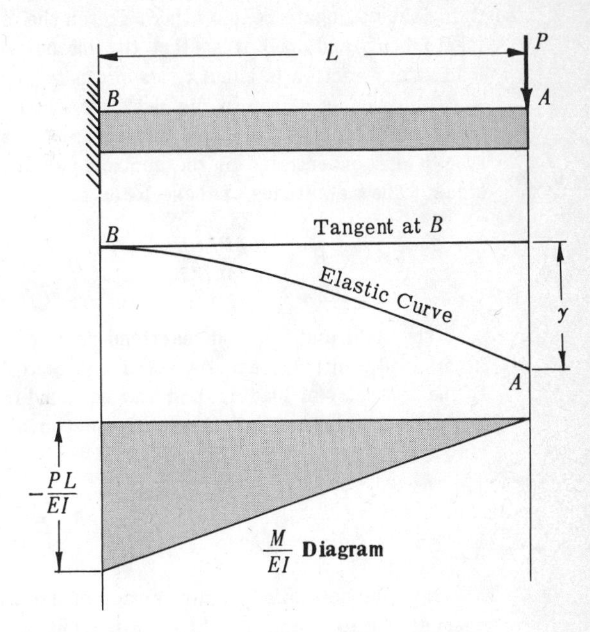

Fig. 5-10

(*c*) **Using the Castigliano theorem.**

The strain energy stored in a straight beam subjected to a bending moment M is

$$U = \int \frac{M^2\,dx}{2EI}.$$

Since the moment is $-Px$,

$$U = \int_0^L \frac{(-Px)^2\,dx}{2EI} = \frac{P^2L^3}{6EI}.$$

Then the deflection is obtained by taking the partial derivative $\frac{\partial U}{\partial P}$: $\quad y = \frac{\partial U}{\partial P} = \frac{2PL^3}{6EI} = \frac{PL^3}{3EI}$

A plus value of deflection means that the deflection is in the direction of the load, which is downward for this problem.

4. Determine that the deflection at the load due to bending of a simply supported beam having a concentrated load of P at its mid-length is $PL^3/48EI$ (*a*) by using the area moment method, (*b*) by using the conjugate beam method, (*c*) by using step functions, (*d*) by using the theorem of Castigliano.

Solution:

(*a*) As shown in Fig. 5-11, sketch the elastic curve, and the M/EI diagram. Then draw a tangent to the elastic curve at its midpoint A, which in this case is the point of maximum deflection. Knowing the slope to be zero at the load simplifies the procedure for this problem.

The deflection Δ is then determined by taking the moment of the area of the M/EI diagram between points A and B with respect to point B.

The area of the M/EI diagram between points A and B is

$$\frac{1}{2}\left(\frac{PL}{4EI}\right)\frac{L}{2} = \frac{PL^2}{16EI}$$

The moment arm to the centroid of the triangular area from point B is $(2/3)(L/2) = L/3$. Then

$$\Delta = \left(\frac{PL^2}{16EI}\right)\left(\frac{L}{3}\right) = \frac{PL^3}{48EI}$$

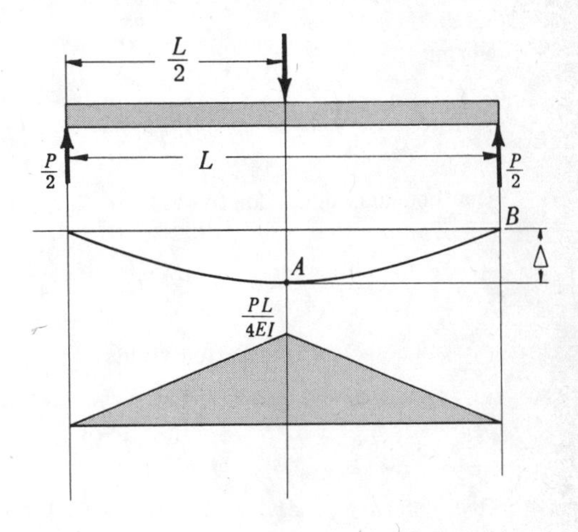

Fig. 5-11

(*b*) Using the conjugate beam method, sketch the conjugate beam and load it so that the intensity of load at any section is equal to the ordinate of the M/EI diagram as shown in Fig. 5-12. Consider the loads on the conjugate beam due to area A and area B as concentrated at the centroids of these areas. The magnitudes of these loads are

$$A = B = \frac{1}{2}\left(\frac{PL}{4EI}\right)\frac{L}{2} = \frac{PL^2}{16EI}$$

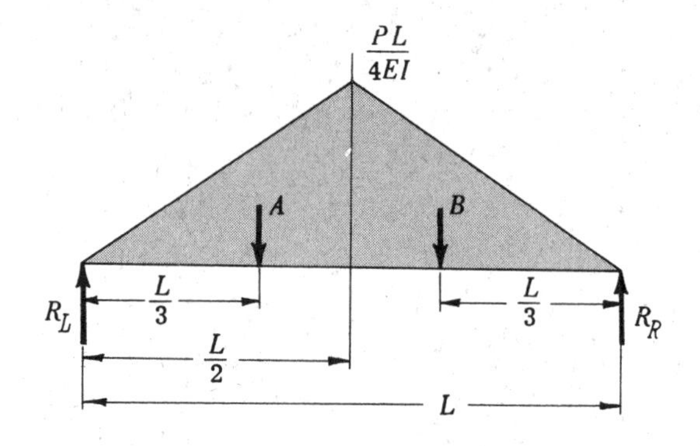

Fig. 5-12

The right and left end reactions may now be determined. In this case they will be equal due to the symmetry of loading, and may be found from a vertical summation of "loads" being equal to zero.

$$R_L = R_R = \frac{PL^2}{16EI}$$

Now the deflection at any section of the original beam is equal to the bending moment of the conjugate beam at that section. The bending moment of the conjugate beam, or the deflection of the original beam, at its midpoint is

$$M_{L/2} = \left(\frac{PL^2}{16EI}\right)\left(\frac{L}{2}\right) - \left(\frac{PL^2}{16EI}\right)\left(\frac{L}{2} - \frac{L}{3}\right) = \frac{PL^3}{48EI}$$

(*c*) The use of step functions in this case is simplified since the beam is taken as one of uniform cross section. We may write the moment equation as

$$EI\frac{d^2y}{dx^2} = M = \frac{P}{2}x - P\left(x - \frac{L}{2}\right)H_{L/2}$$

where the step function: $H_{L/2} = 0$ for $x < L/2$, $H_{L/2} = 1$ for $x \geqq L/2$.

The first integration yields

$$EI\frac{dy}{dx} = \frac{Px^2}{4} - \frac{P(x - L/2)^2}{2}H_{L/2} + C_1$$

noting that

$$\int_0^x P(x - L/2)H_{L/2}\,dx = PH_{L/2}\int_{L/2}^x (x - L/2)\,dx = \frac{P(x - L/2)^2}{2}H_{L/2}$$

One boundary condition to evaluate C_1 is: $dy/dx = 0$ when $x = L/2$; then $C_1 = -PL^2/16$ and

$$EI\frac{dy}{dx} = \frac{Px^2}{4} - \frac{P(x - L/2)^2}{2}H_{L/2} - \frac{PL^2}{16}$$

The second integration yields

$$EIy = \frac{Px^3}{12} - \frac{P(x - L/2)^3}{6}H_{L/2} - \frac{PL^2}{16}x + C_2$$

One boundary condition to evaluate C_2 is: $y = 0$ when $x = 0$; hence $C_2 = 0$. Then substituting $L/2$ for x, the deflection at $x = L/2$ is

$$EIy = \frac{PL^3}{96} - \frac{PL^3}{32} = \frac{-PL^3}{48} \quad \text{and} \quad y = -\frac{PL^3}{48EI}$$

(*d*) Using the theorem of Castigliano, we may write the strain energy equation

$$U = \int \frac{M^2\,dx}{2EI} = \int_0^{L/2} \frac{M^2\,dx}{2EI} + \int_{L/2}^{L} \frac{M^2\,dx}{2EI} = \int_0^{L/2} \frac{(Px/2)^2\,dx}{2EI} + \int_{L/2}^{L} \frac{[Px/2 - P(x-L/2)]^2\,dx}{2EI}$$

from which $U = \dfrac{P^2L^3}{96EI}$. The deflection at the load P is $\dfrac{\partial U}{\partial P} = \dfrac{PL^3}{48EI}$

5. Determine the vertical deflection, due to bending, of point P of a cantilever beam loaded with a horizontal load F, as shown in Fig. 5-13(*a*). Neglect deformation of the vertical member.

Solution:

A problem of this type may be solved by the theorem of Castigliano if we superimpose a vertical load Q at the point where the deflection is to be found, as shown in Fig. 5-13(*b*). The strain energy is

$$U = \int_0^L \frac{(Fh + Qx)^2\,dx}{2EI}$$

$$= \frac{F^2h^2L + FhQL^2 + Q^2L^3/3}{2EI}$$

The vertical deflection is

$$\delta_v = \frac{\partial U}{\partial Q} = \frac{FhL^2 + 2QL^3/3}{2EI}$$

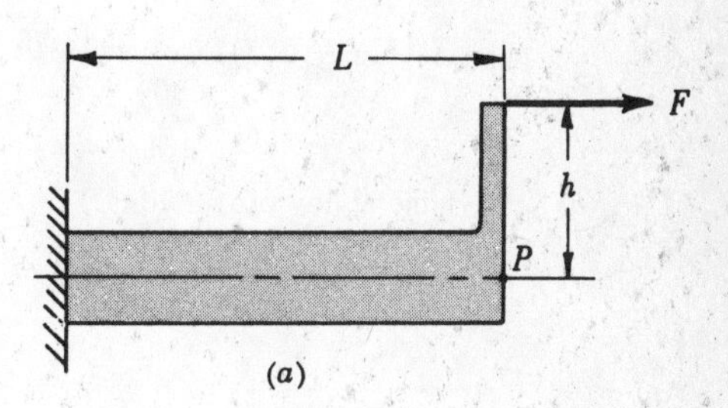

(*a*)

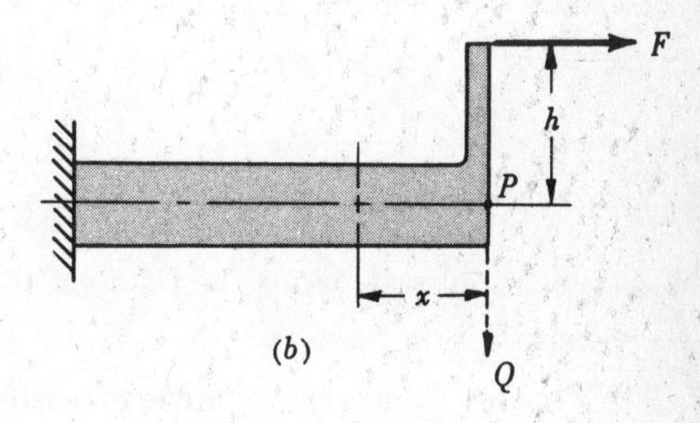

(*b*)

Fig. 5-13

Now setting $Q = 0$, we have the vertical deflection at the point P:

$$\delta_v = \frac{FhL^2}{2EI}$$

6. A shaft is supported by two anti-friction bearings at A and C with loads of 30 lb each acting at points B and F, as shown in Fig. 5-14 below. The portion of the shaft between B and C has a diameter of $2D$ compared to a diameter of D for the portions of the shaft between A and B and between C and F. In connection with a critical speed calculation, it is required to determine the deflection of the shaft at points B and F. Use the area moment method and consider deflections due to bending only. (See the chapter on Shafts for a more extensive deflection analysis.)

Solution:

(*1*) Sketch the elastic curve passing through points of zero deflection at points A and C, and draw the tangent at point A.

(*2*) Sketch the M/EI diagram noting that the moment of inertia of the section having a diameter $2D$ is 16 times that of the sections having a diameter D. The I refers to the smaller diameter portions of the shaft.

(*3*) Determine Δ_1 by taking the moment of the areas of the M/EI diagram between points A and F with respect to point F.

$$\Delta_1 = \left(\frac{180}{EI}\right)\left(\frac{6}{2}\right)(4) + \left(\frac{180}{16EI}\right)(6)(9) + \left(\frac{180}{EI}\right)\left(\frac{6}{2}\right)(14) = \frac{10{,}327.5}{EI}$$

(4) Determine Δ_2 by taking moment of the areas of the M/EI diagram between points A and C with respect to point C.

$$\Delta_2 = \left(\frac{180}{16EI}\right)(6)(3) + \left(\frac{180}{EI}\right)\left(\frac{6}{2}\right)(8) = \frac{4522.5}{EI}.$$

(5) Determine Δ_3 by proportion:

$$\Delta_3 = \frac{18}{12}\Delta_2 = \frac{6783.75}{EI}.$$

Then $y_1 = \Delta_1 - \Delta_3 = \dfrac{3543.75}{EI}$.

(6) Determine Δ_5 by proportion:

$$\Delta_5 = \frac{\Delta_3}{3} = \frac{2261.25}{EI}.$$

(7) Determine Δ_4:

$$\Delta_4 = \left(\frac{180}{EI}\right)\left(\frac{6}{2}\right)(2) = \frac{1080}{EI}.$$

Then $y_2 = \Delta_5 - \Delta_4 = \dfrac{1181.25}{EI}$.

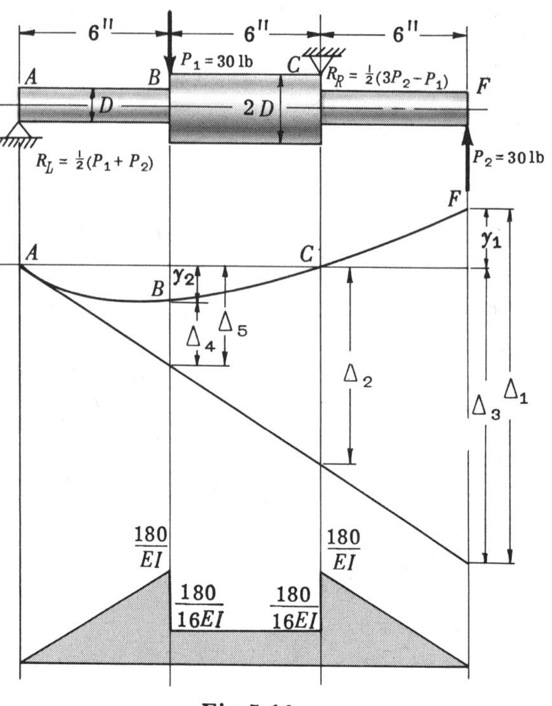

Fig. 5-14

7. Solve Problem 6 using the theorem of Castigliano.

Solution:

The total strain energy U due to bending is

$$U = \int \frac{M^2\,dx}{2EI} = U_1 + U_2 + U_3$$

where
U_1 = energy from $x = 0$ to $x = 6$
U_2 = energy from $x = 6$ to $x = 12$
U_3 = energy from $x = 12$ to $x = 18$.

$$U_1 = \int_0^6 \frac{(R_L x)^2\,dx}{2EI} = \left[\frac{R_L^2 x^3}{6EI}\right]_0^6 = \frac{36R_L^2}{EI} = \frac{36}{EI}\left(\frac{P_1 + P_2}{2}\right)^2$$

Now evaluate U_3:
$$U_3 = \int_{12}^{18} \frac{P_2^2(18-x)^2\,dx}{2EI} = \frac{36P_2^2}{EI}$$

If I is the moment of inertia of a section of diameter D, then the moment of inertia of the section from $x = 6$ to $x = 12$, which has a diameter of $2D$, is $16I$. The strain energy in the center portion is

$$U_2 = \int_6^{12} \frac{[R_L x - P_1(x-6)]^2\,dx}{2E(16I)}$$

Integrating, substituting $\frac{1}{2}(P_1 + P_2)$ for R_L and collecting terms,

$$U_2 = \frac{72}{32EI}\left[7\left(\frac{P_2 - P_1}{2}\right)^2 + 9P_1\left(\frac{P_1 + P_2}{2}\right) - 6P_1^2\right]$$

The total strain energy is $U = U_1 + U_2 + U_3$

$$U = \frac{36}{EI}\left(\frac{P_1+P_2}{2}\right)^2 + \frac{72}{32EI}\left[7\left(\frac{P_2-P_1}{2}\right)^2 + 9P_1\left(\frac{P_1+P_2}{2}\right) - 6P_1^2\right] + \frac{36P_2^2}{EI}$$

The deflection under P_1 is

$$\frac{\partial U}{\partial P_1} = \frac{18}{EI}(P_1+P_2) + \frac{9}{4EI}(P_2+\frac{P_1}{2}) = \frac{1080}{EI} + \frac{101.25}{EI} = \frac{1181.25}{EI}$$

The deflection at P_2 is

$$\frac{\partial U}{\partial P_2} = \frac{18}{EI}(P_1+P_2) + \frac{72}{32EI}\left[14(\frac{P_2-P_1}{2})(\frac{1}{2}) + \frac{9P_1}{2}\right] + \frac{72P_2}{EI} = \frac{1080}{EI} + \frac{303.75}{EI} + \frac{2160}{EI} = \frac{3543.75}{EI}$$

8. (*a*) Using the area moment method, show that the maximum bending deflection of a simply supported member of length L and carrying a uniformly distributed load of w lb per inch, as shown in Fig. 5-15(*a*), is $5wL^4/384EI$. (*b*) Same as (*a*) except use Castigliano's theorem.

Solution:

(*a*) **Using the area moment method.**

1. Sketch the elastic curve as shown in Fig. 5-15(*b*). Draw a horizontal tangent to the elastic curve at point M. Then the deflection y is the moment of the area of the moment diagram between points M and B, with respect to B, divided by EI.

2. Sketch the moment diagram as shown in Figure 5-15(*c*).

3. For a change, let us draw the moment diagram by parts, Fig. 5-15(*d*), to illustrate such a procedure. This procedure in some cases might be expedient in order to simplify the determination of areas and centroids of areas.

4. In this case we are only concerned with the moments of sections I and II.

The area of section I $= (\frac{wL^2}{4})(\frac{L}{4}) = \frac{wL^3}{16}$.

The area of section II $= (\frac{wL^2}{8})(\frac{L}{2})(\frac{1}{3}) = \frac{wL^3}{48}$.

The distance of the centroid of section I to point B is $(2/3)(L/2) = L/3$.

The distance of the centroid of section II to point B is $(3/4)(L/2) = 3L$

Then $EIy = (\frac{wL^3}{16})(\frac{L}{3}) - (\frac{wL^3}{48})(\frac{3L}{8})$

$= \frac{5wL^4}{384}$

and $y = \frac{5wL^4}{384EI}$.

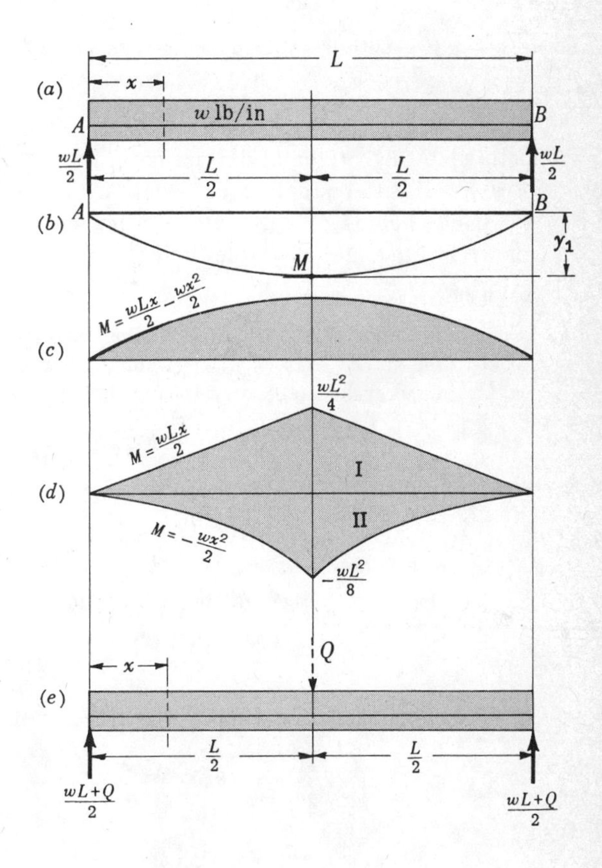

Fig. 5-15

(*b*) **Using Castigliano's theorem.**

1. A load Q must be imagined as acting at the point where the deflection is to be determined, as shown in Fig. 5-15(*e*) above.

2. The bending strain energy is $\int \frac{M^2\,dx}{2EI}$. For the left half of the beam, the strain energy is

$$U_1 = \int_0^{L/2} \frac{\left[\frac{1}{2}(wL+Q)x - \frac{1}{2}wx^2\right]^2 dx}{2EI}$$

Since the strain energy in the left is the same as that for the right portion, the total strain energy in the beam is $U = 2U_1$:

$$U = 2\int_0^{L/2} \frac{\left[\frac{1}{2}(wL+Q)x - \frac{1}{2}wx^2\right]^2 dx}{2EI} = \frac{1}{EI}\left[\left(\frac{wL+Q}{2}\right)^2 \frac{L^3}{24} - \frac{(wL+Q)wL^4}{128} + \frac{w^2L^5}{640}\right]$$

$$y = \frac{\partial U}{\partial Q} = \frac{1}{EI}\left[(wL+Q)\frac{L^3}{48} - \frac{wL^4}{128} + 0\right]$$

When $Q = 0$,

$$y = \frac{1}{EI}\left[\frac{wL^4}{48} - \frac{wL^4}{128}\right] = \frac{5wL^4}{384EI}$$

or if W is the total load and is wL, $y = \frac{5WL^3}{384EI}$.

9. Determine the horizontal deflection of point A of a 2" diameter steel curved beam having a 4" inside radius of curvature and loaded as shown in Fig. 5-16. Consider bending only.

Solution:

At any angle ϕ the bending moment with respect to the gravity axis is $M = P(5\sin\phi)$. Hence the strain energy due to bending is

$$U = \int_0^{\pi} \frac{M^2\,d\phi}{2AeE} = \int_0^{\pi} \frac{(5P\sin\phi)^2\,d\phi}{2AeE}$$

$$= \frac{25}{4}\frac{\pi P^2}{AeE}$$

The deflection in the direction of the load P is

$$\frac{\partial U}{\partial P} = \frac{25}{2}\frac{\pi P}{AeE}$$

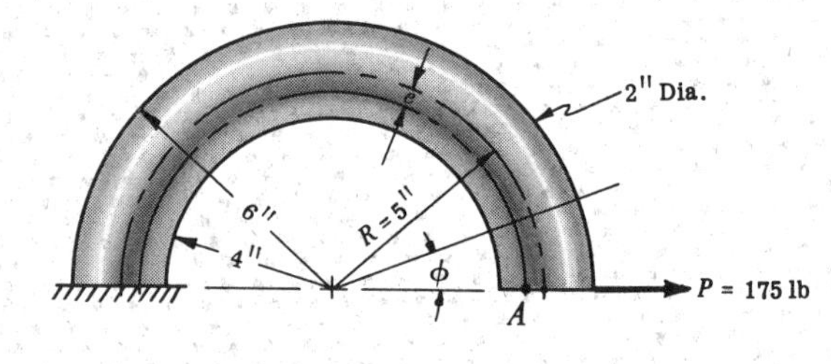

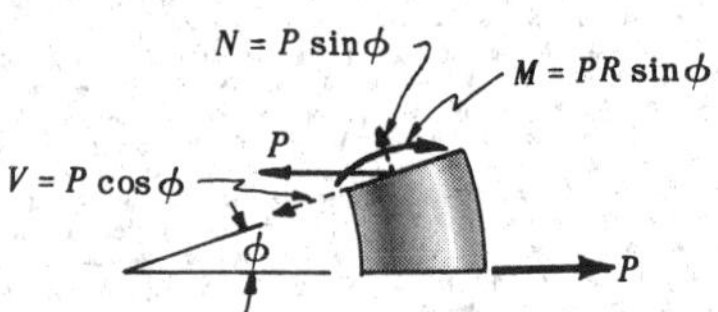

Fig. 5-16

The value of e, the distance from the centroidal axis to the neutral axis for a circular cross section, is

$$e = R - \frac{(\sqrt{r_o} + \sqrt{r_i})^2}{4} = 5 - \frac{(\sqrt{6} + \sqrt{4})^2}{4} = 0.0505$$

The deflection in the direction of the load P is

$$\frac{\partial U}{\partial P} = \frac{25}{2}\frac{\pi P}{AeE} = \frac{25\pi(175)}{2\pi(0.0505)(30\times10^6)}$$

$$= 0.001442''$$

10. For Problem 9, determine the deflections due to (*a*) shear and (*b*) combined effects of bending, shear, and normal load components.

Solution:

(*a*) At any section, the value of the transverse shearing force V is $V = P\cos\phi$. The strain energy is

$$U = \int_0^{\pi} \frac{KV^2 R\,d\phi}{2AG} \qquad \text{(where } K = \tfrac{4}{3} \text{ for a circular cross section)}$$

$$= \int_0^{\pi} \frac{4(P\cos\phi)^2(5)\,d\phi}{3(2)(\pi)(12)(10^6)} = \frac{0.0884P^2}{10^6}\int_0^{\pi}(\cos\phi)^2\,d\phi = \frac{0.0884P^2}{10^6}\left[\frac{\sin 2\phi}{4}+\frac{\phi}{2}\right]_0^{\pi} = \frac{0.0884P^2}{10^6}\left(\frac{\pi}{2}\right)$$

The deflection due to shear in the direction of the force is

$$\frac{\partial U}{\partial P} = \frac{0.0884P\pi}{10^6} = \frac{0.0884(175)\pi}{10^6} = 0.0000486''$$

compared with a deflection of 0.001442'' due to bending only.

(*b*) The normal load component of P which produces axial elongation at any section is $N = P\sin\phi$. The rotation of a section due to the normal force N is opposed by the moment $M = PR\sin\phi$. The strain energy due to the normal load component in the presence of bending is

$$U = \int_0^{\pi}\left[\frac{N^2R}{2AE} - \frac{MN}{AE}\right]d\phi = \int_0^{\pi}\frac{5(P\sin\phi)^2\,d\phi}{2\pi(30\times10^6)} - \int_0^{\pi}\frac{(5P\sin\phi)(P\sin\phi)\,d\phi}{\pi(30\times10^6)}$$

$$= \frac{0.0265P^2}{10^6}\int_0^{\pi}(\sin\phi)^2\,d\phi - \frac{0.053P^2}{10^6}\int_0^{\pi}(\sin\phi)^2\,d\phi$$

$$= \frac{0.0265P^2}{10^6}\left(\frac{\pi}{2}\right) - \frac{0.053P^2}{10^6}\left(\frac{\pi}{2}\right)$$

$$\frac{\partial U}{\partial P} = \frac{[0.0265(175) - 0.053(175)]\,\pi}{10^6} = -0.0000145''$$

Then the net deflection due to the combined effects of bending, shear, and normal force is

$$\delta = 0.001442 + 0.0000486 - 0.0000145 = 0.0014761 \text{ in.,} \quad \text{or} \quad 0.0015 \text{ in.}$$

11. Determine the horizontal displacement along the load line of the frame shown in Fig. 5-17. The moment of inertia is the same for all sections. Consider deflection due to bending only.

Solution:

Using the theorem of Castigliano, the strain energy of the frame is the sum of the energy in the three members. For members 1 and 3 the energy is the same.

$$U_{1,3} = 2\int_0^h \frac{M^2\,dy}{2EI} = 2\int_0^h \frac{(Fy)^2\,dy}{2EI} = 2\left(\frac{F^2h^3}{6EI}\right)$$

$$U_2 = \int_0^L \frac{(Fh)^2\,dx}{2EI} = \frac{F^2h^2L}{2EI} \quad \text{for member 2}$$

$$\text{Total } U = 2\left(\frac{F^2h^3}{6EI}\right) + \frac{F^2h^2L}{2EI}$$

$$\frac{\partial U}{\partial F} = \frac{2Fh^3}{3EI} + \frac{Fh^2L}{EI} = \Delta L \text{ in the direction of } F.$$

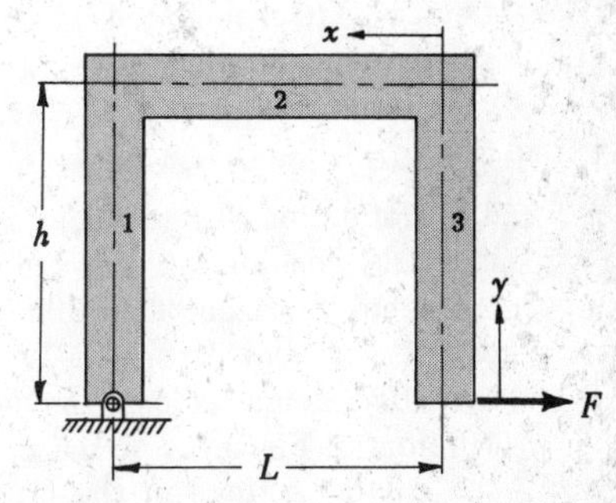

Fig. 5-17

12. For the machine frame as shown in Fig. 5-18, determine both the horizontal and vertical deflection of the lower end of member 1, due to the applied horizontal force F. Consider bending and axial loads.

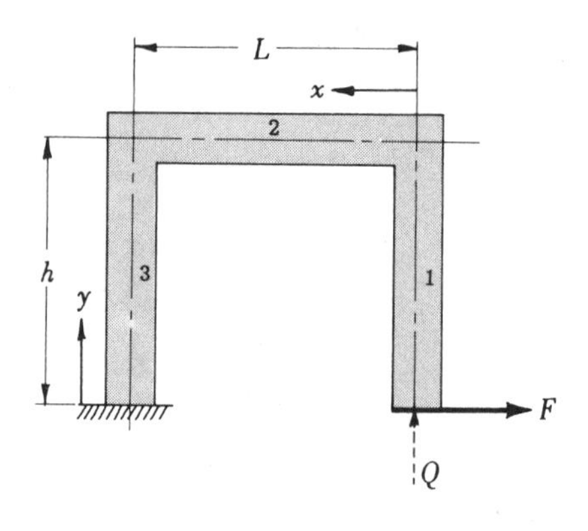

Fig. 5-18

Solution:

The strain energy for bending and axial loading in the various parts of the frame is

$$U_1 = \int_0^h \frac{(Fy)^2}{2EI}\,dy + \int_0^h \frac{Q^2\,dy}{2AE}$$

$$U_2 = \int_0^L \frac{(Qx+Fh)^2}{2EI}\,dx + \int_0^L \frac{F^2\,dx}{2AE}$$

$$U_3 = \int_0^h \frac{(QL+Fy)^2}{2EI}\,dy + \int_0^h \frac{Q^2\,dy}{2AE}$$

The total strain energy $U = U_1 + U_2 + U_3$.

$$U = \left(\frac{F^2h^3}{6EI} + \frac{Q^2h}{2AE}\right) + \left(\frac{Q^2L^3}{6EI} + \frac{QL^2Fh}{2EI} + \frac{F^2h^2L}{2EI} + \frac{F^2L}{2AE}\right) + \left(\frac{Q^2L^2h}{2EI} + \frac{QLFh^2}{2EI} + \frac{F^2h^3}{6EI} + \frac{Q^2h}{2AE}\right)$$

The horizontal deflection is determined by taking the partial derivative of U with respect to F, with Q being zero.

$$\frac{\partial U}{\partial F} = \delta_x = \frac{Fh^2}{EI}\left(\frac{2h}{3} + L\right) + \frac{FL}{AE}$$

The vertical deflection is determined by taking the partial derivative of U with respect to Q, after which Q is set equal to zero.

$$\frac{\partial U}{\partial Q} = \delta_y = \frac{FLh}{2EI}(L+h)$$

13. Derive the shear deflection equation for a beam with several loads and changes of section of the following form:

$$\frac{dy}{dx} = C_1 + \frac{KV}{AG}$$

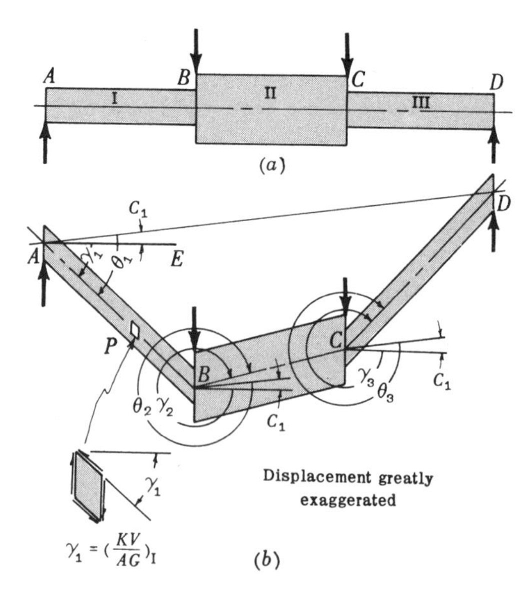

Fig. 5-19

Solution:

1. Consider a beam with forces applied at A, B, C, and D, as shown in Fig. 5-19(a). No restraint is imposed at this time as to what points of the beam are prevented from deflecting. (Concentrated loads are shown, but the procedure could be extended to varying loads in a similar manner as given below.)

2. The deflection due to shear will be determined by considering only the deflection of the neutral surface. This eliminates the necessity of considering the warpage which actually occurs across the section. The differential elements of the cross sections at the neutral axis slide in a direction perpendicular to the neutral surface of the original beam. Then all of the planes containing these elements at the neutral surface remain parallel since they are perpendicular to the neutral surface of the original beam.

3. The parts of the member will deflect due to shear relative to each other as shown (exaggerated) in Fig. 5-19(*b*) above.

4. If it is known that the ends at A and D are prevented from deflecting, the zero deflection line (or base line) AD may be drawn.

5. Now draw the line AE perpendicular to the section at A for a reference line.

6. The angle between the zero deflection line AD and the reference line AE is C_1.

7. The angle between the zero deflection line and the centerline of a member is called θ. $\theta_1 = C_1 + \gamma_1$, $\theta_2 = C_1 + \gamma_2$, $\theta_3 = C_1 + \gamma_3$. Since all these angles are small (close to zero or 360°), we may write

$$\tan\theta_1 = C_1 + \tan\gamma_1, \qquad \tan\theta_2 = C_1 + \tan\gamma_2, \qquad \tan\theta_3 = C_1 + \tan\gamma_3$$

8. The tangent of θ is the slope of the centerline with respect to the zero deflection line.

$$\tan\theta_1 = (dy/dx)_{\text{I}}, \qquad \tan\theta_2 = (dy/dx)_{\text{II}}, \qquad \tan\theta_3 = (dy/dx)_{\text{III}}$$

9. Since shear stress is proportional to shear strain,

$$s_s = \frac{KV}{A} = (\tan\gamma)G, \quad \text{or} \quad \tan\gamma = \frac{KV}{AG}$$

In the above, K is a constant for the particular cross section used (as $K = 4/3$ for a circular cross section or $K = 3/2$ for a rectangular cross section). For the different sections, we have

$$\tan\gamma_1 = (\frac{KV}{AG})_{\text{I}}, \qquad \tan\gamma_2 = (\frac{KV}{AG})_{\text{II}}, \qquad \tan\gamma_3 = (\frac{KV}{AG})_{\text{III}}$$

10. Substituting values from **(9)** and **(8)** into **(7)**, we get

$$\text{Sec. I: } (\frac{dy}{dx})_{\text{I}} = C_1 + (\frac{KV}{AG})_{\text{I}}, \quad \text{Sec. II: } (\frac{dy}{dx})_{\text{II}} = C_1 + (\frac{KV}{AG})_{\text{II}}, \quad \text{Sec. III: } (\frac{dy}{dx})_{\text{III}} = C_1 + (\frac{KV}{AG})_{\text{III}}.$$

11. In using the equations in **(10)**, draw a conventional shear diagram. If the shear force is (+), substitute as such in the equations; if the shear force is (–), substitute as such in the equations. A plus deflection means deflection downward and a minus deflection means deflection upward.

14. Determine the deflection due to shear only in the direction of the applied load P, for Fig. 5-20, (*a*) by applying the strain energy theorem of Castigliano, (*b*) by applying the transverse shear equation combined with a step function. Observe that there is zero deflection due to shear between the fixed supports.

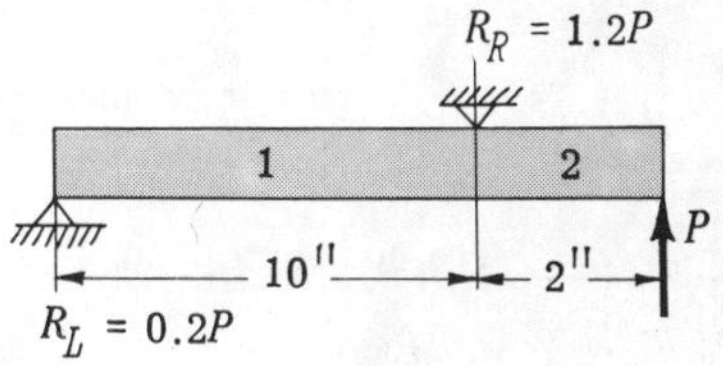

$R_R = 1.2P$

1 2 P

10'' 2''

$R_L = 0.2P$

Fig. 5-20

Solution:

(*a*) The total strain energy stored in the member is the sum of the strain energies in sections 1 and 2.

$$U = U_1 + U_2 = \int_0^{10} \frac{KV^2}{2AG}\,dx + \int_{10}^{12} \frac{KV^2}{2AG}\,dx = \int_0^{10} \frac{K(0.2P)^2}{2AG}\,dx + \int_{10}^{12} \frac{K(-P)^2}{2AG}\,dx = \frac{1.2KP^2}{AG}$$

The vertical deflection at the load P is $\dfrac{\partial U}{\partial P} = \dfrac{2.4KP}{AG}$.

(*b*) The deflection at P may also be obtained by integrating $\dfrac{dy}{dx} = \dfrac{KV}{AG} + C_1$.

It is observed that the value of V between the two reactions is $+0.2P$, and that the value of V is $-P$ between the right reaction and the load P. Using a step function the value of V may be expressed

$$V = 0.2P - 1.2PH_{10} \qquad \text{where } H_{10} = 0 \text{ for } x < 10,\ H_{10} = 1 \text{ for } x \geqq 10.$$

$$\text{Then} \quad \frac{dy}{dx} = \frac{K(0.2P - 1.2PH_{10})}{AG} + C_1$$

$$y = \frac{KP}{AG}\int (0.2 - 1.2H_{10} + C_1)\,dx = \frac{KP}{AG}[0.2x - 1.2H_{10}(x-10) + C_1x + C_2]$$

From the boundary condition $y = 0$ when $x = 0$, $C_2 = 0$.

From the boundary condition $y = 0$ when $x = 10$, $0 = \frac{KP}{AG}(2 + 10C_1)$ and $C_1 = -0.2$.

The general shear deflection equation is $y = \frac{KP}{AG}[0.2x - 1.2H_{10}(x-10) - 0.2x]$.

The shear deflection at $x = 12''$ is $y = \frac{2.4KP}{AG}$.

15. Determine the deflection due to shear only under the load P for the member shown in Fig. 5-21, when there is a change of cross sectional area from A to $2A$ at the midpoint of the member, (a) using the strain-energy method, (b) using the shear deflection equation, (c) same as (b) except using step functions.

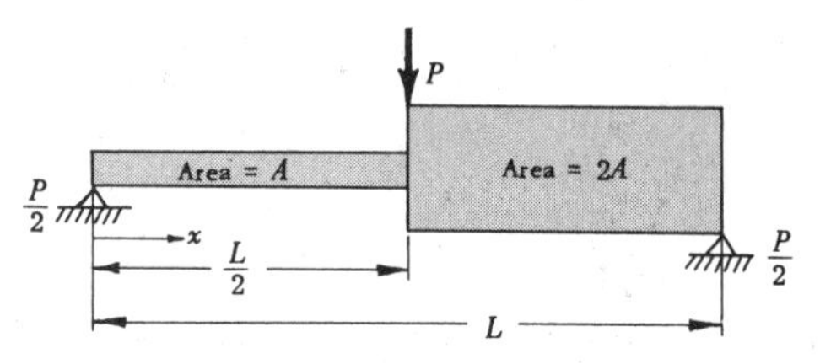

Fig. 5-21

Solution:

(a) The total strain energy due to shear is

$$U = \int_0^{L/2} \frac{K(P/2)^2\,dx}{2AG} + \int_{L/2}^{L} \frac{K(-P/2)^2\,dx}{2(2A)(G)} = \frac{KP^2}{8AG}\left(\frac{L}{2}\right) + \frac{KP^2}{16AG}\left(\frac{L}{2}\right)$$

The shear deflection under the load P is $y = \frac{\partial U}{\partial P} = \frac{KPL}{8AG} + \frac{KPL}{16AG} = \frac{3KPL}{16AG}$

(b) Using transverse shear equation.

1. For $0 \leqq x \leqq \frac{L}{2}$, $\frac{dy}{dx} = C_1 + \frac{KV}{AG}$ where V = shearing force $= \frac{P}{2}$.

Then integrating $\frac{dy}{dx} = C_1 + \frac{K(P/2)}{AG}$, we obtain (1) $y = (C_1 + \frac{KP}{2AG})x + C_2$.

2. For $\frac{L}{2} \leqq x \leqq L$, $\frac{dy}{dx} = C_1 + \frac{KV}{(2A)G}$ where V = shearing force $= -\frac{P}{2}$.

Then integrating $\frac{dy}{dx} = C_1 + \frac{K(-P/2)}{(2A)G}$, we obtain (2) $y = (C_1 - \frac{KP}{4AG})x + C_3$.

3. The boundary conditions are:

a. when $x = 0$, $y = 0$; thus from equation (1), $0 = (C_1 + KP/2AG)0 + C_2$ or $C_2 = 0$.

b. when $x = L$, $y = 0$; thus from equation (2), $0 = (C_1 - KP/4AG)L + C_3$.

c. when $x = L/2$, y from equation (1) = y from equation (2):

$$(C_1 + KP/2AG)L/2 + 0 = (C_1 - KP/4AG)L/2 + C_3.$$

Solving for C_1 and C_3, $C_1 = -\frac{KP}{8AG}$ and $C_3 = \frac{3}{8}\frac{KPL}{AG}$.

The deflection at $x = L/2$ can be found from equation (1) with the constants inserted in the equation:

$$y = \left(-\frac{KP}{8AG} + \frac{KP}{2AG}\right)\frac{L}{2} + 0 = \frac{3KPL}{16AG}$$

(c) Using a step function.

The equation for the slope is, from $\frac{dy}{dx} = \frac{KV}{AG} + C_1$, $\frac{dy}{dx} = \frac{K}{AG}\frac{P}{2} - \frac{3}{4}\frac{KP}{AG}H_{L/2} + C_1$ with the step function $H_{L/2} = 0$ for $x < L/2$ and $H_{L/2} = 1$ for $x \geqq L/2$. Integrating,

$$y = \frac{KP}{2AG}\left[x - \frac{3}{2}H_{L/2}\left(x - \frac{L}{2}\right)\right] + C_1 x + C_2$$

When $x = 0$, $y = 0$, which gives $C_2 = 0$; when $x = L$, $y = 0$, which gives $C_1 = -KP/8AG$. The deflection at $x = L/2$ is

$$y = \frac{KP}{2AG}\left(\frac{L}{2} - 0\right) - \frac{KP}{8AG}\left(\frac{L}{2}\right) + 0 = \frac{3KPL}{16AG}$$

16. Compare the deflection at the load due to transverse shear to the deflection due to bending for the hollow shaft loaded as shown. Determine the total deflection at the load. Refer to Fig. 5-22.

Solution:

(*a*) The deflection due to transverse shear is

$0 \leq x \leq 2$	$2 \leq x \leq 6$
$\frac{dy}{dx} = C_1 + \frac{KV}{AG} = C_1 + \frac{K(800)}{AG}$	$\frac{dy}{dx} = C_1 + \frac{KV}{AG} = C_1 + \frac{K(-400)}{AG}$
Integrating,	Integrating,
(*1*) $y = C_1 x + \frac{K(800)}{AG}x + C_2$	(*2*) $y = C_1 x - \frac{K(400)}{AG}x + C_3$

The boundary conditions are:

1. when $x = 0$, $y = 0$
2. when $x = 6''$, $y = 0$
3. y from (*1*) = y from (*2*) when $x = 2''$

from which $C_1 = 0$, $C_2 = 0$, $C_3 = 2400K/AG$.

Then putting $C_1 = C_2 = 0$ in equation (*1*) and solving for the deflection at $x = 2''$,

$$y = 0 + \frac{K(800)(2)}{AG} + 0 = \frac{1600K}{AG}$$

where K is the factor applied to the average shear stress to find the maximum shear stress at the neutral axis.

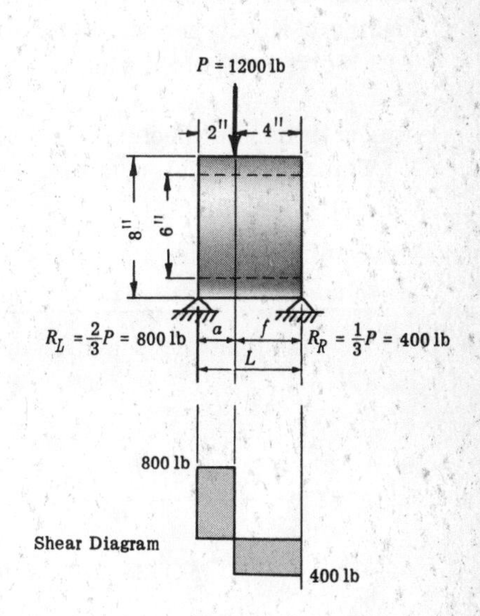

Fig. 5-22

Now $K(\frac{V}{A}) = \frac{VQ}{Ib}$ or $K = \frac{QA}{Ib}$

where

Q = moment of the area above the neutral axis

$= (\frac{\pi D_o^2}{8})\frac{2}{3}\frac{D_o}{\pi} - (\frac{\pi D_i^2}{8})\frac{2}{3}\frac{D_i}{\pi}$

$A = \frac{\pi(D_o^2 - D_i^2)}{4}$, area of the cross section

$I = \frac{\pi(D_o^4 - D_i^4)}{64}$, moment of inertia of a cross section

$b = D_o - D_i$; D_o = outside diameter, 8''; D_i = inside diameter, 6''.

Substituting in $K = \frac{QA}{Ib}$, $K = 1.97$. Then $y = \frac{1600K}{AG} = \frac{1600(1.97)}{\frac{1}{4}\pi(8^2 - 6^2)(12\times 10^6)} = 11.9\times 10^{-6}$ in.

(*b*) Deflection due to bending at the load for the beam loaded as shown is given by

$$y = \frac{Pfx}{6LEI}(L^2 - f^2 - x^2) = \frac{(1200)(4)(2)}{6(6)(30\times 10^6)(\pi/64)(D_o^4 - D_i^4)}(6^2 - 4^2 - 2^2) = 1.035\times 10^{-6} \text{ in.}$$

(*c*) Ratio of shear deflection to bending deflection at the load is $\frac{11.9\times 10^{-6}}{1.035\times 10^{-6}} = 11.5$.

(*d*) Total deflection at the load is $11.9\times 10^{-6} + 1.035\times 10^{-6} = 12.935\times 10^{-6}$ in.

(*e*) Note that the bending stress is quite small: $s = \frac{Mc}{I} = \frac{1600(8/2)}{(\pi/64)(8^4 - 6^4)} = 46.6$ psi.

(*f*) Transverse shear deflection using Castigliano's theorem:

$$U = \int \frac{KV^2\,dx}{2AG} = \int_0^2 \frac{K(2P/3)^2\,dx}{2AG} + \int_2^6 \frac{K(-P/3)^2\,dx}{2AG} = \frac{2KP^2}{3AG}$$

Deflection at the load is $y = \dfrac{\partial U}{\partial P} = \dfrac{4KP}{3AG} = \dfrac{4K(1200)}{3AG} = \dfrac{1600K}{AG}$.

Note that this deflection is the same as obtained by deriving the general equation of transverse shear deflection in (*a*).

17. Determine the shear deflection midway between supports due to the transverse loading of 100 lb per in. Refer to Fig. 5-23. Solve by the following three methods:

(*a*) Castigliano's theorem.
(*b*) Transverse shear equation.
(*c*) Step function.

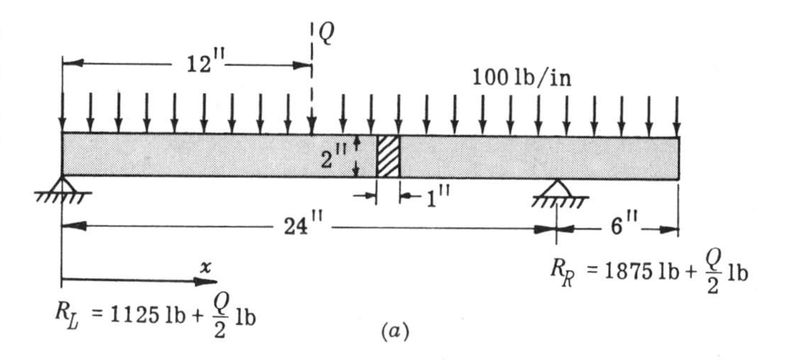

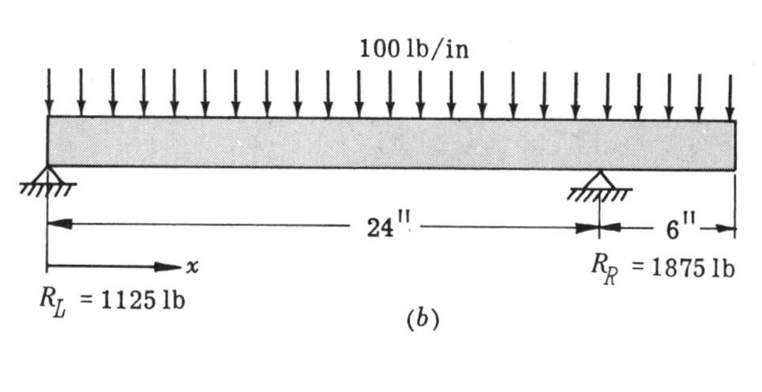

Fig. 5-23

Solution:

(*a*) **Solution using Castigliano's theorem.**

The shear energy is given by

$$U = \int \frac{KV^2\,dx}{2AG}$$

$$= \int_0^{12} \frac{K(1125 + \frac{1}{2}Q - 100x)^2\,dx}{2AG} + \int_{12}^{24} \frac{K(1125 - \frac{1}{2}Q - 100x)^2\,dx}{2AG} + \int_{24}^{30} \frac{K(3000 - 100x)^2\,dx}{2AG}$$

where a load of Q lb is applied at the point where the deflection is to be found. Integrating,

$$U = \frac{-K}{600AG}\left[(\tfrac{1}{2}Q - 75)^3 - (1125 + \tfrac{1}{2}Q)^3 - (\tfrac{1}{2}Q + 1275)^3 + (75 + \tfrac{1}{2}Q)^3 - (600)^3\right]$$

$$y = \frac{\partial U}{\partial Q} = \frac{-K}{400AG}\left[(\tfrac{1}{2}Q - 75)^2 - (1125 + \tfrac{1}{2}Q)^2 - (\tfrac{1}{2}Q + 1275)^2 + (75 + \tfrac{1}{2}Q)^2\right]$$

When $Q = 0$, deflection at Q is $y = 7200K/AG$.

For a rectangular section $2'' \times 1''$, $y = \dfrac{7200K}{AG} = \dfrac{7200(3/2)}{2(12 \times 10^6)} = 450 \times 10^{-6}$ in.

(*b*) **Solution using the transverse shear equation.** See Fig. 5-23(*b*).

$0 \leqq x \leqq 24$

$$\frac{dy}{dx} = C_1 + \frac{KV}{AG} = C_1 + \frac{K(1125 - 100x)}{AG}$$

Integrating,

$$y = C_1 x + \frac{K}{AG}(1125x - 50x^2) + C_2$$

$24 \leqq x \leqq 30$

$$\frac{dy}{dx} = C_1 + \frac{KV}{AG} = C_1 + \frac{K(1125 - 100x + 1875)}{AG}$$

Integrating,

$$y = C_1 x + \frac{K}{AG}(3000x - 50x^2) + C_3$$

Boundary conditions: $x = 0$, $y = 0$; $x = 24''$, $y = 0$ for *both* deflection equations.

Substitution of the boundary conditions into the two deflection equations gives $C_1 = 75K/AG$, $C_2 = 0$, $C_3 = -45{,}000K/AG$. The deflection at $x = 12$ in. is found from

$$y = C_1 x + \frac{K}{AG}(1125x - 50x^2) + C_2 = \frac{75K}{AG}(12) + \frac{K}{AG}\left[1125(12) - 50(12)^2\right] + 0 = \frac{7200K}{AG}$$

(*c*) **Solution using a step function.**

The equation for the shear force, using a step function H_{24}, where $H_{24} = 0$ for $x < 24''$ and $H_{24} = 1$ for $x \geqq 24''$, is $V = 1125 - 100x + 1875H_{24}$.

The shear deflection equation is $\dfrac{dy}{dx} = \dfrac{K}{AG}V + C_1 = \dfrac{K}{AG}(1125 - 100x + 1875H_{24}) + C_1$.

Integrating, $y = \dfrac{K}{AG}\left[1125x - 50x^2 + 1875(x-24)H_{24}\right] + C_1 x + C_2$.

From the boundary conditions ($x = 0$, $y = 0$) and ($x = 24$, $y = 0$), we have $C_1 = 75K/AG$, $C_2 = 0$. The deflection at $x = 12''$ is

$$y = \frac{K}{AG}\left[1125(12) - 50(12)^2 + 0\right] + \frac{75K}{AG}(12) + 0 = \frac{7200K}{AG}$$

18. Determine the shear deflection at P_1 and P_2 for the beam shown in Fig. 5-24 loaded by $P_1 = 30$ lb and $P_2 = 30$ lb. Use the shear deflection equation $dy/dx = C_1 + KV/AG$.

Solution:

$0 \leqq x \leqq 6$

$$\frac{dy}{dx} = C_1 + \frac{K(30)}{AG}$$

Integrating,

$$(1)\quad y = C_1 x + \frac{30K}{AG}x + C_2$$

$6 \leqq x \leqq 12$

$$\frac{dy}{dx} = C_1 + \frac{K(0)}{4AG}$$

Integrating,

$$(2)\quad y = C_1 x + 0 + C_3$$

$12 \leqq x \leqq 18$

$$\frac{dy}{dx} = C_1 + \frac{K(-30)}{AG}$$

Integrating,

$$(3)\quad y = C_1 x - \frac{30K}{AG}x + C_4$$

Boundary conditions:

$x = 0$, $y = 0$
$x = 6$, y from eq. (*1*) $= y$ from eq. (*2*)
$x = 12$, $y = 0$ from eq. (*2*) and from eq. (*3*).

Substitution of the boundary conditions into equations (*1*), (*2*) and (*3*) gives

$$C_1 = -\frac{15K}{AG},\ C_2 = 0,\ C_3 = \frac{180K}{AG},\ C_4 = \frac{540K}{AG}.$$

Thus the deflection at the load P_1 is, from equation (*1*),

$$y = -\frac{15K}{AG}x + \frac{30K}{AG}x + 0 = \frac{15K}{AG}x$$

and for $x = 6''$,

$y = +\dfrac{90K}{AG}$ (the plus sign indicates deflection in the plus direction, that is, downward).

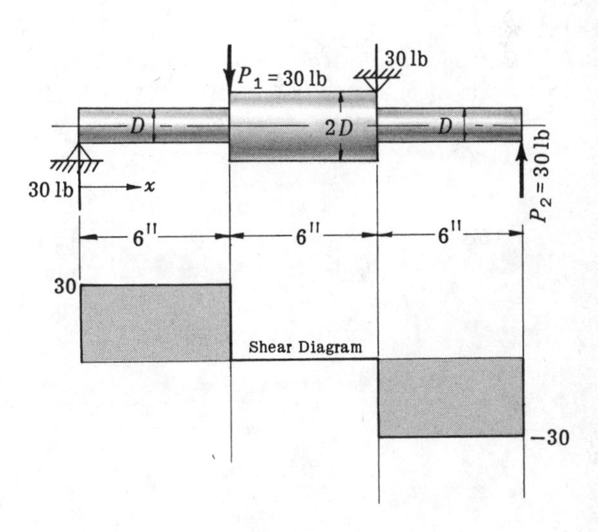

Fig. 5-24

The shear deflection at P_2 is, from equation (3),

$$y = -\frac{15K}{AG}x - \frac{30K}{AG}x + \frac{540K}{AG} = -\frac{45K}{AG}x + \frac{540K}{AG}$$

and for $x = 18''$, $y = -270K/AG$ (the negative sign means deflection in the up direction).

19. Same as previous, except use Castigliano's theorem. See Fig. 5-25.

Solution:

The left reaction is $\frac{1}{2}(P_1+P_2)$ and the right reaction is $\frac{1}{2}(3P_2-P_1)$.

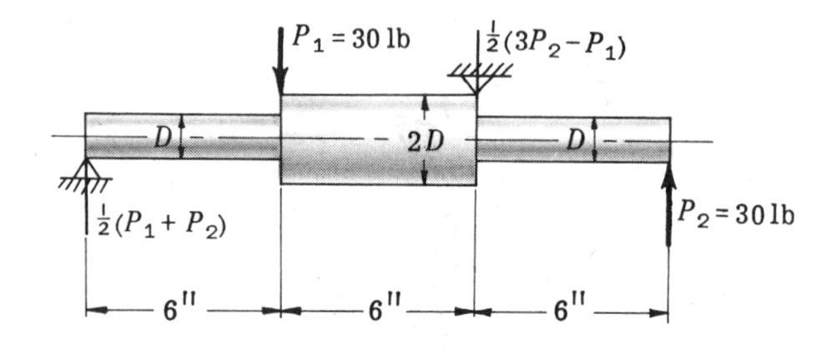

Fig. 5-25

The strain energy is

$$U = \int_0^6 \frac{K[\frac{1}{2}(P_1+P_2)]^2 dx}{2AG} + \int_6^{12} \frac{K[\frac{1}{2}(P_1+P_2)-P_1]^2 dx}{2(4A)G} + \int_{12}^{18} \frac{K(-P_2)^2\,dx}{2AG}$$

Integrating, $$U = \frac{K(P_1+P_2)^2(6)}{8AG} + \frac{K(P_2-P_1)^2(6)}{32AG} + \frac{K(P_2)^2(6)}{2AG}$$

The shear deflection at P_1 is $$y = \frac{\partial U}{\partial P_1} = \frac{3K}{2AG}(P_1+P_2) - \frac{3K}{8AG}(P_2-P_1) + 0$$

and for $P_2 = P_1 = 30$ lb, $y = +\frac{90K}{AG}$ (the plus sign indicates deflection in the direction of P_1, that is, down).

The shear deflection at P_2 is $$y = \frac{\partial U}{\partial P_2} = \frac{3K}{2AG}(P_1+P_2) + \frac{3K}{8AG}(P_2-P_1) + \frac{6K}{AG}P_2$$

and for $P_1 = P_2 = 30$ lb, $y = +\frac{270K}{AG}$ (the plus sign indicates deflection in the direction of P_2, that is, up).

20. Determine the deflection due to shear at the center of a beam of uniform cross section. The loading is uniform and the beam is simply supported at the ends. Use Castigliano's theorem. Refer to Fig. 5-26.

Solution:

Insert a concentrated force Q at the point at which the deflection is to be determined. The shear strain energy is

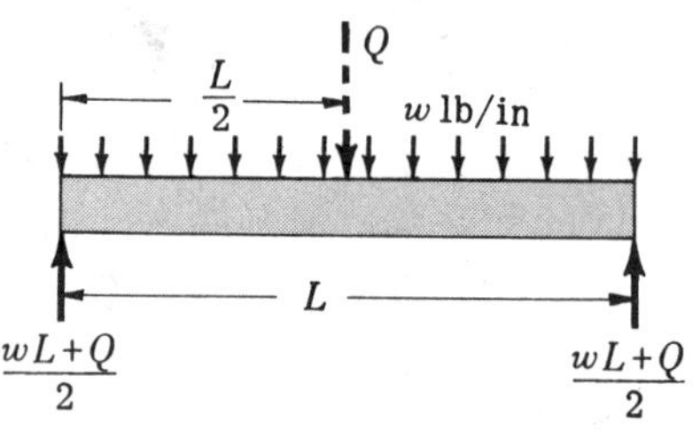

Fig. 5-26

$$U = \int_0^{L/2} \frac{K}{2AG}\left(\frac{wL}{2} + \frac{Q}{2} - wx\right)^2 dx + \int_{L/2}^{L} \frac{K}{2AG}\left(\frac{wL}{2} - \frac{Q}{2} - wx\right)^2 dx$$

$$= -\frac{K}{6AGw}\left[\left(\frac{Q}{2}\right)^3 - \left(\frac{wL}{2}+\frac{Q}{2}\right)^3 + \left(-\frac{wL}{2}-\frac{Q}{2}\right)^3 - \left(-\frac{Q}{2}\right)^3\right]$$

$$y = \frac{\partial U}{\partial Q} = -\frac{K}{6AGw}\left[\frac{3Q^2}{8} - \frac{3}{2}\left(\frac{wL}{2}+\frac{Q}{2}\right)^2 - \frac{3}{2}\left(-\frac{wL}{2}-\frac{Q}{2}\right)^2 + \frac{3}{2}\left(-\frac{Q}{2}\right)^2\right]$$

and for $Q = 0$, $y = KwL^2/8AG$.

21. Two rotors are to be mounted on three bearings and coupled together as illustrated in Fig. 5-27(*a*). It is required that, after installation, the bending moment in shaft B at the center bearing be very nearly zero. The installation procedure is shown in Fig. 5-27(*b*). Shaft B will be mounted in its bearings. Shaft A will be mounted in its bearing (No. 1) and temporarily supported at the coupling. The support for bearing No. 1 will be adjusted vertically to give the angle ϕ, between faces of the coupling halves, the proper value. The coupling halves will then be bolted tightly together and the temporary support removed. Determine the necessary value of the angle ϕ.

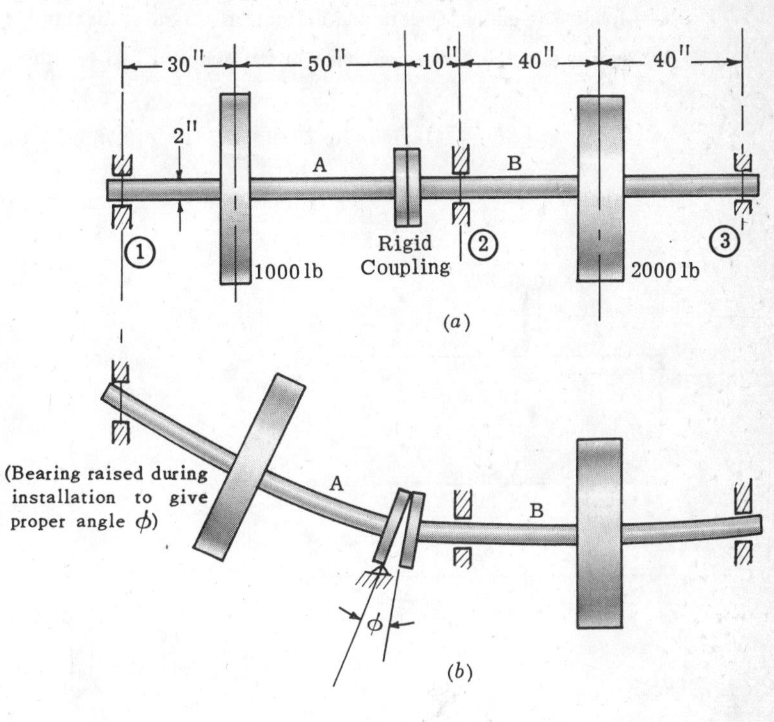

Fig. 5-27

Solution:

(*a*) Freebody diagrams of the two rotors will be as shown in Fig. 5-28 below. M_C is the bending moment set up at the coupling when it is bolted together. F is the vertical force that one coupling half exerts on the other.

(*b*) Taking moments around the left end of shaft A,

$$M_C + 80F = (1000)(30).$$

The bending moment in shaft B at bearing No. 2 must be zero:

$$M_C - 10F = 0.$$

(*c*) Solving the above two equations simultaneously,

$$F = 333.3 \text{ lb},$$
$$M_C = 3333 \text{ in-lb}.$$

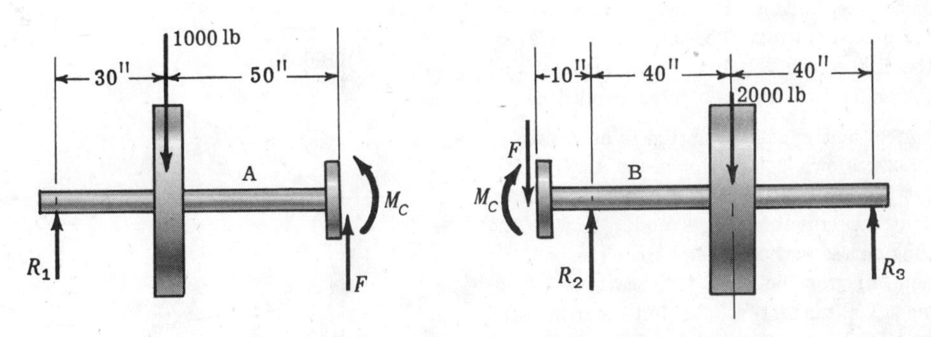

Fig. 5-28

(*d*) We now study the elastic curve of shaft A before and after bolting of the coupling halves. Fig. 5-29 below shows loading, bending moment and deflection diagrams for this shaft before bolting.

The slope of the deflection curve at the coupling end is $Z_1/80$. By the area-moment theorem we calculate

$$Z_1EI \;=\; (18{,}750)(50/2)(30+50/3) + (18{,}750)(30/2)(20) \;=\; 27.50\times10^6$$

Hence angle $\gamma_1 \approx \dfrac{Z_1}{80} = \dfrac{27.50\times10^6}{80EI}$ radians ($\tan\gamma_1 \approx \gamma_1$ since the angle is small).

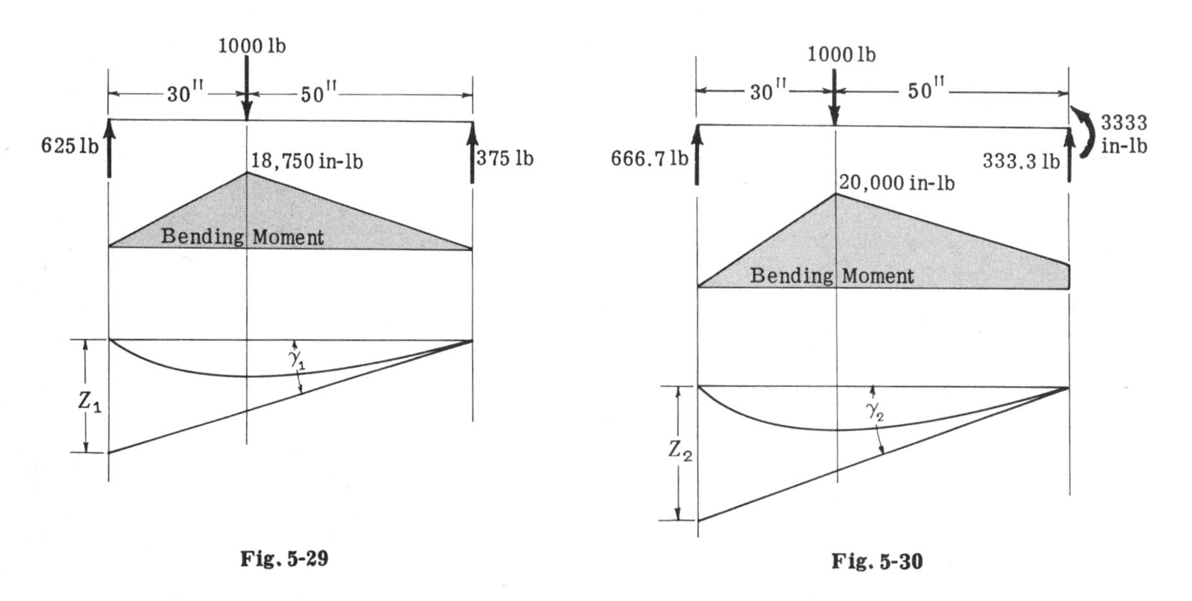

Fig. 5-29 **Fig. 5-30**

Fig. 5-30 above shows the loading, bending moment and deflection diagrams for shaft A after bolting. Calculation by the area-moment theorem yields $Z_2EI = 34.61\times10^6$; then $\gamma_2 = \dfrac{34.61\times10^6}{80EI}$ radians.

(*e*) The angle through which the coupling half attached to shaft A must be rotated upon bolting is

$$\gamma_2 - \gamma_1 \;=\; \left(\frac{(34.61-27.50)10^6}{80EI}\right)\frac{180}{\pi} \text{ degree}$$

Since $E = 3\times10^7$ psi for steel and $I = \pi 2^4/64$ in^4, $\gamma_2-\gamma_1 = 0.215$ deg.

(*f*) We now study the elastic curve for shaft B before and after bolting. Fig. 5-31 shows the situation before bolting. The portion of the shaft to the left of the left bearing is straight and makes angle γ_3 with the bearing centerline.

After bolting, the situation is as shown in Fig. 5-32 below. The portion of the shaft to the left of the left bearing is now curved and a tangent at the left end makes angle γ_4 with the bearing centerline. However, since the bending moment diagram between the bearings is unchanged, a tangent at the left bearing still makes angle γ_3 with the bearing centerline. The angle through which the coupling half must be turned upon bolting is $(\gamma_4-\gamma_3)$.

But $EI(\gamma_4-\gamma_3)$ = the area of the bending

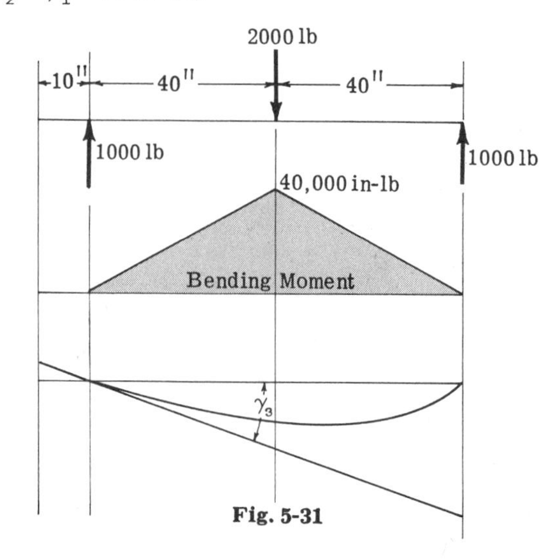

Fig. 5-31

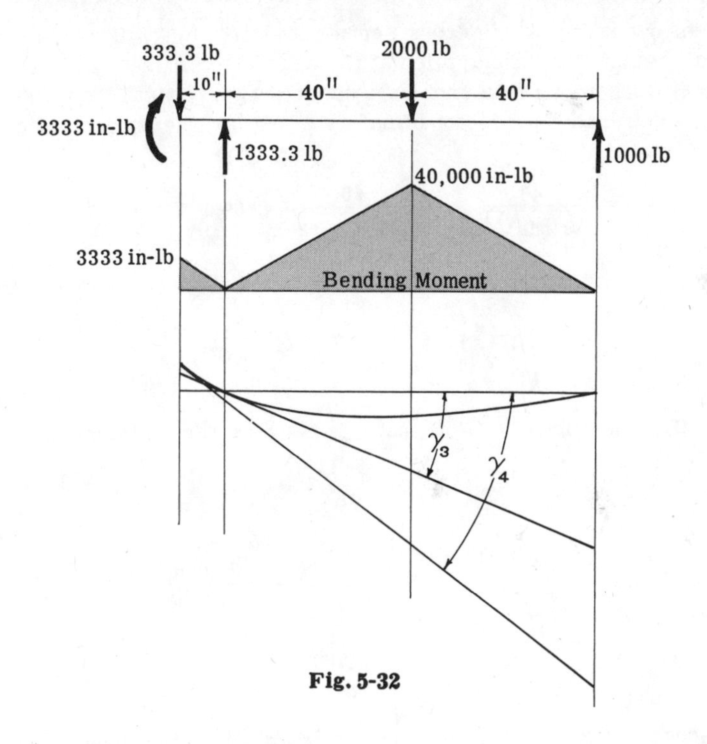

Fig. 5-32

moment diagram between the left shaft end and the left bearing.

$$\gamma_4 - \gamma_3 = \frac{(3333/2)(10)}{EI}\left(\frac{180}{\pi}\right) = 0.041 \text{ deg.}$$

(*g*) Then, finally, the angle between coupling halves before bolting should be

$$\phi = 0.215 + 0.041 = 0.256 \text{ deg.}$$

22. A tapered shaft section shown in Fig. 5-33(*a*) is sometimes more conveniently analyzed if replaced by an approximately equivalent stepped section as shown in Fig. 5-33(*b*). For approximately equivalent stiffness, the step diameters should be determined as follows:

$$(D_1')^4 = \frac{D_0^4 + D_1^4}{2},$$

$$(D_2')^4 = \frac{D_1^4 + D_2^4}{2},$$

$$(D_3')^4 = \frac{D_2^4 + D_3^4}{2}$$

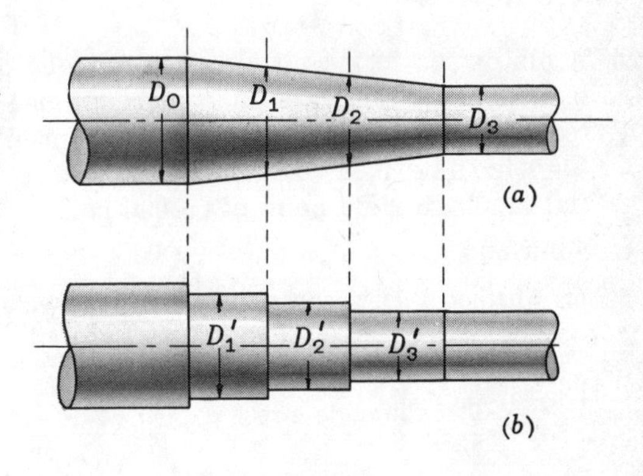

Fig. 5-33

23. In the vicinity of shoulders and grooves, not all the material is effective in stiffening the shaft. A rough rule is to ignore the material shaded as shown in Fig. 5-34.

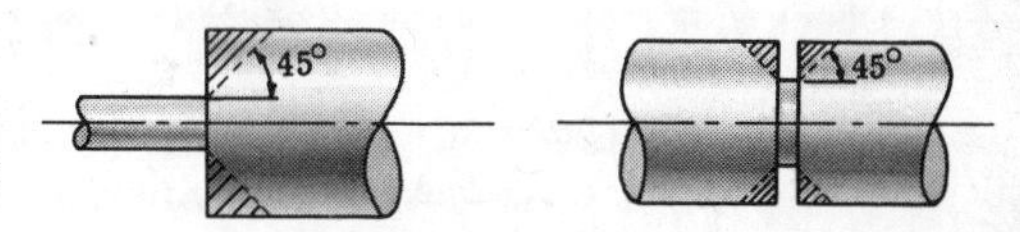

Fig. 5-34

24. A rectangular steel bar is 2"×3" in cross section and 40" long. The yield point of the material used is 50,000 psi. Axial loads are applied at the ends. Determine: (*a*) the L/k ratio; (*b*) whether the Euler or the J.B. Johnson formula should be used; (*c*) the critical load, the ends being relatively rigid; (*d*) the safe axial load for a factor of safety $N = 3$; (*e*) the equivalent compressive stress.

Solution:

(*a*)
$$\frac{L}{k} = \frac{40}{\sqrt{I(\min)/A}} = \frac{40}{\sqrt{(bh^3/12)/bh}} = 69.3 \quad \text{for } h = 2''$$

(*b*) The value of L/k below which the J.B. Johnson formula and above which the Euler formula is to be used is

$$\frac{L}{k} = \sqrt{\frac{2C\pi^2 E}{s_y}} = \sqrt{\frac{2(1)(\pi^2)(30)(10^6)}{50,000}} = 109$$

Thus, use the J.B. Johnson formula. Note that C is taken as 1, even though the ends are considered relatively rigid.

(*c*) The critical load is

$$F_{cr} = s_y A\left[1 - \frac{s_y (L/k)^2}{4C\pi^2 E}\right] = 50,000(6)\left[1 - \frac{50,000(69.3)^2}{4(1)(\pi^2)(30)(10^6)}\right] = 239,000 \text{ lb.}$$

(*d*) The safe axial load $F = F_{cr}/N = 239,000/3 = 79,700$ lb.

(*e*) The equivalent compressive stress $s_{eq} = \dfrac{F}{A}\left[\dfrac{1}{1 - \dfrac{s_y (L/k)^2}{4C\pi^2 E}}\right] = 16,700$ psi.

Note that the above stress is the same as would have been gotten from

$$\frac{s_y}{s_{eq}} = N, \quad \frac{50,000}{s_{eq}} = 3, \quad \text{or} \quad s_{eq} = 16,700 \text{ psi.}$$

Note also that just using F/A gives $79,700/6 = 13,800$ psi for a stress, which has no meaning since column effect is present.

25. A piston rod for an air cylinder is to be designed for an axial load of 6000 lb. The rod when extended has a length of 20". Although one end of the rod is fastened more or less rigidly to the piston and the other end of the rod is pinned to a member which is constrained in a guide, the value of $C = 1$ is to be used. Determine the size of rod to be used for a factor of safety of 2.5 with a material having a yield point of 40,000 psi.

Solution:

(*a*) Whether Euler's equation or J.B. Johnson's equation is to be used cannot be determined at start, since the diameter is unknown. A trial and error procedure is in order. Let's try Euler's equation and check at the end, using the equation in the equivalent stress form.

The allowable stress $s_{eq} = s_y/N = 40,000/2.5 = 16,000$ psi.

$$s_{eq} = \frac{F}{A}\left[\frac{s_y (L/k)^2}{C\pi^2 E}\right] \quad \text{or} \quad 16,000 = \frac{6000}{\frac{1}{4}\pi D^2}\left[\frac{40,000(20/\frac{1}{4}D)^2}{(1)\pi^2(30\times 10^6)}\right]$$

from which $D = 0.802''$. Try $D = 13/16''$.

(*b*) Check L/k: $\dfrac{L}{k} = \dfrac{L}{\frac{1}{4}D} = \dfrac{20}{\frac{1}{4}(13/16)} = 98.5$

For $C = 1$, $E = 30\times 10^6$ psi, and a yield point of 40,000 psi, Euler's equation should be used if L/k is larger than 121. Therefore J.B. Johnson's equation should have been used.

(*c*) Using J.B. Johnson's formula, $D = 0.833''$. Hence use $D = 7/8''$. Final check: $\dfrac{L}{k} = \dfrac{L}{\frac{1}{4}D} = \dfrac{20}{\frac{1}{4}(7/8)} = 91.4$.

26. A 1" square threaded screw is 15" long between the nut and collar. The axial load is 5000 lb and the torque in the screw between the nut and collar is 1000 in-lb. Using $C = 1$ and neglecting the threads, determine the factor of safety if a steel with a yield point in tension of 50,000 psi is used. (Consider steady loading.)

Solution:

(*a*) Root diameter of a 1" square threaded screw is 0.783". $\frac{L}{k} = \frac{15}{0.783/4} = 76.6.$

(*b*) The value of L/k which determines whether we use J.B. Johnson's formula or Euler's formula:

$$\frac{L}{k} = \sqrt{\frac{2C\pi^2 E}{s_y}} = \sqrt{\frac{2(1)(\pi^2)(30)(10^6)}{50,000}} = 109$$

Therefore use J.B. Johnson's formula with $L/k = 76.6$.

(*c*) The equivalent compressive stress is

$$s_{eq} = \frac{F}{A}\left[\frac{1}{1 - \dfrac{s_y (L/k)^2}{4C\pi^2 E}}\right] = \frac{5000}{\frac{1}{4}\pi(0.783)^2}\left[\frac{1}{1 - \dfrac{50,000(76.6)^2}{4(1)(\pi^2)(30)(10^6)}}\right] = 13,900 \text{ psi}$$

(*d*) The shearing stress due to torsion is $s_s = \frac{Tc}{J} = \frac{1000(0.783/2)}{(\pi/32)(0.783)^4} = 10,600$ psi.

(*e*) The maximum shear stress is $\tau(\max) = \sqrt{(s_{eq}/2)^2 + s_s^2} = \sqrt{(13,900/2)^2 + (10,600)^2} = 12,650$ psi.

(*f*) The yield point in shear is about $0.5 s_y = 0.5(50,000) = 25,000$ psi.

The factor of safety is 25,000/12,650 = 1.98.

27. Same as Problem 26, except the load is applied repetitively from zero to maximum. Take the actual stress concentration factor K_f for the threads in axial loading as 2.8 and the actual stress concentration factor K_f' for the threads in torsion as 2.0 (assumed). The endurance limit for the material for reversed bending is 32,000 psi.

Solution:

(*a*) From Problem 26, the maximum equivalent column compressive stress is 13,900 psi and the maximum torsional stress is 10,600 psi.

(*b*) The equivalent normal stress due to the variable loading, with a maximum stress of 13,900 psi, a mean stress of 13,900/2 or 6950 psi and a variable stress of 6950 psi, is

$$s_e = s_m + \frac{s_y K_f s_v}{s_n ABC} = 6950 + \frac{(50,000)(2.8)(6950)}{(32,000)(.7)(.85)(1)} = 58,000 \text{ psi}$$

where $A = 0.7$ (axial loading), $B = .85$ (size effect), $C = 1$ (since actual stress concentration factor is used).

(*c*) The equivalent shear stress due to the variable loading, with a maximum of 10,600 psi, a mean stress of 5300 psi, and a variable stress of 5300 psi, is

$$s_{es} = s_{ms} + \frac{s_y K_f' s_{vs}}{s_n ABC} = 5300 + \frac{(50,000)(.6)(2.0)(5300)}{(32,000)(.6)(.85)(1)} = 24,800 \text{ psi}$$

(*d*) The equivalent shear stress due to the variable loading is

$$\tau_e = \sqrt{(s_e/2)^2 + (s_{es})^2} = \sqrt{(58,000/2)^2 + (24,800)^2} = 38,200 \text{ psi}$$

(*e*) The safe design stress τ_e treating τ_e as a static stress is

$$\frac{s_{ys}}{N} = \frac{0.5(50,000)}{N} = 38,300 \text{ psi}$$

from which $N = 0.65$. A suitable value of N for safe design may be taken as 1.5, or the proposed design is unsatisfactory.

Note that in this problem there are two "equivalent" stresses, one due to an equivalent compressive stress and the other due to variable loading.

28. Derive the equivalent column stress relation for the Euler formula.

Solution:

$$F_{cr} = \frac{C\pi^2 EA}{(L/k)^2}, \qquad \frac{F_{cr}}{NA} = \frac{C\pi^2 E}{N(L/k)^2}, \qquad \frac{F}{A} = \frac{C\pi^2 E}{N(L/k)^2}$$

where N is the factor of safety, A is the area, and the safe load $F = F_{cr}/N$.

Put $N = \dfrac{s_y}{s_{eq}}$ in the last equation and solve for $s_{eq} = \dfrac{F}{A}\left[\dfrac{s_y\,(L/k)^2}{C\pi^2 E}\right]$.

29. Derive the equivalent column stress relation for the J.B. Johnson formula.

Solution:

$$F_{cr} = s_y A\left[1 - \frac{s_y (L/k)^2}{4C\pi^2 E}\right], \qquad \frac{F_{cr}}{NA} = \frac{s_y}{N}\left[1 - \frac{s_y (L/k)^2}{4C\pi^2 E}\right], \qquad \frac{F}{A} = \frac{s_y}{N}\left[1 - \frac{s_y (L/k)^2}{4C\pi^2 E}\right]$$

where N is the factor of safety, A is the area, and the safe load $F = F_{cr}/N$.

Put $N = \dfrac{s_y}{s_{eq}}$ in the last equation and solve for $s_{eq} = \dfrac{F}{A}\left[\dfrac{1}{1 - \dfrac{s_y\,(L/k)^2}{4C\pi^2 E}}\right]$.

SUPPLEMENTARY PROBLEMS

30. Show that the bending deflection at the end of a cantilever beam of length L, due to uniformly distributed load of w lb per unit length is $wL^4/8EI$
(a) using the area moment method, (b) using the theorem of Castigliano.

31. Using a step function, set up the equation for $EI(d^2y/dx^2)$ and by double integration show that the maximum deflection of a cantilever beam of length L, due to a concentrated load P at a distance a units from the free end and at a distance b units from the fixed end is $\dfrac{Pb^2}{6EI}(2b + 3a)$ at the free end.

32. Determine the vertical deflection due to bending at $x = a$, for a horizontal member of length L when subjected to a horizontal force F acting to the left and at a distance h units above the neutral axis at the section where $x = a$, as shown in Fig. 5-35.
(a) Use the conjugate beam method.
(b) Use a step function and apply double integration.
Ans. $y = \dfrac{Fha}{3EIL}(L-a)(L-2a)$

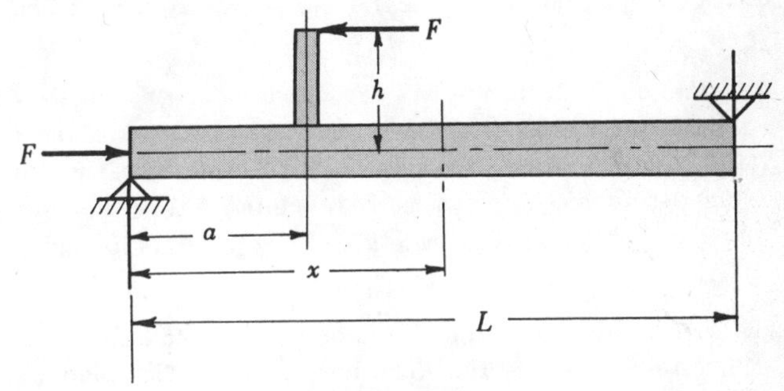

Fig. 5-35

33. A 2 inch diameter steel shaft is freely supported on two bearings 30 inches apart. The shaft operates at 1800 rpm and carries a flywheel mounted midway between the bearings. What should be the weight of the flywheel if it is desired to operate at 50% of the critical speed of the shaft? Use the conjugate beam method of solution for deflection.
Ans. y = 0.00271 in. required. (See Chapter 8 for critical speed.) Weight of flywheel = 113.5 lb.

34. A shaft of constant diameter is simply supported at the ends. The distance between supports is 20 in. and a mass weighing 50 lb is located 4 in. to the right of the left bearing. The shaft must operate at 1800 rpm and it is known that a minimum critical speed or whirling speed of 2500 rpm would give satisfactory operation. What is the minimum diameter of shaft that can be used so that the minimum critical speed is 2500 rpm?
Ans. Deflection at the load = $3412/EI$. Minimum shaft diameter = 0.81 in.

35. A steel shaft, freely supported at its ends, is made up of three sections. The first section, 12 in. long, has a constant diameter. The second section, 24 in. long, has a diameter twice that of the first section. The third section, 12 in. long, has a diameter the same as that of the first section. Equal concentrated loads of 200 lb are applied at the sections where the diameters change. Show that the deflection under each concentrated load is $0.0929/D^4$, where D is the diameter of the first and third sections.

36. A steel shaft, freely supported on bearings 2 feet apart, carries a concentrated load of 200 lb 8 in. from the right bearing and a load of 100 lb 10 in. from the left bearing. The diameter of the shaft is constant. Show that the deflection under the 100 lb load is $0.00244/I$ and that the deflection under the 200 lb load is $0.00228/I$.

37. A 4 inch steel shaft is supported on bearings 5 feet apart and carries a 3000 lb disk $1\frac{1}{2}$ feet from the left bearing. The shaft has a 2 inch hole extending from the right bearing to the centerline of the 3000 lb disk. Determine the deflection at the disk. *Ans.* y = 0.027 in.

38. A shaft, of constant cross section and diameter 2 in., is freely supported by two bearings 30 in. apart. The shaft carries two masses, each weighing 400 lb. One mass is located 9 in. to the right of the left bearing, and the other mass is 9 in. to the left of the right bearing. Determine the deflection under each mass and the critical speed of the shaft. *Ans.* y = 0.0124 in. Critical speed = 1680 rpm. (See Chap. 8.)

39. The steel shaft of an engine is 24 in. long between bearings. For a distance of 8 in. from the left hand bearing the diameter is 2 in. The remainder of the shaft is 3 in. in diameter. A load of 1000 lb is concentrated at a point 10 in. from the left bearing, and a load of 2000 lb is concentrated at a point 15 in. from the left bearing. What is the deflection under each load?

Ans. y = 0.011 in. under 1000 lb, y = 0.0094 in. under 2000 lb

40. A 4 inch diameter shaft is freely supported in bearings 48 in. apart. In the center is a gear weighing 3000 lb. A 2 inch diameter hole in the center of the cross section extends 18 in. toward the gear from the left bearing. At this point the hole diameter decreases to $1\frac{1}{2}$ in. and the hole is continued through the remaining length of the shaft. Determine the deflection under the gear by three different methods, and compute the critical speed of the shaft.

Ans. y = 0.0189 in. Critical speed = 1365 rpm. (See Chap. 8.)

41. A steel shaft, 30 in. long, is supported on bearings at the ends. From the left bearing to a point 12 in. to the right of it the shaft diameter is 2 in. The remainder of the shaft is $1\frac{1}{2}$ in. in diameter. Two loads, each weighing 400 lb, are located one at the change of section and one at the middle of the smaller portion of the shaft. Using the conjugate beam method, determine the deflection under each load.

Ans. y = 0.0381 in. under left load. y = 0.0374 in. under right load.

42. A steel shaft, simply supported on bearings 45 in. apart, is to be of diameter D over the middle 15 in. and of diameter $0.75D$ over the 15 in. at each end. The shaft will carry a 4000 lb load at each change of diameter. If the static deflections at the points where the loads are located are not to exceed 0.001 in., what will be the maximum deflection of the shaft? Neglect weight of shaft in all calculations.

Ans. D = 6.15 in., y(max) = 0.00108 in. at center of shaft.

43. A steel shaft is simply supported on two bearings 30 in. apart. The shaft is of 3 in. diameter for a length of 10 in. from the left bearing, $2\frac{1}{2}$ in. diameter for the next 8 in., and 2 in. diameter for the remaining 12 in. A 700 lb load is carried at a point 10 in. to the right of the left bearing. Determine the static deflection under the 700 lb load. What will be the critical speed of the shaft?

Ans. y = 0.0056 in. The critical speed will be 2500 rpm. (See Chap. 8.)

44. A shaft, of diameter 2 in. and length 60 in., receives 10,000 in-lb torque from a pulley at the left end. A gear at the mid-length of the shaft delivers 6000 in-lb and another gear at the right end delivers the balance. Calculate the maximum total torsional deflection of the shaft for these conditions, neglecting the effect of keyways. Use $G = 11.5 \times 10^6$ psi. *Ans.* 1.335°

45. Determine the equation for the deflection due to shear for a simply supported uniformly loaded beam of length L. The loading is w lb/in.

Ans. $y = \dfrac{Kw}{2AG}(Lx - x^2)$, $y(\max) = \dfrac{KwL^2}{8AG}$ at $x = \dfrac{L}{2}$

46. A hollow steel shaft, 6" o.d. × $5\frac{1}{2}$" i.d. × 30" long, is supported at its ends and carries four rotors of equal weight and equally spaced 6" apart as shown in Fig. 5-36(a). Each rotor weighs 80 lb which includes $\frac{1}{4}$ of the shaft weight. Then for the loading as shown in Fig. 5-36(b), determine: (a) the shaft deflection due to bending at the two outer rotors, and at the two inner rotors; (b) the shaft deflection due to shear at the two outer rotors, and at the two inner rotors.

Ans. (a) $y = 1.44 \times 10^{-4}$ in. at outer rotors due to bending,
$y = 2.31 \times 10^{-4}$ in. at inner rotors due to bending.
(b) $y = 0.354 \times 10^{-4}$ in. at outer rotors due to shear,
$y = 0.532 \times 10^{-4}$ in. at inner rotors due to shear.

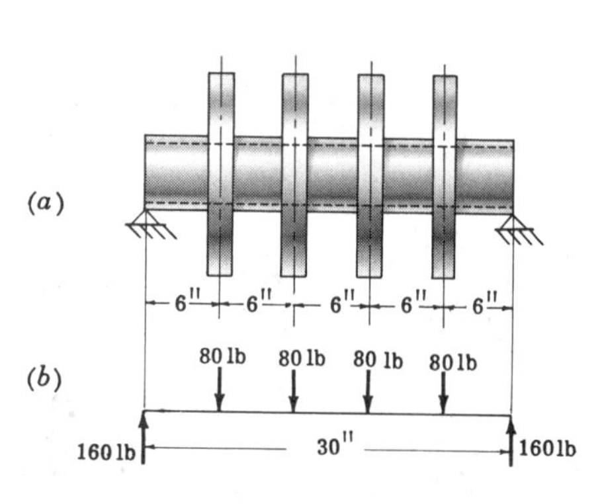

Fig. 5-36

47. Using Castigliano's theorem, derive the general equation for the deflection due to bending at any section of a simply supported beam of uniform cross section having a load P applied as shown in Fig. 5-37. *Hint*: Consider a concentrated imaginary load Q applied at a distance z from the left support. The distance z is variable, although z is considered as a fixed value in determining the strain energy. The distance z is limited to $0 \leqq z \leqq a$ for the bending moment diagram as shown.

Ans. $y = \dfrac{Pbz}{6LEI}[L^2 - b^2 - z^2]$.

This equation is valid for $0 \leqq z \leqq a$. In a similar manner the equation for the deflection to the right of the load P may be determined.

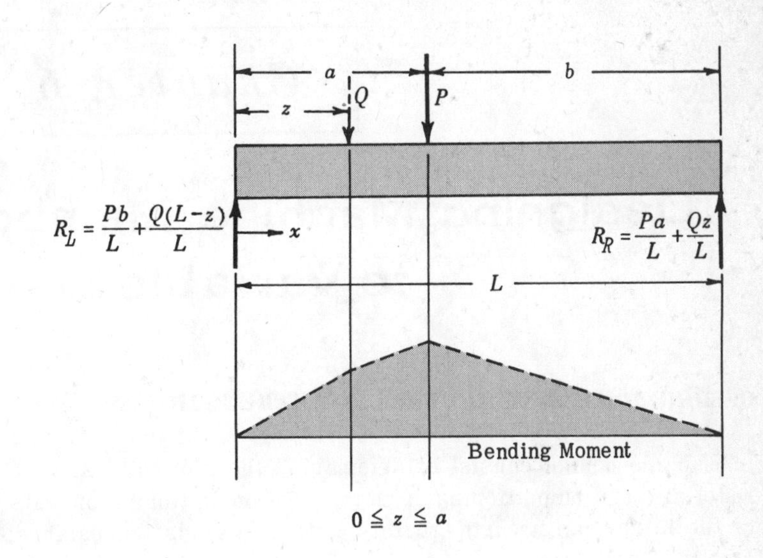

Fig. 5-37

COLUMN PROBLEMS

48. What is the allowable compressive load for a 1" × 2" bar that is 20" long for a factor of safety of 4? The yield point of the material is 40,000 psi. $C = 1$.
Ans. For $L/k = 69.4$, J.B. Johnson's formula applies. $F = 16{,}750$ lb

49. Same as above, except $C = \frac{1}{4}$. *Ans.* For $L/k = 69.4$, Euler's equation applies. $F = 7670$ lb

50. The piston rod of an air cylinder is 60" long. For an axial load of 2000 lb, the material being steel with a yield point of 40,000 psi, determine the size of rod required. Take factor of safety = 4 and $C = 1$.
Ans. Euler's equation applies. $D = 1.58$ in. Use $1\frac{5}{8}$ in.

51. A 1" square threaded screw is 40" long between the nut and collar. The axial load is 2000 lb and the torque in the screw between the nut and collar is 1000 in-lb. Using $C = 1$ and neglecting the threads and stress concentration, determine the factor of safety if a steel with a yield point in tension of 50,000 psi is used. The root diameter is 0.783 in.
Ans. Euler's equation applies. Equivalent column stress = 14,800 psi, torsional stress = 10,600 psi, maximum shear stress = 12,900 psi. The factor of safety for a yield point in shear of 25,000 psi is 1.93.

Chapter 6

Designing Machine Members Subjected to Variable Loads

DESIGNING MACHINE MEMBERS FOR STRENGTH is one of the necessary steps in setting the proportions of a machine member. The usual steps in machine design consist of determining the kinematic arrangement, a force analysis, selection of materials, and proportioning of parts. The proportioning of parts may be controlled by any one or all of the following: strength, rigidity, critical speeds, appearance, corrosion rate, fabrication, foundry practice, stability, etc.

THE STRENGTH OF A MACHINE MEMBER is influenced by many items such as stress concentration, fatigue or variable loading, shock, surface finish, and size of part.

STRESS CONCENTRATION may be caused by any discontinuity (stress raiser) such as holes, abrupt changes in the cross section, notches, grooves, and surface defects. A typical example of a stress raiser is shown in Fig.6-1, where a hole of diameter d is introduced in a tension member. The value of the maximum stress occuring at the edge of the hole may be thought of as the nominal stress multiplied by a stress concentration factor K_t.

$$s(\text{max}) \quad = \quad K_t \frac{P}{A}$$

where

P = total axial load, lb

A = net area at cross section containing the hole, in^2

K_t = theoretical stress concentration factor (*or geometric factor*)

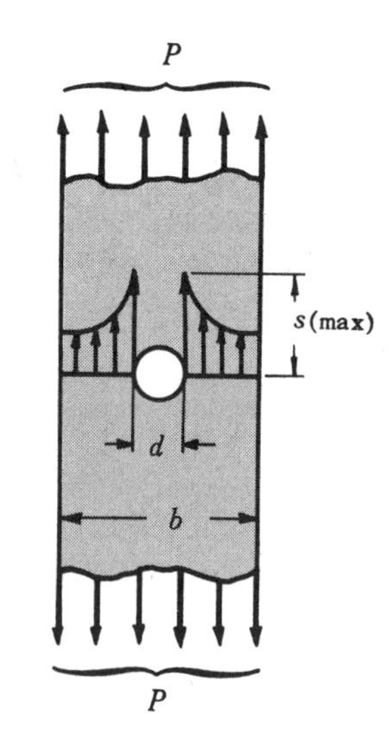

Fig. 6-1

The value of K_t is difficult to calculate in most cases, and is usually determined by some experimental technique such as photoelastic analysis of a plastic model of the part. Under steady loads, ductile materials are not affected by stress raisers to the extent that the photoelastic analysis might indicate due to a redistribution of the stresses in the region of the stress raisers resulting from plastic flow of the material when the maximum stress reaches the yield point. The effect of a stress raiser on brittle material such as cast iron, under steady load, may be as severe as the photoelastic analysis indicates since little or no plastic flow occurs. Under repeated loads, however, the endurance strength of even ductile materials may be greatly decreased due to stress concentration.

THE NOTCH SENSITIVITY q of the material may be used to determine the fatigue strength reduction factor or actual stress concentration factor K_f as a function of the theoretical stress concentration factor for the case of repeated loads. Values for q and K_t may be found in "Stress Concentration Factors" by R.E.Peterson, and in other literature pertaining to this subject.

$$q = \frac{K_f - 1}{K_t - 1} \qquad \text{or} \qquad K_f = 1 + q(K_t - 1)$$

where

q = an experimental notch sensitivity value due to stress concentration. Values range from 0 to 1.0.

K_t = theoretical value of the stress concentration factor. Average values range from 1.0 to 3.0, but could be greater than 3.0.

K_f = the actual stress concentration factor for determining the reduction in the fatigue-strength of the material.

VARIABLE STRESSES may be classified as (*a*) **reversed**, (*b*) **repeated**, (*c*) **fluctuating**, and (*d*) **alternating** as shown in Fig.6-2. The maximum stress is the largest algebraic value and the minimum stress is the lowest algebraic value of a variable stress. The mean stress s_m is the average of the maximum and minimum stress. The variable stress s_v is the increase or decrease in stress above or below the mean stress.

$$s_m = \tfrac{1}{2}\left[s(\max) + s(\min)\right], \qquad s_v = \tfrac{1}{2}\left[s(\max) - s(\min)\right]$$

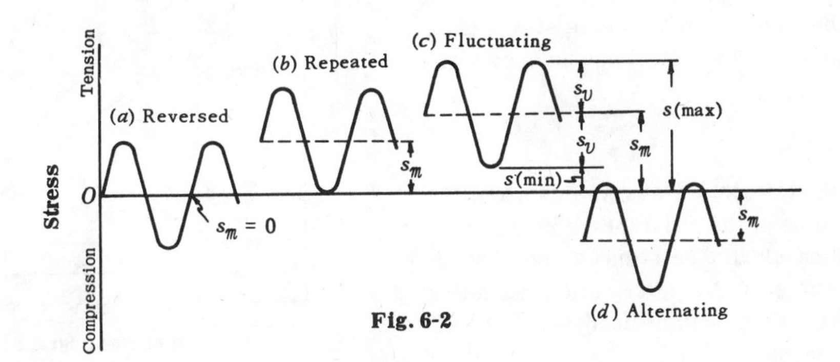

Fig. 6-2

THE ENDURANCE LIMIT of a material is determined experimentally by rotating a test specimen while it is loaded in bending. Typical curves showing the endurance strength of a ferrous and a non-ferrous material are presented in Fig.6-3. Note that the endurance limit of this particular steel specimen is rather sharply defined at about 35,500 psi, while the aluminum specimen has no well defined endurance limit. The value of the endurance limit of 35,500 for the steel specimen is for reversed loading, where a point on the outer fiber is stressed alternately by equal amounts of compression and tension. In order to avoid confusion, the term "endurance limit" will be used for reversed bending only. For other types of loading, the term "endurance strength" will be used when referring

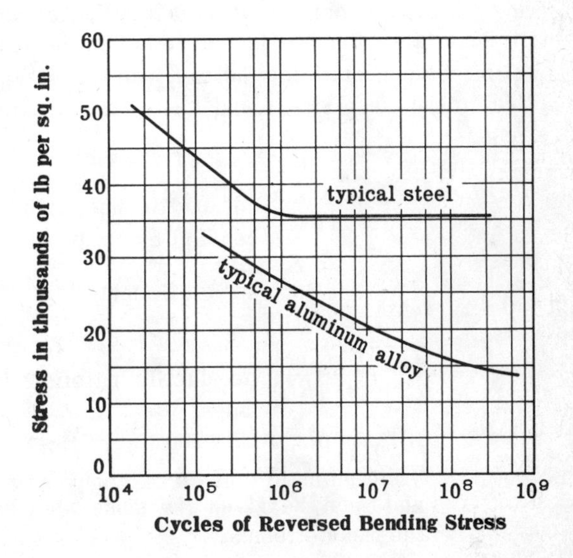

Fig. 6-3

to the fatigue strength of the material. The value of the endurance strength will be different from the endurance limit for other types of loading, and will also be different if the specimen is subjected to variable stresses due to torsion or axial loads. One method of plotting the endurance strength versus the mean stress for various types of loading is the modified Goodman diagram shown in Fig. 6-4. Each material tested would have its own Goodman diagram. However, if no test data are available, approximate Goodman diagrams may be constructed for various ductile materials by assuming that the endurance limit under reversed loading will be approximately equal to one half of the ultimate strength of the material. More recently, endurance strength data have been plotted in the form shown in Fig. 6-5. This plot shows the relationship of the modified Goodman line with the more conservative Soderberg line. In the following discussion we shall use the Soderberg line as our design basis. If we apply a suitable factor of safety N to both the endurance limit and yield strength, we may draw line CD parallel to the Soderberg line AB as shown in Fig. 6-6. Line CD may then be considered as a safe stress line. From the geometry of this plot, it can be shown that

$$\frac{1}{N} = \frac{s_m}{s_y} + \frac{s_v}{s_r}$$

In order to make this into a design equation, the experimental value of the endurance limit s_r under reversed bending should be reduced for size effect, surface effect, and type of variable loading if torsional or axial instead of bending. The calculated variable stress should be increased by the actual stress concentration factor K_f for ductile materials. For brittle materials the theoretical stress concentration factor K_t should be applied to the mean stress and K_f to the variable stress.

$$\frac{1}{N} = \frac{s_m}{s_y} + \frac{K_f s_v}{s_r ABC}$$ for ductile materials in tension or compression

$$\frac{1}{N} = \frac{s_m}{s_y} K_t + \frac{s_v K_f}{s_r ABC}$$ for brittle materials

$$\frac{1}{N} = \frac{s_{ms}}{s_{ys}} + \frac{K_f s_{vs}}{s_r ABC}$$ for ductile materials in shear

where

s_y = yield point in tension or compression and must be given the same sign as the mean stress s_m.

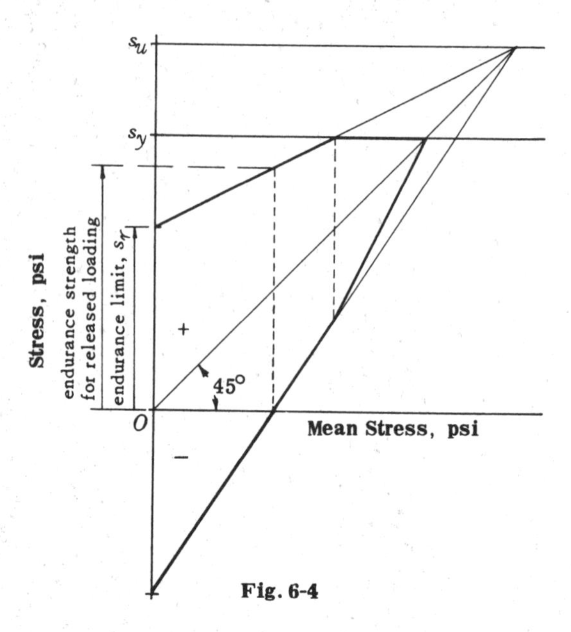

Fig. 6-4

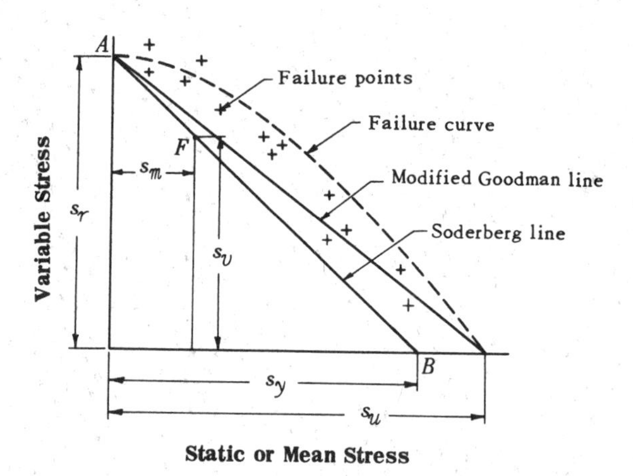

Fig. 6-5

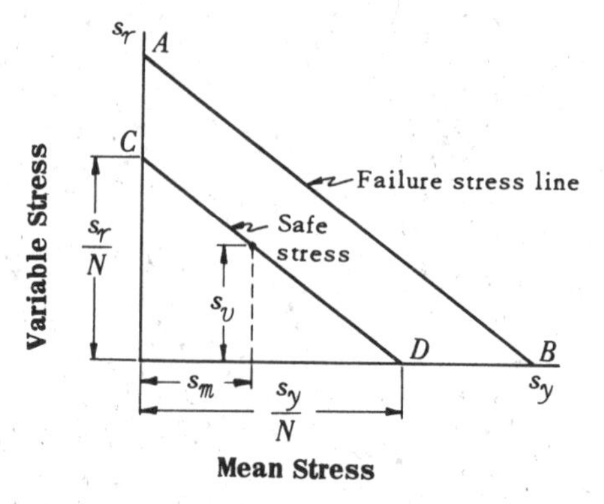

Fig. 6-6

s_m = mean normal stress, psi.
s_{ms} = mean shear stress, psi.
s_v = variable normal stress, psi.
s_{vs} = variable shear stress, psi.
s_r = endurance limit of the material in reversed bending, psi.
K_t = theoretical stress concentration factor.
K_f = actual stress concentration factor based on the notch sensitivity of the material.
A = correction factor for type of loading other than reversed bending.
A = 0.7 for reversed axial loading.
A = 0.6 for reversed torsional loading.
B = a size correction factor, since a standard test specimen has a nominal diameter of 0.3 in.
B = 0.85 for parts ranging in size from $\frac{1}{2}$ in. to 2 in.
C = a surface correction factor, since the test specimen was polished.

Some average values for C for a machined surface and for a hot rolled surface are listed below:

s_u	C **Machined surface**	C **Hot rolled surface**
60,000	0.91	0.72
70,000	0.90	0.68
80,000	0.88	0.62
90,000	0.86	0.58
100,000	0.85	0.55
110,000	0.84	0.50
120,000	0.82	0.48
150,000	0.78	0.38
200,000	0.72	0.30

N = factor of safety to account for such items as variations in material properties, uncertainty of loading, accuracy of assumptions, workmanship, possible loss of life, cost of shutdowns or maintenance, lack or spread of test data, etc. The value of N will range from about 1.25 to 3.0 for ordinary design, depending upon whether the conditions are well defined or if considerable uncertainty exists. Values of N greater than 3 might be used if the uncertainty is quite high and the consequences of failure are serious. The selection of N is a matter of judgment.

THE EQUIVALENT MAXIMUM SHEAR STRESS, τ_{es}(max), when we have both a variable normal stress and a variable shear stress, may be determined by using the theory of combined stresses. The equivalent normal stress s_{en} is

$$s_{en} = s_m + \left(\frac{s_y}{s_r}\right)\frac{K_f s_v}{ABC}$$

The equivalent shear stress, s_{es}, is

$$s_{es} = s_{ms} + \left(\frac{s_{ys}}{s_r}\right)\frac{K_f s_{vs}}{ABC}$$

Note: Put A = 0.6 in this equation when using ductile materials, and use $s_{ys} = (0.6)(s_y)$.

Then the equivalent maximum shear stress $\tau_{es}(\max)$ in designing with ductile materials is

$$\tau_{es}(\max) = \sqrt{(\tfrac{1}{2}s_{en})^2 + (s_{es})^2}$$

This may be equated to s_{ys}/N for use as a design equation,

$$s_{ys}/N = \sqrt{(\tfrac{1}{2}s_{en})^2 + (s_{es})^2}$$

Note: Use $s_{ys} = 0.5\,s_y$ for this equation.

The equivalent maximum normal stress to be used when designing with brittle materials is

$$s_{en}(\max) = \tfrac{1}{2}s_{en} + \sqrt{(\tfrac{1}{2}s_{en})^2 + (s_{es})^2}$$

This may be equated to s_y/N for use as a design equation

$$s_y/N = \tfrac{1}{2}s_{en} + \sqrt{(\tfrac{1}{2}s_{en})^2 + (s_{es})^2}$$

The value of the yield point in shear, s_{ys}, for use in the above equivalent shear stress, s_{es}, equation may be taken as 0.6 times the yield point in tension. This is in close agreement with experimental torsional shear tests. However, the value of the yield point in shear, s_{ys}, should be taken as 0.5 times the yield point in tension for use in the maximum shear design equation. This equation is based on the maximum shear theory of failure which considers a member in simple tension.

SOLVED PROBLEMS

1. A steel connecting rod made of AISI 8650 steel, oil quenched at 1500°F and tempered at 1000°F, is to be subjected to a reversed axial load of 40,000 lb. Determine the required diameter of the rod, using a factor of safety $N = 2$. Assume no column action.

Solution:

The properties of this material are: $s_u = 155{,}000$ psi, $s_y = 132{,}000$ psi. Assume that the endurance limit for reversed bending is half the ultimate tensile strength:

$$s_r = \tfrac{1}{2}(155{,}000) = 77{,}500 \text{ psi.}$$

The mean stress is $s_m = 0$.

The variable stress is $s_v = \dfrac{F}{A} = \dfrac{4F}{\pi d^2} = \dfrac{4(40{,}000)}{\pi d^2}$.

The endurance limit correction factor for axial loading is $A = 0.7$.

The endurance limit correction factor for size, estimating $d > \frac{1}{2}$ in., is $B = 0.85$.

Using the endurance limit correction factor for a machined surface, $C = 0.8$.

Assuming no stress concentration, $K_f = 1$.

Substituting in the design equation

$$\frac{1}{N} = \frac{s_m}{s_y} + \frac{K_f s_v}{s_r ABC}, \quad \frac{1}{2} = 0 + \frac{(1)(4)(40{,}000)}{\pi d^2(77{,}500)(0.7)(0.85)(0.8)}, \quad \text{and } d = 1.66 \text{ in.} \quad \text{Use } d = 1\tfrac{3}{4} \text{ in.}$$

2. A hot rolled AISI 1025 steel rod is to be subjected to a torsional load that will vary from a -1000 in-lb to 4000 in-lb. Determine the required diameter of the rod using a factor of safety $N = 1.75$.

Solution:

The properties of this material are: $s_u = 67{,}000$ psi, $s_y = 45{,}000$ psi.

Assume that the endurance limit for reversed bending is $s_r = \frac{1}{2}(67{,}000) = 33{,}500$ psi. Assume that the yield strength in shear is 0.6 of the yield strength in tension: $s_{ys} = (0.6)(45{,}000) = 27{,}000$ psi. Assuming no stress concentration, $K_f = 1$.

The endurance limit correction factor for torsional loading is $A = 0.6$. The endurance limit correction factor for size, estimating $d > \frac{1}{2}$ in., is $B = 0.85$. The endurance limit correction factor for hot rolled material for $s_u = 67{,}000$ psi is $C = 0.68$.

The mean and variable stresses are based on the mean and variable torques. The mean torque is

$$T_m = \tfrac{1}{2}[T(\max) + T(\min)] = \tfrac{1}{2}[4000 + (-1000)] = 1500 \text{ in-lb.}$$

The variable torque is

$$T_v = \tfrac{1}{2}[T(\max) - T(\min)] = \tfrac{1}{2}[4000 - (-1000)] = 2500 \text{ in-lb.}$$

Then for any point on the outer surface,

$$s_{ms} = \frac{T_m c}{J} = \frac{16T_m}{\pi d^3} = \frac{(16)(1500)}{\pi d^3} = \frac{24{,}000}{\pi d^3}, \qquad s_{vs} = \frac{T_v c}{J} = \frac{16T_v}{\pi d^3} = \frac{(16)(2500)}{\pi d^3} = \frac{40{,}000}{\pi d^3}$$

Substituting in the design equation

$$\frac{1}{N} = \frac{s_{ms}}{s_{ys}} + \frac{K_f s_{vs}}{s_r ABC}, \qquad \frac{1}{1.75} = \frac{24{,}000}{\pi d^3(27{,}000)} + \frac{(1)(40{,}000)}{\pi d^3(33{,}500)(0.6)(0.85)(0.68)},$$

and $d = 1.34$. Use $d = 1\frac{3}{8}$ in.

3. A cantilever beam, made of cold drawn C-1025 steel of circular cross section as shown in Fig. 6-7, is subjected to a load which varies from $-F$ to $3F$. Determine the maximum load that this member can withstand for an indefinite life using a factor of safety $N = 2$. A photoelastic model indicates a theoretical stress concentration factor of $K_t = 1.42$ and the notch sensitivity for a $\frac{1}{8}$ in. radius for this material is $q = 0.9$. Analyze at the change of cross section only.

Solution:

For C-1025 cold drawn material:

$s_u = 80{,}000$ psi.
$s_y = 68{,}000$ psi.
$s_r = 40{,}000$ psi.
$K_f = 1 + q(K_t - 1) = 1 + 0.9(1.42 - 1) = 1.38$.
$A = 1$, since the member is loaded in bending.
$B = 0.85$ correction factor for size effect.
$C = 0.88$ correction factor for surface effect.

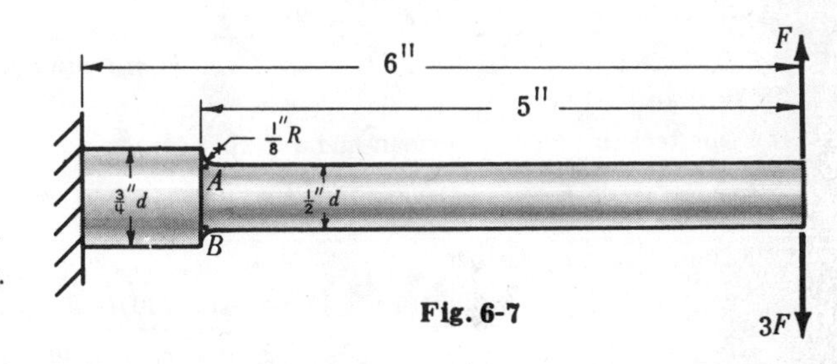

Fig. 6-7

The bending moment at the change in cross section varies from $-5F$ to $15F$. The bending stress at point A in terms of the bending moment is

$$s_b = \frac{32M}{\pi d^3} = \frac{32M}{\pi 0.5^3} = 81.5M$$

Then $\quad s(\min) = (81.5)(-5F) = -407.5F \qquad s_m = \tfrac{1}{2}[1222.5F + (-407.5F)] = 407.5F$

$\quad s(\max) = (81.5)(15F) = 1222.5F \qquad s_v = \tfrac{1}{2}[1222.5F - (-407.5F)] = 815F$

Substituting in $\frac{1}{N} = \frac{s_m}{s_y} + \frac{K_f s_v}{s_r ABC}$, $\frac{1}{2} = \frac{407.5F}{68,000} + \frac{(1.38)(815F)}{(40,000)(0.85)(0.88)}$ and $F = 11.5$ lb.

As a matter of interest, we could have analyzed the stress at point B as follows:

$$s(\text{min}) = -1222.5F \qquad s_m = \tfrac{1}{2}[407.5F + (-1222.5F)] = -407.5F$$

$$s(\text{max}) = +407.5F \qquad s_v = \tfrac{1}{2}[407.5F - (-1222.5F)] = +815F$$

Substituting in $\frac{1}{N} = \frac{s_m}{s_y} + \frac{K_f s_v}{s_r ABC}$ and noting that s_y will be given a negative sign to agree with the negative sign of the mean stress,

$$\frac{1}{2} = \frac{-407.5F}{-68,000} + \frac{(1.38)(815F)}{(40,000)(0.85)(0.88)} \qquad \text{from which} \qquad F = 11.5 \text{ lb.}$$

4. A cold drawn C–1025 steel rod of circular cross section is subjected to a variable bending moment of 5000 in-lb to 10,000 in-lb, as the axial load varies from 1000 lb to 3000 lb. The maximum bending moment occurs at the same instant that the axial load is maximum. Determine the required diameter of the rod for a factor of safety $N = 2$. Neglect any stress concentration and column effect. Design on the basis of the maximum shear stress.

Solution:

For C–1025 cold drawn material:

s_u = 80,000 psi
s_y = 68,000 psi
s_r = 40,000 psi
K_f = 1 for no stress concentration

B = 0.85 correction factor for size effect
C = 0.88 correction factor for surface effect
A = 1.00 for bending
A = 0.70 for axial load

Determine the equivalent normal stress.

(*a*) Due to bending, the mean and variable moments are

$$M_m = \tfrac{1}{2}(5000 + 10,000) = 7500 \text{ in-lb} \quad \text{and} \quad M_v = \tfrac{1}{2}(10,000 - 5000) = 2500 \text{ in-lb.}$$

Then due to bending

$$s_m = \frac{Mc}{I} = \frac{32M}{\pi d^3} = \frac{(32)(7500)}{\pi d^3}, \qquad s_v = \frac{Mc}{I} = \frac{32M}{\pi d^3} = \frac{(32)(2500)}{\pi d^3}$$

and $s_{en} = s_m + \frac{s_y K_f s_v}{s_r ABC} = \frac{(32)(7500)}{\pi d^3} + \frac{(68,000)(1)(32)(2500)}{\pi d^3 (40,000)(1)(0.85)(0.88)} = \frac{134,000}{d^3}$ due to bending

(*b*) Due to axial load, the mean and variable forces are

$$F_m = \tfrac{1}{2}(1000 + 3000) = 2000 \text{ lb} \quad \text{and} \quad F_v = \tfrac{1}{2}(3000 - 1000) = 1000 \text{ lb.}$$

Then due to axial load,

$$s_{en} = \frac{(2000)(4)}{\pi d^2} + \frac{(68,000)(4000)}{\pi d^2 (40,000)(0.70)(0.85)(0.88)} = \frac{6690}{d^2} \quad \text{due to axial load}$$

(*c*) Total equivalent normal stress, $s_{en}(\text{total}) = \frac{134,000}{d^3} + \frac{6690}{d^2}$.

(*d*) Equating the total equivalent normal stress to s_y/N,

$$\frac{134,000}{d^3} + \frac{6690}{d^2} = \frac{s_y}{N} = \frac{68,000}{2}$$

from which by trial and error $d = 1.625$ in.

5. Shaft S_1 is rotating at 1200 rpm clockwise and has a concentrated unbalanced load of W of 8 lb at a radius of 2 in. in a plane midway between supports A and B, as shown in Fig. 6-8. A constant vertical load W_1 of 1500 lb is applied by means of two anti-friction bearings at C and D. If the shaft material has an ultimate strength of 60,000 psi and a yield strength of 45,000 psi, determine the required diameter of the shaft at section A–A for a design factor of safety $N = 2$. Consider only point P.

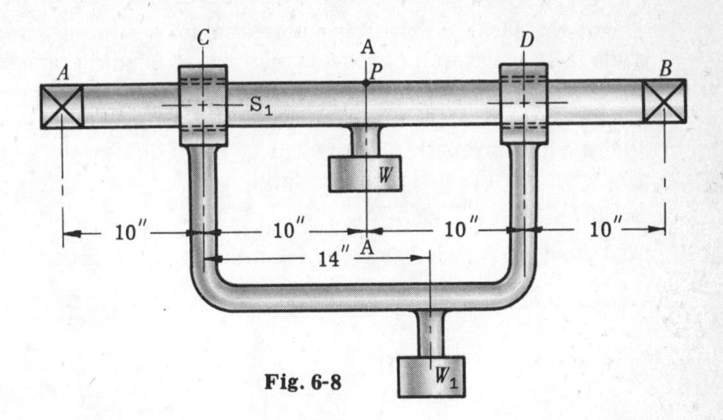

Fig. 6-8

Solution:

(1) Assume: Endurance limit $= s_u/2 = 30{,}000$ psi; stress concentration factor, $K_f = 1$; endurance limit correction factor for size, $A = 0.85$; endurance limit correction factor for machined finish, $C = 0.9$.

(2) Show that the bending moment due to the rotating load varies from −6540 in-lb to 6540 in-lb.

(3) Show that the bending moment due to the constant vertical load is 7500 in-lb.

(4) The combined bending moment then varies from 960 in-lb to 14,040 in-lb.

(5) Now it should be noted that, if we consider point P on the outer fiber in a plane midway between the two supports, the 14,040 in-lb moment will produce a negative or compressive stress, while the 960 in-lb moment will produce a positive or tensile stress.

(6) The maximum, minimum, mean, and variable bending stresses are

$$s(\max) = \frac{-(32)(14{,}040)}{\pi d^3} = \frac{-143{,}000}{d^3}, \qquad s_m = \frac{-143{,}000 + 9775}{2d^3} = \frac{-66{,}610}{d^3}$$

$$s(\min) = \frac{+(32)(960)}{\pi d^3} = \frac{+9775}{d^3}, \qquad s_v = \frac{9775 - (-143{,}000)}{2d^3} = \frac{76{,}390}{d^3}$$

(7) Then $\dfrac{1}{N} = \dfrac{s_m}{s_y} + \dfrac{K_f s_v}{s_r ABC}$, $\dfrac{1}{2} = \dfrac{-66{,}610}{-45{,}000 d^3} + \dfrac{(1)76{,}390}{(30{,}000)(1)(0.85)(0.90)d^3}$, and $d = 2.12$. Use $d = 2\frac{1}{4}$ in.

6. A steel alloy has an ultimate tensile strength of 90,000 psi, a yield strength of 60,000 psi and an endurance limit of 30,000 psi under reversed bending. Sketch a modified Goodman diagram. Indicate on the sketch and give the magnitude of the endurance stress for released loading.

Solution:

Sketch a Goodman diagram as shown in Fig. 6-9. The line NP represents the magnitude of the endurance strength for released loading. The values can be determined from a sketch made to scale, or from a calculation, as follows.

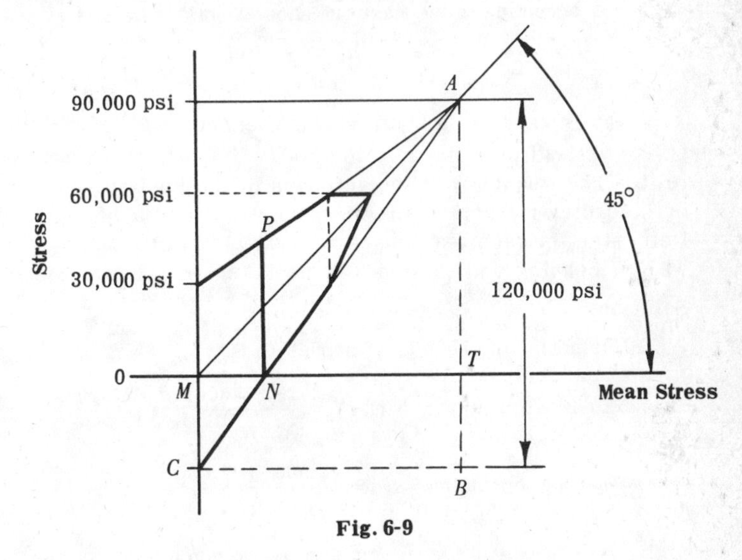

Fig. 6-9

By similar triangles ACB and ANT, $\dfrac{NT}{90{,}000} = \dfrac{90{,}000}{120{,}000}$ or $NT = 67{,}500$ psi.

Then $MN = 22{,}500$ psi, and $NP = 45{,}000$ psi since MA is a mean stress line.

7. A hot rolled steel shaft is subjected to a torsional load that varies from 3000 in-lb clockwise to 1000 in-lb counterclockwise as an applied bending moment at a critical section varies from +4000 in-lb to −2000 in-lb. The shaft is of uniform cross section and no keyway is present at the critical section. Determine the required shaft diameter. The material has an ultimate strength of 80,000 psi and a yield strength of 60,000 psi. Base design on a factor of safety $N = 1.5$. Take the endurance limit as half the ultimate strength.

Solution:

(*a*) Determine the equivalent normal stress due to bending.

$$s(\max) = \frac{(32)(4000)}{\pi d^3} \qquad s_m = \frac{[(32)(4000)] + [-(32)(2000)]}{2\pi d^3} = \frac{10,200}{d^3}$$

$$s(\min) = \frac{-(32)(2000)}{\pi d^3} \qquad s_v = \frac{[(32)(4000)] - [-(32)(2000)]}{2\pi d^3} = \frac{30,600}{d^3}$$

The equivalent normal stress is $[A = 1,\ B = 0.85,\ C = 0.62,\ K_t = 1]$

$$s_{en} = \frac{10,200}{d^3} + \left[\frac{60,000}{40,000}\right]\left[\frac{30,600}{d^3(1)(0.85)(0.62)}\right] = \frac{97,300}{d^3}$$

(*b*) Determine the equivalent shear stress.

$$s_s(\max) = \frac{(16)(3000)}{\pi d^3} \qquad s_{ms} = \frac{(16)(1000)}{\pi d^3} = \frac{5100}{d^3}$$

$$s_s(\min) = \frac{-(16)(1000)}{\pi d^3} \qquad s_v = \frac{(16)(2000)}{\pi d^3} = \frac{10,200}{d^3}$$

The equivalent shear stress is $[A = 0.6,\ B = 0.85,\ C = 0.62,\ s_{ys} = 0.6 s_y]$

$$s_{es} = \frac{5100}{d^3} + \left[\frac{(0.6)(60,000)}{40,000}\right]\left[\frac{10,200}{d^3(0.6)(0.85)(0.62)}\right] = \frac{34,100}{d^3}$$

(*c*) Equate the equivalent maximum shear stress to s_{ys}/N, where $s_{ys} = (0.5)s_y = (0.5)(60,000) = 30,000$ psi.

$$\tau_{es}(\max) = \frac{1}{d^3}\sqrt{\left(\frac{97,300}{2}\right)^2 + (34,100)^2} = \frac{30,000}{1.5} \qquad \text{or} \qquad d = 1.44 \text{ in.}$$

Note. While we used $s_{ys} = 0.6 s_y$ for pure torsional shear, we used $s_{ys} = 0.5 s_y$ for combined stress shear, according to the maximum shear theory of failure.

8. A pulley is keyed to a shaft midway between two anti-friction bearings. The bending moment at the pulley varies from 1500 in-lb to 4500 in-lb as the torsional moment in the shaft varies from 500 to 1500 in-lb. The frequency of the variation of the loads is the same as the shaft speed. The shaft is made of cold drawn steel having an ultimate strength of 78,000 psi and a yield strength of 58,000 psi. Determine the required diameter for an indefinite life. The stress concentration factor for the keyway in bending and torsion may be taken as 1.6 and 1.3 respectively. Use design factor $N = 1.5$.

Solution:

I. Determine the equivalent normal stress, s_{en}

(*a*) Due to bending, $s(\max) = \dfrac{(32)(4500)}{\pi d^3} = \dfrac{45,900}{d^3}$ and $s(\min) = \dfrac{-(32)(1500)}{\pi d^3} = -\dfrac{15,300}{d^3}$.

(*b*) Due to bending, $s_m = \dfrac{45,900 + (-15,300)}{2d^3} = \dfrac{15,300}{d^3}$ and $s_v = \dfrac{45,900 - (-15,300)}{2d^3} = \dfrac{30,600}{d^3}$.

(*c*) Assume $s_r = s_u/2 = 78,000/2 = 39,000$, $A = 1$, $B = 0.85$, $C = 0.88$. The equivalent normal stress is

$$s_{en} = s_m + \left(\frac{s_y}{s_r}\right)\frac{K_f s_v}{ABC} = \frac{15,300}{d^3} + \left(\frac{58,000}{39,000}\right)\frac{(1.6)(30,600)}{(0.85)(0.88)d^3} = \frac{112,600}{d^3}$$

II. Determine the equivalent shear stress, s_{es}.

(a) Maximum and minimum shear stresses:

$$s_s(\max) = \frac{(16)(1500)}{\pi d^3} = \frac{7635}{d^3}, \qquad s_s(\min) = \frac{(16)(500)}{\pi d^3} = \frac{2545}{d^3}.$$

(b) Mean and variable shear stresses:

$$s_{ms} = \frac{7635 + 2545}{2d^3} = \frac{5090}{d^3}, \qquad s_{vs} = \frac{7635 - 2545}{2d^3} = \frac{2545}{d^3}.$$

(c) $s_{ys} = 0.6 s_y = 0.6(58{,}000) = 34{,}800$ psi, $A = 0.6$ for torsion, $B = 0.85$, $C = 0.88$. The equivalent shear stress is

$$s_{es} = s_{ms} + (\frac{s_{ys}}{s_r})\frac{K_f s_{vs}}{ABC} = \frac{5090}{d^3} + (\frac{34{,}800}{39{,}000})\frac{(1.3)(2545)}{(0.6)(0.85)(0.88)d^3} = \frac{11{,}620}{d^3}$$

III. Equating the equivalent maximum shear stress to s_{ys}/N,

$$\tau_{es}(\max) = \sqrt{(\frac{s_{en}}{2})^2 + (s_{es})^2} = \frac{s_{ys}}{N}, \qquad \frac{1}{d^3}\sqrt{(\frac{112{,}600}{2})^2 + (11{,}620)^2} = \frac{(0.5)(58{,}000)}{1.5},$$

$d^3 = 2.97$, $d = 1.44$ in.

9. A cast iron shaft, ASTM-25 with an ultimate tensile strength of 25,000 psi, is subjected to a torsional load which is completely reversed. The load is to be applied an indefinite number of cycles. The shaft is 2" in diameter and is joined to a 3" diameter shaft with a $\frac{1}{2}$" radius fillet. The factor of safety is to be 2. What is the maximum torque that can be applied to the shaft? Solve by two methods: (1) using Soderberg's equation, (2) using $s_s = Tc/J$ directly.

Solution:

(a) The mean shear stress = 0. The variable shear stress is

$$s_{sv} = \frac{16T}{\pi d^3} = \frac{16T}{\pi(2^3)} = \frac{2T}{\pi}, \quad \text{where } T \text{ is the maximum torque, in-lb}$$

(b) The equivalent shear stress s_{es} on a particle on the surface is

$$s_{es} = s_{ms}K_t + K_f s_{vs}\frac{s_{ys}}{s_r ABC}$$

where s_{ms} = mean shear stress = 0.

K_t = theoretical stress concentration factor, which is 1.17 for the given diameter and radius, as found from photoelastic tests for torsion for the shape specified.

K_f = actual stress concentration effect on fatigue, where

$$K_f = 1 + q(K_t - 1) = 1 + 0(1.17 - 1) = 1.$$

The values of notch sensitivity q for cast iron have not been specifically reported in the literature although tests made on cast iron show that the reduction in the endurance limit as the result of notches in test specimens is zero for a tensile strength of 20,000 psi and 26% for a tensile strength of about 43,000 psi. The notch sensitivity factor q is taken as zero for ASTM-25. (Note that whereas the notch sensitivity effect is very low for fatigue, the notch effect is very high on impact loading.)

s_{vs} = variable shear stress = $2T/\pi$ psi.

s_{ys} = the yield strength in shear for cast iron. This value is usually taken equal to the yield strength in tension for cast iron, s_{yp}. The yield strength in tension can be taken as approximately 60% of the ultimate tensile stress. Thus,

$$s_{ys} = s_y = 0.6(25{,}000) = 15{,}000 \text{ psi.}$$

s_r = endurance limit in bending for cast iron. This value has a wider range than found in steels. Tests that have been reported state that the endurance limit in bending vary from 0.33 to 0.6 of the ultimate strength. Results show that the endurance limit in torsion has varied from 0.75 to 1.25 of the endurance limit in bending. The endurance limit in bending will be taken arbitrarily as 0.4 of the ultimate strength. The endurance limit s_r in bending then, is $0.4(25{,}000) = 10{,}000$ psi.

A = 0.75 (the lower value above).

B = size effect, taken as 0.85, the same as for steels.

C = surface finish = 1.

Substitution in the equation for the equivalent shear stress gives

$$s_{es} = 0(1.17) + (1)\left(\frac{2T}{\pi}\right)\frac{15{,}000}{(10{,}000)(.75)(.85)(1)} = 1.5T$$

(c) The equivalent normal stress is zero. From the combined stress equation, the maximum equivalent static tensile stress is

$$s_n(\max) = \tfrac{1}{2}s_{en} + \sqrt{(\tfrac{1}{2}s_{en})^2 + (s_{es})^2} = 0 + \sqrt{0 + (1.5T)^2} = 1.5T \text{ psi}$$

(d) The allowable static tensile stress $= s_y/N = 15{,}000/2 = 7{,}500$ psi.

(e) Setting (c) and (d) equal, $7500 = 1.5T$ or $T = 5000$ in-lb. Thus, the allowable torque = 5000 in-lb.

(f) The preceding solution illustrates the procedure of application of the Soderberg equation in working with cast iron. Since the stress is completly reversed and reversed torsion test data can be applied directly, a quicker solution for this particular problem can be obtained by direct application of $s_s = Tc/J$, where $s_s = (s_r)(A)(B)(C)/N$.

$$\frac{(s_r)(A)(B)(C)}{N} = \frac{Tc}{J}, \qquad \frac{10{,}000(0.75)(0.85)(1)}{2} = \frac{T(1)}{\pi(2^4)/32}$$

or the allowable torque $T = 5000$ in-lb. In the above, the endurance limit in bending of 10,000 psi is multiplied by $A = 0.75$ to correct for torsion, $B = 0.85$ to take care of the size effect, $C = 1$ for surface effect, and the design factor $N = 2$ is used. No stress concentration factor is applied because the notch sensitivity factor for cast iron is taken as zero.

It is to be noted that where test data is available, such should be used directly. If the load is not completely reversed and/or test data is not available, then the use of the Soderberg equation is indicated.

10. In Fig.6-10 below, the shaft transmits 10 horsepower from the pulley P to the gear G at 900 rpm under steady load conditions. The shaft is machined from AISI-1035 steel, hot rolled. The ultimate tensile strength is 85,000 psi and the yield point in tension is 55,000 psi. The pulley diameter is 10.0", and the pitch diameter of the gear is also 10.0". The weight of the pulley P is 30 lb and the weight of the gear G is 30 lb. Neglect the weight of the shaft. The ratio of belt tensions is $T_1/T_2 = 2.5$. The gear pressure angle is 20°.

The shaft size is to be determined, using the Soderberg variable stress equations. (The solution using the ASME Shafting Code equation is on page 121. The design for rigidity and critical speed is on pages 123-127.)

Solution:

(a) The torque M_t on the shaft is found from

$$M_t N/63{,}000 = \text{hp}, \qquad M_t(900)/63{,}000 = 10, \quad \text{or} \quad M_t = 700 \text{ in-lb.}$$

(*b*) The belt forces are found from

$$(T_1 - T_2)(R) = M_t \quad \text{or} \quad (T_1 - T_2)(5) = 700 \quad \text{and} \quad T_1/T_2 = 2.5$$

from which $T_1 = 233$ lb, $T_2 = 93$ lb.

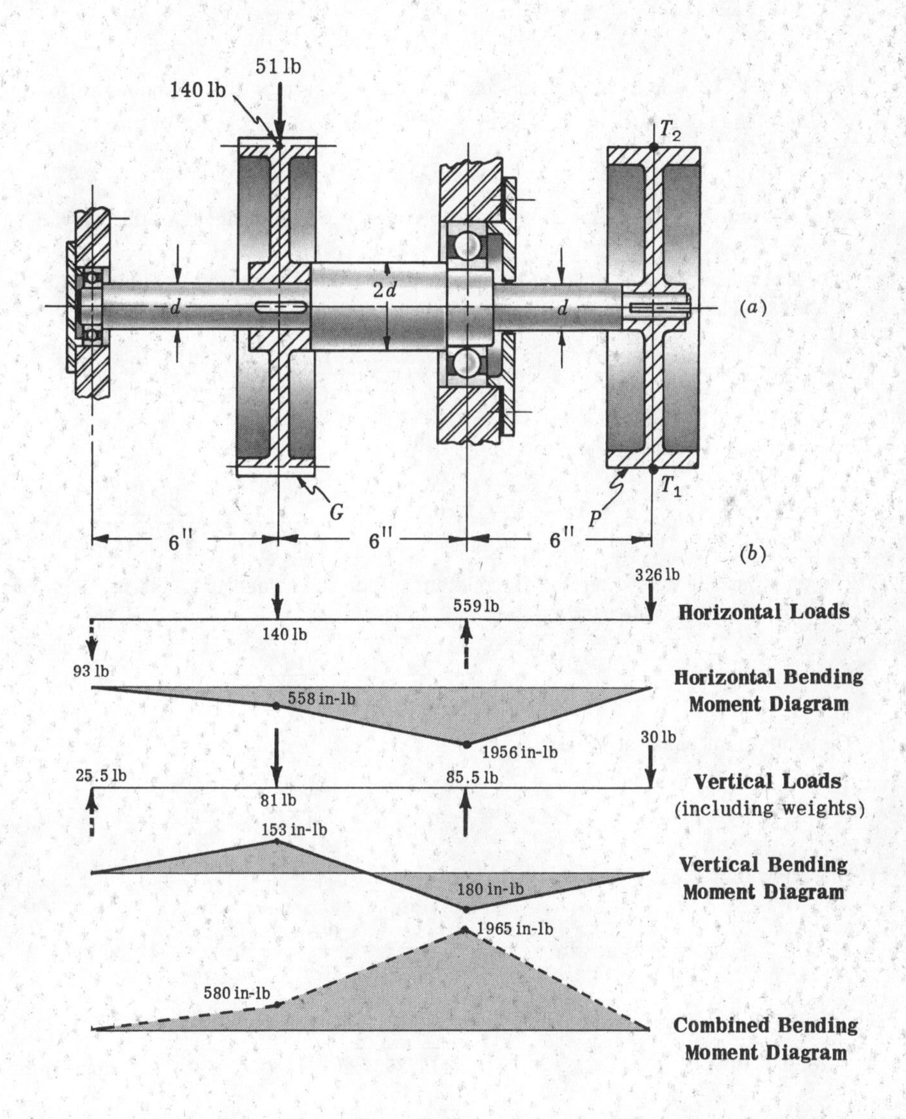

Fig. 6-10

(*c*) The tangential gear force $F_t = M_t/R = 700/5 = 140$ lb.

(*d*) The separating force $F_r = F_t \tan\phi = 140 \tan 20^\circ = 51$ lb.

(*e*) The loading and bending moment diagrams are shown with the figure. The belt forces and gear forces are assumed concentrated as shown. The weight of the pulley and gear is included.

(*f*) Consider the section at the gear first. Even though the bending moment here is less than at the right bearing, the keyway might be the influencing factor.

The stress concentration factor K_f due to the keyway in bending is 1.6.

The stress concentration factor in bending due to the fillet where the shaft portion of diameter

d joins with the shaft of diameter $2d$ depends upon the radius of the fillet. Even if the ratio of the radius of the fillet to the shaft diameter d is specified to obtain the theoretical stress concentration factor K_t, the actual stress concentration factor K_f depends upon the notch sensitivity, which is a function of the radius of the fillet. Thus it is necessary to use a trial and error solution, by approximating the diameter d and the radius of the fillet and checking with the calculated value of d. The values used in the following calculations are those which agree with the final values:

$$r/d = 0.083, \quad \text{for which} \quad r = \frac{1}{16}''$$

For $r/d = 0.083$, and ratio of diameters = 2, the theoretical stress concentration factor K_t in bending is 1.86. The notch sensitivity factor q is 0.78 for annealed steels with the fillet radius of $\frac{1}{16}''$. Then

$$K_f = 1 + q(K_t - 1) = 1 + 0.78(1.86 - 1) = 1.67$$

Thus the radius of the fillet is such as to cause a worse effect than the keyway.

(*g*) The bending is constant, 580 in-lb, but a particle on the surface is subjected to a complete reversal of stress. The mean bending stress = 0. The variable bending stress is

$$s_v = \frac{Mc}{I} = \frac{580(d/2)}{\pi d^4/64} = \frac{5910}{d^3}$$

(*h*) The equivalent normal stress is

$$s_{en} = s_m + K_f s_v \frac{s_y}{s_r ABC} = 0 + 1.67\left(\frac{5910}{d^3}\right)\frac{55{,}000}{(42{,}500)(1)(0.85)(0.87)} = \frac{17{,}300}{d^3}$$

(*i*) The shear stress due to torsion is constant, since the torque is constant. The variable shear stress is zero. The mean shear stress is

$$s_{ms} = \frac{Tc}{J} = \frac{700(d/2)}{\pi d^4/32} = \frac{3570}{d^3}$$

(*j*) The equivalent shear stress is

$$s_{es} = s_{ms} + K_f s_v \frac{s_{ys}}{s_r ABC} = \frac{3570}{d^3} + 0$$

(*k*) The allowable shear stress is

$$\frac{s_{ys}}{N} = \frac{0.5(s_y)}{N} = \frac{0.5(55{,}000)}{1.5} = 18{,}300 \text{ psi}$$

(*l*) Setting the allowable shear stress equal to the maximum shear stress,

$$18{,}300 = \sqrt{(\tfrac{1}{2}s_{en})^2 + (s_{es})^2} = \sqrt{(17{,}300/2d^3)^2 + (3570/d^3)^2} \quad \text{from which} \quad d = 0.796''$$

(*m*) The shaft at the right bearing will be analyzed next. Specifically, the section with diameter d at the fillet will be considered, with the bending moment at the centerline of the bearing taken as acting at the section with the fillet. The mean bending stress $s_m = 0$.

The variable bending stress is

$$s_v = \frac{Mc}{I} = \frac{1965(d/2)}{\pi d^4/64} = \frac{20{,}100}{d^3}$$

The stress concentration factor K_f cannot be determined directly here. The same procedure as used at the section at the gear will be used, trial and error, with final values given. A large value of r/d will be used: $r/d = 0.22$. (d turns out to be about $1\frac{1}{8}''$, and r of about $\frac{1}{4}''$ can be taken.) For $r/d \cong 0.22$, $K_t = 1.37$; for $r = \frac{1}{4}$, $q = 0.95$. Thus $K_f = 1 + q(K_t - 1) = 1 + 0.95(1.37 - 1) = 1.35$. Then the equivalent normal stress s_{en} is

$$s_{en} = s_m + K_f s_v \frac{s_y}{s_r ABC} = 0 + 1.35\left(\frac{20{,}100}{d^3}\right)\frac{55{,}000}{(42{,}500)(1)(0.85)(0.87)} = \frac{47{,}600}{d^3}$$

(*n*) The mean shear stress due to torsion is

$$s_{ms} = \frac{16T}{\pi d^3} = \frac{16(700)}{\pi d^3} = \frac{3570}{d^3}$$

The variable shear stress $s_{vs} = 0$. Hence the equivalent shear stress is

$$s_{es} = s_{ms} + K_f s_{vs}(\frac{s_{ys}}{s_r})\frac{1}{ABC} = \frac{3570}{d^3} + 0$$

(*o*) The allowable shear stress is as found in (*k*): 18,300 psi.

(*p*) From the combined shear stress for the equivalent stress,

$$18{,}300 = \sqrt{(\tfrac{1}{2}s_{en})^2 + (s_{es})^2} = \sqrt{(47{,}600/2d^3)^2 + (3570/d^3)^2} \quad \text{or} \quad d = 1.09''. \text{ Use } d = 1\tfrac{1}{8}''.$$

(*q*) The size of the shaft *d* is thus determined by the stresses acting in the shaft at the right bearing. Final proportions determined from a strength consideration only using the Soderberg equation are: $d = 1\frac{1}{8}''$, $2d = 2\frac{1}{4}''$

11. A steel cantilever member as shown in Fig. 6-11 is subjected to a transverse load at its end that varies from 10 lb up to 30 lb down as an axial load varies from 25 lb (compression) to 100 lb (tension). Determine the required diameter at the change of section for infinite life using a factor of safety of 2. The strength properties of the material are:

s_u = 80,000 psi (ultimate strength),
s_y = 68,000 psi (yield strength),
s_n = 40,000 psi (endurance limit).

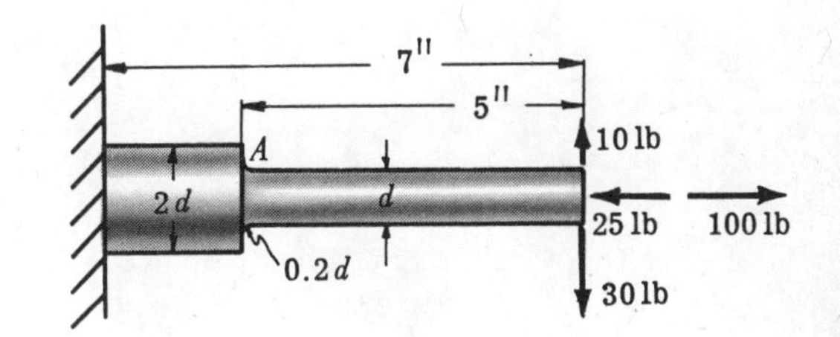

Fig. 6-11

Test data indicate that the theoretical stress concentration factor for bending and axial loads are $K_t = 1.44$ and $K_t = 1.63$ respectively, at the change of cross section.

Solution:

For point *A*, which is critical, determine the equivalent normal stress. It is assumed that the equivalent normal stress at this point will be the algebraic sum of the equivalent normal stress due to bending and the equivalent normal stress due to axial loading.

Due to bending the equivalent normal stress is

$$(s_{en})_b = s_m + \frac{s_y s_v K_f}{s_r ABC} = \frac{510}{d^3} + \frac{(68{,}000)(1020)(1.44)}{(40{,}000)(d^3)(1)(0.85)(0.9)} = \frac{3780}{d^3}$$

where $s(\text{max}) = \dfrac{(32)(150)}{\pi d^3}$, $s(\text{min}) = -\dfrac{(32)(50)}{\pi d^3}$, $s_m = \dfrac{(32)(100)}{2\pi d^3} = \dfrac{510}{d^3}$, $s_v = \dfrac{(32)(200)}{2\pi d^3} = \dfrac{1020}{d^3}$.

Due to axial loading, the equivalent normal stress is

$$(s_{en})_a = \frac{150}{\pi d^2} + \frac{(68{,}000)(250)(1.63)}{(40{,}000)(\pi)(d^2)(0.7)(0.85)(0.9)} = \frac{460}{d^2}$$

where $s(\text{max}) = \dfrac{400}{\pi d^2}$, $s(\text{min}) = -\dfrac{100}{\pi d^2}$, $s_m = \dfrac{150}{\pi d^2}$, $s_v = \dfrac{250}{\pi d^2}$

Then the total equivalent normal stress s_{en} at point *A* is

$$s_{en} = \frac{3780}{d^3} + \frac{460}{d^2} = \frac{s_y}{N} = \frac{68{,}000}{2} \quad \text{from which } d = 0.490 \text{ in.}$$

12. In some instances, it may be more economical to design on the basis of an endurance strength for a finite life rather than for infinite life. As an illustration assume that a fuel pump pusher rod is to be designed for not more than 100,000 cycles while it is being subjected to a released cyclic load of 1750 lb. Test data indicate that the material from which the rod is to be made has a yield strength of 55,000 psi and an endurance limit of 38,000 psi for reversed loading, but has an endurance strength of 50,000 psi for reversed loading at 100,000 cycles. For a factor of safety of 2 determine the required diameter of the pusher rod for both a finite life of 100,000 cycles and for an infinite life.

Solution:

Since we have released loading, $s_m = s_v = F/A = 1750/(\frac{1}{4}\pi d^2) = 2230/d^2$.

Assume $K_t = K_f = 1$, $A = 0.7$, $B = 1$, $C = 0.9$; and substitute in the equation $\frac{1}{N} = \frac{s_m}{s_y} + \frac{K_f s_v}{s_n ABC}$.

(*a*) For a finite life of 100,000 cycles

$$\frac{1}{2} = \frac{2230}{d^2(55{,}000)} + \frac{(1)(2230)}{d^2(50{,}000)(0.7)(1)(0.9)} \quad \text{or} \quad d = 0.475 \text{ in.}$$

(*b*) For an infinite life

$$\frac{1}{2} = \frac{2230}{d^2(55{,}000)} + \frac{(1)(2230)}{d^2(38{,}000)(0.7)(1)(0.9)} \quad \text{or} \quad d = 0.517 \text{ in.}$$

SUPPLEMENTARY PROBLEMS

13. A one inch diameter machined steel cantilever 10 in. long is loaded on the end with a force that varies from 60 lb down to 100 lb up. There is a $\frac{1}{4}''$ fillet where the member is connected to the support which causes a theoretical stress concentration factor $K_t = 1.32$. The notch sensitivity factor q may be taken at 0.92.

If the material has an ultimate stress $s_u = 80{,}000$ psi, an endurance limit in reversed bending $s_r = 35{,}000$, and a yield strength, $s_y = 60{,}000$, determine: (*a*) maximum bending stress, (*b*) minimum bending stress, (*c*) mean stress, (*d*) variable stress, (*e*) design factor N.

Ans. (*a*) 10,200 psi, (*b*) −6120 psi, (*c*) 2040 psi, (*d*) 8160 psi, (*e*) 2.29

14. A force applied to the end of the cantilever bar varies with time in the plane of the paper as shown in Fig. 6-12. A factor of safety $N = 2.5$ is desired for the application, yet proportions dictate the maximum dimensions shown.

The material is AISI–1020 with an ultimate strength of 64,000 psi, an endurance limit of 32,000 psi in reversed bending and a yield point in tension of 48,000 psi. For the section A–A, the theoretical stress concentration factor K_t is 1.37 for the 2" diameter bar with a $\frac{1}{2}''$ fillet radius. The notch sensitivity factor q for an annealed steel is 0.95 for the fillet radius of $\frac{1}{2}''$.

Using a factor $C = 0.90$ for the surface effect, a factor $B = 0.85$ for the size effect, and a factor $A = 1$ since there is no axial load, determine for section A–A: (*a*) the stress concentration factor K_f, (*b*) the mean stress s_m, (*c*) the variable stress s_v, (*d*) the factor of safety N, (*e*) whether

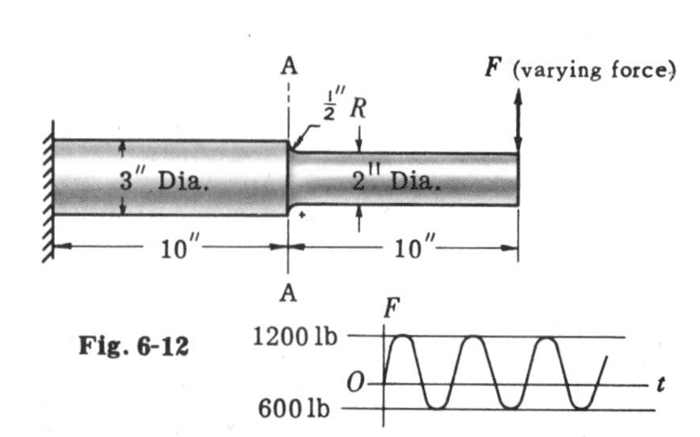

Fig. 6-12

the proportions are satisfactory, (*f*) if the proportions are unsatisfactory, what could be done to give a satisfactory solution without changing the 2" diameter section.

Ans. (*a*) K_f = 1.35, (*b*) s_m = 3820 psi, (*c*) s_v = 11,480 psi, (*d*) N = 1.4. (*e*) Proportions are not satisfactory. (*f*) Use a better material with a higher endurance limit. A larger radius of curvature at the fillet will not give sufficient increase in strength to increase the factor of safety to 2.5. This may be checked by using K_f = 1 as a limiting value.

15. Determine the maximum load for the simply supported beam cyclicly loaded as shown in Fig.6-13. The ultimate strength is 100,000 psi, the yield point in tension is 75,000 psi, the endurance limit for reversed bending is 50,000 psi, and the design factor N is 1.3. Use a size effect factor B = 0.85 and a surface finish factor C = 0.90.

Ans. For a mean stress $32W/\pi$ psi and a variable stress $16W/\pi$ psi, W = 2850 lb and $3W$ = 8550 lb.

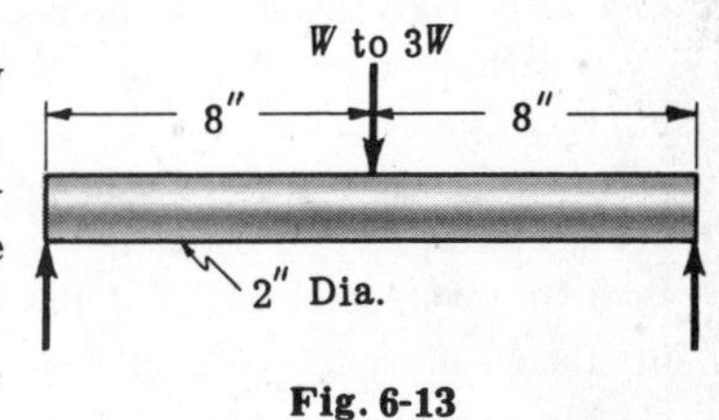

Fig. 6-13

16. A section of a shaft of diameter d is joined to a section of shaft of diameter 1.5 d with a fillet which produces an actual stress concentration factor of K_f = 1.22 for the shaft in torsion.

The material has a yield point in tension of 81,500 psi, and an endurance limit in reversed bending of 54,500 psi; and an endurance limit of 0.6(54,500) = 32,700 psi in reversed torsion.

Using a size effect factor B = 0.85, a surface finish factor C = 0.85, and A = 0.6, determine the size of shaft required for a torque which varies from 0 to 20,000 in-lb in the shaft at the smaller diameter. Use design factor N = 2. *Ans.* d = 1.93"; use $1\frac{15}{16}$"

17. A cantilever beam of circular cross section is subjected to an alternating stress at a point on the outer fiber in the plane of the support that varies from 3000 psi (compression) to 4000 psi (tension). At the same time there is an alternating stress due to axial loading that varies from 2000 psi (compression) to 4000 psi (tension). The material has an ultimate strength s_u = 60,000 psi and a yield strength s_y = 45,000 psi. Assume that K_f = 1, B = 0.85, and C = 0.9. Determine (*a*) the equivalent normal stress due to axial loading, (*b*) the equivalent normal stress due to bending, (*c*) the total equivalent normal stress due to axial loading and bending. *Ans.* (*a*) 9425 psi, (*b*) 7360 psi, (*c*) 16,785 psi

18. A steel member of circular cross section is subjected to a torsional stress that varies from 0 to 5000 psi, and at the same time it is subjected to an axial stress that varies from −2000 psi to +4000 psi. Neglecting stress concentration and column effect, and assuming that the maximum stresses in bending and axial load occur at the same time, determine (*a*) the maximum equivalent shear stress, (*b*) the design factor of safety based upon yield in shear. The material has an endurance limit s_r = 30,000 psi, and a yield strength s_y = 70,000 psi. The diameter of the member is less than $\frac{1}{2}$ inch; B = 1; and the surface has a mirror polish, C = 1. *Ans.* (*a*) τ_{es}(max) = 9100 psi, (*b*) N = 3.85

19. SAE–3125 steel has an ultimate tensile strength 100,000 psi, a yield point 64,000 psi, and a reversed bending endurance limit 32,000 psi. Sketch its modified Goodman diagram and from the sketch determine the magnitude of its endurance strength for released loading in bending. *Ans.* 48,600 psi.

20. The 2 inch diameter bar is bent into the shape shown in Fig.6-14. The force applied to the bar varies from 0 to a maximum of F lb. The bar is made from steel with a yield point in tension of 60,000 psi and an endurance limit of 45,000 psi. What is the maximum load that can be applied for a factor of safety N = 2 based upon the static yield point? Use the Soderberg equations for variable stresses. Surface finish factor C = 0.8. The maximum load is to be found from the variable stresses occuring at section A–A.

Ans. The maximum stress at section A–A due to

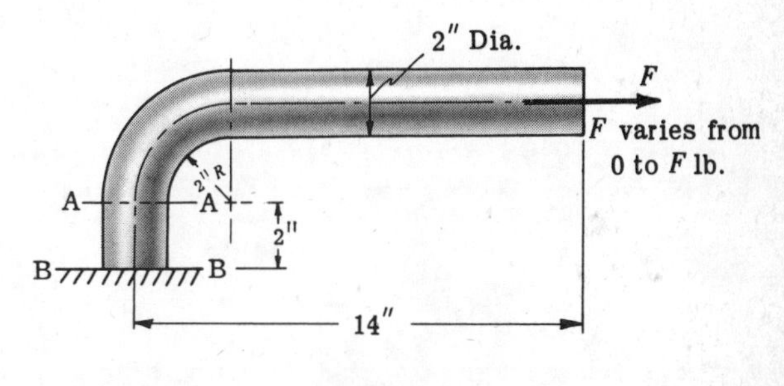

Fig. 6-14

bending and considering the curved beam (see the chapter on curved beams) is $5.08F$. The variable stress is $2.54F$ and the mean stress is $2.54F$. Since the maximum stress has been found from a curved beam analysis, $K_f = 1$. Using $A = 1$, $B = 0.85$, and $C = 0.8$, the maximum load F is 3980 lb.

21. Same as Problem 20, except that the maximum load is to be found from the variable stresses occurring at section B–B.

Ans. The maximum stress at section B–B (for a straight beam) is $7.65F$. Using the Soderberg equation with $A = 1$, $B = 0.85$, and $C = 0.8$, the maximum load F is 2650 lb.

22. A flat steel bar $2'' \times 1''$ is bent into the shape shown in Fig. 6-15. The load F varies from 1000 lb to 4000 lb. The material has an ultimate tensile strength of 80,000 psi, a yield point of 50,000 psi, and an endurance limit (in reversed bending) of 40,000 psi. Determine:

(*a*) the mean bending stress at point P

(*b*) the variable bending stress at P

(*c*) the mean axial stress at P

(*d*) the variable axial stress at P

(*e*) the equivalent bending stress at P using a surface finish factor $C = 0.9$

(*f*) the equivalent tensile stress at P due to axial loading, using $A = 0.7$ for axial loading and $C = 0.9$

(*g*) the total equivalent stress at P

(*h*) the factor of safety at P based on variable stresses

(*i*) the maximum tensile stress at point P using the maximum load and determine the factor of safety as though the load were constant.

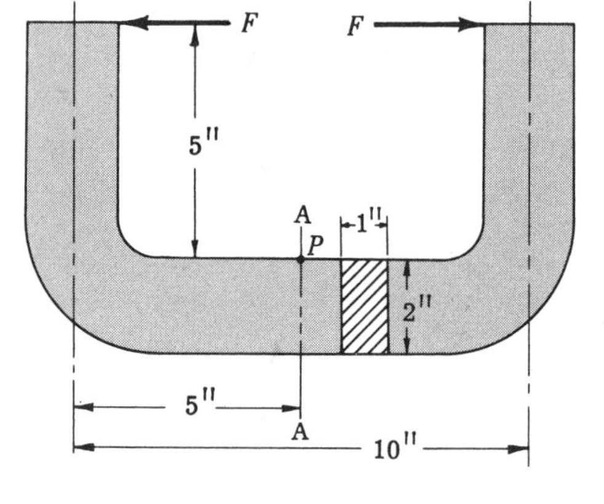

Fig. 6-15

Ans.
(*a*) 22,500 psi
(*b*) 13,500 psi
(*c*) 1250 psi
(*d*) 750 psi
(*e*) 44,600 psi
(*f*) 3000 psi
(*g*) 47,600 psi (tension)
(*h*) $N = 1.05$
(*i*) 38,000 psi, $N = 1.32$

Chapter 7

Machine Vibrations

VIBRATORY MOTIONS in machinery arise when variable forces act on elastic parts. Usually these motions are undesirable although in some cases (vibratory conveyors, for example) they are deliberately designed into the machine.

ANALYSING VIBRATIONS requires the following general procedure:

1. Evaluating masses and elasticity of parts involved.
2. Estimating amount of friction involved.
3. Idealizing the actual mechanical device, replacing it by an approximately equivalent system of masses, springs, and dampers.
4. Writing differential equations of motion for the idealized system.
5. Solving the equations and interpreting the results.

THE SIMPLEST IDEAL SYSTEM consists of a single mass, single spring, and a dashpot, as shown in Fig. 7-1. The differential equation of motion for this system is

$$m\ddot{x} + c\dot{x} + kx = F(t)$$

where

m = the mass.

k = the spring constant (force per unit deflection).

c = the damping (frictional) constant (force per unit of velocity). (Viscous damping, in which the resisting force is proportional to velocity, is assumed.)

$F(t)$ = any external force, a function of time.

x = the displacement of the mass from the static equilibrium position.

$\dot{x}$, $\ddot{x}$ = derivatives, first and second respectively, of x with respect to t.

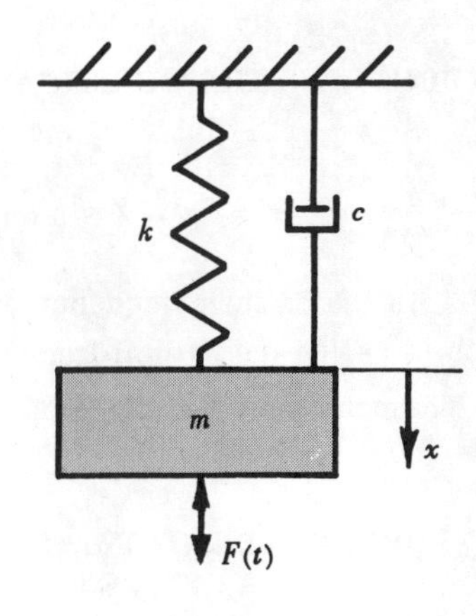

Fig. 7-1

ANY SINGLE-DEGREE-OF-FREEDOM SYSTEM can be described by the same form of differential equation as written above, **if** the restoring force (spring force) is proportional to the displacement and if the frictional force is proportional to the velocity. For the general single-degree-of-freedom system we shall write

$$m_e\ddot{x} + c_e\dot{x} + k_e x = F(t)$$

where m_e, c_e, k_e are respectively the **equivalent** mass, damping constant, and spring constant. The displacement x may be either **linear** or **angular**.

The **forcing function**, $F(t)$, may in practice be of any form. For this analysis it is assumed to be sinusoidal:

$$F(t) = F_o \sin \omega t$$

where F_o is the amplitude of the externally applied force and ω is the frequency.

FREE VIBRATIONS may occur when, after an initial disturbance, no external forcing function is present, i.e. $F(t) = 0$. The differential equation is simply

$$m_e \ddot{x} + c_e \dot{x} + k_e x = 0$$

The solution of this equation can be written

$$x = A_1 e^{s_1 t} + A_2 e^{s_2 t}$$

where $\quad s_1 = -\frac{c_e}{2m_e} + \sqrt{(\frac{c_e}{2m_e})^2 - \frac{k_e}{m_e}} \quad$ and $\quad s_2 = -\frac{c_e}{2m_e} - \sqrt{(\frac{c_e}{2m_e})^2 - \frac{k_e}{m_e}}$

and A_1 and A_2 are constants determined by the initial conditions.

In the special case where $(c_e/2m_e)^2 = k_e/m_e$, $s_1 = s_2 = s$ and the solution is $x = (A + Bt)e^{-st}$.

CRITICAL DAMPING refers to the special case just mentioned for which $(\frac{c_e}{2m_e})^2 = \frac{k_e}{m_e}$, and $c_e = (c_e)_c = 2\sqrt{k_e m_e}$ is called the **critical value** of the damping coefficient.

If the damping is greater than critical, then the solution of the differential equation for free vibration contains no periodic terms. The mass, after an initial disturbance, returns toward the equilibrium position but does not oscillate.

DAMPING LESS THAN CRITICAL. This is the oscillatory situation. The solution of the differential equation for free vibration can be written in the form

$$x = e^{-\alpha t} X \sin(\omega_d t + \gamma) \qquad \text{where } \alpha = \frac{c_e}{2m_e}, \quad \omega_d = \sqrt{\frac{k_e}{m_e} - (\frac{c_e}{2m_e})^2}.$$

ω_d is the **damped frequency** of the system. If damping were zero the frequency would be $\omega_n = \sqrt{\frac{k_e}{m_e}}$, which is called the **natural frequency**.

The constants X and γ are determined by the initial conditions.

FOR FORCED VIBRATIONS, the solution of the differential equation is that given above for free vibrations plus a particular integral. The solution can be written in the form

$$x = e^{-\alpha t} X \sin(\omega_d t + \gamma) + Y \sin(\omega t - \phi)$$

The first part of the above expression represents the **transient** vibration; this dies out with time. The second part is called the **steady state** vibration and is the part which is usually of most interest to the engineer.

THE STEADY STATE AMPLITUDE Y is $\quad Y = \dfrac{F_o}{\sqrt{(k_e - m_e\omega^2)^2 + (c_e\omega)^2}}$. This can be written

$$Y = \frac{(F_o/k)}{\sqrt{(1 - r^2)^2 + (2\xi r)^2}}$$

where $r = \omega/\omega_n$ is the frequency ratio, and $\xi = c_e/(c_e)_c$ is the damping ratio.

MAGNIFICATION FACTOR M is

$$M = \frac{Y}{F_o/k} = \frac{1}{\sqrt{(1-r^2)^2 + (2\xi r)^2}}$$

M is the ratio of steady state displacement amplitude to the displacement which would be caused by a static force equal to F_o.

THE PHASE ANGLE ϕ can be determined from the following.

$$\tan\phi = \frac{c_e\omega}{k_e - m_e\omega^2}, \qquad \sin\phi = \frac{c_e\omega}{\sqrt{(k_e - m_e\omega^2)^2 + (c_e\omega)^2}}$$

THE FORCE TRANSMITTED TO THE BASE is the sum of the spring force and the damping force:

$$k_e x + c_e\dot{x}$$

Using the previously displayed steady state solution for x it can be shown that the transmitted force has the amplitude

$$F_{TR} = \frac{F_o\sqrt{k_e^2 + (c_e\omega)^2}}{\sqrt{(k_e - m_e\omega^2)^2 + (c_e\omega)^2}}$$

TRANSMISSIBILITY RATIO is the ratio of the amplitude of the transmitted force to the amplitude it would have if the mass were bolted to the base (no spring or damper).

$$\text{T.R.} = \frac{F_{TR}}{F_o} = \frac{\sqrt{k_e^2 + (c_e\omega)^2}}{\sqrt{(k_e - m_e\omega^2)^2 + (c_e\omega)^2}}$$

$$= \frac{\sqrt{1 + (2\xi r)^2}}{\sqrt{(1-r^2)^2 + (2\xi r)^2}}$$

THE FORCING FUNCTION, in the previous discussion, was in the form of a periodic force applied to the moving mass. Another important situation is illustrated in Fig. 7-2. Here a periodic motion of the base induces motion of the mass. The usual design problem in this situation is to choose spring and damper such that the amplitude of motion of the mass will be small compared to the amplitude of motion of the base.

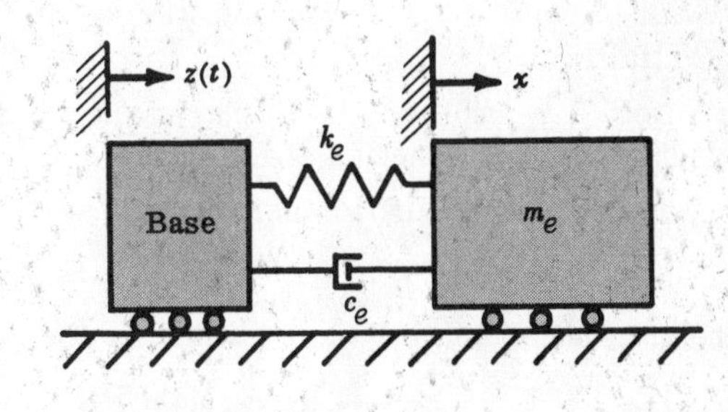

Fig. 7-2

If $z(t)$ is taken to be sinusoidal, i.e.

$$z(t) = z\sin\omega t$$

then the differential equation for motion of the mass is

$$m_e\ddot{x} + c_e\dot{x} + k_e x = z\sqrt{k_e^2 + (c_e\omega)^2}\,\sin(\omega t - \psi)$$

where ψ is a phase angle.

$$\cos\psi = \frac{k_e}{\sqrt{k_e^2 + (c_e\omega)^2}}, \qquad \sin\psi = \frac{-c_e\omega}{\sqrt{k_e^2 + (c_e\omega)^2}}$$

The above differential equation, except for the phase angle ψ, is identical in form with the equation previously discussed. Solution will show that the amplitude of the steady state vibration of the mass is

$$Y = \frac{z\sqrt{k_e^2 + (c_e\,\omega)^2}}{\sqrt{(k_e - m_e\omega^2)^2 + (c_e\,\omega)^2}}$$

TRANSMISSIBILITY RATIO is the ratio of amplitude of the motion of the mass to that of the base.

$$\text{T. R.} = \frac{Y}{z} = \frac{\sqrt{k_e^2 + (c_e\,\omega)^2}}{\sqrt{(k_e - m_e\omega^2)^2 + (c_e\,\omega)^2}}$$

This is identical with the force transmissibility ratio previously discussed.

SYSTEMS WITH MORE THAN ONE DEGREE OF FREEDOM cannot be described by a single second order differential equation. A complete analysis of such a system would, in general, require the simultaneous solution of a set of n second order equations, where n is the number of degrees of freedom of the system. However, relatively simple practical means are available for determining the lowest (or *fundamental*) frequency of vibration. This one piece of information is of great value to the design engineer.

The two-degree-of-freedom system of Fig. 7-3 has two modes of vibration. In the first mode the two masses will move in phase, reaching maximum displacement in the same direction at the same time. In the second mode the two masses will be out of phase, reaching maximum displacements in opposite directions at the same time.

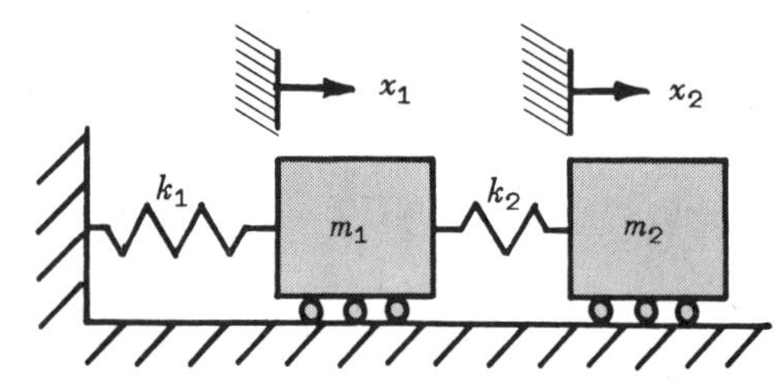

Fig. 7-3

THE ENERGY METHOD for determining the first mode frequency is based on the idea that, neglecting friction, the maximum kinetic energy of the system must equal the maximum potential energy.

Let X_1 = amplitude of displacement of mass m_1, and X_2 = amplitude of displacement of mass m_2. Assume sinusoidal motion of frequency ω.

The maximum kinetic energy of the system will be

$$\text{Max. K.E.} = \tfrac{1}{2}m_1X_1^2\omega^2 + \tfrac{1}{2}m_2X_2^2\omega^2$$

The maximum potential energy stored in the springs will be

$$\text{Max. P.E.} = \tfrac{1}{2}k_1X_1^2 + \tfrac{1}{2}k_2(X_2 - X_1)^2$$

Neglecting friction, $\quad \text{Max. K.E.} = \text{Max. P.E.}$

from which $\quad \omega^2 = \dfrac{k_1X_1^2 + k_2(X_2 - X_1)^2}{m_1X_1^2 + m_2X_2^2} \quad$ or $\quad \omega^2 = \dfrac{k_1 + k_2(X_2/X_1 - 1)^2}{m_1 + m_2(X_2/X_1)^2}$

This equation would give us directly the first, or lowest, natural frequency of vibration if we knew the ratio of amplitudes X_2/X_1. The practical procedure is to *try* a series of values for this ratio. The value which gives the *lowest* result for ω is the most nearly correct.

RESONANCE is variously defined in different textbooks. The term refers generally to operation in the vicinity of maximum forced vibration amplitude. For a frictionless system this means operation at the natural frequency $\omega_n = \sqrt{k_e/m_e}$.

With viscous damping and a forcing function of the form $F_o \sin \omega t$ applied to the mass, maximum amplitude is obtained when the operating frequency ω is

$$\omega_{\max Y} = \omega_n\sqrt{1 - 2\xi^2}$$

Notice that this is different from the damped frequency ω_d.

$$\omega_d = \omega_n\sqrt{1 - \xi^2}$$

In the absence of deliberately built-in damping devices, the factor $\xi = c_e/(c_e)_c$ is usually small enough that ω_n, ω_d and $\omega_{\max Y}$ are very nearly equal. Hence ω_n is ordinarily used for engineering estimates. In the problems to follow, when *resonance* is mentioned, it will mean operation at the natural frequency ω_n.

For a multi-degree-of-freedom system, *resonance* will mean operation at any one of the natural frequencies.

SOLVED PROBLEMS

1. Write the differential equation for the free vibration of the system shown in Fig. 7-4, x being measured from the unstressed spring position.

Solution:

We first make a freebody sketch of the mass and carefully label all forces acting in the x direction. We then apply Newton's second law, setting the sum of the external forces equal to the product of mass and acceleration.

$$-c\dot{x} - kx = m\ddot{x} \qquad \text{or} \qquad m\ddot{x} + c\dot{x} + kx = 0$$

Note that the spring force is properly written $-kx$, because it is opposite in sense to x. Likewise, the damping force is written $-c\dot{x}$ because it is opposite in sense to the velocity $\dot{x}$.

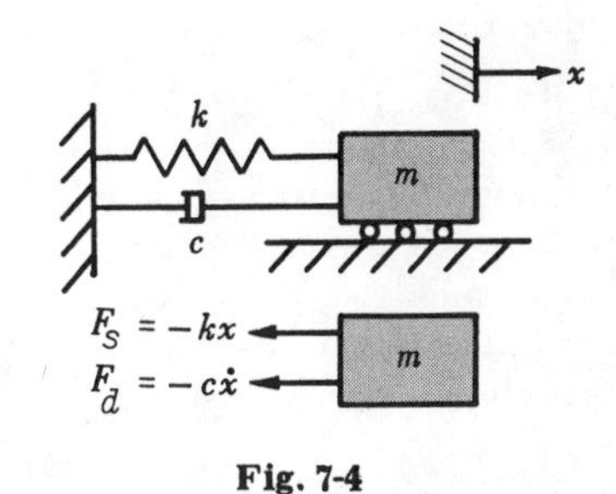

Fig. 7-4

2. Write the differential equation for the free vibration of the system shown in Fig. 7-5. Neglect the mass of the lever.

Solution:

An angular motion is involved. We shall sum moments of external forces around pivot O and set this equal to the product of angular acceleration and moment of inertia with respect to the pivot.

For a *small* displacement θ, the spring force is very nearly $-ka\theta$ and the damping force $-ca\dot{\theta}$. Also, the moment arms for these forces are very nearly equal to a. The moment arm for the weight force is $b \sin\theta$, which will be approximated as $b\theta$. The moment of inertia of the mass with respect to the pivot O is mb^2; hence

$$-(ca\dot{\theta})a - (ka\theta)a - mg(b\theta) = mb^2\ddot{\theta}$$

or

$$mb^2\ddot{\theta} + ca^2\dot{\theta} + (ka^2 + mbg)\theta = 0$$

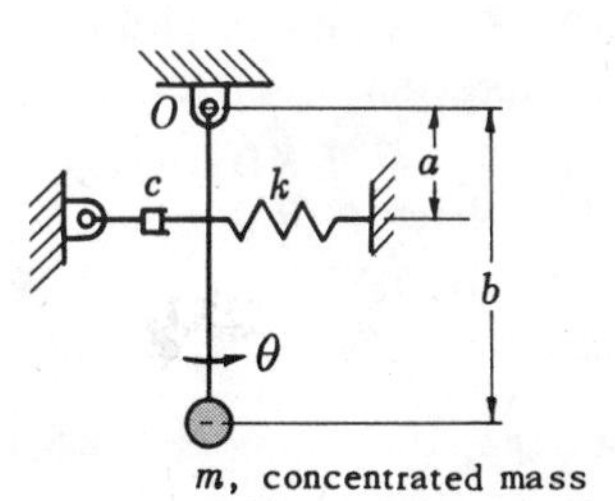

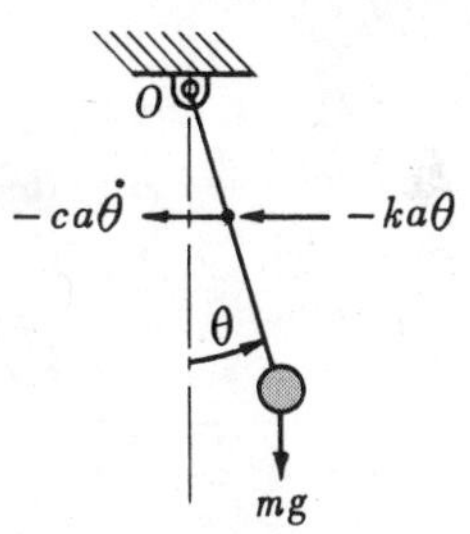

Fig. 7-5

3. For the system of Problem 2 determine
(a) the natural frequency, (b) the damped frequency, (c) c_c, the critical value of damping factor c.

Solution:

Comparing the equation written in Problem 2 with the general single-degree-of-freedom equation discussed earlier, we have

$$x = \theta,\quad \dot{x} = \dot{\theta},\quad \ddot{x} = \ddot{\theta},\quad m_e = mb^2,\quad c_e = ca^2,\quad k_e = ka^2 + mgb$$

Hence

$$(a)\ \omega_n = \sqrt{\frac{k_e}{m_e}} = \sqrt{\frac{ka^2 + mgb}{mb^2}} \qquad (b)\ \omega_d = \sqrt{\frac{k_e}{m_e} - \left(\frac{c_e}{2m_e}\right)^2} = \sqrt{\frac{ka^2 + mgb}{mb^2} - \left(\frac{ca^2}{2mb^2}\right)^2}$$

$$(c)\ (c_e)_c = c_c a^2 = 2\sqrt{k_e m_e} = 2\sqrt{(ka^2 + mgb)mb^2} \quad \text{or} \quad c_c = (2/a^2)\sqrt{(ka^2 + mgb)mb^2}$$

4. Write the differential equation for the system of Fig. 7-6.

Solution:

Again we assume small displacements and make the same approximations as in Problem 2. We define θ to be measured from the **static equilibrium position**. This means that the spring force must initially be large enough to balance the effect of the weight. Taking the moments around pivot O,

$$(-ca\dot{\theta})a + (-ka\theta - \tfrac{b}{a}mg)a + mgb + F_0 b \sin\omega t = mb^2\ddot{\theta}$$

or
$$mb^2\ddot{\theta} + ca^2\dot{\theta} + ka^2\theta = F_0 b \sin\omega t$$

Notice that, with θ measured from the static equilibrium position, the weight force drops out. Although this system is the same as that of Problems 2 and 3, except for the orientation with respect to vertical, the behavior is different. For example, the natural frequency for this system is

$$\omega_n = (a/b)\sqrt{k/m}$$

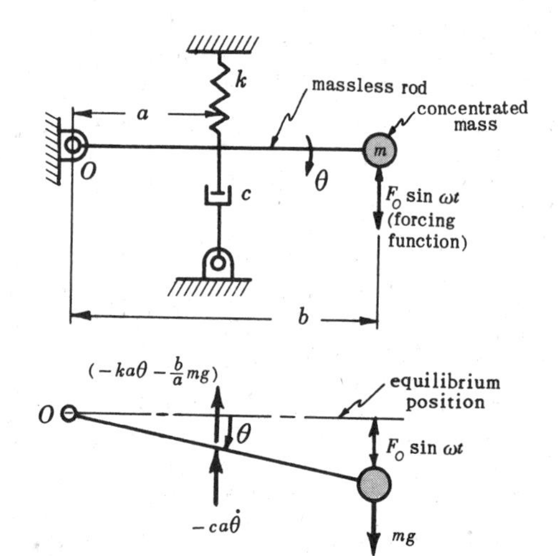

Fig. 7-6

5. A motor is mounted on springs. A small unbalance of the rotor will cause vibration when the motor is operating. Analyze this situation in order that we may be able to decide upon suitable spring characteristics for the mounting. Consider vertical movement only. Refer to Fig. 7-7.

Solution:

We adopt the following symbols:

M = total mass of motor.

me = unbalance of rotor (product of unbalanced mass and radius).

k = spring constant (effect of all springs acting together).

c = damping constant to account for friction (mostly internal frictional effects between parts and within materials, a small value).

ω = motor speed, radians per unit time.

ωt = rotation angle of the unbalanced mass, measured from the horizontal.

x = vertical displacement of the motor, measured from the position of static equilibrium.

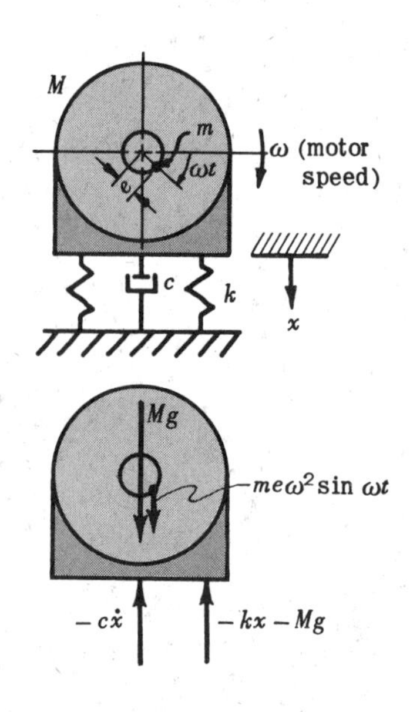

Fig. 7-7

The motor as a whole has vertical acceleration $\ddot{x}$. In addition, the unbalanced mass m has the acceleration $-e\omega^2 \sin \omega t$ in the vertical direction. The external forces are the spring and damping forces plus the weight Mg. Then

$$-c\dot{x} - kx - Mg + Mg = M\ddot{x} - me\omega^2 \sin \omega t$$

or

$$M\ddot{x} + c\dot{x} + kx = +me\omega^2 \sin \omega t$$

(Note: Whether the term on the right hand side of the equation comes out with a positive or negative sign, and whether it be $me\omega^2 \sin \omega t$ or $me\omega^2 \cos \omega t$ depends on the reference for the rotation angle ωt and the sense of rotation ω, as well as the assumed positive sense for displacement x. If, for example, we had chosen to measure ωt clockwise from the positive vertical axis, the forcing function would have been $me\omega^2 \cos \omega t$. This would not change final results of the analysis.)

The above differential equation is of the same form as that discussed earlier for the general case. However, the amplitude of the forcing function, instead of being a simple constant F_0, is a function of ω. We could apply the results listed earlier, but instead will work out the details.

Assume a steady state solution of the form $x = Y \sin(\omega t - \phi)$. Then

$$\dot{x} = Y\omega \cos(\omega t - \phi) \quad \text{and} \quad \ddot{x} = -Y\omega^2 \sin(\omega t - \phi)$$

Substituting into the differential equation, we have

$$M[-Y\omega^2 \sin(\omega t - \phi)] + cY\omega \cos(\omega t - \phi) + kY \sin(\omega t - \phi) = me\omega^2 \sin \omega t$$

or

$$\begin{aligned} &-MY\omega^2 (\sin \omega t \cos \phi - \cos \omega t \sin \phi) \\ &\quad + cY\omega(\cos \omega t \cos \phi + \sin \omega t \sin \phi) \\ &\quad\quad + kY(\sin \omega t \cos \phi - \cos \omega t \sin \phi) = me\omega^2 \sin \omega t \end{aligned}$$

Equating coefficients of $\sin \omega t$, $\quad -MY\omega^2 \cos \phi + cY\omega \sin \phi + kY \cos \phi = me\omega^2$.

Equating coefficients of $\cos \omega t$, $\quad MY\omega^2 \sin \phi + cY\omega \cos \phi - kY \sin \phi = 0$.

Simultaneous solution of the last two equations written yields

$$Y = \frac{me\omega^2}{\sqrt{(k - M\omega^2)^2 + (c\omega)^2}}, \quad \cos \phi = \frac{k - M\omega^2}{\sqrt{(k - M\omega^2)^2 + (c\omega)^2}}, \quad \sin \phi = \frac{c\omega}{\sqrt{(k - M\omega^2)^2 + (c\omega)^2}}$$

Hence the steady state solution of the differential equation is

$$x = \frac{me\omega^2}{\sqrt{(k - M\omega^2)^2 + (c\omega)^2}} \sin(\omega t - \phi)$$

We now investigate the force transmitted to the base. This will be the sum of the spring and damping forces

$$kx + c\dot{x} \quad \text{or} \quad kY \sin(\omega t - \phi) + cY\omega \cos(\omega t - \phi)$$

which can be put in the form $\quad Y\sqrt{k^2 + (c\omega)^2} \sin(\omega t - \phi + \beta)$

where $(-\phi + \beta)$ is the phase angle between the exciting force $me\omega^2 \sin \omega t$ and the transmitted force.

The important thing for our purposes is the amplitude F_{TR} of the transmitted force:

$$F_{TR} = Y\sqrt{k^2 + (c\omega)^2} = \frac{me\omega^2 \sqrt{k^2 + (c\omega)^2}}{\sqrt{(k - M\omega^2)^2 + (c\omega)^2}}$$

A better understanding of this is obtained if we put it into dimensionless form as follows.

Let $r = \dfrac{\omega}{\omega_n} = \dfrac{\omega}{\sqrt{k/M}}$ and $\xi = \dfrac{c}{c_c} = \dfrac{c}{2\sqrt{kM}}$, where ω_n = natural frequency and c_c = critical damping factor. Then

$$\frac{F_{TR}}{me\omega^2} = \frac{\sqrt{1 + (2\xi r)^2}}{\sqrt{(1 - r^2)^2 + (2\xi r)^2}}$$

The ratio of the amplitude of the transmitted force to the amplitude of the forcing function is called **transmissibility ratio**.

The original question posed in this problem was that of deciding upon suitable spring characteristics. We wish the transmitted force to be small in comparison to the force which would be transmitted if the motor frame were bolted directly to the base. This means we wish the quantity

$$\text{T.R.} = \frac{\sqrt{1 + (2\xi r)^2}}{\sqrt{(1-r^2)^2 + (2\xi r)^2}}$$

to be small compared to unity. Friction will be small, unless we deliberately build a damping device into the mounting. Let us estimate $\xi = 0.05$ and solve for r needed to make T.R. = 0.1:

$$0.1 = \frac{\sqrt{1 + 4(.05r)^2}}{\sqrt{(1-r^2)^2 + 4(.05r)^2}} \qquad \text{from which } r = 3.40.$$

Note: If we had assumed zero friction the result would have been $r = 3.41$, so for quick estimates in the kind of situation described here we might as well ignore friction.

If r is to be 3.40, ω_n must be $\omega/3.40$; thus $\sqrt{k/M} = \omega/3.40$ or $k = M\omega^2/11.56$.

Now let us suppose that the motor weighs 42 lb and operates at 1150 rpm. Then k must be

$$k = \frac{M\omega^2}{11.56} = \frac{(42/32.2)(2\pi \times 1150/60)^2}{11.56} = 1635 \text{ lb/ft} = 136 \text{ lb/in}$$

If we use 4 springs in parallel, each spring constant should be $136/4 = 34$ lb/in.

6. Part of a processing operation requires a screening table to be reciprocated with an amplitude of 0.025 in. at a frequency of 6 cycles per sec. The table is to have two spring steel supports, as shown in Fig. 7-8, each with a spring constant k defined as the force on the upper end of a steel support divided by the corresponding deflection at that point. Weight of table will be approximately 80 lb. A solenoid with a sinusoidal force output, $F_o \sin \omega t$, is to be used to drive the device. For what spring constant k should the supports be designed? If effective friction is estimated to be equivalent to $c = 0.05\, c_c$, what peak force F_o must the solenoid provide?

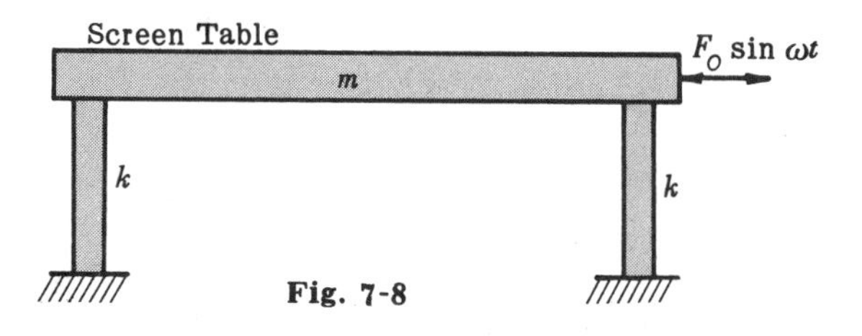

Fig. 7-8

Solution:

This is a forced, steady state vibration situation. The amplitude of vibration is

$$Y = \frac{F_o}{\sqrt{(k_e - m_e\omega^2)^2 + (c_e\omega)^2}}$$

where $m_e = m$, the mass of the table,

$k_e = 2k$ (since there are two springs each having spring constant k),

$c_e = c = 0.05\, c_c = (0.05)(2)\sqrt{k_e m}$,

$\omega = (6)(2\pi) = 12\pi$ rad/sec,

$Y = 0.025$ in., the desired amplitude.

Examination of the above equation for Y shows that Y is near maximum, for a given F_o, at resonance, i.e. when ω equals the natural frequency of the system. Hence we should design so that

$$k_e = 2k = m\omega^2 \quad \text{or} \quad k = \tfrac{1}{2}m\omega^2 = \tfrac{1}{2}(80/32.2)(12\pi)^2 = 1765 \text{ lb/ft} = 147 \text{ lb/in}$$

At resonance, $Y = F_o/c\omega$. Then the peak solenoid force required is

$$F_o = c\omega Y = 0.05\, c_c\omega Y = (0.05)(2\sqrt{k_e m})\omega Y = (0.05)\left(2\sqrt{(2)(1765)(80/32.2)}\right)(12\pi)(0.025/12)$$
$$= 0.74 \text{ lb}$$

7. It is proposed to mount a spin dryer basket as shown in Fig. 7-9. Suitable spring and damper characteristics are to be selected for the following conditions.

Total weight of basket plus contents = 50 lb
Rotational speed = 400 rpm
Maximum unbalance assumed (product of weight and eccentricity) = 20 lb-in
Amplitude of vibration in any direction to be not more than $\frac{1}{2}$ in. at resonance.

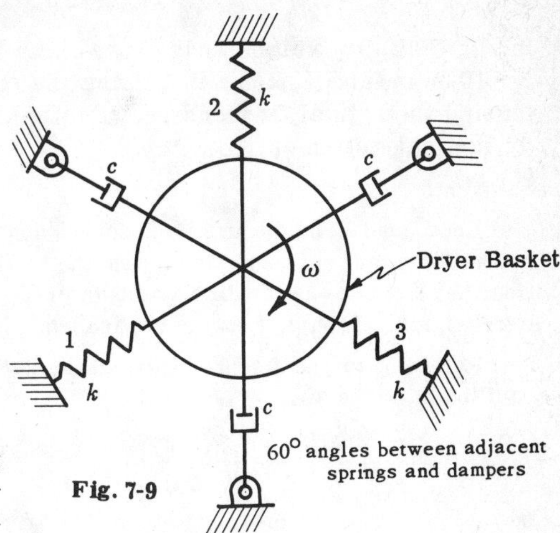

Fig. 7-9

Solution:

Choose X and Y coordinates as shown in Fig. 7-10.

Consider a small deflection x of the basket center. Spring 1 will stretch, spring 3 will compress, and spring 2 will undergo a negligible change of length. The spring forces will be approximately as indicated in Fig. 7-11.

The net spring force in the X direction is

$$F_S = -2\cos 30^\circ\; kx\cos 30^\circ = -1.5kx$$

In other words, the effective spring constant in the X direction is $1.5k$. A similar analysis would yield the same value for the effective spring constant in the Y direction.

If damping forces in the X and Y directions were investigated in the same fashion as above for spring forces, we would find that the effective damping factor in both X and Y directions is $1.5c$.

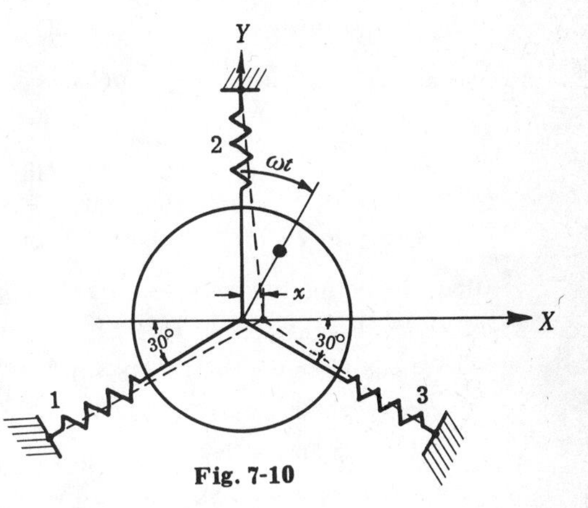

Fig. 7-10

Because all coefficients in the differential equations for X and Y motions will be alike, we need investigate only one equation,

$$M\ddot{x} + 1.5c\dot{x} + 1.5kx = (me)\omega^2 \sin \omega t$$

The displacement amplitude will be

$$Y = \frac{me\omega^2}{\sqrt{(1.5k - M\omega^2)^2 + (1.5c\omega)^2}}$$

by analogy with Prob. 5, for which the differential equation was identical in form; and the amplitude of the transmitted force will be

$$F_{TR} = \frac{me\omega^2\sqrt{(1.5k)^2 + (1.5c\omega)^2}}{\sqrt{(1.5k - M\omega^2)^2 + (1.5c\omega)^2}}$$

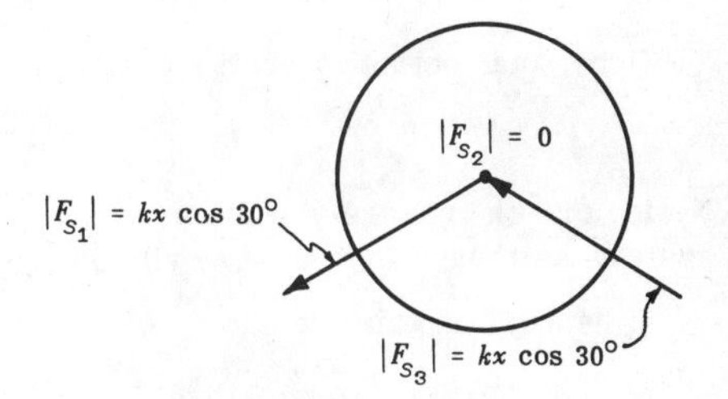

Fig. 7-11

We saw in Prob. 5 that, to keep the transmitted force small, we make the natural frequency low compared to the operating frequency which is specified. For a tentative design we shall choose to make $\omega/\omega_n = 3$. Since in this system the natural frequency is $\omega_n = \sqrt{1.5k/M}$, this means that we shall design so that $1.5k = \omega_n^2 M = (\omega/3)^2 M$ or

$$k = \frac{\omega^2 M}{9(1.5)} = \frac{(400 \times 2\pi/60)^2(50/32.2)}{9(1.5)} = 201 \text{ lb/ft} = 16.8 \text{ lb/in}$$

We now calculate the damping factor c required to limit the displacement amplitude to $\frac{1}{2}$ in. at resonance. At resonance,

$$Y = \frac{me\omega_n^2}{\sqrt{0 + (1.5c\omega_n)^2}} \quad \text{or} \quad c = \frac{me\omega_n}{1.5Y} = \frac{0.0517(13.9)}{1.5(1/24)} = 11.5 \text{ lb-sec/ft} = 0.96 \text{ lb-sec/in}$$

where $Y = 1/24$ ft, $me = (20/32.2)(1/12) = 0.0517$ slug-ft, $\omega_n = (2\pi \times 400/60)/3 = 13.9$ rad/sec.

Answer. Design for $\omega_n = \omega/3$: $k = 16.8$ lb/in, $c = 0.96$ lb-sec/in.

8. In Fig. 7-12, m_1 weighs 10 lb, m_2 weighs 20 lb, $k_1 = 8$ lb/in $k_2 = 10$ lb/in, and $k_3 = 5$ lb/in. Using the energy method, d'-termine the natural frequency of vibration in the first mode, for vertical motion only.

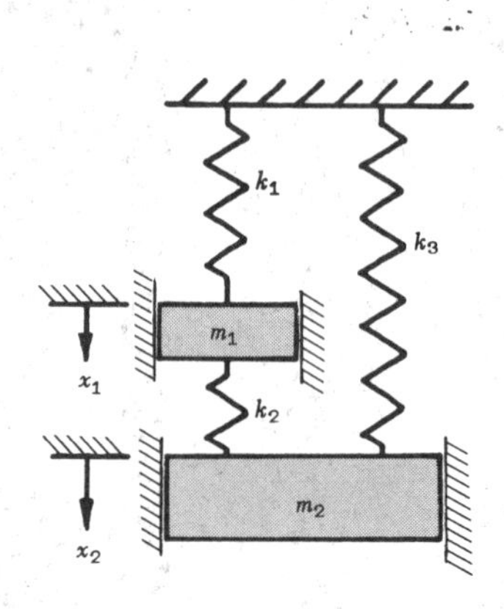

Fig. 7-12

Solution:

Let X_1 and X_2 be the amplitudes of the absolute displacements of masses m_1 and m_2 respectively from the static equilibrium position. Let δ_1 and δ_2 be the displacements of the masses under their own weights, measured from the unstressed spring positions.

Referring to the free body sketches in Fig. 7-13, for static equilibrium we have

$$-k_1\delta_1 + k_2(\delta_2 - \delta_1) + m_1 g = 0$$
$$-k_2(\delta_2 - \delta_1) - k_3\delta_2 + m_2 g = 0$$

or

$$-8\delta_1 + 10(\delta_2 - \delta_1) + 10 = 0$$
$$-10(\delta_2 - \delta_1) - 5\delta_2 + 20 = 0$$

from which $\delta_1 = 2.060$ in., $\delta_2 = 2.708$ in.

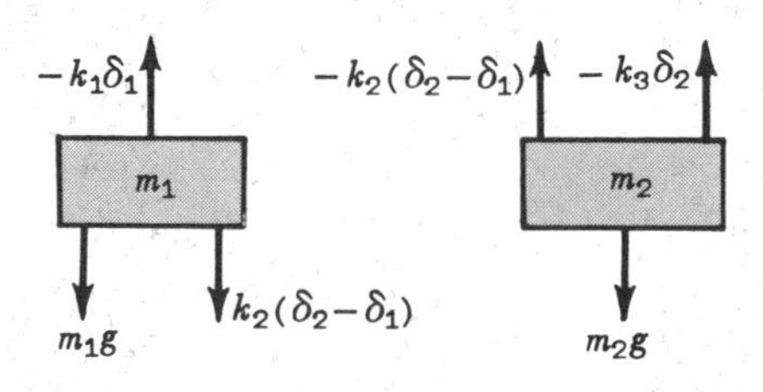

Fig. 7-13

The initial spring forces are then:

Spring No. 1, (8)(2.060) = 16.48 lb
Spring No. 2, (10)(2.708 − 2.060) = 6.48 lb
Spring No. 3, (5)(2.708) = 13.54 lb.

Upon deflection to distances X_1 and X_2 from static equilibrium there will be the following potential energy changes:

Stored in Spring No. 1, $(16.48)X_1 + \frac{1}{2}(8)X_1^2$
Stored in Spring No. 2, $(6.48)(X_2 - X_1) + \frac{1}{2}(10)(X_2 - X_1)^2$
Stored in Spring No. 3, $(13.54)X_2 + \frac{1}{2}(5)X_2^2$
Change of elevation, m_1, $-10X_1$
Change of elevation, m_2, $-20X_2$.

The total potential energy change in moving from the static equilibrium position is then

$$\text{P.E.} = 4X_1^2 + 5(X_2 - X_1)^2 + 2.5X_2^2$$

Notice that the change-of-elevation terms just cancel the initial-spring-force terms. We might have treated the systems as though they were moving in the horizontal plane, without affecting the results.

The maximum kinetic energy of the moving masses, assuming sinusoidal motion at frequency ω, will be

$$\text{K.E.} = \tfrac{1}{2}m_1V_1^2 + \tfrac{1}{2}m_2V_2^2 = \tfrac{1}{2}(10/g)(X_1\omega)^2 + \tfrac{1}{2}(20/g)(X_2\omega)^2 = (5X_1^2 + 10X_2^2)\omega^2/g$$

Equating K.E. and P.E., we obtain $\omega^2 = \dfrac{[4X_1^2 + 5(X_2 - X_1)^2 + 2.5X_2^2]g}{5X_1^2 + 10X_2^2}$ which can be put in the form

$$\omega^2 = \frac{[4 + 5(X_2/X_1 - 1)^2 + 2.5(X_2/X_1)^2]g}{5 + 10(X_2/X_1)^2}$$

The final step is to assume values for the ratio X_2/X_1 and calculate ω. The lowest resulting value for ω is the most nearly correct. (Note: $g = 386$ in/sec^2)

Assumed X_2/X_1	Calculated ω^2	ω
1.6	0.397 g	12.38 rad/sec
1.4	0.394 g	12.33 rad/sec
1.2	0.402 g	12.45 rad/sec

The answer is very nearly 12.33 rad/sec. Notice that the result is not very sensitive to the assumed ratio of X_2/X_1. Usually, a good value to try first is the ratio of static deflections. In this case, $\delta_2/\delta_1 = 2.708/2.060 = 1.31$. If we had chosen $X_2/X_1 = 1.31$, we would have been as close to the final value of $\omega = 12.33$ rad/sec as our sliderule can take us.

SUPPLEMENTARY PROBLEMS

9. Write the differential equations of motion for the systems in Figures 7-14, 7-15, and 7-16. In each case the displacement x is measured from the static equilibrium position.

Ans. Fig. 7-14: $m\ddot{x} + c\dot{x} + \left(\dfrac{k_1 k_2}{k_1 + k_2}\right)x = F(t)$

Fig. 7-15: $m\ddot{x} + c\dot{x} + (k_1 + k_2)x = F(t)$

Fig. 7-16: $m\ddot{x} + c\dot{x} + \left(\dfrac{k_1 k_2}{k_1 + k_2}\right)x = F_o \sin \omega t$

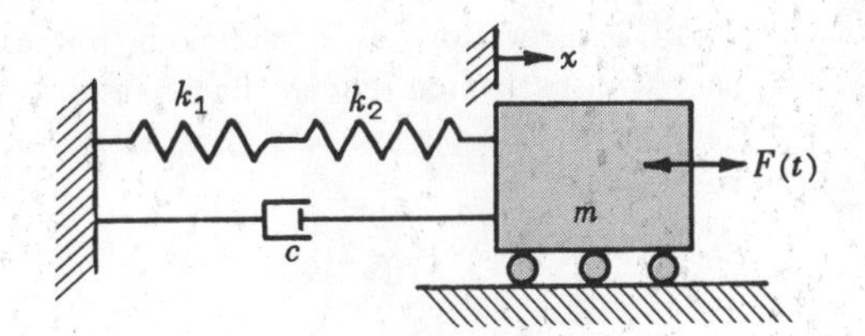

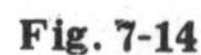

Fig. 7-14

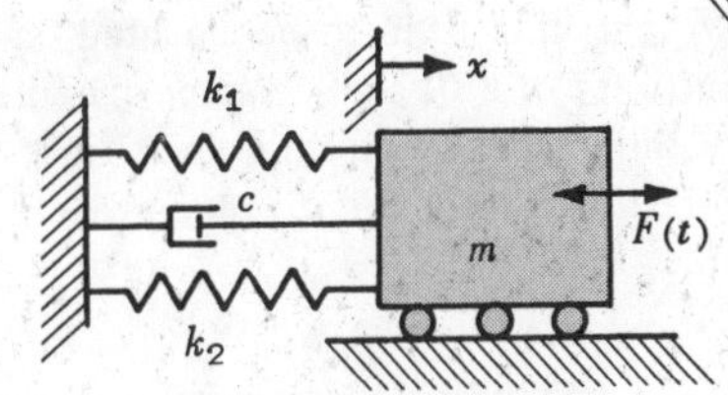

Fig. 7-15

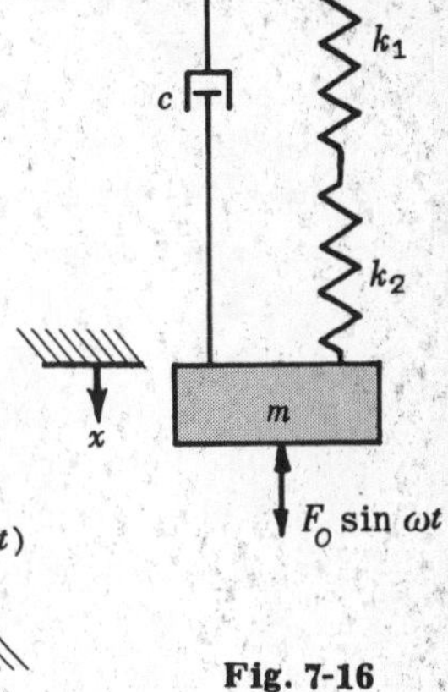

Fig. 7-16

10. Write the differential equations of motion for the systems in Figures 7-17, 7-18 and 7-19. In each case the angular displacement θ is measured from the static equilibrium position. Assume θ to be small and make appropriate linearizing approximations.

Ans.

Fig. 7-17: $mb^2\ddot{\theta} + ca^2\dot{\theta} + ka^2\theta = bF_o \sin \omega t$

Fig. 7-18: $mb^2\ddot{\theta} + ca^2\dot{\theta} + (ka^2 + mgb)\theta = bF_o \sin \omega t$

Fig. 7-19: $m(R^2 + a^2)\ddot{\theta} + ka^2\theta = 0$

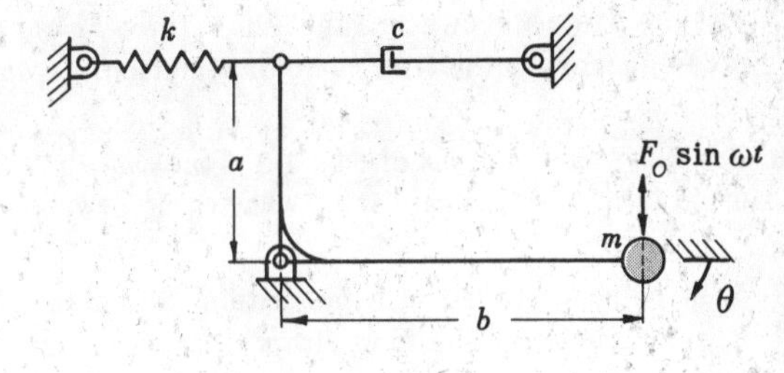

Fig. 7-17

11. What is the natural frequency for each of the systems in Figures 7-14 to 7-19?

Ans. Fig. 7-14: $\sqrt{\dfrac{k_1 k_2}{(k_1 + k_2)m}}$

Fig. 7-15: $\sqrt{\dfrac{k_1 + k_2}{m}}$

Fig. 7-16: $\sqrt{\dfrac{k_1 k_2}{(k_1 + k_2)m}}$

Fig. 7-17: $\dfrac{a}{b}\sqrt{\dfrac{k}{m}}$

Fig. 7-18: $\sqrt{\dfrac{ka^2 + mgb}{mb^2}}$

Fig. 7-19: $\sqrt{\dfrac{ka^2}{m(R^2 + a^2)}}$

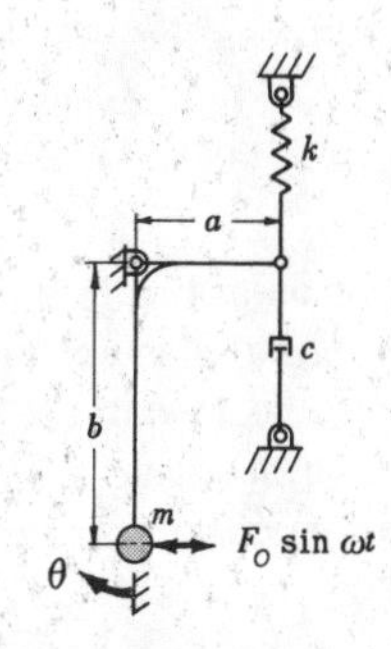

Fig. 7-18

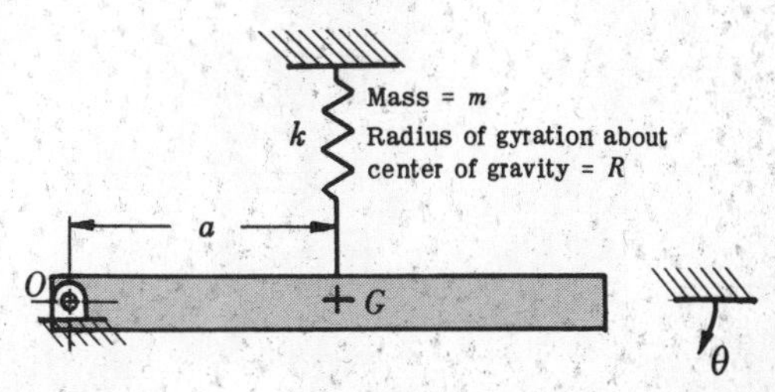

Fig. 7-19

12. The differential equation $10\ddot{x} + 9\dot{x} + 810x = 0$ describes a one-degree-of-freedom system. Units are in., sec, lb. Determine (*a*) the natural frequency ω_n, (*b*) the damped frequency ω_d, (*c*) the damping ratio $\xi = c/c_c$.
Ans. (*a*) $\omega_n = 9$ rad/sec, (*b*) $\omega_d = 9-$ rad/sec (not enough different from ω_n to show on sliderule), (*c*) $\xi = 0.05$

13. The differential equation $10\ddot{x} + 200\dot{x} + 810x = 0$ describes a one-degree-of-freedom system. Units are in., sec, lb. Is this an oscillatory system? *Ans.* No: $c/c_c = 200/180$. Damping is more than critical.

14. The equation $2\ddot{x} + 12\dot{x} + 50x = 8 \sin 10t$ describes a one-degree-of-freedom system in forced vibration. Units are in in., lb, sec. Determine (*a*) the natural frequency ω_n, (*b*) the damped frequency ω_d, (*c*) the damping ratio ξ, (*d*) the amplitude of the steady state vibration.
Ans. (*a*) 5 rad/sec, (*b*) 4 rad/sec, (*c*) 0.60, (*d*) 0.0416 in.

15. An electric motor weighing 25 lb is to be mounted on four springs. The rotating part of the motor weighs 10 lb and has an eccentricity of 0.01 inch. Motor speed is 1200 rpm. It is estimated that the damping ratio will be 0.05. Determine the necessary spring constant if the force transmitted to the base is to be no more than 20 percent of the centrifugal force due to the unbalance of the rotor.
Ans. 41.2 lb/in or less

16. An instrument is to be mounted on a panel subject to vibrations of 0.2 in. amplitude at a frequency of 30 cycles per second. The instrument weighs 2 lb. What spring constant is necessary for the mounting if the amplitude of motion of the instrument is to be not more than 0.02 in.?
Ans. 16.7 lb/in or less

17. For the system shown in Fig. 7-20 below, $k_1 = k_2 = 20$ lb/in and $m_1 = m_2 = 0.1$ lb-sec^2/in. Determine the natural frequency for the first mode of vibration. *Ans.* 8.77 rad/sec

18. For a system like that of Fig. 7-20, $m_1 = m_2 = 0.2$ lb-sec^2/in and $k_1 = k_2 = k$. The natural frequency in the first mode is to be 17.54 rad/sec. What value of k is required? *Ans.* 160 lb/in

19. It is proposed to mount a fan within the cabinet of a piece of cooling equipment as shown schematically in Fig. 7-21 below. The fan (with motor) weighs 20 lb. The cabinet weighs 50 lb. The springs used for isolating the fan from the cabinet have a combined effective constant of 100 lb/in. The springs isolating the cabinet from the base have a combined effective constant of 200 lb/in. The fan operates at 400 rpm. Is there any danger of exciting the first mode vibration system? Use the energy method.
Ans. No danger. Natural frequency is approximately 1.5 rad/sec for first mode vibration. Since fan speed is 41.8 rad/sec (400 rpm), there is no danger of fan unbalance exciting first mode vibration.

20. In an experiment on a simple spring-mass-damper system the frequency of free vibrations was found to be 12 rad/sec. The spring constant and the mass are quite accurately known, from which the natural frequency ω_n was calculated to be 15 rad/sec. (*a*) What is the value of the damping ratio ξ? (*b*) At what frequency should we expect to find maximum amplitude of forced vibration with a forcing function $F_o \sin \omega t$ applied to the mass? *Ans.* (*a*) $\xi = 0.6$ (*b*) $\omega_{\max Y} = 7.95$ rad/sec

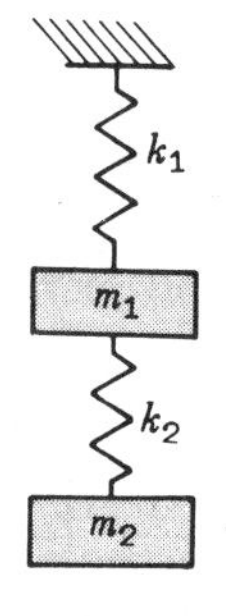

Fig. 7-20

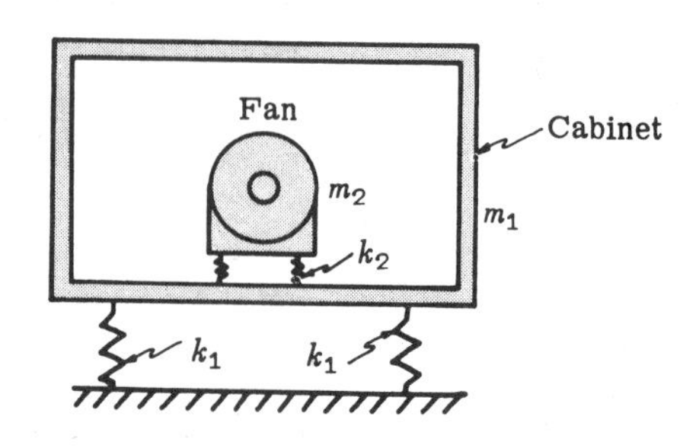

Fig. 7-21

Chapter 8

Critical Speeds of Shafts

ALL ROTATING SHAFTS, even in the absence of external load, deflect during rotation. The magnitude of the deflection depends upon the stiffness of the shaft and its supports, the total mass of shaft and attached parts, the unbalance of the mass with respect to the axis of rotation, and the amount of damping in the system. The deflection, considered as a function of speed, shows maximum values at so-called **critical speeds**. For any shaft there are an infinite number of critical speeds, but only the lowest (first) and occasionally the second are generally of interest to the designer. The others will usually be so high as to be well out of the range of operating speeds.

AT THE FIRST CRITICAL SPEED the shaft will bend to the simplest shape possible. At the second critical speed it will bend to the second simplest shape possible, etc. For example, a shaft supported at its ends and having two relatively large (compared to shaft) masses attached, will bend to the configurations shown in Fig. 8-1(*a*) and Fig. 8-1(*b*) at the first and second critical speeds, respectively.

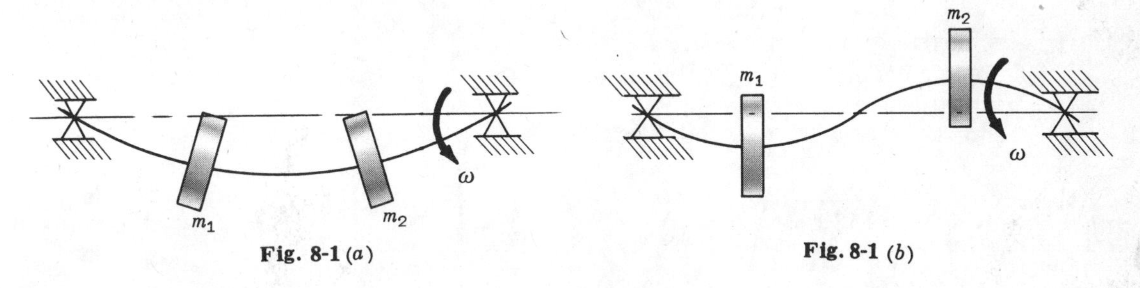

Fig. 8-1 (*a*) **Fig. 8-1** (*b*)

THE NATURAL FREQUENCY of the shaft in bending is very nearly the same as the critical speed, and is usually taken as being the same thing. There is a difference, usually quite small, due to the gyroscopic action of the masses.

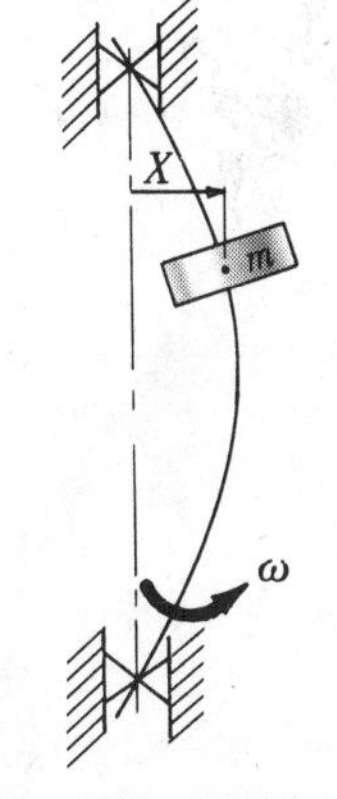

FOR A SHAFT WITH SINGLE ATTACHED MASS (Fig. 8-2 and 8-3), if the shaft mass is small compared to the attached mass, the first critical speed can be calculated approximately as

$$\omega_c = \sqrt{k/m} \quad \text{rad/unit time}$$

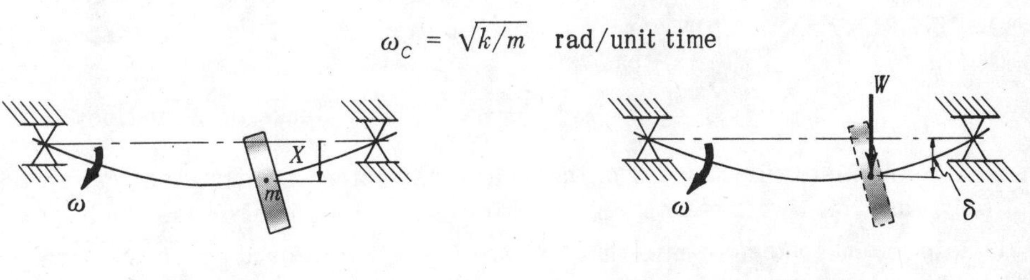

Fig. 8-2(*a*) **Fig. 8-2**(*b*) **Fig. 8-3**

where m is the mass and k is the shaft spring constant (force required for one unit deflection at the mass location). This relation is independent of shaft inclination (horizontal, vertical, or intermediate). Symbol X in Fig. 8-2 represents the shaft deflection, during rotation, at the mass location. Also

$$\omega_c = \sqrt{g/\delta} \quad \text{rad/unit time}$$

where δ is the static deflection (deflection, at the mass location, which would be caused by a force $mg = W$), and g is the gravitational constant (32.2 ft/sec^2 or 386 in/sec^2).

FOR A SHAFT OF CONSTANT CROSS SECTION, simply supported at the ends, with no mass involved other than that of the shaft itself, the first critical speed is very nearly

$$\omega_c = \sqrt{\frac{5}{4}\left(\frac{g}{\delta(\text{max})}\right)} \quad \text{rad/unit time}$$

where $\delta(\text{max})$ is the maximum static deflection caused by a uniformly distributed load equal to the weight of the shaft.

FOR A SHAFT OF NEGLIGIBLE MASS CARRYING SEVERAL CONCENTRATED MASSES, (see Fig. 8-4), the first critical speed is approximately

$$\omega_c = \sqrt{\frac{g \sum_1^j W_n \delta_n}{\sum_1^j W_n \delta_n^2}} \qquad \text{Rayleigh-Ritz Equation}$$

where W_n = weight of nth mass,
δ_n = static deflection at the nth mass,
j = total number of masses.

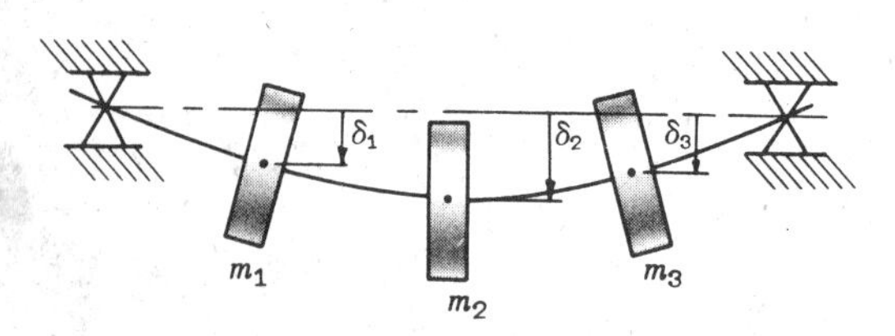

Fig. 8-4

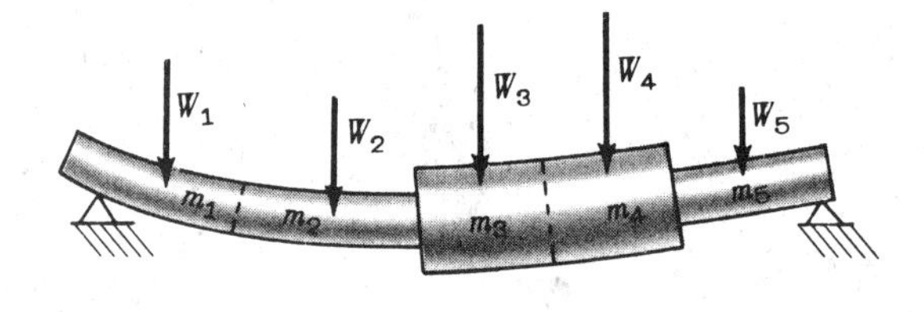

Fig. 8-5

This same equation can be used for estimating the first critical speed of a shaft with distributed mass. Refer to Fig. 8-5 above. Break the distributed mass into a number of pieces, m_1, m_2, m_3, etc. Treat the mass of each piece as though concentrated at its center of gravity. The number of subdivisions to use is a matter to be learned by experience, but it will be found that good accuracy is obtained with rather crude approximations.

THE DUNKERLEY EQUATION, another approximation for the first critical speed of a multimass system, is

$$\frac{1}{\omega_c^2} = \frac{1}{\omega_1^2} + \frac{1}{\omega_2^2} + \frac{1}{\omega_3^2} + \dots \qquad \text{Dunkerley Equation}$$

where ω_c is the first critical speed of the multimass system. ω_1 is the critical speed which would exist if only mass No. 1 were present, ω_2 the critical speed with only mass No. 2, etc.

It is important to keep in mind that both the Rayleigh-Ritz and the Dunkerley equations are approximations to the first natural frequency of vibration, which is assumed to be nearly equal to the critical speed of rotation. In general, the Rayleigh-Ritz equation overestimates and the Dunkerley equation underestimates the natural frequency.

HIGHER CRITICAL SPEEDS for multimass systems require much more extensive calculation than is necessary for the determination of the lowest (first) critical speed. Several different methods have been developed. Here we shall give the equation for a two-mass system only:

$$\frac{1}{\omega^4} - (a_{11}m_1 + a_{22}m_2)\frac{1}{\omega^2} + (a_{11}a_{22} - a_{12}a_{21})m_1m_2 = 0$$

This is a bi-quadratic equation having the positive roots $1/\omega_1$ and $1/\omega_2$, where ω_1 and ω_2 are the first and second critical speeds (or natural frequencies of vibration). The two masses are m_1 and m_2.

The constants a are influence coefficients. a_{12} is the deflection at the location of mass No. 1 that would be caused by a unit load at the location of mass No. 2, a_{11} is the deflection at No.1 caused by unit load at No.1, etc. Maxwell's reciprocity theorem states that $a_{12} = a_{21}$.

FOR ANY MULTIMASS SYSTEM the frequency equation is obtained by setting the following determinant equal to zero.

$$\begin{vmatrix} (a_{11}m_1 - \frac{1}{\omega^2}) & (a_{12}m_2) & (a_{13}m_3) & \cdots \\ (a_{21}m_1) & (a_{22}m_2 - \frac{1}{\omega^2}) & (a_{23}m_3) & \cdots \\ (a_{31}m_1) & (a_{32}m_2) & (a_{33}m_3 - \frac{1}{\omega^2}) & \cdots \\ \cdots & \cdots & \cdots & \cdots \\ \cdots & \cdots & \cdots & \cdots \\ \cdots & \cdots & \cdots & \cdots \end{vmatrix}$$

SOLVED PROBLEMS

1. The shaft shown in Fig. 8-6 has attached to it a gear m_1 weighing 50 lb and a flywheel m_2 weighing 100 lb. Static deflections δ_1 and δ_2 have been found to be .0012 in. and .0003 in. respectively. Determine the first critical speed, ignoring the mass of the shaft itself.

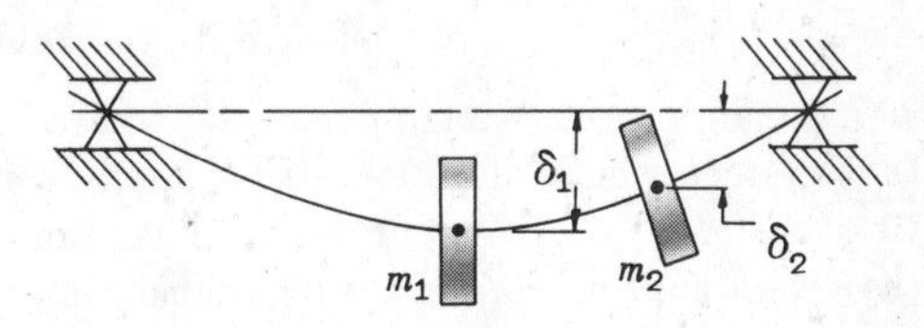

Fig. 8-6

Solution:

$$\Sigma W\delta = (50)(.0012) + (100)(.0003) = .090 \text{ lb-in}$$

$$\Sigma W\delta^2 = (50)(.0012)^2 + (100)(.0003)^2 = 81 \times 10^{-6} \text{ lb-in}^2$$

$$\omega_c = \sqrt{\frac{g\Sigma W\delta}{\Sigma W\delta^2}} = \sqrt{\frac{(386)(.090)}{81\times 10^{-6}}} = 655 \text{ rad/sec} = 6250 \text{ rpm}$$

2. Derive the equation $\omega_c = \sqrt{g/\delta}$ for the critical speed of a shaft carrying a single concentrated mass. Refer to Fig. 8-7 below.

Solution:

We neglect the small tilting of the mass, ignore frictional effects, and presume some small eccentricity e of the mass center of gravity with respect to the shaft center. Then,

$$kX = m(X + e)\omega^2$$

where kX is the spring force which the shaft exerts on the mass, k being the local spring constant for the shaft, i.e. the force required at the location of m to give the shaft one unit of deflection here. $(X+e)\omega^2$ is the acceleration of the center of gravity of the mass. Solving for X, the shaft deflection at m,

$$X(k - m\omega^2) = me\omega^2 \qquad \text{or} \qquad X = me\omega^2/(k - m\omega^2)$$

We see that, under the assumptions made, the deflection X becomes very large when $k = m\omega^2$. Hence the critical speed is $\omega_c = \sqrt{k/m}$. But $m = W/g$; then $k/m = kg/W = g/\delta$. (By definition, the static deflection δ is the deflection which would by caused by a force equal to W; hence $W/k = \delta$.) Thus $\omega_c = \sqrt{g/\delta}$.

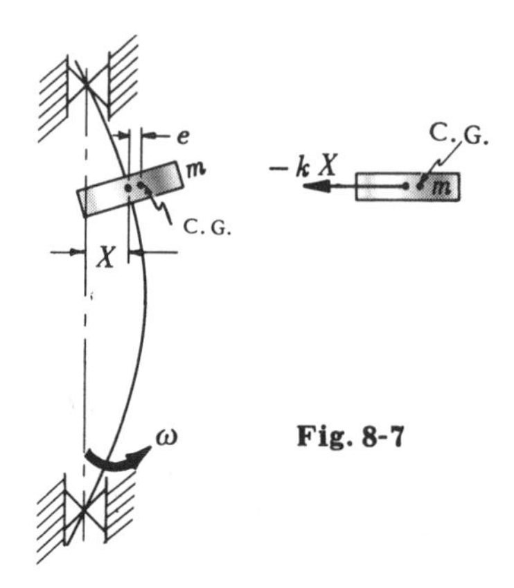

Fig. 8-7

3. Derive the equation $\omega_c = \sqrt{\dfrac{g\sum W\delta}{\sum W\delta^2}}$ for the first critical speed of a shaft with several concentrated masses. Refer to Fig. 8-8.

Solution:

We picture the shaft in free lateral vibration at the fundamental frequency ω (first mode vibration) and reason that the maximum potential energy stored in the shaft must equal the maximum kinetic energy of the moving masses.

$$\text{Max. K.E.} = \tfrac{1}{2}m_1V_1^2 + \tfrac{1}{2}m_2V_2^2 + \ldots$$

The motion of the masses will be sinusoidal. Hence the maximum velocity for any mass will be $X_n\omega$, where X_n is the amplitude of displacement of that mass. Therefore,

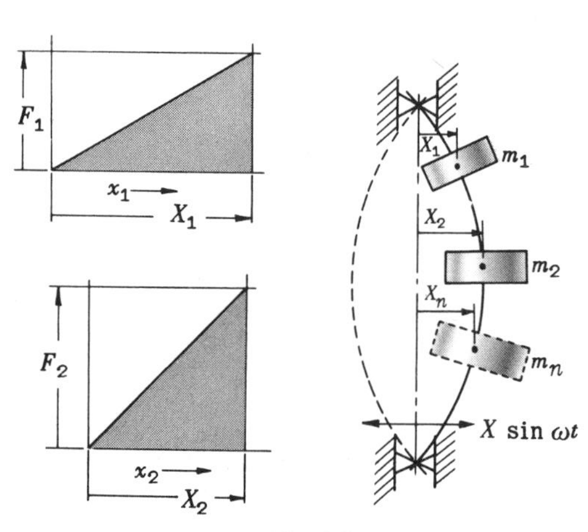

Fig. 8-8

$$\text{Max. K.E.} = \tfrac{1}{2}m_1(X_1\omega)^2 + \tfrac{1}{2}m_2(X_2\omega)^2 + \ldots = \tfrac{1}{2}\omega^2\sum m_nX_n^2$$

The maximum potential energy stored in the shaft is equal to the work necessary to deflect the shaft to the shape defined by the amplitudes X_1, X_2, etc. Hence,

$$\text{Max. P.E.} = \tfrac{1}{2}k_1X_1^2 + \tfrac{1}{2}k_2X_2^2 + \ldots = \tfrac{1}{2}\sum k_nX_n^2$$

where each k is a "spring constant" whose definition can be explained as follows. Let F_1, F_2, F_3, etc., be those forces which, if acting simultaneously at locations 1, 2, 3, etc., respectively, would result in the deflections X_1, X_2, X_3, etc. Now, the shape of the shaft deflection curve depends on these forces, not on how they were built up. We might for example assume F_1 to have been applied first, then F_3, then F_2, ..., in any arbitrary fashion. We choose to assume that the forces were built up *simultaneously* from zero in a *linear* relation to the deflections at the force locations. See the force-deflection diagrams in Fig. 8-8. The work done at each force location is represented by the shaded area under the straight line of slope k.

Equating maximum kinetic and potential energies, we obtain $\omega^2 = \dfrac{\sum k_nX_n^2}{\sum m_nX_n^2}$.

We now *assume* that the shape to which the shaft bends during vibration is the same as the static deflection curve, i.e. we assume $X_1 = C\delta_1$, $X_2 = C\delta_2$, etc. Actually we know this to be incorrect, but it gives a reasonable approximation. Then

$$\omega^2 = \frac{\sum k_n\delta_n^2}{\sum m_n\delta_n^2} = \frac{g\sum W_n\delta_n}{\sum W_n\delta_n^2}$$

since $m_n = W_n/g$ and $k_n\delta_n = W_n$.

Assuming the natural frequency of lateral vibration ω to equal the critical speed of rotation ω_c and dropping the n subscripts for simplicity, we have finally $\omega_c = \sqrt{\dfrac{g\sum W\delta}{\sum W\delta^2}}$.

4. The two masses, m_1 and m_2, attached to the shaft of Fig. 8-9 weigh 140 lb and 60 lb respectively. Through a deflection analysis the influence coefficients for the shaft have been found to be

$$a_{11} = 2\times10^{-6} \text{ in/lb},$$
$$a_{22} = 12\times10^{-6} \text{ in/lb},$$
$$a_{12} = a_{21} = 4\times10^{-6} \text{ in/lb}.$$

(Remember that a_{11} is the deflection at location No. 1 caused by a 1 lb force at that location, a_{12} is the deflection at location No. 1 caused by a 1 lb force at location No. 2, etc.) Determine the first critical speed, ignoring the mass of the shaft.

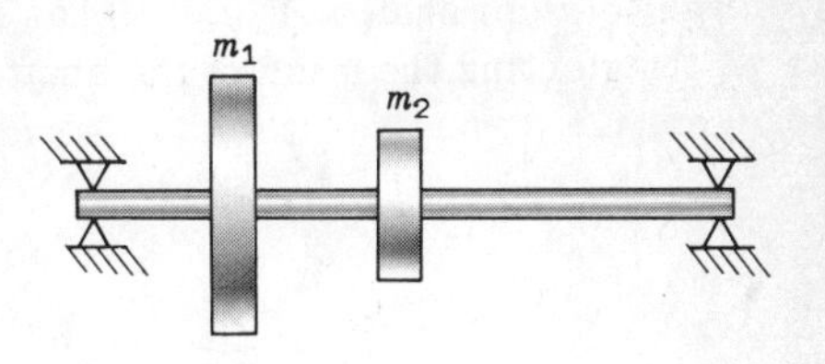

Fig. 8-9

Solutions:

(*a*) **Using the Dunkerley equation.**

$$\omega_1 = \sqrt{\frac{g}{\delta_{11}}} = \sqrt{\frac{g}{W_1 a_{11}}} = \sqrt{\frac{386}{(140)(2)10^{-6}}} = 1174 \text{ rad/sec}$$

$$\omega_2 = \sqrt{\frac{g}{\delta_{22}}} = \sqrt{\frac{g}{W_2 a_{22}}} = \sqrt{\frac{386}{(60)(12)10^{-6}}} = 732 \text{ rad/sec}$$

$$\frac{1}{\omega_c^2} = \frac{1}{\omega_1^2} + \frac{1}{\omega_2^2} = \frac{1}{(1174)^2} + \frac{1}{(732)^2} \quad \text{or} \quad \omega_c = 621 \text{ rad/sec}$$

(*b*) **Using the Rayleigh-Ritz equation.**

$$\omega_c = \sqrt{\frac{g\sum W\delta}{\sum W\delta^2}}$$

$$\delta_1 = W_1 a_{11} + W_2 a_{12} = (140)(2)10^{-6} + (60)(4)10^{-6} = (5.20)10^{-4} \text{ in.}$$
$$\delta_2 = W_2 a_{22} + W_1 a_{21} = (60)(12)10^{-6} + (140)(4)10^{-6} = (12.80)10^{-4} \text{ in.}$$

	$W\delta$			$W\delta^2$	
(*1*)	$(140)(5.20)10^{-4}$	$= (7.28)10^{-2}$	(*1*)	$(7.28)(10^{-2})(5.20)10^{-4}$	$= (37.9)10^{-6}$
(*2*)	$(60)(12.80)10^{-4}$	$= (7.68)10^{-2}$	(*2*)	$(7.68)(10^{-2})(12.80)10^{-4}$	$= (98.3)10^{-6}$
	Σ	$= (14.96)10^{-2}$ lb-in		Σ	$= (136.2)10^{-6}$ lb-in^2

$$\omega_c = \sqrt{\frac{(386)(14.96)10^{-2}}{(136.2)10^{-6}}} = 651 \text{ rad/sec}$$

The two solutions differ, as is to be expected. The Dunkerley equation underestimates and the Rayleigh-Ritz equation overestimates. Hence the true value lies between 621 and 651 rad/sec.

(*c*) **Using the frequency equation.**

$$\frac{1}{\omega^4} - (a_{11}m_1 + a_{22}m_2)\frac{1}{\omega^2} + (a_{11}a_{22} - a_{12}a_{21})m_1 m_2 = 0$$

$$(a_{11}m_1 + a_{22}m_2) = (2)(10^{-6})(\frac{140}{386}) + (12)(10^{-6})(\frac{60}{386}) = (2.59)10^{-6}$$

$$(a_{11}a_{22} - a_{12}a_{21})m_1 m_2 = [(2)(12)-(4)(4)]\frac{(140)(60)10^{-12}}{(386)^2} = (0.451)10^{-12}$$

Hence $\frac{1}{\omega^4} - (2.59)10^{-6}\frac{1}{\omega^2} + (0.451)10^{-12} = 0$, for which the smaller positive root is $\omega_c = 624$ rad/sec.

This is the true value of the critical speed (within sliderule accuracy). Thus for this particular example the Dunkerley equation is a better approximation than the Rayleigh-Ritz equation.

5. The steel shaft in Fig. 8-10 has two gears weighing 50 lb and 100 lb respectively attached as shown. Neglecting the mass of the shaft, determine the first critical speed.

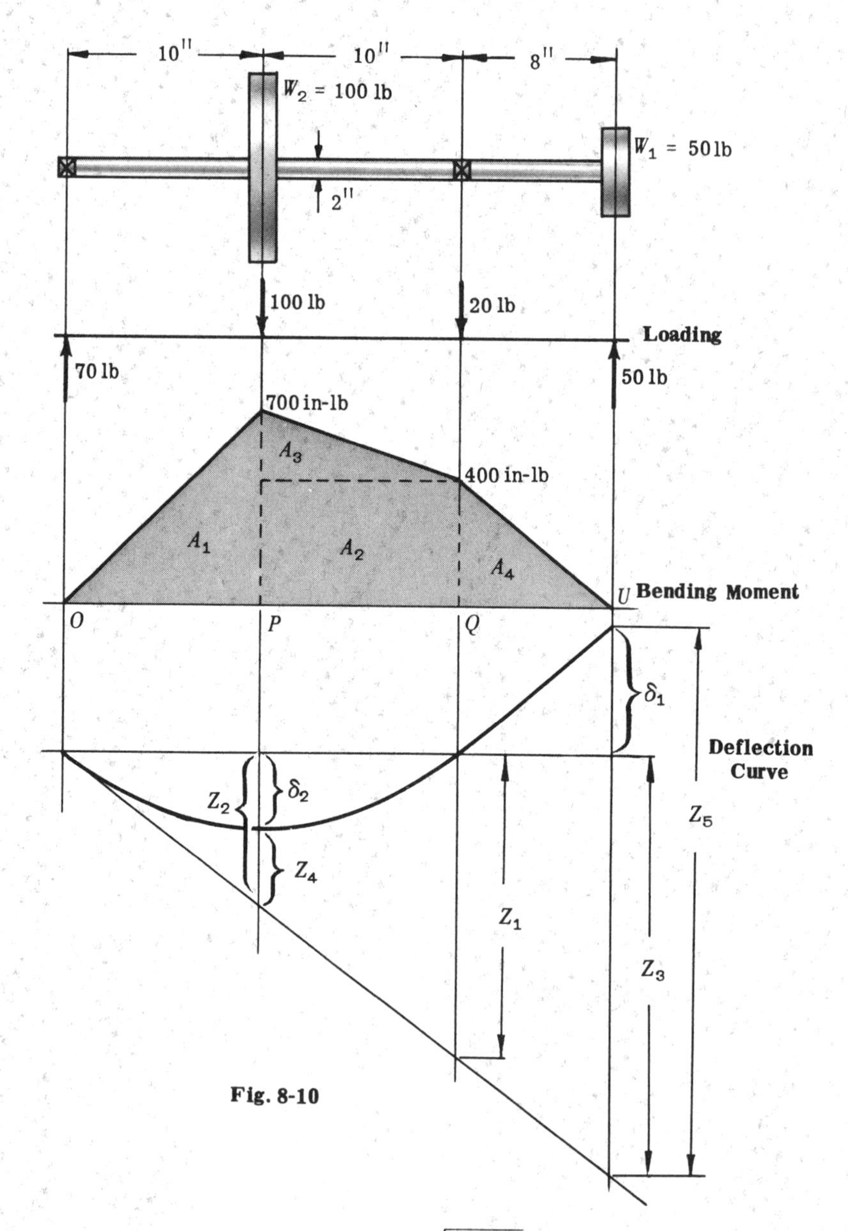

Fig. 8-10

Solution:

We choose to use the Rayleigh-Ritz equation, $\omega_c = \sqrt{\dfrac{g\Sigma W\delta}{\Sigma W\delta^2}}$. Most of the labor of computation lies in determining the δ's. We proceed as illustrated by the diagrams in Fig. 8-10 above.

(*1*) Assume static loading with forces equal in magnitude to W_1 and W_2 and so directed that the shaft will be bent to the simplest form possible (no reversal of curvature). This gives us the loading diagram shown.

(*2*) Calculate the bearing reactions, assuming point supports.

(*3*) Determine bending moments and sketch the bending moment diagram.

(4) Find deflections δ_1 and δ_2 by any suitable technique. Here we shall use the area-moment method. The necessary arithmetic is recorded below.

(a) Z_1EI = moment of areas A_1, A_2, A_3 around Q

$$= \frac{(10)(700)}{2}(10+\frac{10}{3}) + (10)(400)(5) + \frac{(10)(300)}{2}(\frac{20}{3}) = 76{,}667 \text{ lb-in}^3$$

(b) $Z_2EI = 76{,}667(10/20) = 38{,}333 \text{ lb-in}^3$

(c) $Z_3EI = 76{,}667(28/20) = 107{,}334 \text{ lb-in}^3$

(d) $Z_4EI = \text{moment of area } A_1 \text{ around } P = \frac{(10)(700)}{2}(\frac{10}{3}) = 11{,}667 \text{ lb-in}^3$

(e) Z_5EI = moment of areas A_1, A_2, A_3, A_4 around U

$$= \frac{(10)(700)}{2}(18+\frac{10}{3}) + (10)(400)(13) + \frac{(10)(300)}{2}(8+\frac{20}{3}) + \frac{(8)(400)}{2}(\frac{16}{3})$$

$$= 157{,}216 \text{ lb-in}^3$$

(f) $\delta_2EI = Z_2EI - Z_4EI = 38{,}333 - 11{,}667 = 26{,}666$

(g) $\delta_1EI = Z_5EI - Z_3EI = 157{,}216 - 107{,}334 = 49{,}882$

(5) $I = \frac{\pi d^4}{64} = \frac{\pi(2)^4}{64} = 0.785 \text{ in}^4, \qquad E = (3)10^7 \text{ psi (steel)}$

(6) $\delta_1 = 49{,}882/(3)(10^7)(0.785) = (2.118)10^{-3}$ in.
$\delta_2 = 26{,}666/(3)(10^7)(0.785) = (1.132)10^{-3}$ in.

(7) $W_1\delta_1 = (50)(2.118)10^{-3} = (10.59)10^{-2} \qquad W_1\delta_1^2 = (2.243)10^{-4}$
$W_2\delta_2 = (100)(1.132)10^{-3} = (11.32)10^{-2} \qquad W_2\delta_2^2 = (1.282)10^{-4}$
$\Sigma = (21.91)10^{-2} \qquad \Sigma = (3.525)10^{-4}$

$$\omega_c = \sqrt{\frac{g\Sigma W\delta}{\Sigma W\delta^2}} = \sqrt{\frac{(386)(21.91)10^{-2}}{(3.525)10^{-4}}} = 490 \text{ rad/sec}$$

6. Determine both the first and second critical speeds for the system of Fig. 8-10.

Solution:

1. We shall use the frequency equation

$$\frac{1}{\omega^4} - (a_{11}m_1 + a_{22}m_2)\frac{1}{\omega^2} + (a_{11}a_{22} - a_{12}a_{21})m_1m_2 = 0$$

Most of the calculation labor is involved in the determination of the influence coefficients, a_{11}, a_{22}, $a_{12} = a_{21}$. Two deflection analyses must be made.

2. To determine a_{11} and a_{21} we apply a 1 lb load at the location of mass No. 1 and solve for deflections at the locations of masses No. 1 and No. 2 respectively (see Fig. 8-11). Similarly, to determine a_{22} and a_{12} we apply a 1 lb load at the location of mass No. 2 and solve for deflections at the locations of masses No. 2 and No. 1 respectively. The arithmetic will not be reproduced here. The results are

$$a_{12} = a_{21} = (8.50)10^{-6} \text{ in/lb},$$
$$a_{11} = (25.35)10^{-6} \text{ in/lb},$$
$$a_{22} = (7.07)10^{-6} \text{ in/lb}$$

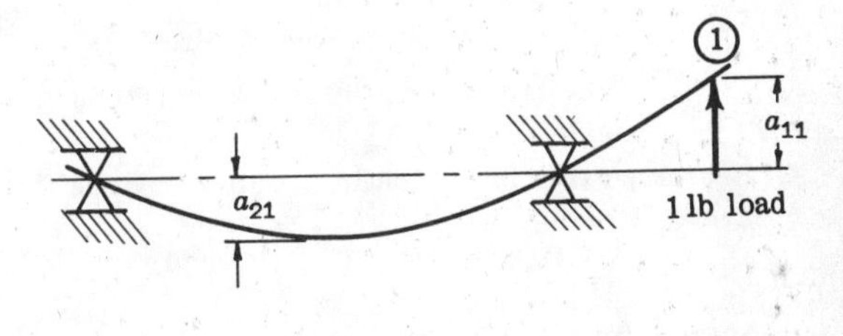

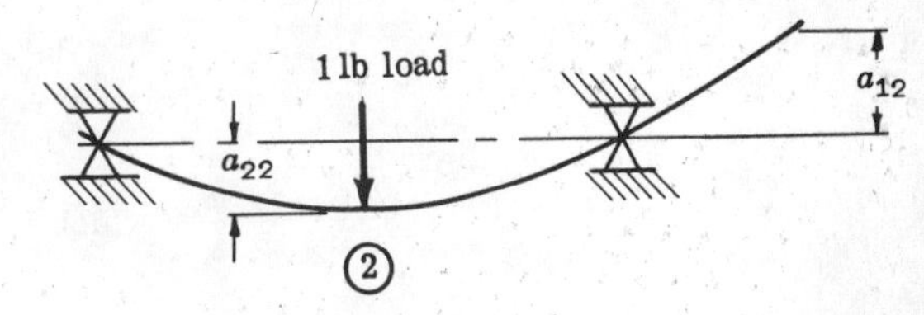

Fig. 8-11

3. $a_{11}m_1 + a_{22}m_2 = (25.35)10^{-6}(50/386) + (7.07)10^{-6}(100/386) = (5.115)10^{-6}$

$(a_{11}a_{22} - a_{12}a_{21})m_1m_2 = [(25.35)(7.07) - (8.50)^2](50)(100)(10^{-12})/(386)^2 = (3.59)10^{-12}$

4. Hence $\frac{1}{\omega^4} - (5.115)(10^{-6})\frac{1}{\omega^2} + (3.59)10^{-12} = 0$ having positive roots $\omega_{c_1} = 483$ and $\omega_{c_2} = 1090$ rad/sec

7. The bearing supports for the shaft shown in Fig. 8-12 have flexibility equivalent to a spring constant k of 250,000 lb/in in any direction perpendicular to the shaft axis. Due to bending, the shaft itself has a deflection δ_b of .0018 in. under the 300 lb load. What effect does the flexibility of the supports have on the critical speed?

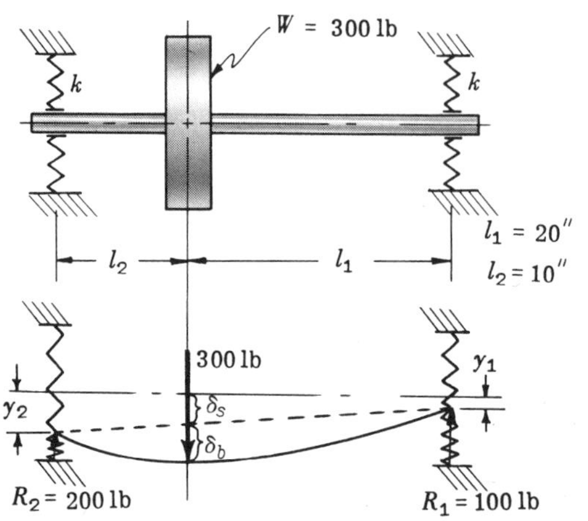

Solution:

1. If the supports were completely rigid, the critical speed would be

$$\omega_c = \sqrt{g/\delta_b} = \sqrt{386/.0018} = 463 \text{ rad/sec}$$

2. The flexibility of the supports increases the deflection at the load, measured with respect to the unloaded shaft centerline. To calculate the critical speed we should use

Fig. 8-12

$$\omega_c = \sqrt{g/(\delta_b + \delta_s)}$$

$$y_1 = R_1/k = 100/250{,}000 = (4)10^{-4} \text{ in.} \qquad \delta_s = y_1 + (y_2 - y_1)\frac{l_1}{l_1 + l_2} = (6.7)10^{-4} \text{ in.}$$

$$y_2 = R_2/k = 200/250{,}000 = (8)10^{-4} \text{ in.} \qquad \delta_b + \delta_s = (18.0 + 6.7)10^{-4} = (24.7)10^{-4} \text{ in.}$$

Then $\omega_c = \sqrt{386/(24.7 \times 10^{-4})} = 395$ rad/sec. The flexibility of the supports reduces the critical speed by

$$\left(\frac{463 - 395}{463}\right)100\% \approx 15\%$$

8. Derive the frequency equation

$$\frac{1}{\omega^4} - (a_{11}m_1 + a_{22}m_2)\frac{1}{\omega^2} + (a_{11}a_{22} - a_{12}a_{21})m_1m_2 = 0$$

for a two-mass system.

Solution:

1. Refer to Fig. 8-13. Consider the shaft rotating and deflected by the centrifugal forces $m_1y_1\omega^2$ and $m_2y_2\omega^2$ on the two masses.

$$y_1 = a_{11}m_1y_1\omega^2 + a_{12}m_2y_2\omega^2,$$

$$y_2 = a_{22}m_2y_2\omega^2 + a_{21}m_1y_1\omega^2$$

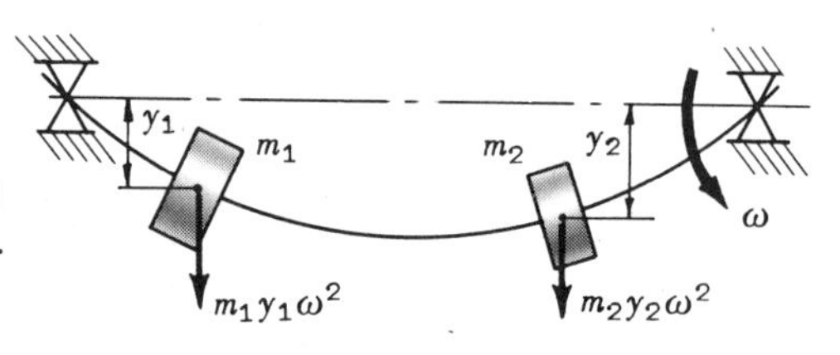

Fig. 8-13

2. Rearrange the above equations, collecting coefficients of y_1 and y_2, and dividing through by ω^2.

$$(a_{11}m_1 - 1/\omega^2)y_1 + (a_{12}m_2)y_2 = 0, \qquad (a_{21}m_1)y_1 + (a_{22}m_2 - 1/\omega^2)y_2 = 0$$

3. Solving for y_1/y_2 in both equations,

$$\frac{y_1}{y_2} = \frac{a_{12}m_2}{1/\omega^2 - a_{11}m_1}, \qquad \frac{y_1}{y_2} = \frac{1/\omega^2 - a_{22}m_2}{a_{21}m_1}$$

Then $\frac{a_{12}m_2}{1/\omega^2 - a_{11}m_1} = \frac{1/\omega^2 - a_{22}m_2}{a_{21}m_1}$, which can be rearranged into the form

$$\frac{1}{\omega^4} - (a_{11}m_1 + a_{22}m_2)\frac{1}{\omega^2} + (a_{11}a_{22} - a_{12}a_{21})m_1m_2 = 0$$

4. We might more simply have said that, in order that the two equations as written in (2) be satisfied, the determinant of the coefficients of y_1 and y_2 must vanish.

$$\begin{vmatrix} (a_{11}m_1 - 1/\omega^2) & (a_{12}m_2) \\ (a_{21}m_1) & (a_{22}m_2 - 1/\omega^2) \end{vmatrix} = 0$$

5. To develop the frequency equation with more masses, we could follow exactly the same procedure, writing one equation for the deflection at each mass. In order that the set of equations be satisfied, the determinant of the coefficients of the y's must vanish.

9. Derive the Dunkerley equation for a two-mass system.

Solution:

1. We start with the frequency equation derived in Problem 8:

$$\frac{1}{\omega^4} - (a_{11}m_1 + a_{22}m_2)\frac{1}{\omega^2} + (a_{11}a_{22} - a_{12}a_{21})m_1 m_2 = 0$$

2. In any equation of the form $x^2 + bx + c = 0$, the sum of the roots is $-b$: $x_1 + x_2 = -b$. Hence in our frequency equation

$$(1/\omega_{c_1}^2 + 1/\omega_{c_2}^2) = a_{11}m_1 + a_{22}m_2$$

where ω_{c_1} and ω_{c_2} are the first and second critical speeds, respectively.

3. ω_{c_2} is larger than ω_{c_1}, usually appreciably larger. Then $1/\omega_{c_1}^2$ will generally be much larger than $1/\omega_{c_2}^2$. Therefore, *approximately*, $1/\omega_{c_1}^2 = a_{11}m_1 + a_{22}m_2$.

4. Now, $a_{11}m_1 = a_{11}W_1/g$; and $a_{11}W_1 = \delta_{11}$, the static deflection at mass No. 1 caused by W_1 acting alone. Hence $a_{11}m_1 = \delta_{11}/g = 1/\omega_1^2$, where ω_1 = critical speed that would exist if only mass No. 1 were present. Similarly, $a_{22}m_2 = 1/\omega_2^2$.

5. Thus $1/\omega_{c_1}^2 = 1/\omega_1^2 + 1/\omega_2^2$, approximately, the Dunkerley equation.

6. We can now see the reason for a previous statement to the effect that the Dunkerley equation *underestimates* the critical speed. The Dunkerley equation assumes $1/\omega_{c_1}^2 = a_{11}m_1 + a_{22}m_2$, whereas actually $1/\omega_{c_1}^2 = a_{11}m_1 + a_{22}m_2 - 1/\omega_{c_2}^2$.

10. A bare steel shaft of diameter D shows a first critical speed of 1200 rpm. If the shaft were bored to make it hollow, with an inside diameter of $\frac{3}{4}D$, what would be the critical speed?

Solution:

1. ω_c^2 is proportional to $1/\delta$; then $\omega_{ch}^2/\omega_{cs}^2 = \delta_s/\delta_h$, where ω_{ch} is the critical speed of the hollow shaft and ω_{cs} that of the solid shaft, δ_s the static deflection of the solid shaft and δ_h that of the hollow shaft (both measured at the same location).

2. Boring out the shaft reduces both the weight and stiffness, thus affecting the deflection in two ways.

The weight is reduced in the ratio $\dfrac{W_h}{W_s} = \dfrac{D^2 - (\frac{3}{4}D)^2}{D^2} = \dfrac{7}{16}$.

The moment of inertia I of the cross section is reduced in the ratio $\dfrac{I_h}{I_s} = \dfrac{D^4 - (\frac{3}{4}D)^4}{D^4} = \dfrac{175}{256}$.

3. Since δ is proportional to W/I, then $\delta_s/\delta_h = (16/7)(175/256) = 1.562$ and

$$\omega_{ch} = \omega_{cs}\sqrt{\delta_s/\delta_h} = 1200\sqrt{1.562} = 1500 \text{ rpm}$$

The reduction of mass tends to raise the critical speed, while the reduction of stiffness tends to lower it. The mass is reduced more than the stiffness; hence the net effect is to raise the critical speed.

SUPPLEMENTARY PROBLEMS

11. A shaft simply supported on two bearings 20 in. apart carries an 80 lb flywheel 7 in. to the right of the left bearing. The static deflection curve shows the following:

Distance from left bearing, in.	0	2	4	6	8	10	12	14	16	18	20
Deflection, in.	0	.001	.003	.005	.007	.008	.009	.008	.006	.002	0

Estimate the critical speed. *Ans.* 2400 rpm approximately

12. A steel shaft 40 in. long is simply supported at the ends and has diameter 3 in. over the mid-20 in. of length. The remainder of the shaft is 2.5 in. in diameter. Masses weighing 300 lb each are attached at the two locations where the diameter changes. Neglecting shaft mass and using the Rayleigh-Ritz equation, estimate the first critical speed. *Ans.* $\delta_1 = \delta_2 = 0.00425$ in., $\omega_c = 30$ rad/sec

13. Determine the critical speed for the steel shaft shown in Fig. 8-14 below. Neglect shaft mass. *Ans.* 1900 rpm

14. The shaft shown in Fig. 8-15 below is to be made of stainless steel ($E = 26 \times 10^6$ psi). Determine a safe diameter to insure that the first critical speed be no less than 3600 rpm. *Ans.* $d = 2\frac{1}{4}$ in.

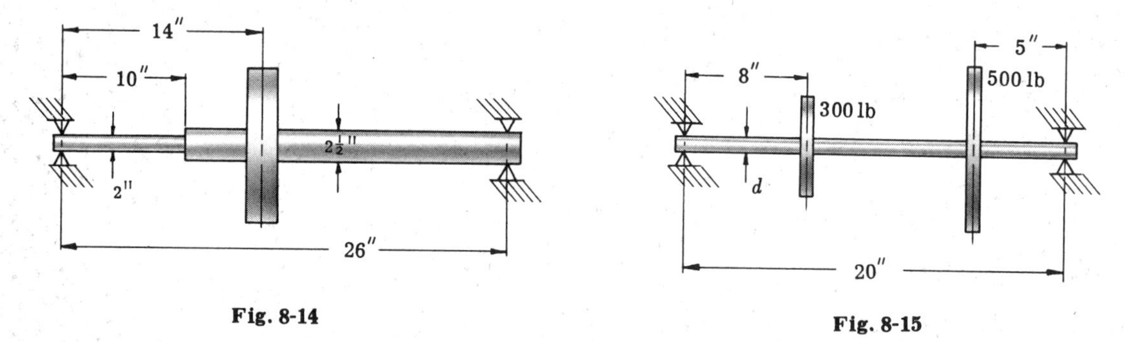

Fig. 8-14

Fig. 8-15

15. For the steel shaft shown in Fig. 8-16 below estimate the first critical speed using the Dunkerley equation. *Ans.* 1800 rpm

16. For the shaft of Fig. 8-10 of Problem 5, determine the first critical speed by the Dunkerley equation. *Ans.* 442 rad/sec

17. Determine the critical speed of the steel shaft shown in Fig. 8-17 below. *Ans.* 1480 rpm

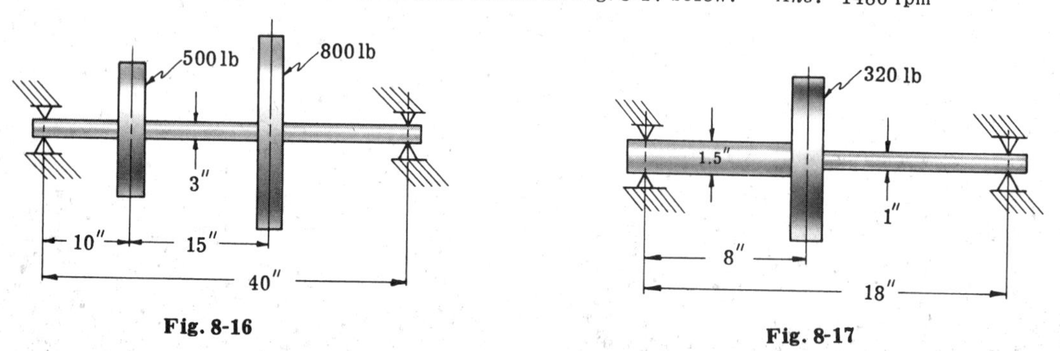

Fig. 8-16

Fig. 8-17

18. The steel shaft shown in Fig. 8-18 below is to be designed for a critical speed not less than 1800 rpm. Determine the smaller diameter d needed. *Ans.* 2 in.

19. A shaft (bare) has a critical speed of 800 rpm. If the shaft diameter were doubled, what would be the critical speed? *Ans.* 1600 rpm

20. A shaft carries two equal concentrated masses in locations 1 and 2 on the shaft. With only mass 1 present, the static deflections at 1 and 2 are .008 in. and .007 in. respectively. With only mass 2 present the static deflections at 1 and 2 are .007 in. and .010 in. respectively. Estimate the first critical speed for the two-mass system. *Ans.* 1400 rpm (Dunkerley), 1480 rpm (Rayleigh-Ritz)

21. For the shaft described in Problem 20 determine the first and second critical speeds by the frequency equation (Note: $m_1 = m_2 = m$, $a_{11} = .008/mg$, $a_{21} = .007/mg = a_{12}$, $a_{22} = .010/mg$.) *Ans.* 1480 rpm, 4280 rpm

22. Determine the first and second critical speeds for the steel shaft shown in Fig. 8-19 below.
Ans. 340 rad/sec, 660 rad/sec

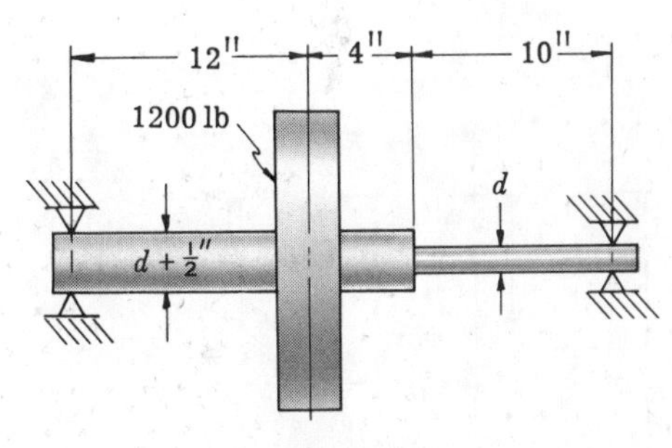

Fig. 8-18

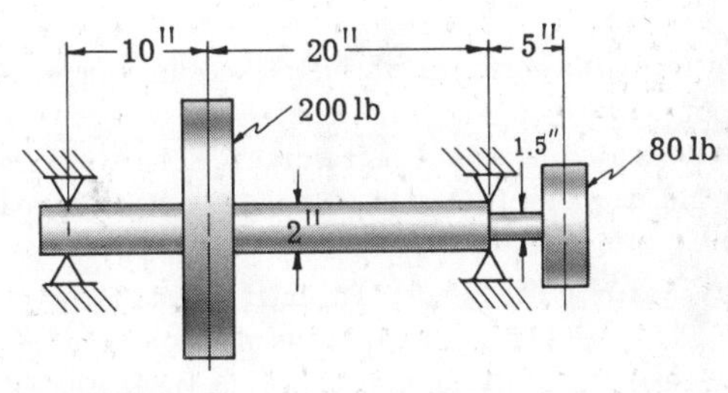

Fig. 8-19

23. Estimate the first critical speed of the steel shaft in Fig. 8-19 above by means of the Dunkerley equation.
Ans. 303 rad/sec

24. It has been determined for the shaft shown in Fig. 8-20 that the static deflections due to shaft bending are $\delta_1 = .0009$ in., $\delta_2 = .0030$ in., $\delta_3 = .0013$ in. The bearing supports have a flexibility in the vertical direction equivalent to a spring constant k = 200,000 lb/in. In the horizontal direction the supports are essentially rigid. Investigate the first mode critical speed (or speeds).

Ans. We should expect two first mode critical speeds, one at which vertical deflections will tend to be large and the other at which horizontal deflections will tend to be large. Our estimates for these, based on the Rayleigh-Ritz equation, are 362 rad/sec and 428 rad/sec respectively.

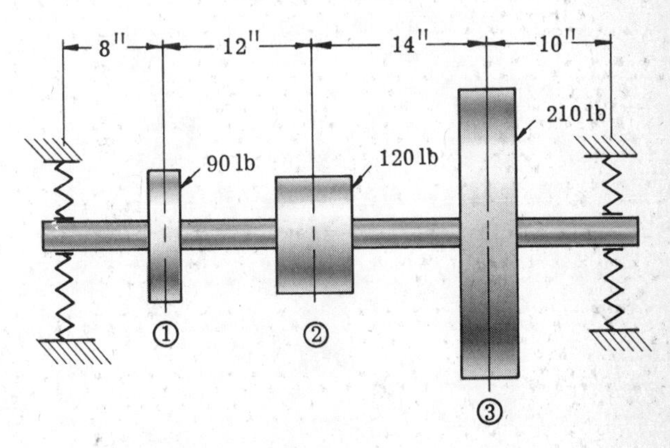

Fig. 8-20

25. (*a*) Determine the first critical speed for the steel shaft shown in Fig. 8-21 below.

Suggestion: Consider the mass of each 10 in. length of shaft as though concentrated at the center of gravity of that 10 in. section.

(Use the Rayleigh-Ritz equation for your estimate.)

(*b*) For the same shaft make a cruder approximation. Treat as a 3-mass system, taking the mass of each 3 in. diameter section to be concentrated at the center of gravity of that section, and the mass of the 6 in. diameter section to be concentrated at the center of that section.

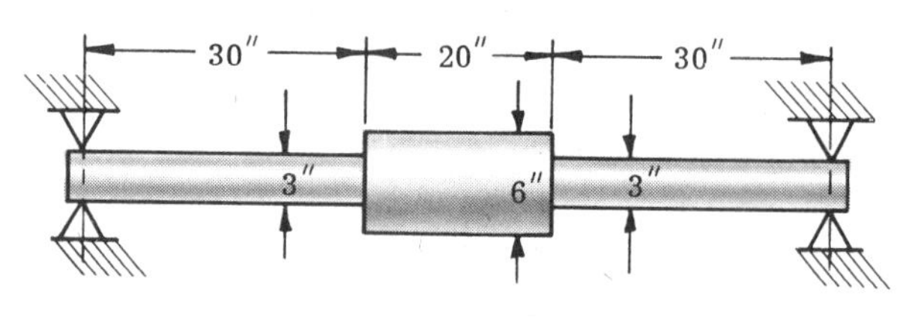

Fig. 8-21

Ans. (*a*) 778 rad/sec (using $E = 30 \times 10^6$ psi and specific weight of steel = 0.283 lb/in^3)

(*b*) Same as for (*a*) within sliderule accuracy.

Discussion: Actually we should expect (*b*) to give a slightly lower answer than (*a*), but the difference was less than could be attributed to differences in sliderule reading. This illustrates a statement made earlier to the effect that distributed masses can be replaced by a rather crudely approximating system of concentrated masses for the purpose of estimating first mode critical speeds. For estimating higher critical speeds it is necessary to use closer approximations.

26. For an example of shaft design in which critical speed is one of the criteria, see Chapter 9, Problem 12.

27. Estimate the critical speed of the air-compressor shown in Fig. 8-22. Each of the four rotors weighs 80 lb (including $\frac{1}{4}$ the shaft weight). The steel shaft is hollow, 6 in. O.D. and 5.5 in. I.D. Neglect stiffening effect of rotors.

Discussion: The shaft is relatively stiff (large I) but of small cross section area. The shaft length is only 5 times the O.D. These conditions may make the shear deflection of some importance in the calculation.

Ans. (*a*) Ignoring the shear deflection and using the Rayleigh-Ritz equation, $\omega_c = 1430$ rad/sec.

(*b*) Including the shear deflection added to the bending deflection and using the Rayleigh-Ritz equation, $\omega_c = 1260$ rad/sec.

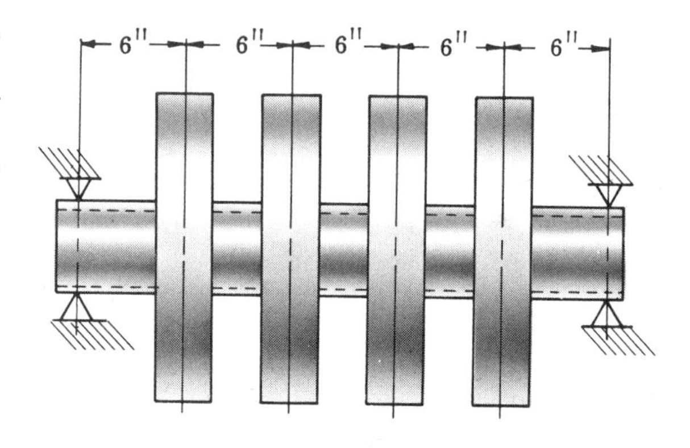

Fig. 8-22

Chapter 9

Power Transmission Shafting

SHAFT DESIGN consists primarily of the determination of the correct shaft diameter to ensure satisfactory strength and rigidity when the shaft is transmitting power under various operating and loading conditions. Shafts are usually circular in cross section, and may be either hollow or solid.

DESIGN OF SHAFTS of ductile materials, based on strength, is controlled by the maximum shear theory. The following presentation is based on shafts of ductile material and circular cross section. Shafts of brittle material would be designed on the basis of the maximum normal stress theory. Shafting is usually subjected to torsion, bending and axial loads. For torsional loads, the torsional stress τ_{xy} is

$$\tau_{xy} = M_t r/J = 16M_t/\pi d^3 \quad \text{for solid shafts}$$

$$\tau_{xy} = 16M_t d_o/\pi(d_o^4 - d_i^4) \quad \text{for hollow shafts}$$

For bending loads, the bending stress s_b (tension or compression) is

$$s_b = M_b r/I = 32M_b/\pi d^3 \quad \text{for solid shafts}$$

$$s_b = 32M_b d_o/\pi(d_o^4 - d_i^4) \quad \text{for hollow shafts}$$

For axial loads, the tensile or compressive stress s_a is

$$s_a = 4F_a/\pi d^2 \quad \text{for solid shafts}$$

$$s_a = 4F_a/\pi(d_o^2 - d_i^2) \quad \text{for hollow shafts}$$

The ASME Code equation for a hollow shaft combines torsion, bending, and axial loads by applying the maximum shear equation modified by introducing shock, fatigue, and column factors as follows:

$$d_o^3 = \frac{16}{\pi s_s(1 - K^4)} \sqrt{\left[K_b M_b + \frac{\alpha F_a d_o(1+K^2)}{8}\right]^2 + (K_t M_t)^2}$$

For a solid shaft having little or no axial loading, the Code equation reduces to

$$d^3 = \frac{16}{\pi s_s} \sqrt{(K_b M_b)^2 + (K_t M_t)^2}$$

where, at the section under consideration,

τ_{xy} = torsional shear stress, psi
d_o = shaft outside diameter, in.
M_t = torsional moment, in-lb
d_i = shaft inside diameter, in.
M_b = bending moment, in-lb
F_a = axial load, lb
$K = d_i/d_o$
K_b = combined shock and fatigue factor applied to bending moment
K_t = combined shock and fatigue factor applied to torsional moment

	K_b	K_t
For stationary shafts:		
Load gradually applied	1.0	1.0
Load suddenly applied	1.5 to 2.0	1.5 to 2.0
For rotating shafts:		
Load gradually applied	1.5	1.0
Load suddenly applied (minor shock)	1.5 to 2.0	1.0 to 1.5
Load suddenly applied (heavy shock)	2.0 to 3.0	1.5 to 3.0

s_b = bending stress (tension or compression), psi

s_a = axial stress (tension or compression), psi

ASME Code specifies that for commercial steel shafting

s_s(allowable) = 8000 psi for shaft without keyway

s_s(allowable) = 6000 psi for shaft with keyway

ASME Code states that for steel purchased under definite specifications

s_s(allowable) = 30% of the elastic limit but not over 18% of the ultimate strength in tension for shafts without keyways. These values are to be reduced by 25% if keyways are present.

α = column-action factor. The column-action factor is unity for a tensile load. For a compression load, α may be computed by:

$$\alpha = \frac{1}{1 - 0.0044(L/k)} \qquad \text{for} \quad L/k < 115$$

$$\alpha = \frac{s_y}{\pi^2 nE}\left(\frac{L}{k}\right)^2 \qquad \text{for} \quad L/k > 115$$

n = 1 for hinged ends

n = 2.25 for fixed ends

n = 1.6 for ends partly restrained, as in bearings

k = radius of gyration = $\sqrt{I/A}$ in.

I = rectangular moment of inertia, in^4

A = cross section area of shaft, in^2

s_y = yield stress in compression, psi

DESIGN OF SHAFTS FOR TORSIONAL RIGIDITY is based on the permissible angle of twist. The amount of twist permissible depends on the particular application, and varies about 0.08 deg per foot for machine tool shafts to about 1.0 deg per foot for line shafting.

$$\theta = 584 M_t L / G(d_o^4 - d_i^4) \qquad \text{for a hollow circular shaft}$$

$$\theta = 584 M_t L / G d^4 \qquad \text{for a solid circular shaft}$$

where

θ = angle of twist, deg

L = length of shaft, in.

M_t = torsional moment, in-lb

G = torsional modulus of elasticity, psi

d = shaft diameter, in.

DESIGN OF SHAFTS FOR LATERAL RIGIDITY is based on the permissible lateral deflection for proper bearing operation, accurate machine tool performance, satisfactory gear tooth action, shaft alignment, and other similar requirements. The amount of deflection may be determined by two successive integrations of

$$d^2y/dx^2 = M_b/EI$$

where

M_b = bending moment, in-lb
E = modulus of elasticity, psi
I = rectangular moment of inertia, in^4.

If the shaft is of variable cross section, a graphical solution of the above expression is practical. (See Chapter 5.)

STANDARD SIZES OF SHAFTING have been tentatively standardized by the American Engineering Standards Committee as follows:

Transmission shafting sizes in inches:

15/16, 1 3/16, 1 7/16, 1 11/16, 1 15/16, 2 3/16, 2 7/16, 2 15/16, 3 7/16, 3 15/16, 4 7/16, 4 15/16, 5 7/16, and 5 15/16.

Machinery shafting sizes in inches:

1/2 in. to 2 1/2 in. by 1/16 in. increments
2 5/8 in. to 4 in. by 1/8 in. increments
4 1/4 in. to 6 in. by 1/4 in. increments.

Standard stock lengths are 16, 20, and 24 ft.

BENDING AND TORSIONAL MOMENTS are the main factors influencing shaft design. One of the first steps in shaft design is to draw the bending moment diagram for the loaded shaft or the combined bending moment diagram if the loads acting on the shaft are in more than one axial plane. From the bending moment diagram, the points of critical bending stress can be determined.

The torsional moment acting on the shaft can be determined from

$$M_t = \frac{\text{hp} \times 33{,}000 \times 12}{2\pi \text{ rpm}} = \frac{63{,}000 \times \text{hp}}{\text{rpm}} \text{ in-lb}$$

For a belt drive, the torque is found from

$$M_t = (T_1 - T_2)R \text{ in-lb}$$

where

T_1 = tight side of belt on pulley, lb
T_2 = loose side of belt on pulley, lb
R = radius of pulley, in.

For a gear drive, the torque is found from

$$M_t = F_t R$$

where

F_t = tangential force at the pitch radius, lb
R = pitch radius, in.

SOLVED PROBLEMS

1. A 3 ft length of commercial steel shafting is to transmit 50 hp at 3600 rpm through flexible coupling from an A.C. motor to a D.C. generator. Determine the required shaft size.

Solution:

In this case the shaft has only torsional stress and K_t is unity assuming that the load is gradually applied.

s_s(allowable) = 6000 psi in accordance with ASME Code for commercial shaft with keyway.

$$s_s(\text{allowable}) = 16 M_t / \pi d^3$$

$$6000 = 16\left(\frac{50 \times 63{,}000}{3600}\right)\left(\frac{1}{\pi d^3}\right) \quad \text{or} \quad d = 0.905 \text{ in.}$$ Use 15/16 in., nearest standard size.

2. A section of commercial shafting 5 ft long between bearings carries a 200 lb pulley at its midpoint, as shown in Fig. 9-1 below. The pulley is keyed to the shaft and receives 20 hp at 150 rpm which is transmitted to a flexible coupling just outside the right bearing. The belt drive is horizontal and the sum of the belt tensions is 1500 lb. Assume $K_t = K_b = 1.5$. Calculate the necessary shaft diameter and determine the angle of twist between bearings. $G = 12 \times 10^6$ psi.

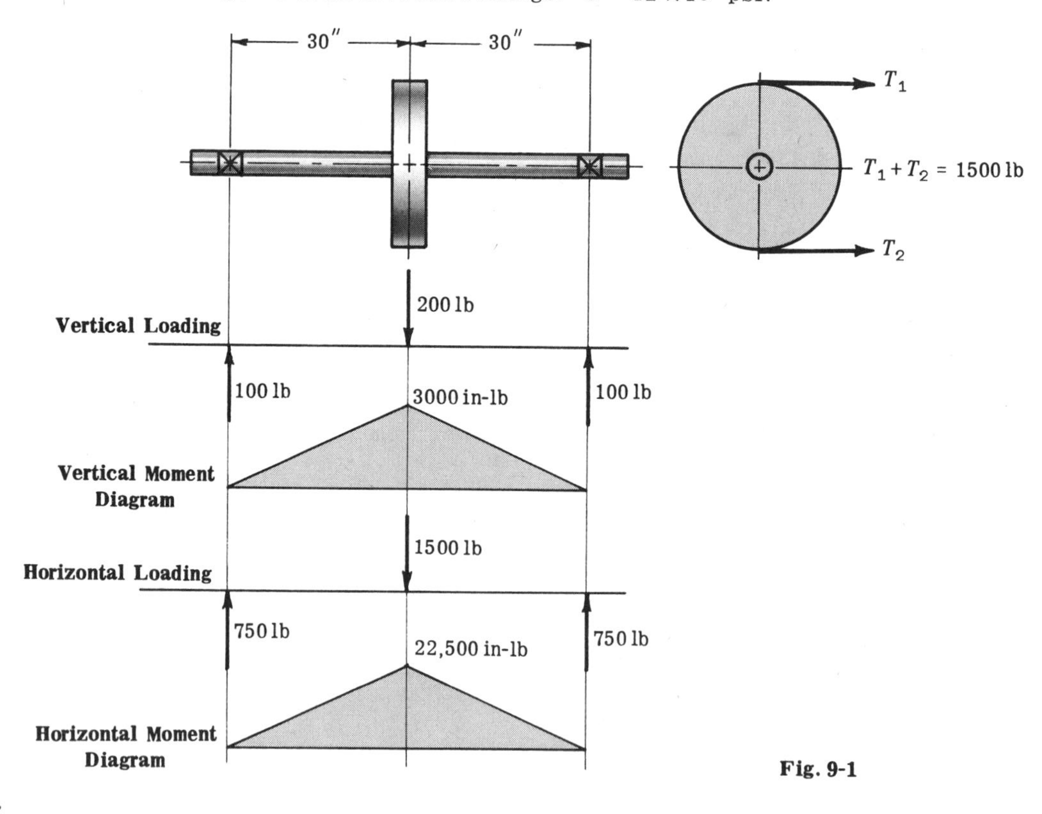

Fig. 9-1

Solution:

It is first necessary to determine the maximum bending and torsional moments acting on the shaft.

$$M_b(\text{max}) = \sqrt{3000^2 + 22{,}500^2} = 22{,}700 \text{ in-lb} \qquad M_t(\text{max}) = 20(63{,}000)/150 = 8400 \text{ in-lb}$$

s_s(allowable) = 6000 psi per ASME Code for shaft with keyway. Then

$$d^3 = \frac{16}{\pi s_s}\sqrt{(K_b M_b)^2 + (K_t M_t)^2} = \frac{16}{\pi 6000}\sqrt{(1.5 \times 22{,}700)^2 + (1.5 \times 8400)^2}$$

from which $d = 3.12$ in. Use 3 1/8 in. shaft, nearest standard size.

$$\theta = \frac{584 M_t L}{G d^4} = \frac{584 \times 8400 \times 30}{(12 \times 10^6)(3.125)^4} = 0.128^\circ \text{ twist}$$

3. Fig. 9-2 shows the forces acting on a steel shaft carrying two gears. The gears are keyed at B and D. A and C are journal bearing centers. Nine hp is transmitted at 650 rpm of the shaft. The allowable stress for an unkeyed section is 12,000 psi according to the ASME Code. $K_b = K_t = 1.5$.
   (a) Sketch horizontal, vertical and resultant bending moment diagrams. Show values at change points.
   (b) Determine the necessary shaft diameter to the nearest 0.01 in. Indicate the critical section.

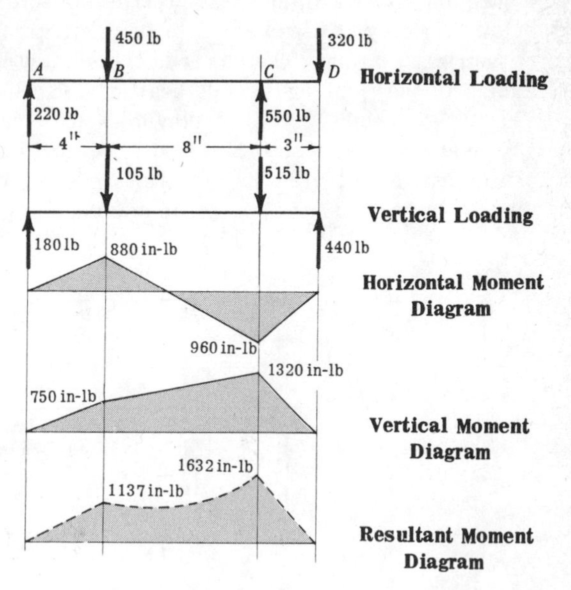

Fig. 9-2

Solution:

At the bearing C:

$$M_t(\text{max}) = 9(63.000)/650 = 873 \text{ in-lb}$$
$$M_b(\text{max}) = 1632 \text{ in-lb at } C$$
$$d^3 = \frac{16}{\pi(12,000)}\sqrt{(1.5\times1632)^2 + (1.5\times873)^2}$$
$$d = 1.07 \text{ in}$$

Just to the right of gear B:

$M_t(\text{max}) = 873$ in-lb, $M_b(\text{max}) = 1132$ in-lb

$$d^3 = \frac{16}{\pi(0.75)(12,000)}\sqrt{(1.5\times1132)^2 + (1.5\times873)^2} \quad \text{and} \quad d = 1.07 \text{ in.}$$

Note: Even though the bending moment at gear B is less than at bearing C, the same size shaft is required as a result of the keyway at B.

4. A 24 inch diameter pulley driven by a horizontal belt transmits power through a solid shaft to a 10 inch diameter pinion which drives a mating gear. The pulley weighs 300 lb to provide some flywheel effect. The arrangement of elements, the belt tensions, and the components of the gear reactions on the pinion are as indicated in Fig. 9-3 below. Determine the necessary shaft diameter using ASME Code stress value for commercial shafting and shock fatigue factors of $K_b = 2$ and $K_t = 1.5$.

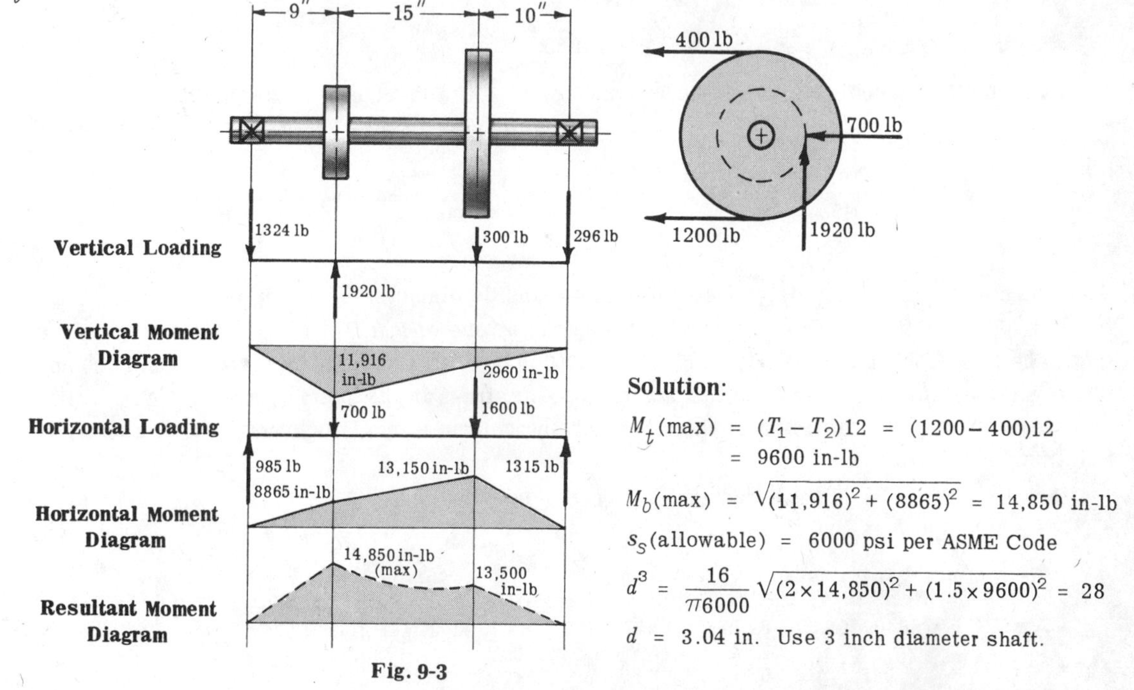

Fig. 9-3

Solution:

$$M_t(\text{max}) = (T_1 - T_2)12 = (1200-400)12 = 9600 \text{ in-lb}$$
$$M_b(\text{max}) = \sqrt{(11,916)^2 + (8865)^2} = 14,850 \text{ in-lb}$$
$$s_s(\text{allowable}) = 6000 \text{ psi per ASME Code}$$
$$d^3 = \frac{16}{\pi 6000}\sqrt{(2\times14,850)^2 + (1.5\times9600)^2} = 28$$

$d = 3.04$ in. Use 3 inch diameter shaft.

5. A machine shaft turning at 600 rpm is supported on bearings 30 inches apart as shown in Fig. 9-4 below. Twenty hp is supplied to the shaft through an 18 inch pulley located 10 inches to the right of the right bearing. The power is transmitted from the shaft through an 8 inch spur gear located 10 inches to the right of the left bearing. The belt drive is at an angle of 60° above the horizontal. The pulley weighs 200 lb to provide some flywheel effect. The ratio of the belt tensions is 3:1. The gear has a 20° tooth form and mates with another gear located directly above the shaft. If the shaft material selected has an ultimate strength of 70,000 psi and a yield point of 46,000 psi, determine the necessary diameter in accordance with the ASME Code using $K_b = 1.5$ and $K_t = 1.0$.

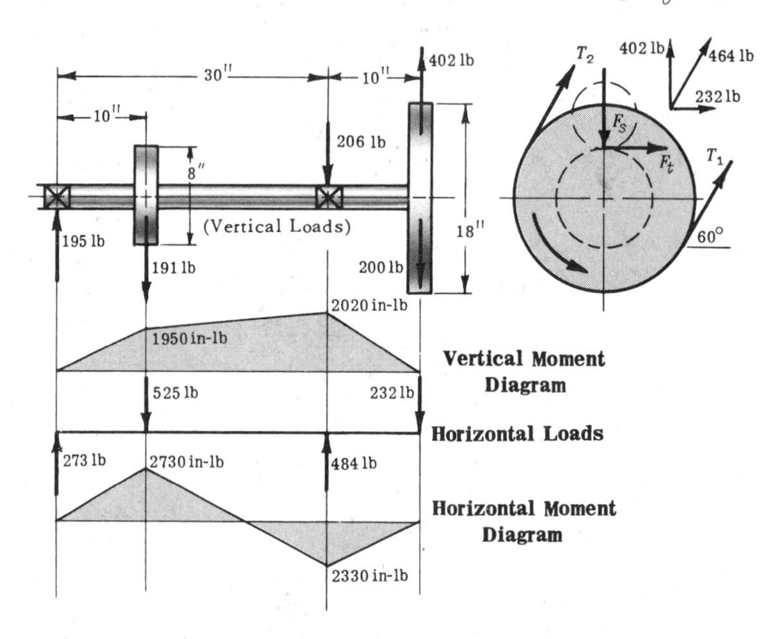

Fig. 9-4

Solution:

$M_t = 20(63,000)/600 = 2100$ in-lb

From $(T_1 - T_2)9 = 2100$ and $3T_1 = T_2$ we have

$T_2 = 116$ lb, $T_1 = 348$ lb, $(T_1 + T_2) = 464$ lb.

$4F_t = 2100$, $F_t = 525$ lb. $F_s = 525 \tan 20° = 191$ lb.

$18\% \times 70,000 = 12,600$ psi. $30\% \times 46,000 = 13,800$ psi. s_s(allowable) $= 75\% \times 12,600 = 9450$ psi.

$M_b(\max) = \sqrt{1950^2 + 2730^2} = 3360$ in-lb

$$d^3 = \frac{16}{\pi 9450}\sqrt{(3360 \times 1.5)^2 + (2100)^2} \quad \text{or} \quad d = 1.44 \text{ in.} \quad \text{Use } 1\tfrac{1}{2} \text{ in. shaft.}$$

6. A hollow shaft, 20 in. outside diameter and 12 in. inside diameter, is supported by two bearings 20 ft apart. The shaft is driven by a flexible coupling at one end and drives a ship's propeller at 100 rpm. The maximum thrust on the propeller is 120,000 lb when the shaft is transmitting 8000 hp. The shaft weighs 15,000 lb. Determine the maximum shear stress in the shaft by means of the ASME Code equation considering the weight of the shaft and the column effect. Assume $K_b = 1.5$ and $K_t = 1.0$.

Solution:

$M_b(\max) = WL/8 = (15,000)(240)/8 = 450,000$ in-lb

$M_t(\max) = (8000 \times 63,000)/100 = 5,040,000$ in-lb.

$I = \pi(20^4 - 12^4)/64 = 6840 \text{ in}^4$. $A = \pi(20^2 - 12^2)/4 = 201 \text{ in}^2$.

$k = \sqrt{I/A} = \sqrt{6840/201} = 5.84$ in. $L/k = 240/5.84 = 41.2$, which is < 115. Then

$$\alpha = \frac{1}{1 - 0.0044(240/5.84)} = 1.222$$

$d_o = 20$ in., $d_i = 12$ in., and $K = d_i/d_o = 12/20 = 0.6$.

$$s_s = \frac{16}{\pi d_o^3(1-K^4)} \sqrt{\left[K_b M_b + \frac{\alpha F_a d_o(1+K^2)}{8}\right]^2 + (K_t M_t)^2}$$

$$= \frac{16}{\pi\, 20^3(1-0.6^4)} \sqrt{\left[(1.5 \times 450{,}000) + \frac{1.222 \times 120{,}000 \times 20\,(1+0.6^2)}{8}\right]^2 + (1 \times 5{,}040{,}000)^2} = 3800 \text{ psi}$$

7. A shaft 48 in. long receives 10,000 in-lb torque from a pulley located at the center of the shaft, as shown in Fig. 9-5. A gear at the left end of the shaft transmits 6000 in-lb of this torque from the shaft while the remainder is transmitted through a gear located at the right end of the shaft. Calculate the angular deflection of the left end of the shaft with respect to the right end of the shaft if the shaft is 2 in. in diameter and is made of steel. Neglect the effect of the keyways in the calculation.

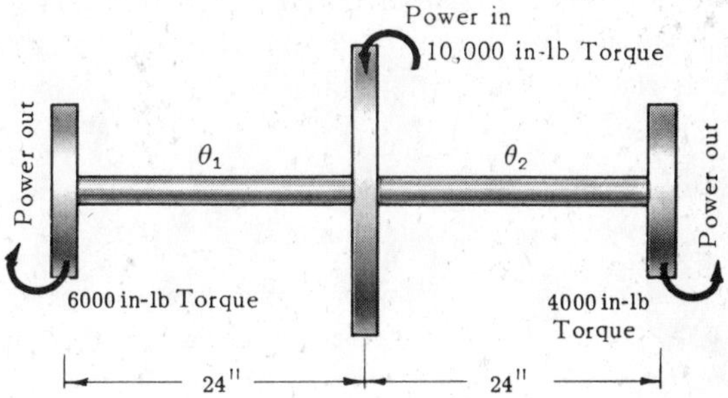

Fig. 9-5

Solution:

The angular deflection of one end of the shaft with respect to the other is the difference of the anular deflection of the ends with respect to the center.

$$\theta_1 - \theta_2 = \frac{584(6000)(24)}{Gd^4} - \frac{584(4000)(24)}{Gd^4} = \frac{584(24)(6000-4000)}{(12 \times 10^6)(2^4)} = 0.146^\circ$$

8. Thirty horsepower is supplied to the 30 in. sprocket by means of a chain drive as shown in Fig. 9-6. Twenty horsepower is taken off at the 24 in. pulley which weighs 1000 lb, and 10 hp is taken off at the 8 in. crank. The force in the chain on the tight side is represented by T_c. The tension in the slack side is so small that it can be neglected. The ratio of the tensions in the belt is 4:1. The shaft is rotating at 300 rpm. The loads are applied with moderate shock, $K_b = 2$ and $K_t = 1.5$. Determine the size of shaft necessary if s_s(allowable) = 8000 psi. It is assumed that the sprocket and pulley are keyed to the shaft.

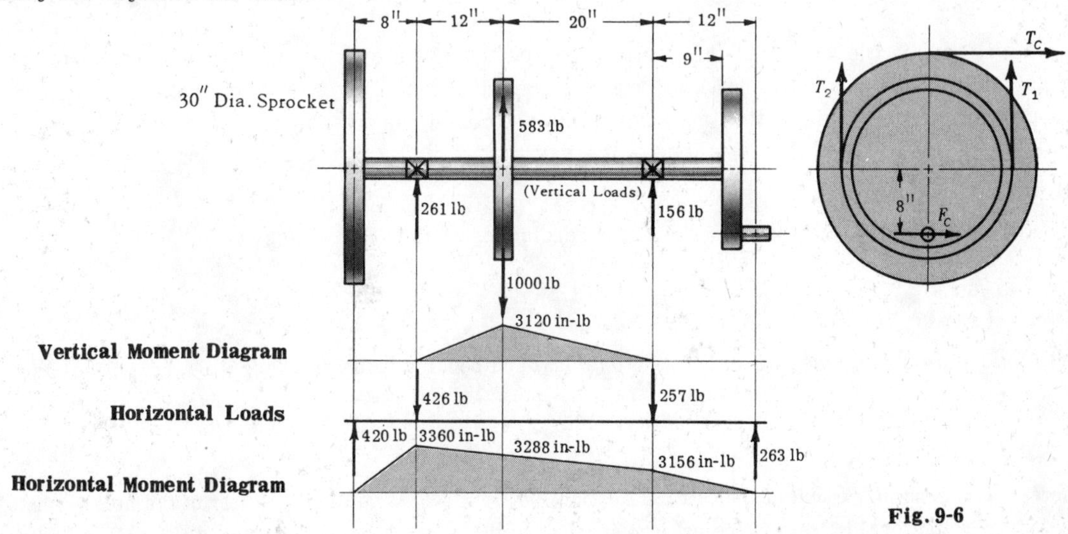

Fig. 9-6

From $(T_1 - T_2)12 = 4200$ and $T_1 = 4T_2$ we have $T_1 = 466$ lb, $T_2 = 117$ lb, and $(T_1 + T_2) = 583$ lb. $F_c = 2100/8 = 263$ lb.

M_t(sprocket) = $63{,}000 \times 30/300 = 6300$ in-lb, M_t(pulley) = $2M_t$(crank) = 4200 in-lb, M_t(crank) = 2100 in-lb.

$M_b(\max) = \sqrt{3288^2 + 3120^2} = 4490$ in-lb at pulley, $M_t(\max) = 6300$ in-lb at pulley.

$$d^3 = \frac{16}{\pi s_s(0.75)}\sqrt{(K_b M_b)^2 + (K_t M_t)^2} = \frac{16}{\pi(8000)(0.75)}\sqrt{(2\times 4490)^2 + (1.5\times 6300)^2} = 11.06$$

from which $d = 2.23$ in. Use $2\frac{3}{16}$ in. shaft.

9. Determine the diameter below which the angle of twist of a shaft, and not the maximum stress, is the controlling factor in design of a solid shaft in torsion. The allowable shear stress is 8000 psi and the maximum allowable twist is 1/12 degree per foot. (Consider a shaft with no key). $G = 12 \times 10^6$ psi.

Solution:

$$s_s(\text{allowable}) = 16M_t/\pi d^3, \qquad \theta(\text{allowable}) = 584 M_t L/Gd^4.$$

$M_t = \theta d^4 G/584L$ moment that can be transmitted in allowable twist.

$M_t = s_s \pi d^3/16$ moment that can be transmitted in allowable stress.

Then $\dfrac{\theta d^4 G}{584L} = \dfrac{s_s \pi d^3}{16}$ or $\dfrac{(1/12)(d^4)(12\times 10^6)}{584(12)} = \dfrac{8000\pi d^3}{16}$, from which $d = 11.0$ in.

10. Shafts AB and CD are connected by spur gears as shown in Fig. 9-7. A couple applied at A stresses the shaft AB to 8000 psi. Determine the diameter of the shaft CD if the shearing stress therein must not exceed 8000 psi. Neglect keyways and any bending action. $G = 12 \times 10^6$ psi.

Solution:

M_t on shaft CD is 3 times M_t on shaft AB.

Let diameter of shaft $AB = d_1$, of shaft $CD = d_2$. Then

$$s_s \pi d_1^3/16 = s_s \pi d_2^3/(16\times 3)$$

and, since $d_1 = 2$ in., the required diameter $d_2 = 2.88$ in.

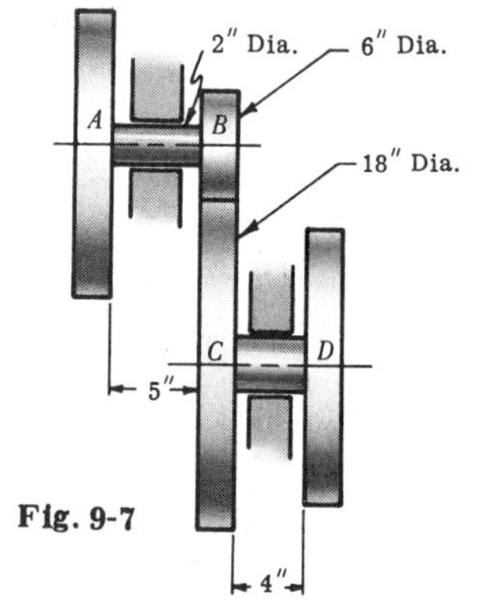

Fig. 9-7

11. In order to reduce the weight of the control and power plant facilities used in a certain aircraft, it is planned to use all hollow shafting for power transmission. Develop an expression to determine the percent weight savings that may be effected through the use of hollow shafting in place of equal strength solid shafting for such an application.

Solution:

For a solid shaft subjected to torsional and bending loads, the shear stress is

$$s_s = \frac{16}{\pi d^3}\sqrt{M_b^2 + M_t^2}$$

And for a hollow shaft subjected to the same torsional and bending loads as above, the shear stress is

$$s_s = \frac{16\, d_o}{\pi(d_o^4 - d_i^4)}\sqrt{M_b^2 + M_t^2}$$

where M_b = bending moment at the critical section, in-lb; M_t = torsional moment at the critical section, in-lb; d_o = outside diameter of the hollow shaft, in.; d_i = inside diameter of the hollow shaft, in.

Since it is assumed that the hollow shafting will be of equal strength to that of the solid shafting, we may equate the right sides of the two above equations and obtain

$$\frac{16}{\pi d^3} = \frac{16 d_o}{\pi(d_o^4 - d_i^4)} \qquad \text{from which} \qquad (1) \quad 1 - (\frac{d}{d_o})^3 = (\frac{d_i}{d_o})^4$$

From a weight consideration, the hollow shafting will be lighter than the solid shafting by a factor of $(1 - N/100)$, where N is the percent weight savings to be effected through the use of hollow vs solid shafting. Then

$$\frac{\pi}{4}(d_o^2 - d_i^2)L\lambda = (1 - \frac{N}{100})\frac{\pi}{4}d^2 L\lambda \qquad \text{or} \qquad (2) \quad (d_o^2 - d_i^2) = (1 - \frac{N}{100})d^2$$

where L = length of shafting, in.
λ = specific weight of shafting material, lb/in^3

Substituting the value of d_i from (1) into (2) and solving for N, we obtain

$$N = \left[1 - (d_o/d)^2 + \sqrt{(d_o/d)^4 - d_o/d}\,\right]100$$

12. The shaft shown in Fig. 9-8 (a) is to be designed from the standpoint of strength, critical speed, and rigidity. Power is supplied to the pulley P by means of a flat belt and power is taken from the shaft through spur gear G. The shaft is supported by two deep groove ball bearings.

The following information has been established:

Horsepower = 10 (steady load conditions)
Speed of shaft = 900 rpm
Shaft is to be machined from hot rolled AISI 1035 (s_u = 85,000 psi and s_y = 55,000 psi)
Diameter of pulley = 10 in.
Pitch diameter of the gear = 10 in.
Weight of the pulley = 30 lb
Weight of the gear = 30 lb
Ratio of belt tensions $T_1/T_2 = 2.5$
Gear pressure angle = 20°
The pulley and gear are assembled with press fits and keys.
Dimension $A = B = C = 6$ in.

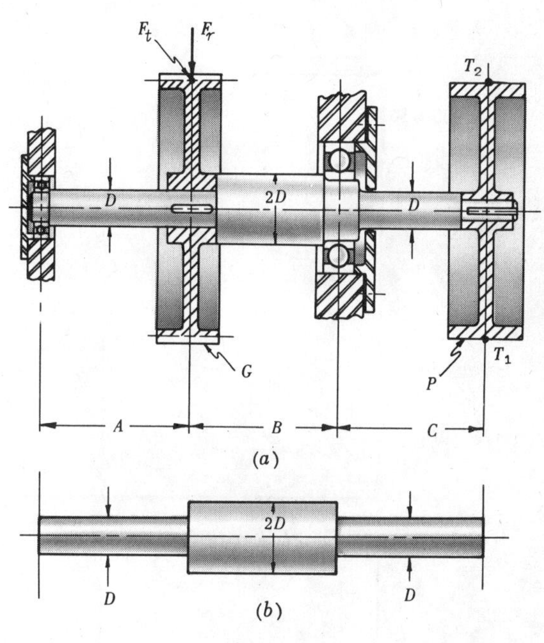

Fig. 9-8

The belt forces are perpendicular to the paper with the tight side being T_1 and the slack side T_2. The tangential force on the gear is F_t and the separating force is F_r. F_t is perpendicular to the paper.

The following limitations have been imposed:
(a) The shaft at the gear shall not deflect more than 0.001 in.
(b) The slope of the shaft through the bearings shall not exceed 1°.
(c) The operating speed of the shaft shall not be more than 60% of the lowest critical speed.

Solution:

The hub of the gear and of the pulley contribute to the stiffness of the shaft, as well as the inner race of each bearing. If a hub is relatively long, its effect is different than if the hub is short. For purposes of this problem, half lengths of hubs and inner races of the bearings will be considered effective in stiffening the shaft. The effect of the web of the pulley and gear can be neglected in deflection analysis. Design will then be based upon the simplified shaft as shown in Fig. 9-8 (b). We will first determine the required diameter D for strength in accordance with the ASME shafting code.

The torque between the pulley and gear is $M_t = (10)(63{,}000)/900 = 700$ in-lb.

The sum of the belt tensions may be determined from

$$(T_1 - T_2)(5) = 700 \quad \text{and} \quad T_1 = 2.5\,T_2$$

from which $T_1 = 233.3$ lb, $T_2 = 93.3$ lb, and $(T_1 + T_2) = 326.6$ lb.

The transmitted force $F_t = 700/5 = 140$ lb.

The separating force $F_r = 140 \tan 20^\circ = 51$ lb.

From the above information the moment diagrams for vertical and horizontal loadings may be combined to obtain the resultant moment diagram as shown in Fig. 9-9 below.

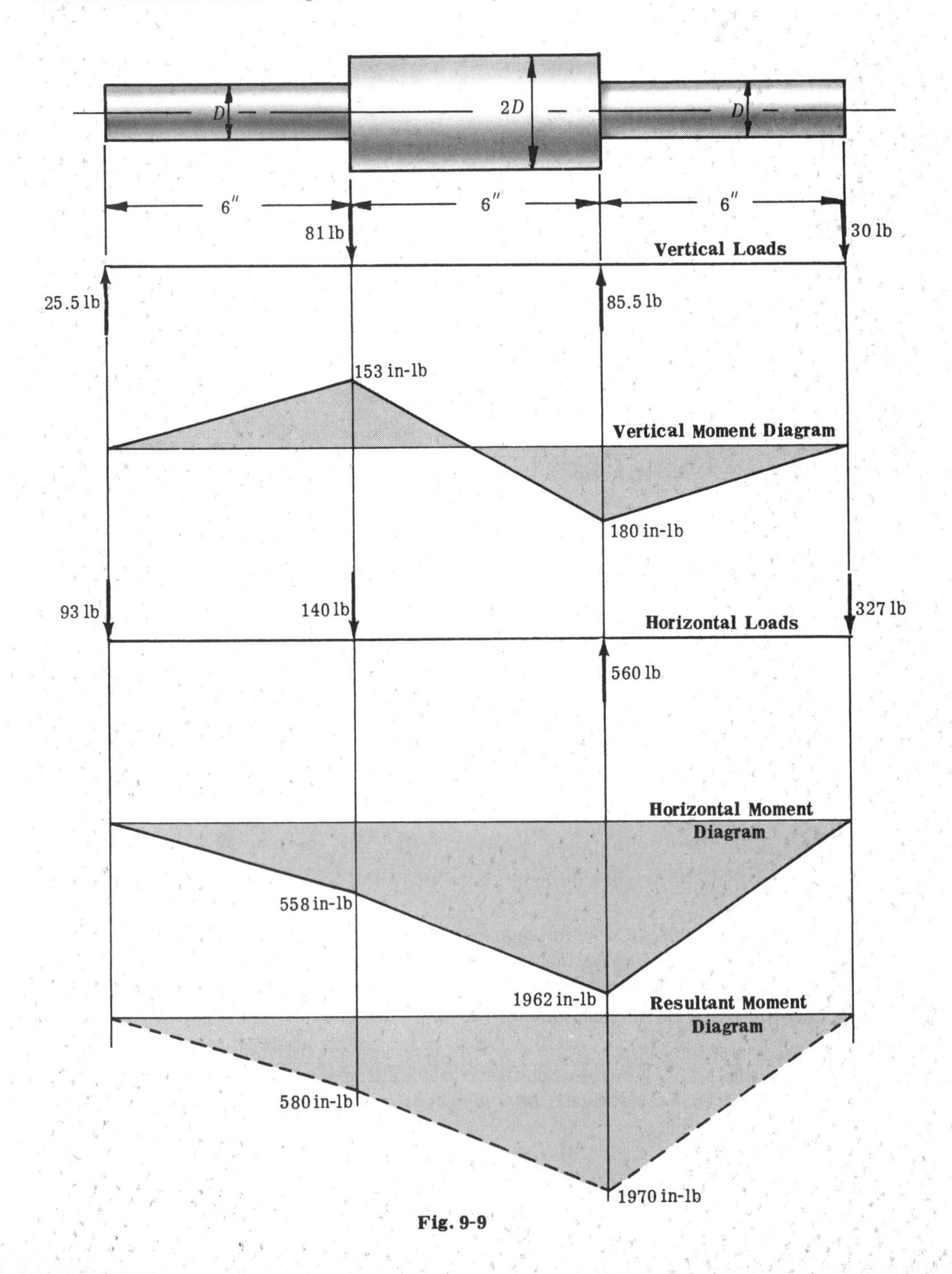

Fig. 9-9

The allowable shear stress is determined by: $18\% \times 85{,}000 = 15{,}300$ psi, $30\% \times 55{,}000 = 16{,}500$ psi. Use s(allowable) = 15,300 psi.

As seen from Fig. 9-9, the maximum resultant bending occurs at the right bearing: $M_b = 1970$ in-lb, $M_t = 700$ in-lb.

For steady load, $K_b = 1.5$ and $K_t = 1.0$.

$$D^3 \quad = \quad \frac{16}{\pi(15{,}300)}\sqrt{(1.5\times 1970)^2 + (1\times 700)^2} \quad = \quad 1.01$$

from which $D = 1.00$ in., and $2D = 2.00$ in. required for strength.

Next, in order to determine the required diameter for operating below 60% of the first critical speed, it is necessary to compute the static deflections at the gear and pulley locations due only to the weights of the gear and pulley. It is important to note that in order to obtain the first critical speed, the weight of the pulley at the right end of the shaft has to be considered acting upward in order to satisfy the first mode of vibration. The shaft with its elastic curve and moment diagram for this purpose is shown in Fig. 9-10 below. Note that it is expedient to draw the tangent to the elastic curve at the left end in order to employ the area moment method for determining the required deflections. Instead of drawing the M/EI diagram for the following deflections, we will simply note that the moment of inertia for the $2D$ section is 16 times the moment of inertia of the D sections.

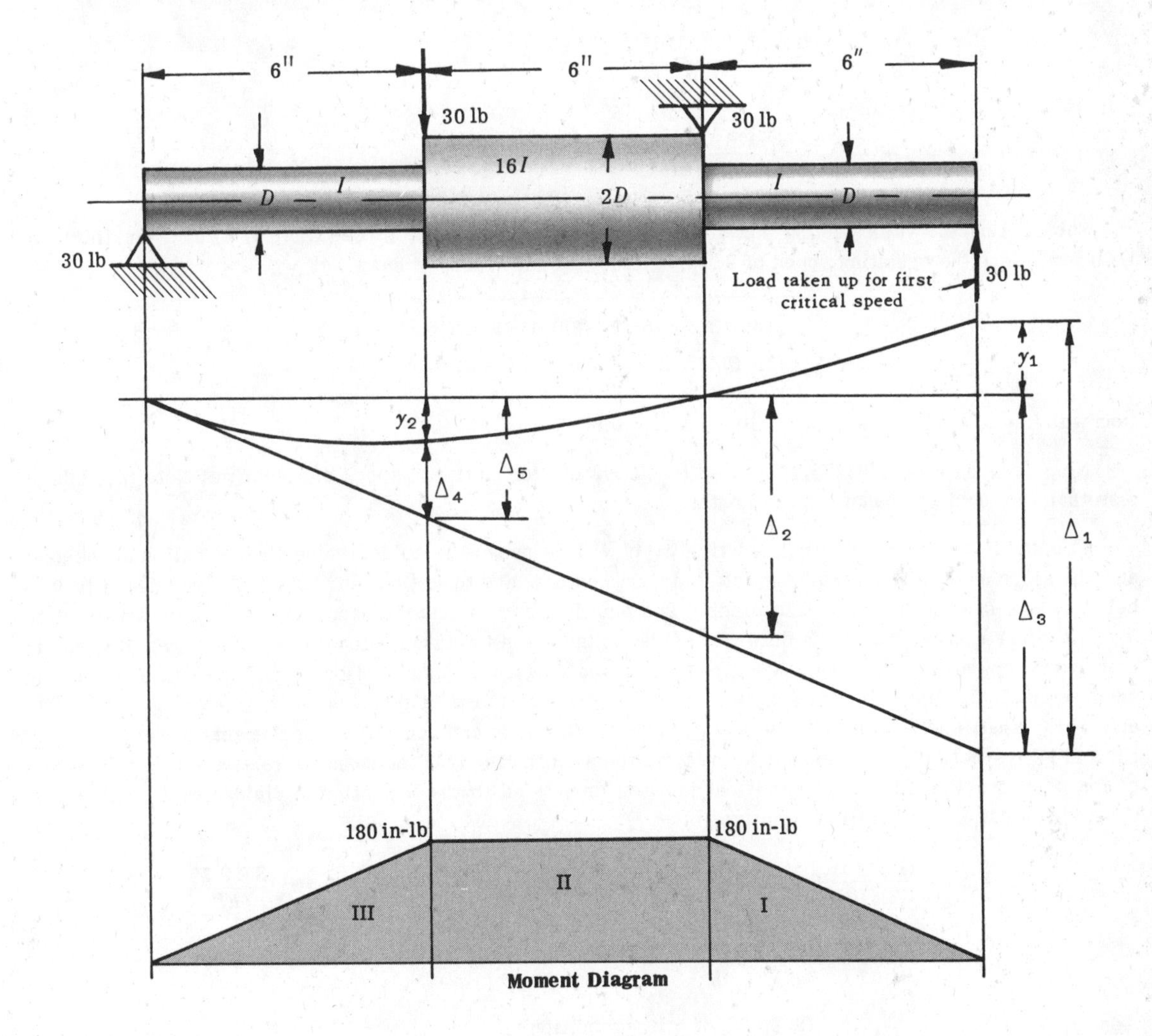

Fig. 9-10

We find Δ_1 by taking moments at the right end of the moment diagram, and letting I be the moment of inertia of the sections having diameter D. Using calculator and rounding off final results,

$$\Delta_1 = \frac{(180)(6)(4)}{2EI} + \frac{(180)(6)(9)}{16EI} + \frac{(180)(6)(14)}{2EI} = \frac{10{,}327.5}{EI}$$

Δ_2 is found by taking moments at the right bearing:

$$\Delta_2 = \frac{(180)(6)(3)}{16EI} + \frac{(180)(6)(8)}{2EI} = \frac{4522.5}{EI}$$

Δ_3 is found by proportion:

$$\Delta_3 = \frac{18}{12}\Delta_2 = \frac{18}{12}\frac{(4522.5)}{EI} = \frac{6783.75}{EI}$$

$$y_1 = \frac{10{,}327.5 - 6783.75}{EI} = \frac{3543.75}{EI}$$

$$\Delta_4 = \frac{(180)(6)(2)}{2EI} = \frac{1080}{EI}$$

$$\Delta_5 = \frac{\Delta_3}{3} = \frac{6783.75}{3EI} = \frac{2261.25}{EI} \quad \text{(by proportion)}$$

$$y_2 = \Delta_5 - \Delta_4 = \frac{2261.25 - 1080}{EI} = \frac{1181.25}{EI}$$

Substituting the values for y_1 and y_2 in the critical speed equation (see Chapter 8) and equating it to 1500 rpm, since the operating speed of 900 rpm is 60% of 1500 rpm, we have

$$1500 = 187.7\sqrt{\frac{[(30)(3543.75) + (30)(1181.25)]/(EI)}{[(30)(3543.75)^2 + (30)(1181.25)^2]/(EI)^2}} = 187.7(0.0184)\sqrt{EI}$$

from which $\sqrt{EI} = 434$; and for $E = 30\times10^6$, $I = 0.006275$ in^4.

Now $I = \pi D^4/64 = 0.006275$ in^4 gives $D = 0.598$ in. for a critical speed of 1500 rpm. Note that this is less than the required diameter for strength.

In order to design for the required rigidity it will be necessary to determine the deflection at the gear and the slope of the shaft at both the left and right bearings due to vertical and horizontal loadings. Fig. 9-11 below is based upon the vertical loadings. The elastic curve is sketched and tangents are drawn at points A and B. The moment diagram is drawn. In order to facilitate the taking of moments, the moment diagram is then drawn by parts, consisting of four triangular and one rectangular sections. The moment diagram was drawn by parts by first going from the left reaction across to the right reaction and then starting at the right end of the shaft and returning to the right reaction. Δ_1 is determined by taking moments of sections I, II, III, and IV respectively with respect to the right reaction, noting that the moments related to the $2D$ section of the shaft are divided by $16EI$ and that the moment related to the D section is divided by EI. Also note that the moment of section III is negative.

$$\Delta_1 = \frac{(153)(6)(2)}{(2)(16)EI} + \frac{(153)(6)(3)}{16EI} - \frac{(486)(6)(2)}{(2)(16)EI} + \frac{(153)(6)(8)}{2EI} = \frac{3719.25}{EI}$$

$$\Delta_2 = \frac{(153)(6)(2)}{2EI} = \frac{918}{EI}$$

$$\Delta_3 = \tfrac{1}{2}\Delta_1 = 1859.625/EI \quad \text{by proportion}$$

$$y_v = \Delta_3 - \Delta_2 = 942/EI \quad \text{(deflection at gear in vertical plane)}$$

$\tan\theta_1 = 1859.625/6EI = 310/EI$ (slope at left bearing in vertical plane)

Δ_4 is determined by taking moment of sections IV, I, II, and III respectively with respect to the left bearing.

$$\Delta_4 = \frac{(153)(6)(4)}{2EI} + \frac{(153)(6)(10)}{(2)(16)EI} + \frac{(153)(6)(9)}{16EI} - \frac{(486)(6)(10)}{(2)(16)EI} = \frac{1728}{EI}$$

$\tan\theta_2 = \Delta_4/12 = 144/EI$ (slope at right bearing in vertical plane)

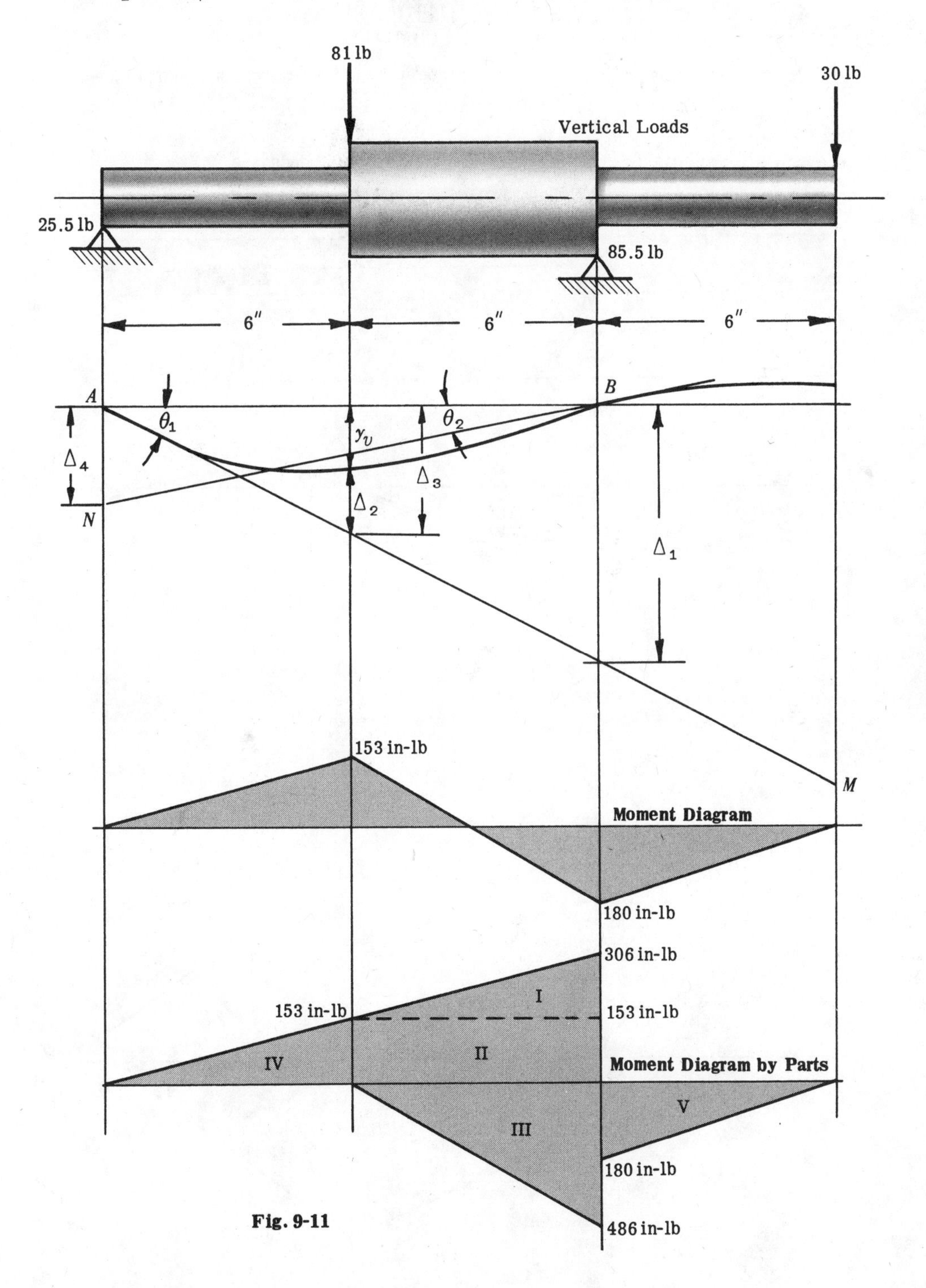

Fig. 9-11

Fig. 9-12 below is based upon horizontal loadings. The elastic curve is sketched and tangents are drawn at points A and B. The moment diagram is drawn and divided into sections I, II, III, and IV. Δ_1 is determined by taking moments of sections II, III, and IV respectively with respect to the right bearing.

$$\Delta_1 = \frac{(558)(6)(3)}{16\,EI} + \frac{(1404)(6)(2)}{(2)(16)\,EI} + \frac{(558)(6)(8)}{2\,EI} = \frac{14{,}546.25}{EI}$$

$$\tan\theta_1 = 14{,}546.25/12EI = 1212/EI \quad \text{(slope at left bearing in horizontal plane)}$$

$$\Delta_2 = \frac{(558)(6)(4)}{2\,EI} + \frac{(558)(6)(9)}{16\,EI} + \frac{(1404)(6)(10)}{(2)(16)\,EI} = \frac{11{,}211.75}{EI}$$

$$\tan\theta_2 = 11{,}211.75/12EI = 934/EI \quad \text{(slope at right bearing in horizontal plane)}$$

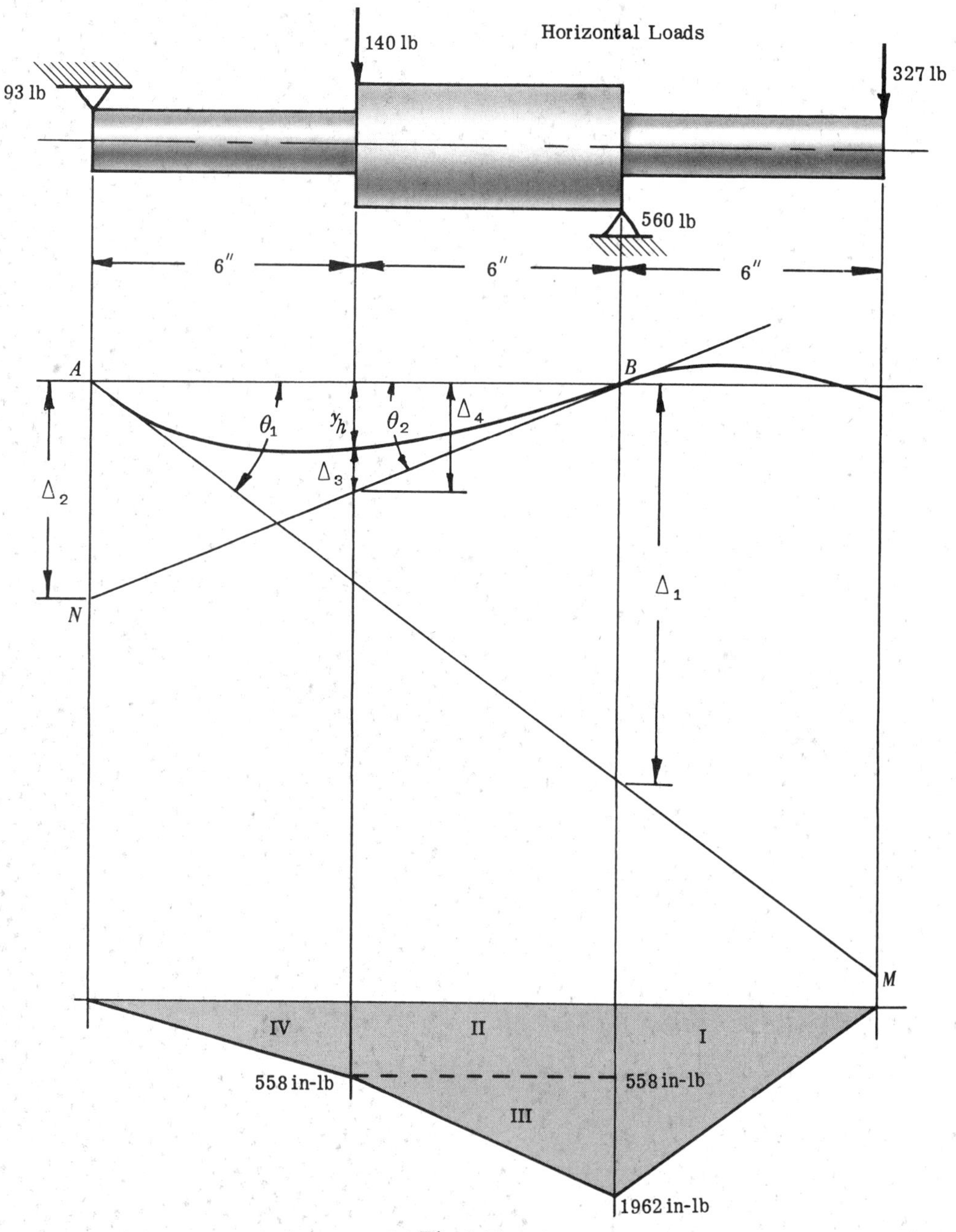

Fig. 9-12

$$\Delta_3 = \frac{(558)(6)(3)}{16EI} + \frac{(1404)(6)(4)}{(2)(16)EI} = \frac{1680.75}{EI}$$

$$\Delta_4 = \frac{11.211,75}{2EI} = \frac{5605.875}{EI} \text{ by proportion}$$

$$y_h = \Delta_4 - \Delta_3 = \frac{5605.875 - 1680.75}{EI} = \frac{3925}{EI} \text{ (deflection at gear in horizontal plane)}$$

The resultant deflection at the gear is equal to the vector sum of the deflections in the vertical and horizontal planes.

$$y \text{ (gear)} = \frac{1}{EI}\sqrt{942^2 + 3925^2} = \frac{4040}{EI}$$

The deflection at the gear is limited to 0.001 in. Then

$$\frac{4040}{EI} = 0.001 \quad \text{or} \quad I = \frac{4040}{(30 \times 10^6)(0.001)} = 0.1347 \text{ in}^4, \text{ required moment of inertia}$$

$$\frac{\pi D^4}{64} = 0.1347 \quad \text{or} \quad D = 1.285 \text{ in. to limit gear deflection to } 0.001 \text{ in.}$$

The resultant slope at the bearing is equal to the vector sum of the slopes at the vertical and horizontal planes. At the left bearing,

$$\text{slope} = \frac{1}{EI}\sqrt{310^2 + 1212^2} = \frac{1250}{EI} \quad \text{which is limited to } \tan 1^\circ$$

Then $\tan 1^\circ = 0.0175 = 1250/EI$ from which

$$I = 0.00238 \text{ in}^4 \text{ and } D = 0.47 \text{ in. required at left bearing.}$$

At the right bearing,

$$\text{slope} = \frac{1}{EI}\sqrt{144^2 + 934^2} = \frac{946}{EI} \quad \text{which is less than at left bearing.}$$

A summary of the above calculations is as follows:

	Vertical	Horizontal	Resultant
Deflection at gear	$942/EI$	$3925/EI$	$4040/EI$
Slope at left bearing	$310/EI$	$1212/EI$	$1250/EI$
Slope at right bearing	$144/EI$	$934/EI$	$946/EI$

Required Size Shaft				
	For strength based on ASME Code	Based on gear deflection	Based on slope at bearings	Based on critical speed
D =	1 in.	1.285 in.	0.47 in.	0.598 in.
$2D$ =	2 in.	2.57 in.	0.94 in.	1.196 in.

SUPPLEMENTARY PROBLEMS

13. A 24 inch pulley driven by a horizontal belt transmits power through a solid steel shaft to a 10 inch pinion which drives a mating gear. The pulley weighs 300 pounds to provide some flywheel effect. The arrangement of elements, the belt tensions, and the components of the gear reaction on the pinion are as shown in Fig.9-13 below.

(*a*) Sketch in order the following: vertical loading, vertical bending moment, horizontal loading, horizontal bending moment, and combined bending moment.

(*b*) Determine the necessary shaft diameter using code stress values for commercial shafting and shock and fatigue factors of $K_b = 2.0$ and $K_t = 1.5$.

Ans. $M_t(\text{max}) = 9600$ in-lb, $M_b(\text{max}) = 16{,}350$ in-lb, $d = 2.83$ in.

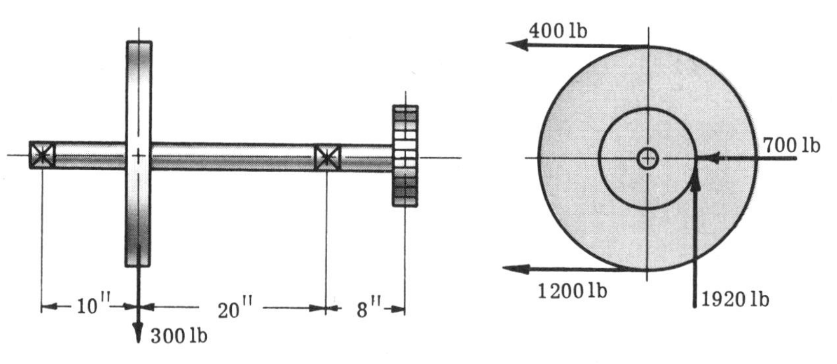

Fig. 9-13

14. Power is transmitted to a shaft, supported on bearings 36 inches apart, by a belt running on an 18 inch pulley which overhangs the right bearing by 10 inches. Power is transmitted from the shaft by a belt running on a 10 inch pulley located midway between the bearings. The belt drives are at right angles to each other and the belt tensions are 3 to 1 with the total pull on the tight side of either belt being limited to 600 pounds.

(*a*) Draw the moment diagrams.

(*b*) Determine the necessary size of SAE 1045 transmission shafting (ultimate tensile strength 97,000 psi, tensile elastic limit 58,000 psi). Assume $K_b = 1.5$ and $K_t = 1.0$.

(*c*) Calculate the torsional deflection in degrees.

Ans. $M_t(\text{max}) = 2000$ in-lb, $M_b(\text{max}) = 7520$ in-lb, $d = 1.64$ in., $\theta° = 0.377°$

15. A steel shaft 60 in. long has applied to it a 10,000 in-lb torque by a pulley located at the center of the shaft. A gear at the left end of the shaft applies 8000 in-lb of torque to the shaft while a gear located 9 in. to the left of the right end of the shaft applies 2000 in-lb of torque. Calculate the angular deflection of the shaft if the shaft is 2 in. in diameter for a length of 36 in. from the left end of the shaft and 1.5 in. in diameter in the remainder of the shaft. Neglect the effect of the keyways in the calculations. *Ans.* 0.424°

16. A horizontal piece of commercial shafting is supported by two bearings 5 feet apart. A keyed gear, 20° involute and 7 inches in diameter, is located 16 inches to the left of the right bearing and is driven by a gear directly behind it. A 24 inch diameter pulley is keyed to the shaft 20 inches to the right of the left bearing and drives a pulley with a horizontal belt directly behind it. The tension ratio of the belt is 3 to 1 with the slack side on top. The drive transmits 60 hp at 330 rpm. $K_b = K_t = 1.5$.

(*a*) Draw moment diagrams showing values at the change points.

(*b*) Calculate the necessary shaft diameter.

(*c*) Calculate the angular deflection in degrees.

Ans. $M_t(\text{max}) = 11{,}450$ in-lb, $M_b(\text{max}) = 38{,}500$ in-lb, $D = 3.72$ in., $\theta = 0.0677°$

17. A solid shaft and a hollow shaft are to be of equal strength in torsion. The hollow shaft is to be 10% larger in diameter than the solid shaft. What will be the ratio of the weight of the hollow shaft to that of the solid shaft? Both shafts are to be made of the same material.

Ans. The hollow shaft will weigh 0.6 that of the solid shaft.

18. The coefficient of friction between the cam and follower disk in Fig. 9-14 below is 0.3. The torque required to turn the cam under these conditions is supplied at the right end of the cam shaft. If the cam shaft is made of SAE 1020 steel quenched and tempered to an ultimate tensile strength of 80,000 psi and a yield point of 56,000 psi, what is the required minimum diameter of the cam shaft under the ASME Shafting Code? The shock and fatigue factors selected for the loading condition present are $K_b = 2.0$ and $K_t = 1.5$. Neglect the weight of the shaft and assume it is continuous from bearing to bearing. It is also assumed that the maximum effective torque occurs when the follower is at the top of its travel, where it is shown in Fig. 9-14.
Ans. $d = 1.01$ in.

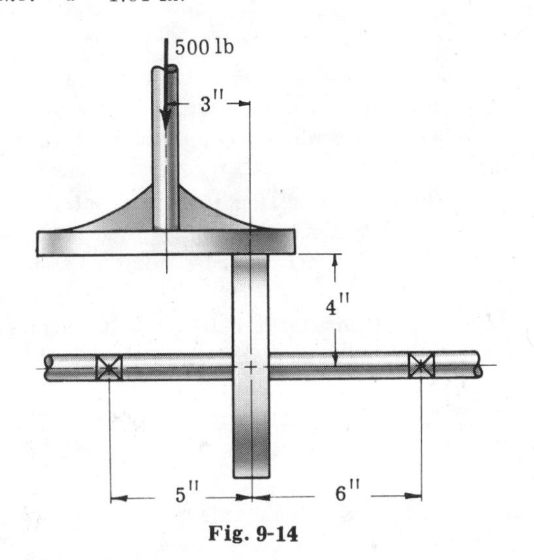

Fig. 9-14

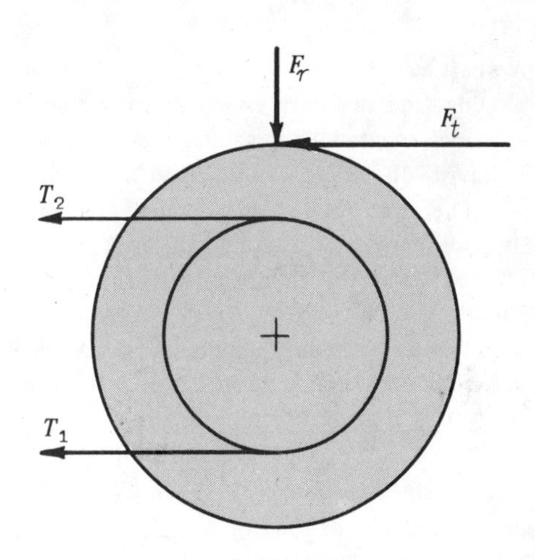

Fig. 9-15

19. Two bearings located 36 in. apart support a section of commercial shafting. A 500 lb, 30 in. diameter, 20 degree involute gear is keyed to the shaft 8 in. to the right of the right bearing. A 12 in. diameter sprocket is keyed to the shaft 20 in. to the right of the left bearing. The combined weight of the sprocket and that part of the chain weight taken by the shaft is 210 lb downward. Assume no tension on the slack side of the chain. The gear receives 9 hp at 210 rpm from a gear located above. Five hp is taken from the shaft at the sprocket and the remainder is taken from the shaft through a flexible coupling located 6 in. to the left of the left bearing. Fig. 9-15 above shows an end view of the arrangement as observed from the right.

(*a*) Draw the bending moment diagrams showing values at the change points.

(*b*) Calculate the diameter of commercial steel shafting based upon strength.

(*c*) Calculate the angular deflection in degrees of the right end of the shaft with respect to the left end of the shaft when under load, neglecting the effect of the keyways and stiffening effect of the pulley and sprocket hubs.

Ans. $M_t(\text{max}) = 2700$ in-lb, $M_b(\text{max}) = 4700$ in-lb, $d = 1.86$ in., $\theta = 0.389°$

20. A shaft is mounted between bearings located 31 ft apart and transmits 13,000 hp at 90 rpm. The shaft weighs 14,850 lb, has an outside diameter of 18 in. and an inside diameter of 12 in. Determine the stress induced in shaft and the angular deflection between bearings. Do not neglect the weight of the shaft.
Ans. $s_s = 9920$ psi, $\theta = 1.95°$

21. Fig. 9-16 shows an arrangement for a motor and exciter with a pinion on the same shaft. The pinion drives a gear with the gear directly below the pinion. The motor develops 75 hp at 200 rpm. The exciter absorbs 5 hp, the remainder going to the pinion. The motor and exciter are assembled to the shaft by means of a force fit while the pinion is keyed to the shaft.

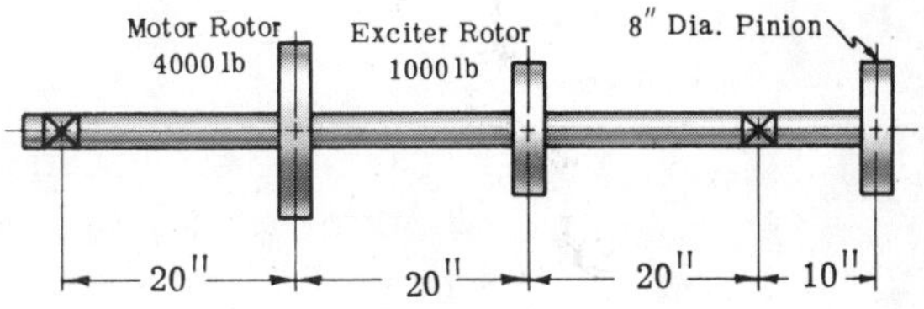

For this unit, what is the required diameter of shaft (a constant diameter of shaft will be used)? The shaft is to be made of SAE 1035, which has an ultimate strength of 75,000 psi and a yield point of 48,000 psi. The pressure angle of the gears is 20 degrees, and the stub form of tooth is to be used. Neglect stress concentration due to force fits.

Motor Rotor 4000 lb — Exciter Rotor 1000 lb — 8" Dia. Pinion — 20" 20" 20" 10"

Fig. 9-16

Draw all moment diagrams, showing the values at change points. $K_b = 1.5$ and $K_t = 1.5$.
Ans. $M_t = 23{,}600$ in-lb, $M_b(\text{max}) = 69{,}200$ in-lb, $s_s(\text{allowable}) = 13{,}500$ psi, $d = 3.81$ in.

22. A line shaft, 18 feet long and $1\frac{3}{8}$ inches in diameter, is rotating at 500 rpm and has 10 hp input at one end. Six hp is taken out at a point 8 feet from the input end and the remaining 4 hp is taken out at the opposite end. Using $G = 12 \times 10^6$ psi, find the angular deflection of one end relative to the other due to this loading.
Ans. $\theta = 2.49^\circ$

23. A 9 inch diameter solid shaft is used to drive the propeller of a marine vessel. It is necessary to reduce the weight of the shaft by 70%. What would be the dimensions of a hollow shaft made of the same material as the solid shaft? *Ans.* $d_o = 15.771$ in., $d_i = 14.980$ in.

24. A shaft has a constant diameter, with the distance between bearings equal to 32 in. Located between the bearings are two pulleys which are keyed to the shaft. One pulley, which has a diameter of 8 in. and weighs 20 lb, is located 8 in. to the right of the left bearing; the other pulley, which has a diameter of 16 in. and weighs 60 lb, is located 22 in. to the right of the left bearing.

The shaft rotates at 900 rpm. The tight and slack sides of the belt are horizontal and parallel. Twenty-five horsepower is supplied to the 8 in. pulley. Power is transmitted from the 16 in. pulley to another pulley located so as to give a smaller bending moment in the shaft, with the belt strands horizontal as already stated.

The belt stress is limited to a maximum of 300 psi. The ratio of diameter of pulley to belt thickness is limited to a minimum of 30. A belt thickness of 1/4 in. will be used. The coefficient of friction for the belt and pulley may be taken as 0.3.

The shaft is made from hot rolled SAE 1035, for which the ultimate strength may be taken as 80,000 psi and the yield point may be taken as 49,000 psi. The shaft is fitted in journal bearing with a class 2 fit.

Conditions of loading are steady, with no shock.

Determine the necessary diameter of shaft based on strength, deflection in the bearings and critical speed. Neglect the weight of the shaft and pulleys for strength and deflection calculations.

Ans. Shaft diameter = 1.5 in. based on strength in accordance with ASME Code. For this diameter the critical speed is 2720 rpm which is safely above the operating speed. The static deflection under the 20 lb pulley is 0.0039 in., and the static deflection under the 60 lb pulley is 0.005 in. A shaft diameter of 2.25 in. is required to prevent excessive deflection in the bearings based on an L/D ratio of 1.5.

Chapter 10

Coupling Design

COUPLINGS are used to connect sections of shafts or to connect the shaft of a driving machine to the shaft of a driven machine. This affords a permanent connection, contrasted with clutches which provide for engagement or disengagement at will. Clutches are treated in a different section.

CLASSIFICATION of couplings can be made on the basis of rigid or flexible designs.

(A) Rigid couplings:

Illustrated by a flange coupling, compression coupling, or tapered-sleeve coupling. This type of coupling is suitable for low speeds, accurately aligned shafts.

(B) Flexible couplings:

Illustrated by the Falk flexible coupling, Oldham coupling, gear type of flexible coupling, roller or silent chain coupling, etc.

Flexible couplings are used:

(*a*) To take care of a small amount of unintentional misalignment.

(*b*) To provide for "end float", that is, axial movement of a shaft.

(*c*) To alleviate shock by providing transfer of power through springs or to absorb some of the vibration in the coupling.

Coupling may be classified also as to use, specified by the relation of axes of the connected shafts:

(*1*) Axes of the shafts are collinear.

(*2*) Axes of the shafts intersect. (A universal joint of the many types available might be used.)

(*3*) Axes of the shafts are parallel but not collinear. (A coupling of the Oldham type might be used with its central sliding member. This type is to be avoided where possible with heavy loads because of friction due to sliding.)

Since rigid couplings can transmit bending in a shaft, stresses may be induced which can cause fatigue failure. It is therefore desirable to provide for good alignment and location of the coupling where the bending moment is practically zero. Thus rigid couplings, as well as flexible couplings, are usually analyzed for torsion only.

Although standardized couplings may be purchased from manufacturers, the analysis and proportioning of the various parts afford illustration of machine design procedures applied to a single machine element.

SOLVED PROBLEMS

1. A rigid flange coupling has a bore diameter of $\frac{2.000}{2.002}$ in. Four machined bolts on a bolt circle of 5 in. diameter are fitted in reamed holes. If the bolts are made from the same material as the shaft, SAE 1030, with an ultimate tensile strength of 80,000 psi and a yield point in tension of 50,000 psi, determine the necessary size of bolts to have the same capacity as the shaft in torsion. Refer to Fig. 10-1 which shows half a coupling.

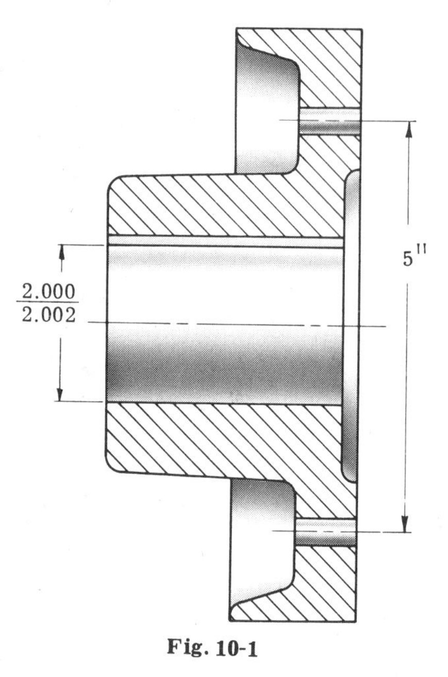

Fig. 10-1

Solution:

(*a*) The shaft capacity, as determined from the ASME Shafting Code, is found from

$$D^3 = \frac{16}{\pi s_s} M_t K_t$$

the shafting equation for a solid shaft in torsion only. Then

$$(2)^3 = \frac{16}{\pi(14{,}400)(0.75)} M_t K_t \qquad \text{or} \qquad M_t K_t = 17{,}000 \text{ in-lb}$$

where s_s is the smaller of $(0.18)s_u = 0.18(80{,}000) = 14{,}400$ psi and $(0.3)s_{yp} = 0.3(50{,}000) = 15{,}000$ psi

and the allowance for the keyway effect is 0.75.

(*b*) The coupling can be designed for shock and fatigue K_t, equal to 1, or $(M_t K_t)$ can be left as a product and carried through the analysis. The same final result is obtained.

(*c*) The analysis of the bolts can be made in any one of several different ways:

(*1*) Assume that the bolts are just finger-tight, and the load is transferred from one half of the coupling to the other half by a uniform shear stress in the shank of the bolt.

(*2*) Assume that the bolts are just finger-tight, and the load is transferred from one half of the coupling to the other half with a maximum shear stress in the shank of the bolt equal to 4/3 times the average shear stress.

(*3*) Assume that the bolts are tightened sufficiently so that power is transmitted from one half of the coupling to the other by means of friction.

(*4*) Assume that the bolts are tightened and that part of the power is transmitted by means of friction, and the rest of the power is transmitted by shear in the bolts.

In (*1*) and (*2*), it is usual practice to assume that all the bolts share the load proportionally for finished bolts in drilled and reamed holes. (If the bolts are set in clearance holes, it is also usual practice to assume that half the bolts are effective.)

(*d*) Using arbitrarily (*1*) above, which gives the most conservative design,

$$M_t K_t = s_s(\tfrac{1}{4}\pi d^2)(\tfrac{1}{2}D_{BC})(n) \qquad \text{or} \qquad 17{,}000 = 14{,}400(\tfrac{1}{4}\pi d^2)(\tfrac{1}{2}\times 5)(4), \qquad \text{and} \qquad d = 0.387 \text{ in.}$$

where s_s = allowable shear stress, psi

d = diameter of bolt, inches, (shank diameter)

D_{BC} = diameter of bolt circle, inches

n = total number of bolts for drilled and reamed holes.

(Note that s_s for the bolt is the same as obtained from the ASME Shafting Code.) Hence use a 3/8 in. bolt or a 7/16 in. bolt.

(*e*) Using (*2*) above, $M_t K_t = \frac{3}{4}s_s(\frac{1}{4}\pi d^2)(\frac{1}{2}D_{BC})(n)$, from which $d = 0.447$ in.; a 7/16 in. bolt may be used.

(*f*) The next problem will illustrate a solution by (*3*) above.

2. In the design of rigid flange couplings, it is quite customary in this country to assume that the bolts are loosened in service and the capacity of the coupling is based, in part, upon the stresses set up in the bolts due to shearing of the bolts. The tightening effect of the bolts, with friction as the basis of power transmission, is generally neglected. However the purpose of this problem is to evaluate the capacity of a particular coupling **based upon friction**.

Assume that a flange coupling has the following specifications:

Number of bolts, 6

Size of bolts, $\frac{1}{2}$ in. diameter

Preloading of bolts, 5000 lb in each bolt

Inner diameter of contact, 7 in.

Outer diameter of contact, 8 in.

Speed of rotation of coupling, 300 rpm

Coefficient of friction, 0.15

Shaft diameter, 2 in.

Shaft material: SAE 1045, annealed with an ultimate tensile strength of 85,000 psi and a yield point in tension of 45,000 psi.

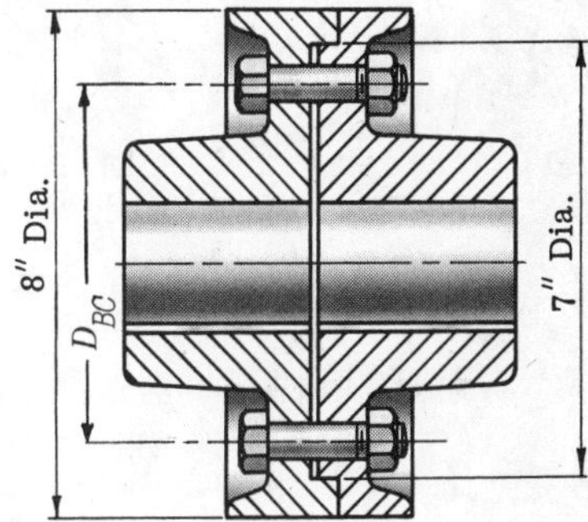

Fig. 10-2

The bolts are set in large clearance holes in the coupling. Refer to Fig. 10-2.

Determine:

(*1*) The maximum power capacity based upon friction such that slip occurs between faces of contact.

(*2*) Compare the shaft horsepower capacity with the friction horsepower capacity. Assume steady load conditions and that the shaft is in torsion only.

Solution:

(*a*) The torque capacity based on friction is (see chapter on Clutches)

$$M_t = FfR_f = 30{,}000(0.15)(3.75) = 16{,}900 \text{ in-lb}$$

where F = axial force caused by bolt loading = 30,000 lb

f = coefficient of friction

$$R_f = \text{friction radius} = \frac{2}{3}\left(\frac{R_o^3 - R_i^3}{R_o^2 - R_i^2}\right) = \frac{2}{3}\left(\frac{4^3 - 3.5^3}{4^2 - 3.5^2}\right) = 3.75 \text{ in.}$$

This assumes that the pressure is uniformly distributed.

$$\text{Friction horsepower} = \frac{M_t N}{63{,}024} = \frac{16{,}900(300)}{63{,}024} = 80.4 \text{ hp}$$

(*b*) Shaft torque capacity,

$$M_t = s_s \pi D^3/16 = 13{,}500(0.75)\pi D^3/16 = 15{,}900 \text{ in-lb}$$

where s_s is the smaller of 0.18(85,000) = 15,300 psi and 0.3(45,000) = 13,500 psi.

Note the factor 0.75 to take care of stress concentration.

$$\text{Shaft horsepower capacity} = \frac{M_t N}{63{,}024} = \frac{15{,}900(300)}{63{,}024} = 75.7 \text{ hp}$$

(*c*) For the data given, the coupling has greater horsepower capacity based on friction (80.4 hp) than the shaft capacity (75.7 hp).

3. Problems 1 and 2 have dealt with the diameter of the bolt necessary to transmit power through a flange coupling. This problem is concerned with the necessary proportions for the various parts of a flange coupling. Set up the equations or relations necessary to determine (*a*) diameter D_H of hub, (*b*) thickness t of web, (*c*) thickness h of the flange. Refer to Fig. 10-3.

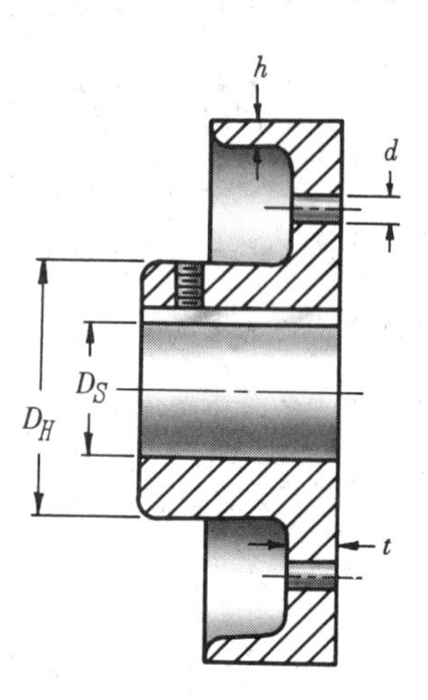

Fig. 10-3

Solution:

(*a*) The diameter of the hub is established on the basis of proportions. The diameter of the hub should be about $1\frac{3}{4}$ to 2 times the diameter of the shaft. Thus

$$D_H \approx 1\tfrac{3}{4} D_S \text{ to } 2D_S$$

(*b*) The minimum thickness t is based on two considerations: (*1*) shear of the web, (*2*) bearing of the web and bolt assuming that the bolts are finger-tight and the bolts are pressed against the web.

(*1*) **Shear of the web:** The torque capacity of the web is based on the shear of the minimum area, which occurs at the junction of the hub and web.

$$M_t = s_s(\pi D_H t)\frac{D_H}{2} \quad \text{or} \quad t = \frac{2M_t}{\pi s_s D_H^2}$$

Usually, t determined from the above equation is very small and the difficulty of casting necessitates using a thickness much larger than calculated.

(*2*) **Bearing of the bolt and web:** The torque capacity based on bearing is

$$M_t = s_B(dt)\frac{D_{BC}}{2}n \quad \text{or} \quad t = \frac{2M_t}{s_B d D_{BC} n}$$

where s_B = allowable bearing pressure for the bolt or web (whichever is weaker), psi of projected area

d = bolt diameter, inches

D_{BC} = diameter of bolt circle, inches

n = number of effective bolts, taken as all the bolts if finished bolts are used in reamed holes and taken as half the total number of bolts if bolts are set in clearance holes. Note that this assumption is arbitrary, but a very conservative design results.

(*c*) Thickness of flange is based upon proportions and casting requirements.

4. A coupling of the Falk type is keyed to two 1 in. transmission shafts (with s_s allowable = 8000 psi for unkeyed shafts, 6000 psi for keyed shafts) as shown in Fig. 10-4. The shafts rotate at 950 rpm. If the connecting strip is 1.50 in. from the center of the shafts, how many folds of 0.010 by 0.100 inch steel (SAE 1045, quenched in water and drawn at 600°F) are required? The connector is to have 95% of the strength of the shaft according to its ASME Code rating. Under what conditions could you rate this coupling at 13.5 hp? SAE 1045 steel, quenched in water and drawn at 600°F, may be considered to have an ultimate tensile strength of 150,000 psi and a yield point in tension of 114,000 psi.

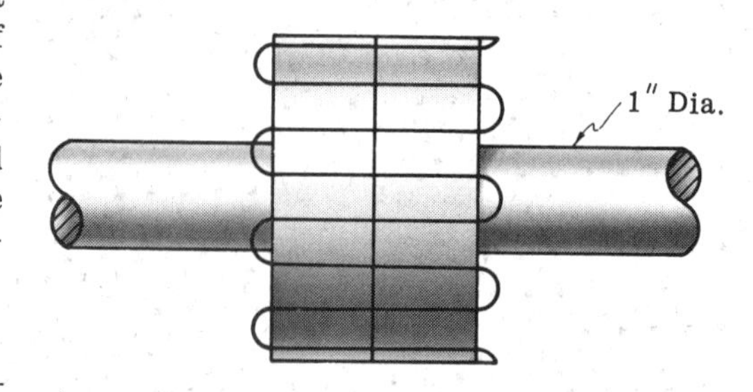

Fig. 10-4

Solution:

(*a*) Shaft torque capacity, using s_s = 6000 psi, with allowance for the keyway:

$$M_t = s_s \pi d^3/16 = 6000\pi(1^3)/16 = 1180 \text{ in-lb}$$

(*b*) Assume that the folds are subjected to shear only. The torque capacity of the folds is

$$M_t = s_s t h R_f n \quad \text{or} \quad 0.95(1180) = (27{,}000)(0.010)(0.100)(1.5)(n)$$

where s_s = allowable shear stress, taken as 0.18 of ultimate tensile strength, as suggested in ASME Code, or 0.18(150,000) = 27,000 psi.

t = thickness of steel strip, 0.010 in.

h = height of steel strip, 0.100 in.

R_f = radius from shaft center to fold

n = number of folds.

Solving, n = 27,6; use 28 folds.

(*c*) For 28 folds, the torque capacity is

$$M_t = s_s t h R_f n = (27{,}000)(0.010)(0.100)(1.5)(28) = 1140 \text{ in-lb}$$

The safe horsepower capacity is $= \dfrac{M_t N}{63{,}024} = \dfrac{1140(950)}{63{,}024} = 17.2$ hp. Hence one could rate the coupling at 13.5 hp with possibility of about 30% overload.

5. A universal coupling (universal joint, or Hooke's joint) is used to connect two shafts which intersect but which are not necessarily in the same straight line, as shown in Fig. 10-5 below. The angular velocity of the output shaft is not equal to the angular velocity of the input shaft, unless the input and output shafts are in line. The ratio of speeds is given by

$$\frac{N_{S_2}}{N_{S_1}} = \frac{\cos\theta}{1 - \cos^2\alpha \sin^2\theta}$$

where N_{S_2} = angular velocity of the driven shaft

N_{S_1} = angular velocity of the driver shaft

θ = angle between axes of the shafts

α = angle of the driving shaft from the position where the pins of the drive shaft yoke are in the plane of the two shafts.

A torque of 360 in-lb is applied to shaft S_1 of a universal joint in which S_1 and the output shaft S_2 are in the same horizontal plane.

(*a*) Determine the torque on shaft S_2 for the position shown in Fig. 10-5.

(*b*) Determine the size of the pins of the connecting cross for an allowable bearing stress of 2000 psi (per projected area), an allowable tensile stress of 20,000 psi, and an allowable shear stress of 10,000 psi.

(*c*) Calculate the maximum shear stress on section E-E, which is 2 in. from axis Y-Y.

Solution:

(*a*) There are several ways the torque on S_2 can be determined. One method is to examine the cross, by application of the equations of equilibrium, and to determine that the only forces which can be applied are as shown in the plane of the cross. Consider each of the forces acting on the cross as F. The components of F, acting on the shaft S_1, are $F\cos 20^\circ$ and $F\sin 20^\circ$. The torque acting on the shaft S_1 due to the action of the cross is $M_t = 360 = (F\cos 20^\circ)(2)$, from which $F = 191.4$ lb. The torque on the shaft S_2 is $F(2) = (191.4)(2) = 383$ in-lb. Note that, for the position shown, shaft S_2 is in torsion only, while shaft S_1 is in bending as well as torsion. If shaft S_1 is rotated 90°, shaft S_1 will be in torsion only, while shaft S_2 will be subjected to bending and torsion.

A second method is to use the relation of angular speeds to obtain the torque. For no friction loss the power in must equal the power out, i. e.,

$$\frac{T_{S_1} N_{S_1}}{63{,}024} = \frac{T_{S_2} N_{S_2}}{63{,}024} \quad \text{or} \quad T_{S_1} N_{S_1} = T_{S_2}\left(N_{S_1} \frac{\cos\theta}{1 - \cos^2\alpha \sin^2\theta}\right)$$

Then for $T_{S_1} = 360$ in-lb, $\theta = 20^\circ$, and $\alpha = 90^\circ$ for position shown, we obtain $T_{S_2} = 360/(\cos 20^\circ) = 383$ in-lb, the torque output. This agrees with the force analysis.

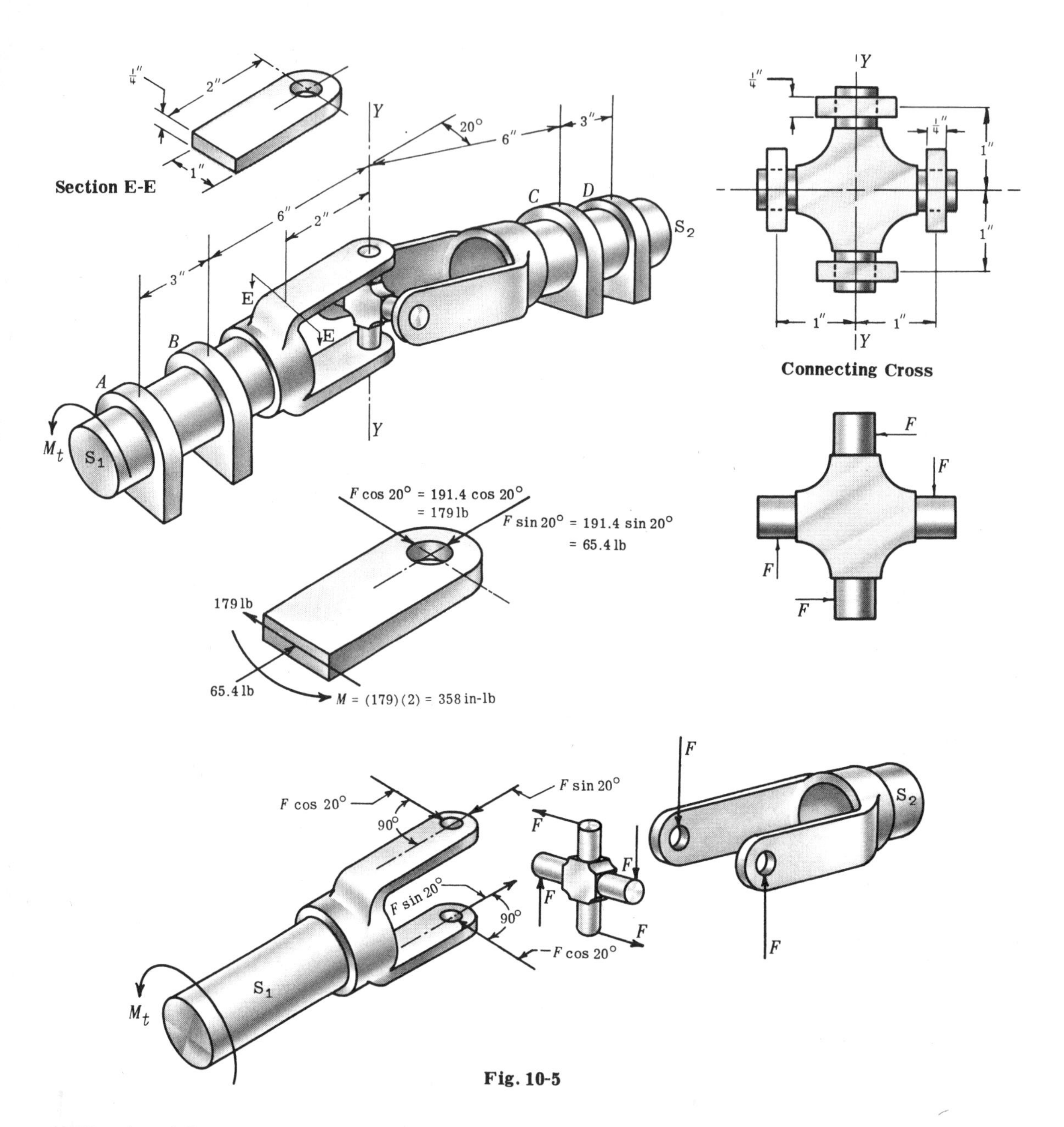

Fig. 10-5

(*b*) The size of the pins will depend on the maximum load, which occurs for the position shown. The maximum pin load is 191 lb.

(*1*) Diameter of pin based on bearing: $s_b = \dfrac{F}{A} = \dfrac{F}{\frac{1}{4}d}$, $2000 = \dfrac{191}{\frac{1}{4}d}$, $d = 0.384$ in.

(*2*) Diameter of pin based on bending: $s = \dfrac{Mc}{I}$, $20{,}000 = \dfrac{(191\times\frac{1}{4})(\frac{1}{2}d)}{(\pi/64)d^4}$, $d = 0.29$ in.

(*3*) Diameter of pin based on transverse shear: $s_s = (\frac{4}{3})\dfrac{F}{A}$, $10{,}000 = (\frac{4}{3})(\dfrac{191}{\frac{1}{4}\pi d^2})$, $d = 0.18$ in.

Therefore bearing dictates the minimum size of pin; a $\frac{7}{16}$ in. diameter pin should be satisfactory.

(*c*) Maximum compressive stress at section E-E is $s = \dfrac{Mc}{I} + \dfrac{P}{A} = \dfrac{(179\times 2)(\frac{1}{2})}{\frac{1}{4}(1^3)/12} + \dfrac{65.4}{\frac{1}{4}(1)} = 8850$ psi.

Maximum shear $= \frac{1}{2}(8850) = 4425$ psi

SUPPLEMENTARY PROBLEMS

6. A rigid flange coupling is assembled with five finished bolts in reamed holes on a 6 in. diameter bolt circle. The shafts are commercial steel (with the allowable shear stress = 8000 psi, 6000 psi taking into account the keyway effect) and are $1\frac{15}{16}$ in. in diameter. Determine a standard bolt diameter to transmit the ASME Code strength of the shaft

(*a*) on the basis of the bolts having loosened and the shear stress is uniformly distributed.

(*b*) on the basis of the bolts having loosened and the maximum shear stress in the bolt is 4/3 times the average.

The allowable shear stress in the bolt is 10,000 psi.

Ans. (*a*) d = 0.270 in.; use $\frac{5}{16}$ in. (*b*) d = 0.312 in.; use $\frac{5}{16}$ in.

7. A flange coupling connects two 2 in. diameter lengths of commercial shafting. The coupling webs are bolted together with four bolts of the same material as the shaft. The bolts are set in clearance holes. The diameter of the bolt circle is 9.5 in. and the web thickness is 7/8 in.

(*a*) Determine the minimum bolt diameter required to transmit the same torque that the shaft can transmit.

(*b*) What horsepower may be transmitted at 200 rpm under steady load conditions?

Base calculations on the assumption that the bolt nuts may loosen during operation.

Ans. (*a*) Diameter of bolt = 0.398 in.; use $\frac{3}{8}$ in. or $\frac{7}{16}$ in. diameter (based upon shear stress being uniform). The diameter of the bolt based upon bearing is 0.0708 in., with allowable bearing pressure twice the allowable shear. Bearing does not control the design.

(*b*) 29.9 hp under steady load conditions (torque capacity = 9420 in-lb).

8. Each half of a rigid flange coupling with fitted bolts for a shaft of diameter D is to be installed on the shaft with a square key $1.25D$ long. Five bolts are to be used on a bolt circle of diameter $5D$. Assume coupling, bolts, shaft, and key to be of the same material.

(*a*) What should be the diameter d of the bolts in terms of D to make the coupling as strong as the shaft in torsion?

(*b*) What should be the dimension of the key in terms of D if the key is to transmit the full capacity of the shaft in torsion?

Ans. (*a*) Based on shear being uniform, $d = 0.122D$. Based on maximum shear = 4/3 average, $d = 0.141D$.

(*b*) Width = thickness = $0.236D$.

9. Two halves of a flange coupling fitted on 4 in. steel shafts are bolted together with six 3/4 in. bolts fitted into drilled holes with clearance on a bolt circle 10 in. in diameter. The ultimate tensile and compressive strength of the shaft and bolt material is 64,000 psi and the yield strength is 48,000 psi. Assuming that the allowable stress for the bolt may be determined using the ASME Shafting Code specifications, calculate the horsepower that may be safely transmitted by this shaft-coupling combination at 180 rpm. Assume the bending load on the shafting is negligible and that steady load conditions prevail.

Ans. Hp = 217 (with torque capacity of bolts = 76,000 in-lb, using a uniform shear stress distribution, and a torque capacity of the shaft of 108,000 in-lb).

10. A torque of M_t = 360 in-lb is applied to shaft S_1 of a universal joint. Determine

(*a*) the torque on shaft S_2,

(*b*) the force on the pins of the connecting cross,

(*c*) the bearing reactions at A, B, C, and D.

Refer to Fig. 10-5 and rotate shaft S_1 90° from that shown.

Ans. (*a*) 348 in-lb

(*b*) 180 lb

(*c*) Force at A = 0, at B = 0, at C = 41.1 lb, at D = 41.1 lb.

Chapter 11

Keys, Pins, and Splines

KEYS are used to prevent relative motion between a shaft and the connected member through which torque is being transmitted. Even though gears, pulleys, etc., are assembled with an interference fit, it is desirable to use a key designed to transmit the full torque.

COMMON TYPES OF KEYS are the square key as shown in Fig. 11-1 (*a*), the flat key as shown in Fig. 11-1 (*b*), the Kennedy key as shown in Fig. 11-1 (*c*), and the Woodruff key as shown in Fig. 11-1 (*d*).

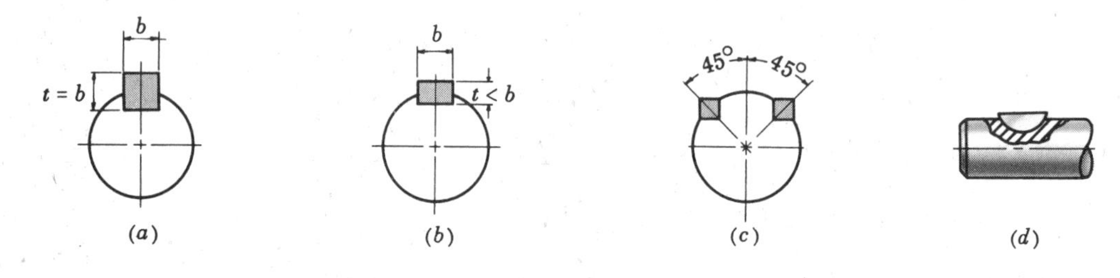

Fig. 11-1

The width of the square and the flat key is usually one fourth the diameter of the shaft. These keys may be either straight or tapered approximately $\frac{1}{8}$ in. per ft. A Gib-Head key is shown in Fig. 11-2. Feather keys and splines are used when it is necessary to have relative axial motion between the shaft and mating member. ASME and ASA standards for key and spline dimensions are available.

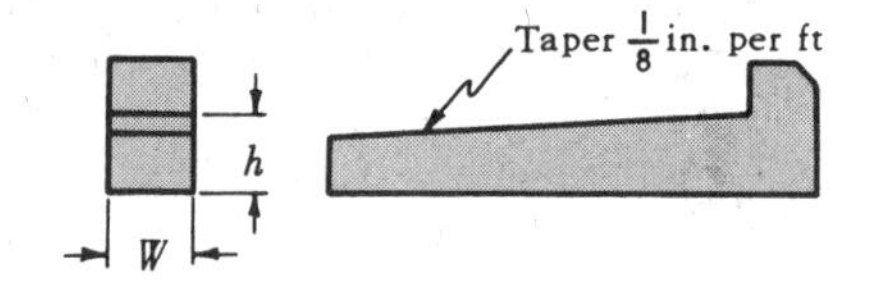

Fig. 11-2

DESIGN OF SQUARE AND FLAT KEYS may be based on the shear and compressive stresses induced in the key as a result of the torque being transmitted. The forces acting on the key are shown in Fig. 11-3. The forces F' act as a resisting couple to prevent the key from tending to roll in the fitted keyway. The exact location of the force F is not known and it is convenient to assume that it acts tangent to the surface of the shaft. This force produces both shear and compression stresses in the key.

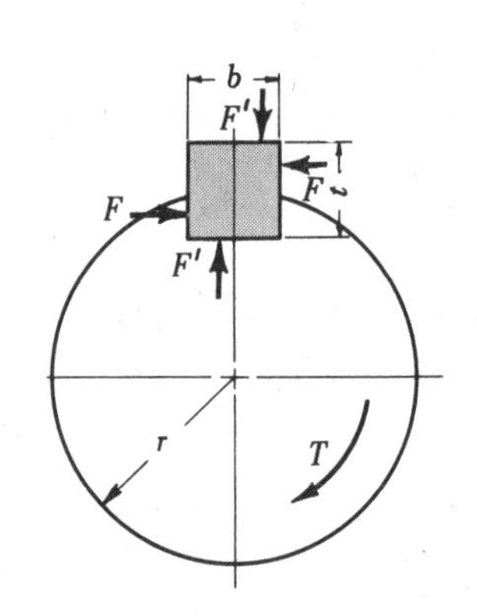

Fig. 11-3

Resistance to the shaft torque T may then be approximated by $T = Fr$, where r is the radius of the shaft. The shearing stress s_s in the key is

$$s_s = \frac{F}{bL} = \frac{Fr}{bLr} = \frac{T}{bLr}$$

where L is the length of the key.

The shaft torque that the key can sustain from the standpoint of shear is

$$T_s = s_s bLr$$

The compressive stress s_c in the key is

$$s_c = \frac{F}{(t/2)L} = \frac{Fr}{(t/2)Lr} = \frac{T}{(t/2)Lr}$$

The shaft torque that the key can sustain from the standpoint of compression is

$$T_c = s_c(t/2)Lr$$

A square key can sustain the same shaft torque from the standpoint of shear as it can from the standpoint of compression. This is proved as a solved problem by equating the two torque equations and making use of the approximate relation $s_c = 2s_s$ for ductile steels. On this same basis, flat keys which are wider than they are deep will fail in compression, and feather keys which are deeper than they are wide will fail in shear.

PINS are used in knuckle joints which connect two rods or bars loaded in either tension or compression as shown in Fig. 11-4 (a). An excessive load F may cause the joint to fail due to any of the following induced stresses.

1. Tensile stress in the rod:

$$s_t = \frac{4F}{\pi D^2}$$

2. Tensile stress in the net area of the eye, see Fig. 11-4(b):

$$s_t = \frac{F}{(d_o - d)b}$$

3. Shear stress in the eye due to tear out, see Fig. 11-4(c):

$$s_s = \frac{F}{b(d_o - d)} \quad \text{approx.}$$

4. Tensile stress in the net area of the clevis or fork:

$$s_t = \frac{F}{(d_o - d)2a}$$

5. Shear stress in the fork due to tear out:

$$s_s = \frac{F}{2a(d_o - d)} \quad \text{approx.}$$

6. Compressive stress in the eye due to bearing pressure of the pin:

$$s_c = \frac{F}{db}$$

7. Compressive stress in the fork due to bearing pressure of the pin:

$$s_c = \frac{F}{2da}$$

8. Shear stress in the pin:

$$s_s = \frac{F}{A} = \frac{2F}{\pi d^2}$$

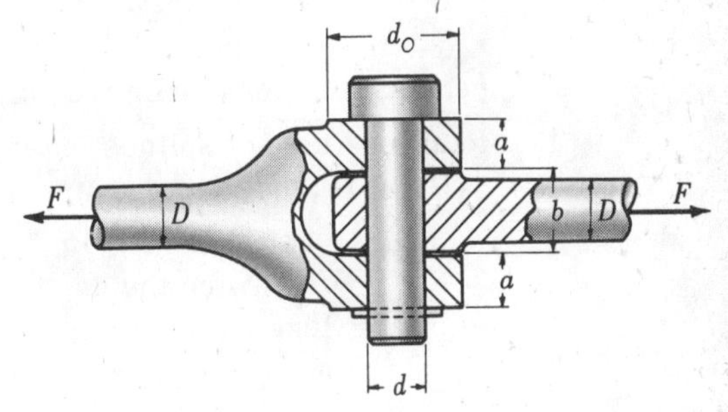

(a)

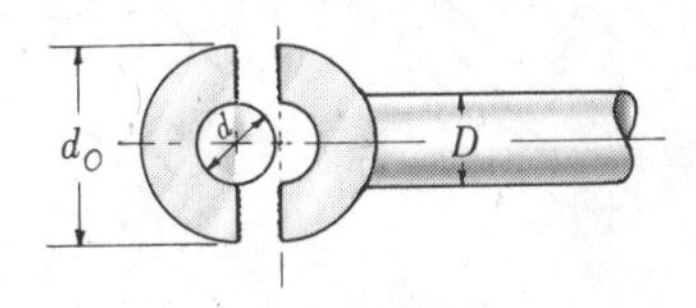

(b)

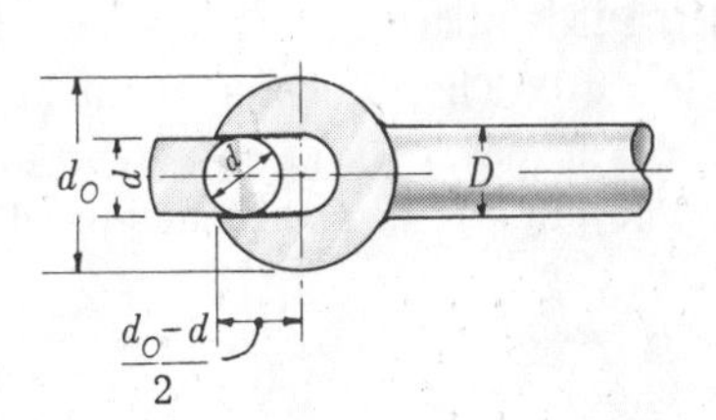

(c)

Fig. 11-4

9. Bending stress in the pin, based on assumption that the pin is supported and loaded as shown in Fig. 11-5. The maximum bending moment M_b occurs at the center of the pin. $M_b = Fb/8$, $I = \pi d^4/64$, $c = d/2$, and

$$s_b = \frac{Mc}{I} = \frac{4Fb}{\pi d^3}$$

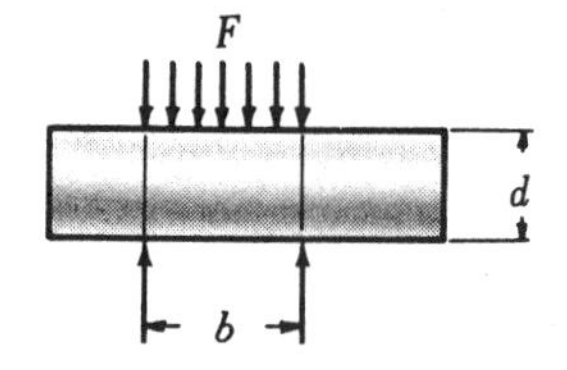

Fig. 11-5

10. Compressive stress in the pin due to the eye: $s_c = \dfrac{F}{db}$

11. Compressive stress in the pin due to the fork: $s_c = \dfrac{F}{2ad}$

SPLINED CONNECTIONS as shown in Fig. 11-6 below are used to permit relative axial motion between the shaft and hub of the connected member. The splines are keys made integral with the shaft and usually consist of four, six, or ten in number. The keyways are broached in the hub to the required fit. The splines are usually made with straight sides or cut with an involute profile. When there is relative axial motion in a splined connection, the side pressure on the splines should be limited to about 1000 psi. The torque capacity of a splined connection is

$$T = pAr_m$$

where

p = permissible pressure on the splines, <1000 psi

A = total load area of splines, sq in.

= $\frac{1}{2}(D-d)(L)$(number of splines), sq in.

D = shaft diameter, in.

d = D − twice the depth of the spline, in.

L = length of hub, in.

r_m = mean radius, in.

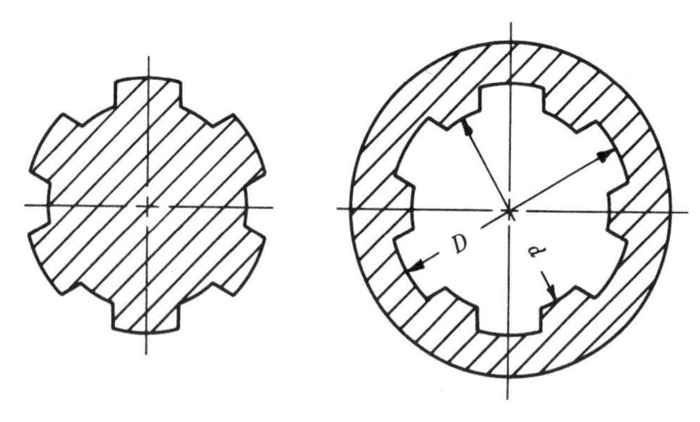

Fig. 11-6

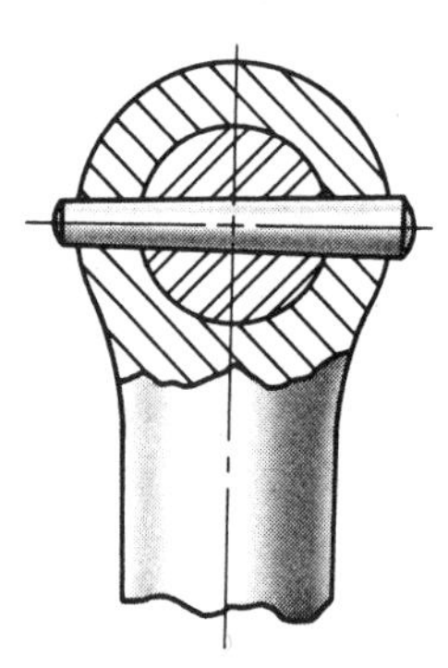

Fig. 11-7

TAPERED PINS similar to that shown in Fig. 11-7 above are frequently used to key hubs to shafts. The diameter of the large end of the pin is usually about one-fourth the diameter of the shaft. The capacity of this type of pin key connection is determined by the two shear areas of the pin. The pin key is sometimes used as a shear pin.

SOLVED PROBLEMS

1. Prove that a square key is equally strong in shear and compression.

Solution:

From the standpoint of compression a key can sustain the following torque; $T_c = s_c(t/2)Lr$.

From the standpoint of shear a key can sustain the following torque: $T_s = s_s bLr$.

Equating the two torque equations to establish equal strength in shear and compression, and assuming that $s_c = 2s_s$, we have $T_c = T_s$, $2s_s(t/2)Lr = s_s bLr$, and $t = b$ (a square key).

2. Determine the required length of a square key if the key and shaft are to be of the same material and of equal strength.

Solution:

The torque that a shaft of diameter d can transmit allowing for a 25% reduction due to stress concentration is $T = 0.75\pi d^3 s_s/16$. Equating this torque to the torque that a square key can sustain from the standpoint of shear, we have

$$0.75\pi d^3 s_s/16 \quad = \quad s_s bLr$$

Substitute $d/4$ for b and solve for $L = 1.18d$; use $L = 1.25d$.

3. A square key is to be used to key a gear to a $1\frac{7}{16}$ in. diameter shaft. The hub length of the gear is $2\frac{1}{2}$ in. Both shaft and key are to be made of the same material, having an allowable shear stress of 8000 psi. What are the minimum dimensions for the sides of the square key if 3490 in-lb of torque is to be transmitted?

Solution:

Equate the expression for the torque that the key can sustain from the standpoint of shear to 3490 in-lb and solve for b.

$rLbs_s = 3490$, $(1.4375/2)(2.5)(b)(8000) = 3490$, $b = 0.243$ in. Use a standard 0.25 in. square key.

4. A feather key is $\frac{1}{2}$ in. wide by $\frac{3}{8}$ in. deep and is to transmit 6000 in-lb of torque from a $1\frac{1}{2}$ in. diameter shaft. The steel key has an allowable stress in tension and compression of 16,000 psi and an allowable stress in shear of 8000 psi. Determine the required length of the key.

Solution:

Since the key is wider than it is deep, it will fail in compression before it will fail in shear.

$s_c(t/2)Lr = 6000$, $(16{,}000)(0.375/2)(L)(0.75) = 6000$, $L = 2.66$ in. Use $L = 2\frac{3}{4}$ in.

5. If the key in Problem 4 had been 3/8 in. wide and $\frac{1}{2}$ in. deep, what would have been the required length for the same load and material?

Solution:

In this case the key is weaker in shear than it is in compression.

$$s_s bLr = 6000, \quad (8000)(0.5)(L)(0.75) = 6000, \quad L = 2 \text{ in.}$$

6. A pin in a knuckle joint as shown in Fig.11-4(a) is subjected to an axial load of 20,270 lb. Assume that the thickness of the eye is to be 1.5 times the diameter of the pin. The allowable stress of the material in tension and compression due to bending is 9000 psi, and the allowable stress in shear is 4500 psi. The allowable bearing stress is 3000 psi. Determine the required pin diameter.

Solution:

Check the pin for (a) bending, (b) shear, and (c) bearing.

(*a*) **Bending:** $s_b = \frac{Mc}{I} = \frac{(FL/8)(d/2)}{\pi d^4/64}$, $9000 = \frac{(20,270 \times 1.5d/8)(d/2)}{\pi d^4/64}$, and

d = 2.08 in. required for bending.

(*b*) **Shear:** $s_s = \frac{F}{A} = \frac{F}{2\pi d^2/4}$, $4500 = \frac{20,270}{2\pi d^2/4}$, and

d = 1.7 in. required for shear.

(*c*) **Bearing:** $s_b = \frac{F}{Ld} = \frac{F}{(1.5d)d}$, $3000 = \frac{20,270}{1.5d^2}$, and

d = 2.1 in. required for bearing. Use $d = 2\frac{1}{8}$ in.

7. A splined connection in an automobile transmission consists of 10 splines cut in a $2\frac{1}{4}$ in. diameter shaft. The height of each spline is 0.214 in. and the keyways in the hub are 1.75 in. long. Determine the horsepower that may be transmitted at 2500 rpm if the allowable normal pressure on the splines is limited to 700 psi.

Solution:

Total surface area of splines = (0.214)(1.75)(10) = 3.74 in^2.

Torque = (3.74×700)(1.018) = 2660 in-lb. Power = (2660)(2500)/63,000 = 106 hp.

8. A Woodruff key $\frac{3}{16}$ in. by 1 in., is used to key a gear on a $1\frac{3}{16}$ in. shaft made of SAE 1035 steel. The key extends into the gear hub $\frac{3}{32}$ in. The key is made of SAE 1035 cold drawn steel (s_u = 92,000 psi and s_y = 78,000 psi). Determine the torque capacity of the shaft in accordance with the ASME Shafting Code. Calculate the torque capacity of the key using a factor of safety of 1.5 based upon the yield strength of the material.

Solution:

The allowable shear stress for the shaft is $0.18 s_u$ or $0.30 s_y$, whichever is the smaller. In this case the allowable stress will be s_s = 0.18(92,000) = 16,560 psi. Then the torque capacity of the shaft, using a 25% reduction for its keyway will be

$$T = 0.75\pi D^3 s_s/16 = 0.75\pi(1.1875)^3(16,560)/16 = 4100 \text{ in-lb}$$

The torque capacity of the key in shear, using a shear area A_s of 0.178 sq in., will be

$$T = s_s A_s r = \frac{(0.6)(78,000)}{1.5}(0.178)(\frac{1.1875}{2}) = 3290 \text{ in-lb}$$

The torque capacity of the key in compression will be (the key extends into the hub $t/2$)

$$T = s_c(\frac{t}{2})Lr = (\frac{78,000}{1.5})(\frac{0.1875}{2})(1)(\frac{1.1875}{2}) = 2900 \text{ in-lb}$$

Thus the torque capacity of the keyed connection is controlled by the torque capacity of the key in compression.

SUPPLEMENTARY PROBLEMS

9. Fig. 11-8 below shows a knuckle joint made from SAE 1020 steel. Assuming an allowable tensile stress of 15,000 psi, an allowable shear stress of 7500 psi, and an axial load of 5000 lb, determine:

(*1*) An algebraic expression for each of the following.

(*a*) Tensile stress at section A-A.
(*b*) Shearing stress in the pin.
(*c*) Bearing stress between the pin and rod.
(*d*) Bearing stress between the pin and yoke.
(*e*) Tensile stress across hole in the rod.
(*f*) Tensile stress across hole in the yoke.
(*g*) Bending stress in the pin.
(*h*) Tearout of the rod by the pin.
(*i*) Tearout of the yoke by the pin.

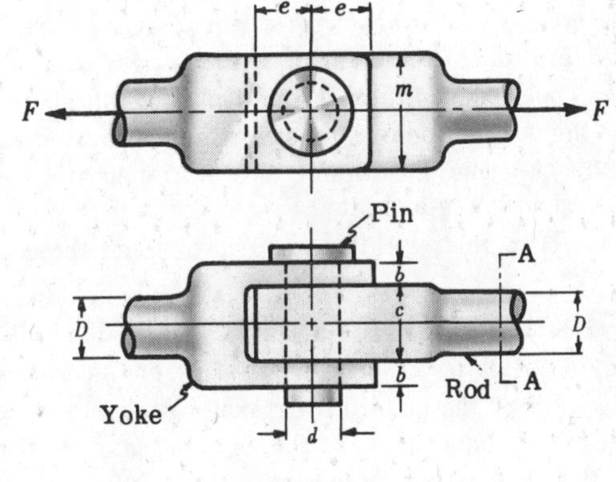

Fig. 11-8

Ans. (*a*) $s_t = 4F/\pi D^2$
(*b*) $s_s = 2F/\pi d^2$
(*c*) $s_c = F/dc$
(*d*) $s_c = F/2db$
(*e*) $s_t = F/[c(m-d)]$
(*f*) $s_t = F/[2b(m-d)]$
(*g*) $s_b = 4Fc/\pi d^3$
(*h*) $s_s = F/2ce$
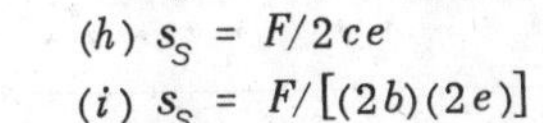
(*i*) $s_s = F/[(2b)(2e)]$

(*2*) The dimensions of the various parts.
Ans. $D = 0.652$ in., $d = 0.652$ in., $c = 0.66$ in., $b = 0.33$ in., $m = 1.306$ in., $e = 0.505$ in.

10. A key is sometimes used as a shear pin for economical reasons in case of extreme overloads. A shaft made of SAE 1045 steel with an ultimate tensile strength of 97,000 psi and a yield point in tension of 58,000 psi is transmitting maximum power in torsion. The shaft is 2 in. in diameter. A non-standard (for a 2 in. shaft) key $\frac{1}{4} \times \frac{1}{4}$ in. is to be used, if feasible. How long should the key be if it is to have 60% of the maximum strength capacity of the shaft? The key is to be made from SAE 1030 cold rolled stock, with an ultimate tensile strength of 80,000 psi and a yield point in tension of 55,000 psi.
Ans. $\frac{1}{4} \times \frac{1}{4} \times 3\frac{1}{2}$ in.

11. A sliding gear transmits 6000 in-lb torque to a length of $1\frac{1}{2}$ in. diameter shaft through a feather key $\frac{1}{2}$ in. wide by $\frac{3}{8}$ in. thick. Assuming the key to be made of the same material as the shaft and to be as strong as the shaft, what is the necessary hub length? Note that the hub length is not equal to the key length in this case.
Ans. Hub length = 1.77 in. based on compression

12. A square key, $\frac{1}{2} \times \frac{1}{2}$ in., is used to transmit power from a 2 in. shaft to a gear through a hub. A torque of 15,000 in-lb is applied to the gear. What is the necessary length of the key if the loading is steady? The key is made from cold rolled SAE 1035 steel with an ultimate tensile strength of 95,000 psi and a yield point of 60,000 psi. Use the ASME Code procedure for determining allowable stresses.
Ans. Length of key = 1.75 in. Use 2 in. since the length of the key should be at least equal to the shaft diameter for a satisfactory proportion.

13. If a key and shaft are made from the same material, determine the necessary length of the key for equal strength of the shaft and key. The key is rectangular, with a width of $D/4$ and a height of $3D/16$. The shaft is under torsion only. *Ans.* Key length = $1.57D$

14. A gear keyed to a 2 in. shaft is to transmit 12,000 in-lb of torque under steady load. A square key $\frac{1}{2} \times \frac{1}{2}$ in. having an allowable stress in shear of 9000 psi is to be used. How long should the key be? Would an SAE 1035 steel having an ultimate tensile strength of 80,000 psi and a yield point of 50,000 psi be satisfactory for the shaft? Base calculations on the ASME Shafting Code.

Ans. Length of key = 2.67 in. The shaft would be stressed below its allowable stress of 14,400 psi in accordance with the code.

15. Determine the horsepower capacity ratio for the two systems: a 1 in. diameter shaft with a $\frac{1}{4} \times \frac{1}{4} \times 2$ in. key and a 1 in. diameter shaft with a $\frac{1}{4}$ in. diameter pin key. The pin key is perpendicular to the axis of the shaft and passes through the center of the shaft. The stress concentration factor for the shaft is that given by the ASME Code. The stress concentration factor for the 1 in. diameter shaft with a $\frac{1}{4}$ in. radial hole is 1.75. Assume that torsion only is transmitted and that the material of the shaft is the same as used for the rectangular key and pin.

Ans. The shaft with the key can transmit three times as much power as the shaft with the pin key.

16. A $\frac{1}{2} \times 1\frac{1}{4}$ in. Woodruff key made of SAE 1035 cold drawn steel (s_u = 92,000 psi and s_y = 78,000 psi) is used to key a pulley on a $1\frac{3}{4}$ in. shaft made of the same material. Using a factor of safety of 1.5 based on the yield strength of the material, determine the torque capacity of the key in shear and in compression. The shear area is 0.296 sq in., and the key extends into the hub of the pulley 0.25/2 in. Calculate the torque capacity of the shaft in accordance with the ASME Shafting Code.

Ans. Capacity of the key in shear = 8075 in-lb
Capacity of the key in compression = 7172 in-lb
Capacity of the shaft = 13,100 in-lb

Chapter 12

Power Screws and Threaded Fasteners

POWER SCREWS provide a means for obtaining large mechanical advantage in such applications as screw jacks, clamps, presses, and aircraft control-surface actuators. Occasionally they are used in reverse for such applications as **push drills**.

THREADED FASTENERS include through bolts, stud bolts, cap screws, machine screws, set screws, and a variety of more special devices using the screw principle.

TERMINOLOGY OF SCREW THREADS is illustrated in Figure 12-1. Thread form is ordinarily described in axial section. The square and the Acme forms are commonly used for power screws (Fig. 12-2 below). For threaded fasteners, the Unified and American standard thread form has the basic shape and proportions shown in Fig. 12-3 below. This basic shape has maximum metal content. Variations for different classes of fit are made in the direction of greater metal removal. For detailed tables of standard sizes, thread series, and information on classes of fit see any standard Machine Design text or Mechanical Engineers handbook.

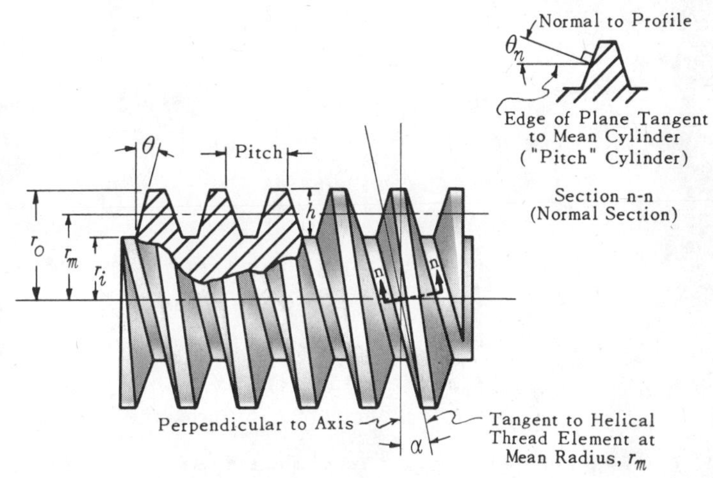

Fig. 12-1

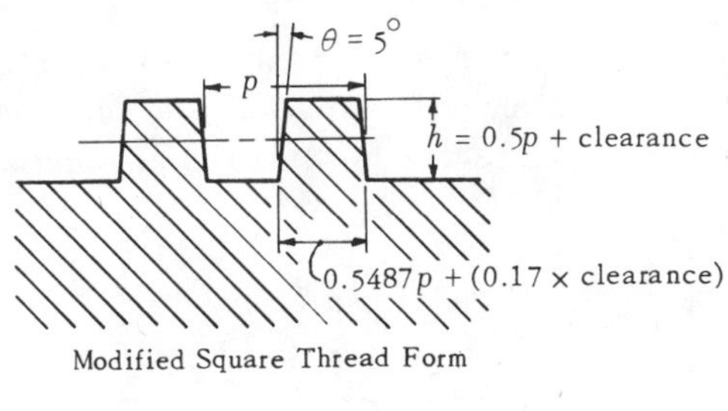

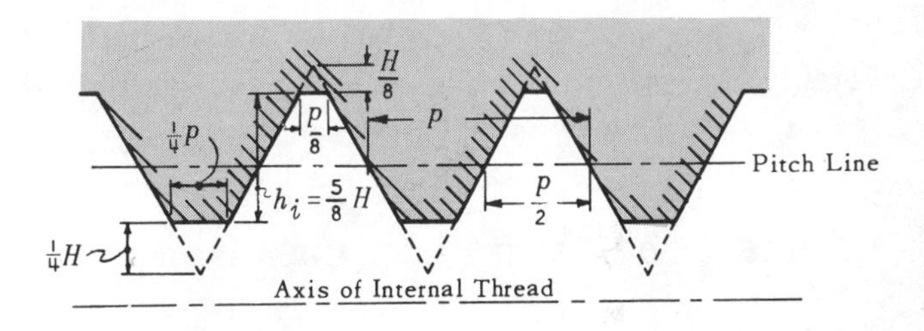

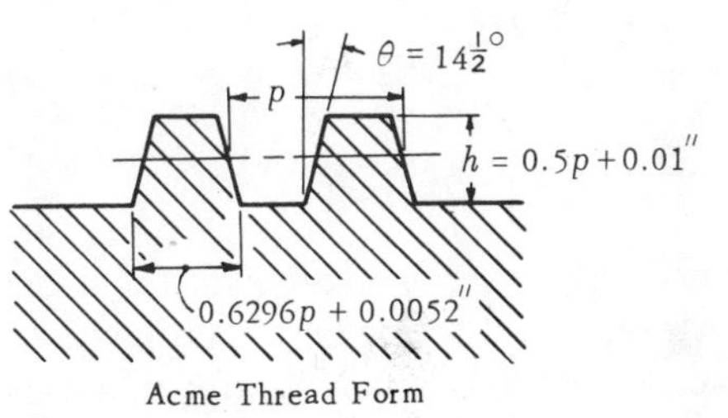

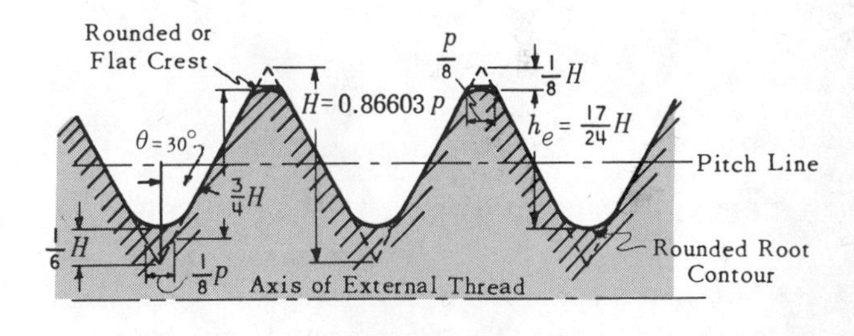

Fig. 12-2

Fig. 12-3

Pitch is the distance from a point on one thread to the corresponding point on the next adjacent thread, measured parallel to the axis.

Lead is the distance the screw would advance relative to the nut in one rotation. For a single-thread screw, lead is equal to pitch. For a double-thread screw, lead is equal to twice the pitch, etc.

Helix angle α is related to the lead and the mean radius r_m by the equation

$$\tan\alpha = \frac{\text{lead}}{2\pi r_m}$$

In some calculations we shall make use of the angle θ_n measuring the slope of the thread profile in the normal section. This is related to the angle θ in the axial section and to the helix angle as follows:

$$\tan\theta_n = \tan\theta\cos\alpha$$

Note: Where $\cos\theta_n$ appears in the equations to follow, it is frequently replaced by $\cos\theta$. This yields an approximate equation but, for the usual small values of α, introduces no great error.

TURNING MOMENT AND AXIAL LOAD are related to each other through the following equation for advance **against load** (or *raising* the load):

$$T = W\left[r_m\left(\frac{\tan\alpha + f/\cos\theta_n}{1 - f\tan\alpha/\cos\theta_n}\right) + f_c r_c\right]$$

where

T = torque applied to turn screw or nut, whichever is being rotated

W = load parallel to screw axis

r_m = mean thread radius

r_c = effective radius of rubbing surface against which load bears, called *collar radius*

f = coefficient of friction between screw and nut threads

f_c = coefficient of friction at *collar*

α = helix angle of thread at mean radius

θ_n = angle between tangent to tooth profile (on the loaded side) and a radial line, measured in plane normal to thread helix at mean radius.

The torque required to advance the screw (or nut) **in the direction of the load** (or *lowering* the load) is

$$T = W\left[r_m\left(\frac{-\tan\alpha + f/\cos\theta_n}{1 + f\tan\alpha/\cos\theta_n}\right) + f_c r_c\right]$$

This torque may be either positive or negative. If positive, work must be done to advance the screw. If negative, the meaning is that, for equilibrium, the torque must retard rotation, i.e. the axial load alone will cause rotation (the *push drill* situation). In this case the screw is said to be *overhauling*.

EFFICIENCY OF A SCREW MECHANISM is the ratio of work output to work input.

$$\text{Efficiency} = \frac{100(W)(\text{lead})}{2\pi T}\,\% = \frac{100\tan\alpha}{\left(\dfrac{\tan\alpha + f/\cos\theta_n}{1 - f\tan\alpha/\cos\theta_n}\right) + \dfrac{f_c r_c}{r_m}}\,\%$$

STRESSES IN THE THREAD are estimated by considering the thread to be a short cantilever beam projecting from the root cylinder. (See Fig. 12-4 below) The beam load is taken to be the axial screw load W, presumed concentrated at the mean radius, i.e. at one-half the thread depth h. The beam width is the length of thread (measured at mean radius) subject to load.

With these assumptions the bending stress at the root of the thread is, very nearly,

$$s_b = \frac{3Wh}{2\pi n r_m b^2}$$

and the mean transverse shear stress is

$$s_s = \frac{W}{2\pi n r_m b}$$

where n is the number of thread turns subject to load and b is the width of thread section at the root.

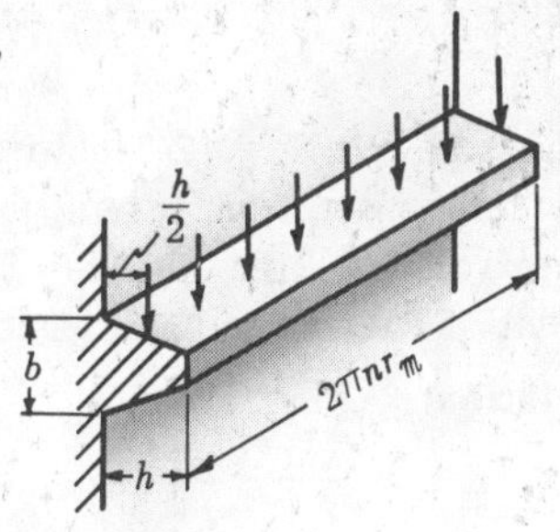

Fig. 12-4

The stress picture at the junction of the thread and root cylinder is actually very complicated, and the above expressions are only rough approximations which serve as design guides. In place of r_m in these expressions, many designers will use r_i for the screw and r_o for the nut, a somewhat better approximation in that it recognizes the nut threads to be less likely to *strip* than the screw threads.

BEARING PRESSURE between the surfaces of screw and nut threads may be a critical factor in design, especially for power screws. It is given approximately by

$$P = \frac{W}{2\pi n r_m h}$$

This estimate will be on the low side because (*1*) clearances between root and crest of internal and external threads mean that load is not carried over full depth h and (*2*) load is not uniformly distributed over thread length.

STRESSES IN THE ROOT CYLINDER of the screw may be estimated by considering loads and torques carried by the bare cylinder (neglecting strengthening effect of thread). The torsional shear stress is

$$s_s = \frac{2T}{\pi r_i^3}$$

where r_i is the root radius of the screw. T is the appropriate torque, i.e. the torque to which the section under consideration is subjected. This may be the total applied torque, only the collar friction torque, or only the *screw* torque (total minus collar friction torque). Each case must be examined carefully to see which applies.

The direct stress, which may be either tensile or compressive, is

$$s_n = \frac{W}{\text{root area}} = \frac{W}{\pi r_i^2}$$

A modification of the above formula is sometimes used in calculations on threaded fastenings to account approximately for the strengthening effect of the threads. Basically the modification consists of presuming the cylinder to be larger in radius than it really is. (See Chapter 13.) Then

$$s_n = \frac{W}{\text{stress area}}$$

Stress areas, as well as root areas, are tabulated in many textbooks and handbooks.

SOLVED PROBLEMS

1. The screw in Fig.12-5 below is operated by a torque applied to the lower end. The nut is loaded and prevented from turning by guides. Assume friction in the ball bearing to be negligible. The screw has a 2 in. outside diameter and a triple Acme thread, 3 threads per inch. Thread coefficient of friction is 0.15. Determine the load which could be raised by a torque T of 400 in-lb.

Solution:

$$T = W\left[r_m\left(\frac{\tan\alpha + f/\cos\theta_n}{1 - f\tan\alpha/\cos\theta_n}\right) + f_c r_c\right]$$

where:

$$\text{thread depth} = 0.18 \text{ in.}$$

$$r_m = 1.00 - 0.18/2 = 0.91 \text{ in.}$$

$$\tan\alpha = \frac{\text{lead}}{2\pi r_m} = \frac{1.00}{2\pi(0.91)} = 0.175$$

$$\alpha = 9.92^\circ$$

$$\theta = 14.5^\circ \text{ for Acme thread}$$

$$\tan\theta_n = (\tan\theta)(\cos\alpha)$$

$$= (\tan 14.5^\circ)(\cos 9.92^\circ) = 0.255$$

$$\theta_n = 14.2^\circ.$$

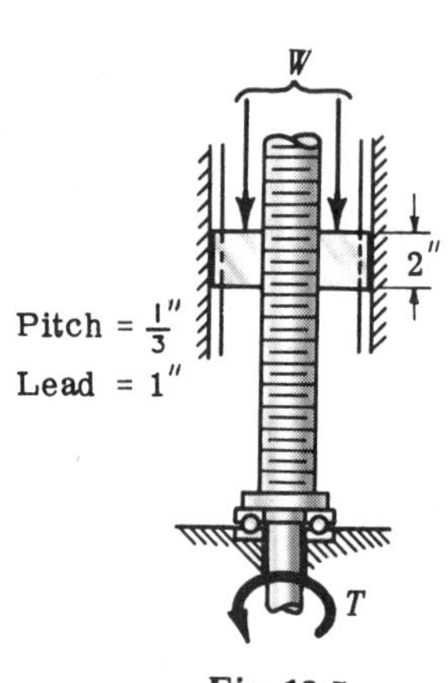

Fig. 12-5

Note that the difference between θ_n and θ is so slight that we might as well use θ. Then

$$400 = W\left[0.91\left(\frac{0.175 + 0.15/0.968}{1 - (0.15)(0.175)/0.968}\right) + 0\right] \quad \text{or} \quad W = 1290 \text{ lb}$$

2. Would the screw of Problem 1 be overhauling?

Solution:

The screw will be overhauling if the torque in the following equation is negative.

$$T = W\left[r_m\left(\frac{-\tan\alpha + f/\cos\theta_n}{1 + f\tan\alpha/\cos\theta_n}\right) + f_c r_c\right]$$

Since $f_c = 0$ for this problem, T will be negative if $(-\tan\alpha + f/\cos\theta_n)$ is negative.

From Problem 1, $\tan\alpha = 0.175$ and $f/\cos\theta_n = 0.15/0.968 = 0.155$. Hence the screw will overhaul, i.e. to prevent screw rotation when a load W is applied, a holding torque must be applied.

3. For the screw of Problem 1 determine the average bearing pressure between the screw and nut thread surfaces.

Solution:

$$P = \frac{W}{2\pi n r_m h} = \frac{1290}{2\pi(6)(0.91)(0.18)} = 210 \text{ psi}$$

where $n = \dfrac{\text{nut length}}{\text{pitch}} = \dfrac{2}{1/3} = 6$ thread turns sharing the load.

4. Derive the equation for torque T required to advance a screw **against** a load W.

Solution:

Refer to Fig.12-6 below. The total normal force exerted by the threads of the nut against the threads of the screw is F_n. This is distributed over the length of thread in engagement and over the thread depth, but for the purposes of this analysis may be considered concentrated at a point at the mean screw radius, r_m.

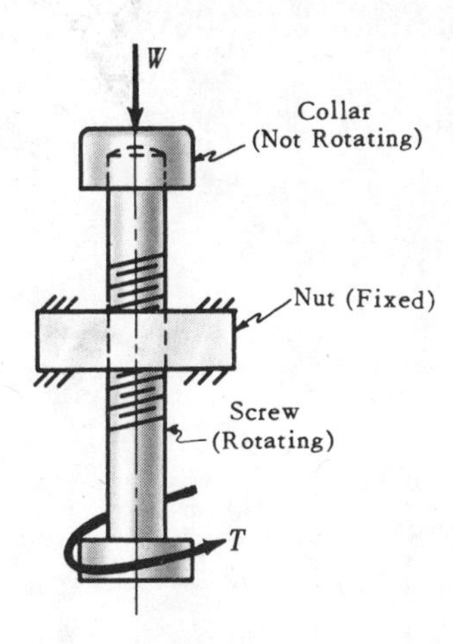

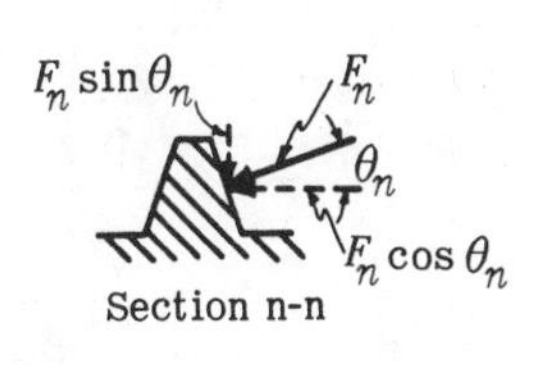

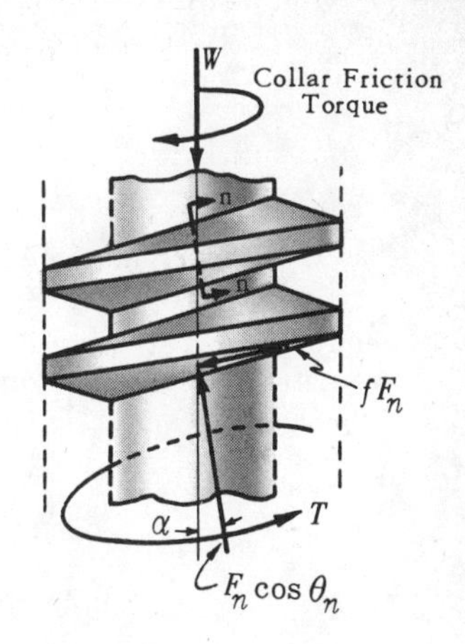

Fig. 12-6

The normal force vector F_n appears in true length in the normal section. Component $F_n \cos\theta_n$ is tangent to the pitch cylinder and at angle α (helix angle) with the screw axis. Component $F_n \sin\theta_n$ is radial.

The friction force is fF_n, acting along the thread helix.

Also acting on the screw is the axial load W, the collar friction torque $Wf_c r_c$, and the applied torque T.

Summing forces parallel to the screw axis yields

$$W - F_n \cos\theta_n \cos\alpha + fF_n \sin\alpha = 0$$

Summing moments around the screw axis yields

$$T - F_n r_m \cos\theta_n \sin\alpha - fF_n r_m \cos\alpha - Wf_c r_c = 0$$

Eliminating F_n between these two equations yields

$$T = W\left[r_m\left(\frac{\tan\alpha + f/\cos\theta_n}{1 - f\tan\alpha/\cos\theta_n}\right) + f_c r_c\right]$$

5. The following data apply to the C-clamp of Fig. 12-7.

American Standard Threads
13 threads per inch (single-threaded)
Outside diameter = $\frac{1}{2}$ in.
Root diameter = 0.4001 in.
Root area = 0.1257 in^2
Coefficient of thread friction = 0.12 (= f)
Coefficient of collar friction = 0.25 (= f_c)
Mean collar radius = 0.25 in.
Load W = 1000 lb
Operator can comfortably exert a force of 20 lb at the end of the handle.

(*a*) What length of handle, L, is needed?

(*b*) What is the maximum shear stress in the body of the screw and where does this exist?

(*c*) What is the bearing pressure P on the threads?

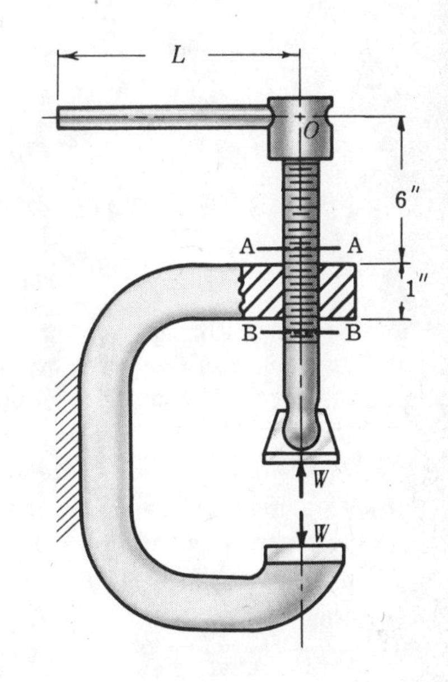

Fig. 12-7

Solution:

(*a*) The torque required is

$$T = W\left[r_m\left(\frac{\tan\alpha + f/\cos\theta_n}{1 - f\tan\alpha/\cos\theta_n}\right) + f_c r_c\right]$$

where $r_m = \frac{1}{4}(0.5000 + 0.4001) = 0.225$ in., $\tan\alpha = \dfrac{\text{lead}}{2\pi r_m} = \dfrac{1/13}{2\pi(0.225)} = 0.0544.$

We shall take $\theta_n = \theta = 30°$, since the helix angle is so small. Then

$$T = 1000\,[0.225\,(\frac{0.0544 + 0.12/0.866}{1-(0.12)(0.0544)/0.866}) + (0.25)(0.25)\,]$$

$$= 43.8 \text{ (screw torque)} + 62.5 \text{ (collar torque)} = 106.3 \text{ in-lb}$$

To develop this torque with a 20 lb force, we need $L = 106.3/20 = 5.32$ in.

(*b*) Section A-A, just above the nut, is subjected to torque and bending. Section B-B, just below the nut, is subjected to torque and direct compressive load. It will be necessary to check both sections for maximum shear stress.

At A-A

$$\text{Torsional shear stress, } s_s = \frac{Tr}{J} = \frac{(106.3)(0.200)}{0.00251} = 8470 \text{ psi}$$

where $T = 106.3$ in-lb (from above), $r = r_i = 0.200$ in., $J = \frac{1}{2}\pi r_i^4 = 0.00251$ in^4.

$$\text{Bending stress, } s_t = \frac{M_b c}{I} = \frac{(120)(0.200)}{0.00126} = 19{,}100 \text{ psi}$$

where $M_b = (20)(6) = 120$ in-lb, $c = r_i = 0.200$ in., $I = \frac{1}{4}\pi r_i^4 = 0.00126$ in^4.

$$\text{Maximum shear stress, } \tau(\max) = \sqrt{(\tfrac{1}{2}s_t)^2 + s_s^2} = 12{,}750 \text{ psi}$$

At B-B

This section is subjected to the collar friction torque $W f_c r_c$. Hence the torsional shear stress is

$$s_s = \frac{(W f_c r_c) r_i}{J} = \frac{(1000)(0.25)(0.25)(0.200)}{0.00251} = 4970 \text{ psi}$$

The direct compressive stress is $s_c = \dfrac{W}{A} = \dfrac{1000}{0.1257} = 7960$ psi.

Hence the maximum shear stress is $\tau(\max) = \sqrt{(7960/2)^2 + (4970)^2} = 6370$ psi

Our conclusion, then, is that the maximum shear stress occurs at section A-A and is 12,750 psi.

(*c*)
$$P = \frac{W}{2\pi n r_m h} = \frac{1000}{2\pi(13)(0.225)(0.050)} = 1090 \text{ psi}$$

where $n = \dfrac{\text{nut length}}{\text{pitch}} = \dfrac{1}{1/13} = 13$ threads, and $h = r_o - r_i = 0.250 - 0.200 = 0.050$ in.

6. It is proposed to make a screw jack in accordance with the sketch of Fig. 12-8. Neither screw rotates. Outside screw diameter is 2 in. Thread is square (depth = $\frac{1}{2}$ pitch), single thread, and coefficient of thread friction is estimated to be 0.15.

(*a*) What would be the efficiency of the jack?

(*b*) What load can be raised if the shear stress in the bodies of the screws is limited to 4000 psi? Assume torque applied to nut in such a way as to cause no bending stress in the lower screw.

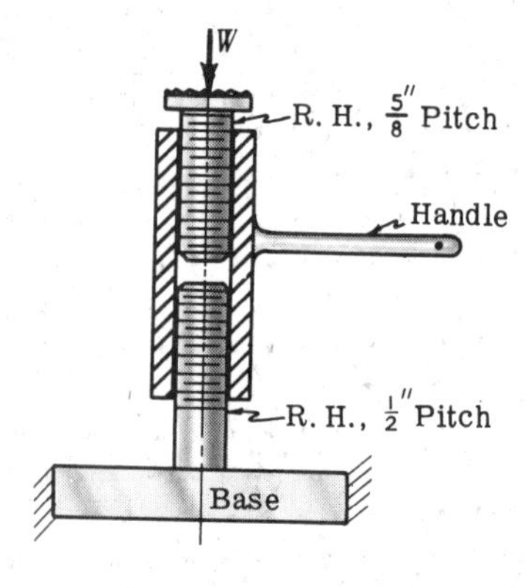

Fig. 12-8

Solution:

(*a*) A differential screw action is involved. In one turn of the nut the load is raised an amount equal to the difference in leads of the two screws. Hence the output work in one turn is

Output work per turn $= W$ (lead of upper screw − lead of lower screw) $= W(\frac{5}{8} - \frac{1}{2}) = W/8$ in-lb

No collar friction is involved since there is no rotation of the screw to which the load is applied.

To turn the nut relative to the upper screw requires the following torque T':

$$T' = W\left[r_m'\left(\frac{\tan\alpha' + f/\cos\theta_n'}{1-f\tan\alpha'/\cos\theta_n'}\right)\right] = W\left[\frac{27}{32}\left(\frac{0.118 + 0.15}{1-(0.15)(0.118)}\right)\right] = 0.230W \text{ in-lb (upper screw)}$$

where $r_m' = r_o' - \dfrac{\text{thread depth}}{2} = 1 - \dfrac{5}{32} = \dfrac{27}{32}$ in., $\tan\alpha' = \dfrac{\text{lead}}{2\pi r_m'} = \dfrac{5/8}{2\pi(27/32)} = 0.118$

To turn the nut relative to the lower screw requires the following torque T''. Note that in this case the nut advances in the direction of the load applied to the nut.

$$T'' = W\left[r_m''\left(\frac{-\tan\alpha'' + f/\cos\theta_n''}{1 + f\tan\alpha''/\cos\theta_n''}\right)\right] = W\left[\frac{7}{8}\left(\frac{-0.0910 + 0.15}{1 + (0.15)(0.0910)}\right)\right] = 0.051W \text{ in-lb (lower screw)}$$

where $r_m'' = r_o'' - \dfrac{\text{thread depth}}{2} = 1 - \dfrac{1}{8} = \dfrac{7}{8}$ in., $\tan\alpha'' = \dfrac{\text{lead}}{2\pi r_m''} = \dfrac{1/2}{2\pi(7/8)} = 0.0910$,

and we take $\theta_n'' = \theta'' = 0°$.

Hence the total torque T to be applied to the nut is $T = T' + T'' = 0.281W$ in-lb.

$$\text{Efficiency} = \frac{\text{output work per turn}}{\text{input work per turn}} = \frac{W/8}{2\pi(0.281W)} = 0.071 = 7.1\%$$

(*b*) The upper screw will be critical, since it is subjected to the larger torque and has the smaller root area. There is a direct compressive stress s_c and a torsional shear stress s_s to be taken into account.

$$s_c = \frac{W}{\text{root area}} = \frac{W}{\pi r_i^2} = \frac{W}{\pi(11/16)^2} = 0.674W$$

where $r_i = r_o - \text{thread depth} = 1 - \frac{5}{16} = \frac{11}{16}$ in.

$$s_s = \frac{Tr}{J} = \frac{(0.230W)(11/16)}{0.350} = 0.452W$$

where $r = r_i = \frac{11}{16}$ in., $J = \frac{1}{2}\pi r_i^4 = 0.350$ in^4, and $T = T'$ of part (*a*) $= 0.230W$.

$$\text{Maximum shear stress, } \tau(\text{max}) = \sqrt{(s_c/2)^2 + s_s^2}$$

$$4000 = \sqrt{(0.674W/2)^2 + (0.452W)^2} \quad \text{or} \quad W = 7100 \text{ lb}$$

7. A hand-operated valve grinding device is to be operated by forcing a nut downward along the stem which is provided with helical grooves square in axial section. The *overhauling* action thereby causes the stem to rotate and turn the valve in its seat either by means of a screwdriver tip or by means of a suction cup, depending on the type of valve. Assume the following data in addition to that shown on the sketch, Fig.12-9 below.

Coefficient of friction f between nut and stem = 0.10.
Coefficient of friction f_c between valve and seat = 0.35.
Mean friction radius between valve and seat = 1.0 in.

Determine the minimum helix angle α which could be used in the device under the conditions assumed.

Solution:

The helix angle must be at least large enough to guarantee *overhauling* action. This would be the value which makes $T = 0$ in the equation

$$T = W\left[r_m\left(\frac{-\tan\alpha + f/\cos\theta_n}{1 + f\tan\alpha/\cos\theta_n}\right) + f_c r_c\right]$$

Then $\tan\alpha = \dfrac{r_m f + r_c f_c \cos\theta_n}{r_m \cos\theta_n - r_c f_c f} = \dfrac{(0.17)(0.1) + (1.0)(0.35)(1)}{(0.17)(1) - (1.0)(0.35)(0.1)} = 2.72$ and $\alpha(\text{min}) = 69.8°$.

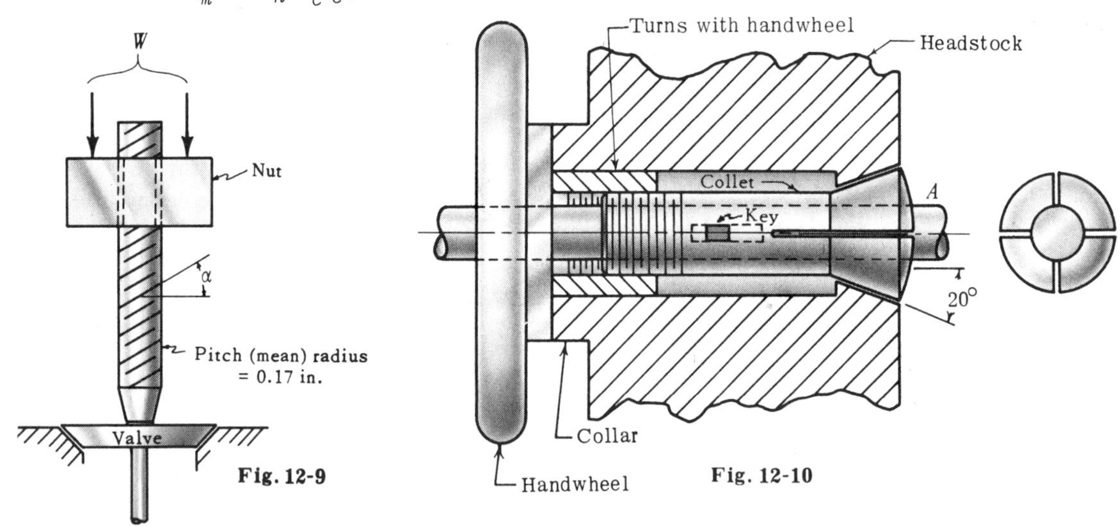

Fig. 12-9

Fig. 12-10

8. The collet chuck in Fig.12-10 above is operated by turning the handwheel to draw the collet into the conical seat in the headstock. This tightens the four collet pieces against the workpiece, clamping it in place. Assume the following data:

Coefficient of friction between collet and conical seat = 0.20.
Coefficient of friction at collar = 0.15.
Coefficient of thread friction = 0.10.
Effective radius of collar, r_c = 0.75 in.
Thread, 60°– V, 1 in. outside diameter, 0.84 in. root diameter, and 16 threads per inch.

If each collet piece is to exert a force of 100 lb against the workpiece, what torque is required on the handwheel?

Solution:

If we neglect the stiffness of the collet pieces, then a freebody sketch of one collet piece will be as shown in Fig.12-11.

W is the total axial force on the collet. P is the normal force of the conical seat against the collet piece. We may write the following equations for equilibrium of forces parallel and perpendicular to the collet axis:

$$W/4 = P \sin 20° + 0.20P \cos 20°$$
$$P \cos 20° - 0.20P \sin 20° = 100$$

Simultaneous solution yields $W = 243$ lb. This is the axial force which must be developed by the screw mechanism.

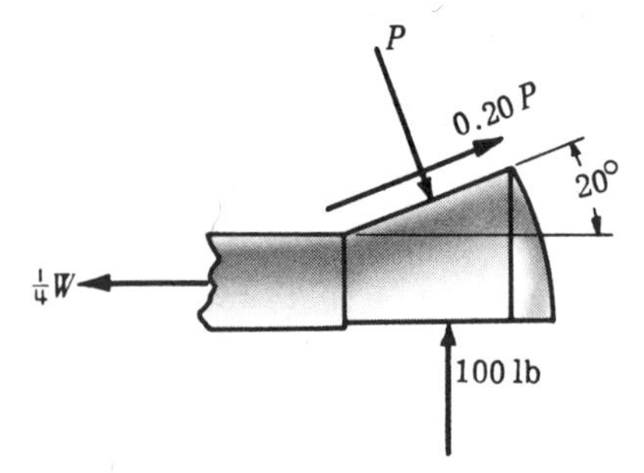

Fig. 12-11

The torque required on the handwheel (the nut of the screw mechanism) is

$$T = W\left[r_m\left(\frac{\tan\alpha + f/\cos\theta_n}{1 - f\tan\alpha/\cos\theta_n}\right) + f_c r_c\right]$$

where $r_m = \dfrac{1 + 0.84}{4} = 0.460$ in. and $\tan\alpha = \dfrac{\text{lead}}{2\pi r_m} = \dfrac{1/16}{2\pi(0.460)} = 0.0216.$

Using also $\theta_n = \theta = 30°$ and the given values of f_c and r_c, we obtain $T = 43$ in-lb.

9. Estimate the maximum wrench torque which can be applied in tightening a $\frac{3}{4}$ in. bolt if the shear stress in the body of the bolt is not to exceed 20,000 psi.

Outside bolt diameter = 0.7500 in.

Root diameter = 0.6201 in.

Thread section has 60° included angle (θ = 30°). Threads per inch = 10.

Effective friction radius under nut, r_c = 0.50 in.

Thread and collar friction coefficient estimated at 0.10.

Solution:

Maximum shear stress in body of bolt, $\tau(\max) = \sqrt{(\frac{1}{2}s_t)^2 + s_s^2}$

where s_t = direct tensile stress $= \dfrac{W}{\pi r_i^2} = \dfrac{W}{\pi(0.3100)^2} = 3.31\,W$

$s_s = \dfrac{T'r_i}{J} = \dfrac{T'r_i}{\frac{1}{2}\pi r_i^4} = 21.35\,T'$, and

T' = screw torque = wrench torque − collar friction torque.

However
$$T = W\left[r_m\left(\frac{\tan\alpha + f/\cos\theta_n}{1 - f\tan\alpha/\cos\theta_n}\right) + r_c f_c\right]$$

where $r_m = \dfrac{0.7500 + 0.6201}{4} = 0.3425$ in., $\tan\alpha = \dfrac{\text{lead}}{2\pi r_m} = \dfrac{1/10}{2\pi(0.3425)} = 0.0465$

$f = f_c = 0.10$, $r_c = 0.50$ in.

Taking $\theta_n = \theta = 30°$, we have

$$T = W\left[0.3425\left(\frac{0.0465 + 0.10/0.866}{1-(0.10)(0.0465)/0.866}\right) + (0.50)(0.10)\right]$$

$$= 0.056\,W + 0.050\,W = 0.106\,W$$

Then $s_s = 21.35\,T' = (21.35)(0.056\,W) = 1.195\,W$.

Solving now for W in the $\tau(\max)$ equation, W = 9800 lb.

Hence the wrench torque $T = 0.106\,W = (0.106)(9800) = 1040$ in-lb.

SUPPLEMENTARY PROBLEMS

10. The following data apply to the machinists clamp shown in Fig.12-12.

Outside diameter of screw = $\frac{1}{2}$ in.
Root diameter = 0.4350 in.
Pitch (single thread) = 0.0500 in.
Collar friction radius = 0.200 in.
Collar friction coefficient = 0.15
Screw friction coefficient = 0.15
Assume that the machinist can comfortably exert a maximum force of 30 lb on the handle.

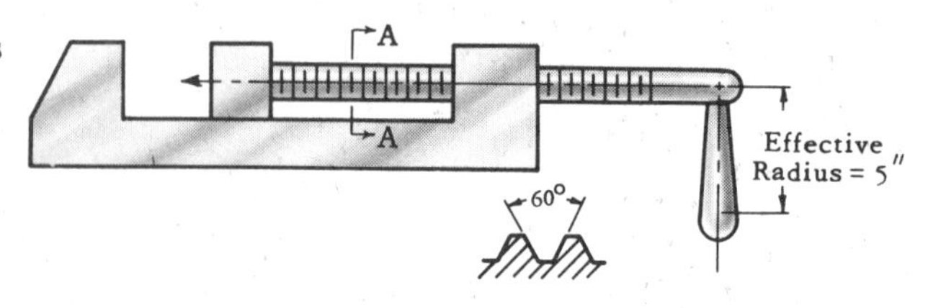

Fig. 12-12

Determine (*a*) the clamping force developed between the jaws of the clamp
(*b*) the efficiency of the clamp
(*c*) the torque in the screw body at section A-A

Ans. (*a*) 1905 lb, (*b*) 10%, (*c*) 57 in-lb

11. Derive the expression for torque required to advance a screw or nut *in the direction of the load.* (Hint: Use a sketch like Fig.12-6, but reverse the senses of collar friction torque T and friction force fF_n.)

12. Four different situations are shown in Fig.12-13 below, as regards location of load and torque application. In each case the axial load W is 1000 lb, the externally applied torque is 90 in-lb and the collar friction torque is 30 in-lb.

(1) For each case state the value of the axial force and the torque to be used in calculating stresses in the body of the screw for a section just above the nut.

(2) Same, but for a section just below the nut.

Ans. (1)		*Ans.* (2)	
(*a*)	1000 lb, 60 in-lb	(*a*)	0 lb, 0 in-lb
(*b*)	1000 lb, 30 in-lb	(*b*)	0 lb, 90 in-lb
(*c*)	0 lb, 90 in-lb	(*c*)	1000 lb, 30 in-lb
(*d*)	0 lb, 0 in-lb	(*d*)	1000 lb, 60 in-lb

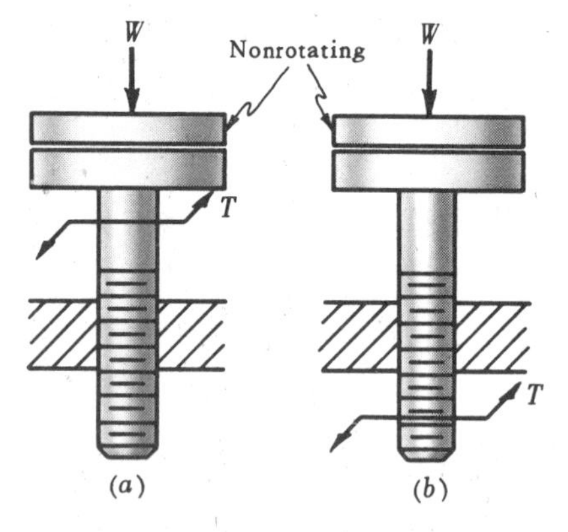

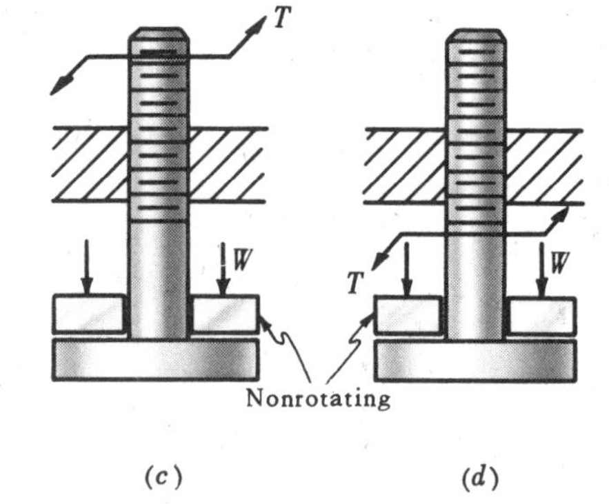

Fig. 12-13

13. A 1 in. bolt is tightened to develop an initial axial force of 10,000 lb. Using the data listed below, determine
(*a*) the necessary tightening torque to be applied to the nut
(*b*) the maximum shear stress in the body of the bolt
Outside bolt diameter, 1 in.; root diameter, 0.8376 in.; 8 threads per in.; $f_c = f = 0.15$; $r_c = 0.625$ in.
Ans. (*a*) 1938 in-lb, (*b*) 12,650 psi

14. Using data of Problem 13, what coefficient of friction is needed under the bolt head in order that it not be necessary to hold the head while tightening? Assume the same effective friction radius as for the nut.
Ans. 0.16

15. In a large gate valve used in a high pressure water line, the gate weighs 1500 lb and friction force due to water pressure, resisting opening, is 500 lb. The valve stem is non-rotating and is raised by a rotating wheel with internal threads acting as a rotating nut on the valve stem. The wheel presses against a supporting collar of $1\frac{5}{8}$ in. inside diameter and 3 in. outside diameter. The valve stem is fitted with 3 square threads (single threaded) per inch. Assuming the coefficient of friction for the collar 0.25 and for the threads 0.10, determine

(*a*) the torque that must be applied to the wheel to raise the valve gate
(*b*) the efficiency of the screw and collar mechanism
(*c*) the maximum shear stress in the body of the screw

Ans. (*a*) 818 in-lb, (*b*) 13%, (*c*) 1215 psi

16. A turnbuckle is used to tighten a wire rope. The threads are single right and left hand and square in section. The outside diameter of the screw is $1\frac{1}{2}$ in. and the pitch is $\frac{1}{3}$ in. The coefficient of friction between the screws and nuts is 0.15. What torque on the turnbuckle is necessary if the rope is to be tightened to a tension of 2000 lb? *Ans.* 618 in-lb

17. A steel screw driving a bronze nut is to develop an axial load of 80,000 lb in an extrusion press. The screw has an outside diameter of 4 in. and a single square thread (depth = $\frac{1}{2}$ pitch) with a lead of $\frac{2}{3}$ in. The length of nut is to be chosen so that the bearing pressure between screw and nut threads will not exceed 2300 psi and the shearing stress on the nut threads will not exceed 4000 psi. Determine a suitable nut length. *Ans.* 6 in. (bearing pressure controls)

18. Fig.12-14 shows a type of window latch. Assuming the coefficients of friction to be 0.3 and 0.2 on the ramp and collar respectively, what force F on the handle is required to develop a force of 70 lb clamping the window? *Ans.* 10 lb

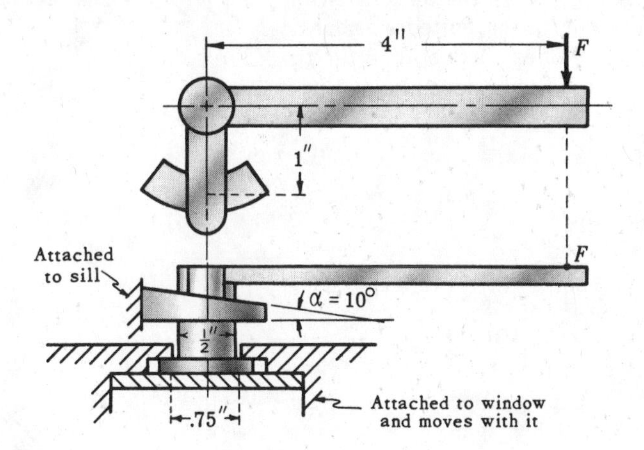

Fig. 12-14

Chapter 13

Bolt Loading

BOLTED JOINTS LOADED IN TENSION are frequently encountered in the design of fasteners. The bolt is subjected to an initial load in tension, W_1, often followed by the application of an external load, W_2, as shown in Fig. 13-1. The resultant load W on the bolt is determined by

$$W = W_1 + W_2\left(\frac{m_1 + m_2 + m_3 + \ldots + m_n}{b + m_1 + m_2 + m_3 + \ldots + m_n}\right)$$

or

$$W = W_1 + W_2\left(\frac{m}{m+b}\right)$$

where W_1 = initial load on bolt due to tightening, lb

W_2 = external load, lb

W = resultant load on bolt due to W_1 and W_2, lb

m_1, m_2 and m_3 are defined as the deflection in in. per lb of load for the bolted members, m_1, m_2 and m_3. These symbols refer to all parts in the bolted assembly, including the gasket.

m = the sum of m_1, m_2, etc.

b is defined as the deflection in in. per lb of load for the bolt.

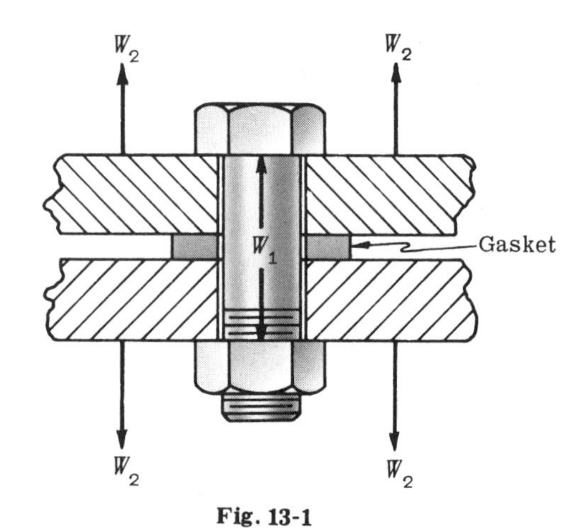

Fig. 13-1

SEPARATION OF THE BOLTED JOINT will occur if $W_2 = W$. The equation given above is that of a straight line having slope $m/(m+b)$ and ordinate intercept W_1. The plot of this line, as shown in Fig. 13-2, provides a quick method for determining when separation of the members will occur. Line AC is the extreme situation of zero slope which occurs when the members have practically no deflection per lb of load as compared to the bolt, i.e. $m/b = 0$. Line AB represents the extreme situation when the bolt has practically no deflection per lb of load as compared to the members, i.e. $b/m = 0$. The actual situation occurs between these two extremes, as indicated by lines AD and DE.

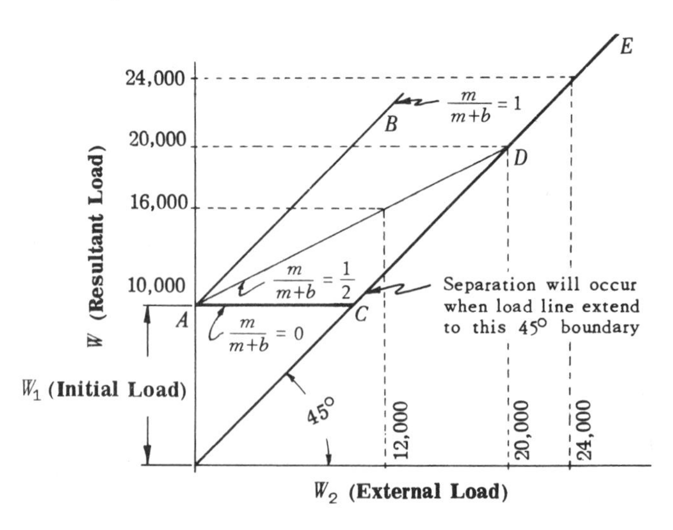

Fig. 13-2

THE INITIAL TENSION IN THE BOLT due to tightening may result from the use of a torque wrench or may depend upon the judgment of an experienced mechanic. Experimental results indicate that the initial bolt load W_1 in a bolt tightened by an experienced mechanic may be estimated by

$$W_1 = Kd$$

where d = nominal bolt diameter and K ranges from about 10,000 to 16,000.

If a torque wrench is used to tighten the bolt, the value of the initial bolt load W_1 may be approximated by

$$W_1 = T/0.2d$$

where T = applied tightening torque and d = nominal bolt diameter. The above equation is obtained by using the screw thread torque equation (Chapter 12), neglecting the helix angle, assuming a coefficient of friction 0.15 for both threads and nut, and assuming the friction collar radius of the nut is approximately 2/3 of the pitch diameter of the bolt. For well lubricated threads, the initial bolt load might be as much as double that indicated by the above expression. The use of the screw thread torque equation is preferred to the above approximation.

The initial bolt load may also be calculated from the theoretical expression

$$T = \text{thread torque} + \text{collar torque} = W_1 r_m \left(\frac{\tan\alpha + f/\cos\theta_n}{1 - f\tan\alpha/\cos\theta_n}\right) + W_1 f_c r_c$$

where
r_m = mean radius of thread, in. $\quad$ α = helix angle
f = coefficient of thread friction $\quad$ θ_n = one-half of thread angle
f_c = coefficient of collar friction $\quad$ r_c = collar friction radius, in.

STRESSES INDUCED IN TENSION BOLTS are the result of torsional shear combined with resultant axial bolt load. The maximum shear stress in a tension bolt may be calculated by

$$\tau(\text{max}) = \sqrt{(W_1/2A_r)^2 + (16T_f/d_r^3\pi)^2}$$

where
$\tau(\text{max})$ = maximum shear stress in the body of the screw, psi
A_r = root area, in^2
T_f = thread torque, in-lb
d_r = root diameter of thread, in.
W = resultant axial bolt load, lb.

For a less conservative design A_r and d_r may be replaced by A_s and d_s based on the stress area A_s, which is a mean of the average pitch diameter area and the average minor diameter area for Class 3A tolerances, and $d_s = \sqrt{4A_s/\pi}$.

In general for static loading, the maximum shear stress induced in the bolt should not exceed about 3/4 of the shear yield strength of the material; however, there are times, especially in the case of small bolts ($\frac{1}{2}$ in. and less), where the yield point is exceeded. For variable loading the bolt should be designed for endurance. It should also be noted that bolts usually lose their initial torsional stress when they are subjected to dynamic loading. This is due to the fact that the bolt head and/or nut will slip back if there is insufficient frictional collar resistance.

IMPACT STRESSES result when bolts are subjected to suddenly applied or impact loads. The bolt has to absorb the energy of impact.

$$U = \tfrac{1}{2}F\delta$$

where F = force caused by impact, lb; δ = deformation caused by impact, in.; U = energy of impact, in-lb.

REQUIRED HEIGHT OF THE NUT may be estimated assuming that each turn of the thread supports an equal part of the resultant load W, as shown in Fig. 13-3.

The strength of the bolt in tension should equal the strength of the threads in shear. For the bolt in tension, $W = \frac{1}{4}\pi d_r^2 s_t$; for the threads in shear, $W = \pi d_r h s_s$; for ductile materials, $s_s = \frac{1}{2} s_t$. Then

$$\tfrac{1}{4}\pi d_r^2 = \tfrac{1}{2}\pi d_r h \qquad \text{or} \qquad h = \tfrac{1}{2} d_r$$

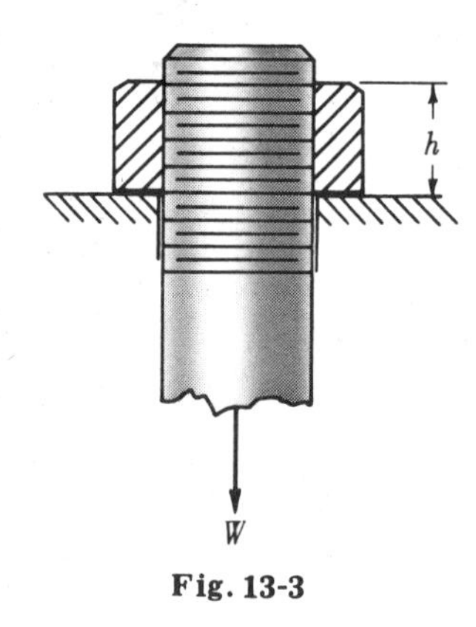

Fig. 13-3

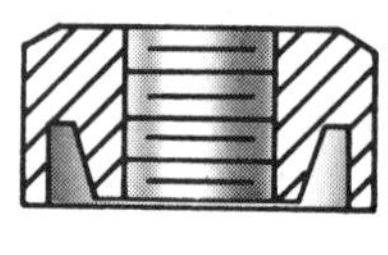

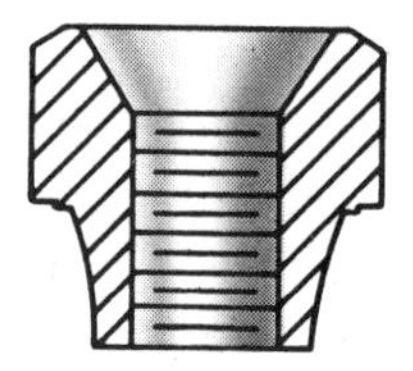

Fig. 13-4

The assumption that each thread takes its share of the load is not true. Since the nut is under compression and the bolt is under tension, the load will shift toward the bottom threads of the nut. For heavily loaded bolts, special nuts are sometimes used in order to obtain better load distribution as shown in Fig. 13-4 above.

THE FATIGUE STRENGTH OF A BOLT depends upon the maximum and minimum loads to which it is subjected. When the external load W_2 is fluctuating, the initial bolt load W_1 should be sufficient to prevent separation with a reasonable factor of safety. Separation will be pending when the external load W_2 is equal to the resultant bolt load W. Then

$$W_2 = W_1 + W_2\left(\frac{m}{m+b}\right)$$

or W_1 must be $\geqq W_2\left(1 - \frac{m}{m+b}\right)$ to prevent separation. When no separation occurs, the load may vary between W_1 and $W_1 + W_2\left(\frac{m}{m+b}\right)$.

STRESS CONCENTRATION AT THE ROOT of a standard coarse thread is high. Photoelastic tests indicate static stress concentration factors as high as 5.62. This may not be too serious for bolts made of ductile material when subject to static loads. However, the stress concentration factor has been found to lower the endurance limit of standard coarse threads by factors ranging from 2 to 4. Therefore the fluctuating stress in a threaded bolt must be multiplied by a suitable stress concentration factor.

SOLVED PROBLEMS

1. Derive the equation for the resultant bolt load W in terms of the initial load W_1 and the applied external load W_2.

Solution:

Consider two members bolted together. Fig. 13-5 below shows the members and the bolt as free bodies due to the initial tightening load W_1 only. Fig. 13-6 shows the members and the bolt as free bodies after an external load W_2 has been applied. Note that the change in length of the bolt is equal to the change in length of the bolted members if there is no separation of the parts. Then

$$(\Delta L)_b = (\Delta L)_1 + (\Delta L)_2$$

and
$$(W - W_1)b = [W_1 - (W - W_2)]m_1 + [W_1 - (W - W_2)]m_2$$

or
$$W = W_1 + W_2\left(\frac{m_1 + m_2}{b + m_1 + m_2}\right) = W_1 + W_2\left(\frac{m}{m + b}\right)$$

where the symbols are the same as previously given. (Note: external load is assumed to be applied to the bolt.)

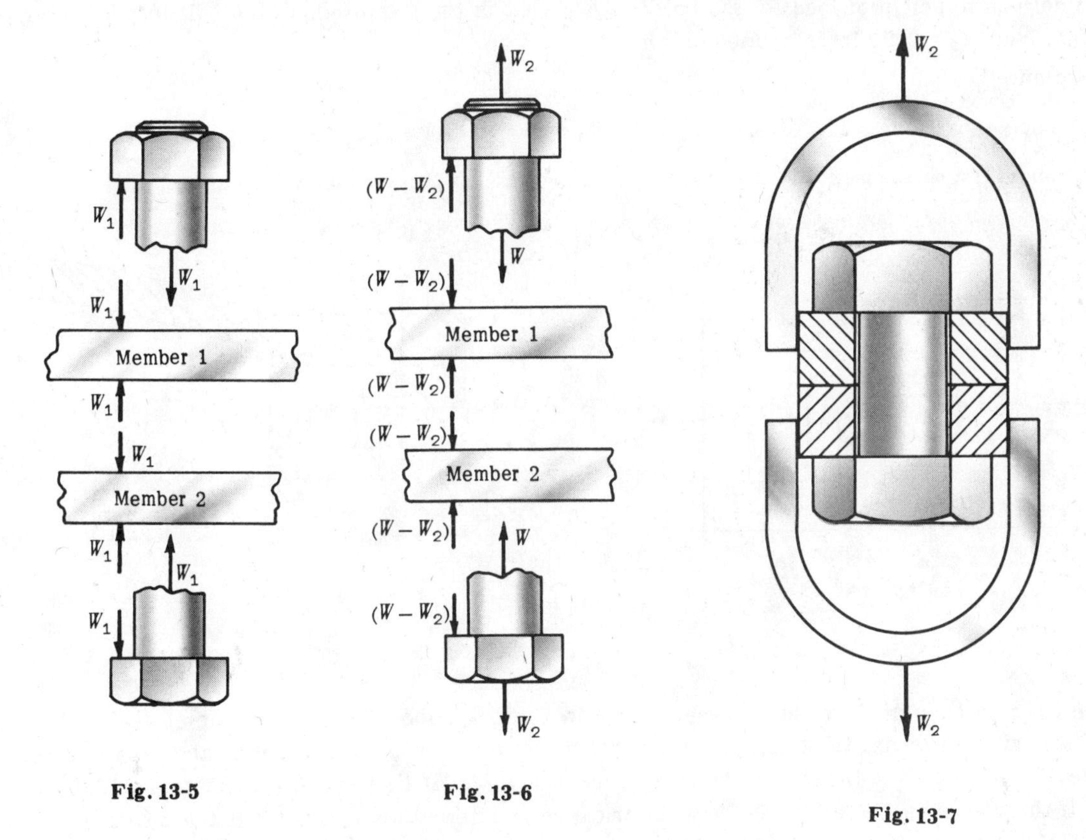

Fig. 13-5 Fig. 13-6 Fig. 13-7

2. A bolt is used to fasten two members together as shown in Fig. 13-7 above. The members and the bolt are of the same material and have the same cross section area. Determine what external load W_2 will cause separation of the members to occur if the initial tightening load W_1 is 5000 lb.

Solution:

Since the connected members and bolt are of the same material and have the same cross section area, they have the same deflection per lb of load. Thus $m = b$ and $W = W_1 + W_2(\frac{m}{m+b}) = W_1 + \frac{1}{2}W_2$.

Separation will occur when $W = W_2$; then $W_2 = 5000 + \frac{1}{2}W_2$, or $W_2 = 10{,}000$ lb before separation occurs.

3. Several members are bolted together in such a manner that the deflection per lb of load for the bolted members is the same as for the bolt, i.e. $m = b$ or $m/(m+b) = \frac{1}{2}$. Determine the following graphically using Fig. 13-2.
   (*a*) If the initial tightening load on the bolt is 10,000 lb, what axial external load has to be applied to the bolt to cause separation of the bolted members?
   (*b*) What is the resultant bolt load for an external load of 12,000 lb?
   (*c*) What is the resultant bolt load for an external load of 24,000 lb?

Solution: Refer to Fig. 13-2.

(*a*) Separation occurs at point D for which an external load W_2 = 20,000 lb will just cause separation.
(*b*) For an external load W_2 = 12,000 lb, the resultant bolt load W = 16,000 lb.
(*c*) For an external load W_2 = 24,000 lb, the resultant bolt load W = 24,000 lb (separation has occured).

4. The bolted assembly shown in Fig. 13-8 below has been preloaded by tightening the nut so that the bolt has an initial load of 1200 lb. If the ratio of the deflection per lb of load for the members to the deflection per lb of load for the bolt is 1/3, what is the magnitude of the bolt load when an external load W_2 = 2000 lb is applied as shown?

Solution:

Since $m/b = 1/3$, $\quad W = W_1 + W_2(\frac{m}{m+b}) = W_1 + \frac{1}{4}W_2 = 1200 + \frac{1}{4}(2000) = 1700$ lb.

Since $W_2 > W$, the members have separated and the final load on the bolt will be 2000 lb.

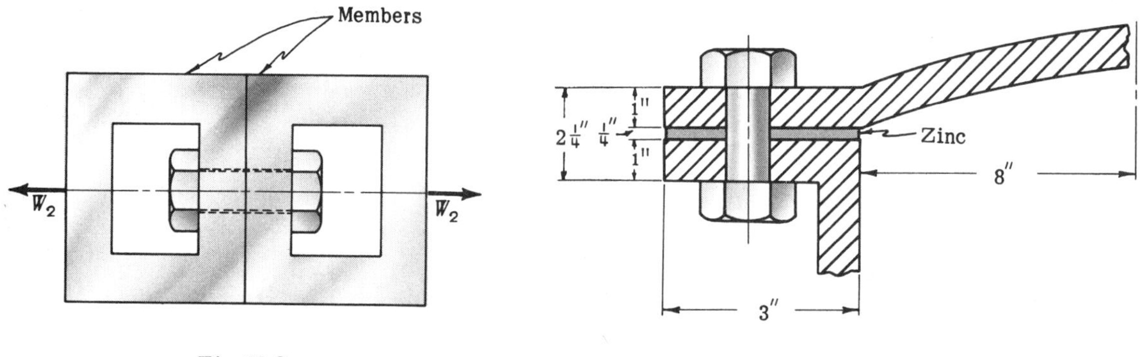

Fig. 13-8

Fig. 13-9

5. The lid of a cast iron pressure vessel shown in Fig. 13-9 above is held in place by ten $\frac{1}{2}$ in. steel bolts having an initial tightening load of 5000 lb, when the vessel is at 70°F and the initial pressure is atmospheric. Determine the load in each bolt (*a*) if the pressure is increased to 200 psi, (*b*) if the vessel is heated to 250°F with atmospheric internal pressure, (*c*) if the vessel is heated to 250°F with an internal pressure of 200 psi.

E for steel = 30×10^6 psi, for cast iron = 12×10^6 psi, for zinc = 12×10^6 psi.

Linear expansion coefficient for steel = $6.6 \times 10^{-6}/°F$, for cast iron = $5.6 \times 10^{-6}/°F$, for zinc = $17.8 \times 10^{-6}/°F$.

Solution:

(*a*) Cross section area of the flange and zinc gasket per bolt is

$$A = \frac{1}{10}(\pi D_m t) = \frac{1}{10}\pi(\frac{16+22}{2})(3) = 17.9 \text{ in}^2$$

Cross section area of $\frac{1}{2}$ in. bolt = 0.196 in^2.

Hence the net area for zinc and cast iron flange = 17.9 − 0.196 = 17.7 in^2/bolt.

From $s = \frac{\Delta L}{L} E = \frac{P}{A}$, we have $\frac{\Delta L}{P} = \frac{L}{AE}$ inches deflection per lb of load.

$$(L/AE)_{zinc} = \frac{0.25}{(17.7)(12)(10^6)} = \frac{1}{(850)(10^6)} \text{ in/lb of load}$$

$$(L/AE)_{CI} = \frac{2.0}{(17.7)(12)(10^6)} = \frac{1}{(106)(10^6)} \text{ in/lb of load}$$

$$(L/AE)_{bolt} = \frac{2.25}{(0.196)(30)(10^6)} = \frac{1}{(2.62)(10^6)} \text{ in/lb of load}$$

$$m = \frac{1}{(850)(10^6)} + \frac{1}{(106)(10^6)} \text{ in/lb of load}, \quad b = \frac{1}{(2.62)(10^6)} \text{ in/lb of load}, \quad \frac{m}{m+b} = \frac{1}{37}.$$

$$W_2 = \frac{\pi(16^2)}{4}\left(\frac{200}{10}\right) = 4020 \text{ lb per bolt, and } W = 5000 + \frac{4020}{37} = 5110 \text{ lb.}$$

(*b*)

$$(\Delta L)_{zinc} \text{ due to temp. change} = \frac{(0.25)(180)(17.8)}{10^6} = \frac{(180)(4.45)}{10^6} \text{ in.}$$

$$(\Delta L)_{CI} \text{ due to temp. change} = \frac{(2)(180)(5.6)}{10^6} = \frac{(180)(11.2)}{10^6} \text{ in.}$$

$$(\Delta L)_{bolt} \text{ due to temp. change} = \frac{(2.25)(180)(6.6)}{10^6} = \frac{(180)(14.9)}{10^6} \text{ in.}$$

$$(\Delta L)_{zinc} + (\Delta L)_{CI} = \frac{180}{10^6}(4.45 + 11.2) = \frac{180}{10^6}(15.65) \text{ in.}$$

$(\Delta L)_{bolt} = (\Delta L)_{members}$. $(\Delta L)_{bolt}$ will increase due to both an increase in temperature and an increase in load. Let W_1' be the new load on the bolt, remembering that $W_1 = 5000$ lb.

$$(\Delta L)_{bolt} = \frac{(W_1' - 5000)(2.25)}{(0.196)(30)(10^6)} + \frac{(180)(14.9)}{10^6}$$

$(\Delta L)_{members}$ will tend to decrease due to an increase in load, but will tend to increase due to the temperature rise; thus

$$(\Delta L)_{members} = -\frac{(W_1' - 5000)(2.25)}{(17.7)(12)(10^6)} + \frac{(180)(15.65)}{10^6}$$

Equating $(\Delta L)_{bolt} = (\Delta L)_{members}$, we obtain $W_1' = 5360$ lb. This is the new initial bolt load.

(*c*) After the external pressure has been applied the resultant bolt load will be $W = 5360 + 4020/37 = 5469$ lb.

6. A $\frac{1}{2}$ in. 12 UNC by 10 in. long steel bolt is subjected to an impact load. The kinetic energy to be absorbed is 35 in-lb. (*a*) Determine the stress in the shank of the bolt if there is no threaded portion between the nut and the bolt head. (*b*) Find the stress in the shank if the area of the shank is reduced to that of the root area of the threads.

Solution:

(*a*) The energy of impact will be absorbed by elongation of the $\frac{1}{2}$ in. shank which has an area of 0.196 in^2.

$$U = \frac{F}{2}\delta = \frac{F}{2}\left(\frac{FL}{AE}\right) = \frac{F^2 L}{2AE} \quad \text{or} \quad F = \sqrt{\frac{2AEU}{L}} = \sqrt{\frac{(2)(0.196)(30)(10^6)(35)}{10}} = 6400 \text{ lb (impact load)}$$

The root area $A_r = 0.1257$ in^2. The stress based on the root area is $s = 6400/0.1257 = 50{,}900$ psi. This value has neglected stress concentration.

(*b*) If the diameter of the shank of the bolt is reduced to the root diameter,

$$F = \sqrt{\frac{(2)(0.1257)(30)(10^6)(35)}{10}} = 5140 \text{ lb} \quad \text{and} \quad s = \frac{5140}{0.1257} = 40{,}900 \text{ psi}$$

This illustrates how the stress due to impact may be reduced by making the shank diameter equal to the root diameter of the thread. The impact stress may also be reduced by increasing the length of the bolt.

7. A 1″–8NC–2 tie bolt is 15 in. long between the bolted members. It is tightened to an initial load of 10,000 lb. Assume a coefficient of friction for both the threads and collar of 0.15, and a collar radius of 0.625 in. (*a*) Determine the necessary tightening torque applied to the nut, using the theoretical screw thread torque equation. (*b*) Determine the maximum shear stress in the bolt.

Solution:

(*a*) For the specified thread: $d_o = 1''$, $d_i = 0.8466''$, $d_m = 0.9233''$, $r_m = 0.4617''$, $\tan\alpha = \dfrac{\text{lead}}{\pi d_m} = \dfrac{0.125}{\pi(0.9233)} = 0.04312$

$$T = 10{,}000\left[0.4617\left(\frac{0.15/0.866 + 0.04312}{1 - (0.15)(0.04312)/0.866}\right) + (0.625)(0.15)\right] = 1080 + 938 = 2018 \text{ in-lb}$$

Note that the portion of the applied torque absorbed by the threads is 1080 in-lb and the portion of the total torque absorbed by the collar is 938 in-lb.

(*b*) $s_x = \dfrac{(10{,}000)(4)}{\pi(0.8466)^2} = 17{,}750 \text{ psi}$, $\tau_{xy} = \dfrac{(1080)(16)}{\pi(0.8466)^3} = 9050 \text{ psi}$, and $\tau(\max) = \sqrt{8875^2 + 9050^2} = 12{,}700 \text{ psi}$.

8. Derive an expression for the maximum stress induced in the shank of a horizontal bolt when the head is subjected to an impact of a concentric weight W with a velocity V. Neglect bending due to W and stress concentration. See the adjoining figure.

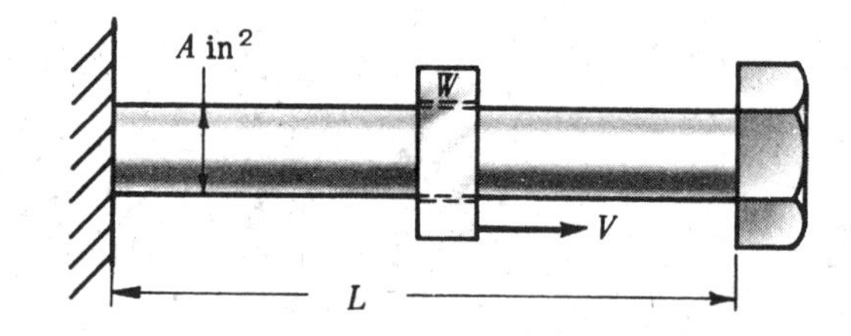

Fig. 13-10

Solution:

The kinetic energy of the moving weight must be absorbed by the bolt upon impact. Using lb, in. and sec units,

$$\tfrac{1}{2}MV^2 = \tfrac{1}{2}P\delta, \quad (W/g)V^2 = (sA)(sL/E), \quad \text{and} \quad s = V\sqrt{WE/gAL} \text{ psi (tension)}$$

9. The external load applied to a bolted joint fluctuates between zero and 1600 lb. The ratio of the inches deflection per lb of load for the bolt to that for the members is 3. The endurance limit s_r of the bolt material in reversed axial loading is 30,000 psi and the yield point is 50,000 psi. The root area of the thread is 0.1257 sq. in. Assume a stress concentration factor $K_f = 2.5$ and a factor of safety $N = 2$ based on the yield strength of the material. In this case K_f includes surface and size effects. Determine:

(*a*) The minimum initial tightening load that must be applied to prevent separation.

(*b*) The average, s_m, and the variable stress range, s_v, based on the initial load as determined in part (*a*).

(*c*) Plot the Soderberg working stress diagram for the material and determine if the bolt is safely loaded based on an initial load as determined in part (*a*).

Solution:

(a) $W_1 \geqq W_2(1 - \frac{m}{m+b})$ to prevent separation, where $\frac{m}{m+b} = \frac{1}{4}$. Then

$$W_1(\text{min}) = 1600(1 - \tfrac{1}{4}) = 1200 \text{ lb}$$

(b) $W(\text{max}) = 1200 + 1600/4 = 1600$ lb

$W(\text{min}) = 1200 + 0 = 1200$ lb

$W_m = 1400$ lb (mean load)

$W_v = 200$ lb (variable load)

$s_m = 1400/0.1257 = 11{,}150$ psi

$K_f s_v = 2.5(200/0.1257) = 3980$ psi

(c) The sum of the average and variable stress is shown at point A of Fig. 13-11. Since point A falls below the working–stress line, the bolt is safely loaded. Note that the stress concentration factor was applied only to the variable stress, and not to the average stress which may be considered as static.

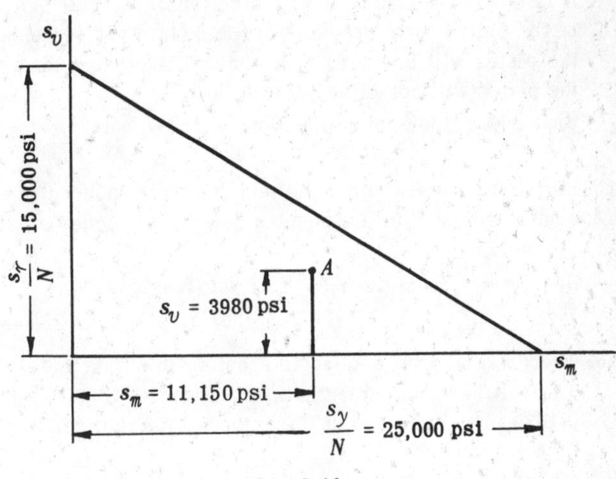

Fig. 13-11

SUPPLEMENTARY PROBLEMS

10. The cover of a pressure vessel is held in place by ten $\frac{3}{4}''$ UNC bolts. The pressure is 200 psi and the effective area of the cover exposed to the pressure is 314 in^2. The ratio of the stiffness of the bolts to the connected parts is 1/4, where stiffness is defined as inches of deflection per pound of load. Each bolt is tightened initially, before the pressure is applied, to 6000 lb. (a) Will the joint separate as a result of the load due to internal pressure? (b) If the joint does not separate, determine the tensile stress in each bolt due to the axial load.
Ans. (a) The members will not separate. (b) $s = 33{,}000$ psi

11. An oil cylinder has two ends held in place with four through bolts, each with an area of 0.2 in^2 and each tightened to an initial load of 3000 lb. The cross section area of the cylinder is 2 in^2. The effective length of the bolts and cylinder may be taken as the same and equal to 18 in. Considering the end plates as very rigid, determine the load in each bolt if an internal pressure is applied to cause a force of 6000 lb on the head and piston, in the position where the piston rod is fully extended. Material of the bolt and cylinder is SAE 1030 steel with an ultimate strength of 80,000 psi and a yield point of 50,000 psi. *Ans.* 3430 lb

12. One through steel bolt, $\frac{3}{4}$–10 UNC – 2A, is used to tighten up two end plates against a cylinder with an o.d. of 4 in. and an i.d. of 3 in. The initial tightening force in the bolt is 12,000 lb. The root area of the bolt is 0.3020 in^2. Tests made on a compression machine to measure the flexibility of the cylinder and end plates, without the bolt, show that a deflection of 0.001 in. results with a load of 32,000 lb. If an internal oil pressure of 3000 psi is applied inside the cylinder, what will be the bolt load? *Ans.* 20,344 lb

13. A cast iron cylinder head is fastened to a 20 in. (inside diameter) cylinder by means of 8 bolts. Consider the bolt to be extremely flexible as compared to the bolted parts. For an internal pressure of 200 psi, what is the axial force on each bolt if the bolts were tightened just enough to prevent the joint opening under a pressure of 300 psi? *Ans.* 11,775 lb per bolt

14. A through bolt is used to fasten two plates with a gasket between the two plates. It is known that the ratio of deflection of the bolt per unit load to the deflection of the bolted parts per unit load is 1/4. What percentage of the applied load to the plates will be added to the initial tightening load of the bolt? Assume that the plates will not separate under load.

Ans. 80% of the applied load goes into the bolt.

15. Derive an expression for the tensile stress induced in a vertical bolt when a concentric weight W falls through a height of h inches as shown in Fig. 13-12.

Ans. $s = \frac{W}{A}\left(1 + \sqrt{\frac{2AEh}{WL} + 1}\right)$ psi (tension)

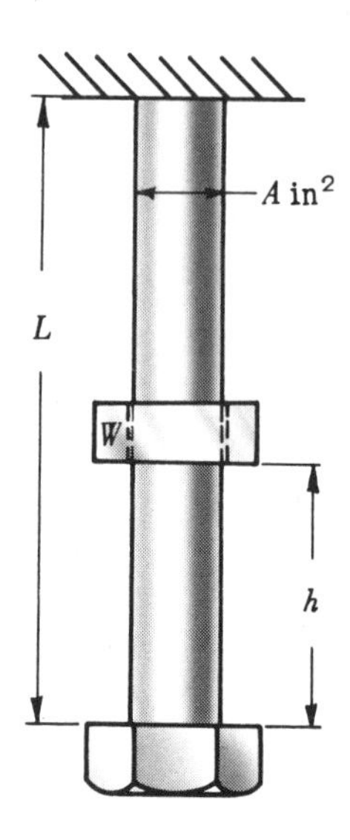

Fig. 13-12

16. The external load applied to a bolted joint fluctuates between zero and 1400 lb. The bolt is tightened with an initial load of 1300 lb. The root area of the bolt is 0.1620 in^2. The ratio of the inches deflection per lb of load for the bolt to that for the members is 3.

(*a*) Determine the maximum and minimum bolt loads.

(*b*) Determine the average stress and the variable stress, assuming a stress–concentration factor of 2.8 which includes surface and size effects.

(*c*) Plot the Soderberg working–stress diagram and determine if the bolt is safely loaded for a factor of safety of 1.8. The material has a yield point of 40,000 psi, and an endurance limit in reversed axial loading of 20,000 psi.

Ans. (*a*) W(max) = 1650 lb, W(min) = 1300 lb

(*b*) s_m = 9260 psi, s_v = 3030 psi

(*c*) The bolt is safely loaded.

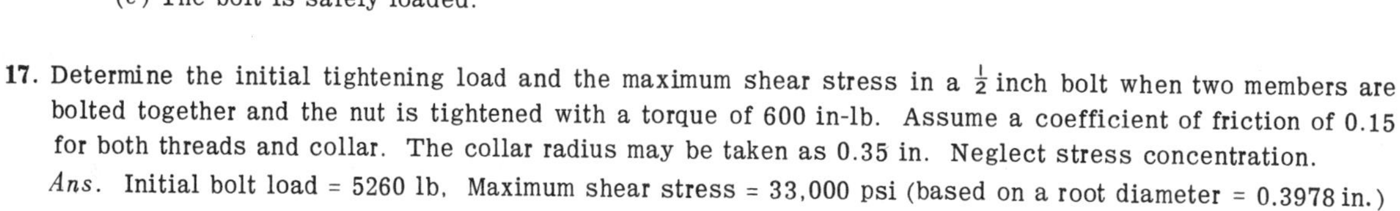

17. Determine the initial tightening load and the maximum shear stress in a $\frac{1}{2}$ inch bolt when two members are bolted together and the nut is tightened with a torque of 600 in-lb. Assume a coefficient of friction of 0.15 for both threads and collar. The collar radius may be taken as 0.35 in. Neglect stress concentration.

Ans. Initial bolt load = 5260 lb, Maximum shear stress = 33,000 psi (based on a root diameter = 0.3978 in.)

Chapter 14

Clutches

A CLUTCH is a friction device which permits the connection and disconnection of shafts. The designs of clutches and brakes are comparable in many respects. This is well illustrated by a multiple disk clutch which is used also as a brake. One problem of design much more evident in brake design compared to clutch design is that of heat generation and dissipation. Friction clutches generate heat as a result of relative motion of the parts, but the amount of sliding is not ordinarily as great as in a brake. It is quite customary in the analysis of a clutch to picture that the parts are in impending motion with respect to each other, although one must not lose sight of the fact that transmission of power through friction usually involves some slip. For this reason, when it is necessary to have positive power transmission one must resort to a positive device, as a jaw type of clutch.

PLATE OR DISK CLUTCHES

A MULTIPLE DISK clutch is shown in Fig. 14-1. The plates shown as A are usually steel and are set on splines on shaft C to permit axial motion (except for the last disk). The plates shown as B are usually bronze and are set in splines of member D.

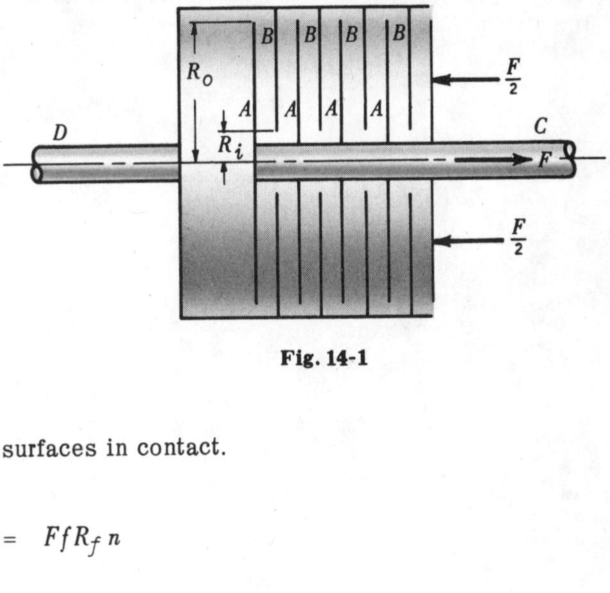

The number of pairs of surfaces transmitting power is one less than the sum of the steel and bronze disks, and is also an even number if the design is such that no thrust bearings are needed.

Fig. 14-1

$$n = n_{\text{steel}} + n_{\text{bronze}} - 1$$

For the system shown, $n = 5+4-1 = 8$ pairs of surfaces in contact.

The torque capacity is given by

$$T = FfR_f n$$

where T = torque capacity, in-lb

F = axial force, lb

f = coefficient of friction

R_f = friction radius $= \frac{2}{3}\left(\frac{R_o^3 - R_i^3}{R_o^2 - R_i^2}\right)$ if the contact pressure is assumed uniform

$= \frac{R_o + R_i}{2}$ if wear is assumed uniform

R_o = outside radius of contact of surfaces, inches

R_i = inside radius of contact of surfaces, inches

n = number of pair of surfaces in contact.

The axial force F is given by

$$F = p\pi(R_o^2 - R_i^2)$$

where p is the average pressure.

The horsepower capacity is

$$\text{Hp} = TN/63{,}000$$

where T = shaft torque, in-lb; and N = speed of rotation, rpm.

For uniform wear, the pressure variation is given by

$$p = \frac{C}{r} = \frac{F}{2\pi(R_o - R_i)\,r}$$

where C is a constant and r is radius to differential element shown in Fig. 14-3, on page 168.

CONE CLUTCHES

A CONE CLUTCH achieves its effectiveness by the wedging action of the cone part in the cup part.

(a) The torque capacity of a cone clutch with the parts engaged based on uniform pressure is

$$T = \frac{Ff}{\sin\alpha}\left[\frac{2}{3}\left(\frac{R_o^3 - R_i^3}{R_o^2 - R_i^2}\right)\right]$$

The torque capacity can also be written in an alternate form as

$$T = Ff\left(\frac{R_o^3 - R_i^3}{3R_m b \sin^2\alpha}\right)$$

where T = torque, in-lb
F = axial force, lb
f = coefficient of friction
R_o = outside radius of contact, in.
R_i = inside radius of contact, in.
R_m = mean radius = $\frac{1}{2}(R_o + R_i)$, in.
b = face width, in.
α = pitch cone angle.

Fig. 14-2

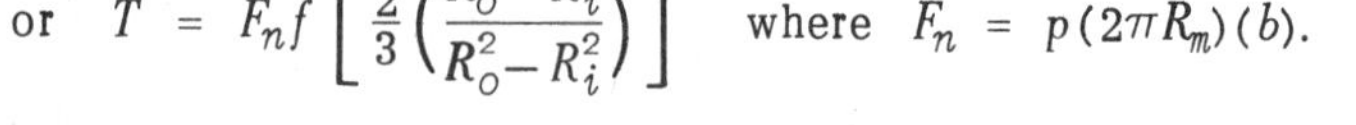

or $T = F_n f\left[\frac{2}{3}\left(\frac{R_o^3 - R_i^3}{R_o^2 - R_i^2}\right)\right]$ where $F_n = p(2\pi R_m)(b)$.

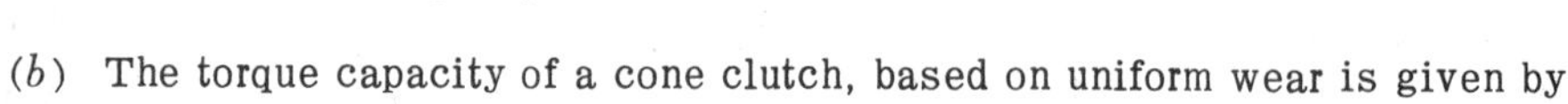

(b) The torque capacity of a cone clutch, based on uniform wear is given by

$$T = \frac{FfR_m}{\sin\alpha} \quad \text{or} \quad T = F_n f R_m$$

The pressure variation, where uniform wear is assumed, is

$$p = \frac{F}{2\pi(R_o - R_i)\,r}$$ See Fig. 14-8

The maximum pressure occurs at the smallest radius: $p_{max} = \dfrac{F}{2\pi(R_o - R_i)R_i}$.

The minimum pressure occurs at the largest radius: $p_{min} = \dfrac{F}{2\pi(R_o - R_i)R_o}$.

The average pressure $= \dfrac{F}{\pi(R_o^2 - R_i^2)}$.

ENGAGING CONE CLUTCHES. A problem encountered with cone clutches not encountered with multi-disk clutches is the possibility of a larger force to engage a clutch than that required during operation when the cup and cone are rotating at the same speed. The analysis is complicated by the fact that the direction of the frictional forces depends upon the manner of engagement, that is, the ratio of the relative rotary motion to the relative axial motion of the cup and cone. A conservative procedure is to assume that **no relative rotary motion occurs** during engagement, for which the maximum axial force F_e necessary to engage the cup and cone is

$$F_e = F_n(\sin\alpha + f\cos\alpha)$$

This force is the maximum required to obtain the desired normal force F_n which in turn develops the frictional force to give the desired frictional torque.

AXIAL FORCE TO HOLD CUP AND CONE IN ENGAGEMENT. The force to hold the cup and cone in engagement, with friction taken into account, will vary between

$$F = F_n \sin\alpha \qquad \text{and} \qquad F = F_n(\sin\alpha - f\cos\alpha)$$

Because of vibration, friction may not be very dependable and it is conservative to assume that the axial force to hold the parts together is the larger value of F: $F = F_n \sin\alpha$.

AXIAL FORCE REQUIRED TO DISENGAGE CUP AND CONE. Ordinarily, with the cone angles commonly used, no force is necessary to disengage the parts, although it is possible that if $f\cos\alpha > \sin\alpha$, an axial force F_d may be necessary to disengage the parts:

$$F_d = F_n(f\cos\alpha - \sin\alpha)$$

HORSEPOWER CAPACITY FOR A CONE CLUTCH is as follows, depending upon whether uniform wear or uniform pressure is assumed:

Uniform Wear: $$\text{Hp} = \frac{TN}{63{,}000} = \frac{(F_n f D_m/2)N}{63{,}000} = \frac{FfR_m}{\sin\alpha}\left(\frac{N}{63{,}000}\right)$$

Uniform Pressure: $$\text{Hp} = \frac{TN}{63{,}000} = F_n f(\tfrac{2}{3})\left(\frac{R_o^3 - R_i^3}{R_o^2 - R_i^2}\right)\frac{N}{63{,}000} = \frac{Ff}{\sin\alpha}(\tfrac{2}{3})\left(\frac{R_o^3 - R_i^3}{R_o^2 - R_i^2}\right)\frac{N}{63{,}000}$$

where F = axial force, lb
f = coefficient of friction
R_o = outside radius, in.
R_i = inside radius, in.
N = speed, rpm
α = cone pitch angle
$F_n = p(2\pi R_m)(b)$, where p is the average pressure, R_m is the mean cone radius, and b is the face width.

SOLVED PROBLEMS

1. Derive the torque capacity for *one pair* of surfaces pressed together with an axial force F. Assume uniform pressure. Refer to Fig. 14-3 below.

Solution:

Consider a differential area $dA = 2\pi r\,dr$. The differential normal force $= dN = p\,dA = p(2\pi r\,dr)$. The differential frictional force $= dQ = f\,dN = f(p2\pi r\,dr)$. The differential frictional torque $= dT = r\,dQ = r(fp2\pi r\,dr)$; integrating with p and f as constants, the total torque is

$$T = 2\pi fp\int_{R_i}^{R_o} r^2\,dr = 2\pi fp\left(\frac{R_o^3 - R_i^3}{3}\right)$$

The axial force $F = p(\pi)(R_o^2 - R_i^2)$, from which the average pressure $p = \dfrac{F}{\pi(R_o^2 - R_i^2)}$.

Substituting this value of p into $T = 2\pi fp\left(\dfrac{R_o^3 - R_i^3}{3}\right)$, we obtain $T = Ff\left[\dfrac{2}{3}\left(\dfrac{R_o^3 - R_i^3}{R_o^2 - R_i^2}\right)\right] = FfR_f$.

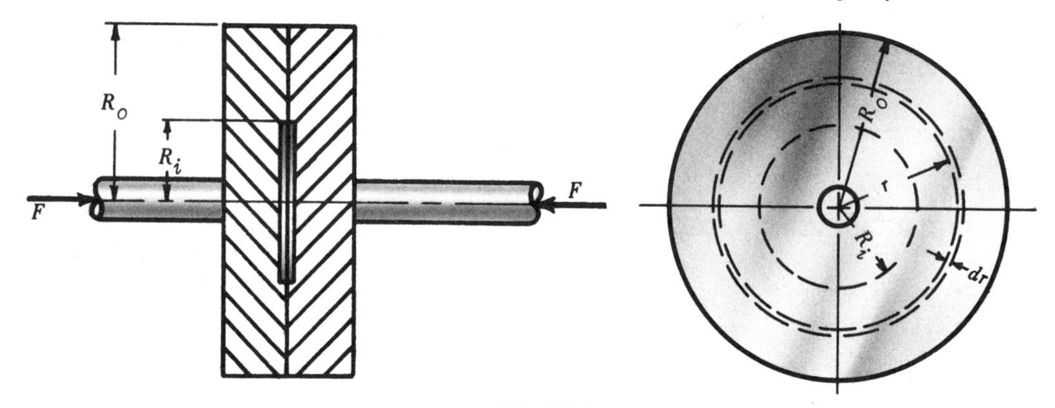

Fig. 14-3

2. Derive the torque capacity for *one pair* of surfaces pressed together with an axial force F. Assume uniform wear. Refer to Fig. 14-3 above.

Solution:

When a clutch is new, it is perhaps true that the pressure may be rather uniform. If the surfaces are relatively rigid, the outer portion, where the velocity is high, will wear more than the inner portion. After initial wearing-in, it is reasonable to assume that the curve of the profile will maintain its shape; or, the wear thereafter may be considered to be uniform.

Uniform wear can be expressed in a different way by saying that in any time interval the work done per unit area is constant:

$$\frac{\text{(frictional force)(velocity)}}{\text{area}} = \frac{(fp2\pi r\,dr)(r\omega)}{2\pi r\,dr} = \text{constant } C'$$

or $p = C'/fr\omega$. Then since f and ω are constants, $p = C/r$, where C is a constant.

An alternate method of showing that pressure varies inversely as the radius is to consider that wear δ is proportional to pressure p and velocity V. Thus $\delta = KpV = Kp(r\omega)$, or $p = C/r$ since δ and K are constants and ω is fixed for a given clutch.

As in Problem 1, the differential frictional torque $dT = r(fp2\pi r\,dr)$; the total torque is

$$T = \int_{R_i}^{R_o} rf\left(\frac{C}{r}\right)2\pi r\,dr = 2\pi fC\left(\frac{R_o^2 - R_i^2}{2}\right)$$

To find C: $F = \displaystyle\int_{R_i}^{R_o} p(2\pi r\,dr) = \int_{R_i}^{R_o} (C/r)(2\pi r\,dr) = 2\pi C(R_o - R_i)$, or $C = \dfrac{F}{2\pi(R_o - R_i)}$.

Substituting this value of C in the equation for T, $T = Ff\left(\dfrac{R_o + R_i}{2}\right) = FfR_f$.

3. Compare the friction radius based upon uniform pressure and uniform wear for two cases: (1) $R_o = 4$ in., $R_i = 3.5$ in.; (2) $R_o = 4$ in., $R_i = 1$ in.

Solution:

(1) Uniform pressure, $R_f = \frac{2}{3}\left(\frac{R_o^3 - R_i^3}{R_o^2 - R_i^2}\right) = \frac{2}{3}\left(\frac{4^3 - 3.5^3}{4^2 - 3.5^2}\right) = 3.76$ in. Uniform wear, $R_f = \frac{R_o + R_i}{2} = \frac{4 + 3.5}{2} = 3.75$ in.

(2) Uniform pressure, $R_f = \frac{2}{3}\left(\frac{R_o^3 - R_i^3}{R_o^2 - R_i^2}\right) = \frac{2}{3}\left(\frac{4^3 - 1^3}{4^2 - 1^2}\right) = 2.8$ in. Uniform wear, $R_f = \frac{R_o + R_i}{2} = \frac{4 + 1}{2} = 2.5$ in.

Thus for low values of R_o/R_i the difference between uniform wear and uniform pressure is very small As R_o/R_i increases, the difference becomes larger.

4. Plot the ratio of friction radius to outside radius (R_f/R_o) versus the ratio of inside radius to outside radius (R_i/R_o) for uniform pressure and uniform wear assumptions. Refer to Fig. 14-4 for solution.

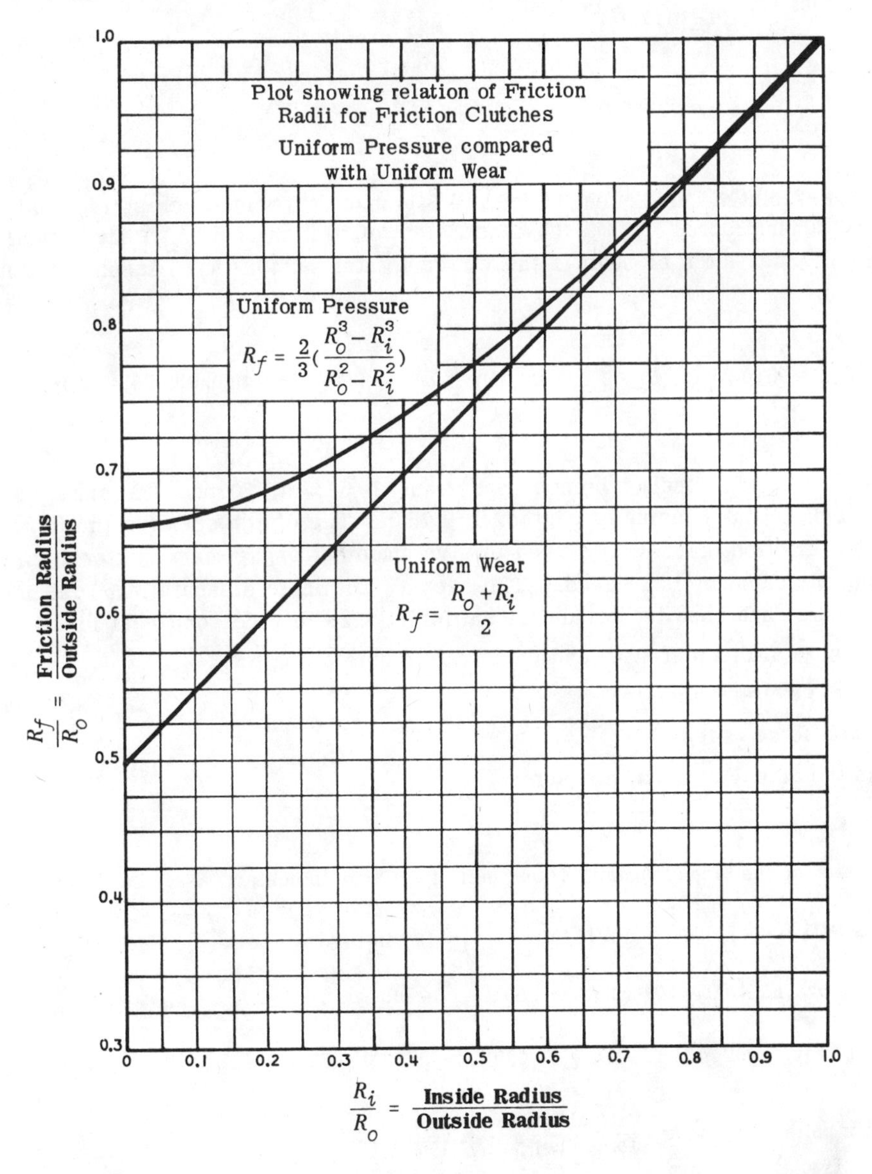

Fig. 14-4

5. Determine the maximum, minimum, and average pressure in a plate clutch where the axial force is 1000 lb, the inside radius of contact is $R_i = 2$ in., the outside radius is $R_o = 4$ in. Uniform wear is assumed. Refer to Fig. 14-5.

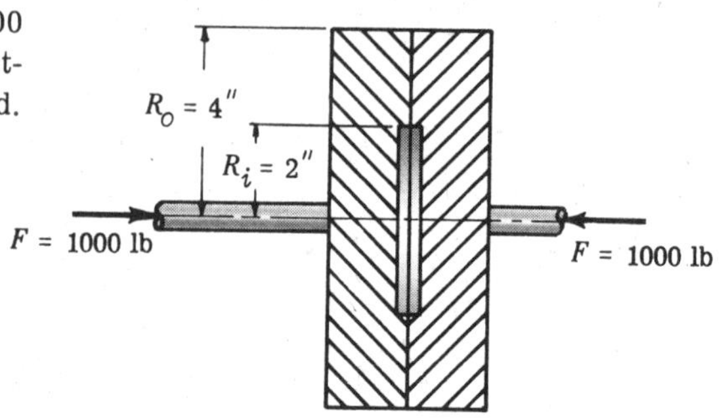

Fig. 14-5

Solution:

The pressure variation is given by

$$p = \frac{C}{r} = \frac{F}{2\pi(R_o - R_i)(r)}.$$

The maximum pressure occurs where $r = R_i$

$$p(\text{max}) = \frac{1000}{2\pi(4-2)(2)} = 39.8 \text{ psi}.$$

The minimum pressure occurs at $r = R_o$

$$p(\text{min}) = \frac{1000}{2\pi(4-2)(4)} = 19.9 \text{ psi}.$$

$$\text{Average pressure } p = \frac{\text{force}}{\text{area of contact}} = \frac{F}{\pi(R_o^2 - R_i^2)} = \frac{1000}{\pi(4^2 - 2^2)} = 26.5 \text{ psi}.$$

6. A multiple disk clutch has 4 steel disks and 3 bronze disks and each surface has a contact area of 4 in^2 and a mean radius of 2 in. The coefficient of friction is 0.25. What is the horsepower capacity for an axial force of 90 lb if the clutch rotates at 400 rpm? Assume uniform wear in the clutch plates.

Solution:

$T = FfR_f n = 90(0.25)(2)(6) = 270$ in-lb. Hp $= TN/63{,}000 = 270(400)/63{,}000 = 1.71$.

7. A multiple disk clutch, steel on bronze, is to transmit 5 hp at 750 rpm. The inner radius of contact is 1.50 in. and the outer radius of contact is 2.75 in. The clutch operates in oil with an expected coefficient of friction 0.10. (Oil is used to give smoother engagement, better dissipation of heat, even though the capacity is reduced.) The average allowable pressure is 50 psi, maximum. (Low design pressures are used to provide for sufficient size to give good heat dissipation capacity.)

(*1*) How many total disks of steel and bronze are required?

(*2*) What is the average pressure?

(*3*) What axial force is required?

(*4*) What is the actual maximum pressure?

Solution:

(*a*) First determine the torque capacity of *one* pair of surfaces in contact, assuming uniform wear.

$$T = Ff\left(\frac{R_o + R_i}{2}\right) = 834(0.10)\left(\frac{2.75 + 1.50}{2}\right) = 177 \text{ in-lb}$$

where $F = p\pi(R_o^2 - R_i^2) = 50\pi(2.75^2 - 1.50^2) = 834$ lb.

(*b*) The total torque applied is $T = (\text{hp})(63{,}000)/N = 5(63{,}000)/750 = 420$ in-lb.

(*c*) Number of pairs of surfaces $= \dfrac{\text{total torque}}{\text{torque per pair}} = \dfrac{420}{177} = 2.37$.

Since the number must be even, use 4 pairs of surfaces with 3 steel and 2 bronze disks.

(*d*) Using 4 pairs of surfaces, we can use a reduced pressure.

The actual torque per pair of surfaces = $\dfrac{\text{total torque}}{\text{pairs of surfaces}} = \dfrac{420}{4} = 105$ in-lb.

(*e*) To find the actual force required: $T' = Ff\left(\dfrac{R_o+R_i}{2}\right)$, $105 = F(0.1)\left(\dfrac{2.75+1.50}{2}\right)$, $F = 495$ lb.

The average pressure is $\dfrac{F}{A} = \dfrac{495}{\pi(2.75^2 - 1.50^2)} = 29.6$ psi.

(*f*) Maximum pressure occurs where $r = R_i$: $p(\max) = \dfrac{F}{2\pi(R_o - R_i)r} = \dfrac{495}{2\pi(2.75-1.50)(1.50)} = 42$ psi.

Answers: (*1*) Four pairs of surfaces giving 3 steel and 2 bronze disks, or a total of 5 disks. (*2*) Average pressure = 29.6 psi. (*3*) Axial force = 495 lb. (*4*) Actual maximum pressure = 42 psi.

8. A multiple disk clutch is composed of 5 steel and 4 bronze disks. The clutch is required to transmit 160 in-lb of torque. If the inner *diameter* is restricted to 2 in., determine (*1*) the necessary outer diameter of the disks and (*2*) the necessary axial force. The coefficient of friction may be taken as 0.1 and the *average* pressure is not to exceed 50 psi. Assume uniform wear.

Solution:

Torque per pair of surfaces = 160/8 = 20 in-lb. Then

$$20 = Ff\left(\frac{D_o+D_i}{4}\right) = \left[\frac{\pi}{4}(D_o^2 - D_i^2)p\right] f\left(\frac{D_o+D_i}{4}\right) = \left[\frac{\pi}{4}(D_o^2 - 2^2)(50)(0.1)\left(\frac{D_o+2}{4}\right)\right]$$

from which, by trial and error, $D_o \cong 2\frac{7}{8}$ in.

For $D_o = 2\frac{7}{8}$ in., $F = \dfrac{T}{f(D_o+D_i)/4} = 164$ lb (and average pressure = $\dfrac{164}{\frac{1}{4}\pi[(2\frac{7}{8})^2 - 2^2]} = 49$ psi).

9. Under what conditions would uniform pressure be a more appropriate assumption than uniform wear in a clutch analysis?

Solution:

Uniform pressure assumption would be more appropriate where the plates are flexible to permit deflection when wear occurs.

10. A motor rotating at *constant* speed ω drives a load through a reversing gear arrangement and clutch as shown in Fig. 14-6 below. A brake is available to bring the load to rest. A comparison of two methods of operation is to be made:

(*1*) In the first method, the clutch is engaged and the load is brought up to motor speed ω in time t

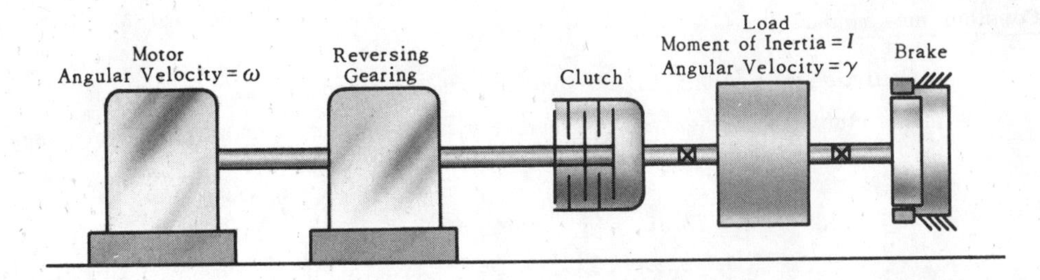

Fig. 14-6

seconds. The clutch is disengaged and the brake brings the load to rest. The reversing gear is shifted to reverse the direction of rotation and the load is accelerated to $-\omega$ speed.

(*2*) In the second method, the clutch is engaged and the load is brought up to speed ω in t seconds. The reversing of direction of rotation of the load is accomplished by disengaging the clutch, shifting the reverse gear, and re-engaging the clutch. The motor rotates until the load rotates at $-\omega$.

Compare the friction work dissipated in heat in the two different methods of operation.

Solution:

A. Consider method (*1*) first.

Let T = the friction torque developed by the clutch (which is also the motor torque) and $d\theta$ = the differential angle of rotation of the motor. Then the work done by the motor in bringing the load up to speed ω is

$$W_m = \int_0^t T\,d\theta = \int_0^t T\omega\,dt$$

since $d\theta/dt = \omega$ (the constant motor speed). But the torque by the clutch on the load causes an angular acceleration α of the load. Then $T = I\alpha$, where I is the polar mass moment of inertia of the load, and

$$W_m = \int_0^t I\alpha\omega\,dt = I\omega \int_0^t \alpha\,dt$$

Since $d\gamma/dt = \alpha$, where γ is the angular speed of the load, varying from 0 to the motor speed ω, the work done by the motor is

$$W_m = I\omega \int_0^{\omega} d\gamma = I\omega[\omega - 0] = I\omega^2$$

The friction work dissipated as heat, W_f, is the energy put in by the motor less the kinetic energy of rotation:

$$W_f = W_m - \tfrac{1}{2}I\omega^2 = I\omega^2 - \tfrac{1}{2}I\omega^2 = \tfrac{1}{2}I\omega^2$$

If the brake is applied to the load with the clutch disengaged, the energy lost in friction is the kinetic energy of the rotating parts, or $\frac{1}{2}I\omega^2$. If the reverse gear is shifted and the load is brought up to motor speed $-\omega$, the work done in friction is obtained in a similar way to the above, and is $\frac{1}{2}I\omega^2$.

The total energy lost is made up of three parts: (*a*) Energy lost in friction in the clutch when the load goes from zero speed to ω, $\frac{1}{2}I\omega^2$. (*b*) Energy lost in braking, $\frac{1}{2}I\omega^2$. (*c*) Energy lost in the clutch when the load goes from zero speed to $-\omega$, $\frac{1}{2}I\omega^2$. Thus the total energy lost in method (*1*) is $(3/2)I\omega^2$.

The time for the complete reversal is t seconds to go from zero to ω, plus t seconds to go from ω to zero, plus t seconds to go from zero to $-\omega$. (This assumes that the braking time is equal to the accelerating time and no allowance is made for engagement and disengagement of the clutch or for shifting the reverse gear.) The total time is $3t$ seconds in method (*1*).

B. Consider, now, method (*2*).

The friction work in bringing the load up to motor speed ω is as before, $\frac{1}{2}I\omega^2$.

If the clutch is disengaged, the reverse gear is shifted, and the clutch re-engaged, the motor running at constant speed ω, the work done by the motor is

$$\text{Work} = \int_{t_1}^{t_2} T\omega\,dt = \int_{t_1}^{t_2} -I\alpha\omega\,dt = -I\omega \int_{+\omega}^{-\omega} d\gamma = 2I\omega^2$$

Note that the motor torque is applied to the input of the reverse gear; hence the direction of the motor torque is opposite to the torque applied to the load, i.e. $T = -I\alpha$.

Since the kinetic energy when the load is rotating at ω is the same as when the load is rotating at $-\omega$, all the work done by the motor appears as heat in slipping of the clutch. Hence the total energy used in friction work in method (2) is $(\frac{1}{2}I\omega^2 + 2I\omega^2) = (5/2)I\omega^2$.

The total time for a complete cycle by method (2) is t seconds to get the load from 0 to ω speed, plus $2t$ seconds to go from ω to $-\omega$, or a total of $3t$ seconds.

Thus the time for a complete cycle is the same for both methods, but method (1) is more efficient than method (2). Method (1) loses $(3/2)I\omega^2$ in friction work, while method (2) loses $(5/2)I\omega^2$ in friction work.

Reversing by method (2) would actually be faster than (1) because of less time needed for the manipulation of brake, clutch, and reverse gear.

11. Derive the torque capacity of a cone clutch based upon the assumption that the pressure between the cup and cone part is uniform. Refer to Fig. 14-7.

Solution:

(*a*) Consider a differential element bounded by circles of radii r and $(r+dr)$. The area of the differential fustrum of a cone is $dA = 2\pi r(\frac{dr}{\sin\alpha})$.

(*b*) The integral of the differential torques is

$$\int dT = \int_{R_i}^{R_o} (2\pi r \frac{dr}{\sin\alpha})pfr$$

or

$$T = \frac{2\pi pf}{\sin\alpha}\left(\frac{R_o^3 - R_i^3}{3}\right)$$

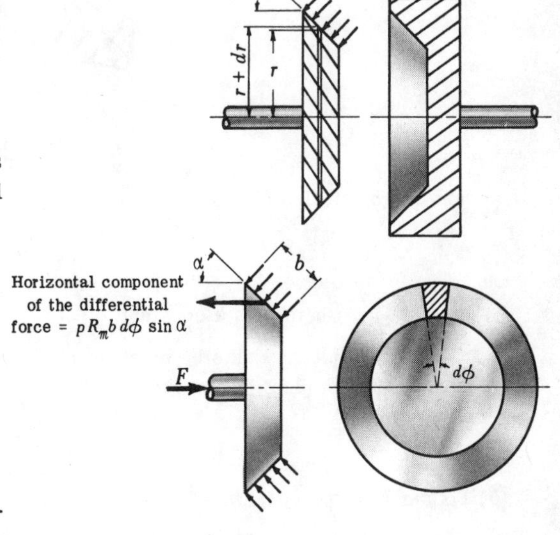

Fig. 14-7

(*c*) Define the force F_n as that due to the pressure applied to the area as if it were stretched out into a plane:

$$F_n = p(2\pi R_m b)$$

(*d*) To relate F_n to the axial force F, consider a differential element with central angle $d\phi$. The differential area is

$$dA = 2\pi R_m b\,(d\phi/2\pi) = R_m b\,d\phi$$

The differential normal force is $dN = pR_m b\,d\phi$. The horizontal component of the differential force is dF; then

$$\int dF = \int_0^{2\pi} pR_m b\,d\phi \sin\alpha \quad \text{or} \quad F = 2\pi pR_m b \sin\alpha = F_n \sin\alpha$$

(*e*) Substitution of the pressure p from the equation of (*c*) into the equation of (*b*) gives

$$T = \frac{F_n f}{R_m b \sin\alpha}\left(\frac{R_o^3 - R_i^3}{3}\right) = F_n f\left[\frac{2}{3}\left(\frac{R_o^3 - R_i^3}{R_o^2 - R_i^2}\right)\right] = \frac{Ff}{\sin\alpha}\left[\frac{2}{3}\left(\frac{R_o^3 - R_i^3}{R_o^2 - R_i^2}\right)\right]$$

since $R_m = \frac{1}{2}(R_o + R_i)$, $(b\sin\alpha) = R_o - R_i$, and $F_n = F/(\sin\alpha)$.

12. Derive the torque capacity of a cone clutch based upon a uniform wear assumption. Refer to Fig. 14-8 below.

Solution:

(*a*) For wear to be uniform, the work done per unit area must be constant. Consider a differential element

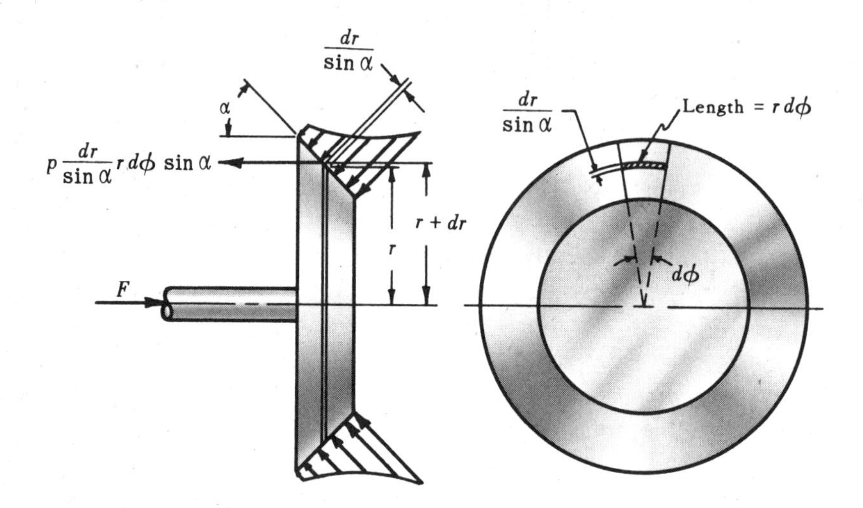

Fig. 14-8

bounded by circles of radii r and $(r + dr)$.

$$\frac{\text{Work done in } N \text{ rev}}{\text{area}} = \frac{pf[2\pi r\,(dr/\sin\alpha)]\,(2\pi rN)}{2\pi r\,(dr/\sin\alpha)} = \text{constant}$$

or $p = C/r$, where C is a constant.

This result may also be obtained by considering that the wear at any point is constant and is proportional to the product of pressure and velocity. Thus, wear $= KpV = Kp\,(\omega r) =$ constant, or $p = C/r$ since ω is constant.

(*b*) Torque $T = \int_{R_i}^{R_o} pf\,(2\pi r \frac{dr}{\sin\alpha})\,r = 2\pi Cf\left(\frac{R_o^2 - R_i^2}{2\sin\alpha}\right)$,

where $C = pr$.

(*c*) $F_n = \int_{R_i}^{R_o} p\,(2\pi r \frac{dr}{\sin\alpha}) = \frac{2\pi C}{\sin\alpha}(R_o - R_i)$

(*d*) To eliminate C, substitute the value of C from the equation of (*c*) into the equation of (*b*) and obtain

$$T = F_n f R_m$$

(*e*) The relation of F_n and F can be obtained by first setting up the differential normal force on the differential area considered as a rectangle with differential dimensions $dr/(\sin\alpha)$ and $r(d\phi)$:

$$dF_n = p\,(dr/\sin\alpha)\,r\,d\phi$$

(*f*) The sum of the horizontal components of the differential forces is F:

$$F = \int_{R_i}^{R_o}\int_0^{2\pi} p\,\frac{dr}{\sin\alpha}\,r\,d\phi\,\sin\alpha = \int_{R_i}^{R_o}\int_0^{2\pi} \frac{C}{r}(dr)\,r\,d\phi$$

$$= 2\pi C\,(R_o - R_i)$$

From (*c*), $2\pi C\,(R_o - R_i) = F_n \sin\alpha$; hence $F = F_n \sin\alpha$, the same as for uniform pressure.

Substituting $F_n = F/(\sin\alpha)$ into the equation of (*d*), the torque is given by

$$T = F_n f R_m = \frac{F}{\sin\alpha} f R_m$$

13. A soft surface cone clutch must handle 1865 in-lb of torque at 1250 rpm. The large diameter of the clutch is 13.75 in., the cone pitch angle is $6\frac{1}{4}^\circ$, the face width b is 2.50 in., and the coefficient of friction is 0.20. Referring to Fig. 14-9, determine:

(*a*) The axial force F required to transmit the torque.

(*b*) The axial force required to engage the clutch, F_e, engagement taking place when the clutch is not rotating.

(*c*) The average normal pressure p on the contact surfaces when the maximum torque is being transmitted.

(*d*) The maximum normal pressure assuming uniform wear.

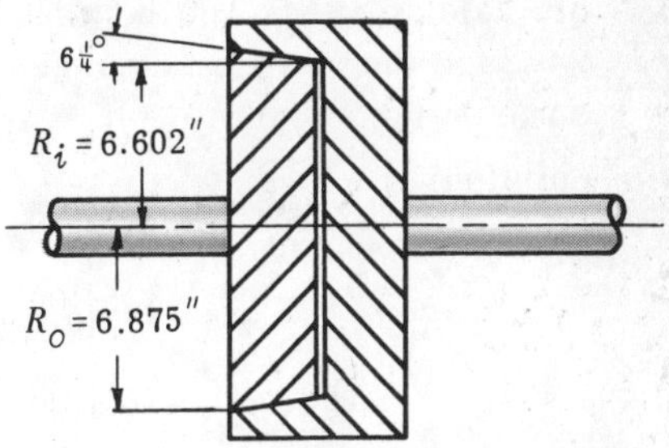

$6\frac{1}{4}^\circ$

$R_i = 6.602''$

$R_o = 6.875''$

Fig. 14-9

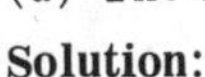

Solution:

(*a*) $R_m = R_o - \frac{1}{2}b\sin\alpha = \frac{1}{2}(13.75) - \frac{1}{2}(2.50\sin 6\frac{1}{4}^\circ) = 6.74$ in.

$$T = \frac{F}{\sin\alpha}fR_m, \qquad 1865 = \frac{F}{\sin 6\frac{1}{4}^\circ}(0.20)(6.74), \qquad F = 151 \text{ lb}$$

(*b*) $$F_e = F_n(\sin\alpha + f\cos\alpha) = \frac{T}{fR_m}(\sin\alpha + f\cos\alpha) = \frac{1865}{0.20(6.74)}(\sin 6\tfrac{1}{4}^\circ + 0.20\cos 6\tfrac{1}{4}^\circ) = 428 \text{ lb}$$

(*c*) $$p = \frac{F}{\pi(R_o^2 - R_i^2)} = \frac{151}{\pi(6.875^2 - 6.60^2)} = 13.0 \text{ psi}, \text{ where } R_i = R_o - b\sin\alpha = 6.60 \text{ in.}$$

(*d*) $$p(\max) = \frac{F}{2\pi(R_o - R_i)R_i} = \frac{151}{2\pi(6.875 - 6.60)(6.60)} = 13.3 \text{ psi.}$$

14. Consider the same clutch and conditions as in Problem 13, but assume uniform pressure. Determine:

(*a*) The axial force F required to transmit the torque.

(*b*) The axial force required to engage the clutch, F_e, engagement taking place when the clutch is not rotating.

(*c*) The average normal pressure p on the contact surfaces when the maximum torque is being transmitted.

Solution:

(*a*) $$T = Ff\left(\frac{R_o^3 - R_i^3}{3R_m b\sin^2\alpha}\right), \qquad 1865 = F(0.20)\left[\frac{6.875^3 - 6.60^3}{3(6.74)(2.50)(0.109^2)}\right], \qquad F = 148 \text{ lb}$$

(*b*) $F_e = F_n(\sin\alpha + f\cos\alpha) = 1360(\sin 6\frac{1}{4}^\circ + 0.20\cos 6\frac{1}{4}^\circ) = 421$ lb, where $F_n = F/\sin\alpha = 1360$ lb.

(*c*) $F_n = p(2\pi R_m b)$, $\quad 1360 = p(2\pi)(6.74)(2.50)$, $\quad p = 12.9$ psi

15. Compare the horsepower capacity of two clutches: one a multiple disk clutch and the other a cone type of clutch. Both clutches operate at the same speed, both have the same mean diameter, and the same axial load is exerted in both clutches. The coefficient of friction is the same for both clutches. The multiple disk clutch has 4 steel disks and 3 bronze disks. The total cone angle of the cone clutch is 20° (pitch angle = 10°). Assume uniform wear in both clutches.

Solution:

$$\frac{T\text{ (disk clutch)}}{T\text{ (cone clutch)}} = \frac{6FfR_m}{(F/\sin\alpha)fR_m} = 6\sin\alpha = 6\sin 10^\circ = 1.044$$

Hence, for dimensions given, hp capacity of disk clutch = 1.044 × hp capacity of cone clutch.

16. A cone clutch, asbestos lined, is to transmit 900 in-lb after engagement. If the maximum available axial force is 200 lb, what is the required width of face? The total included cone angle is 24°, and the maximum average pressure is limited to 16 psi. Coefficient of friction is 0.20. Assume uniform wear.

Solution:

Force to engage clutch, $F_e = F_n(\sin\alpha + f\cos\alpha)$, $200 = F_n(\sin 12^\circ + 0.20\cos 12^\circ)$, $F_n = 496$ lb

$T = F_n f R_m$, $900 = 496(0.20)R_m$, $R_m = 9.07$ in. Use $R_m = 9\frac{1}{8}$ in.

$F_n = p(2\pi R_m b)$, $496 = 16(2\pi)(9\frac{1}{8})b$, $b = 0.54$ in. Use $b = \frac{9}{16}$ in.

SUPPLEMENTARY PROBLEMS

17. In a multiple disk clutch, the radial width of the friction material is to be $\frac{1}{5}$ of the maximum radius. The coefficient of friction is 0.25. (*a*) How many disks are required to transmit 70 hp at 3000 rpm? The maximum diameter of the clutch cannot exceed 10 in. The axial force is limited to 150 lb. (*b*) What is the mean unit pressure on each contact surface? *Ans.* 11 disks, 4.64 psi

18. A multiple disk clutch has 9 plates having contact surfaces of 2 in. inside diameter and 4 in. outside diameter. If the coefficient of friction is 0.2 and the maximum average permissible normal pressure is 40 psi, what is the required operating force and how much horsepower can the clutch deliver at 500 rpm?
Ans. 377 lb, 7.2 hp

19. A disk clutch consists of two steel disks in contact with one asbestos fabric-faced disk having an outside diameter of 10 in. and an inside diameter of 8 in. Determine the horsepower that can be transmitted at 1000 rpm if the coefficient of friction is 0.35 and the disks are pressed together by an axial force of 2000 lb.
Ans. 100 hp

20. A multiple disk clutch has six pairs of contact surfaces of alternate steel and asbestos-lined steel. The outside and inside diameters of the contact surfaces are 10 and 7 inches respectively. How much horsepower can be transmitted at 600 rpm if the coefficient of friction is 0.2 and the axial force is 100 pounds?
Ans. 4.86 hp

21. A leather-faced cone clutch transmits power at 1200 rpm. The total cone angle is 20° (cone pitch angle is 10°). The face width of the contact surfaces is $3\frac{1}{2}$ in. The coefficient of friction is 0.25. Determine the necessary mean diameter of the clutch to transmit 22 hp. The maximum average pressure is 10 psi.
Ans. Mean diameter = 9.13 in., use $9\frac{1}{8}$ in.

22. A leather-faced cone clutch must transmit 20 hp at a speed of 1000 rpm. The cone pitch angle is $10^\circ (\alpha = 10^\circ)$ and the mean diameter of the bearing surfaces is 8 in. Coefficient of friction is 0.3. Determine (*a*) the required width b to limit the bearing pressure to a maximum average value of 10 psi, (*b*) the necessary axial load to engage the clutch, with both parts stationary, to obtain the required torque capacity. Assume uniform wear. *Ans.* (*a*) 4.17 in., use $4\frac{1}{4}$ in. (*b*) 493 lb

23. A cone clutch with cast iron surfaces and coefficient of friction of 0.2 is to transmit 40 hp at 500 rpm. The maximum diameter is limited to 12 in. The cone pitch angle, α, is 15°. The average pressure is limited to about 50 psi. Determine (*a*) the face width b and (*b*) the force required to hold the clutch in engagement. Assume uniform wear. *Ans.* (*a*) $b = 2.32$ in. (trial and error solution), use $b = 2\frac{3}{8}$ in. which gives an average pressure of 52 psi. (*b*) 1150 lb

24. A soft cone clutch has a cone pitch angle of 10°, a mean diameter of 12 in., and a face width of 4 in. Using a coefficient of friction 0.2, the assumption that uniform wear exists, and an average pressure of 10 psi for a speed of 500 rpm, determine (*a*) the force required to engage the clutch and (*b*) the horsepower that can be transmitted. *Ans.* 560 lb, 14.3 hp

25. A soft surface cone clutch must handle 1900 in-lb of torque at 1200 rpm. The large diameter of the clutch is 14 in. and the included angle is 20°. The width of face is 3 in. Using a coefficient of friction 0.2, determine (*a*) the axial force required to engage the clutch, (*b*) the normal unit pressure required when the clutch is operating at capacity. Assume uniform pressure.
Ans. 523 lb, 11.1 psi

26. A soft surface cone clutch must handle 1865 in-lb of torque at 1250 rpm. The large diameter of the clutch is 13.75 in. and the included angle is 12.5°. The face width of the bearing surfaces is 2.5 in. Using a coefficient of friction 0.20, determine (*a*) the force (F_e) to engage the clutch, (*b*) the required normal unit pressure on the contact surfaces when operation is at capacity.
Ans. 428 lb, 13.15 psi

27. A cone clutch is mounted on a shaft which transmits power at 225 rpm. The small diameter of the cone is 9 in., the cone face is 2 in., and the cone face makes an angle of 15 degrees with the horizontal. Determine the axial force necessary to engage the clutch to transmit 6 hp if the coefficient of friction of the contact surfaces is 0.25. What is the maximum pressure on the contact surfaces assuming uniform wear?
Ans. 706 lb, 24.9 psi

28. A soft surface cone clutch has an included angle of 20 degrees, a mean diameter of 12 inches, and a face width of 4 inches. Using a coefficient of friction 0.2 and an allowable average pressure of 10 psi, determine the force required to engage clutch and the horsepower that can be transmitted at 500 rpm.
Ans. 560 lb, 14.4 hp

29. An engine developing 40 hp at 1250 rpm is fitted with a cone clutch built into the flywheel. The cone has a face angle of 12.5 degrees and a mean diameter of 14 in. The coefficient of friction is 0.20 and the normal pressure on the clutch face is not to exceed 12 psi. Determine the required face width and the force necessary to engage the clutch, assuming uniform wear.
Ans. 2.96 in., 592 lb

30. A leather-faced cone clutch has a contact surface with a mean diameter of 15 in. and transmits 20 hp when turning at 800 rpm. For a cone angle of 20 degrees and a coefficient of friction 0.30, determine the axial force required to keep the surface in contact.
Ans. 121.5 lb

Chapter 15

Brake Design

BRAKES are machine elements that absorb either kinetic or potential energy in the process of slowing down or stopping a moving part. The absorbed energy is dissipated as heat. Brake capacity depends upon the unit pressure between the braking surfaces, the coefficient of friction, and the ability of the brake to dissipate heat equivalent to the energy being absorbed. The performance of brakes is similar to that of clutches except that clutches connect one moving part to another moving part, whereas brakes connect a moving part to a frame.

EXTERNAL SHOE OR BLOCK BRAKES consist of shoes or blocks pressed against the surface of a rotating cylinder called the brake drum. The shoe may be rigidly mounted to a pivoted lever as shown in Fig. 15-1, or the shoe may be pivoted to the lever as shown in Fig. 15-2.

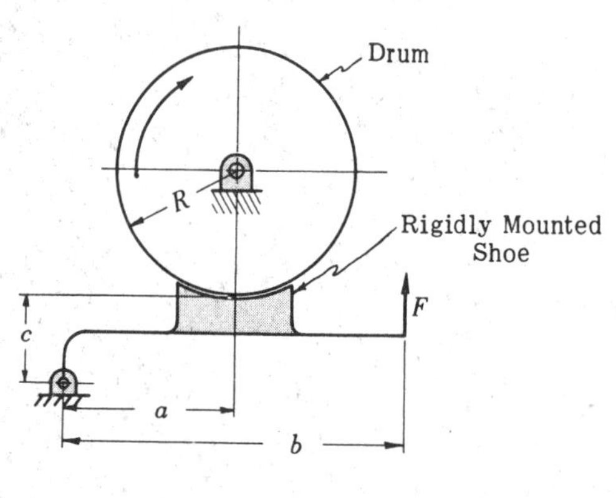

Fig. 15-1

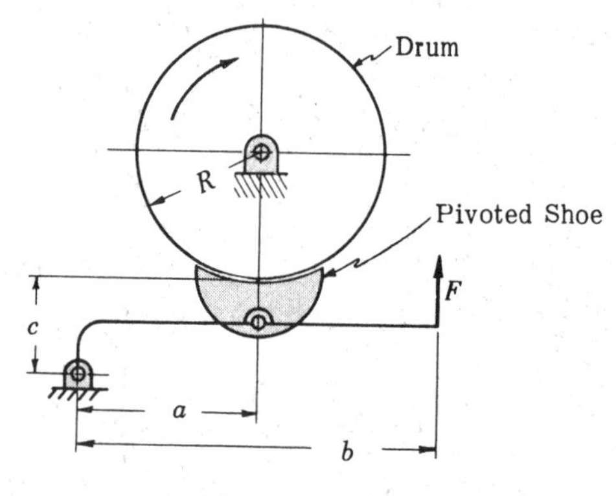

Fig. 15-2

SINGLE BLOCK BRAKE design may be based on the force and torque analysis of the lever and shoe as a free body, as shown in Fig. 15-3. The normal force N and the frictional force fN may be shown acting at the midpoint of contact of the shoe without appreciable error for angles of θ not greater than 60°. Summing moments about the fixed pivot O,

$$(N+W)a - fNc - Fb = 0 \qquad \text{or} \qquad F = \frac{(N+W)a - fNc}{b}$$

Note that for a clockwise rotation of the drum, the friction force fN aids the force F in applying the brake and the brake is partially **self-actuating**. For a given coefficient of friction the brake may be designed to be wholly self-actuating (or self-locking). For this condition to exist, $F=0$ or negative in the above equa-

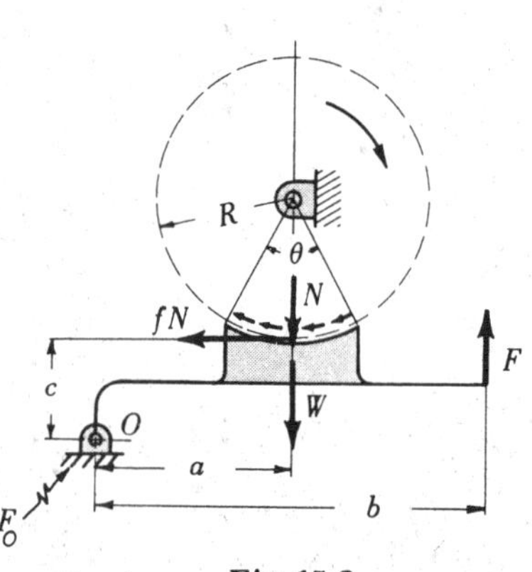

Fig. 15-3

tion. We may also assume that the weight W is negligible; then

$$F = \frac{Na - fNc}{b} \leqq 0$$

i.e. when $\frac{a}{c} \leqq f$ the brake is self-locking.

The braking torque T for a non-self-locking situation is

$$T = fNR \text{ in-lb}$$

where f = coefficient of friction; N = total normal force, lb; R = radius of brake drum, in.

When the angle of contact is large, say 60° or more, an appreciable error might result from assuming that the frictional and normal forces act at the midpoint of contact of the shoe. A more precise analysis shows that the frictional force fN is shifted away from the surface of the drum to a point D at a distance h from the center of the drum as shown in Fig. 15-4 for a *pivoted* shoe. The pivoted shoe is the more usual construction when using long external shoes. The braking torque T is now

$$T = fNh = fN\left(\frac{4R \sin \frac{1}{2}\theta}{\theta + \sin\theta}\right) \quad \text{(See Problem 5.)}$$

where $h = \dfrac{4R \sin \frac{1}{2}\theta}{\theta + \sin\theta}$. This is based on assuming that wear in the direction of the resultant normal force N is uniform, which means that the normal pressure p_n varies as the cosine of the angle ϕ, or

$$p_n = C \cos\phi$$

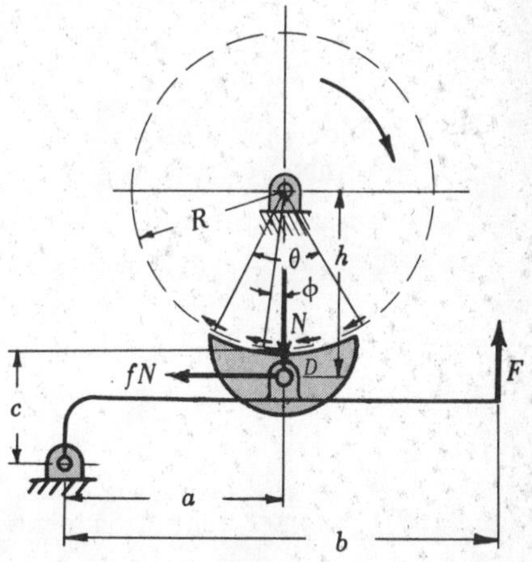

Fig. 15-4

where C is a constant $= \dfrac{2N}{wR(\theta + \sin\theta)}$, w being the width of the brake shoe in inches.

The magnitude of h then determines the location of the pivot for the pivoted shoe. Two conditions have been satisfied: (1) the shoe is a two force member, and the resultant of the normal force and frictional force must pass through the pivot; (2) the pressure distribution is as assumed. If the pivot of the shoe is located at a distance other than h, as calculated, the moment of the resultant normal force and frictional force would still be zero about the pivot, but now the assumed pressure distribution cannot exist. Consequently the pressure must change and greater wear will occur at either the trailing or leading edge. However, if the pivot is located at a small distance from the theoretical value of h, based upon the pressure distribution $p_n = C \cos\phi$, the above equations may still be used without appreciable error. Also the pivot may be located anywhere along the resultant of the frictional and normal forces without affecting the assumed pressure distribution.

The average pressure, $p_{av} = \dfrac{2C \sin \frac{1}{2}\theta}{\theta}$.

DOUBLE SHOE BRAKES are commonly used in order to reduce shaft and bearing loads, to obtain greater capacity, and to reduce the amount of heat generated per sq in. See Fig. 15-5. The normal force N_L on the left shoe is not necessarily equal to the normal force N_R on the right shoe. For double block brakes whose shoes have small contact angles, of say less than 60°, the braking torque may be approximated by

$$T = f(N_L + N_R)R$$

If the shoe contact angle is greater than about 60°, then a more precise evaluation of the braking torque for pivoted shoes is

$$T = f(N_L + N_R)\left(\frac{4R \sin \frac{1}{2}\theta}{\theta + \sin\theta}\right)$$

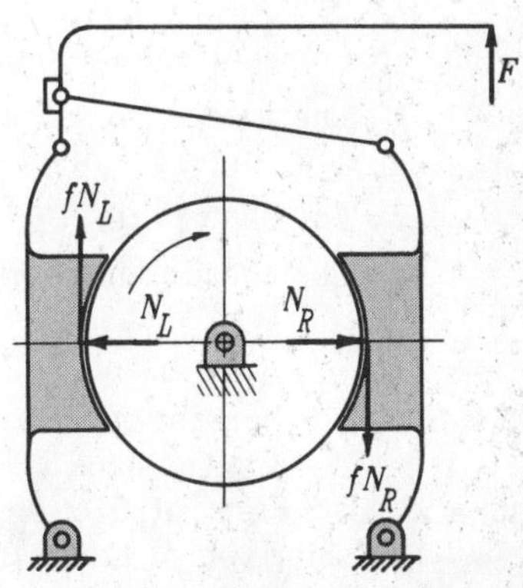

Fig. 15-5

If long rigid shoes are to be used, an analysis similar to that for internal shoes as presented on the following page would apply.

INTERNAL SHOE BRAKE design of the symmetrical type shown in Fig. 15-6 may be approximated by the equations given below.

The braking torque T may be determined by

$$T = fwr^2 \left(\frac{\cos\theta_1 - \cos\theta_2}{\sin\theta_m}\right)(p_m + p_m')$$

where f = coefficient of friction

w = face width of shoe, in.

r = internal radius of drum, in.

θ_1 = center angle from shoe pivot to heel of lining, degrees

θ_2 = center angle from shoe pivot to toe of lining, degrees

p_m = maximum pressure, psi (right shoe)

p_m' = maximum pressure, psi (left shoe) $= \dfrac{cFp_m}{M_n + M_f}$

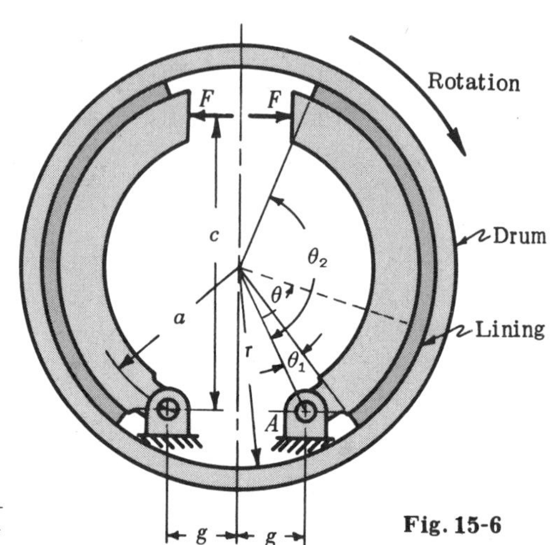

Fig. 15-6

The above is based on the assumed pressure distribution

$$p = p_m \frac{\sin\theta}{\sin\theta_m}$$

where θ_m = center angle from shoe pivot to point of maximum pressure, psi

$\theta_m = 90°$ if $\theta_2 > 90°$, $\theta_m = \theta_2$ if $\theta_2 < 90°$.

The moment M_f of the frictional forces with respect to the shoe pivot may be determined by

$$M_f = \frac{fp_m wr}{\sin\theta_m}\int_{\theta_1}^{\theta_2} \sin\theta(r - a\cos\theta)\,d\theta$$

where a = distance from the center of the drum to the shoe pivot, in.

The moment M_n of the normal forces with respect to the shoe pivot may be determined by

$$M_n = \frac{p_m wra}{\sin\theta_m}\int_{\theta_1}^{\theta_2} \sin^2\theta\,d\theta$$

The actuating force F may be determined by setting the summation of moments about the pin joint equal to zero. For clockwise rotation of the drum, the right shoe has self actuating properties and

$F = \dfrac{M_n - M_f}{c}$; for the left shoe, $F = \dfrac{M_n' + M_f'}{c}$

where c = the moment arm, in inches, of the actuating force F, $M_n' = \dfrac{M_n p_m'}{p_m}$, $M_f' = \dfrac{M_f p_m'}{p_m}$.

The above equations are based on the following assumptions:

1) The normal pressure at any contact point on the shoe is proportional to its vertical distance from the pivot point.
2) The shoe is rigid.
3) The coefficient of friction does not vary with pressure and velocity.

BAND BRAKES consist of a flexible band wrapped partly around the drum. They are actuated by pulling the band tightly against the drum. The brake capacity depends upon the angle of wrap, the coefficient of friction, and the band tensions. A simple band brake is shown in Fig.15-7 below. For this type of brake the direction of rotation of the drum is such that the band anchored to the frame is the tight side F_1, as shown.

As for belts at zero velocity, the relationship between the tight and loose sides of the band is

$$F_1/F_2 = e^{f\alpha}$$

where F_1 = tension in tight side of band, lb
F_2 = tension in loose side of band, lb
e = natural logarithm base
f = coefficient of friction
α = angle of wrap, radians.

The torque braking capacity T is

$$T = (F_1 - F_2)r \text{ in-lb}$$

where r = radius of brake drum, in. This type of band brake does not have self-actuating properties.

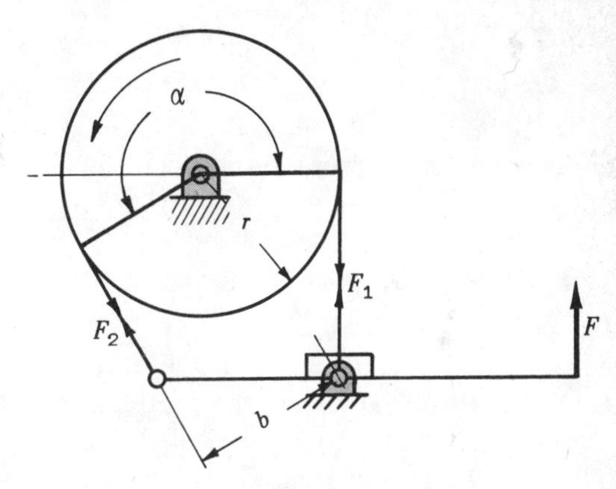

Fig. 15-7

A simple two-way band brake is shown in Fig. 15-8 below. This type of design functions equally well for either direction of rotation since the moment arms of the tight and loose tensions are equal.

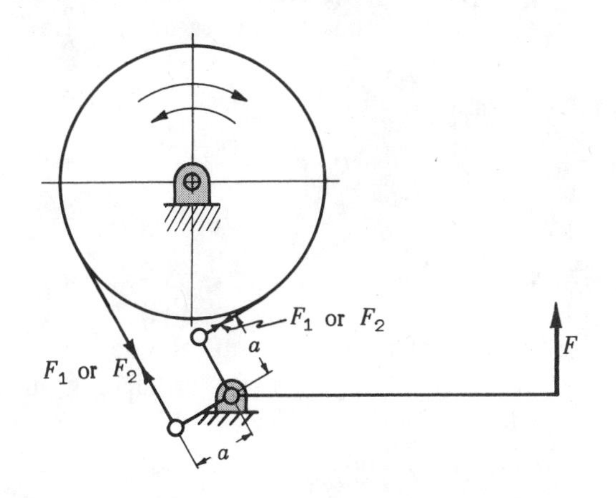

Fig. 15-8

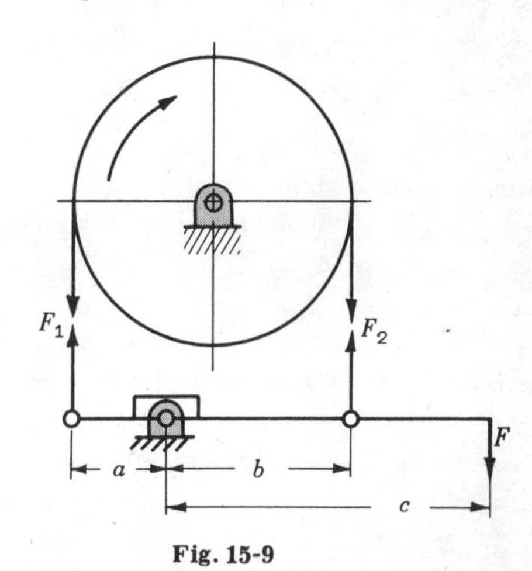

Fig. 15-9

The differential band brake as shown in Fig. 15-9 above is one that has self-actuating properties and may be designed to be self-locking. The differential band brake is usually designed so that the direction of drum rotation permits the tight side of the band to aid in applying the brake. Referring to Fig. 15-9, if we take the summation of moments with respect to the pivot, we have

$$Fc + F_1 a - F_2 b = 0 \quad \text{or} \quad F = \frac{F_2 b - F_1 a}{c}$$

Substituting $F_1 = F_2 e^{f\alpha}$,

$$F = \frac{F_2(b - e^{f\alpha}a)}{c}$$

from which it can be seen that for a self-locking brake, i.e. when $F = 0$ or negative,

$$b \leqq ae^{f\alpha} \quad \text{or} \quad b/a \leqq e^{f\alpha}$$

It should be noted that the differential band brake may be made self-locking for one direction of rotation only. A self-locking brake of this type is used to allow motion in one direction only and to prevent a reversed motion, as might occur when a conveyor or hoist is acted upon by gravity. If a brake is self-locking, it requires a force in the opposite direction of applying the brake in order to have it released. Also, after the brake has locked and additional torque is applied, the band tensions F_1 and F_2 will increase, but the ratio of F_1 to F_2 will no longer equal $e^{f\alpha}$ since this relationship prevails only when the brake is slipping or when slip is pending.

The maximum unit pressure p_m occurs at the tight end of the band and is determined by

$$p_m = \frac{F_1}{w\,r}$$

The average normal pressure between the band and the drum (which is used in heat generated calculations) is

$$p_{av} = \frac{F_1}{w\,r\,f\,\alpha}\left(\frac{e^{f\alpha}-1}{e^{f\alpha}}\right)$$

HEAT GENERATED during the application of a brake must be dissipated by heat transfer or the brake will overheat and perhaps burn out the lining. The rate of heat generated, H_g, is equal to the rate of frictional work:

$$H_g = p_{av} A_c f V/778 \text{ Btu/min}$$

where p_{av} = average contact pressure, psi; f = coefficient of friction
A_c = contact area, in^2; V = peripheral velocity of drum, ft/min.

The heat generated may also be determined by considering the amount of kinetic or potential energy that is being absorbed:

$$H_g = (E_p + E_k)/778 \text{ Btu/min}$$

where E_p = total potential energy absorbed, ft-lb/min
E_k = total kinetic energy absorbed, ft-lb/min.

The heat dissipated, H_d, may be estimated by

$$H_d = C\Delta t A_r \text{ Btu/min}$$

where C = coefficient of heat transfer, Btu per in^2 per min per °F temperature difference
Δt = temperature difference between the exposed radiating surface and the surrounding air
A_r = area of radiating surface, in^2.

C may be of the order of 0.0006 for a Δt of 100°F and increase up to 0.0009 for a Δt of 400°F.

The expressions for heat dissipated are quite approximate and should serve only as an indication of the capacity of the brake to dissipate heat. The exact performance of the brake should be determined by test. Another convenient indicator of brake capacity is hp/wd which is limited to about 0.3, where w = width of band or shoe and d = diameter of drum in inches.

Experience has also shown that the product of the average pressure p_{av} (psi of projected area) and the rubbing velocity V (ft/min) should be limited as follows: $p_{av}V \leqq 28{,}000$ for continuous application of load, as in lowering operations, and poor dissipation of heat; $p_{av}V \leqq 55{,}000$ for intermittent application of load, with comparatively long periods of rest, and poor dissipation of heat; $p_{av}V \leqq 83{,}000$ for continuous application of load and good dissipation of heat, as in an oil bath.

Some permissible average values for operating temperatures, coefficient of friction, and maximum contact pressure for brake materials are given below.

Material	Max. Temp., °F	f	p_{max}, psi
Metal on metal	600	0.25	200
Wood on metal	150	0.25	70
Leather on metal	150	0.35	25
Asbestos on metal in oil	500	0.40	50
Sintered metal on cast iron in oil	500	0.15	400

SOLVED PROBLEMS

1. A 14 in. radius brake drum contacts a single shoe as shown in Fig. 15-10 below and sustains 2000 in-lb of torque at 500 rpm. For a coefficient of friction of 0.3 determine:
   (*a*) The total normal force N on the shoe.
   (*b*) The required force F to apply the brake for clockwise rotation.
   (*c*) The required force F to apply the brake for counterclockwise rotation.
   (*d*) The dimension c required to make the brake self-locking, assuming the other dimensions remain as shown.
   (*e*) The rate of heat generated, Btu/min.

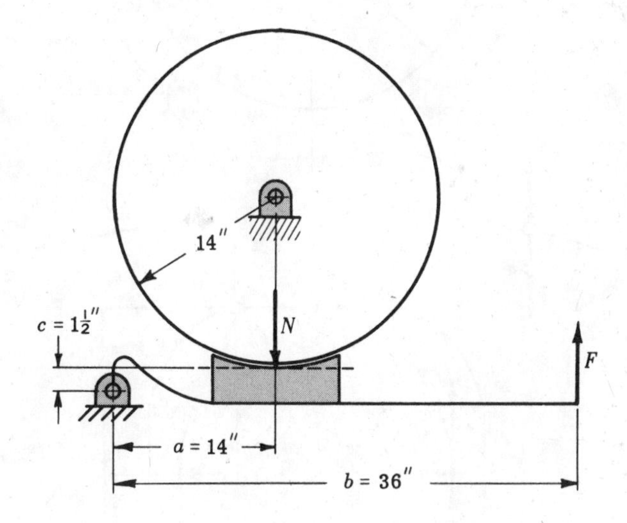

Fig. 15-10

Solution:

(*a*) Torque = fNr = $0.3N(14)$ = 2000, N = 476 lb
Frictional force = fN = 2000/14 = 143 lb

(*b*) For clockwise rotation, take summation of moments about the pivot equal to zero:

$$(1.5)(143) + 36F - (14)(476) = 0, \quad F = 179 \text{ lb}$$

(*c*) For counterclockwise rotation, take summation of moments about the pivot equal to zero:

$$(14)(476) + (1.5)(143) - 36F = 0, \quad F = 191 \text{ lb}$$

(*d*) For self-locking, which can only occur for clockwise rotation of the drum,

$$a \leqq fc \quad \text{or} \quad c \geqq a/f = 14/0.3 = 46.7 \text{ in.}$$

(*e*)
$$H_g = \frac{fNV}{778} = \frac{(0.3)(476)[\pi 28(500)/12]}{778} = 674 \text{ Btu/min}$$

2. A double shoe block brake as shown in Fig. 15-11 below has a force of 300 lb applied at the end of the operating lever. Determine the amount of torque that the brake can sustain for clockwise rotation of the drum and a coefficient of friction of 0.3.

Solution:

First consider the operating lever as a free body and evaluate the horizontal and vertical components of the forces on the pin joints A and B by taking summation of forces and moments as required.

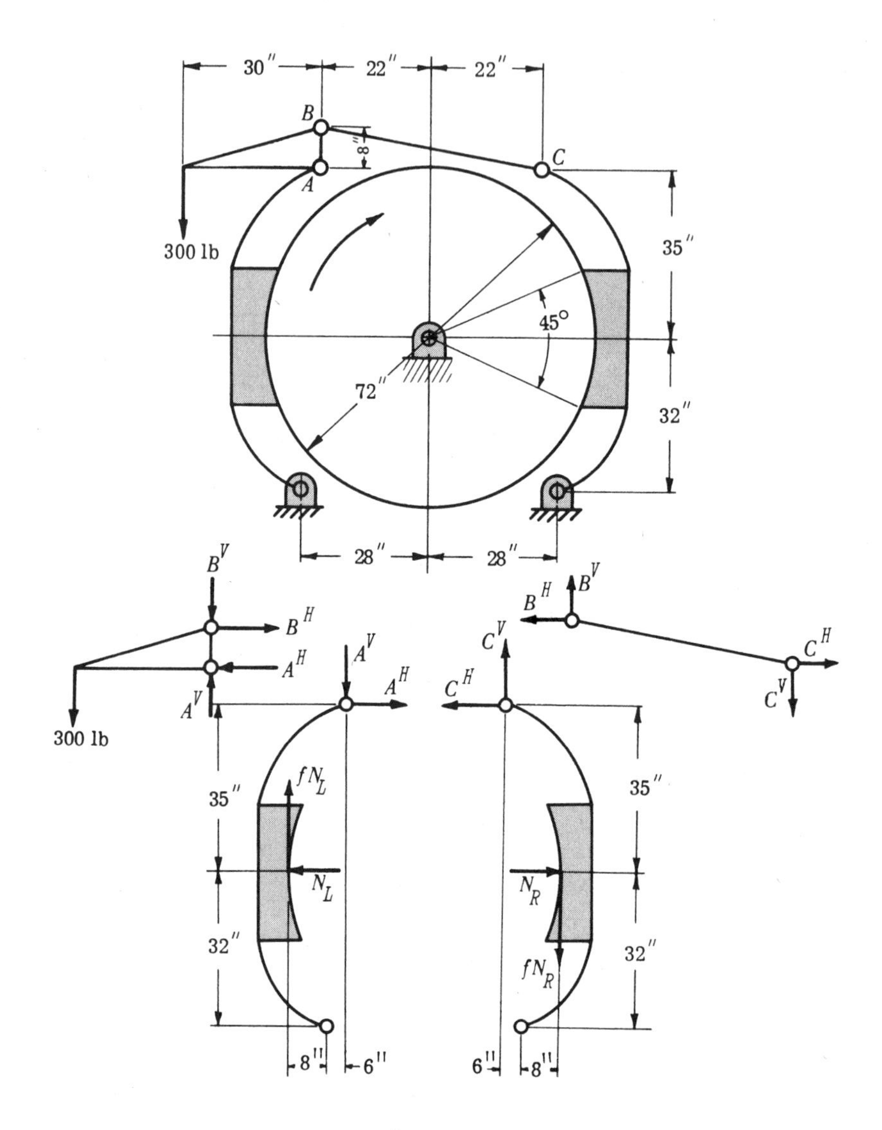

Fig. 15-11

$$A^H = B^H, \quad A^V - B^V - 300 = 0, \quad 8B^H = 300(30) \text{ or } B^H = 1125 \text{ lb}$$

Next consider link BC as a free body and make further evaluations of the horizontal and vertical forces at pin joints B and C.

$$B^H = C^H, \quad B^V = C^V, \quad 44B^V = 8B^H \text{ or } B^V = 204.3 \text{ lb}$$

Finally consider the right and left side shoe levers as free bodies and determine the magnitude of the normal forces on the right and left shoes. Taking summation of moments about the pivot of the left lever,

$$N_L(32) - (0.3N_L)(8) - 1125(67) - 504.3(6) = 0, \quad N_L = 2650 \text{ lb}$$

Taking summation of moments about the pivot of the right lever,

$$N_R(32) + (0.3N_R)(8) - 1125(67) + 204.3(6) = 0, \quad N_R = 2150 \text{ lb}$$

The braking torque is

$$T = (0.3)(2650+2150)(6/2) = 4320 \text{ ft-lb.}$$

3. A simple band brake has the tight side of the band attached to a fixed pivot. The angle of wrap is 280° about an 18 inch diameter drum. A torque of 1500 in-lb is sustained at 900 rpm and the coefficient of friction is 0.2. Determine the required belt tensions.

Solution:

From $F_1/F_2 = e^{f\alpha} = e^{(0.2)(280\pi/180)} = e^{0.98} = 2.665$ and $9(F_1 - F_2) = 1500$ we obtain

$$F_1 = 266.5 \text{ lb}, \quad \text{and} \quad F_2 = 100 \text{ lb}$$

4. A differential band brake has a force of 50 lb applied at the end of the lever as shown in Fig. 15-12. The coefficient of friction is 0.4.

(*a*) If a clockwise torque of 4000 in-lb is applied to the drum, determine the maximum and minimum force in the band.

(*b*) What is the maximum torque that the brake may sustain for counterclockwise rotation of the drum?

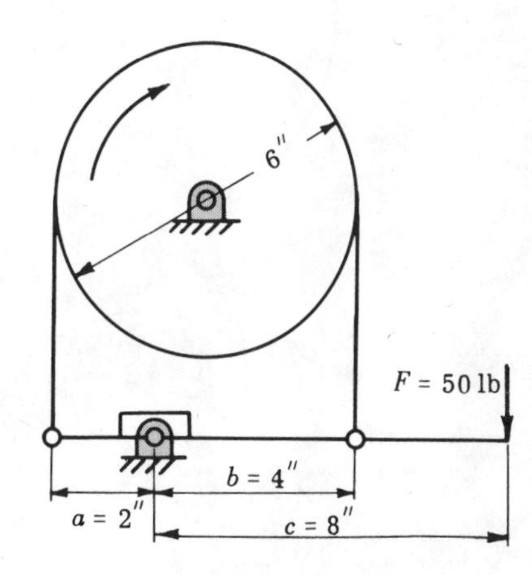

Fig. 15-12

Solution:

(*a*) For clockwise rotation, check to see if the brake is self-locking. The brake is self-locking if $b/a \leq e^{f\alpha}$, where $e^{f\alpha} = e^{0.4\pi} = 3.5$. Here $b/a = 4/2 = 2$, which is less than 3.5; hence the brake is self-locking and $F_1/F_2 = e^{f\alpha}$ does not apply.

Taking summation of moments about the fixed pivot equal to zero and using the torque relationship,

$$2F_1 + 8(50) - 4F_2 = 0 \quad \text{and} \quad 3(F_1 - F_2) = 4000,$$

from which $F_1 = 2866$ lb, $F_2 = 1533$ lb.

(*b*) For counterclockwise rotation the brake is not self-locking and $F_1'/F_2' = e^{f\alpha}$ does apply. Then

$$4F_1' - 8(50) - 2F_2' = 0 \quad \text{and} \quad F_1'/F_2' = e^{f\alpha} = 3.5, \quad \text{from which} \quad F_1' = 116 \text{ lb}, \; F_2' = 33 \text{ lb}$$

The amount of torque that may be sustained is $T = 3(116 - 33) = 249$ in-lb.

5. For a symmetrical brake shoe pressed against a brake drum as shown in Fig. 15-13(*a*) below, determine: the resultant normal force, the resultant frictional force, the location of these forces, and the moment about the center of the drum. Assume uniform wear.

Solution:

(*a*) For uniform wear, the removal of material from the face of the lining must be such that the radius of curvature of the brake shoe face be constant and equal to the radius of the drum, as shown in figure 15-13(*b*) below. The radial wear W is proportional to the product of the pressure p_n and velocity V:

$$W = Kp_n V$$

where K is a constant for a given material.

After the radial wear has taken place a point such as M moves to M' to maintain contact of the shoe with the drum. The horizontal displacement δ of point M is

$$\delta = Kp_n V/\cos\phi$$

But since δ is to be the same for every point, or constant, then

$$p_n = C\cos\phi$$

where $C = \delta/KV$. C is also the maximum pressure, occuring at $\phi = 0$.

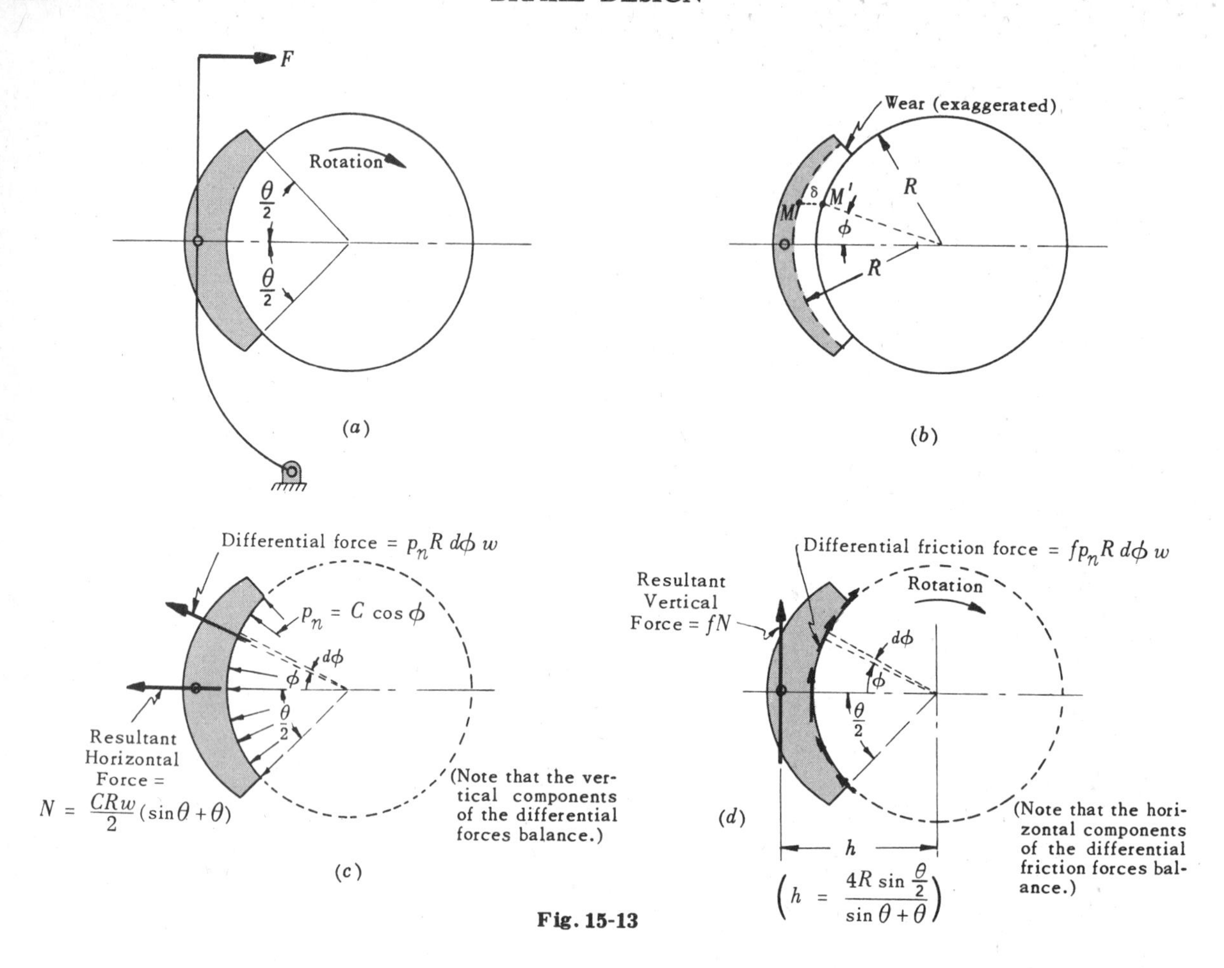

Fig. 15-13

(*b*) Since the brake shoe is symmetrical, and since the normal pressure is symmetrical, the resultant horizontal force is the sum of horizontal components of the differential normal forces and the resultant vertical force is the sum of the vertical components of the differential friction forces. See Fig.15-13(*c*) and 15-13(*d*) above.

$$\text{Resultant horizontal force} = N = 2\int_0^{\frac{1}{2}\theta} (C\cos\phi)\,R\,d\phi\,w\cos\phi = \frac{CRw}{2}(\sin\theta + \theta)$$

(*c*) Resultant vertical force $= 2\int_0^{\frac{1}{2}\theta} f(C\cos\phi)\,R\,d\phi\cos\phi = fN$

(*d*) The location of the resultant force N is seen from the symmetry of the loading: N passes through the center of the pin of the shoe on the horizontal axis of symmetry. See Fig.15-13(*c*) above.

(*e*) The location of the vertical force fN can be obtained by equating the moment of the resultant force to the moment of the differential friction forces, about any reference point. Take the center of the drum as a convenient reference point.

$$fNh = 2\int_0^{\frac{1}{2}\theta} f(C\cos\phi)\,R\,d\phi\,w\,R = 2fCR^2w\sin\tfrac{1}{2}\theta$$

where h is the distance from the center of the drum to the location of fN.

Now put $C = \dfrac{2N}{Rw(\sin\theta + \theta)}$ into the above equation and obtain $h = \dfrac{4R\sin\frac{1}{2}\theta}{\sin\theta + \theta}$.

(*f*) The moment of the resultant frictional force fN about the center of the drum is the braking torque T.

$$T = fNh = fN\left(\frac{4R\sin\frac{1}{2}\theta}{\sin\theta + \theta}\right)$$

(*g*) If the pin of the shoe is located at the distance h from the center of the drum, then the free body can be made with the normal force N passing through the center of the pin and the friction force fN also passing through the center of the pin of the shoe to satisfy the pressure distribution $p_n = C \cos\phi$. See Fig. 15-13(*e*). The force analysis can then be made without regard for the distributed loading on the shoes. If the pin is located at a distance other than h as calculated above, the resultant force must still pass through the center of the pin, although the assumption of $p_n = C \cos\phi$ cannot be satisfied. It would be satisfactory to assume the force components N and fN to act at the center of the pin without appreciable error. Note: the pivot could be located anywhere along the resultant of N and fN without affecting the pressure distribution.

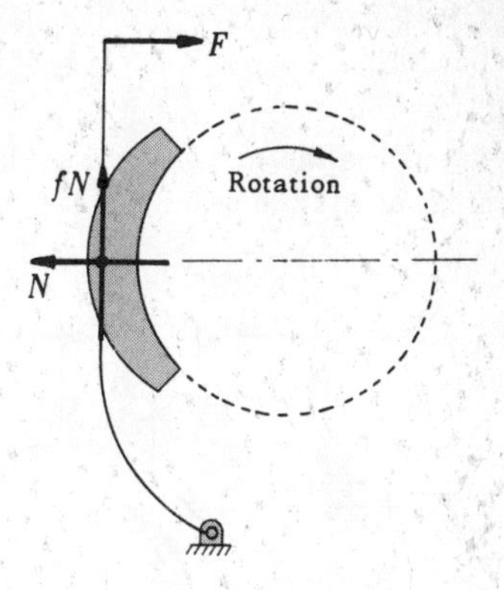

Fig. 15-13 (*e*)

6. A pivoted symmetrical shoe subtends an angle of 90° on a 20 inch diameter drum. How far from the center of the drum should the pivot be placed in order to avoid a turning moment due to the resultant frictional force, assuming uniform wear? Assume pivot located along the normal force.

Solution: Distance h to pivot from center of drum is $h = \dfrac{4R\sin\frac{1}{2}\theta}{\theta + \sin\theta} = \dfrac{(4)(10)(0.707)}{\frac{1}{2}\pi + 1} = 11$ in.

7. An internal brake of the type shown in Fig. 15-6 has a diameter of 12 in. The actuating forces F are equal and the shoes have a face width of 1.5 in. For a coefficient of friction of 0.3 and a maximum permissible pressure of 150 psi, with $\theta_1 = 0$, $\theta_2 = 130°$, $\theta_m = 90°$, $a = 5$ in. and $c = 9$ in., determine the value of the actuating forces F and the brake torque capacity.

Solution: The moment of the frictional forces about the right hand pivot is

$$M_f = \frac{fp_m wr}{\sin\theta_m}\int_0^{\theta_2}(\sin\theta)(r - a\cos\theta)\,d\theta = \frac{fp_m wr}{\sin\theta_m}\left[r - r\cos\theta_2 - \tfrac{1}{2}a\sin^2\theta_2\right]$$

$$= (0.3)(150)(1.5)(6)\left[6 + 6(0.643) - 2.5(0.766)^2\right] = 3400 \text{ in-lb}$$

The moment of the normal forces about the right hand pivot is

$$M_n = \frac{p_m wra}{\sin\theta_m}\int_0^{\theta_2}\sin^2\theta\,d\theta = \frac{p_m wra}{\sin\theta_m}\left[\tfrac{1}{2}\theta_2 - \tfrac{1}{4}\sin 2\theta_2\right] = 9300 \text{ in-lb}$$

$$F = (M_n - M_f)/c = (9300 - 3400)/9 = 656 \text{ lb}$$

The brake torque capacity of the right shoe, $T = fp_m wr^2\left(\dfrac{\cos\theta_1 - \cos\theta_2}{\sin\theta_m}\right) = 4000$ lb.

For left shoe, $T = 1860$ in-lb based on $p'_m = 69.7$ psi from $p'_m = \dfrac{Fcp_m}{M_n + M_f}$.

Total torque = 4000 + 1860 = 5860 in-lb

8. An 18 in. diameter drum has two shoes that subtend angles of 90° each. The face width of the shoe is 4 in., and 4000 Btu/min is being generated. Will the brake overheat if an allowable temperature difference between the surface of the drum and the surrounding air is 300°F?

Solution:

Equate the heat being generated to the heat dissipated, and solve for the required area A_r.

$$4000 = C\Delta t A_r, \quad 4000 = (0.0008)(300)A_r, \quad A_r = 16{,}700 \text{ in}^2 \text{ (required)}$$

where $C = 0.0008$ (Btu per in² per min per °F temp. difference) for a Δt of 300°F.

Not counting the web, the actual area A of the drum surface exposed to the air is

$A = \frac{1}{2}\pi(18)(4) = 113$ in². The drum will overheat.

SUPPLEMENTARY PROBLEMS

9. Determine the torque that may be resisted by the single block brake shown in Fig.15-14 below for a coefficient of friction of 0.3. *Ans.* 438 in-lb

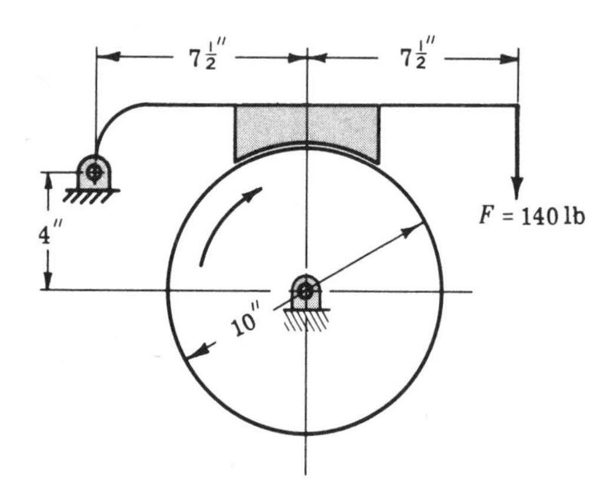

Fig. 15-14

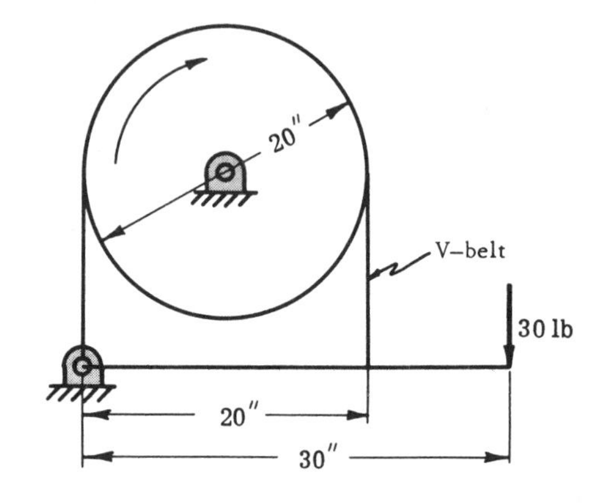

Fig. 15-15

10. A band brake uses a V–belt. The pitch diameter of the V–grooved sheave is 20 in. The groove angle is 45° and the coefficient of friction is 0.25. For the dimensions shown in Fig.15-15 above, determine the maximum horsepower rating for 300 rpm. *Ans.* 14.5 hp

11. A band brake is designed as shown in Fig.15-16 below. For the coefficient of friction used, the ratio between the band tensions is 1.75. The belts are fastened normal to the operating lever.

(*a*) What must be the distance a in order that the bands be fastened normal to the operating lever?

(*b*) How much horsepower can the brake absorb?

Ans. (*a*) 4.85 in., (*b*) 8.82 hp

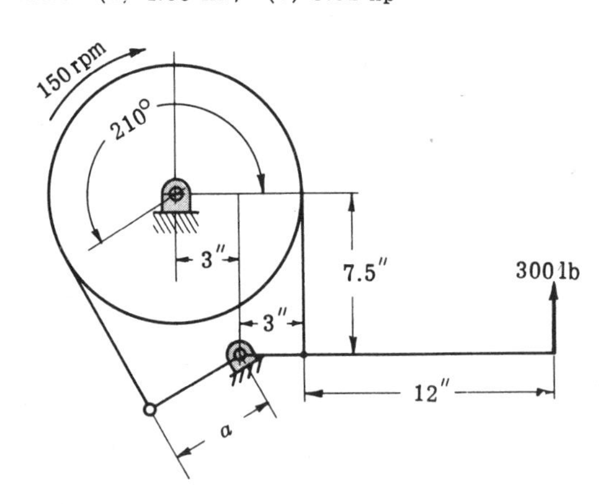

Fig. 15-16

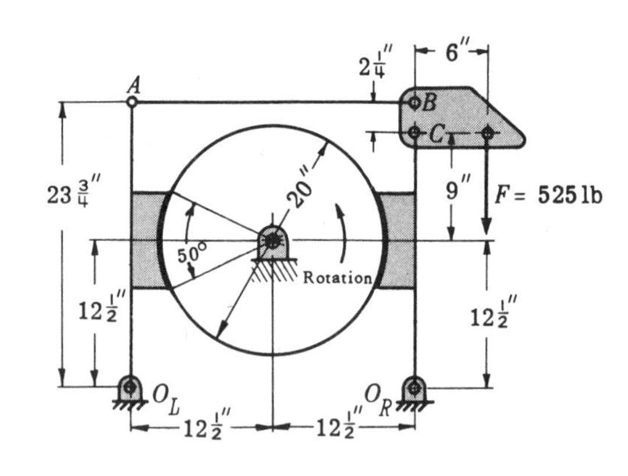

Fig. 15-17

12. A double block brake is actuated as shown in Fig.15-17 above. The drum rotates at 80 rpm when the applied force F is 525 lb and the coefficient of friction is 0.3. Employing free body force analysis, determine the braking torque and the amount of heat being generated in Btu per minute.

Ans. T = 15,300 in-lb, H_g = 825 Btu/min

13. Refer to Fig.15-6. Derive an expression for the braking torque of a symmetrically arranged internal brake.

Ans. $$T = fwr^2\left(\frac{\cos\theta_1 - \cos\theta_2}{\sin\theta_m}\right)(p_m + p'_m), \quad \text{where } p'_m = \frac{cFp_m}{M_n + M_f}$$

14. For an internal brake similar to that shown in Fig.15-6 where $\theta_1 = 15°$, $\theta_2 = 150°$, $f = 0.35$, $p_m = 125$ psi, $w = 2$ in., $r = 6$ in., $c = 10$ in. and $a = 5$ in., determine the braking torque.
Ans. $T = 7960$ in-lb

15. A double block brake with wooden shoes on a cast iron drum ($f = 0.3$) is arranged as shown in Fig. 15-18 below.
(*a*) Draw a free body diagram of each part and label all forces.
(*b*) Determine the operating force F required to absorb 35 horsepower with a drum speed of 300 rpm counterclockwise.
Ans. $F = 103$ lb

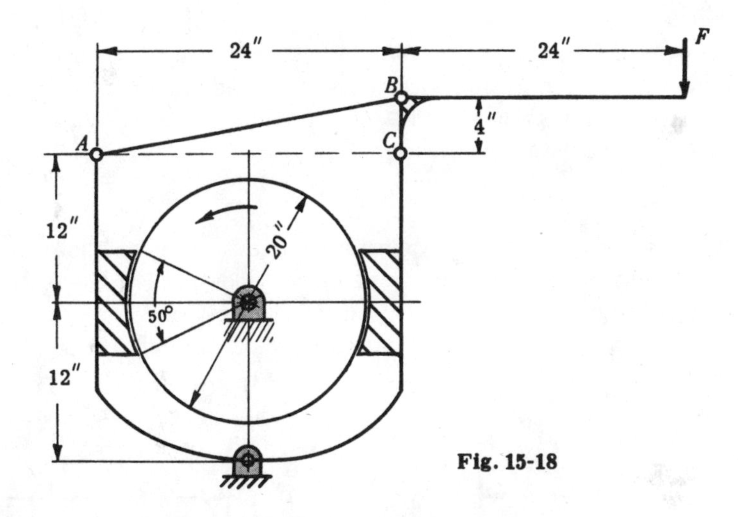

Fig. 15-18

16. The double block brake as shown in Fig.15-19 below has wooden brake shoes applied to a cast iron drum. The coefficient of friction for these two materials is 0.3. The drum rotates at 1500 rpm. Determine the power lost as heat. *Ans.* 62.3 hp

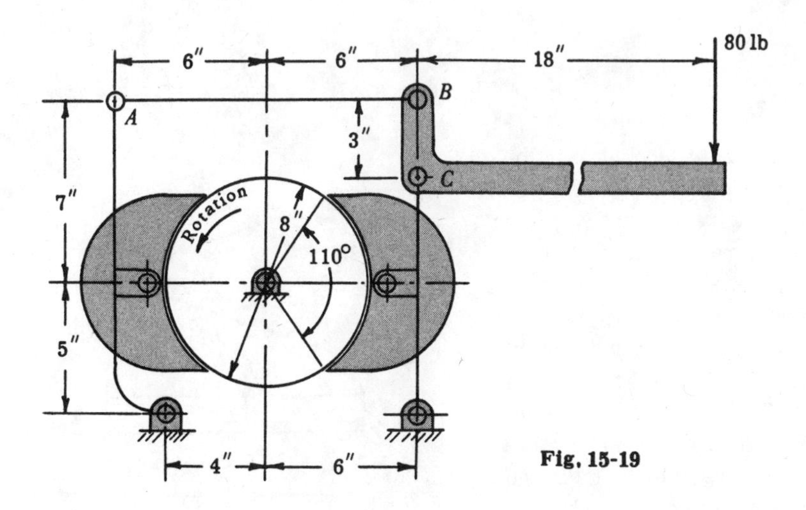

Fig. 15-19

Chapter 16

Springs

SPRING DESIGN involves the relationship between force, torque, deflection, and stress. Springs have many uses in connection with machine design, such as to cushion impact and shock loading, to store energy, to maintain contact between machine members, for force measuring devices, to control vibration, and other related functions.

MULTI-LEAF SPRINGS may be of either the simple cantilever type as shown in Fig. 16-1(a), or the semi-elliptic leaf spring design as shown in Fig. 16-1(b). The design of these springs is usually based upon the force, deflection, and stress relationships that apply to beams of constant strength and uniform thickness. Such beams are of triangular profile.

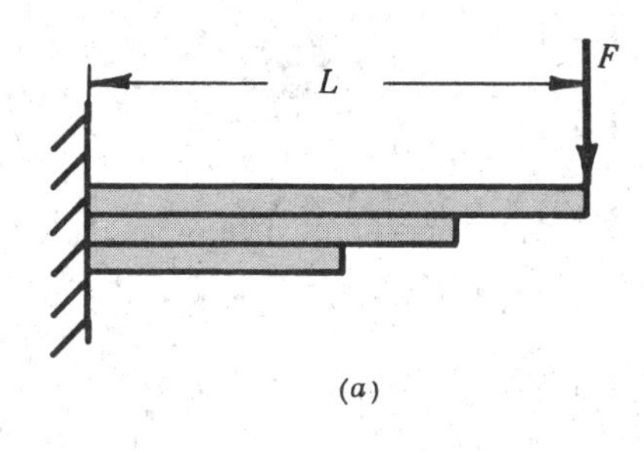

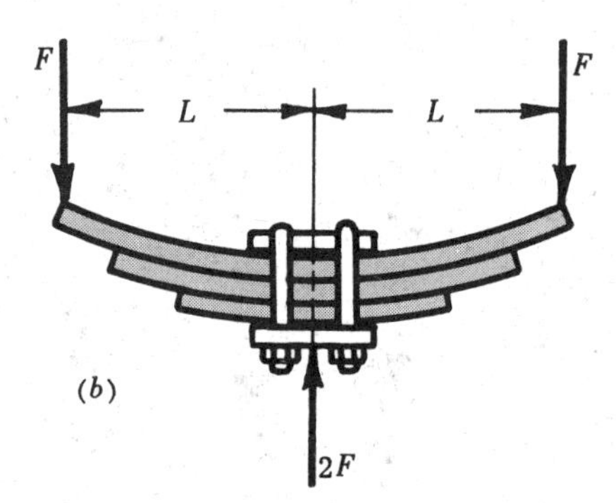

Fig. 16-1

Basically, the multi-leaf spring may be considered as a triangular plate as shown in Fig. 16-2(a) cut into n strips of width b, and stacked in a graduated manner as shown in Fig. 16-2(b). A graduated spring made from a triangular beam comes to a point at its end, which is satisfactory from the standpoint of bending stress. However, sufficient metal must be provided to support transverse shear and to provide for load connections which in turn are sometimes called upon to carry end thrust and twisting action. This may be accomplished by adding one or more extra full length leaves, n_e, of uniform width and thickness on top of the graduated stack, as shown in Fig. 16-3 below.

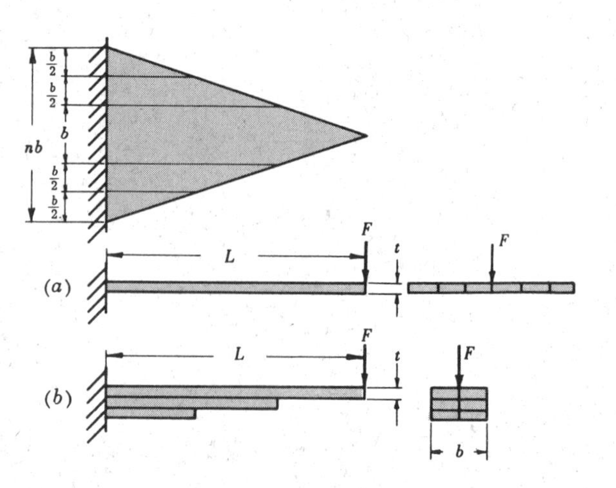

Fig. 16-2

Note that the number of extra full length leaves, n_e, is always one less than the total

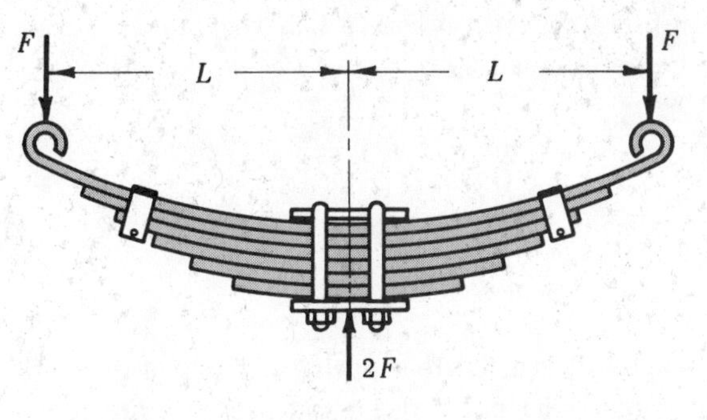

Fig. 16-3

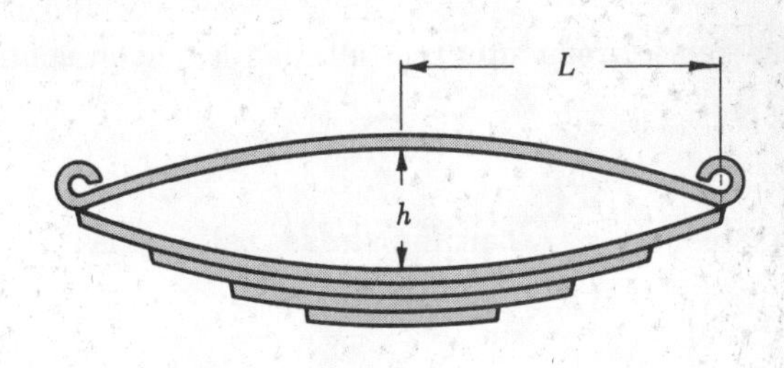

Fig. 16-4

number of full length leaves, n. The extra full length leaves are not beams of constant strength and will have a bending stress approximately 50% greater than the graduated leaves unless they are pre-stressed during assembly. Pre-stressing can be accomplished by having extra full length leaves formed with a different radius of curvature than the graduated leaves. This will leave a gap h between the extra full length leaves and the graduated leaves before assembly, as shown in Fig. 16-4 above. Then, upon assembly, the extra full length leaves will have an initial stress of opposite sign to that which occurs when the load is applied. The gap may be determined so that all of the leaves will be equally stressed after the full load F is applied.

THE BENDING STRESS, s_e, in the extra full length leaves if they are installed without an initial pre-stress will be

$$s_e = \frac{18FL}{bt^2(3n_e + 2n_g)}$$

where
F = total applied load at the end of the spring, lb
L = length of the cantilever or half the length of the semi-elliptic spring, in.
b = width of each spring leaf, in.
t = thickness of each spring leaf, in.
n_e = number of extra full length leaves
n_g = number of graduated leaves.

THE BENDING STRESS, s_g, in the graduated leaves if they are assembled with extra full length leaves without an initial pre-stress will be

$$s_g = \frac{12FL}{bt^2(3n_e + 2n_g)} = \frac{2s_e}{3}$$

THE DEFLECTION OF A MULTI-LEAF SPRING composed of graduated and extra full length leaves will be

$$y = \frac{12FL^3}{bt^3E(3n_e + 2n_g)}$$

where y = deflection at the end of the spring, in., E = modulus of elasticity, psi.

This equation will determine the deflection if $n_e = 0$, and also if the extra full length leaves are pre-stressed or if they are not pre-stressed.

THE BENDING STRESS, s, in multi-leaf springs without extra full length leaves or with extra full length leaves which have been pre-stressed so that all of the leaves have the same stress after the full load has been applied can be determined by

$$s = \frac{6FL}{nbt^2}$$

where s = bending stress, psi, and n = total number of leaves.

THE BENDING STRESS will be the same in all of the leaves of a multi-leaf spring composed of graduated and extra full length leaves if the extra full length leaves are pre-stressed by having the leaves pre-formed so that the gap h as shown in Fig. 16-4 above is

$$h = \frac{2FL^3}{nbt^3E}$$

where h = the gap between pre-assembled graduated leaves and extra full length leaves, in.

HELICAL SPRINGS are usually made of circular cross section wire or rod as shown in Fig. 16-5. These springs are subjected to a torsional shear stress and to a transverse shear stress. There is also an additional stress effect due to the curvature of the helix. In order to take into account the effects of transverse shear and curvature, it is customary to multiply the torsional shear stress by a correction factor K, called the Wahl factor.

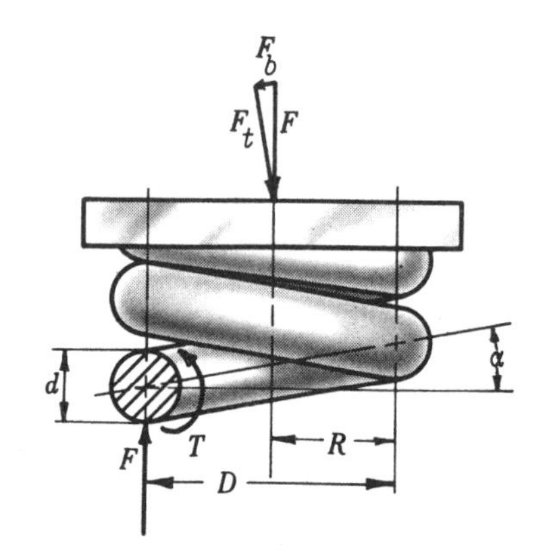

Fig. 16-5

THE SHEAR STRESS induced in a helical spring due to an axial load F is

$$s_s = K\frac{8FD}{\pi d^3} = K\frac{8FC}{\pi d^2}$$

where s_s = total shear stress, psi; F = axial load, lb;
D = mean diameter of coil, in.; d = diameter of wire, in.;
$K = \frac{4C-1}{4C-4} + \frac{0.615}{C}$, called the Wahl factor; $C = \frac{D}{d}$, called the spring index.

THE DEFLECTION of a helical spring due to an axial load F is

$$y = \frac{8FD^3n}{d^4G} = \frac{8FC^3n}{dG}$$

where n = number of active coils; y = axial deflection, in.; G = modulus of rigidity, psi.

THE SPRING RATE, or spring constant, is defined as the pounds per inch of deflection.

$$k = \frac{F}{y}$$

$$k = \frac{Gd}{8C^3n} \quad \text{for a helical spring under axial load}$$

THE SPRING RATE for springs in parallel having individual spring rates as shown in Fig. 16-6(a) below is

$$k = k_1 + k_2 + k_3$$

THE SPRING RATE for springs in series as shown in Fig. 16-6(b) below is

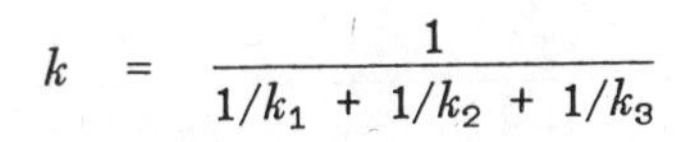

$$k = \frac{1}{1/k_1 + 1/k_2 + 1/k_3}$$

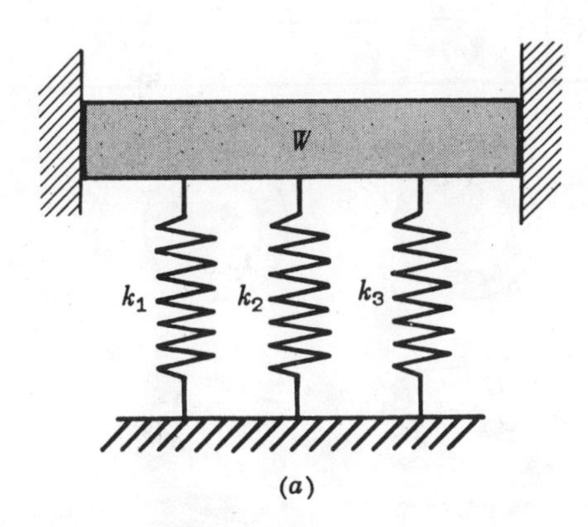

(a)

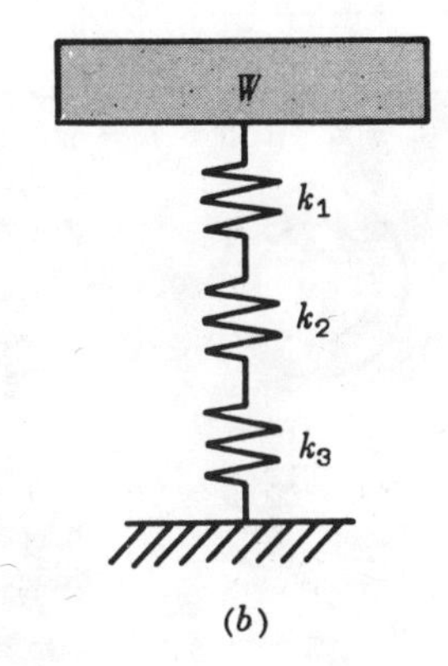

(b)

Fig. 16-6

THE ENERGY STORED, $(\text{Eng})_s$, in springs having a linear force deflection relationship and obeying Hooke's law, can be determined by

$$(\text{Eng})_s = \tfrac{1}{2}Fy \qquad \text{or} \qquad (\text{Eng})_s = \tfrac{1}{2}T\theta$$

For a helical spring subjected to an axial load F, the energy stored is

$$(\text{Eng})_s = \frac{s_s^2}{4G} \text{ in-lb per in}^3$$

For a helical spring subjected to a torsional load, the energy stored is

$$(\text{Eng})_s = \frac{s^2}{8E} \text{ in-lb per in}^3 \quad \text{(for round wire)}$$

$$(\text{Eng})_s = \frac{s^2}{6E} \text{ in-lb per in}^3 \quad \text{(for rectangular wire)}$$

For a cantilever beam of constant strength subjected to a bending force at the end, the amount of energy stored is

$$(\text{Eng})_s = \frac{s^2}{6E} \text{ in-lb per in}^3$$

For a spiral spring subjected to a torsional load, the energy stored is

$$(\text{Eng})_s = \frac{s^2}{6E} \text{ in-lb per in}^3$$

where

s_s = shear stress, psi

s = bending stress, psi

T = torque, in-lb

E = modulus of elasticity, psi

G = modulus of rigidity, psi

y = linear deflection, in.

θ = angular deflection, rad.

SPRING ENDS for helical springs may be either plain, plain ground, squared, or squared and ground as shown in Fig. 16-7 below. This results in a decrease of the number of active coils and affects the free length and solid length of the spring as shown below.

Type of Ends	Total Coils	Solid Length	Free Length
Plain	n	$(n+1)d$	$np+d$
Plain ground	n	nd	np
Squared	$n+2$	$(n+3)d$	$np+3d$
Squared and ground	$n+2$	$(n+2)d$	$np+2d$

p = pitch, n = number of active coils, d = wire diameter

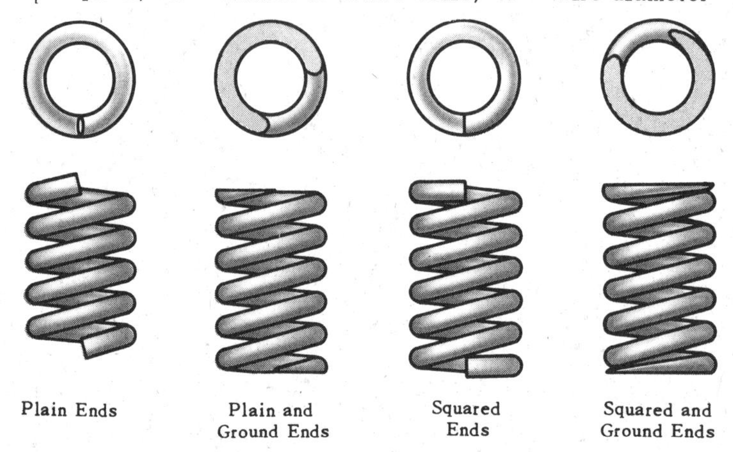

Fig. 16-7

BUCKLING MAY OCCUR IN COMPRESSION SPRINGS if the free length is over 4 times the mean diameter unless the spring is properly guided. The critical axial load that will cause buckling may be approximated by

$$F_{cr} = kL_f K_L$$

where F_{cr} = axial load to produce buckling, lb
k = spring rate, lb/in. of axial deflection
L_f = free length of the spring, in.
K_L = a factor depending on the ratio L_f/D.

Hinged Ends		Built-in Ends	
L_f/D	K_L	L_f/D	K_L
1	0.72	1	0.72
2	0.63	2	0.71
3	0.38	3	0.68
4	0.20	4	0.63
5	0.11	5	0.53
6	0.07	6	0.38
7	0.05	7	0.26
8	0.04	8	0.19

SURGING may occur in helical springs which have loads applied repetitively at a rate close to the natural frequency of the spring. To avoid this possibility it is advisable that the natural frequency of the spring be at least 20 times the frequency of the applied load. The natural frequency of a steel coil, f_n, in cycles per minute can be determined by

$$f_n = \frac{761{,}500\,d}{nD^2}$$

ALLOWABLE STRESSES FOR HELICAL SPRINGS SUBJECTED TO STATIC LOADING may be based on the elastic limit in torsion. For static loading a factor of safety of 1.5 has been recommended to be applied to the torsional yield strength of the material. In determining the maximum stress induced in the spring, one method is to apply the portion of the Wahl factor that corrects for the transverse shear effect, but not the portion that corrects for curvature, since the latter has the nature of a stress concentration and is not serious in ductile materials subjected to static loads.

In the Wahl factor, $K = \dfrac{4C-1}{4C-4} + \dfrac{0.615}{C}$, the $\dfrac{4C-1}{4C-4}$ corrects for curvature and the $\dfrac{0.615}{C}$ corrects for transverse shear. The use of the full value of K for static loading would result in a conservative design. The Wahl factor may be considered as composed of two sub-factors, K_s and K_c. The K_s shear stress sub-factor to be applied to the mean stress may be determined, according to Wahl, by

$$K_s = 1 + 0.5/C$$

which is based on a uniform transverse shear stress distribution. Then the design equations are

$$\frac{s_{ys}}{1.5} = K_s\frac{8FD}{\pi d^3} \qquad \text{or} \qquad \frac{s_{ys}}{1.5} = K\frac{8FD}{\pi d^3} \quad \text{for more conservative design}$$

ALLOWABLE STRESSES FOR HELICAL SPRINGS SUBJECTED TO FATIGUE LOADING are based on the endurance strength of the material. Wahl suggests two methods which are essentially as follows. In the first method use is made of a modified Soderberg line. Spring materials are usually tested for torsional endurance strength under a repeated stress that varies from zero to a maximum. Since test data for this released loading is available and since springs are ordinarily loaded in one direction only, more accurate results can be obtained by using the modified Soderberg diagram, as shown in Figure 16-8; the endurance limit for released loading, s_{rel}, is shown at a point A (where the mean stress is equal to $\frac{1}{2}s_{rel}$ and the variable stress is also equal to $\frac{1}{2}s_{rel}$). A line drawn from point A to point B, the yield point in shear, will give the failure line for fatigue and will correspond to test data better than the line from the endurance strength in reversed shear to the yield point in shear. The design line CD is drawn parallel to the line AB, with point D being located at s_{ys}/N. The mean stress s_m is plotted as the abscissa and the variable stress s_v is plotted as the ordinate.

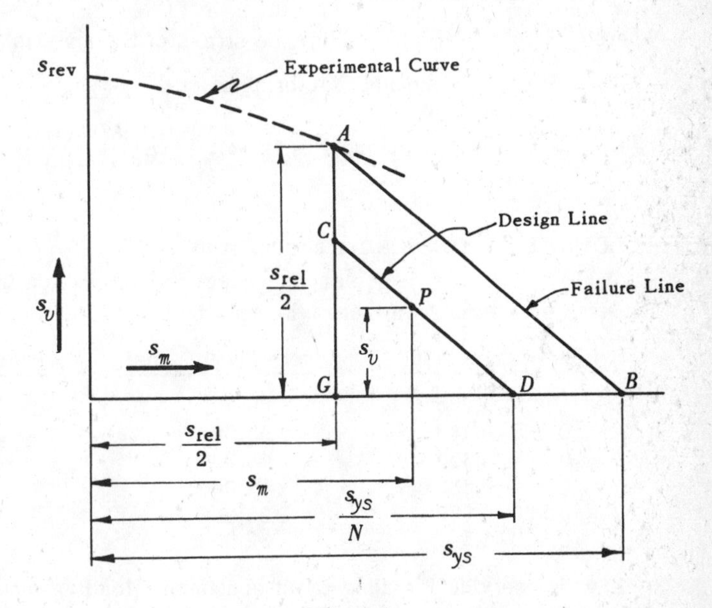

Fig. 16-8

The variable stress s_v may be calculated using the full value of the Wahl factor, $K = K_c K_s$, or the K_c may be reduced if information is available regarding the sensitivity of the material to this stress concentration effect due to curvature. Some materials are less sensitive than others.

$$s_v = K\frac{8F_v D}{\pi d^3} \qquad \text{where} \quad F_v = \frac{F(\max) - F(\min)}{2}$$

The average stress s_m may be calculated using only the static portion of the Wahl factor, K_s, which agrees with experimental evidence.

$$s_m = K_s\frac{8F_m D}{\pi d^3} \qquad \text{where} \quad F_m = \frac{F(\max) + F(\min)}{2}$$

Referring to the fatigue-stress diagram, line AB is the failure line. Hence we may construct line CD parallel to and below line AB to allow for a reasonable factor of safety N based on the yield shear strength. An equation may be written for line CD. With the origin at G, the coordinates of P are $[(s_m - \frac{1}{2}s_{rel}),\ s_v]$; the slope of CD = slope of $AB = -\dfrac{\frac{1}{2}s_{rel}}{s_{ys} - \frac{1}{2}s_{rel}}$; and intercept $CG = AG(\dfrac{GD}{GB}) = \frac{1}{2}s_{rel}\left(\dfrac{s_{ys}/N - \frac{1}{2}s_{rel}}{s_{ys} - \frac{1}{2}s_{rel}}\right)$. Then

$$s_v = -\left(\frac{\frac{1}{2}s_{rel}}{s_{ys} - \frac{1}{2}s_{rel}}\right)(s_m - \tfrac{1}{2}s_{rel}) + \tfrac{1}{2}s_{rel}\left(\frac{s_{ys}/N - \frac{1}{2}s_{rel}}{s_{ys} - \frac{1}{2}s_{rel}}\right)$$

from which

$$N = \frac{s_{ys}}{s_m - s_v + 2s_v s_{ys}/s_{rel}}$$

This may be used as a design equation, since all points on line CD represent a combination of variable and mean stress conditions which are safe. The factor of safety may be taken as 1.8, more or less, depending upon operating conditions. Values for s_{rel} are not very complete, but based on various current sources a value of $36{,}000/d^{0.2}$ seems to be a good approximation for oil-tempered carbon steel for wire diameters up to 0.625 in.

In the second method suggested by Wahl, one condition is that the stress range is calculated using the full value of the Wahl factor K. Also, a second condition is that the peak stress calculated using only K_s must not exceed the yield strength of the material divided by a suitable factor of safety.

First condition: $$s_s(\max) - s_s(\min) = K\frac{8D[F(\max) - F(\min)]}{\pi d^3} = \frac{s_{rel}}{N}$$

where s_{rel} = limiting endurance stress of the material

N = a suitable factor of safety.

Second condition: $$s_s(\max) = K_s\frac{8DF(\max)}{\pi d^3} = \frac{s_{ys}}{N}$$

ALLOWABLE STRESSES for helical steel springs, for one specific material, as published by the Westinghouse Electric Corporation for SAE 6150 oil-tempered hot wound springs heat-treated after forming, are tabulated below.

Wire Diameter, in.	Severe Service, psi	Average Service, psi	Light Service, psi
up to 0.085	60,000	75,000	93,000
0.085 - 0.185	55,000	69,000	85,000
0.185 - 0.320	48,000	60,000	74,000
0.320 - 0.530	42,000	52,000	65,000
0.530 - 0.970	36,000	45,000	56,000
0.970 - 1.5	32,000	40,000	50,000

Severe service includes rapid continuous loading where the ratio of minimum to maximum stress is one-half or less. Average service is the same as severe except for intermittent operation. Light service includes springs subjected to static loads or to infrequently varied loads.

BELLEVILLE SPRINGS are made up from tapered washers as shown in Fig. 16-9 (*a*) below. The washers may be stacked in series, parallel, or a combination of parallel-series as shown in Fig. 16-9 (*b*) below. The load-deflection and stress-deflection formulas for one washer as given by Almen and Laszlo (ASME transactions, May 1936, Volume 58, No. 4) are:

$$P = \frac{Ey}{(1-\mu^2)M(d_o/2)^2}[(h-y/2)(h-y)t + t^3]$$

$$s = \frac{Ey}{(1-\mu^2)M(d_o/2)^2}[C_1(h-y/2) + C_2 t]$$

where

P = axial load, lb
y = deflection, in.
t = thickness of washer, in.
h = free height minus thickness, in.
E = modulus of elasticity, psi
s = stress at inside circumference, psi
d_o = outside diameter of washer, in.
d_i = inside diameter of washer, in.
μ = Poisson's ratio (0.3 for steel)

$$M = \frac{6}{\pi \log_e(d_o/d_i)}\left[\frac{d_o/d_i - 1}{d_o/d_i}\right]^2$$

$$C_1 = \frac{6}{\pi \log_e(d_o/d_i)}\left[\frac{d_o/d_i - 1}{\log_e(d_o/d_i)} - 1\right]$$

$$C_2 = \frac{6}{\pi \log_e(d_o/d_i)}\left[\frac{d_o/d_i - 1}{2}\right]$$

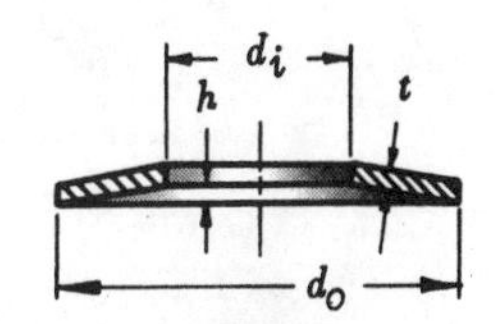

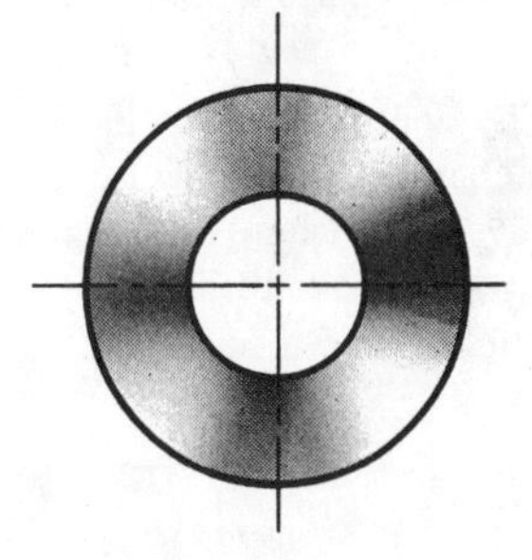

Fig. 16-9 (*a*)

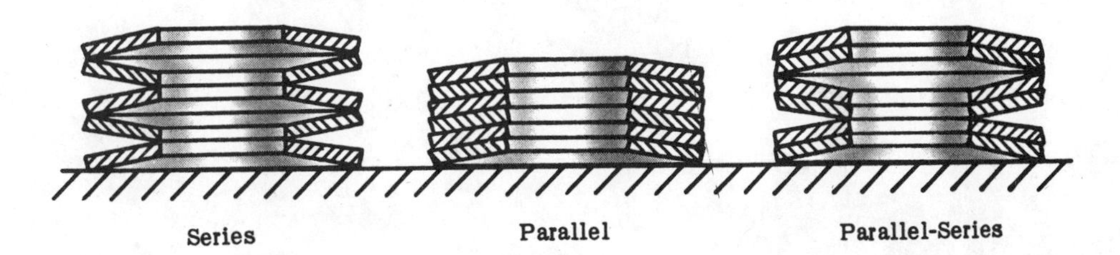

Fig. 16-9 (*b*)

SOLVED PROBLEMS

1. Derive the stress, force, and deflection relationships for multi-leaf springs.

Solution:

Consider a cantilever beam of constant strength and uniform thickness t, as shown in Fig. 16-2(a), to be cut into n strips of width b and stacked in a graduated manner as shown in Fig. 16-2(b).

The bending stress is the same at all sections of the triangular beam. We will assume that this situation prevails after the strips are stacked, even though this is not entirely true.

$$s = \frac{Mc}{I} = \frac{FL(\frac{1}{2}t)12}{nbt^3} = \frac{6FL}{nbt^2}$$

The deflection of a beam of constant strength and uniform thickness is

$$y = \frac{FL^3}{2EI_{(max)}} = \frac{6FL^3}{Ebnt^3}$$

These equations also apply to the semi-elliptic leaf spring, which may be considered as two cantilevers supported at its center as shown in Fig. 16-3.

The addition of one or more extra full length leaves, n_e, of constant width and thickness on top of the graduated stack is approximately equivalent to having beam e of constant width loaded in parallel with beam g of constant strength, as shown in Fig. 16-10. The deflections of beams e and g are

$$y_e = \frac{F_e L^3}{3EI_{(max)e}} \quad \text{and} \quad y_g = \frac{F_g L^3}{2EI_{(max)g}}$$

where F_e and F_g represent the portions of the total force F absorbed by beams e and g. Since the deflections are equal, we may equate $y_e = y_g$ or

$$\frac{F_e L^3}{3EI_{(max)e}} = \frac{F_g L^3}{2EI_{(max)g}}$$

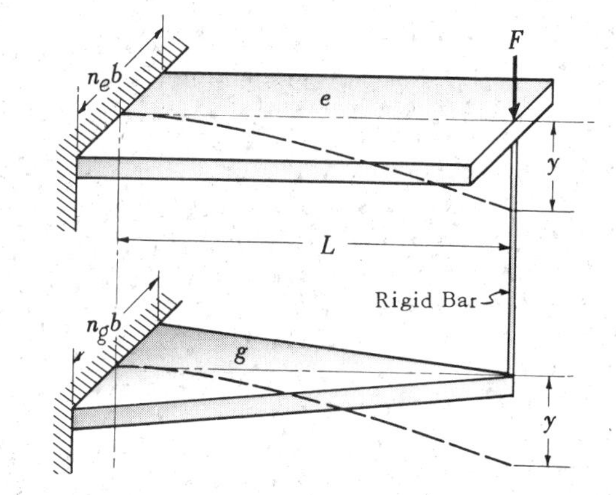

Fig. 16-10

Let n_g and n_e equal the number of graduated leaves and extra full length leaves respectively. Then $I_{(max)e} = n_e bt^3/12$ and $I_{(max)g} = n_g bt^3/12$. Substituting these values in the previous equation, $\frac{F_e}{3n_e} = \frac{F_g}{2n_g}$ or $F_e = \frac{3n_e F_g}{2n_g}$. Now

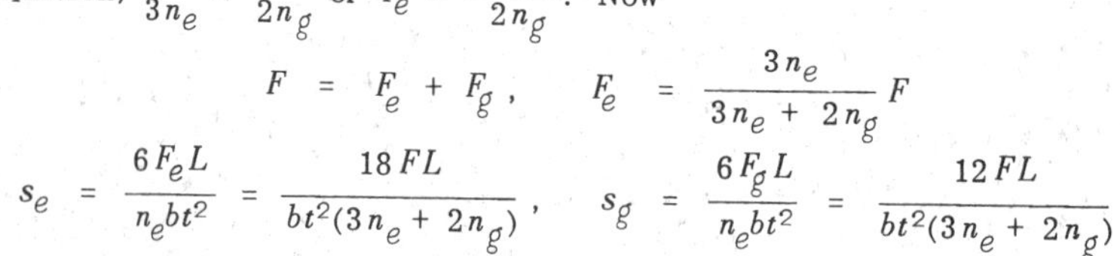

$$F = F_e + F_g, \qquad F_e = \frac{3n_e}{3n_e + 2n_g}F$$

$$s_e = \frac{6F_e L}{n_e bt^2} = \frac{18FL}{bt^2(3n_e + 2n_g)}, \qquad s_g = \frac{6F_g L}{n_g bt^2} = \frac{12FL}{bt^2(3n_e + 2n_g)}$$

The deflection of the composite spring is $y = \dfrac{12FL^3}{bt^3E(3n_e + 2n_g)}$

2. Derive the stress, force, and deflection relationship for a helical coil spring for a concentric axial load.

Solution:

Referring to Fig. 16-5, the F_b component of the axial force F produces a bending stress s,

$$s = \frac{16FD\sin\alpha}{\pi d^3} \quad \text{(neglecting curvature effects)}$$

This stress may be neglected for small helix angles α. The axial force F produces torsional stress s_s. Since $T = \frac{1}{2}FD\cos\alpha \approx \frac{1}{2}FD$ for small helix angles,

$$s_s = \frac{TR}{J} = \frac{8FD}{\pi d^3}$$

where F = axial load, lb; D = mean diameter of the coil, in.; d = diameter of the wire, in.; y = axial deflection, in.; s_s = shearing stress, psi.

In addition to the torsional shear stress, there is a transverse shear and an additional stress due to the curvature of the coil. In order to include both of these effects, a stress factor K, called the Wahl factor, may be used.

$$s_s = K\frac{8FD}{\pi d^3}$$

where $K = \dfrac{4C-1}{4C-4} + \dfrac{0.615}{C}$ and the spring index $C = D/d$.

An equation for the deflection of a helical spring may be obtained by equating the work required to deflect the spring to the torsional energy absorbed by the twisted wire. The helical spring having n active coils is developed into a straight rod of diameter d and length $n\pi D/(\cos\alpha)$, as shown in Fig. 16-11. Cos α may be taken as unity since the helix angle is usually small. Then

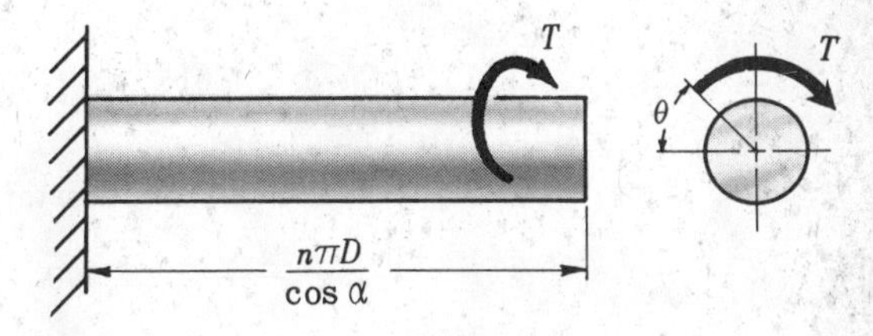

Fig. 16-11

Work in = energy absorbed

$$\tfrac{1}{2}Fy = \tfrac{1}{2}T\theta = \tfrac{1}{2}(\tfrac{1}{2}FD)\theta \quad \text{or} \quad y = \tfrac{1}{2}D\theta$$

Since $\theta = \dfrac{Tn\pi D}{JG} = \dfrac{16FD^2n}{d^4G}$, where G = torsional modulus of elasticity (psi),

$$y = \frac{8FD^3n}{d^4G} = \frac{8FC^3n}{dG}$$

The value of G for spring steel is approximately 11.5×10^6 psi.

3. A 35 in. long cantilever spring is composed of 8 graduated leaves and one extra full length leaf. The leaves are $1\frac{3}{4}$ in. wide. A load of 500 lb at the end of the spring causes a deflection of 3 in. Determine the thickness of the leaves and the maximum bending stress in the full length leaf assuming first that the extra full length leaf has been pre-stressed to give the same stress in all the leaves, and then determine the stress in the full extra length leaf assuming no pre-stress.

Solution:

$$y = \frac{12FL^3}{bt^3(2n_g + 3n_e)E}, \quad 3 = \frac{(12)(500)(35)^3}{(1.75)(t^3)(16+3)(3\times10^7)}, \quad t = 0.442 \text{ in.}$$

With extra full length leaf pre-stressed, $s = \dfrac{6FL}{nbt^2} = \dfrac{6(500)(35)}{9(1.75)(0.442)^2} = 34{,}300$ psi.

With no pre-stress, $s_e = \dfrac{18FL}{bt^2(2n_g+3n_e)} = \dfrac{(18)(500)(35)}{(1.75)(0.442)^2(16+3)} = 48{,}500$ psi.

4. Determine the required number of coils and permissible deflection in a helical spring made of 1/16 inch diameter steel wire, assuming a spring index of 6 and an allowable stress of 50,000 psi in shear. The spring rate is to be 10 lb/in.

Solution:

Spring index $C = \dfrac{D}{d}$, $6 = \dfrac{D}{1/16}$, $D = 0.375$ in., Wahl factor $K = \dfrac{4C-1}{4C-4} + \dfrac{0.615}{C} = 1.25$.

$$\frac{F}{y} = \frac{dG}{8C^3n}, \quad 10 = \frac{(1/16)(11.5\times10^6)}{8(6^3)n}, \quad n = 41.6 \text{ turns}$$

Find force and deflection: $s_s = K\dfrac{8FD}{\pi d^3}$, $50{,}000 = 1.25\dfrac{8F(0.375)}{\pi(1/16)^3}$, $F = 10.2$ lb.

The deflection should be limited to 1 in. for a spring rate of 10 lb/in.

5. Design a coil spring to have a mean diameter of 5 in. and a spring rate of 400 lb/in. The total axial load is 1900 lb and the allowable shear stress is 40,000 psi.

Solution:

Design requires that the number of turns n and diameter d of the wire be determined.

Using $s_s = K\dfrac{8FD}{\pi d^3}$ with $d = \dfrac{D}{C}$, $KC^3 = \dfrac{s_s \pi D^2}{8F} = \dfrac{40,000\pi(5^2)}{8(1900)} = 207$ (allowed).

Try $C = 5.5$ in $(\dfrac{4C-1}{4C-4} + \dfrac{0.615}{C})C^3 = 207$: $(1.165 + 0.112)(5.5)^3 = 212$, close to 207.

Then $d = 5/5.5 = 0.91$; use 1 in. diameter wire.

$$\frac{F}{y} = \frac{d^4 G}{8D^3 n}, \qquad 400 = \frac{(1^4)(11.5\times 10^6)}{8(5^3)n}, \qquad n = 28.8 \text{ turns}$$

6. When a coil spring with a spring scale of 100 lb/in. is compressed $1\frac{1}{4}$ in., the coils are closed. The allowable shear stress is 50,000 psi, the spring index $C = 8$, the ends are squared and ground, and $G = 12\times 10^6$ psi. Calculate the required wire diameter d, the required coil diameter D, and the closed length of the spring.

Solution:

$K = \dfrac{4C-1}{4C-4} + \dfrac{0.615}{C} = 1.184$. Then $s_s = K\dfrac{8FC}{\pi d^2}$, $50,000 = 1.184\dfrac{8(125)8}{\pi d^2}$, $d = 0.246$ in.

$D = dC = (0.246)(8) = 1.968$ in.

$$\frac{F}{y} = \frac{d^4 G}{8D^3 n} = \frac{dG}{8C^3 n}, \qquad 100 = \frac{(0.246)(12\times 10^6)}{8(8^3)n}, \qquad n = 7.22$$

Closed length $= (n+2)d = (7.22+2)(0.246) = 2.26$ in.

7. At the bottom of an elevator shaft a group of 8 identical springs are set in parallel to absorb the shock of the elevator in case of a failure. The elevator weighs 6400 lb. Assuming that the elevator has a free fall of 4 ft from rest, determine the maximum stress in each spring if each spring is made from 1 in. diameter rod. For each spring the spring index is 6 and the number of active turns is 15. Neglect any effects of counterweights in the system and take $G = 12\times 10^6$ psi.

Solution:

Energy absorbed per spring $= (\dfrac{6400}{8})(48+y) = \frac{1}{2}Fy$, from which $y = \dfrac{76,800}{F-1600}$, where F is the maximum spring force. Then

$$y = \frac{8FC^3 n}{dG} = \frac{8F(6^3)15}{1(12\times 10^6)} = \frac{76,800}{F-1600} \quad \text{which gives} \quad F = 6840 \text{ lb}$$

Now using $K = \dfrac{4C-1}{4C-4} + \dfrac{0.615}{C} = 1.25$, we obtain $s_s = K\dfrac{8FC}{\pi d^2} = 1.25\dfrac{8(6840)6}{\pi(1^2)} = 130,500$ psi.

8. The free end of a horizontal, constant strength steel cantilever beam is directly over and in contact with a vertical coil spring as shown in Fig. 16-12. The width of the beam at its fixed end is 24 in., its length is 30 in., and its thickness is 0.5 in. The coil spring has 10 active coils of 0.5 in. diameter wire and has an outside diameter of 4 in. Take $G = 12\times 10^6$ psi.

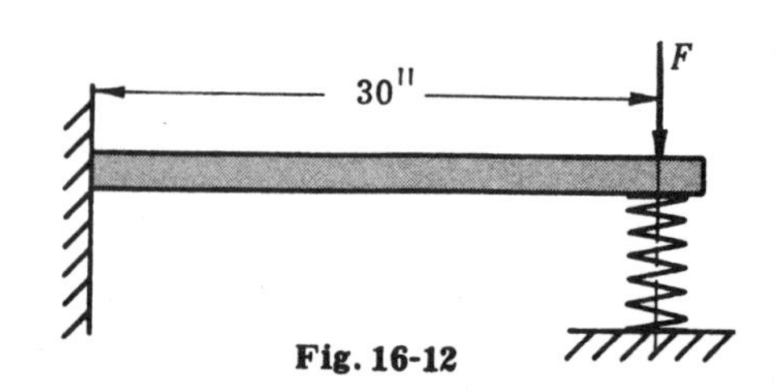

Fig. 16-12

(*a*) What force Q, if gradually applied to the end of the cantilever beam, is required to cause a deflection of 1.5 in.?

(*b*) What is the bending stress in the beam at a section 15 in. from the fixed end?

(*c*) How much energy is absorbed by the coil spring?

Solution:

Both springs have the same deflection. For the coil spring,

$$y = \frac{8FD^3n}{d^4G}, \quad 1.5 = \frac{8F(3.5)^3(10)}{(0.5)^4(12\times10^6)}, \quad F = 328 \text{ lb}$$

For the cantilever spring: $y = \dfrac{F'L^3}{2EI_{(max)}}, \quad 1.5 = \dfrac{F'(30)^3}{2(30\times10^6)[(24)(0.5)^3/12]}, \quad F' = 833$ lb.

(*a*) $Q = 328 + 833 = 1161$ lb (*b*) $s = \dfrac{Mc}{I} = \dfrac{(833\times15)(0.25)}{12(0.5)^3/12} = 25{,}000$ psi

(*c*) Energy absorbed by the coil spring $= \frac{1}{2}Fy = \frac{1}{2}(328)(1.5) = 246$ in-lb

9. One helical spring is nested inside another; the dimensions are as tabulated. Both springs have the same free length and carry a total maximum load of 550 lb.

	Outer Spring	**Inner Spring**
No. active coils	6	10
Wire diameter	0.5 in.	0.25 in.
Mean coil diameter	3.5 in.	2.25 in.

Determine:

(*a*) the maximum load carried by each spring, (*b*) the total deflection of each spring, (*c*) the maximum stress in the outer spring. Take $G = 12\times10^6$ psi.

Solution:

Since both springs have the same deflection,

$$y = \frac{8F_iD_i^3n_i}{Gd_i^4} = \frac{8F_oD_o^3n_o}{Gd_o^4}, \quad \frac{8F_i(3.5)^3(6)}{G(0.5)^4} = \frac{8F_o(2.25)^3(10)}{G(0.25)^4}, \quad F_i = 7.08F_o$$

(*a*) The simultaneous solution of $F_i = 7.08F_o$ and $F_i + F_o = 550$ lb is $F_i = 482$ lb, $F_o = 68$ lb.

(*b*) $y = \dfrac{8(482)(3.5)^3(6)}{(12\times10^6)(0.5)^4} = 1.325$ in.

(*c*) $C = \dfrac{3.5}{0.5} = 7, \quad K = \dfrac{28-1}{28-4} + \dfrac{0.615}{7} = 1.213$, and $s_s = K\dfrac{8FD}{\pi d^3} = 1.213\dfrac{8(482)(3.5)}{\pi(0.5)^3} = 41{,}700$ psi.

10. The load on an oil-tempered carbon steel helical compression spring varies from 150 to 400 lb. The mean diameter of the coil is to be 2 inches, and the desired design factor of safety is 1.3 based on the variable stresses. Determine the required wire size. $s_{ys} = 100{,}000$ psi.

Solution:

First method.

$$F_m = \tfrac{1}{2}(400+150) = 275 \text{ lb}, \qquad F_v = \tfrac{1}{2}(400-150) = 125 \text{ lb}$$

$$s_m = K_s\frac{8F_mD}{\pi d^3} = K_s\frac{8(275)(2)}{\pi d^3} = K_s\frac{1400}{d^3}, \qquad s_v = K\frac{8F_vD}{\pi d^3} = K\frac{8(125)(2)}{\pi d^3} = K\frac{636}{d^3}$$

The problem is now solved by trial and error. Let us try No. 4-0 W and M wire, $d = 0.3938$ in.; then

$$C = \frac{2}{0.3938} = 5.07, \qquad K_s = 1 + \frac{0.5}{C} = 1.099, \qquad K = \frac{4C-1}{4C-4} + \frac{0.615}{C} = 1.306$$

$$s_m = 1.099\frac{1400}{(0.3938)^3} = 25{,}200 \text{ psi}, \qquad s_v = 1.306\frac{636}{(0.3938)^3} = 13{,}650 \text{ psi}$$

Assuming $s_{(rel)} = \dfrac{36{,}800}{(0.3938)^{0.2}} = 44{,}400$ psi, $N = \dfrac{s_{ys}}{s_m - s_v + 2s_v s_{ys}/s_{(rel)}} = 1.37$ (satisfactory).

Use No. 4-0 oil-tempered carbon steel wire.

Second method. Try No. 4-0 wire.

$$s_s(\max) - s_s(\min) = K\frac{8D[F(\max) - F(\min)]}{\pi d^3} = \frac{s_{(rel)}}{N}$$

$$= 1.306\frac{8(2)(250)}{\pi(0.3938)^3} = 27{,}000 = \frac{44{,}400}{N}$$

from which $N = 1.64$ (based on endurance).

$$s_s(\max) = K_s\frac{8DF(\max)}{\pi d^3} = \frac{s_{ys}}{N}$$

$$= 1.099\frac{8(2)(400)}{\pi(0.3938)^3} = 36{,}800 = \frac{100{,}000}{N}$$

from which $N = 2.72$ (based on yield).

Factor of safety is satisfactory for No. 4-0 wire.

SUPPLEMENTARY PROBLEMS

11. A laminated semi-elliptic leaf spring under a central load of 3000 lb is to have an effective length of 36 in. and is to deflect not more than 3 in. The spring has 10 leaves, two of which are full length, and all leaves have the same width and thickness. The maximum stress in the leaves is not to exceed 50,000 psi. Calculate the width and thickness of the leaves. *Ans.* $b = 11$ in., $t = 0.172$ in.

12. A helical compression spring is made from steel wire. It has an allowable shear stress of 130,000 psi, with a modulus of elasticity in shear of 11.5×10^6 psi. The mean diameter of the spring is 5 in., and a load of 1110 lb is applied. What size wire should be used, assuming the spring is stressed to the maximum? *Ans.* $d = 0.5$ in.

13. Calculate the diameter of wire required for a coil spring made to the following specifications: mean diameter of the spring = 6 in., spring rate = 500 lb/in., working load = 1800 lb, design stress = 40,000 psi. *Ans.* Use 1 in. wire.

14. What thickness of leaf is required for a cantilever leaf spring designed to the following specifications?

Load on the spring = 500 lb	Design stress in tension = 50,000 psi
Total number of leaves = 8	Length of spring = 20 in.
Width of each leaf = 2 in.	Number of extra full length leaves = 2

Ans. $t = 0.274$ in.

15. A helical spring is set inside another, the outer spring having a free length of $1\frac{1}{2}$ in. greater than the inner spring. The dimensions of each spring are as follows:

	Outer Spring	**Inner Spring**
Mean diameter	4 in.	$2\frac{1}{2}$ in.
Wire diameter	$\frac{1}{2}$ in.	$\frac{1}{2}$ in.
Inactive turns	2	2
Active turns	20	15
Material	SAE 1060	SAE 1090

Determine the combined spring rate of the two springs after sufficient load has been applied to deflect the outer spring $2\frac{1}{2}$ in. Use $G = 12 \times 10^6$ psi. *Ans.* 473 lb/in.

16. A 4 in. o.d. steel coil spring having 10 active coils of 0.5 in. diameter wire is in contact with a 30 in. long steel cantilever spring having six graduated leaves 4 in. wide and 0.25 in. thick as shown in Fig. 16-13.

(*a*) What force F if gradually applied to the top of the coil spring will cause the cantilever spring to deflect 1 in.?

(*b*) What will be the maximum shear stress in the coil spring?

Ans. F = 69.5 lb, s_s = 6000 psi

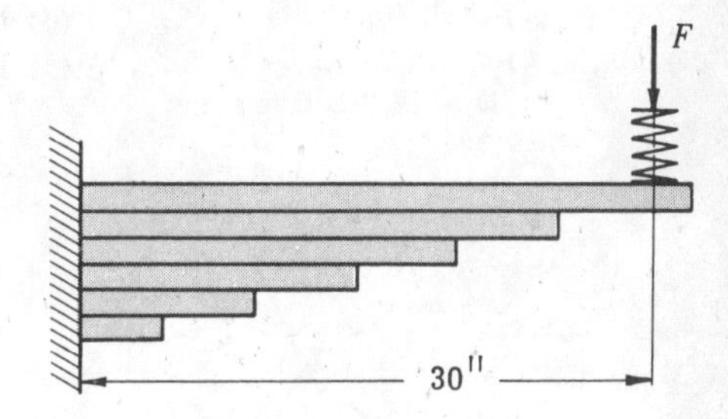

Fig. 16-13

17. A weight W = 2400 lb is supported by a spring (or springs) as shown in Fig. 16-14. A certain natural frequency of vibration of the weight is desired, and the spring rate necessary for the prescribed frequency is found to be 1500 lb/in.

A junk yard has a group of identical steel springs available with the following specifications:

Mean diameter = 3 in.
Spring index = 6
Number of active coils = 8
Modulus of elasticity in shear = 12×10^6 psi
Modulus of elasticity in tension = 30×10^6 psi

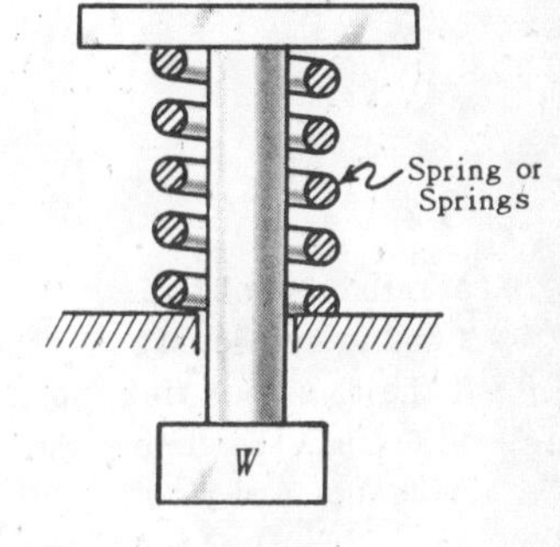

Fig. 16-14

(*a*) How many springs should be used and how should the springs be arranged to have the spring rate as close to the desired value as possible?

(*b*) Assuming that each spring may be modified by cutting off as many turns as necessary and refinishing the end of each spring, how many active coils must be removed from each spring to give the desired spring rate of 1500 lb/in.?

(*c*) What is the maximum stress in each spring for (*a*) and (*b*) above?

Ans. (*a*) Use 3 or 4 springs in parallel.
(*b*) Cut off one active turn of each spring, if 3 springs are used.
(*c*) s_s = 61,000 psi for either case.

18. Refer to Fig. 16-15. A semi-elliptic leaf spring has an effective length of 60 in. The spring seat, midway between the shackles, carries a helical spring upon which is imposed an impact equivalent to 1500 ft-lb of energy. The laminated spring is composed of 10 graduated leaves and two extra full length leaves, each $\frac{1}{4}$ in. thick and 2 in. wide. The coil spring is composed of 6 effective turns of 5/8 in. wire. The mean coil diameter is 4 in. Calculate the maximum stress induced in each spring.

Ans. s_s = 107,000 psi in coil spring
s = 125,000 psi in leaf spring

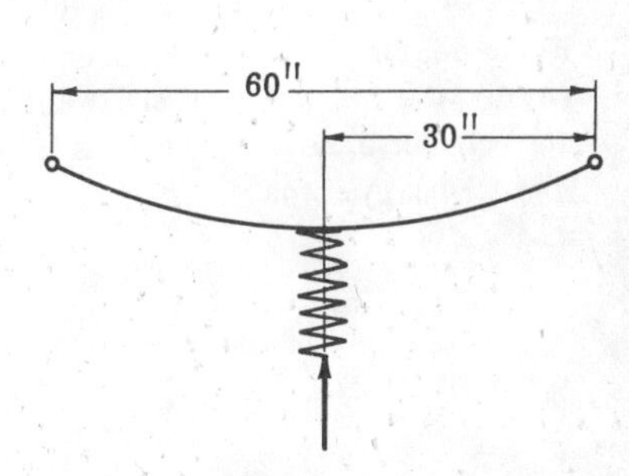

Fig. 16-15

19. A spring-loaded flyball governor with dimensions as shown in Fig. 16-16(*a*) below requires a spring force of 42 lb to permit the proper speed with the balls at a 5 in. radius. Assume the limiting position to be that as shown in Fig. 16-16(*b*) below with the balls at a 7 in. radius. For proper speed regulation the spring force must be 129 lb in that position.

(*a*) Determine the required spring rate.

(*b*) For maximum shear stress of 50,000 psi and spring index of 8, determine the required wire and mean coil diameters.

(*c*) Using a shear modulus $G = 11.6 \times 10^6$ psi, determine the number of active turns required.

(*d*) Allowing one ineffective turn at each end, determine the free length needed so that the spring will be closed in position as shown in Fig. 16-16(*b*).

(*e*) What is the spring length in position as shown in Fig. 16-16(*a*)?

Ans. (*a*) 50 lb/in. (*d*) free length = 6.63 in.
(*b*) d = 0.25 in., D = 2 in. (*e*) length = 5.79 in.
(*c*) n = 14.2 active turns

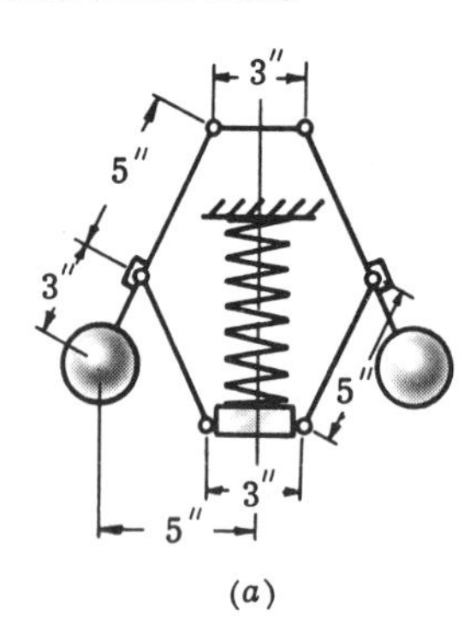

(*a*)

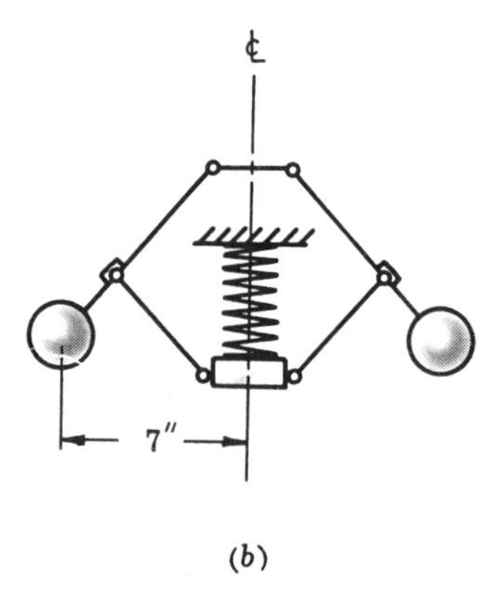

(*b*)

Fig. 16-16

20. A carbon steel coil spring has a mean diameter of 1.5 in. and is formed of $\frac{1}{2}$ in. bar. It has a spring index of 3 and is subjected to a continuously alternating load between a maximum of 1800 lb and a minimum of 1300 lb. If the torsional yield point of the material is 110,000 psi and the endurance limit due to released loading is 44,000 psi, determine the factor of safety under which the spring is operating from both the standpoint of endurance and yield.

Ans. N = 1.82 based upon endurance, N = 1.58 based upon yield

21. A compression spring will be used in a service where the maximum value of the varying load is three times the minimum value. The spring specified below is available in stock and a check of capacity under these load conditions must be made to determine whether it is suitable. The spring specifications are:

Material is oil-tempered carbon steel, s_{ys} = 100,000 psi.
Mean coil diameter = 2 in.
Wire size = No. 4-0 = 0.394 in. diameter.
Active coils = 11; inactive coils = 2 (one on each end).
Free length of spring = 7 in.

For a design factor of 1.3 based on the variable stresses, what is the value of the peak load to be permitted? (Apply the full value of the Wahl factor to the variable stress; but only the portion of the Wahl factor that corrects for transverse shear is to be applied to the mean stress.)

Ans. F(max) = 406 lb

Chapter 17

Gear Forces

THE COMPONENTS OF GEAR FORCES are usually determined rather than the resultant gear force, although the latter can be found by the vector sum of the components. The components are used in calculating bearing reactions, shaft size, etc.

FRICTION LOSSES in spur, helical, and bevel gears are usually so small that these gears are considered as operating at 100% efficiency. There are situations where the friction in spur gearing, even though low, must be taken into account, as in the case of circulating power in planetary gearing.

Worm and worm gears, however, are usually not as efficient as spur, bevel, and helical gears; hence friction is usually taken into account in determining the force components on worm and worm gears.

SPUR GEAR force components are (see Fig. 17-1 below)

(1) Tangential force $F_t = M_t/r$, where M_t = gear torque and r = pitch radius of the gear.

(2) Separating or radial force $F_r = F_t \tan \phi$ where ϕ is the pressure angle.

Note that the radial force is always directed towards the center of the gear.

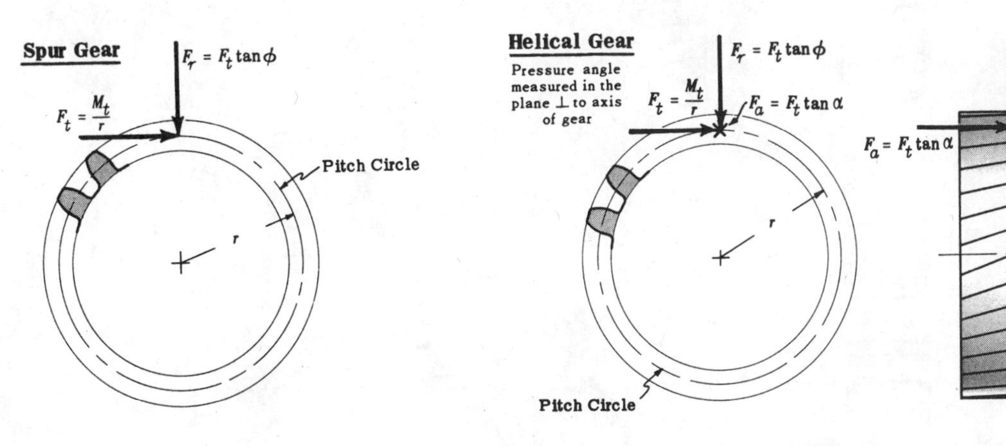

Fig. 17-1 Fig. 17-2

HELICAL GEAR force components are expressed in two different ways depending upon how the pressure angle is defined. There are two standards: (1) the pressure angle ϕ is measured in the plane perpendicular to the axis of the gear and (2) the pressure angle ϕ_n is measured in a plane normal to a tooth. See Fig. 17-2 above and Fig. 17-3 below.

(1) If the pressure angle is measured in a plane perpendicular to the axis of the gear, the components are (see Fig. 17-2 above):

a. Tangential force $F_t = M_t/r$

b. Separating force $F_r = F_t \tan\phi$

c. Thrust force $F_a = F_t \tan\alpha$

where r = gear pitch radius,

ϕ = pressure angle measured in a plane perpendicular to the axis of the gear,

α = helix angle measured from the axis of the gear.

(2) If the pressure angle is measured in a plane perpendicular to a tooth, the components are (see Fig. 17-3):

a. Tangential force $F_t = M_t/r$

b. Separating force $F_r = \dfrac{F_t \tan\phi_n}{\cos\alpha}$

c. Thrust force $F_a = F_t \tan\alpha$

where ϕ_n = pressure angle measured in a plane perpendicular to a tooth,

α = helix angle measured from the axis of the gear.

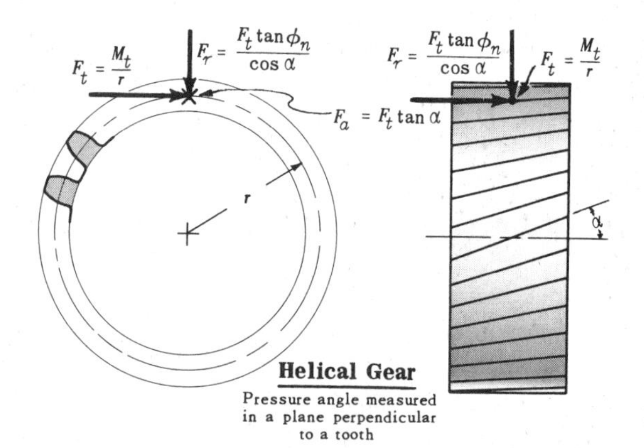

Fig. 17-3

The direction of the thrust force depends on the direction of rotation and the hand of the gear teeth. Four possibilities of combinations of right and left hand helical gears with different combinations of rotation are shown in Fig. 17-4 below, with the direction of thrust. Reversing the direction of rotation of the driver will reverse the direction of thrust from that shown.

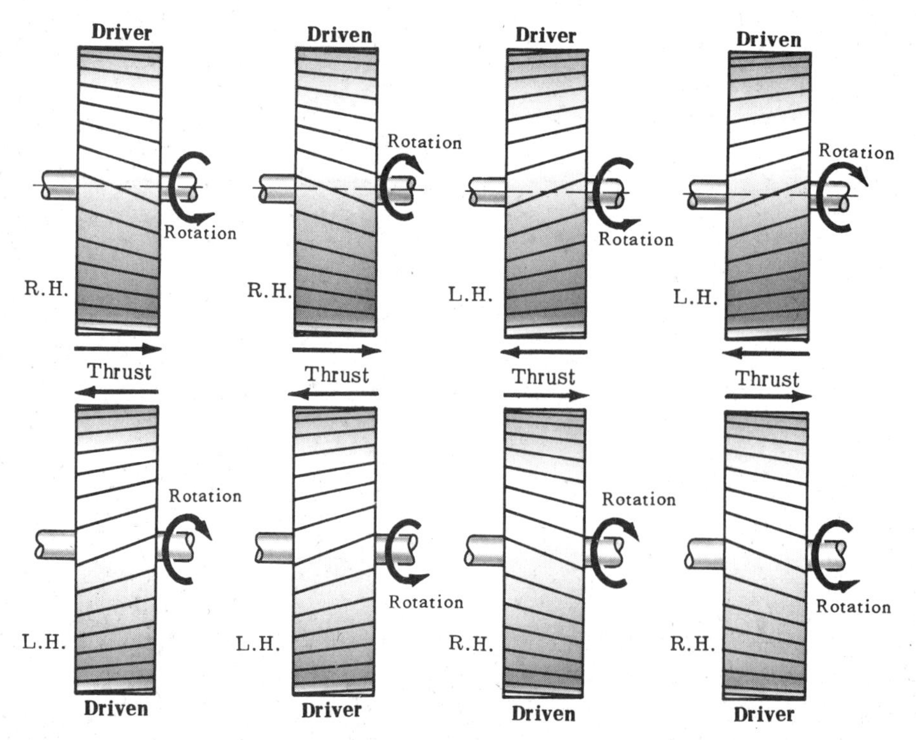

Fig. 17-4

STRAIGHT TOOTH BEVEL GEAR force components, shown in Fig. 17-5 (*a*) below, are:

(1) Tangential force $F_t = M_t/r$.
This force is considered acting at the mean pitch radius r.

(2) Separating force $F_r = F_t \tan\phi$
where ϕ is the pressure angle. The separating force can be resolved into two components; the force component along the shaft axis of the pinion is called the pinion thrust force F_p, and the force component along the shaft axis of the gear is called the gear thrust force F_g.

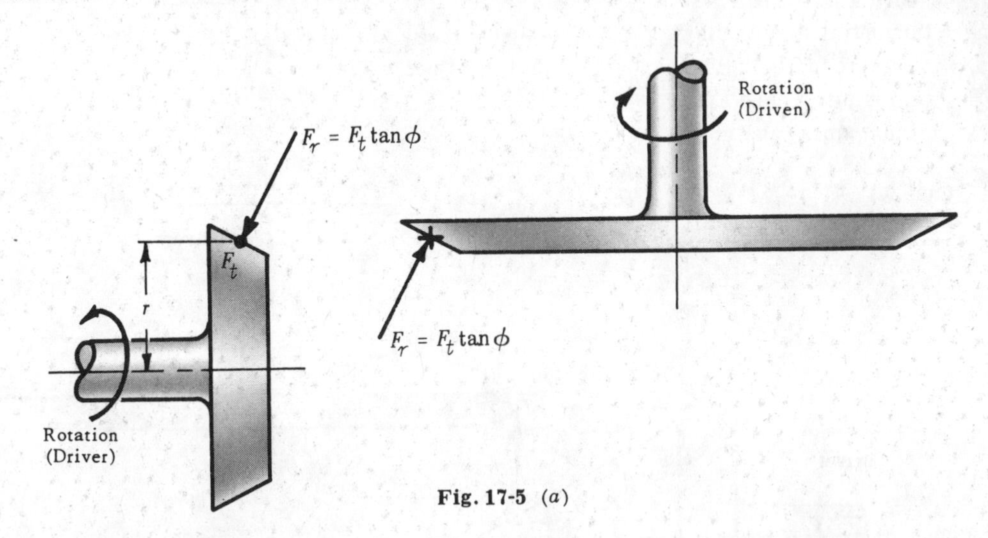

Fig. 17-5 (*a*)

The three mutually perpendicular components, shown in Fig. 17-5 (*b*) below, are:

a. The tangential force $F_t = M_t/r$ acting at the mean pinion pitch radius r, where M_t is the pinion torque.

b. The pinion thrust force $F_p = F_t \tan\phi \sin\beta$, where β is the pitch cone angle of the pinion.

c. The gear thrust force $F_g = F_t \tan\phi \cos\beta$.

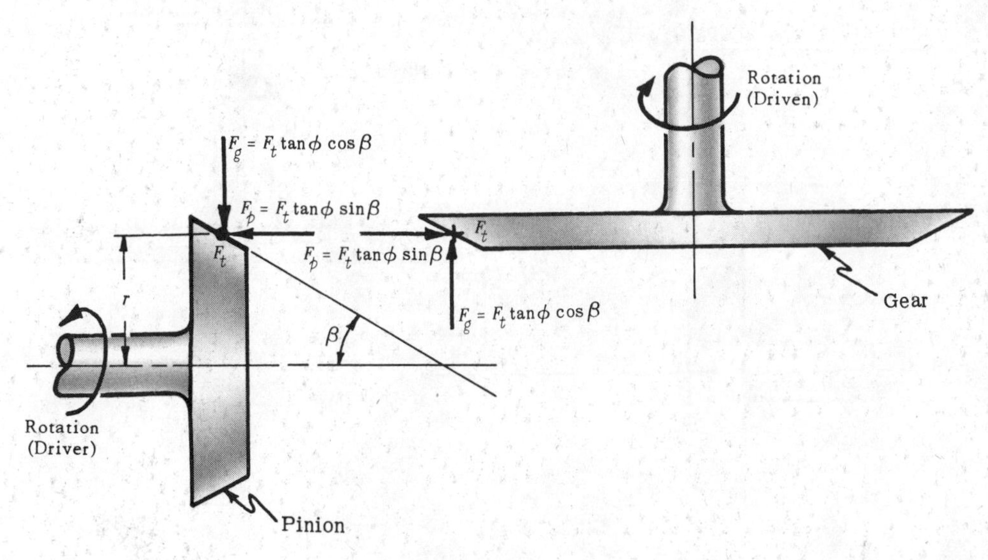

Fig. 17-5 (*b*)

SPIRAL BEVEL GEAR force components are more involved than those for a straight tooth bevel gear.

The tangential force at the mean pitch radius r is $F_t = M_t/r$, where M_t is the torque.

The pinion thrust force F_p and the gear thrust force F_g can be expressed in different ways, depending on how the pressure angle is measured. Pinion and gear thrust forces, with the pressure angle ϕ_n measured in the plane normal to the tooth are shown in Fig. 17-6(*a* to *d*) for different hand of spirals (that is, left hand and right hand) and for different directions of rotation. The symbols are:

F_p = pinion thrust force
F_g = gear thrust force
F_t = tangential force causing the torque at the mean radius r
ϕ_n = tooth pressure angle measured in the plane normal to a tooth
β = pinion pitch cone angle
γ = pinion spiral angle.

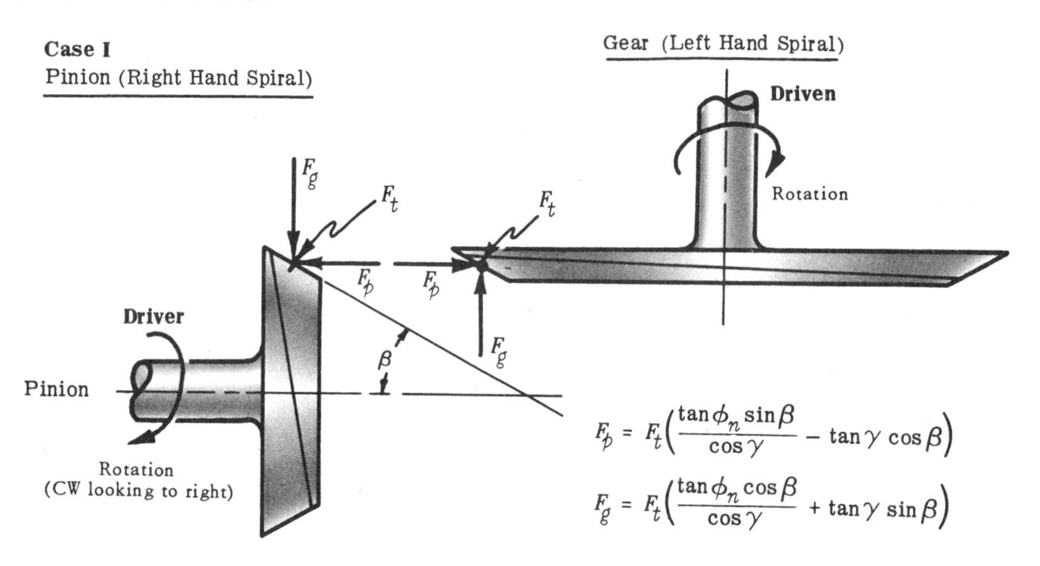

Fig. 17-6(*a*)

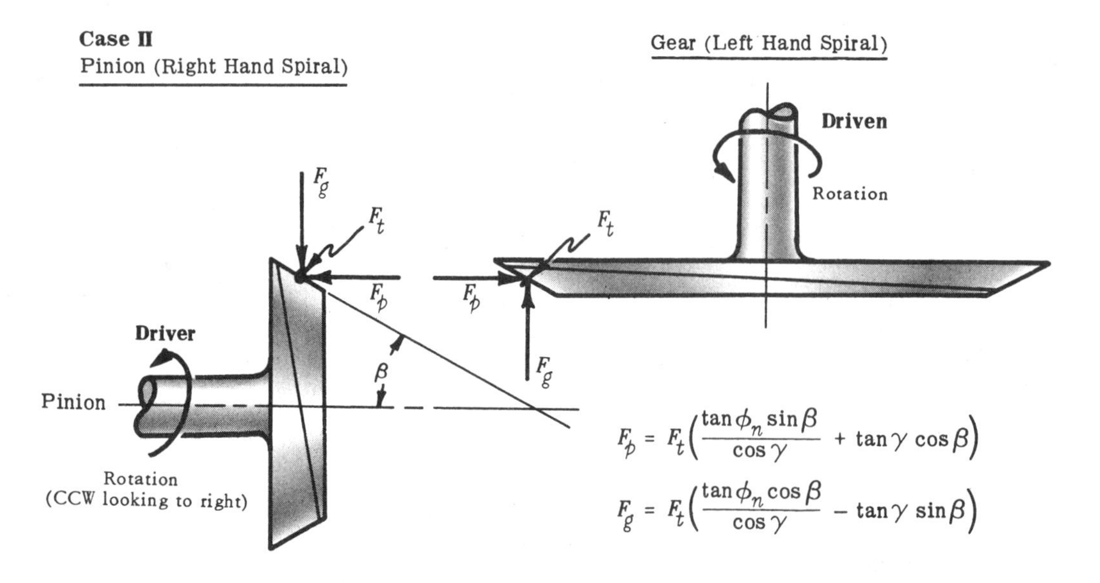

Fig. 17-6(*b*)

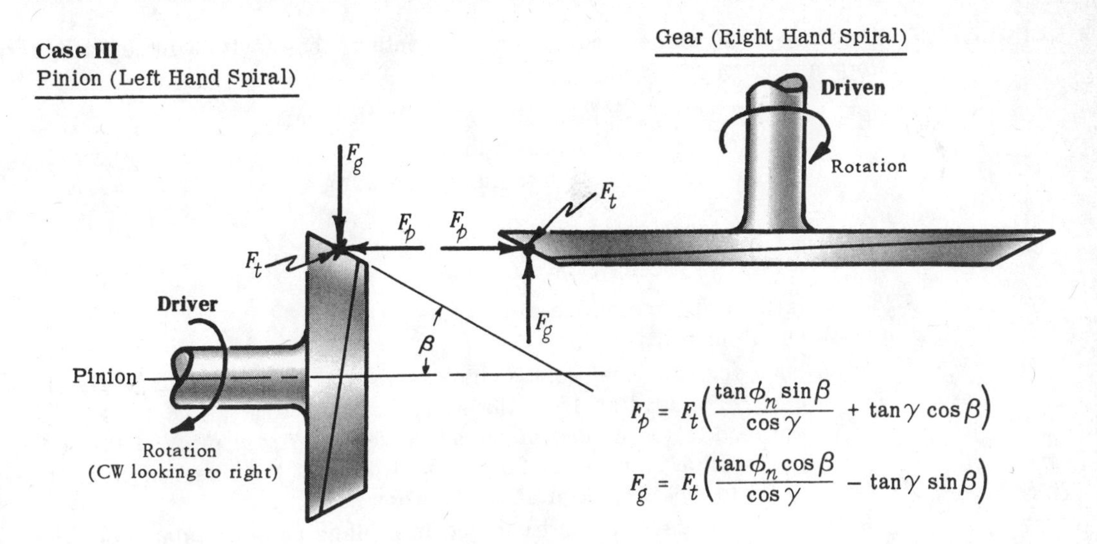

Fig. 17-6(*c*)

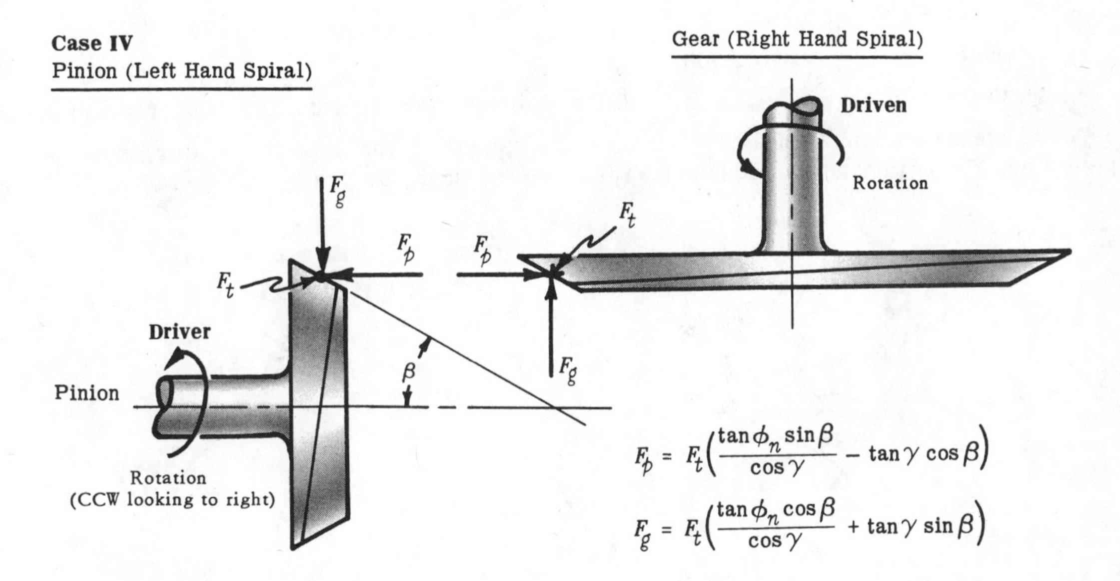

Fig. 17-6(*d*)

The spiral angle is measured as shown in Fig. 17-7.

If the forces are found to be positive, they are directed as shown in the figure; if negative, they are opposite in direction to that shown.

If the pressure angle ϕ is measured in a plane normal to a pitch cone element, the equations given with the figure are changed by substituting

$$\tan\phi = \frac{\tan\phi_n}{\cos\gamma}$$

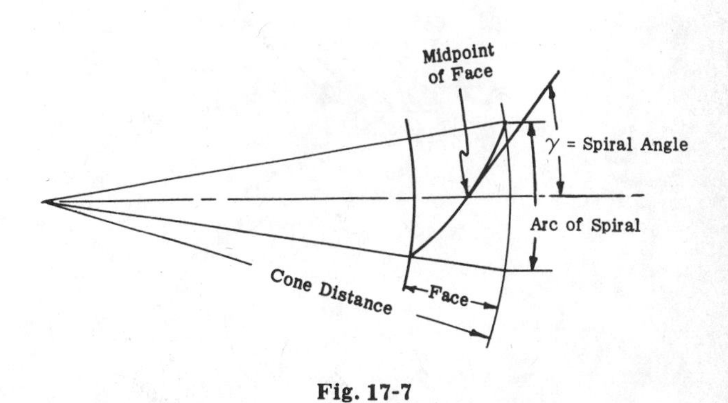

Fig. 17-7

WORM GEARING. The three mutually perpendicular components of the resultant force acting between a worm and worm gear are:

(1) $F_{t(\text{worm})} = M_t/r_w$ where $F_{t(\text{worm})}$ = tangential force on the worm
M_t = torque on the worm
r_w = pitch radius of the worm.

(2) $$F_{t(\text{gear})} = F_{t(\text{worm})}\left(\frac{1 - f\tan\alpha/\cos\phi_n}{\tan\alpha + f/\cos\phi_n}\right)$$

where $F_{t(\text{gear})}$ = tangential force on the worm gear
f = coefficient of friction
α = lead angle of the worm (which is the same as the helix angle of the worm gear). The lead angle of the worm is found from $\tan\alpha = \text{lead}/(\pi D_w)$, where the lead is the number of threads times the linear pitch of the worm and D_w is the pitch diameter of the worm. Note that the linear pitch of the worm is equal to the circular pitch of the worm gear.
ϕ_n = normal pressure angle measured in a plane perpendicular to a tooth (usually $14\frac{1}{2}°$ for a single or double thread and 20° for a triple or quadruple thread).

(3) $$F_r = F_{t(\text{gear})}\left(\frac{\sin\phi_n}{\cos\phi_n\cos\alpha - f\sin\alpha}\right) = F_{t(\text{worm})}\left(\frac{\sin\phi_n}{\cos\phi_n\sin\alpha + f\cos\alpha}\right)$$

where F_r is the separating force.

Fig. 17-8 below, shows the forces for different directions of rotation and hand of worm threads.

The pressure angle ϕ measured in the plane containing the axis of the worm is related to the pressure angle ϕ_n measured in a plane normal to a worm thread by $\tan\phi_n/\cos\alpha$.

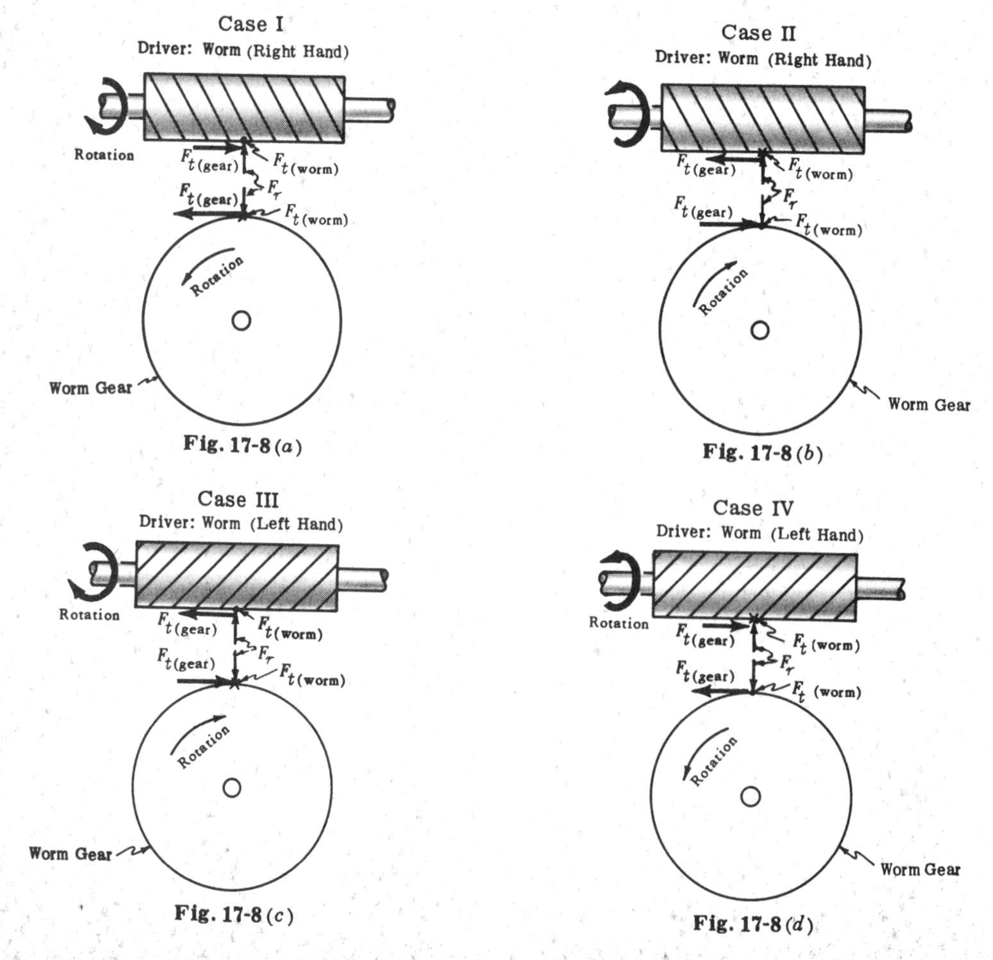

Fig. 17-8 (a) Fig. 17-8 (b) Fig. 17-8 (c) Fig. 17-8 (d)

THE FORCES IN PLANETARY GEAR TRAINS are obtained by the application of the basic equations of mechanics. These are illustrated in solved problems.

A problem encountered in planetary gearing with branch control circuits is the circulating power, which might be less or greater than the power input. The design of such a system can be simplified by the application of appropriate equations. Fig. 17-9 below, shows an arbitrary planetary gear system with a branch control circuit.

The circulating power ratio is given by

$$\gamma = \frac{r(1-R)}{1-r}$$

where $r = \omega_2/\omega_1$, $R = \omega_1/\omega_3$; and ω_1, ω_2 and ω_3 are respectively the angular velocities of elements 1, 2 and 3 as defined below.

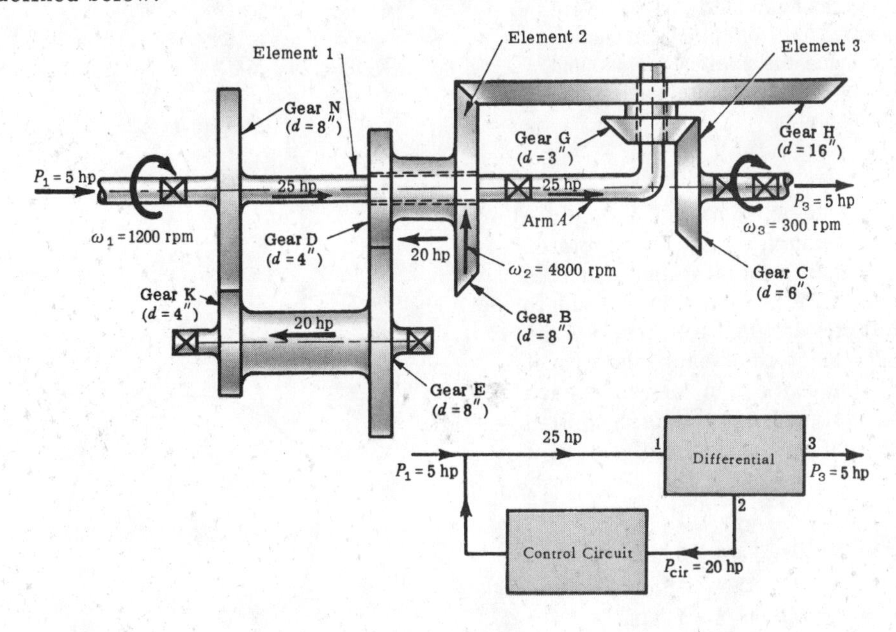

Fig. 17-9

Isolate the three basic elements of the planetary gear part, as shown in Fig. 17-10.

Element 3 is defined as that rotating element projecting from the differential directly to outside the system (gear C in the illustrative example) which has no connection with the control circuit. In some cases element 3 will be the arm; in other cases it may be one of the two gears which project from the differential.

Element 1 will always be that element, projecting from the differential to outside the system, that is connected to rotating element 2 by means of the branch control circuit.

Element 2 will always be that member which transmits power to or from the differential from or to the branch control circuit, but does not transmit power directly to or from the outside of the system. Thus, gear C is element 3, gear B is element 2, and the arm is element 1 for the example chosen.

The circulating power, P_{cir}, is

$$P_{cir} = \gamma P_3$$

where γ is defined above, and P_3 is the power through element 3.

The circulating power is the power in the branch control circuit, element 2.

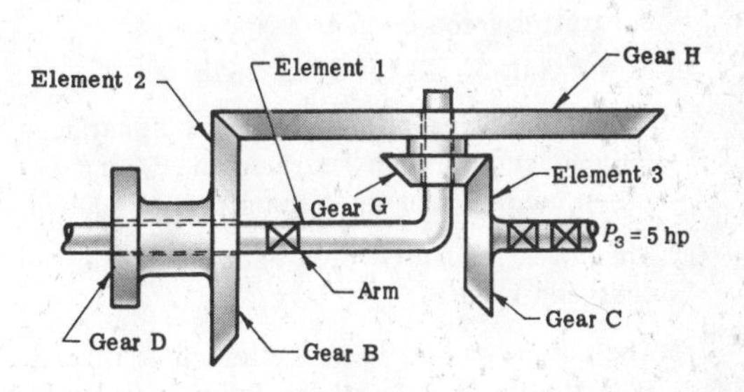

Fig. 17-10

SOLVED PROBLEMS

1. A spur pinion 4 in. in diameter has a torque of 2000 in-lb applied to it. The spur gear in mesh with it is 10 in. in diameter. The pressure angle is 20°. Determine the tangential force F_t and the separating force F_r, and show in position.

Solution:

$$F_t = M_t/r = 2000/2 = 1000 \text{ lb}$$

$$F_r = F_t \tan\phi = 1000 \tan 20^\circ = 364 \text{ lb}$$

The forces are shown in Fig. 17-11. Note that the tangential force on the pinion causes a torque to balance the applied torque, and the pinion separating force is directed towards the center of the pinion.

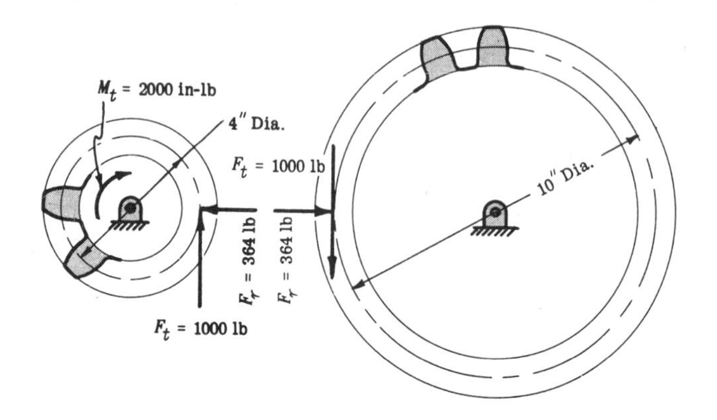

Fig. 17-11

2. Referring to Fig. 17-12, spur gear A receives 4 hp at 600 rpm through its shaft and rotates clockwise. Gear B is an idler and gear C is the driven gear. The teeth are 20° full depth. (The pitch circles are shown in the sketch.) Determine (*1*) the torque each shaft must transmit, (*2*) the tooth load for which each gear must be designed, (*3*) the force applied to the idler shaft as a result of the gear tooth loads.

Solution:

(*a*) Gear diameters: $D_A = 35/4 = 8\frac{3}{4}$ in.

$D_B = 65/4 = 16\frac{1}{4}$ in.

$D_C = 45/4 = 11\frac{1}{4}$ in.

(*b*) Torque on shaft of gear A

$= (\text{hp})(63{,}024)/N = 4(63{,}024)/600$

$= 420$ in-lb.

Torque on shaft of gear B = 0.

Torque on shaft of gear C

$= 4(63{,}024)/600(35/45) = 540$ in-lb,

where gear C rotates at 600(35/45) rpm.

(*c*) Tangential force on gear A

$$= F_t = \frac{M_t}{r} = \frac{420}{\frac{1}{2}(8\frac{3}{4})} = 96 \text{ lb.}$$

Separating force on gear A

$$= F_t \tan\phi = 96 \tan 20^\circ = 35 \text{ lb.}$$

(*d*) The same tangential force and separating force occur between gears A and B and between gears B and C, in the direction shown.

(*e*) The tooth load for which each gear must be designed is 96 lb.

(*f*) The force applied to the idler shaft of gear B is the vector sum of the forces applied to gear B by gears A and C:

$$F_B = \sqrt{(96+35)^2 + (96+35)^2} = 185 \text{ lb.}$$

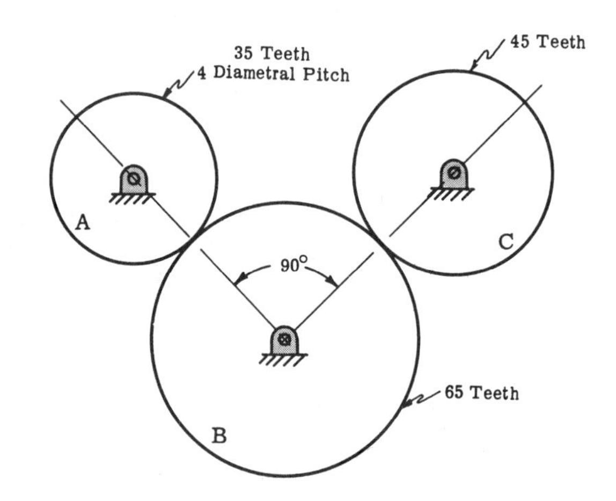

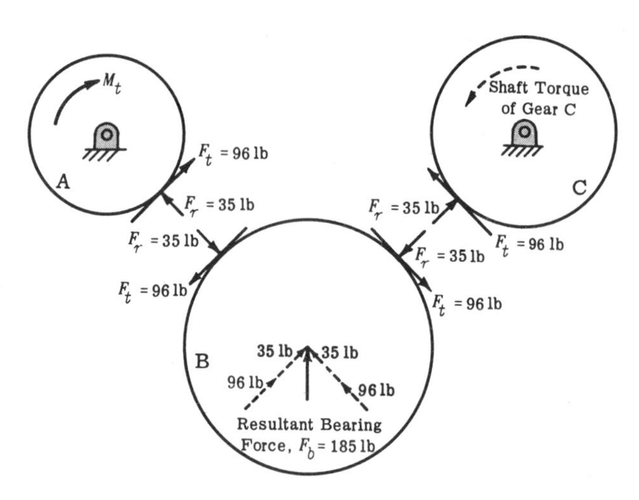

Fig. 17-12

3. A helical gear 9.00 in. in diameter has applied to it through its shaft a torque of 1800 in-lb. There are 45 teeth on the gear. The pressure angle, measured in a plane perpendicular to the axis of the gear, is 20°. The helix angle is 30°. Determine (*a*) the tangential force component F_t, (*b*) the separating force component F_r, (*c*) the axial thrust force component F_a. The helical gear has left hand teeth, and meshes with a right handed gear whose axis is directly above the axis of the left hand gear. Refer to Fig.17-13.

Solution:

(*a*) $F_t = M_t/r = 1800/4.5 = 400$ lb

(*b*) $F_r = F_t \tan\phi = 400 \tan 20^\circ = 146$ lb

(*c*) $F_a = F_t \tan\alpha = 400 \tan 30^\circ = 231$ lb

The directions are as shown in Fig.17-13.

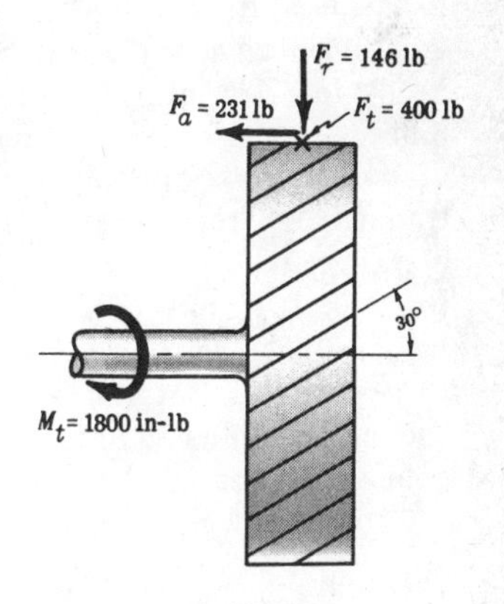

Fig. 17-13

4. Repeat Problem 3, except that the pressure angle, measured in a plane perpendicular to the tooth, is 20°. Refer to Fig.17-14.

Solution:

(*a*) $F_t = M_t/r = 1800/4.5 = 400$ lb

(*b*) $F_r = \dfrac{F_t \tan\phi_n}{\cos\alpha} = \dfrac{400 \tan 20^\circ}{\cos 30^\circ} = 168$ lb

(*c*) $F_a = F_t \tan\alpha = 400 \tan 30^\circ = 231$ lb

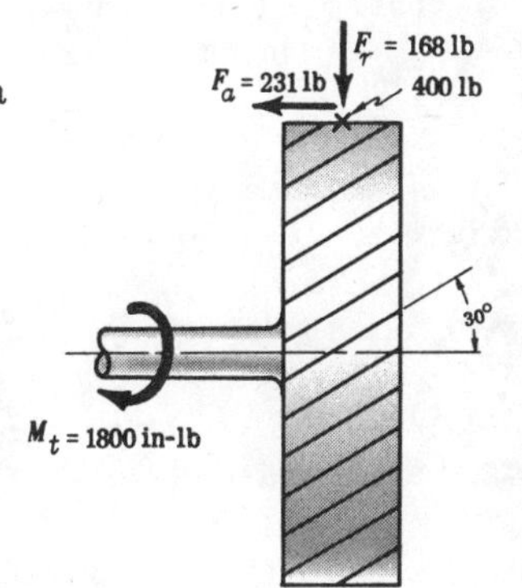

Fig. 17-14

5. In Fig.17-15 a pair of straight tooth bevel gears has a velocity ratio of 4/3. The pitch diameter of the pinion is 6 in. The face width is $1\frac{1}{2}$ in. The pinion rotates at 240 rpm. The teeth are 5 diametral pitch, $14\frac{1}{2}^\circ$ involute. If 8 hp is transmitted, determine (*1*) the tangential force F_t at the mean radius, (*2*) the pinion thrust force F_p, (*3*) the gear thrust force F_g.

Solution:

(*a*) Diameter of the gear = 6(4/3) = 8 in.

(*b*) Slant height L of the pitch cone

$= \sqrt{R_p^2 + R_g^2} = \sqrt{3^2 + 4^2} = 5$ in.

(*c*) Mean radius of the pinion,

$r_m = R_p - \frac{1}{2} b \sin\beta = 3 - \frac{1}{2}(3/2)(3/5) = 2.55$ in.

(*d*) Pinion torque M_t

$= (\text{hp})(63{,}024)/N = 8(63{,}024)/240 = 2100$ in-lb.

(*e*) Tangential force at the mean radius, F_t

$= M_t/r_m = 2100/2.55 = 825$ lb.

(*f*) Pinion thrust force F_p

$= F_t \tan\phi \sin\beta = 825(\tan 14\frac{1}{2}^\circ)(3/5) = 129$ lb.

(*g*) Gear thrust force F_g

$= F_t \tan\phi \cos\beta$

$= 825(\tan 14\frac{1}{2}^\circ)(4/5) = 171$ lb.

The forces are shown in the free body diagrams.

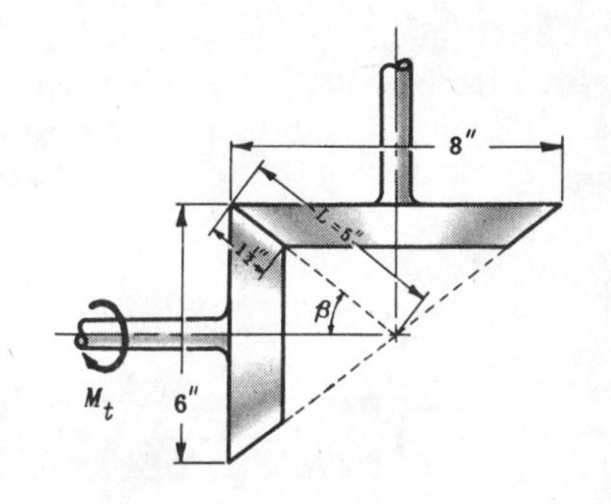

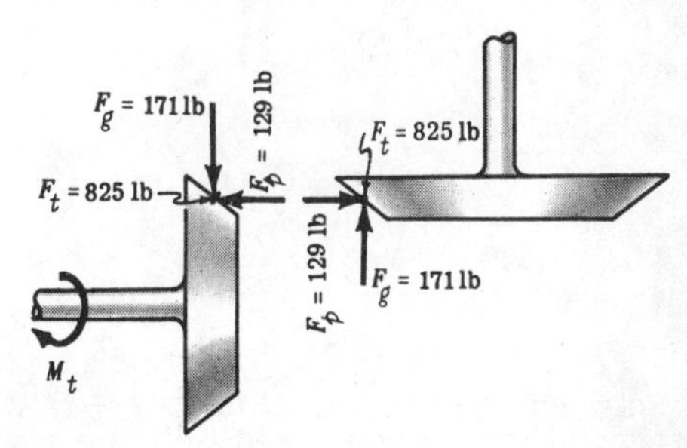

Fig. 17-15

6. A pair of spiral tooth bevel gears has a 4/3 velocity ratio. The pitch diameter of the pinion is 6 in. The face width is $1\frac{1}{2}$ in. The pinion rotates at 240 rpm. The teeth are 5 diametral pitch with a pressure angle ϕ_n of $14\frac{1}{2}°$ measured in a plane normal to a tooth. Eight horsepower is transmitted from the pinion to the gear. The pinion has a right hand spiral and the rotation is clockwise (looking towards the apex of the pitch cone). The spiral angle is $\gamma = 30°$. This corresponds to Case I for spiral bevel gear forces. Determine (*1*) the tangential force F_t at the mean radius, (*2*) the pinion thrust load F_p, (*3*) the gear thrust load F_g.

Refer to Fig. 17-16.

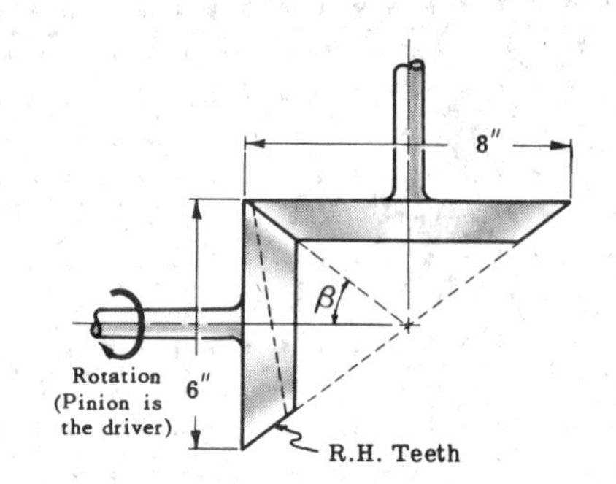

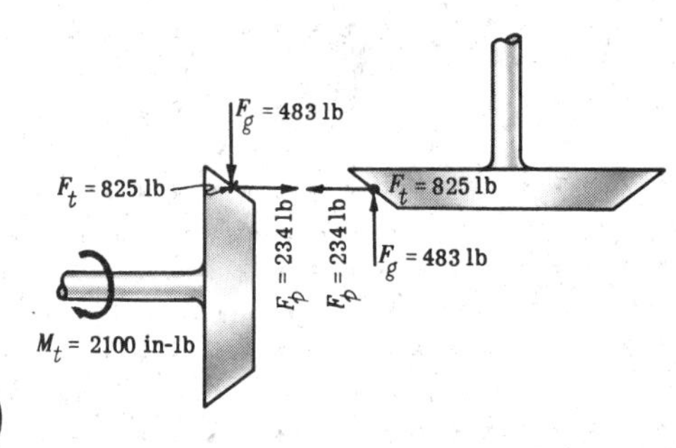

Fig. 17-16

Solution:

(*a*) The values found in Problem 5 that are applicable to this problem are: diameter of gear = 8 in.; slant height of pitch cone = 5 in.; mean radius of pinion = 2.55 in.; pinion torque = 2100 in-lb; tangential force at the mean radius = 825 lb; $\sin\beta = 3/5$, $\cos\beta = 4/5$.

(*b*) Pinion thrust force $F_p = F_t\left(\dfrac{\tan\phi_n \sin\beta}{\cos\gamma} - \tan\gamma\cos\beta\right)$

$$= 825\left[\frac{(\tan 14\frac{1}{2}°)(3/5)}{\cos 30°} - (\tan 30°)(4/5)\right] = -234\text{ lb}.$$

(*c*) Gear thrust force $F_g = F_t\left(\dfrac{\tan\phi_n\cos\beta}{\cos\gamma} + \tan\gamma\sin\beta\right) = 825\left[\dfrac{(\tan 14\frac{1}{2}°)(4/5)}{\cos 30°} + (\tan 30°)(3/5)\right] = +483\text{ lb}.$

The force components are shown in the correct directions in the free body diagrams of Fig. 17-16.

7. A worm transmitting 9 hp at 1200 rpm drives a worm gear rotating at 60 rpm. The pitch diameter of the worm is 2.68 in. and the worm is triple threaded. The circular pitch of the worm gear is $\frac{3}{4}$ in. (which is the same as the axial pitch of the worm). The worm gear has 60 teeth which are 20° stub. The coefficient of friction f is 0.10. The worm is right handed and rotates as shown in Fig. 17-17 below. (Note that the figure corresponds to Case I under Worm Gearing. Also note that the power output is not equal to the power input because of friction.) Calculate (*1*) the tangential force $F_{t\,(worm)}$ on the worm, (*2*) the tangential force $F_{t\,(gear)}$ on the gear, (*3*) the separating force F_r.

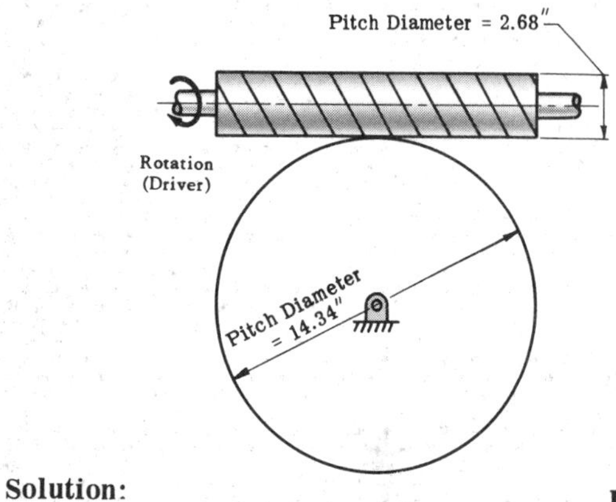

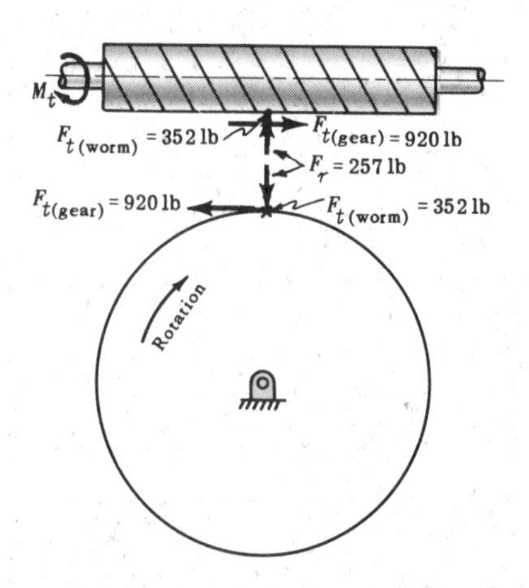

Fig. 17-17

Solution:

(*a*) Torque on the worm, M_t = (hp)(63,024)/N = 9(63,024)/1200 = 472 in-lb.

(*b*) $F_{t\,(\text{worm})} = M_t/r = 472/(2.68/2) = 352$ lb

(*c*) $$F_{t(\text{gear})} = F_{t(\text{worm})} \frac{1 - f\tan\alpha/\cos\phi_n}{\tan\alpha + f/\cos\phi_n} = 352\left(\frac{1 - 0.1(0.268)/\cos 20^\circ}{0.268 + 0.1/\cos 20^\circ}\right) = 920 \text{ lb}$$

where $\tan\alpha = \text{lead}/(\pi D_w) = (3)(\frac{3}{4})/(2.68\pi) = 0.268 \quad (\alpha = 15^\circ)$.

(*d*) $$F_r = F_{t(\text{gear})}\left(\frac{\sin\phi_n}{\cos\phi_n\cos\alpha - f\sin\alpha}\right) = 920\left(\frac{\sin 20^\circ}{\cos 20^\circ \cos 15^\circ - 0.1\sin 15^\circ}\right) = 257 \text{ lb}$$

(*e*) Another method of calculating the tangential force on the gear is to employ the efficiency equation for worm gearing to find the output horsepower. The efficiency *e* for worm gearing is

$$e = (\tan\alpha)\left(\frac{\cos\phi_n - f\tan\alpha}{\cos\phi_n\tan\alpha + f}\right) = 0.268\left(\frac{\cos 20^\circ - 0.1\tan 15^\circ}{\cos 20^\circ\tan 15^\circ + 0.1}\right) = 69.8\%$$

$$\text{Gear torque} = (\text{output hp})(63{,}024)/N = (9 \times 0.698)(63{,}024)/60 = 6600 \text{ in-lb}$$

$$F_{t(\text{gear})} = M_t/r = 6600/(14.34/2) = 920 \text{ lb, as in } (c).$$

8. A differential planetary gear system is shown in Fig. 17-18. Gear B rotates at a constant speed, while the speed of gear H is varied to permit variations in speed of gear I. However, for this problem, consider that all gears rotate at a constant speed. Neglect friction.

Power is applied to gear B and either applied to or taken from gears H and I. Determine how much power must be applied to or taken from gear H if 3 horsepower is supplied to gear B at 1800 rpm of gear B, the direction of rotation of gear B being clockwise as viewed from the right. Gear H is rotating at 700 rpm counterclockwise as viewed from the right. Determine also the power supplied to or taken from gear I and the angular velocity of gear I.

All gears have a pressure angle of $14\frac{1}{2}^\circ$. The diameter of each gear is as follows:

gear A: 4.0"
gear B: 5.0"
gear C: 7.0"
gear D: 9"(mean dia.)
gear E: 6.0"(mean dia.)
gear F: 6.0"(mean dia.)
gear G: 10.0"(mean dia.)
gear H: 12.0"
gear I: 3.0"

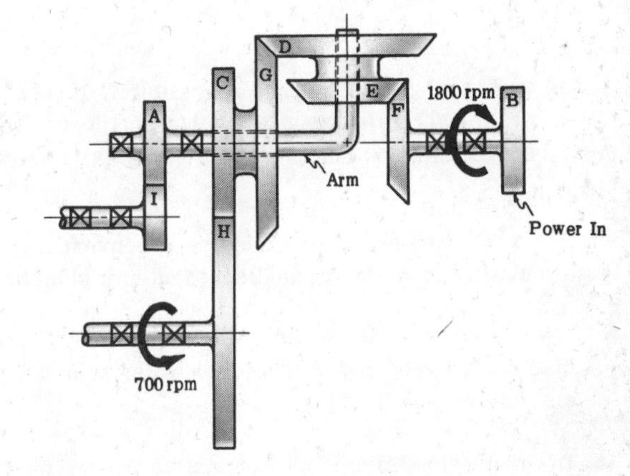

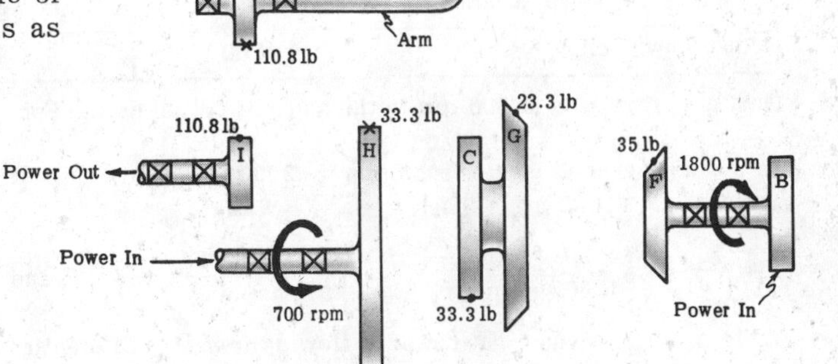

Fig. 17-18

Solution:

(*a*) The forces shown in the free body diagrams are the tangential forces causing torque about the centerline axis of the corresponding gear.

Torque on gear B = torque on gear F: $M_t = \frac{(hp)(63{,}024)}{N} = \frac{3(63{,}024)}{1800} = 105$ in-lb.

Force exerted on gear F by gear E $= M_t/r = 105/3 = 35$ lb.

(*b*) The moment about the axis of gears D and E must be zero for constant speed:

$$F_{GD} R_D = F_{FE} R_E, \quad F_{GD}(4.5) = 35(3), \quad F_{GD} = 23.3 \text{ lb}$$

where F_{GD} = tangential force exerted by gear G on D, R_D = radius of gear D
F_{FE} = tangential force exerted by gear F on E, R_E = radius of gear E.

(*c*) Consider gears C and G: $F_{DG} R_G = F_{HC} R_C$, $23.3(5) = F_{HC}(3.5)$, $F_{HC} = 33.3$ lb.

The direction of rotation is opposite the direction of the torque exerted on gear H; hence power must be supplied to the shaft of gear H as shown.

Power supplied to gear H $= M_t N/63{,}024 = (33.3 \times 6)(700)/63{,}024 = 2.22$ hp.

Since power is supplied to gear B and also supplied to gear H, the power that must be taken out through gear I is $(3 + 2.22) = 5.22$ hp.

(*d*) Since power is taken out through gear I, the direction of rotation must correspond to the direction of torque on gear I. The torque is counterclockwise, looking from right to left; hence the rotation is counterclockwise looking from right to left.

Speed of gear I is $N_I = (hp)(63{,}024)/M_t = (5.22)(63{,}024)/(110.8 \times 1.5) = 1980$ rpm.

9. Refer to Fig. 17-9 and Fig. 17-10. Gear N rotates at 1200 rpm clockwise looking from right to left. Five horsepower is transmitted through the unit. Find the horsepower for which gears K, E and D must be designed, assuming no power loss in friction.

Solution:

A solution can be obtained by a conventional force analysis, but this problem will be solved using the circulating power factor as discussed with planetary gearing forces.

(*a*) A velocity analysis is made first: Gear K rotates at 1200(8/4) = 2400 rpm counterclockwise, and gear E also makes 2400 rpm counterclockwise; gear D rotates at 2400(8/4) = 4800 rpm clockwise, and gear B also makes 4800 rpm clockwise.

(*b*) In the differential unit, the angular velocities can be obtained quickly by:

Angular Velocity Calculations (rpm)

	Element 1, arm A	Element 2, gear B	Element 3, gear C
Angular velocity of arm	+ 1200	+ 1200	+ 1200
Ang. vel. relative to arm	0	+ 3600	− 3600(8/16)(3/6)
Angular velocity	+ 1200	+ 4800	+ 300

Thus gear C rotates at 300 rpm in the same direction as the arm.

(*c*) As defined, gear C is element 3 ($\omega_3 = +300$ rpm); gear B is element 2 ($\omega_2 = +4800$ rpm); the arm is element 1 ($\omega_1 = +1200$ rpm). Then

$$r = \frac{\omega_2}{\omega_1} = \frac{+4800}{+1200} = +4, \quad R = \frac{\omega_1}{\omega_3} = \frac{+1200}{+300} = +4, \quad \text{and} \quad \gamma = \frac{r(1-R)}{1-r} = \frac{+4(1-4)}{1-4} = +4$$

where a + sign means that power is flowing **from** the differential unit through both elements 2 and 3.

(*d*) Power through element 2, the circulating hp, is $P_{cir} = \gamma P_3 = +4(5) = 20$ hp.

(*e*) Thus gears K, D and E must be designed for 20 hp. Note that even though the power is larger than the input and output power, it **cannot** be tapped to give perpetual motion.

SUPPLEMENTARY PROBLEMS

10. A spur pinion of 3 in. pitch diameter drives a 9 in. gear. The pinion shaft has 600 in-lb of torque applied, and the pressure angle is 20°. Determine the tangential force, the separating or radial force, and the gear torque.
Ans. F_t = 400 lb, F_r = 146 lb, $M_{t(\text{gear})}$ = 1800 in-lb

11. The helical gear train shown in Fig.17-19 below transmits 10 hp from gear C to gear A at 900 rpm of gear C. The overall velocity ratio is 2. Calculate the total radial load on the shaft of gear B, and the total thrust load in the shaft of gear B. What are the tangential and separating forces between A and B and between B and C?
Ans. Total radial load on shaft of gear B = 127 lb.
Resultant thrust force = 0.
Tangential force between A and B is the same as between B and C: 140 lb.
Separating force between A and B is the same as between B and C: 51 lb.

12. An 18 pitch helical pinion with 20° stub teeth, helix angle of 23°, pitch diameter of 3 in., and face width of $1\frac{1}{8}$ in. transmits 20 hp at 10,000 rpm. If the pressure angle is measured in the plane of rotation, determine the tangential force, the separating force component, and the axial or thrust force.
Ans. 84 lb, 30.6 lb, 35.6 lb

13. Refer to Fig.17-20 below. Gear A receives 6 hp at 500 rpm through its shaft and rotates counterclockwise. Gear B is an idler and gear C is the driven gear. The teeth are 20° full depth form. (*a*) What is the torque on the shaft of each gear? (*b*) What is the tangential force for which each gear must be designed? (*c*) What force is applied to the idler shaft as a result of the gear tooth loads?
Ans. (*a*) M_{tA} = 756 in-lb, M_{tB} = 0, M_{tC} = 864 in-lb (*b*) 173 lb (same for each gear) (*c*) 156 lb

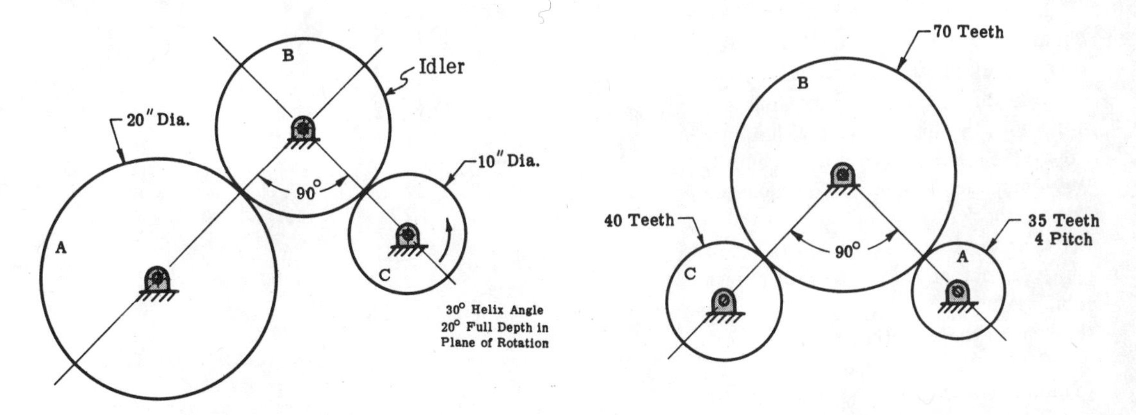

Fig. 17-19 **Fig. 17-20**

14. A 20° full depth straight tooth bevel gear has a pitch of 3, a face width of $3\frac{3}{4}$ in., a pitch diameter of 12.0 in., and a cone pitch angle of $37\frac{1}{2}°$. If the torque on the gear is 6500 in-lb, what is the axial component, or thrust component, of the tooth force? What is the mean diameter of the gear? What is the tangential force at the mean radius?
Ans. 297 lb, 4.86 in., 1340 lb

15. A 30 tooth bevel gear meshes with a 60 tooth bevel gear with straight teeth. The angle between shafts is 90°. The torque on the pinion is 400 in-lb and the *mean* radius of the pinion is 2 in. The pressure angle is 20°. Determine the pinion thrust force. *Ans.* 32.6 lb

16. A pair of straight tooth bevel gears connects a pair of shafts at 90°. The velocity ratio is 3 to 1. What is the cone pitch angle of each gear?
Ans. 18.4° for pinion, 71.6° for gear.

17. A spiral bevel pinion with a left hand spiral rotates clockwise (looking toward the apex of the pitch cone) and transmits 4 hp at 1200 rpm to a mating gear (Case III of spiral bevel gear forces). The mean diameter of the pinion is 3.00 in. The pressure angle ϕ_n measured in the plane perpendicular to a tooth is 20°, the spiral angle is 20°, and the velocity ratio is 2 to 1. Determine (*a*) the pitch angle of the pinion, (*b*) the tangential force F_t at the mean radius, (*c*) the pinion thrust force F_p, (*d*) the gear thrust force F_g.
Ans. (*a*) $\beta = 26.55°$ (*c*) $F_p = +70$ lb (directed as shown in figure of Case III)
(*b*) $F_t = 140$ lb (*d*) $F_g = +25.8$ lb (directed as shown in figure of Case III)

18. A worm rotating at 1150 rpm drives a worm gear. The velocity ratio is 15 to 1. The worm is double threaded and has a pitch diameter of 3.000 in. The circular pitch of the worm gear is $1\frac{1}{8}$ in. (The axial pitch of the worm is also $1\frac{1}{8}$ in. with the lead being $2\frac{1}{4}$ in., since the worm is double threaded.) The worm has left hand threads, as shown in Case III of worm gear forces, and rotates clockwise as indicated. The normal pressure angle is $14\frac{1}{2}°$, and the coefficient of friction is 0.2. If 10 hp is supplied to the worm, determine (*a*) the tangential force on the worm, (*b*) the tangential force on the gear, (*c*) the separating force, (*d*) the efficiency. (The directions are as shown in Case III.) *Ans.* (*a*) 365 lb, (*b*) 778 lb, (*c*) 218 lb, (*d*) 50.8%

19. Referring to Fig.17-21, find the torque on each of the two output shafts for an input torque of 1600 in-lb applied to gear G. The gears rotate at a constant speed. Diameter of gear B = 8", of gear C = 6". Mean diameter of gear D = 12", of gear E = 6", of gear F = 3", of gear G = 6".
Ans. Torque on gear B = 2130 in-lb,
Torque on gear arm A = 3200 in-lb.

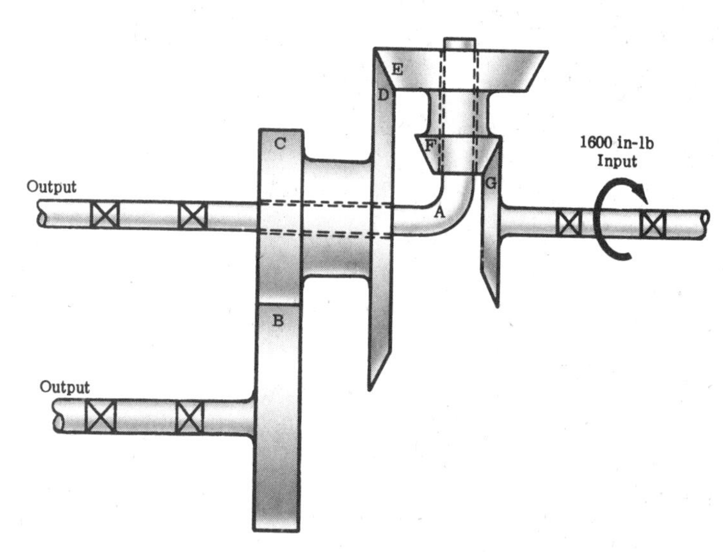

Fig. 17-21

20. The induction motor of Fig.17-22 below, supplies 20 hp at 1800 rpm and drives shaft E through a planetary gear system, with the internal gear *F* held stationary. There are two planet gears D. Determine the tangential force on gear C and the velocity of engagement of the gear teeth between gears C and D. The velocity of engagement is the velocity of the pitch line of the gears relative to the arm; this is the velocity with which the teeth mesh. Assume the planet gears D share the load equally.
Ans. 70 lb, 2900 ft/min

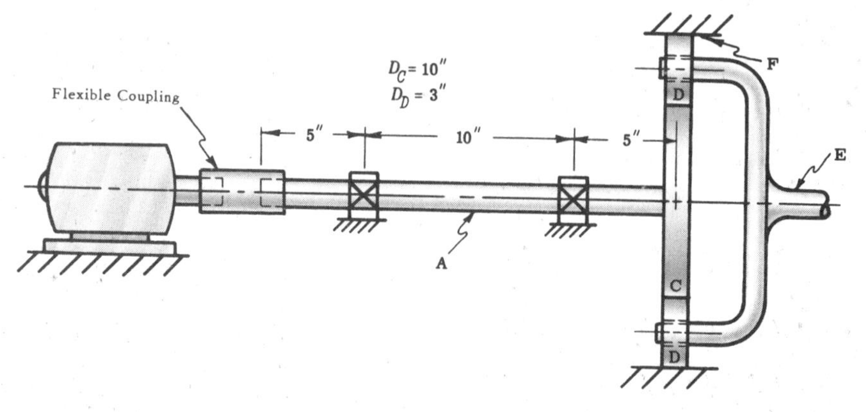

Fig. 17-22

21. The gear train of Fig.17-23 transmits 50 hp. Gear E is held stationary. The input shaft A rotates at 1000 rpm. The pitch of each gear is 6. The arm carrying gears B, D, and F has diameter 2 in. The gears are spaced 3 in. apart and are 20° full depth. Consider the loads concentrated at the centers of the gears and neglect stress concentration. Calculate the torque applied to gear E and the maximum shear stress in the arm whose axis is the axis of gears B, D, and F.

Ans. 15,750 in-lb; 30,500 psi (maximum bending moment = 48,000 in-lb)

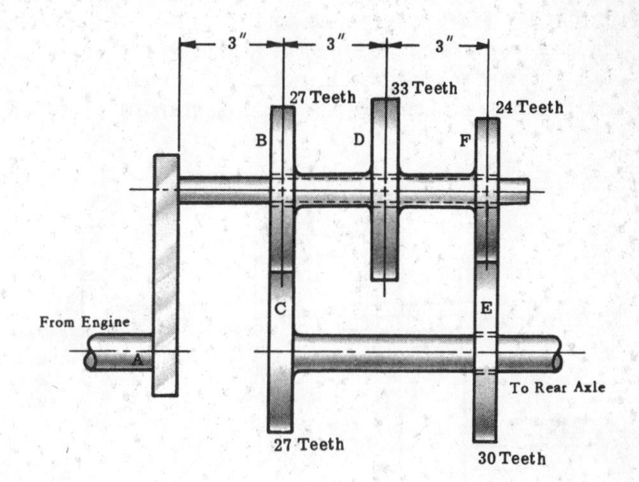

Fig. 17-23

22. The input shaft of the gear train shown in Fig.17-24 below drives gear 2 at 10 rpm with an input torque of 900 in-lb. Gears 4 and 5 are integral. All gears have 20° involute form teeth. Determine the reactions at bearings G and H. Power is taken from the output shaft through a flexible coupling.

Ans. R_G = 70 lb, R_H = 30 lb

Gear	No. of Teeth
1	120
2	60
3	30
4	30
5	50
6	40

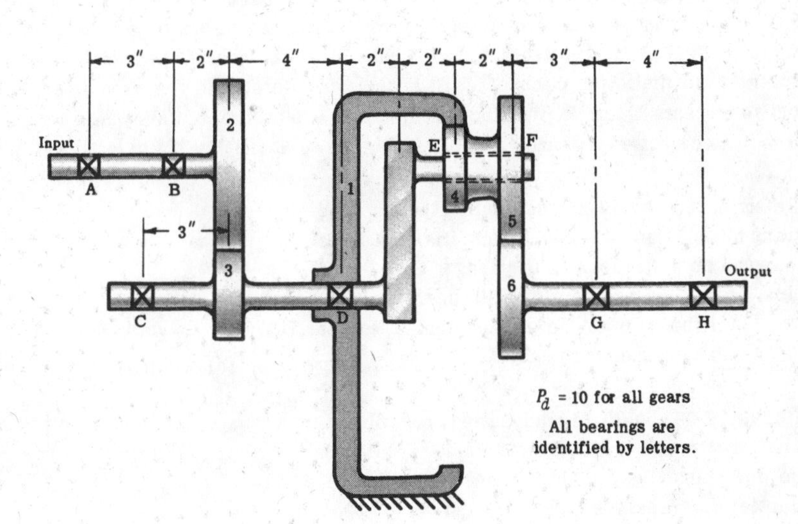

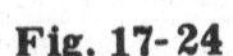

Fig. 17-24

23. Refer to Fig.17-25. A radial engine uses an epicyclic gear train of the form shown in Fig.17-1 to convert the reciprocating motion of the pistons to the rotation of the crankshaft which is collinear with the stationary axis X-X. Gears B and E have 144 and 72 teeth respectively, and the diametral pitch of all gears is 6. (*a*) If the angular velocity of each of the gears B and E is zero, how many teeth are on gears C and D? (*b*) Assuming the engine delivers 2125 hp when the crankshaft is rotating at 400 rpm, determine, by drawing a free body diagram for each element of the train, the tangential force acting at each mesh and the required tangential connecting rod force at G. (*c*) Determine the required crank pin force at G for part (*b*) by some method other than a force analysis as made in part (*b*) above.

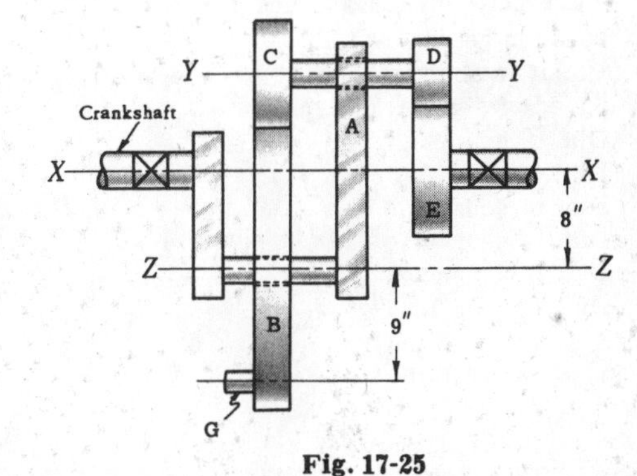

Fig. 17-25

Ans. (*a*) Teeth on C = 48, on D = 24.

(*b*) Force between gears E and D = 63,000 lb; force between C and B = 31,500 lb; force on G = 42,000 lb.

24. In Fig.17-26 below, power is applied to shaft I and either taken off or applied to shafts II and III. If 600 in-lb of torque is applied to shaft I, what torque must be applied to shaft II and shaft III if each gear rotates at a constant velocity and if friction is neglected.

Ans. Torque on shaft II = 263 in-lb; on shaft III = 820 in-lb.

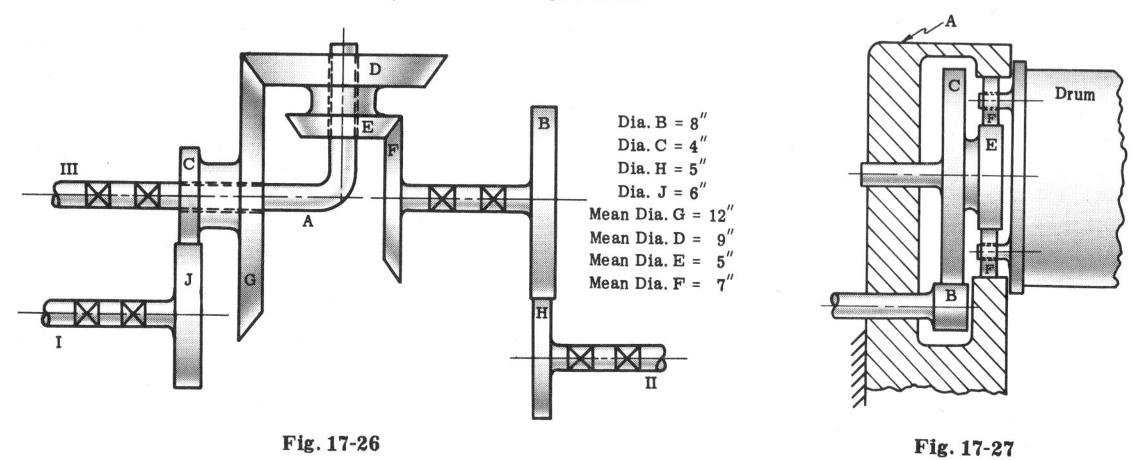

Fig. 17-26

Fig. 17-27

25. Refer to Fig.17-27 above. The drum of a concrete mixer has 5 hp supplied to it and the drum rotates at 200 rpm. The drum has fastened integrally to it two pins on which are located gears F. Gears C and E are integral. Gear B has 18 teeth, gear C has 75 teeth, gear E has 35 teeth, and the internal gear of A has 65 teeth. The diametral pitch of each gear is 5. Determine the tangential force between gears B and C and between gears E and F. Neglect friction and assume each planet gear takes its proportional part of the load.

Ans. Force between B and C = 73.7 lb, between E and F = 79 lb.

26. Referring to Fig.17-28, determine the horsepower transmitted through gear C and through gear B. Assume no power loss in friction.

Ans. Power through gear C = 50 hp, through gear B = 40 hp. (Power flows from gear C to gear D and from gear B to gear A.)

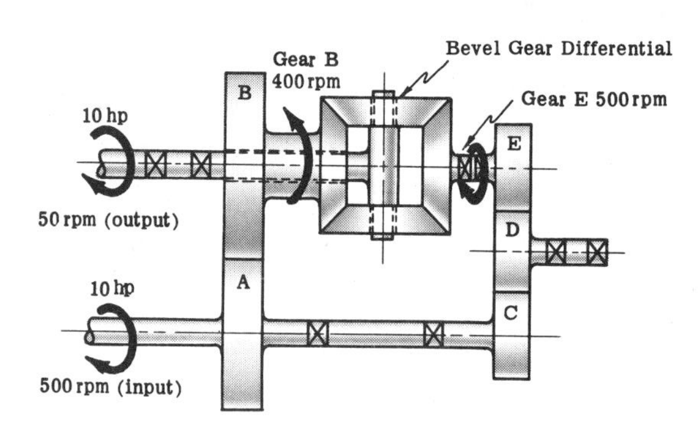

Fig. 17-28

27. In Fig.17-29, power is transmitted from shaft A to shaft B through the differential shown. Assuming no power loss due to friction, determine (*a*) the tangential force between gears 2 and 3, (*b*) the tangential force between gears 2 and 4, (*c*) the torque in the shaft between gears 3 and 5, (*d*) the torque in C between gears 4 and 7, (*e*) the power in the shaft between gears 3 and 5, (*f*) the power in C between gears 4 and 7.

Power in shaft A: 6 hp
Speed of shaft A: 600 rpm
Dia. of gear 2: 2″
Dia. of gear 3: 6″
Dia. of gear 4: 10″
Dia. of gear 5: $7\frac{1}{2}$″
Dia. of gear 6: 2″
Dia. of gear 7: $11\frac{1}{2}$″

Ans. (*a*) 7875 lb
(*b*) 7245 lb
(*c*) 23,625 in-lb
(*d*) 36,225 in-lb
(*e*) 75 hp
(*f*) 69 hp
(Note the presence of circulating power.)

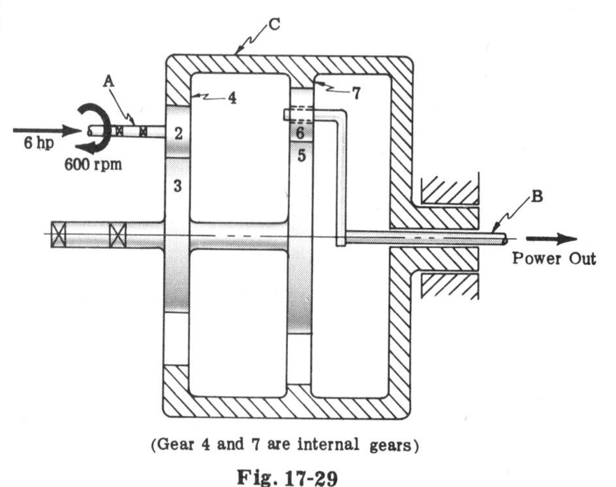

(Gear 4 and 7 are internal gears)

Fig. 17-29

28. Repeat Problem 27, except that the gear diameters are as follows:

Dia. of gear 2: 2″ Dia. of gear 5: 6″
Dia. of gear 3: $7\frac{1}{2}$″ Dia. of gear 6: 2″
Dia. of gear 4: $11\frac{1}{2}$″ Dia. of gear 7: 10″

Ans. (*a*) 7250 lb (*b*) 7880 lb (*c*) 27,190 in-lb (*d*) 45,300 in-lb (*e*) 69 hp (*f*) 75 hp

29. The data and figure for this problem are the same as for Problem 27. In designing a gear for strength, one must know the tangential force acting on the gear and the proper velocity at the pitch point. When a gear rotates about its axis (as gear 2 or 3), the velocity is obtained by $V = r\omega$, where r is the pitch radius and ω is the angular velocity; when a gear is part of the planetary system (as gears 5, 6, and 7), the velocity to be used in the Lewis strength equation and Buckingham dynamic load equation is the velocity of the gear at the pitch point relative to the arm. This velocity relative to the arm can be obtained by $V = r\omega_{ga}$, where r is the pitch radius and ω_{ga} is the angular velocity of the gear with respect to the arm. Determine the force and velocity to be used in designing the following gears for strength; gear 3, gear 4, gear 5, gear 6, gear 7.
Ans. Gear 3: 7875 lb, 314 fpm. Gear 4: 7245 lb, 314 fpm.
Each of gears 5, 6 and 7: 6300 lb, 304 fpm.

30. Refer to Fig.17-30 below. The pitch diameter of helical gear A is 8.00 in. The pressure angle measured in a plane normal to the tooth is 20°, and the helix angle is 30°. The teeth on gear A are left hand. The torque on the output shaft is 1600 in-lb. (*a*) Calculate the tangential, thrust, and separating forces on gear A. (*b*) What is the bending moment at section B-B?
Ans. (*a*) 400 lb, 231 lb, 168 lb (*b*) 3080 in-lb

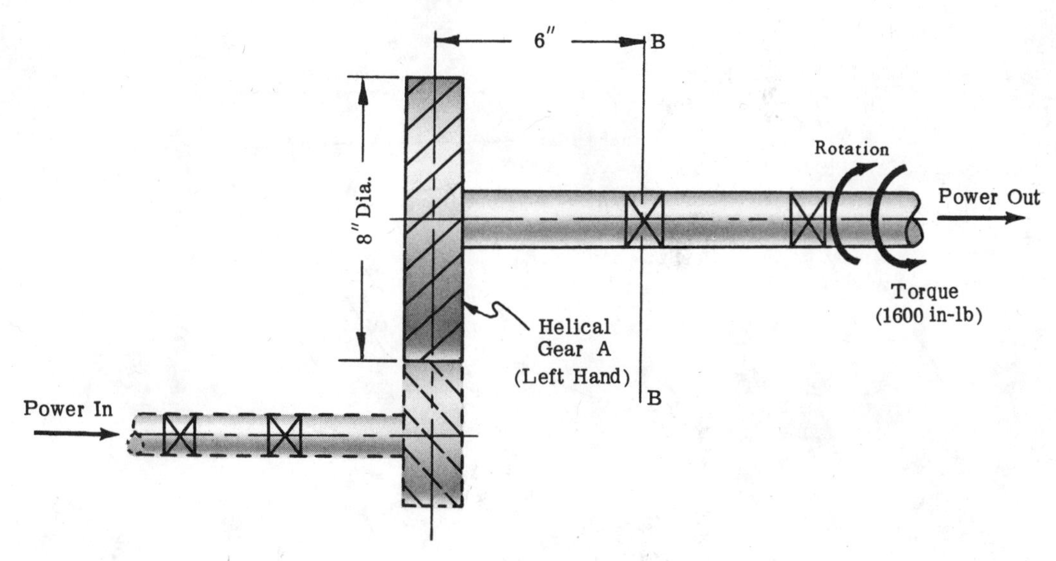

Fig. 17-30

Chapter 18

Spur Gears

SPUR GEARS provide a positive means of transmitting power between parallel shafts at a constant angular velocity ratio. The value of the velocity ratio is the same as would be obtained by two imaginary cylinders pressed together and rotating without slippage at their line of contact.

GEAR TOOTH TERMINOLOGY

The principal parts of gear teeth are denoted as shown in Fig. 18-1 below.

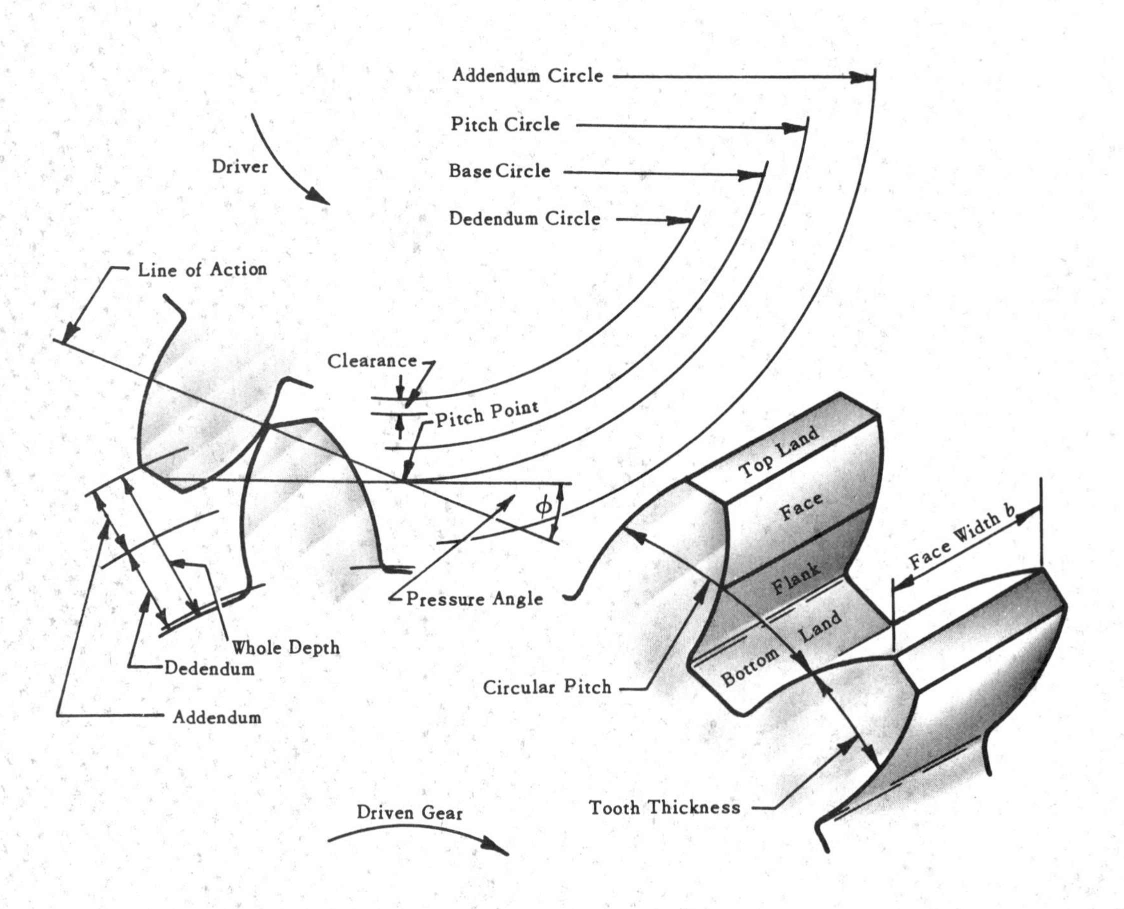

Fig. 18-1

DEFINITIONS

Circular pitch P_c is the distance from a point on one tooth to the corresponding point on an adjacent tooth measured on the pitch circle.

$$P_c = \pi D/N$$

where D = pitch diameter in inches and N = number of teeth on the gear.

Diametral pitch P_d is the number of teeth on a gear per inch of its diameter.

$$P_d = N/D \qquad \text{Note that } P_c \times P_d = \pi.$$

Line of action is a line normal to a pair of mating tooth profiles at their point of contact.

Pressure angle ϕ is the angle between the line of action and the common tangent to the pitch circles.

Pitch point is the point of tangency of the pitch circles.

Angular velocity ratio (or transmission ratio) is the ratio of the angular velocity of the pinion to the angular velocity of its mating gear. It is inversely proportional to the number of teeth on the two gears, and for spur gears it is also inversely proportional to the pitch diameters.

$$\text{Angular velocity ratio} = N_g/N_p = D_g/D_p$$

FUNDAMENTAL LAW OF GEARING. The common normal to the tooth profile at the point of contact must always pass through a fixed point called the pitch point in order to maintain a constant angular velocity ratio of the two gears. The involute curve satisfies the law of gearing and is most commonly used for gear teeth profiles. Frequently a combination of the involute and cycloid curves is used for a gear tooth profile in order to avoid interference. In this composite form, approximately the middle third of the profile has an involute shape while the remainder is cycloidal.

INTERFERENCE. Under certain conditions involute profiles overlap or cut into the mating teeth. This interference can be avoided if the maximum addendum radius for each gear is equal to or less than

$$\sqrt{(\text{radius of base circle})^2 + (\text{center distance})^2(\sin\phi)^2}$$

PROPORTIONS OF STANDARD GEAR TEETH

	$14\frac{1}{2}°$ Composite	$14\frac{1}{2}°$ Full Depth Involute	20° Full Depth Involute	20° Stub Involute
Addendum	$\frac{1}{P_d}$	$\frac{1}{P_d}$	$\frac{1}{P_d}$	$\frac{0.8}{P_d}$
Minimum dedendum	$\frac{1.157}{P_d}$	$\frac{1.157}{P_d}$	$\frac{1.157}{P_d}$	$\frac{1}{P_d}$
Whole depth	$\frac{2.157}{P_d}$	$\frac{2.157}{P_d}$	$\frac{2.157}{P_d}$	$\frac{1.8}{P_d}$
Clearance	$\frac{0.157}{P_d}$	$\frac{0.157}{P_d}$	$\frac{0.157}{P_d}$	$\frac{0.2}{P_d}$

STANDARD PITCHES. Standard diametral pitches in common use are: 1 to 2 varying by 1/4 pitch, 2 to 4 by 1/2 pitch, 4 to 10 by 1 pitch, 10 to 20 by 2 pitch, and 20 to 40 by 4 pitch.

DESIGN OBJECTIVES. Gear tooth design involves primarily the determination of the proper **pitch** and **face width** for adequate strength, durability, and economy of manufacture.

STRENGTH OF GEAR TEETH – Lewis Equation.

At the beginning of action between a pair of gear teeth, the flank of the driver tooth makes contact with the tip of the driven tooth. Neglecting friction, the total load W_n is normal to the tooth profile and the load is assumed to be carried by this one tooth. W, the load component of W_n perpendicular to the centerline of the tooth, produces a bending stress at the base of the tooth. The radial component W_r is neglected. The parabola shown in Fig. 18-2 outlines a beam of uniform strength. Hence the weakest section of the gear tooth is at section A–A where the parabola is tangent to the tooth outline. The load is assumed to be uniformly distributed across the face of the gear.

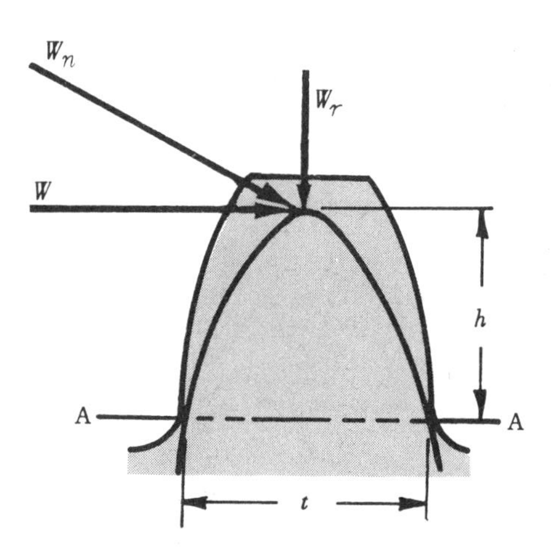

Fig. 18-2

The induced bending stress s is

$$s = \frac{Mc}{I} = \frac{6M}{bt^2} = \frac{6Wh}{bt^2}$$

and

$$W = sb(t^2/6h) = sb(t^2/6hP_c)P_c$$

where $c = t/2$, $I = bt^3/12$, and $M = Wh$.

The ratio $t^2/6hP_c$ is a dimensionless quantity called the form factor y, values for which are tabulated in Table I on page 227. This form factor y is a function of the tooth shape, which depends primarily on the tooth system and the number of teeth on the gear.

For convenience, W is approximated by the transmitted force F, which is defined as the torque divided by the pitch radius. Therefore, substituting F for W and y for $t^2/6hP_c$, we have the usual form of the Lewis equation

$$F = sbP_c y$$

For ordinary design conditions, the face width b is limited to a maximum of 4 times the circular pitch. Letting $b = kP_c$, where $k \leqq 4$,

$$F = sP_c^2 ky = s\pi^2 ky/P_d^2$$

In the design of a gear for strength, the pitch diameter is either known or unknown. If the pitch diameter is known, the following form of the Lewis equation may be used:

$$P_d^2/y = sk\pi^2/F$$

where s = allowable stress; $k = 4$, upper limit; F = transmitted force, $2M_t/D$. Then the above expression gives an **allowable** numerical value for the ratio P_d^2/y which controls the design, since it is based on an allowable stress.

If the pitch diameter is unknown, the following form of the Lewis equation may be used:

$$s = 2M_t P_d^3/k\pi^2 yN$$

where s = stress $\leqq$ allowable stress; M_t = torque on weaker gear; $k = 4$, upper limit; N = number of teeth on weaker gear. This expression gives a value for the induced stress in terms of the diametral pitch. The minimum number of teeth, N, is usually limited to 15.

In both of the above cases, the largest possible diametral pitch will provide the most economical design. In general, where the diameters are known, design for the largest number of teeth possible; where the diameters are unknown, design for the smallest pitch diameters possible.

ALLOWABLE TOOTH STRESSES. The allowable stress for gear tooth design depends upon the selected material and pitch line velocity. For spur gears,

$$\text{Allowable } s = s_o\left(\frac{600}{600+V}\right) \quad \text{for } V \text{ less than 2000 fpm}$$

$$= s_o\left(\frac{1200}{1200+V}\right) \quad \text{for } V \text{ 2000 to 4000 fpm}$$

$$= s_o\left(\frac{78}{78+\sqrt{V}}\right) \quad \text{for } V \text{ greater than 4000 fpm}$$

where s_o is the endurance strength for released loading corrected for average stress concentration values of the gear material, psi, and V is the pitch line velocity, fpm.

VALUES OF s_o. The values of s_o for various gear materials are listed in publications of the American Gear Manufacturers Association, various engineering handbooks, and most design textbooks. The s_o values for cast iron and bronze are 8000 psi and 12,000 psi respectively. Carbon steels range from 10,000 psi to 50,000 psi depending upon their carbon content and degree of heat treatment. In general, s_o may be taken as approximately one-third of the ultimate strength of the material.

BASE DESIGN ON WEAKER GEAR. The amount of force that can be transmitted to a gear tooth is a function of the $s_o y$ product as shown by the Lewis equation. For two mating gears, the weaker will have the smaller $s_o y$ value.

When two mating gears are to be made of the same material, the smaller gear (pinion) will be the weaker and control design.

DYNAMIC TOOTH LOADS – Buckingham Equation. Inaccuracies of the tooth profiles, spacing, misalignments in mounting, and tooth deflection under load result in velocity changes which produce dynamic forces on the teeth greater than the transmitted force. The dynamic load F_d as generally used for average mass conditions approximates a more detailed dynamic analysis, as proposed by Buckingham.

$$F_d = \frac{0.05\,V(bC+F)}{0.05\,V+\sqrt{bC+F}} + F$$

where F_d = dynamic load, lb
V = pitch line velocity, fpm
b = face width, in.
F = $\dfrac{\text{gear torque}}{\text{pitch radius of gear}} = 2M_t/D$
C = a constant which depends on the tooth form, material, and the degree of accuracy with which the tooth is cut. Some values for C have been tabulated in Table II on page 228. Curves showing the relation of errors in tooth profiles vs pitch line velocity and diametral pitch are shown in Fig.18-3 and Fig.18-4 below.

F_d must be less than the allowable endurance load F_o, where $F_o = s_o\, b y P_c$. In this equation, s_o is based on average stress concentration values.

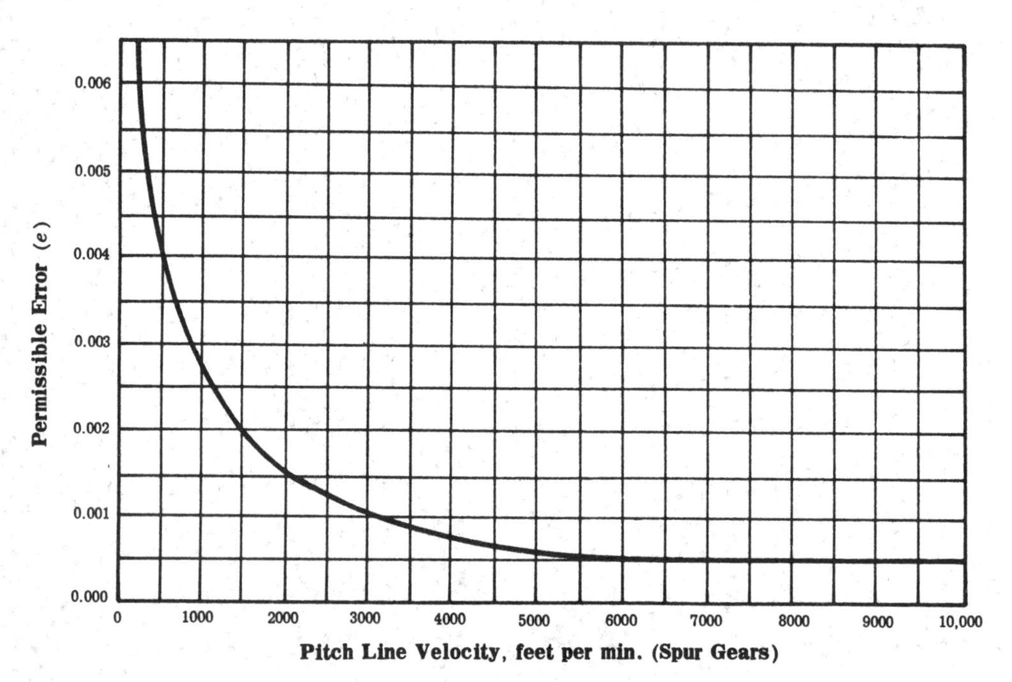

Fig. 18-3

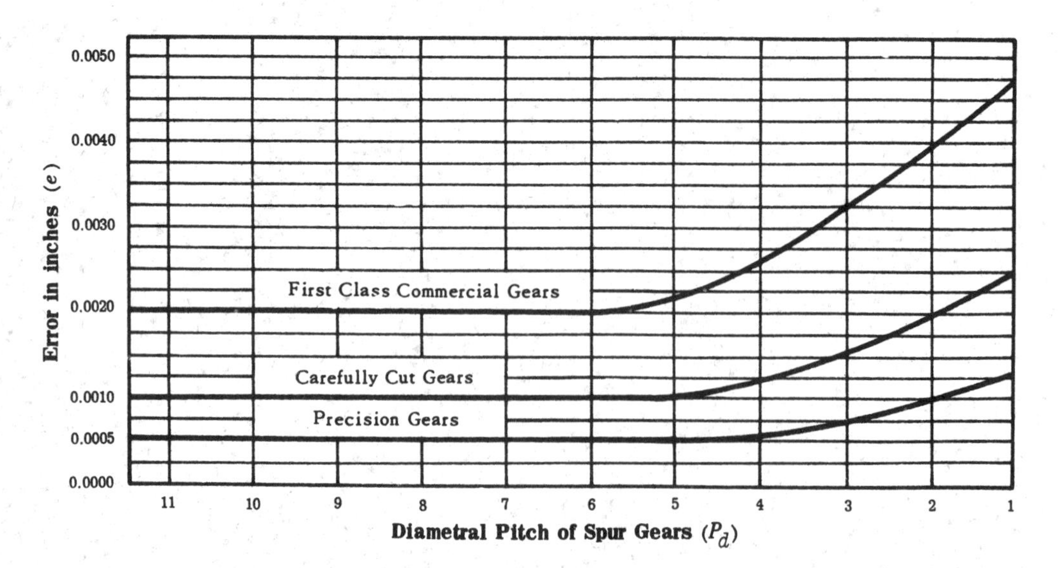

Fig. 18-4

WEAR TOOTH LOADS – Buckingham Equation. To insure the durability of a gear *pair*, the tooth profiles must not have excessive contact stress as determined by the wear load F_w.

$$F_w = D_p b K Q$$

where D_p = pitch diameter of smaller gear (pinion)
b = face width of gear, in.
K = stress factor for fatigue
$Q = 2N_g/(N_p + N_g)$
N_g = number of teeth on gear
N_p = number of teeth on pinion

and
$$K = \frac{s_{es}^2(\sin\phi)(1/E_p + 1/E_g)}{1.4}$$

where s_{es} = surface endurance limit of a gear pair, psi
E_p = modulus of elasticity of the pinion material, psi
E_g = modulus of elasticity of the gear material, psi
ϕ = pressure angle.

The surface endurance limit may be estimated from

$$s_{es} = (400)(\text{BHN}) - 10{,}000 \text{ psi}$$

where BHN may be approximated by the average brinell hardness number of the gear and pinion up to a BHN of about 350 for steels.

The wear load F_w is an *allowable* load and must be greater than the dynamic load F_d.

Several values of K for various materials and tooth forms have been tabulated in Table III on page 228 as tentative values recommended by Buckingham.

The above procedures will establish preliminary or tentative gear design, but as is the case in most machine design work, final design is contingent upon laboratory tests and/or test runs under actual operating conditions.

TABLE I – Form Factors y – for use in Lewis strength equation.

Number of Teeth	$14\frac{1}{2}°$ Full-Depth Involute or Composite	20° Full-Depth Involute	20° Stub Involute
12	0.067	0.078	0.099
13	0.071	0.083	0.103
14	0.075	0.088	0.108
15	0.078	0.092	0.111
16	0.081	0.094	0.115
17	0.084	0.096	0.117
18	0.086	0.098	0.120
19	0.088	0.100	0.123
20	0.090	0.102	0.125
21	0.092	0.104	0.127
23	0.094	0.106	0.130
25	0.097	0.108	0.133
27	0.099	0.111	0.136
30	0.101	0.114	0.139
34	0.104	0.118	0.142
38	0.106	0.122	0.145
43	0.108	0.126	0.147
50	0.110	0.130	0.151
60	0.113	0.134	0.154
75	0.115	0.138	0.158
100	0.117	0.142	0.161
150	0.119	0.146	0.165
300	0.122	0.150	0.170
Rack	0.124	0.154	0.175

TABLE II – Values of Deformation Factor C – for dynamic load check

Materials		Involute tooth form	Tooth Error – inches			
Pinion	Gear		0.0005	0.001	0.002	0.003
cast iron	cast iron	$14\frac{1}{2}°$	400	800	1600	2400
steel	cast iron	$14\frac{1}{2}°$	550	1100	2200	3300
steel	steel	$14\frac{1}{2}°$	800	1600	3200	4800
cast iron	cast iron	20° full depth	415	830	1660	2490
steel	cast iron	20° full depth	570	1140	2280	3420
steel	steel	20° full depth	830	1660	3320	4980
cast iron	cast iron	20° stub	430	860	1720	2580
steel	cast iron	20° stub	590	1180	2360	3540
steel	steel	20° stub	860	1720	3440	5160

TABLE III

Values for s_{es} as used in the wear load equation depend upon a combination of the gear and pinion materials. Some values for various materials for both s_{es} and K are tabulated.

Average Brinell Hardness Number of steel pinion and steel gear		Surface Endurance Limit s_{es}	Stress Fatigue Factor K	
			$14\frac{1}{2}°$	20°
150		50,000	30	41
200		70,000	58	79
250		90,000	96	131
300		110,000	144	196
400		150,000	268	366
Brinell Hardness Number, BHN				
Steel pinion	**Gear**			
150	C.I.	50,000	44	60
200	C.I.	70,000	87	119
250	C.I.	90,000	144	196
150	Phosphor Bronze	50,000	46	62
200	Phosphor Bronze	65,000	73	100
C.I. Pinion	**C.I. Gear**	80,000	152	208
C.I. Pinion	**C.I. Gear**	90,000	193	284

SOLVED PROBLEMS

1. A pair of mating spur gears have $14\frac{1}{2}°$ full depth involute teeth of $2\frac{1}{2}$ diametral pitch. The pitch diameter of the smaller gear is 6.4 inches. If the transmission ratio is 3 to 2, calculate: (*a*) number of teeth for each gear, (*b*) addendum, (*c*) whole depth, (*d*) clearance, (*e*) outside diameters, (*f*) root diameters, (*g*) dedendum, (*h*) base circle diameters and (*i*) check for interference.

Solution:

(*a*) $D_p = 6.4$ in., $D_g = 6.4(3/2) = 9.6$ in., $N_p = 6.4(2.5) = 16$ teeth, and $N_g = 9.6(2.5) = 24$ teeth.

(*b*) Addendum $= 1/P_d = 1/2.5 = 0.4$ in.

(*c*) Whole depth $= 2.157/P_d = 2.157/2.5 = 0.862$ in.

(*d*) Clearance $= 0.157/P_d = 0.157/2.5 = 0.0628$ in.

(*e*) Outside diameter = pitch diameter + 2 × addendum
Outside diameter of pinion $= 6.4+2(0.4) = 7.2$ in., of gear $= 9.4+2(0.4) = 10.2$ in.

(*f*) Root diameter = outside diameter − 2 × whole depth
Root diameter of pinion $= 7.2-2(0.862) = 5.476$ in., of gear $= 10.2-2(0.862) = 8.476$ in.

(*g*) Dedendum $= 1.157/P_d = 1.157/2.5 = 0.462$ in.

(*h*) Radius of base circle = pitch radius × cos $14\frac{1}{2}°$.
For pinion: $R_b = (6.4/2)(0.968) = 3.1$ in., and diameter of base circle = 6.2 in.
For gear: $R_b = (9.6/2)(0.968) = 4.65$ in., and diameter of base circle = 9.3 in.

(*i*) Interference is avoided if the addendum radius of the gear is

$$\leqq \sqrt{(\text{base circle radius})^2 + (\text{center distance})^2(\sin\phi)^2} = \sqrt{(4.65)^2 + [\tfrac{1}{2}(6.4+9.6)]^2(\sin 14\tfrac{1}{2}°)^2} = 7.85.$$

Since the addendum radius of the gear $= 9.8/2 = 4.9$, no interference will exist.

2. A bronze spur pinion ($s_o = 12{,}000$ psi) rotating at 600 rpm drives a cast steel spur gear ($s_o = 15{,}000$ psi) at a transmission ratio of 4 to 1. The pinion has 16 standard 20° full depth involute teeth of 3 diametral pitch. The face width of both gears is $3\frac{1}{2}$ inches. How much power can be transmitted from the standpoint of strength?

Solution:

It is first necessary to determine which is weaker, the gear or pinion.

	Number of teeth	s_o	Form factor y	$s_o y$
Pinion	16	12,000 psi	0.094	1130
Gear	64	15,000 psi	0.135	2020

Since the load carrying capacity of the tooth is a function of the $s_o y$ product, the pinion is the weaker.

The pitch line velocity V is next determined in order to select the correct velocity factor required for calculating the allowable stress: $V = \pi(5.33)(600)/12 = 840$ fpm. Since V is less than 2000 fpm, allowable stress $s = 12{,}000\left(\dfrac{600}{600+840}\right) = 5000$ psi. Hence the amount of force that can be transmitted in accordance with the Lewis equation is

$$F = sbyP_c = 5000(3.5)(.094)(\pi/3) = 1722 \text{ lb.}$$

The horsepower that can be transmitted $= FV/33{,}000 = 1722(840)/33{,}000 = 44$ hp.

3. A spur pinion of cast steel ($s_o = 20{,}000$ psi) is to drive a spur gear of cast iron ($s_o = 8000$ psi). The transmission ratio is to be $2\frac{1}{3}$ to 1. The diameter of the pinion is to be 4 inches and 30 hp will be transmitted at 900 rpm of the pinion. The teeth are to be 20° full depth involute form. Design for the greatest number of teeth. Determine the necessary diametral pitch and face width of the gears for strength only.

Solution:

First determine the probable weaker of the two gears by assuming a set of arbitrary tooth numbers, such as 15 and 35, which satisfy $2\frac{1}{3}$ to 1 ratio. Then, for pinion $s_o y = 20{,}000(.092) = 1840$, and for gear $s_o y = 8000(.119) = 952$; the gear is probably weaker since 952 is less than 1840.

$D_p = 4$ in., $D_g = 9\frac{1}{3}$ in. Since the diameters are known, use the following form of the Lewis equation:

$$P_d^2/y = sk\pi^2/F$$

Torque transmitted by pinion $= 30(63{,}000)/900 = 2100$ in-lb. Transmitted force $F = 2100/2 = 1050$ lb.

Pitch line velocity $V = 4\pi(900)/12 = 942$ fpm. Allowable stress $s = 8000\left(\frac{600}{600+942}\right) = 3110$ psi.

$$P_d^2/y = 3110(4)\pi^2/1050 = 117 \text{ allowable}$$

Assuming $y \approx 0.1$, $P_d \approx \sqrt{11.7} \approx 3$. Try $P_d = 3$: then $N_g = 3(9\frac{1}{3}) = 28$ teeth, $y = 0.112$ (from table), and $P_d^2/y = 9/0.112 = 80.4$; the gear is strong.

A P_d of 4 or 5 cannot be used due to the required velocity ratio. A P_d of 6 would give a gear too weak. Hence reduce k to $k = 4(80.4/117) = 2.75$. Then $b = 2.75(\pi/3) = 2.88$ in.

Use $b = 2\frac{7}{8}$ in., $P_d = 3$, $N_p = 12$, $N_g = 28$.

A final check to determine the weaker of the two gears based on the tooth numbers selected: pinion $s_o y = 20{,}000(.078) = 1560$; gear $s_o y = 8000(.112) = 896$ (weaker).

4. A bronze spur gear ($s_o = 12{,}000$ psi) is to drive a mild steel pinion ($s_o = 15{,}000$ psi). The angular velocity ratio is to be $3\frac{1}{2}$ to 1. The pressure angle is to be $14\frac{1}{2}°$. Determine the smallest diameter gears that can be used and the necessary face width to transmit 6 hp at 1800 rpm of the pinion. Design for strength only. No less than 15 teeth are to be used on either gear.

Solution:

Minimum $N_p = 16$ teeth for an angular velocity ratio $= 3\frac{1}{2}$. Then $N_g = 16(3\frac{1}{2}) = 56$ teeth.

For gear, $s_o y = 12{,}000(.112) = 1340$; for pinion, $s_o y = 15{,}000(.081) = 1220$. The pinion is weaker.

The torque $M_t = 6(63{,}000)/1800 = 210$ in-lb. Since the diameters are unknown, the induced stress is

$$s = 2M_t P_d^3/k\pi^2 yN = 2(210)P_d^3/4\pi^2(.081)(16) = 8.23P_d^3$$

Assume allowable stress $s \approx \frac{1}{2}s_o \approx 15{,}000/2 = 7500$ psi; this assumption permits the determination of an approximate P_d. Then $P_d^3 \approx 7500/8.23$ and $P_d \approx 10$.

Try $P_d = 10$; then $D_p = 16/10 = 1.6$ in., $V = 1.6\pi(1800)/12 = 754$ fpm, allowable $s = 15{,}000\left(\frac{600}{600+754}\right) = 6640$ psi, and induced $s = 8.23(10^3) = 8230$ psi. The pinion is weak since $8230 > 6640$.

Try a stronger tooth, $P_d = 9$: then $D_p = 16/9 = 1.78$ in., $V = 1.78\pi(1800)/12 = 838$ fpm, allowable $s = 15{,}000\left(\frac{600}{600+838}\right) = 6260$ psi, and induced $s = 8.23(9^3) = 6000$ psi. Now the pinion is slightly strong. Hence reduce k to $k = 4(6000/6260) = 3.83$; then the face width $b = 3.83(\pi/9) = 1.34$ in.

Use $P_d = 9$, $b = 1\frac{3}{8}$ in., $D_p = 1.78$ in., $D_g = 1.78(3.5) = 6.23$ in.

5. A cast steel pinion ($s_o = 15{,}000$) rotating at 900 rpm is to drive a cast iron gear ($s_o = 8000$) at 144 rpm. The teeth are to have standard 20° stub involute profiles and the maximum power to be transmitted is 35 hp. Determine the proper diametral pitch, number of teeth, and the face width for these gears from the standpoint of strength, dynamic load, and wear. Pinion is surface hardened to BHN 250.

Solution:

The diameters of the gears are *unknown*. The number of teeth will be assumed, selecting not less than 15 for the pinion. Note that the minimum number of teeth the pinion can have is 16 in order to satisfy the required transmission ratio; the gear would then have $16(900/144) = 100$ teeth.

For pinion, $s_o y = 15{,}000(0.115) = 1725$; for gear, $s_o y = 8000(0.161) = 1288$. The gear is the weaker since $1288 < 1725$. As the diameters are unknown, the form of the Lewis equation in terms of moment will be used and design will be based on the gear.

$M_t = 35(63{,}000)/144 = 15{,}300$ in-lb. For the initial trial design, always let $k=4$. Then the induced stress is

$$s = 2M_t P_d^3/k\pi^2 y N_g = 2(15{,}300)P_d^3/4\pi^2(0.161)(100) = 48P_d^3$$

Assume allowable stress $s \approx \frac{1}{2}s_o = 8000/2 = 4000$ psi. Then $P_d^3 \approx 4000/48$ and $P_d \approx 4$ or 5. From the standpoint of economy, it is desirable to use the largest diametral pitch possible; hence we will *try* $P_d = 5$.

For $P_d = 5$: $D_g = 100/5 = 20$ in., $V = 20\pi(144)/12 = 754$ fpm, allowable stress $s = 8000\left(\frac{600}{600+754}\right)$ $= 3540$ psi, induced stress $s = 48P_d^3 = 48(5^3) = 6000$ psi. The gear is too weak since $6000 > 3540$. We will now try the next larger standard tooth having a $P_d = 4$.

For $P_d = 4$: $D_g = 100/4 = 25$ in., $V = 25\pi(144)/12 = 943$ fpm, allowable stress $s = 8000\left(\frac{600}{600+943}\right)$ $= 3110$ psi, induced $s = 48(4^3) = 3080$ psi. Thus for a $P_d = 4$ the gear would be slightly stronger than necessary. Reducing k to $k = 4(3080/3110) = 3.96$, the required face width $b = kP_c = 3.96(\pi/4) = 3.11$ in. Then from the standpoint of strength, use $P_d = 4$ and $b = 3\frac{1}{8}$ in.

Next check the tentative design from the standpoint of dynamic load and wear effects. The endurance load F_o and the wear load F_w are allowable values.

$$F_o = s_o b y P_c = 8000(3.125)(0.161)(\pi/4) = 3160 \text{ lb}$$
$$F_w = D_p b K Q = 4(3.125)(196)(172.5) = 4225 \text{ lb}$$

where $D_p = 25(144/900) = 4$ in., $K = 196$ from table III, $Q = 2N_g/(N_g+N_p) = 2(100)/(100+16) = 172.5$

F_o and F_w must each be greater than F_d.

$$F_d = \frac{0.05V(bC+F)}{0.05V + \sqrt{bC+F}} + F$$

where $V = 943$ fpm, $b = 3.125$ in., and $F = M_t/(\frac{1}{2}D) = 15{,}300/12.5 = 1224$ lb. From Fig.18-3 we find that for $V = 943$ fpm, an error of 0.0028 in. could be tolerated from a noise standpoint. Referring to Fig.18-4, try a first class commercial gear having an error of 0.0025 in. for $P_d = 4$. Then from Table II, $C = 2950$. Substituting values in the above equation, $F_d = 4520$ lb. Hence $F_w = 4225 < 4520$ and $F_o = 3160 < 4520$, i.e. the design will be unsatisfactory both from the standpoint of durability or wear and from the standpoint of strength.

We must then select a carefully cut gear, say one having an error of action of 0.0012 in., as shown in Fig. 18-4; this gives a C value of 1416. Recalculating F_d for $C = 1416$, we find $F_d = 3394$. Now $F_w = 4225 > 3394$, $F_o = 3160 \approx 3394$ (within 7%), and the design will probably be satisfactory without going to a precision cut gear.

6. A 3 in. diameter steel pinion ($s_o = 20{,}000$ psi) drives a gray iron 9 in. diameter gear ($s_o = 12{,}000$ psi). The pinion operates at 1200 rpm and transmits 6 hp. The teeth are 20° stub. Determine the greatest number of teeth (to provide the smoothest operation and cheapest machining) and the necessary face width. Base design on the Lewis strength equation. An alternate procedure for the solution will be followed.

Solution:

Not knowing which is the weaker, we will design for the gear and make a final check to see if it is weaker after a solution has been established. We will compare the allowable endurance load based on the Lewis equation to the approximate actual dynamic load using the Barth velocity factor.

Compare allowable load $F_o = \dfrac{s_o b \pi y}{P_d} = \dfrac{12{,}000(4\pi/P_d)\pi y}{P_d} = \dfrac{473{,}000y}{P_d^2}$ lb with

actual load (approx.) $F_d = \dfrac{F}{\text{velocity factor}} = \dfrac{210}{600/(600+942)} = 540$ lb.

If y is approximated as around 0.1, $P_d \approx \sqrt{473{,}000(0.1)/540}$ or $P_d \approx 10$.

Try $P_d = 10$: $N_g = 90$, $y = 0.160$, and $F_o = 473{,}000(0.160)/10^2 = 758$ lb (too strong).

Try a weaker gear, $P_d = 12$: $N_g = 108$, $y = 0.161$, and $F_o = 530$ lb (close enough to $F_d = 540$ lb).

Now check $s_o y$ for pinion $= 20{,}000(0.143) = 2860$
$s_o y$ for gear $= 12{,}000(0.161) = 1930$ (weaker, as initially assumed).

The face width $b = 4\pi/12 = 1.05$ in.; use 1 in.

7. An alternate application of the design equations will be used to solve the previous Problem 4. A bronze spur gear ($s_o = 12{,}000$ psi) is to drive a mild steel pinion ($s_o = 15{,}000$ psi). The angular velocity ratio is to be $3\frac{1}{2}$ to 1. The pressure angle is to be $14\frac{1}{2}°$. Determine the smallest diameter gears that can be used and the necessary face width to transmit 6 hp at 1800 rpm of the pinion. Design for strength only. No less than 15 teeth are to be used on either gear.

Solution:

Minimum number of teeth on pinion = 16 for a velocity ratio of $3\frac{1}{2}$. The gear would then have $16(3\frac{1}{2}) = 56$ teeth.

Check which gear is weaker: for the gear, $s_o y = 12{,}000(0.112) = 1340$
for pinion, $s_o y = 15{,}000(0.081) = 1220$ (weaker).

Torque on the pinion $= 6(63{,}000)/1800 = 210$ in-lb.

The Lewis equation may be expressed in terms of the torque, $FR = sb\pi yR/P_d = M_t$.

Allowable torque, using endurance strength, is
$$M_o = \frac{s_o b\pi yR}{P_d} = \frac{s_o b\pi yN_p}{P_d(2P_d)} = \frac{15{,}000(4\pi/P_d)\pi(0.081)(16)}{2P_d^2} = \frac{383{,}000}{P_d^3}.$$

Actual dynamic torque
$$M_d = \frac{FR}{\text{velocity factor}} = \frac{M_t}{\text{velocity factor}} = \frac{210}{\text{velocity factor}}.$$

If the velocity factor is approximated as $\frac{1}{2}$, then $383{,}000/P_d^3 \approx 210/\frac{1}{2}$ or $P_d \approx 10$.

Try $P_d = 10$: $D_p = 16/10 = 1.6$ in., $V = 1.6\pi(1800)/12 = 754$ fpm; then

$$M_o = \frac{383{,}000}{10^3} = 383 \text{ in-lb} \quad \text{and} \quad M_d = \frac{210}{600/(600+754)} = 475 \text{ in-lb}$$

which indicates that $P_d = 10$ is slightly weak.

Try $P_d = 9$: $D_p = 16/9 = 1.78$ in., $V = 1.78\pi(1800)/12 = 838$ fpm; then

$$M_o = \frac{383{,}000}{9^3} = 526 \text{ in-lb} \quad \text{and} \quad M_d = \frac{210}{600/(600+838)} = 504 \text{ in-lb}$$

which indicates that $P_d = 9$ is strong.

Reduce the face width from $b = 4\pi/P_d$ to $b = 4\pi(504/526)/9 = 1.34$ in.; use $1\frac{3}{8}$ in.

SUPPLEMENTARY PROBLEMS

8. A spur steel pinion (s_o = 30,000 psi) is to drive a spur steel gear (s_o = 20,000 psi). The diameter of the pinion is to be 4 in. and the center distance 8 in. The pinion is to transmit 6 hp at 900 rpm. The teeth are to be 20° full depth. Determine the necessary diametral pitch and width of face to give the greatest number of teeth. Design for strength only, using the Lewis equation.

Ans. $b = \frac{7}{8}$ in., $P_d = 14$

9. Two spur gears are to be used for a rock crusher drive and are to be of minimum size. The gears are to be designed for the following requirements: power to be transmitted 25 hp, speed of pinion 1200 rpm, angular velocity ratio 3.5 to 1, tooth profile 20° stub, s_o value for pinion 15,000 psi, s_o value for gear 10,000 psi. Determine the necessary face width and diametral pitch for strength requirements only, using the Lewis equation.

Ans. b = 2.25 in., $P_d = 5$

10. A pair of spur gears transmitting power from a motor to a pump impeller shaft is to be designed with as small a center distance as possible. The forged steel pinion (s_o = 23,000 psi) is to transmit 5 hp at 600 rpm to a cast steel gear (s_o = 15,000 psi) with a transmission ratio of $4\frac{1}{2}$ to 1, and 20° full depth involute teeth are to be used. Determine the necessary face width and diametral pitch for strength only, using the Lewis equation.

Ans. $P_d = 9$, $b = 1\frac{1}{4}$ in.

11. A pair of spur gears for a crane hoist drive is to be made to the following specifications: 20° full depth teeth; s_o pinion = 12,000 psi, s_o gear = 8000 psi; N_p = 20 teeth, N_g = 80 teeth.

(*a*) What standard diametral pitch and width of face will satisfy these conditions with a minimum center distance? Use the Lewis equation.

(*b*) If the dynamic load for this pair is computed to be 760 lb, determine whether or not the design is safe from the standpoint of strength.

(*c*) Check the design for wear or surface fatigue if the fatigue constant K = 198.

Ans. (*a*) $P_d = 5$, b = 2.32 in. (use $2\frac{3}{8}$ in.)

(*b*) F_o = 1650 lb, F_d = 760 lb (satisfactory)

(*c*) F_w = 3010 lb, F_d = 760 lb (satisfactory)

12. A cast steel 24 tooth spur pinion operating at 1150 rpm transmits $3\frac{1}{2}$ hp to a cast steel 56 tooth spur gear. The gears have the following specifications: diametral pitch of 8, s_o value of 15,000 psi, face width of $1\frac{1}{2}$ in., C factor of 1600 for dynamic load, K factor of 40 for wear load. Determine (*a*) induced stress in weaker gear, (*b*) dynamic load, (*c*) wear load, (*d*) allowable static load.

Ans. s = 5670 psi, F_d = 1330 lb, F_w = 252 lb, F_o = 848 lb.
Unsatisfactory from the standpoint of wear and dynamics effects.

13. In the layout of the drive for a packaging machine, a pair of 20° full depth spur gears is to transmit 5 hp at a transmission ratio of 2.5 to 1. The pinion operates at 1200 rpm. For initial design, a forged steel pinion (s_o = 15,000 psi) and a semi-steel gear (s_o = 9000 psi) have been selected. The gears are to be carefully cut and from data tables the C factor for dynamic load is 1140 and the K factor for wear is 156.

(*a*) Determine diameters, face width and tooth numbers for minimum size gears of adequate strength, using the Lewis equation.

(*b*) Solve for dynamic and wear loads, stating whether the gears are satisfactory or not.

(*c*) If the gears are not satisfactory from the standpoint of wear and strength, state what changes should be made.

Ans. (*a*) $b = 1\frac{1}{4}''$, $P_d = 8$

(*b*) F_d = 997 lb, F_w = 558 lb, F_o = 548 lb.

(*c*) The gears are not satisfactory from the standpoint of strength and wear because F_d is greater than the allowable values F_o and F_w. One or more of the following changes would be required: decrease the tooth error, decrease the diametral pitch, increase the face width, or case harden.

Chapter 19

Helical Gears

HELICAL GEARS differ from spur gears in that they have teeth that are cut in the form of a helix on their pitch cylinders instead of parallel to the axis of rotation. Helical gears may be used to connect either parallel or non-parallel shafts. The discussion in this chapter will be limited to helical gears connecting parallel shafts. In this case a right hand helix will always mesh with a left hand helix. A helical gear with a left hand helix is shown in Fig. 19-1 below.

ψ = helix angle, degrees
F = transmitted force (torque producing force), lb
F_e = end thrust = $F \tan\psi$, lb
P_c = circumferential circular pitch, in.
P_{nc} = normal circular pitch, in.
b = face width, in.
P_d = diametral pitch in plane of rotation
P_{nd} = normal diametral pitch in plane normal to tooth
Note that: $P_{nc} = P_c \cos\psi$, $P_{nd} = P_d/\cos\psi$, $P_{nc} \times P_{nd} = \pi = P_c P_d$

In order that contact on the face of the tooth shall always contain at least one point on the pitch line, the minimum face width of the tooth is

$$b_{\text{min}} = \frac{P_c}{\tan\psi}$$

THE PRESSURE ANGLE ϕ_n in the normal plane is distinguished from the pressure angle ϕ in the transverse plane as shown in Fig. 19-2 below, the relationship being

$$\tan\phi_n = \tan\phi \cos\psi$$

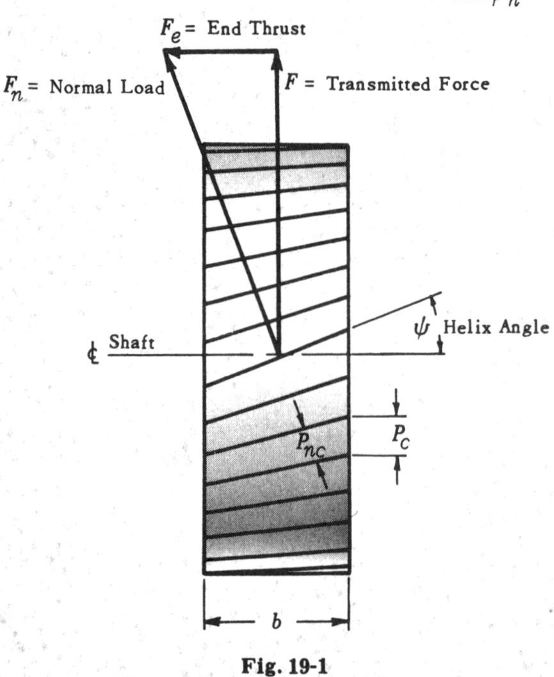

Fig. 19-1

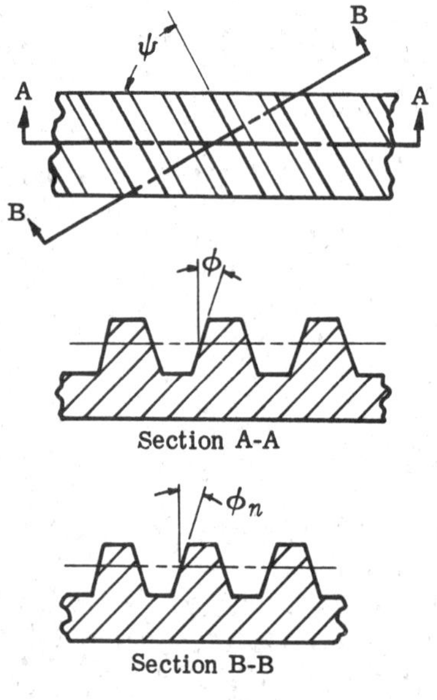

Section A-A

Section B-B

Fig. 19-2

THE VIRTUAL OR FORMATIVE number of teeth, N_f, on a helical gear is defined as the number of teeth that could be generated on the surface of a cylinder having a radius equal to the radius of curvature at a point at the tip of the minor axis of an ellipse obtained by taking a section of the gear in the normal plane.

$$N_f = \frac{N}{\cos^3 \psi}$$

where N = actual number of teeth and ψ = helix angle.

STRENGTH DESIGN for helical gears may be handled by employing design methods similar to those used for spur gears. Assuming that the load is distributed as for a spur gear, and looking at the tooth normal to the helix, the normal load F_n using the Lewis equation is

$$F_n = s\left(\frac{b}{\cos\psi}\right)\frac{\pi y}{P_{nd}}$$

Substituting the tangential force $F = F_n \cos\psi$, and $P_{nd} = P_d/\cos\psi$,

$$F = \frac{sby\pi}{P_{nd}} = \frac{sk\pi^2 y}{P_{nd}^2 \cos\psi} \quad \text{(use where standard pitch is in normal plane)}$$

or

$$F = \frac{sby\pi\cos\psi}{P_d} = \frac{sk\pi^2 y\cos\psi}{P_d^2} \quad \text{(use where standard pitch is in diametral plane)}$$

where $k = b/P_c$ (limited to a maximum of about 6)
P_d = diametral pitch in the plane of rotation
y = the form factor based on the virtual or formative number of teeth. If the pressure angle is standard in the normal plane, use y from the spur gear table. If the pressure angle in the diametral plane is standard, use y from the spur gear table as an approximation. A more accurate evaluation of y for the latter case could be obtained from a graphical solution.

The allowable stress s may be taken as approximately equal to the endurance limit of the material in released loading, corrected for stress concentration effects and multiplied by a velocity factor:

$$s = s_o\left(\frac{78}{78+\sqrt{V}}\right) \quad \text{allowable stress, psi}$$

where s_o = about one-third of the ultimate strength of the material, psi. This allows for an average stress concentration correction.
V = pitch line velocity, fpm.

A more accurate evaluation of s_o could be made if data regarding endurance limit and fatigue stress-concentration effects for the material are available. However, in view of other approximations, design based on the above expressions should, in general, be adequate since it must also be checked for dynamic load and wear load as explained later.

In the design check for strength, the pitch diameter is either known or unknown. If the pitch diameter is known, the following form of the Lewis equation may be used:

$$\frac{P_d^2}{y} = \frac{s_o k\pi^2\cos\psi}{F}\left(\frac{78}{78+\sqrt{V}}\right)$$

where $k = b/P_c$
F = tangential force = torque/(pitch radius), lb
V = pitch line velocity, fpm.

Then the above expression gives an *allowable* numerical value for the ratio P_d^2/y which controls the strength check.

If the pitch diameter is unknown, the following form of the Lewis equation may be used:

$$s = \frac{2TP_d^3}{ky\pi^2 N\cos\psi}$$

where s = actual induced stress, psi
T = resisting torque of the weaker gear
N = actual number of teeth on the weaker gear

This expression gives a numerical value of the actual induced stress in terms of the diametral pitch.

The above procedures based on strength design should be considered only as a first approximation in arriving at a possible pitch and face width which must be checked for wear load and dynamic load.

THE LIMITING ENDURANCE BEAM STRENGTH LOAD, F_o, is based on the Lewis equation without a velocity factor.

$$F_o = \frac{s_o b y \pi \cos\psi}{P_d}$$

where the symbols are the same as above.

The limiting endurance strength load, F_o, must be equal to or greater than the dynamic load F_d.

THE LIMITING WEAR LOAD, F_w, for helical gears may be determined by the Buckingham equation for wear.

$$F_w = \frac{D_p b Q K}{\cos^2\psi}$$

where D_p = pitch diameter of pinion, in.

$$Q = \frac{2D_g}{D_p + D_g} = \frac{2N_g}{N_p + N_g}$$ (N_p and N_g are actual numbers of teeth)

$$K = s_{es}^2(\sin\phi_n)(1/E_p + 1/E_g)/1.4$$

s_{es} = surface endurance limit. (See Chapter 18 on spur gears.)

The limiting wear load F_w must be equal to or greater than the dynamic load F_d.

THE DYNAMIC LOAD, F_d, for helical gears is the sum of the transmitted load and an incremental load due to dynamic effects:

$$F_d = F + \frac{0.05V(Cb\cos^2\psi + F)\cos\psi}{0.05V + \sqrt{Cb\cos^2\psi + F}}$$

where the symbols are the same as before. Values for C, which is a function of the amount of effective error in tooth profiles, may be obtained from Chapter 18 on spur gears.

F_w must be $\geqq F_d$ and F_o must be $\geqq F_d$

Note that F_o and F_w are allowable values which cannot be exceeded.

SOLVED PROBLEMS

1. For a helical gear derive an expression for the virtual number of teeth N_f in terms of the helix angle ψ and the actual number of teeth N.

Solution:

Fig.19-3 below shows one tooth of a helical gear of pitch diameter D. Consider section A–A in the normal plane. This section will be that of an ellipse whose minor diameter is D. The radius of curvature at point B is

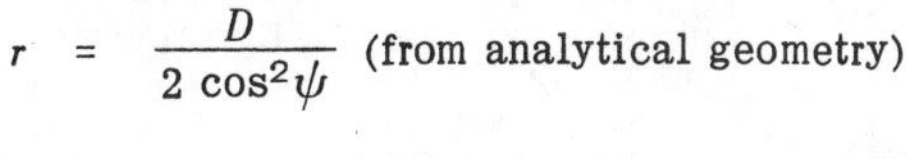

$$r = \frac{D}{2\cos^2\psi} \quad \text{(from analytical geometry)}$$

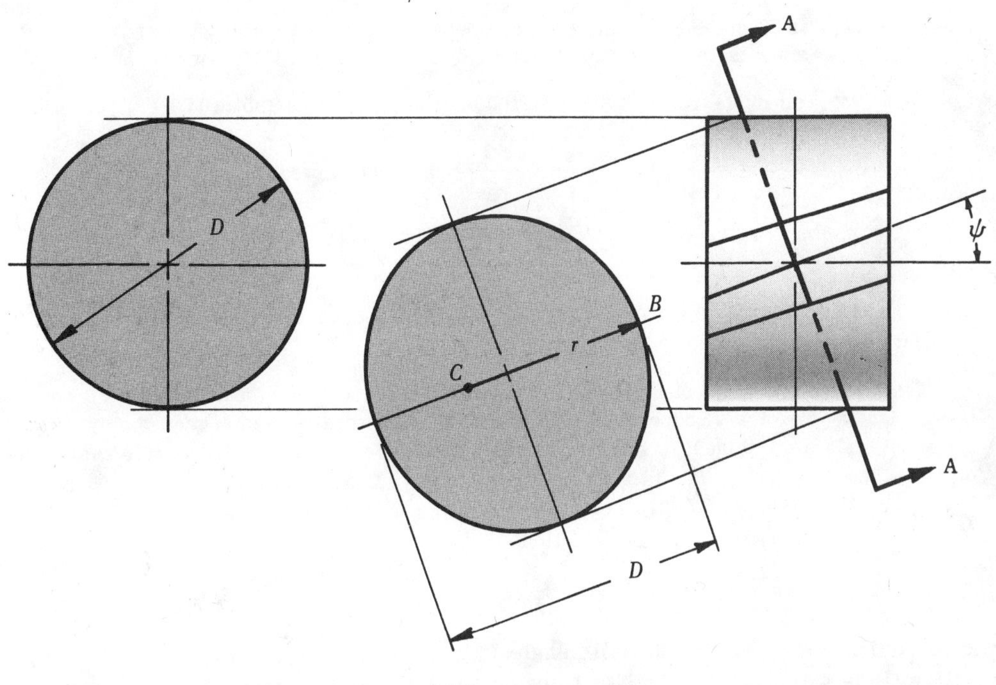

Fig. 19-3

The shape of the tooth at B would be that of one generated on the surface of a pitch cylinder of radius r, and the number of teeth on this surface is defined as the virtual or formative number of teeth N_f.

$$N_f = \frac{2\pi r}{P_{nc}} = 2rP_{nd} = \frac{2rP_d}{\cos\psi} = \frac{2DP_d}{2\cos^3\psi} = \frac{N}{\cos^3\psi}$$

2. A pair of helical gears are to transmit 20 hp. The teeth are 20° stub in diametral plane and have a helix angle of 45°. The pinion has a 3 inch pitch diameter and operates at 10,000 rpm. The gear has a 12 inch pitch diameter. If the gears are made of cast steel (SAE 1235, s_o = 15,000 psi), determine a suitable diametral pitch and face width. The pinion is heat treated to a brinell of 300 and the gear has a brinell hardness of 200.

Solution:

(*a*) For a strength check, s_o = 15,000 psi. Since the diameters are known, we find

$$\frac{P_d^2}{y} = \frac{s_o k \pi^2 \cos\psi}{F}\left(\frac{78}{78+\sqrt{V}}\right) = 3500 \text{ (allowed)}$$

where V = 7850 fpm, assumed k = 6, $\cos\psi$ = 0.707, and F = 20(33,000)/7850 = 84 lb.

The pinion is the weaker gear since the two gears are of the same material.

If $y \approx 0.15$, $P_d \approx 24$; try $P_d = 24$. Now $N_p = 3(24) = 72$, $N_f = N/\cos^3\psi = 72/(0.707)^3 = 204$, $y = 0.168$ (approximated by using a 20° pressure angle), and $P_d^2/y = (24)^2/0.168 = 3430$ which is satisfactory since the allowed value is 3500.

The k value may be reduced to $k = 6(3430/3500) = 5.9$. Then $b = 5.9(\pi/24) = 0.772$ in.; use $\frac{7}{8}$ in. face width.

(*b*) For a dynamic check determine the wear load F_w, the endurance beam load F_o, and compare with the dynamic load F_d.

$$F_w = \frac{D_p bQK}{\cos^2\psi} = 803 \text{ lb (allowed)}$$

where $\tan\phi_n = \tan 20^\circ \cos 45^\circ$, $\phi_n = 14.43^\circ$; $b = 0.875$ in.; $D_p = 3$ in.; $Q = 2D_g/(D_p + D_g) = 2(12)/(3+12) = 1.6$; $s_{es} = 90{,}000$ psi since the average brinell number of the two gears is 250; and

$$K = s_{es}^2 (\sin\phi_n)(1/E_p + 1/E_g)/1.4 = (90{,}000)^2(\sin 14.43^\circ)[2/(30\times10^6)]/1.4 = 95.5.$$

$$F_o = \frac{s_o b y \pi \cos\psi}{P_d} = 204 \text{ lb (allowed)}$$

$$F_d = F + \frac{0.05V(Cb\cos^2\psi + F)\cos\psi}{0.05V + \sqrt{Cb\cos^2\psi + F}} = 391 \text{ lb}$$

where $s_o = 15{,}000$ psi, $b = 0.875$ in., $y = 0.168$, $P_d = 24$, $F = 84$ lb, $V = 7850$ fpm, and $C = 860$ for a precision cut gear having a profile error of 0.0005 in.

The preliminary design of $P_d = 24$ is not satisfactory since F_d *is* greater than F_o. However, the design is satisfactory from the standpoint of wear since the wear load is greater than the dynamic load. If the same materials are retained, it will be necessary to reduce the pitch. Successive trials establish a required standard pitch of $P_d = 14$. Now let $b = 6\pi/14 = 1.345$ in.; use $b = 1.25$ in. Then $N_p = 3(14) = 42$, $N_f = 42/(0.707)^3 = 119$, $y = 0.162$ (approximated by using a 20° pressure angle), and we obtain $F_o = 481$ lb and $F_d = 412$ lb. This a satisfactory solution.

3. A pair of helical gears with a 23° helix angle is to transmit $3\frac{1}{2}$ hp at 10,000 rpm of the pinion. The velocity ratio is 4 to 1. Both gears are to be made of hardened steel, with an allowable $s_o = 15{,}000$ psi for each gear. The gears are 20° stub and the pinion is to have 24 teeth. Determine the minimum diameter gears that may be used, and the required BHN.

Solution:

(*a*) Check for strength first. The pinion is the weaker of the two mating gears.

Since the diameters are unknown, use the following form of the Lewis equation and find

$$s = \frac{2TP_d^3}{ky\pi^2 N \cos\psi} = 0.242\,P_d^3$$

where the torque on the pinion is $T = 3.5(63{,}000)/10{,}000 = 22$ in-lb, assumed $k = 6$, $N = 24$, $N_f = N/\cos^3\psi = 31$, $y = 0.139$ (approximated by using a 20° pressure angle), and $\psi = 23^\circ$.

Assuming a velocity factor $\approx \frac{1}{2}$, $0.242P_d^3 \approx \frac{1}{2}(15{,}000)$ and $P_d \approx 31$. Try a standard pitch of 32; then $D_p = 24/32 = 0.75$ in. and $V = 0.75\pi(10{,}000)/12 = 1965$ fpm.

$$s_{\text{allowable}} = 15{,}000\left(\frac{78}{78 + \sqrt{1965}}\right) = 9550 \text{ psi}, \qquad s_{\text{induced}} = 0.242(32)^3 = 7930 \text{ psi}$$

The design is satisfactory from the standpoint of strength.

The k value may be reduced to $k = 6(7930/9550) = 5$. Now $b = 5\pi/32 = 0.49$; use $b = \frac{1}{2}$ in.

(*b*) Check for wear load and endurance beam load. Assume average brinell hardness of 250 for first trial.

$$F_w = \frac{D_p bQK}{\cos^2\psi} = \frac{(0.75)(0.5)(1.6)(122)}{\cos^2 23^\circ} = 86.7 \text{ lb (allowed)}$$

$$F_o = \frac{s_o by\pi \cos\psi}{P_d} = \frac{(15,000)(0.5)(0.139)\pi(0.92)}{32} = 94.5 \text{ lb (allowed)}$$

where $\tan\phi_n = \tan 20^\circ \cos 23^\circ$, $\phi_n = 18.5^\circ$, $Q = 2(96)/(24+96) = 1.6$, $K = 122.0$ (based on ϕ_n).

(c) Check for dynamic load. Assume $C = 860$ (precision cut gears).

$$F_d = F + \frac{0.05V(Cb\cos^2\psi + F)\cos\psi}{0.05V + \sqrt{Cb\cos^2\psi + F}} = 380.6 \text{ lb}$$

where $F = 22/0.375 = 58.6$ lb, $b = 0.5$, $V = 1965$ fpm, $\cos 23^\circ = 0.92$.

The design is unsatisfactory from the standpoint of wear, since the dynamic load is greater than the wear load and the endurance strength beam load. It will probably be necessary to increase the diameters and change the material to one having a higher surface endurance limit.

Starting with the wear load equation, $F_w = D_p b(1.6)K/(0.92)^2$, let $b = 6P_c = \pi D_p/4$ for a 24 tooth pinion; then $F_w = 1.485 D_p^2 K$.

The dynamic load equation may also be set up in terms of the pinion diameter using $F = 2T/D_p = 44/D_p$, $0.05V = 131 D_p$ for 10,000 rpm, and assuming $C = 860$.

$$F_d = \frac{44}{D_p} + \frac{131 D_p[(860\pi D_p/4)(0.92)^2 + 44/D_p](0.92)}{131 D_p + \sqrt{(860\pi D_p/4)(0.92)^2 + 44/D_p}}$$

Now by successive trials determine a satisfactory combination of D_p and K. Try $P_d = 10$ or $D_p = 2.4$ in., $K = 250$, $b = \pi(2.4)/4 = 1.885$; then

$$F_w = 1.485 D_p^2 K = 2140 \text{ lb}, \quad F_d = 1164 \text{ lb}, \quad F_o = (15,000)(1.885)(0.139)\pi(0.92)/10 = 1138 \text{ lb}$$

This will give a solution, since F_d is only slightly (2.3%) greater than F_o.

4. A pair of precision cut helical steel gears on parallel shafts with a center distance of 7.5 in. transmits power with a velocity ratio of 4 to 1. The pinion rotates at 10,000 rpm. Both gears are made from the same material, having $s_o = 15,000$ psi. The teeth are 20° stub, with a 45° helix angle. The face width is 0.75 in. and the diametral pitch is 24. Determine the maximum horsepower that can be transmitted safely, considering wear and strength. Both gears have a brinell hardness of 400.

Solution:

(a) Determine the wear load.

$$F_w = \frac{D_p bQK}{\cos^2\psi} = \frac{3(0.75)(1.6)(268)}{(0.707)^2} = 1930 \text{ lb}$$

where $D_p = 3$, $b = 0.75$, $Q = 1.6$, $\tan\phi_n = \tan 20^\circ \cos 45^\circ$, $\phi_n = 14.43^\circ$, and

$$K = s_{es}^2(\sin\phi_n)(1/E_p + 1/E_g)/1.4 = (150,000)^2(0.25)[2/(30\times 10^6)]/1.4 = 268$$

(b) Determine the endurance load.

$$F_o = \frac{s_o by\pi\cos\psi}{P_d} = \frac{(15,000)(0.75)(0.139)\pi(0.92)}{24} = 188.5 \text{ lb}$$

(c) The dynamic load may not exceed 188.5 lb. $V = 7850$ ft/min.

$$F_d = F + \frac{(0.05)(7850)(860\times 0.75\times 0.92^2 + F)(0.92)}{(0.05)(7850) + \sqrt{860(0.75)(0.92)^2 + F}}$$

Putting $F = 0$ in this equation, we obtain $F_d = 474$ lb, which is greater than F_o.

Buckingham equations indicate that the above design will not be satisfactory from the standpoint of endurance even with zero horsepower. Based on average mass conditions, the gear life would be limited.

SUPPLEMENTARY PROBLEMS

5. Prove: $\phi_n = \tan^{-1}[\tan\phi\cos\psi]$.

6. Two precision cut forged steel helical gears have the following specifications:

$$s_o = 10{,}000 \text{ psi}, \quad s_{es} = 90{,}000 \text{ psi}, \quad P_d = 8, \quad b = 1.25 \text{ in.}$$

The pinion makes 600 rpm, the transmission ratio is 25/9, $\phi = 20^\circ$ (full depth teeth), and helix angle $\psi = 23^\circ$. Determine the transmitted load F, the wear load F_w, the dynamic load F_d, and the end thrust F_e.
Ans. $F = 386$ lb, $F_w = 440$ lb, $F_d = 773$ lb, $F_e = 164$ lb

7. Two helical steel gears, having a $14\frac{1}{2}^\circ$ normal pressure angle and a helix angle of 23°, connect two parallel shafts. The pinion has 48 teeth, the gear has 240 teeth, and the diametral pitch is 8. The pinion has a brinell hardness of 250 and the gear has a brinell hardness of 200. The face width is 10 inches. Determine the wear load. *Ans.* $K = 76$, $Q = 1.67$, $F_w = 9000$ lb

8. Two parallel shafts are connected by a pair of steel helical gears. The pinion transmits 15 hp at 4000 rpm of the pinion. Both gears are made of the same material, hardened steel with an allowable $s_o = 15{,}000$ psi. If the velocity ratio is $4\frac{1}{2}$ to 1, determine the smallest diameter gears that may be used having sufficient strength. No less than 30 teeth are to be used on either gear, the teeth are of 20° stub in diametral plane, and the helix angle is 45°. Use the Lewis equation.
Ans. $P_d = 16$, $b = 1.25$

9. For Problem 8, determine the required average brinell hardness of the two gears to provide a satisfactory design from the standpoint of wear. Assume a precision cut gear. $C = 860$.
Ans. $K = 89.5$, $s_{es} = 86{,}600$ psi, average BHN = 242

10. For Problem 8, determine if the gears are designed satisfactorily to withstand dynamic effects. Use $K = 89.5$. Calculate F_w, F_o, and F_d.
Ans. $F_w = 687$ lb, $F_o = 362$ lb, $F_d = 686$ lb. F_o should be $\geqq F_d$.

Chapter 20

Bevel Gears

BEVEL GEARS are usually used to connect intersecting shafts, and may be classified according to the magnitude of their pitch angle. Those having a pitch angle α less than 90° are external bevels as shown in Fig. 20-1 below. Those having a pitch angle of 90° are called crown gears as shown in Fig. 20-2 below. Those having a pitch angle α greater than 90° are internal bevels as shown in Fig. 20-3 below. The sum of the pitch angles of two mating bevel gears is equal to the angle between the intersecting shafts. The Hypoid bevel gear is used to connect non-intersecting shafts. The teeth may be either straight or spiraled with respect to the cone element. The discussion in this chapter will be limited to straight tooth bevel gears connecting shafts intersecting at 90° as shown in Fig. 20-4 below.

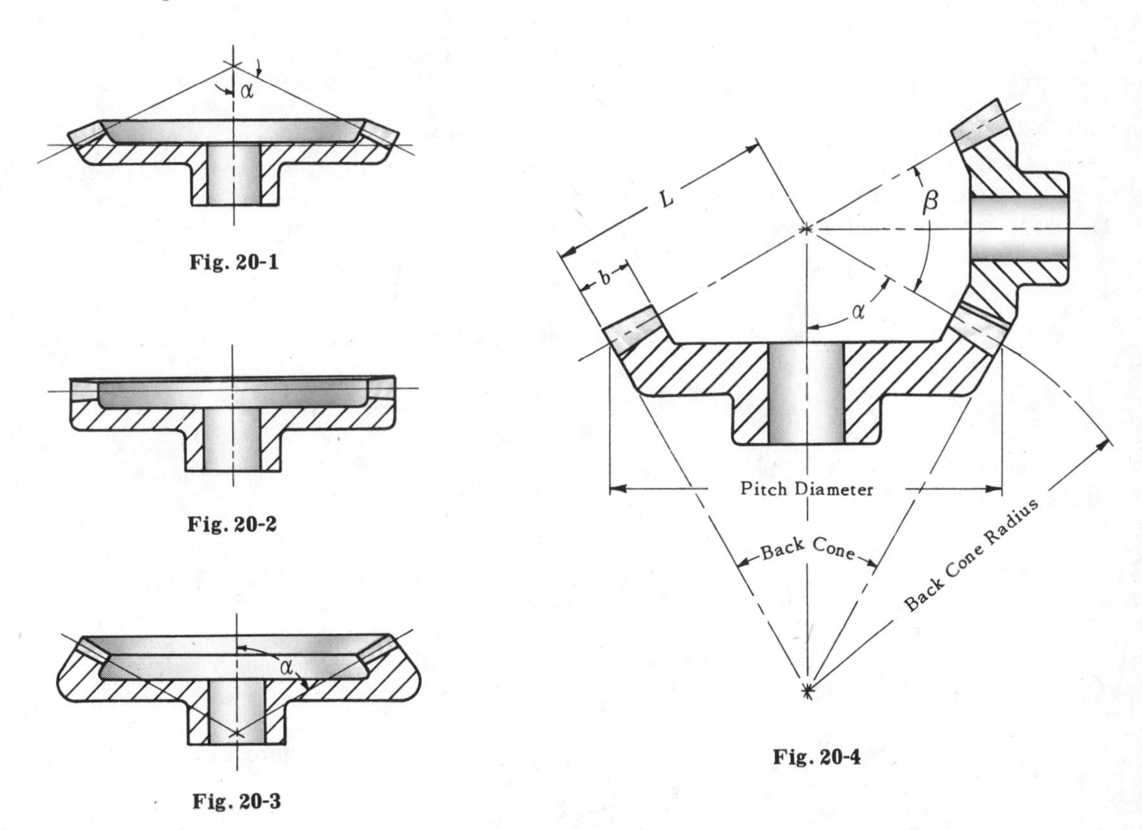

As is true in the design of most other machine elements, there are numerous approaches to gear design. No firm rules can be established since there are so many variables. Most engineers follow procedures by Buckingham, Gleason, or those recommended by the AGMA (American Gear Manufacturers Association). Any procedure for gear design should be considered as preliminary until proved by experiment to satisfy specific requirements.

As for the case of spur and helical gears, design of bevel gears is based on beam strength, dynamic load, and wear.

STRENGTH DESIGN of a straight tooth bevel gear may be based on the Lewis equation. It should be noted that the tooth tapers and becomes smaller in cross section as it converges to the apex of the cone. The Lewis equation is modified as follows to correct for this situation.

The permissible force F that may be transmitted is

$$F = \frac{sby\pi}{P_d}\left(\frac{L-b}{L}\right)$$

where s = allowable bending stress, psi
y = form factor based on the formative number of teeth and the type of tooth profile
L = the cone distance, in., and is equal to the square root of the sum of the squares of the pitch radii of the mating gears (for shafts intersecting at 90°)
b = the face width of the gear, in.
P_d = the diametral pitch based on the largest tooth cross section.

For ease of manufacture and satisfactory operation of bevel gears, it is recommended that the face width be limited to between $L/3$ and $L/4$, where L is the cone distance. In general we will design the face width close to, but never greater than, $L/3$. When designing for strength the diameter of the gear may be either known or unknown. When the diameter is known, it is convenient to use the modified Lewis equation in this form:

$$\frac{P_d}{y} = \frac{sb\pi}{F}\left(\frac{L-b}{L}\right) = \text{an allowed value}$$

Note that all the terms on the right side of the above equation can be determined after the material has been specified. The transmitted force F is determined by dividing the torque on the weaker gear by its pitch radius. The face width b may be taken as $L/3$ rounded out to the nearest 1/8 in. under this value. The allowable stress s is evaluated as explained in the following section. The above equation then yields an allowable value of P_d/y which must be satisfied by selecting a suitable value for P_d.

When the diameter is unknown, it is convenient to use the following form of the Lewis equation:

$$s = \frac{2TP_d^2}{b\pi yN}\left(\frac{L}{L-b}\right) = \text{actual stress} \leq \text{allowed stress}$$

This equation will yield a value for the actual stress in terms of P_d^3 after making the following substitutions:

$$\text{Let } b = \frac{L}{3} = \frac{N_p}{6P_d}\sqrt{1+R^2} \qquad \text{and} \qquad \text{Let } \frac{L}{L-b} = \frac{3}{2}$$

where N = actual number of teeth on the weaker gear
N_p = number of teeth on the pinion
R = ratio of the angular velocity of the pinion to the angular velocity of the gear.

Design from a standpoint of strength may be considered as a first approximation which must be checked for wear and dynamic effects as explained later.

THE ALLOWABLE STRESSES, s, for the average conditions may be taken as

$$s = s_o\left(\frac{1200}{1200+V}\right) \text{ psi for cut teeth} \qquad \text{or} \qquad s = s_o\left(\frac{78}{78+\sqrt{V}}\right) \text{ psi for generated teeth}$$

where s_o is the endurance limit of the gear material for released loading, corrected for average stress concentration, psi. An approximate value for s_o is 1/3 of the ultimate strength, based on an average value for stress concentration. V is the pitch line velocity, fpm.

THE FORMATIVE OR VIRTUAL number of teeth, N_f, for a bevel gear is the number of teeth, having the same pitch as the actual gear, that could be cut on a gear having a pitch radius equal to the radius of the back cone.

$$N_f = N/\cos\alpha$$

where N = actual number of teeth on the gear and α = pitch angle or half of the cone angle.

THE LIMITING WEAR LOAD, F_w, may be approximated from

$$F_w = \frac{0.75\,D_p bKQ}{\cos\alpha} \quad \text{(an allowed value)}$$

where D_p, b, K, and Q are the same as for spur gears, except that Q is based on the formative number of teeth, and α is the pitch angle of the pinion.

THE LIMITING ENDURANCE LOAD, F_o, may be approximated from

$$F_o = \frac{s_o b y \pi}{P_d}\left(\frac{L-b}{L}\right) \quad \text{(an allowed value)}$$

THE DYNAMIC LOAD, F_d, which is the transmitted load plus an incremental load due to dynamic effects, may be approximated from

$$F_d = F + \frac{0.05V(bC+F)}{0.05V + \sqrt{bC+F}}$$

where the symbols are the same as for spur gears. F_d must be $\leqq F_w$, F_d must be $\leqq F_o$.

Note that F_o and F_w are allowed values which must not be exceeded by the dynamic load.

THE AMERICAN GEAR MANUFACTURERS ASSOCIATION (AGMA) STANDARDS recommend the following horsepower rating, for peak load, for both straight and spiral bevel gears:

$$\text{hp} = \frac{snD_p by\pi(L-0.5b)}{126{,}000P_d L}\left(\frac{78}{78+\sqrt{V}}\right)$$

where s = 250 times the Brinell hardness number of the weaker gear for gears hardened and also not hardened after cutting.

s = 300 times the Brinell hardness number of the weaker gear if the gear is case hardened.

n = speed of pinion, rpm.

All other symbols are the same as before.

THE AGMA STANDARDS FOR WEAR (DURABILITY) recommend the following horsepower ratings:

$$\text{hp} = 0.8\,C_m C_B b \quad \text{for straight bevel gears}$$

$$\text{hp} = C_m C_B b \quad \text{for spiral bevel gears}$$

where C_m = a material factor as listed below

$$C_B = \frac{D_p^{1.5}\,n}{233}\left(\frac{78}{78+\sqrt{V}}\right)$$

n = rpm of the pinion.

PARTIAL LIST, MATERIAL FACTOR C_m

Gear		Pinion		
Material	Brinell	Material	Brinell	C_m
I	160-200	II	210-245	0.30
II	245-280	II	285-325	0.40
II	285-325	II	335-360	0.50
II	210-245	III	500	0.40
II	285-325	IV	550	0.60
III	500	IV	550	0.90
IV	550	IV	550	1.00

I = Annealed steel   III = Oil or surface-hardened steel
II = Heat-treated steel   IV = Case-hardened steel

It has been found by experience that generally, if cast iron teeth are strong enough they will not fail by wear, and that if steel teeth satisfy the wear requirements they will be strong enough.

SOLVED PROBLEMS

1. A cast iron bevel gear has a pitch diameter D of 24 in. and a pitch angle α of 30°. The diametral pitch P_d is 10. Determine the permissible endurance load F_o. The teeth are 20° full depth.

Solution:

$$F_o = \frac{s_o by\pi}{P_d}\left(\frac{L-b}{L}\right) = \frac{(8000)(8)(0.149)\pi}{10}\left(\frac{24-8}{24}\right) = 1996 \text{ lb}$$

where s_o = 8000 psi for cast iron, $L = D/(2\sin 30^\circ) = 24$ in., $b = L/3 = 8$ in.,

$y = 0.149$ (form factor based on $N_f = \dfrac{N}{\cos\alpha} = \dfrac{P_d D}{\cos\alpha} = \dfrac{10(24)}{\cos 30^\circ} = 277$ teeth).

2. Two steel bevel gears, both having a brinell hardness of 250, connect shafts at 90°. The teeth are $14\frac{1}{2}^\circ$ full depth and the diametral pitch is 6. The number of teeth on the pinion and gear are 30 and 48. The face width is 1.5 in. Determine the wear load F_w.

Solution:

$$F_w = \frac{0.75\,D_p bKQ}{\cos\alpha} = \frac{(0.75)(5)(1.5)(96)(1.44)}{0.846} = 918 \text{ lb}$$

where $D_p = N_p/P_d = 30/6 = 5$ in., $D_g = N_g/P_d = 48/6 = 8$ in., $b = 1.5$ in.

$$K = \frac{s_{es}^2(\sin\phi)(1/E_p + 1/E_g)}{1.4} = \frac{(90{,}000)^2(0.25)[2/(30\times 10^6)]}{1.4} = 96$$

$$s_{es} = (\text{BHN})(250) - 10{,}000 = (400)(250) - 10{,}000 = 90{,}000 \text{ psi}$$

$$Q = \frac{2N_f\text{ (gear)}}{N_f\text{ (pinion)} + N_f\text{ (gear)}} = \frac{2(90.5)}{35.4 + 90.5} = 1.44$$

$$N_f\text{ (gear)} = \frac{N_g}{\cos\alpha\text{ (gear)}} = \frac{48}{0.53} = 90.5, \quad N_f\text{ (pinion)} = \frac{N_p}{\cos\alpha\text{ (pinion)}} = \frac{30}{0.847} = 35.4$$

$$\cos\alpha\text{ (gear)} = \frac{R_p}{L} = \frac{2.5}{4.72} = 0.53, \quad \cos\alpha\text{ (pinion)} = \frac{R_g}{L} = \frac{4}{4.72} = 0.847, \quad L = \sqrt{R_p^2 + R_g^2} = 4.72$$

3. Two cast iron bevel gears transmit 3 hp with a pitch line velocity of 860 fpm. The face width of the gears is 0.75 in. Determine the dynamic load F_d. The teeth are $14\frac{1}{2}°$ involute and precision cut.

Solution:

$$F_d = F + \frac{0.05V(Cb+F)}{0.05V + \sqrt{Cb+F}} = 115 + \frac{(0.05)(860)(400\times 0.75+115)}{(0.05)(860) + \sqrt{400\times 0.75+115}} = 397 \text{ lb}$$

where $F = (\text{hp})(33{,}000)/V = (3)(33{,}000)/860 = 115$ lb

$C = 400$ for precision cut gears (same as for spur gears)

$V = 860$ fpm, $b = 0.75$ in.

4. Two cast iron bevel gears having pitch diameters of 3 in. and 4 in. respectively are to transmit 3 hp at 1100 rpm of the pinion. The tooth profiles are of $14\frac{1}{2}°$ composite form.

(*a*) Determine the face width b and the required P_d from the standpoint of strength using the Lewis equation.

(*b*) Check design from the standpoint of dynamic load and wear.

Solution:

The pinion is the weaker since both gear and pinion are of the same material.

(*a*) Design for strength.

$$\frac{P_d}{y} = \frac{sb\pi}{F}\left(\frac{L-b}{L}\right) = \frac{(4650)(0.75)\pi}{115}\left(\frac{2.5-0.75}{2.5}\right) = 66.5 \quad \text{(allowed)}$$

where $s = s_o\left(\frac{1200}{1200+V}\right) = 8000\left(\frac{1200}{1200+860}\right) = 4650$ psi, $V = \frac{3\pi}{12}(1100) = 860$ fpm

$b = L/3 = 2.5/3 = 0.83$ in. (use 0.75 in.), $L = \sqrt{R_p^2+R_g^2} = \sqrt{1.5^2+2^2} = 2.5$ in.

$s_o = 8000$ psi for cast iron, $F = (3)(33{,}000)/860 = 115$ lb.

Then if $y \approx 0.1$ and $P_d/y = 66.5$, $P_d \approx 6$ or 7.

Try $P_d = 7$: $N_p = (3)(7) = 21$, N_f (pinion) $= 21/\cos\alpha = 21/(2/2.5) = 26.2$ (formative teeth), $y = 0.098$ for 26.2 teeth. Now $P_d/y = 7/0.098 = 71.5$ (too weak since $71.5 > 66.5$).

Next try $P_d = 6$: $N_p = (3)(6) = 18$, N_f (pinion) $= 18/\cos\alpha = 18/(2/2.5) = 22.5$, $N_g = (4)(6) = 24$, N_f (gear) $= 24/\cos\alpha = 24/(1.5/2.5) = 40$, $y = 0.094$ for 22.5 teeth. Now $P_d/y = 6/0.094 = 63.8$ (satisfactory since $63.8 < 66.5$).

(*b*) Check for wear and dynamic effects using $P_d = 6$.

$$F_w = \frac{0.75D_p bKQ}{\cos\alpha \text{ (pinion)}} = \frac{(0.75)(3)(0.75)(193)(1.28)}{0.8} = 522 \text{ lb} \quad \text{(allowed)}$$

where $K = 193$ based on $s_{es} = 90{,}000$ psi for cast iron on cast iron (Table III, Chap. 18), and

$$Q = \frac{2N_f \text{ (gear)}}{N_f \text{ (pinion)} + N_f \text{ (gear)}} = \frac{(2)(40)}{22.5+40} = 1.28.$$

$$F_o = \frac{s_o by\pi}{P_d}\left(\frac{L-b}{L}\right) = \frac{(8000)(0.75)(0.094)\pi}{6}\left(\frac{2.5-0.75}{2.5}\right) = 207 \text{ lb} \quad \text{(allowed)}$$

Both F_o and F_w must be equal to or greater than F_d.

$$F_d = F + \frac{0.05V(Cb+F)}{0.05V + \sqrt{Cb+F}} = 115 + \frac{(0.05)(860)(400\times 0.75+115)}{(0.05)(860) + \sqrt{400\times 0.75+115}} = 397 \text{ lb}$$

The design is satisfactory from the standpoint of wear, but the dynamic load is greater than the endurance load. Better material should be specified for the pinion in order to increase the endurance load to at least 397 lb.

5. A pair of bevel gears is to be used to transmit 12 hp. Determine the required diametral pitch and gear diameters for the following specifications:

	Pinion	Gear
No. of teeth..............	21	60
Material....................	Semi-steel	Cast iron
s_o	12,000 psi	8000 psi
Brinell Hardness	200	160
Speed	1200 rpm	420 rpm
Tooth Profile	$14\frac{1}{2}°$ composite	Same

Solution:

(*a*) Design for strength using the Lewis equation.

First determine which of the mating gears is weaker. The strength of the gears is a function of the product of s_o and y.

$$\text{Gear } N_f = \frac{60\sqrt{21^2+60^2}}{21} = 182,\ y = 0.120. \qquad \text{Pinion } N_f = \frac{21\sqrt{21^2+60^2}}{60} = 22.2,\ y = 0.093.$$

$s_o y$ (gear) $= 8000 \times 0.120 = 960$ (weaker). $s_o y$ (pinion) $= 12{,}000 \times 0.093 = 1120$.
Base design on the gear since it is the weaker.

Since the diameters are unknown, we will use the following form of the Lewis equation:

$$s_{actual} = \frac{2TP_d^2}{b\pi yN}\left(\frac{L}{L-b}\right) \leqq s_{allowed}$$

where $T = \dfrac{12 \times 63{,}000}{420} = 1800$ in-lb for gear, and $L = \dfrac{N_p}{2P_d}\sqrt{1+R^2} = \dfrac{21}{2P_d}\sqrt{1+(20/7)^2} = \dfrac{31.8}{P_d}$.

Let $b = \dfrac{L}{3} = \dfrac{31.8}{3P_d} = \dfrac{10.6}{P_d}$ and $\dfrac{L}{L-b} = \dfrac{3}{2}$. Then $s = \dfrac{(2)(1800)P_d^2(3)}{(31.8/3P_d)\pi(0.120)(60)(2)} = 22.6P_d^3$.

Assuming a velocity factor $\approx \frac{1}{2}$, $s_{allowed} \approx 8000(\frac{1}{2}) \approx 4000$; $22.6P_d^3 \approx 4000$, $P_d \approx 5$.

Try $P_d = 5$. Then $D_g = 12$ in., $V = (12\pi/12)(420) = 1320$ fpm, and

$$s_{allowed} = 8000\left(\frac{1200}{1200+1320}\right) = 3810 \text{ psi}, \qquad s_{actual} = 22.6(5^3) = 2820 \text{ psi}.$$

$P_d = 5$ is therefore satisfactory. $b = 10.6/5 = 2.12$ in.; use $b = 2$ in.

(*b*) Check for wear and dynamic effects.

$$F_w = 0.75\,D_p bKQ/\cos\alpha = (0.75)(4.2)(2)(193)(1.78)/0.945 = 2290 \text{ lb}$$

where $Q = (2)(182)/(22.2+182) = 1.78$.

$$F_o = \frac{s_o b y\pi}{P_d}\left(\frac{L-b}{L}\right) = \frac{(8000)(2)(0.120)\pi}{5}\left(\frac{6.35-2}{6.35}\right) = 825 \text{ lb}$$

$$F_d = F + \frac{0.05V(Cb+F)}{0.05V+\sqrt{Cb+F}} = 300 + \frac{(0.05)(1320)(400\times 2+300)}{(0.05)(1320)+\sqrt{400\times 2+300}} = 1030 \text{ lb}$$

The design is satisfactory from the standpoint of wear since $F_w > F_d$, but F_o will have to be increased to equal F_d. This may be accomplished by using a smaller diametral pitch or better materials.

6. Check Problem 5 by means of the procedure recommended by AGMA using $P_d = 5$.

Solution:

(*a*) The horsepower rating from the standpoint of strength for the values calculated in Problem 5 may be determined by the AGMA equation.

$$\text{hp} = \frac{snD_p by\pi(L - 0.5b)}{126{,}000 P_d L}\left(\frac{78}{78 + \sqrt{V}}\right)$$

$$= \frac{(8000)(1200)(4.2)(2)(0.120)(\pi)(6.35-1.0)}{(126{,}000)(5)(6.35)}\left(\frac{78}{78 + \sqrt{1320}}\right) = 27.8 \text{ hp}$$

(*b*) For durability the AGMA horsepower rating is

$$\text{hp} = 0.8(C_m C_B b) = (0.8)(0.3)(30.1)(2) = 14.4$$

where $C_m = 0.3$, $C_B = \frac{D_p^{1.5} n}{233}\left(\frac{78}{78 + \sqrt{V}}\right) = \frac{(4.2^{1.5})(1200)}{233}\left(\frac{78}{78 + \sqrt{1320}}\right) = 30.1$, $b = 2$ in.

The above equations indicate that a $P_d = 5$ and a face width of 2 in. is more than safe for 12 hp according to AGMA.

7. Two steel bevel gears have been designed for strength to transmit 25 hp. If the gears have the following specifications, find their required hardness to satisfy the AGMA durability recommendation.

	Gear	**Pinion**
Diameter............	8 inches	5.76 inches
s_o	20,000 psi	25,000 psi
Speed	900 rpm	1250 rpm
No. of teeth.........	32	23
Face.................	1.5 inches	1.5 inches
P_d	20	20
Form.................	$14\frac{1}{2}°$ full depth	$14\frac{1}{2}°$ full depth

Solution:

The required material is a function of C_m.

$$C_m = \frac{\text{hp}}{0.8 C_B b} = \frac{25}{(0.8)(47.75)(1.5)} = 0.4375 \text{ needed}$$

where $C_B = \left(\frac{D_p^{1.5} n}{233}\right)\left(\frac{78}{78 + \sqrt{V}}\right) = \frac{(5.76^{1.5})(1250)}{233}\left(\frac{78}{78 + \sqrt{1884}}\right) = 47.75$.

This material indicates a required brinell hardness of 285 for the gear and 325 for the pinion. These values correspond to a $C_m = 0.5$ from the material factor table (Page 244).

8. Two $14\frac{1}{2}°$ composite tooth, steel bevel gears are to transmit 20 hp with a transmission ratio of 3. The speed of the pinion is 1800 rpm. If the gears are to be hardened to give a material factor of 0.4, determine the probable minimum pinion diameter starting with the AGMA durability equation.

Solution:

$$\text{hp} = 0.8(C_m C_B b) = 0.8(0.4)\left(\frac{D_p^{1.5} \times 1800}{233}\right)(\text{V.F.})\frac{D_p}{6}\sqrt{1 + 3^2} = 20$$

Assume a V.F. (velocity factor) $\approx \frac{1}{2}$ and solve for $D_p \approx 3.94$ in., say 4 in.

Then $V = \frac{\pi 4}{12}(1800) = 1885$ fpm, and V.F. $= \frac{78}{78 + \sqrt{1885}} = 0.642$ instead of the assumed $\frac{1}{2}$ which is on the safe side.

SUPPLEMENTARY PROBLEMS

9. A cast steel (s_o=15 000 psi) bevel gear pinion has a pitch diameter of 9 in. and a pitch angle of 30°. The diametral pitch is 6. The gear rotates at 600 rpm. From the standpoint of strength only, using the AGMA recommendations, how much power should this gear be capable of transmitting? Also calculate the endurance load F_o. The tooth is $14\frac{1}{2}°$ composite. *Ans.* 18.2 hp based on AGMA, F_o = 1752 lb

10. Two steel bevel gears connect shafts at 90°. The pinion has a brinell hardness of 300 and the gear has a hardness of 200. The teeth are $14\frac{1}{2}°$ full depth and the diametral pitch is 8. The number of teeth on the pinion is 40 and the gear has 64 teeth. The face width is 1.5 in. Determine the wear load F_w.
Ans. F_w = 916 lb

11. Two cast iron bevel gears connect shafts at right angles and transmit a tangential force of 300 lb. The teeth are of 20° full depth and are carefully cut with an error of 0.001 in. Their pitch line velocity is 3000 ft/min, and their face width is 2 in. Calculate the dynamic load F_d. *Ans.* F_d = 1820 lb

12. A right angle speed reducer uses hardened alloy steel precision cut bevel gears. The transmission ratio is 5 to 1 and the pinion rotates at 900 rpm while transmitting 50 hp. If the teeth are of 20° full depth form and the pinion has a diameter of $4\frac{1}{2}$ in., what must be the diametral pitch and width of the face of the gears, using the Lewis equation? s_o = 30,000 psi for both gears. What brinell hardness is required for satisfactory wear? Determine the endurance load, wear load, and dynamic load.
Ans. P_d = 10, $b = 3\frac{3}{4}$ in., F_d = 3590 lb, F_o = 3050 lb, F_w = 3590 for K = 145

13. Two shafts at right angles are to be connected with a pair of bevel gears having 20° full depth teeth. The velocity ratio is to be $4\frac{1}{2}$ to 1. The pinion is to be made of steel (s_o = 15,000 psi) and the gear is to be made of semi-steel (s_o = 12,000 psi). The pinion is to transmit 5 hp at 900 rpm. Determine the minimum diameters, diametral pitch, and face width that should be used based on strength only. Then using the AGMA durability equation estimate the minimum diameter that would be required for wear, assuming a material factor of 0.4.
Ans. For strength: P_d = 8, N_p = 16, N_g = 72, D_p = 2 in., D_g = 9 in. For wear, D_p = 2.5 in.

14. A pair of straight tooth bevel gears at right angles is to transmit 2 hp at 1200 rpm of the pinion. The diameter of the pinion is 3 in. and the velocity ratio is $3\frac{1}{2}$ to 1. The tooth form is $14\frac{1}{2}°$ composite type. Both pinion and gear are cast iron (s_o = 8000 psi). Determine the pitch and face width from the standpoint of strength only, using the Lewis equation. *Ans.* P_d = 28, b = 1.75 in.

15. A pair of straight tooth bevel gears have 20° full depth teeth and are generated from SAE 1030 steel blanks. Eight horsepower at 100 rpm of the pinion is transmitted through shafts at right angles with a velocity ratio of 5 to 3. If the pinion diameter is 6 in., what is the greatest number of teeth that can be used, based on AGMA strength and wear? The gears are heat treated to a brinell hardness of 225. Use C_m = 0.3.
Ans. P_d = 16. For durability, hp = 10.45.

Chapter 21

Worm Gears

WORM GEARING is widely used to transmit power at high velocity ratios between non-intersecting shafts that are usually, but not necessarily, at right angles. The worm drive consists of a threaded worm in mesh with a gear, sometimes called the worm wheel, as shown in Fig.21-1 below. The worm may have a single, double, triple or more threads. The axial pitch P_a of the worm is equal to the circular pitch P_c of the gear. The lead is the distance the worm helix advances along the axis per revolution.

If we develop one turn of the worm thread, it forms the hypotenuse of a right triangle whose base is equal to the pitch circumference of the worm and whose altitude is equal to the lead of the worm, as shown in Fig. 21-2 below.

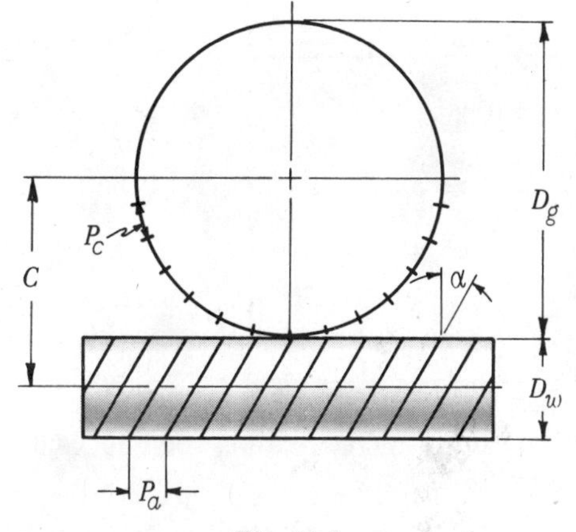

Fig. 21-1

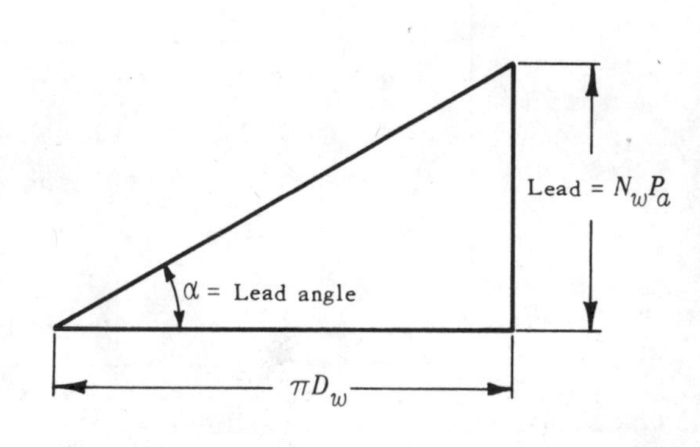

Fig. 21-2

The following relationships are noted:

$$\tan\alpha = \frac{\text{lead}}{\pi D_w} = \frac{P_c N_w}{\pi D_w} \qquad \text{and} \qquad \frac{(\text{rpm})_w}{(\text{rpm})_g} = \frac{N_g}{N_w} = \frac{D_g}{D_w \tan\alpha}$$

where the subscript g applies to the worm-gear, and the subscript w applies to the worm.

STRENGTH DESIGN of the worm wheel is based on the Lewis equation,

$$F = sbyP_{nc} = \frac{sby\pi}{P_{nd}}$$

where F (lb) = permissible tangential load, s (psi) = allowable stress = $s_o(\frac{1200}{1200 + V_g})$

s_o (psi) = about $\frac{1}{3}$ of the ultimate strength, based on an average value for stress concentration

V_g (fpm) = pitch line velocity of the gear.

DYNAMIC LOAD, F_d, for the worm gear may be estimated by

$$F_d = \left(\frac{1200 + V_g}{1200}\right)F$$

where F = actual transmitted tangential load.

ENDURANCE LOAD, F_o, for the gear, based on the Lewis equation is

$$F_o = \frac{s_o b y \pi}{P_{nd}}$$

WEAR LOAD, F_w, for the worm gear may be estimated by

$$F_w = D_g b B$$

where D_g = pitch diameter of the gear, in.
b = gear face width, in.
B = a constant depending upon the combination of the materials used for the worm and gear, as listed below.

Worm	Gear	B
Hardened steel	Cast iron	50
Steel, 250 BHN	Phosphor bronze	60
Hardened steel	Phosphor bronze	80
Hardened steel	Chilled phosphor bronze	120
Hardened steel	Antimony bronze	120
Cast iron	Phosphor bronze	150

The above values for B are suitable for lead angles up to 10°. For angles between 10° and 25°, increase B by 25%. For lead angles greater than 25°, increase B by 50%.

As for spur, helical and bevel gears, F_o and F_w are allowable values which must not be exceeded by the dynamic load F_d.

AGMA HORSEPOWER RATING EQUATIONS are based on wear and the heat dissipation capacity of the worm gear unit. From the standpoint of wear,

$$\text{hp} = \frac{n}{R} K Q m \qquad \text{(wear check)}$$

where hp = input horsepower
n = rpm of worm
R = transmission ratio = $(\text{rpm})_w/(\text{rpm})_g$
K = a pressure constant depending upon center distances, as listed below
Q = $R/(R + 2.5)$
m = velocity factor depending upon the center distance, transmission ratio, and worm speed. m may be estimated by

$$m = \frac{450}{450 + V_w + 3V_w/R}$$

where V_w = pitch line velocity of worm, fpm.

Center Distance C (in.)	K
1	0.0125
2	0.025
3	0.04
4	0.09
5	0.17
6	0.29
7	0.45
8	0.66
9	0.99

Center Distance C (in.)	K
10	1.20
15	4.0
20	8.0
30	29.0
40	66.0
50	120.0
60	200.0
70	320.0
80	320.0

The AGMA recommendations further include the following design equations:

$$D_w \approx \frac{C}{2.2} \approx 3P_c, \qquad b \approx 0.73 \times \text{worm pitch diameter}, \qquad L \approx P_c\left(4.5 + \frac{N_g}{50}\right)$$

where D_w = pitch diameter of the worm, in.
C = center distance between axis of worm and axis of gear, in.
b = face width of gear, in.
P_c = circular pitch of gear, in.
L = axial length of worm, in.

These equations are for estimating the approximate proper proportions of the gear unit.

Based on AGMA recommendations, the limiting input horsepower rating of a plain worm gear unit from the standpoint of heat dissipation, for worm gear speeds up to 2000 rpm, may be estimated by

$$\text{hp} = \frac{9.5C^{1.7}}{R + 5} \qquad \text{(heat check)}$$

where hp = permissible horsepower input
C = center distance, in.
R = transmission ratio.

The efficiency of a worm gear unit, assuming square threads, may be approximated by

$$\text{Efficiency} = \frac{1 - f\tan\alpha}{1 + f/\tan\alpha}$$

where f = coefficient of friction
α = lead angle.

SOLVED PROBLEMS

1. A triple threaded worm has a pitch diameter of 4 in. and an axial pitch of 0.75 in. Determine the lead angle α.

Solution:

$$\tan\alpha = \frac{\text{lead}}{\pi D_w} = \frac{(0.75)(3)}{\pi(4)} = 0.179, \qquad \alpha = 10.16^\circ$$

2. A worm gear reducer unit is to have a 16 inch center distance. What should be the approximate worm diameter and axial pitch of the worm in accordance with AGMA recommendations?

Solution:

$$D_w \approx \frac{C^{0.875}}{2.2} = \frac{16^{0.875}}{2.2} = 5.14\text{ in.} = 3P_c. \quad \text{Then } P_c \approx \frac{5.14}{3} = 1.71; \text{ use } 1\tfrac{3}{4}\text{ in.}$$

Standard circular pitches are: $\frac{1}{8}, \frac{5}{16}, \frac{3}{8}, \frac{1}{2}, \frac{5}{8}, \frac{3}{4}, 1, 1\frac{1}{4}, 1\frac{1}{2}, 1\frac{3}{4}$, and 2 inches.

3. A worm gear speed reducer unit has a gear center distance of 10 in. and a transmission ratio of 14. Estimate the horsepower input without the gear overheating, assuming that the strength and wear capacity are not exceeded.

Solution:

From standpoint of heat dissipation, permissible horsepower input $= \dfrac{9.5\,C^{1.7}}{R+5} = \dfrac{9.5(10)^{1.7}}{14+5} = 25$ hp.

4. A hardened steel worm and phosphor bronze gear reducer unit has a transmission ratio of 40 to 1 and a center distance of 12 in. The worm speed is 1500 rpm and its diameter is 4.9 in. What is the safe power input based on AGMA from the standpoint of wear?

Solution:

$$\text{hp} = \frac{n}{R}KQm = 14.5\text{ hp}$$

where $n = 1500$ rpm, $R = 40$, $K = 2.3$ (by interpolation in table)

$Q = R/(R+2.5) = 0.94$

$m = \dfrac{450}{450 + V_w + 3V_w/R} = 0.179$, and V_w = pitch line velocity of worm $= (1500)(4.9\pi)/12 = 1925$ fpm.

5. Complete the design and determine the input horsepower capacity of a worm gear speed reducer unit composed of a hardened steel worm and a phosphor bronze gear having 20° stub involute teeth. The center distance C is to be 8 inches, the transmission ratio R is to be 10, and the worm speed is to be 1750 rpm.

Solution:

(*a*) Determine D_w, D_g, P_c, N_w, N_g, α, b, and L.

$D_w \approx C^{0.875}/2.2 = 2.81 \approx 3P_c$. Thus $P_c \approx 2.81/3 = 0.94$ in.; use a standard pitch of 1 in. Then if the worm diameter is to be approximately 3", the gear diameter D_g desired will be approximately $D_g = 2C - D_w = 2(8) - 3 = 13$ in.

Now $N_g/N_w = 10 = \pi D_g/P_c N_w$ or $D_g = 10P_c N_w/\pi$. Then for various values of N_w the exact D_g can be determined.

N_w	1	2	3	4	5
D_g	3.19	6.38	9.57	12.76	15.95

Thus the diameter of the gear will be taken as 12.76'' (closest to 13'') and the worm diameter will be 3.24'', which are close to desired proportions.

Since the worm will have a quadruple thread, $\tan\alpha = \text{lead}/\pi D_w = (1)(4)/3.24\pi = 0.393$, $\alpha = 21\frac{1}{2}^\circ$. Then $P_{nc} = P_c \cos\alpha = (1)(\cos 21\frac{1}{2}^\circ) = 0.93''$.

The face width $b \approx 0.73 D_w = (0.73)(3.24) = 2.4''$; use $2\frac{1}{2}''$.

(*b*) We can estimate the capacity of the gear as follows:

$$F \;=\; sbyP_{nc} \;=\; 1830 \text{ lb} \quad \text{(safe transmitted load)}$$

where $P_{nc} = 0.93''$ (above), $y = 0.146$ (from table of form factors), $b = 2\frac{1}{2}''$ (above); and $s = s_o(\frac{1200}{1200+V_g})$ in which $s_o = 8000$ psi (for phosphor bronze) and $V_g = \pi D_g(\text{rpm})_g/12 = \pi(12.76)(175)/12 = 584$ fpm.

For a transmitted load $F = 1830$ lb, the dynamic load will be approximately $(\frac{1200+V_g}{1200})F \approx 2720$ lb. However, the allowable wear load is $F_w = D_g bB = 3200$ lb, where $B = (80)(1.25) = 100$ for hardened steel on phosphor bronze and a lead angle between 10° and 25°. Since the dynamic load does not exceed the allowable wear load, the safe transmitted load calculated above governs. Hence the allowable power, from the standpoint of gear tooth strength and wear, is

$$\text{hp} \;=\; FV_g/33{,}000 \;=\; (1830)(584)/33{,}000 \;=\; 32.4 \text{ hp}$$

(*c*) According to the AGMA formula for wear, the input capacity of the unit is

$$\text{hp} \;=\; \frac{n}{R}KQm \;=\; 17.5 \text{ hp}$$

where $n = 1750$ rpm, $R = 10$, $K = 0.66$ (from table, for $C = 8''$), $Q = R/(R+2.5) = 0.8$; and $m = \dfrac{450}{450+V_w+3V_w/R}$ in which $V_w = \pi D_w n/12 = 1485$ fpm.

(*d*) The input horsepower from the standpoint of heat dissipation may be estimated:

$$\text{hp} \;=\; \frac{9.5C^{1.7}}{R+5} \;=\; \frac{9.5(8)^{1.7}}{15} \;=\; 21.5 \text{ hp}$$

The above analysis indicates the input horsepower should be limited to 17.5 in accordance with AGMA wear recommendations.

6. A speed reducer unit is to be designed for an input of 1 hp with a transmission ratio of 27. The speed of the hardened steel worm is 1750 rpm. The worm wheel is to be made of phosphor bronze. The tooth form is to be $14\frac{1}{2}^\circ$ involute.

Solution:

(*a*) It is necessary to choose a center distance for trial. Assume that from previous experience the center distance for this size unit should be about 4 in. Then $D_w \approx 4^{0.875}/2.2 = 1.53 \approx 3P_c$ and $D_g \approx 8 - 1.53 = 6.47''$; these are desired proportions.

N_g must be some multiple of 27; that is, $\pi(6.47)/P_c = 27, 54, 81$, etc.

Also,. $P_c \approx \pi(6.47)/N_g$ should be about $\frac{1}{3}$ of D_w or about 0.5.

For $N_g = 27$, $P_c = 0.75''$; for $N_g = 54$, $P_c = 0.375''$. Use $P_c = 0.375''$ and $N_w = 2$.

Then $D_g = (0.375)(54)/\pi = 6.45''$, $D_w = (2)(4) - 6.45 = 1.55''$, and face width $b \approx (0.73)(1.55) = 1.13''$. Use $b = 1.125''$.

(*b*) Check design for gear tooth strength and wear. Permissible transmitted load F is

$$F \;=\; sbyP_c \;=\; 381 \text{ lb}$$

where $P_c = 0.375''$ (above), $y = 0.111$ (from form factor table, for 54 $14\frac{1}{2}^\circ$ involute teeth), $b = 1.125''$ (above); and $s = s_o(\frac{1200}{1200+V_g})$ in which $s_o = 8000$ psi (for phosphor bronze) and $V_g = \pi D_g(\text{rpm})_g/12 = 109.5$ fpm.

Required transmitted load, F = (hp transmitted)(33,000)/V_g = 301 lb.

Estimated dynamic load = $F(\frac{1200+V_g}{1200}) = 301(\frac{1200+109.5}{1200}) = 328$ lb.

Allowable wear load, $F_w = D_g bB = (6.45)(1.125)(80) = 581$ lb.

Since the allowable wear load is greater than the estimated dynamic load, and since the allowable transmitted load is greater than the required transmitted load, the design is satisfactory from the standpoint of strength and wear of the gear teeth. In fact, the permissible power is

$$FV_g/33{,}000 = (344)(109.5)/33{,}000 = 1.14 \text{ hp}$$

(*c*) Check AGMA rating for wear.

$$\text{Input power} = \frac{n}{R}KQm = 1.94 \text{ hp}$$

where n = 1750 rpm, R = 27, K = 0.09 (from table, for 4'' center distance), $Q = R/(R+2.5) = 0.915$; and $m = \frac{450}{450+V_w+3V_w/R} = 0.364$ in which $V_w = \pi D_w n/12 = 710$ fpm.

(*d*) Check for heat dissipation. Permissible input power $= \frac{9.5C^{1.7}}{R+5} = \frac{(9.5)(4)^{1.7}}{27+5} = 3.15$ hp

(*e*) In summary:

Safe Power	Based on
1.14 hp	Gear tooth strength and wear
1.94 hp	AGMA wear rating
3.15 hp	Heat dissipation capacity

The unit as designed is good for 1.14 hp according to our estimates. It could be redesigned for a slightly smaller center distance.

SUPPLEMENTARY PROBLEMS

7. A double threaded worm has a lead angle of 20°. For a pitch of 1.25'', what is the diameter of the worm?
Ans. D_w = 2.19 in.

8. A worm gear reducer unit is to have a 10 inch center distance. What should be the worm diameter and axial pitch of the worm in accordance with AGMA recommendations?
Ans. D_w = 3.40 in., P_c = 1.25 in.

9. A worm gear speed reducer unit has a gear center distance of 8.5 inches, and a transmission ratio of 20. What is its approximate horsepower input rating in order to prevent overheating? *Ans.* 14.4 hp

10. A hardened steel worm and phosphor bronze gear reducer unit has a transmission ratio of 20 to 1. The speed of the worm is 1200 rpm and its diameter is 2.68 inches. What is the approximate permissible power input from the standpoint of the AGMA wear equation? *Ans.* 17.8 hp

11. A hardened steel worm transmits power to a phosphor bronze gear with a velocity ratio of 20 to 1. The center distance is 15 inches. Determine the standard circular pitch and the lead angle, for proportions as close as possible to AGMA recommendations.
Ans. P_c = 1.75 in., lead angle = 8.15°

12. A hardened steel worm rotating at 1250 rpm transmits power to a phosphor bronze gear with a transmission ratio of 15 to 1. The center distance is 9 inches. Determine the remaining design and give estimated horsepower input ratings from the standpoint of strength, endurance, and heat dissipation. The teeth are of $14\frac{1}{2}°$ involute, full depth, form.

Ans.

D_g = 14.3 in.	b = 2.75 in.
D_w = 3.7 in.	hp = 15.3 (strength)
N_w = 3	hp = 15.2 (endurance)
N_g = 45	hp = 19.9 (heat)
P_c = 1 in.	

Chapter 22

Rolling Bearings

INTRODUCTION. Rolling bearing application involves the proper selection, mounting, lubrication, and possibly shielding in order that the bearings function satisfactorily under specified operating conditions.

The selection of a rolling bearing is made from a manufacturer's catalog. Unfortunately, the catalogs of different manufacturers do not necessarily use the same methods of arriving at a bearing selection, principally because of differences in interpretation of test data and service conditions. However, the rating of bearings is based upon certain general theory as outlined in this chapter and modified by various companies according to their experiences.

The mounting of bearings may be based on one of several recommended procedures, the arrangement used quite often being controlled by the economics.

Rolling bearings are also called anti-friction bearings, although the friction in rolling bearings is comparable to that in well designed journal bearings operating under thick film conditions. The decision as to the kind of bearing to use, that is, whether to use a rolling bearing or journal bearing, can be influenced by one or several of the following:

(*1*) Rolling bearings have an advantage where starting torques are high because of the rolling action of the balls, or rollers.

(*2*) Rolling bearings, especially at high speeds, are not as quiet in operation as journal bearings.

(*3*) Where space limitations are present, rolling bearings are preferable if the axial dimension is limited; and journal bearings are preferable if the radial dimension is limited, although the use of a ring or collar oiled bearing with the oil reservoir might require a large radial dimension.

(*4*) Where electrical insulation is desirable, the oil film in perfect lubrication will help provide insulation.

(*5*) Rolling bearings give warning (by becoming noisy) when failure is imminent; whereas, when failure occurs in journal bearings, the failure is sudden with more disastrous results.

(*6*) Rolling bearings can take a combination of radial and thrust loads (except for straight roller bearings).

(*7*) Rolling bearings can be preloaded, when desirable, to reduce deflections in the bearing and to provide for more accuracy, as in machine tools.

(*8*) Clearances in rolling bearings need be much less than in journal bearings, providing for accurate positioning of machine parts such as gears.

(*9*) Rolling bearings can be prepacked with grease to provide for a maintenance-free installation. Where oil is used for lubrication in rolling bearings, the lubrication problem is usually much simpler than for journal bearings. Failure of the lubricating system with rolling bearings is not calamitous, as it might be with journal bearings.

(*10*) Rolling bearings can take high overloads for short periods.

COEFFICIENT OF FRICTION in rolling bearings varies with speed, load, amount of lubrication, assembly, temperature of operation. A constant coefficient can be used for approximate calculations under favorable lubrication and what might be called normal operating conditions. The values listed are as recommended by SKF Industries, Inc.:

f = 0.0010 for self aligning bearings (radial load)
f = 0.0011 for cylindrical roller bearings with flange-guided short rollers (radial load)
f = 0.0013 for thrust ball bearings (thrust load)
f = 0.0015 for single row ball bearings (radial load)
f = 0.0018 for spherical roller bearings (radial load)
f = 0.0018 for tapered roller bearings

The coefficients of friction due to use of oils of high viscosity, more than the optimum amount of lubrication, or new bearings will be greater than those listed. Seal frictions should not be ignored. The values of coefficient of friction, as found by tests by New Departure, have been found to vary from 0.0005 to 0.003, with a general average of about 0.001.

It should be pointed out that improper assembly, as might occur with an interference between the shaft and inner race greater than recommended by the bearing manufacturers, can cause excessive binding and excessive friction.

The friction torque is given by

$$M_t = Ff(D/2)$$

where M_t = friction torque, in-lb; F = radial or axial load as specified, lb; f = coefficient of friction; D = diameter of the *bore* of the bearing. (It is usual practice to refer the frictional force to the bore of the bearing, or shaft diameter.)

STATIC CAPACITY OF BEARINGS depends on the conditions subsequent to static loading, as well as the various physical dimensions. The static capacity of a bearing which is *not* rotated subsequently to static loading will be much higher than one which is rotated; very small loads will cause permanent deformations in the rolling element and raceways which may prevent quiet operation at high speed even though friction is not affected appreciably and the bearing is not damaged.

A light, medium, and heavy series bearing of the same bore is shown in Fig. 22-1.

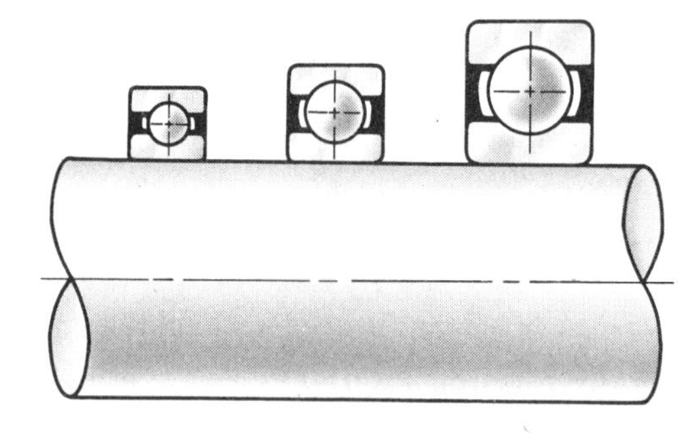

Fig. 22-1

The initial work done by Stribeck on static capacity of bearings served for many years as the basis of rating bearings. Later experience and test data gave added information as to the proper rating of bearings, and modifications were made by Palmgren with subsequent modifications made by the Anti-Friction Bearing Manufacturers Association (AFBMA) to suit dynamic conditions. Stribeck's work still serves as a basis for static rating of bearings.

Stribeck's equation for the static capacity C_o for ball bearings is

$$C_o = \frac{KZD^2}{5}$$

where K is a constant depending upon ball diameter, Z = number of balls, D = diameter of the balls; and for the static capacity of a straight roller bearing the equation is

$$C_o = \frac{KZDL}{5}$$

where K = a constant, Z = numbers of rollers, D = diameter of rollers, L = length of rollers.

The following definitions and data for method of evaluating static load ratings of radial ball bearings is taken from the AFBMA Standards – *Methods of Evaluating Load Ratings of Ball Bearings* published by the Anti-Friction Bearing Manufacturers Association, Inc. and reproduced with permission.

I. METHOD OF EVALUATING STATIC LOAD RATINGS FOR RADIAL BALL BEARINGS

A. Definitions

(1) The *static load* is defined as a load acting on a non-rotating bearing.

(2) Permanent deformations appear in balls and raceways under static load of moderate magnitude and increase gradually with increasing load. The permissible static load is therefore dependent upon the permissible magnitude of permanent deformation.

Experience shows that a total permanent deformation of 0.0001 of the ball diameter, occurring at the most heavily loaded ball and race contact, can be tolerated in most bearing applications without impairment of bearing operation.

In certain applications where subsequent rotation of the bearing is slow and where smoothness and friction requirements are not too exacting, a much greater total permanent deformation can be permitted. Likewise, where extreme smoothness is required or friction requirements are critical, less total permanent deformation may be tolerated.

For purposes of establishing comparative ratings, the *basic static load rating* therefore is defined as that static radial load which corresponds to a total permanent deformation of ball and race at the most heavily stressed contact of 0.0001 of the ball diameter.

In single row angular contact ball bearings the basic static load rating relates to the radial component of that load, which causes a purely radial displacement of the bearing rings in relation to each other.

(3) The *static equivalent load* is defined as that static, radial load which, if applied, would cause the same total permanent deformation at the most heavily stressed ball and race contact as that which occurs under the actual condition of loading.

B. Calculation of Basic Static Load Rating and Static Equivalent Load

(1) **Basic Static Load Rating:** The magnitude of the basic static load rating C_o is

$$C_o = f_o i Z D^2 \cos \alpha$$

where i = number of rows of balls in any one bearing

α = nominal angle of contact = the nominal angle between the line of action of the ball load and a plane perpendicular to the bearing axis

Z = number of balls per row

D = ball diameter.

Values of the factor f_o for different kinds of bearings as commonly designed and manufactured and made of hardened steel are given in Table I-1.

Table I-1

Factor f_o

Bearing Type	f_o	
	Units kg, mm	**Units** pound, inch
Self-aligning ball bearings	0.34	484
Radial and angular contact groove ball bearings	1.25	1780

(2) **Static Equivalent Load:** The magnitude of the static equivalent load P_o, for radial bearings under combined radial and thrust loads, is the greater of

$$P_o = X_o F_r + Y_o F_a$$

$$P_o = F_r$$

where X_o = a radial factor F_r = the radial load

Y_o = a thrust factor F_a = the thrust load.

Values of X_o and Y_o are given in Table I-2.

Table I-2
Factors X_o and Y_o

Bearing Type		Single Row Bearings (1)		Double Row Bearings (3)	
		X_o	Y_o	X_o	Y_o
Radial Contact Groove Ball Bearings (1)		0.6	0.5	0.6	0.5
Angular Contact Groove Ball Bearings (2)	$\alpha = 20^\circ$	0.5	0.42	1	0.84
	$\alpha = 25^\circ$	0.5	0.38	1	0.76
	$\alpha = 30^\circ$	0.5	0.33	1	0.66
	$\alpha = 35^\circ$	0.5	0.29	1	0.58
	$\alpha = 40^\circ$	0.5	0.26	1	0.52
Self-aligning Ball Bearings		0.5	$0.22 \cot \alpha$	1	$0.44 \cot \alpha$

Notes: (1) P_o is always $\geq F_r$

(2) For two similar single row angular contact ball bearings mounted "face-to-face" or "back-to-back", use the values of X_o and Y_o which apply to a double row angular contact ball bearing. For two or more similar single row angular contact ball bearings mounted "in tandem", use the values of X_o and Y_o which apply to a single row angular contact ball bearing.

(3) Double row bearings are presumed to be symmetrical.

(4) Permissible maximum value of F_a/C_o depends on the bearing design (groove depth and internal clearance).

DYNAMIC CAPACITY OF A BEARING is based on the fatigue life of the material, contrasted with the static capacity which is based on permanent deformation or brinelling. *It is significant to note that, in general, a bearing rotating at low speed has a higher rating than the static rating since the brinelling that takes place is more evenly distributed; consequently, a greater amount of permanent deformation may be tolerated with rotation.*

Life of a bearing can be defined either in terms of hours of rotation at a certain speed, or life can be defined in terms of number of revolutions. It is necessary to define life in terms of the performance of a group of bearings, since the life of a single bearing cannot be predicted. Bearings are rated on either of two bases, depending upon the manufacturer:

(*1*) the average life of a group of bearings

(*2*) the life which 90% of the bearings will reach or exceed. The ratings as given by the AFBMA are based upon a life which 90% of the bearings in a group will reach or exceed.

The longest life of a single bearing is seldom longer than 4 times the average life. The life which 50% of a group of bearings will complete or exceed is approximately 5 times the life which 90% of the bearings will complete or exceed. The maximum life of a single bearing is about 30 to 50 times the minimum life. Thus, where dependability and reliability are essential for a single bearing, larger factors of safety must be used, since there is no way of predicting beforehand how far away from average a given bearing may be.

The specific dynamic capacity C of a bearing is defined as the constant radial load in a radial bearing (or constant thrust load in a thrust bearing) that can be carried for a minimum life of 1,000,000 revolutions (which is equivalent to 500 hours of operation at 33.3 rpm); the minimum life in the definition is that life which 90% of the bearings of a group will reach or exceed. Specific dynamic capacity is based upon the inner ring rotating and the outer ring stationary. (Note that the average life would then correspond to about 5 times as much, or 5,000,000 revolutions, which would correspond to 2500 hours at 33.3 rpm.)

The following information on the method of evaluating dynamic load ratings of radial ball bearings, furnished by the Anti-Friction Bearing Manufacturers Association, Inc. and reproduced with their permission gives the definitions, methods of calculations of the basic load ratings, rating life, and equivalent load, and necessary constants for radial ball bearings, which have been selected to serve as illustration of the procedures used in rating all bearings. Similar information for other bearings has been prepared by the AFBMA, but is not given here. Note that the information can be used to determine the basic load rating for a given bearing, but the selection of a bearing requires the tabulation of the results for a series of bearings since the ball diameter and number of balls is variable.

II. METHOD OF EVALUATING DYNAMIC LOAD RATINGS FOR RADIAL BALL BEARINGS

A. Definitions

(1) The *life* of an individual ball bearing is defined as the number of revolutions (or hours at some given constant speed) which the bearing runs before the first evidence of fatigue develops in the material of either ring or of any of the rolling elements.

(2) The *rating life* of a group of apparently identical ball bearings is defined as the number of revolutions (or hours at some given constant speed) that 90 percent of a group of bearings will complete or exceed before the first evidence of fatigue develops. As presently determined, the life which 50 percent of the group of ball bearings will complete or exceed is approximately five times this rating life.

(3) The *basic load rating* is that constant stationary radial load which a group of apparently identical ball bearings with stationary outer ring can endure for a rating life of one million revolutions of the inner ring. In single row angular contact ball bearings, the basic load rating relates to the radial component of the load, which results in a purely radial displacement of the bearing rings in relation to each other.

(4) Load ratings, if given for specific speeds, are to be based on a rating life of 500 hours.

(5) The *equivalent load* is defined as that constant stationary radial load which, if applied to a bearing with rotating inner ring and stationary outer ring, would give the same life as that which the bearing will attain under the actual conditions of load and rotation.

B. Calculation of Basic Load Rating, Rating Life and Equivalent Load

(1) It is recognized that revisions of this recommendation may be required from time to time as the result of improvements or new developments.

(2) **Basic Load Rating**: The magnitude of the basic load rating C, for radial and angular contact ball bearings, except filling slot bearings, with balls not larger than 25.4 mm or 1 inch in diameter, is

$$C = f_c (i \cos \alpha)^{0.7} Z^{2/3} D^{1.8};$$

with balls larger than 25.4 mm in diameter when kg and mm units are used,

$$C = f_c (i \cos \alpha)^{0.7} Z^{2/3}\, 3.647 D^{1.4};$$

with balls larger than 1 inch in diameter when pound and inch units are used,

$$C = f_c (i \cos \alpha)^{0.7} Z^{2/3} D^{1.4}$$

where i = number of rows of balls in any one bearing

α = nominal angle of contact = nominal angle between the line of action of the ball load and a plane perpendicular to the bearing axis

Z = number of balls per row

D = ball diameter

f_c = a factor which depends on the units used, the geometry of the bearing components, the accuracy to which the various bearing parts are made and the material.

Values of f_c are obtained by multiplying the value of f_c/f from the appropriate column of Table II-1 by a factor f, covered in Appendix 1 (page 262).

Table II-1

Factor $\frac{f_c}{f}$

$\frac{D \cos \alpha}{d_m}$ (1)	$\frac{f_c}{f}$		
	Single row radial contact, single and double row angular contact groove ball bearings (2)	Double row radial contact groove ball bearings	Self-aligning ball bearings
0.05	0.476	0.451	0.176
0.06	0.500	0.474	0.190
0.07	0.521	0.494	0.203
0.08	0.539	0.511	0.215
0.09	0.554	0.524	0.227
0.10	0.566	0.537	0.238
0.12	0.586	0.555	0.261
0.14	0.600	0.568	0.282
0.16	0.608	0.576	0.303
0.18	0.611	0.579	0.323
0.20	0.611	0.579	0.342
0.22	0.608	0.576	0.359
0.24	0.601	0.570	0.375
0.26	0.593	0.562	0.390
0.28	0.583	0.552	0.402
0.30	0.571	0.541	0.411
0.32	0.558	0.530	0.418
0.34	0.543	0.515	0.420
0.36	0.527	0.500	0.421
0.38	0.510	0.484	0.418
0.40	0.492	0.467	0.412

Notes: (1) d_m denotes the pitch diameter of the ball set. For values of $\frac{D \cos \alpha}{d_m}$ other than given in the table, f_c/f is obtained by linear interpolation.

(2) a. When calculating the basic load rating for a unit consisting of two similar single row radial contact ball bearings in a duplex mounting, the pair is considered as one double row radial contact ball bearing.

b. When calculating the basic load rating for a unit consisting of two similar single row angular contact ball bearings in a duplex mounting, "face-to-face" or "back-to-back", the pair is considered as one double row angular contact ball bearing.

c. When calculating the basic load rating for a unit consisting of two or more similar single row angular contact ball bearings mounted "in tandem", properly manufactured and mounted for equal load distribution, the rating of the combination is the number of bearings to the 0.7 power times the rating of a single row ball bearing. If for some technical reason the unit may be treated as a number of individually interchangeable single row bearings, this footnote (2)c does not apply.

(3) **Rating Life:** The approximate magnitude of the rating life L for ball bearings, except filling slot bearings, is

$$L = (C/P)^3 \text{ million revolutions}$$

where P = the equivalent load.

(4) **Equivalent Load:** The magnitude of the equivalent load P for radial and angular contact ball bearings of conventional types, except filling slot bearings, under combined constant radial and constant thrust loads, is

$$P = XVF_r + YF_a$$

where X = a radial factor, Y = a thrust factor, F_a = the thrust load, V = a rotation factor, F_r = the radial load

Values of X, V and Y are given in Table II-2. The factor V, due to lack of sufficient experimental evidence, is used as a matter of precaution.

Table II-2
Factors X, V and Y

Bearing Type			In Relation to the Load the Inner Ring is		Single Row Bearings(2)		Double Row Bearings (3)				e
			Rotating	**Stationary**	$\frac{F_a}{VF_r} > e$		$\frac{F_a}{VF_r} \leqq e$		$\frac{F_a}{VF_r} > e$		
			V	V	X	Y	X	Y	X	Y	
Radial Contact Groove Ball Bearings(4)	$\frac{F_a}{C_0}$ (1)	$\frac{F_a}{iZD^2}$ **Units** lb, in.									
	0.014	25				2.30				2.30	0.19
	0.028	50				1.99				1.99	0.22
	0.056	100				1.71				1.71	0.26
	0.084	150	1	1.2	0.56	1.55	1	0	0.56	1.55	0.28
	0.11	200				1.45				1.45	0.30
	0.17	300				1.31				1.31	0.34
	0.28	500				1.15				1.15	0.38
	0.42	750				1.04				1.04	0.42
	0.56	1000				1.00				1.00	0.44
Angular Contact Groove Ball Bearings with Contact Angle(4):	$\frac{iF_a}{C_0}$ (1)	$\frac{F_a}{ZD^2}$ **Units** lb, in.			For this type use the X, Y and e values applicable to single row radial contact bearings						
	0.014	25						2.78		3.74	0.23
	0.028	50						2.40		3.23	0.26
	0.056	100						2.07		2.78	0.30
	0.085	150	1	1.2			1	1.87	0.78	2.52	0.34
5°	0.11	200						1.75		2.36	0.36
	0.17	300						1.58		2.13	0.40
	0.28	500						1.39		1.87	0.45
	0.42	750						1.26		1.69	0.50
	0.56	1000						1.21		1.63	0.52
	0.014	25				1.88		2.18		3.06	0.29
	0.029	50				1.71		1.98		2.78	0.32
	0.057	100				1.52		1.76		2.47	0.36
	0.086	150				1.41		1.63		2.29	0.38
10°	0.11	200	1	1.2	0.46	1.34	1	1.55	0.75	2.18	0.40
	0.17	300				1.23		1.42		2.00	0.44
	0.29	500				1.10		1.27		1.79	0.49
	0.43	750				1.01		1.17		1.64	0.54
	0.57	1000				1.00		1.16		1.63	0.54
	0.015	25				1.47		1.65		2.39	0.38
	0.029	50				1.40		1.57		2.28	0.40
	0.058	100				1.30		1.46		2.11	0.43
	0.087	150				1.23		1.38		2.00	0.46
15°	0.12	200	1	1.2	0.44	1.19	1	1.34	0.72	1.93	0.47
	0.17	300				1.12		1.26		1.82	0.50
	0.29	500				1.02		1.14		1.66	0.55
	0.44	750				1.00		1.12		1.63	0.56
	0.58	1000				1.00		1.12		1.63	0.56
20°			1	1.2	0.43	1.00	1	1.09	0.70	1.63	0.57
25°			1	1.2	0.41	0.87	1	0.92	0.67	1.41	0.68
30°			1	1.2	0.39	0.76	1	0.78	0.63	1.24	0.80
35°			1	1.2	0.37	0.66	1	0.66	0.60	1.07	0.95
40°			1	1.2	0.35	0.57	1	0.55	0.57	0.93	1.14
Self-aligning Ball Bearings			1	1	0.40	0.4 cot α	1	0.42 cot α	0.65	0.65 cot α	1.5 tan α

Notes: (1) C_o is the static basic load rating.

(2) For single row bearings, when $\frac{F_a}{VF_r} \leqq e$, use $X = 1$ and $Y = 0$.

Two similar single row angular contact ball bearings mounted "face-to-face" or "back-to-back" are considered as one double row angular contact bearing.

For two or more similar single row ball bearings mounted "in tandem", use the values of X, Y and e which apply to one single row ball bearing. When α is smaller than 20°, F_r and F_a are not the total loads but the loads per single row bearing. C_o and i also refer to one single row bearing.

(3) Double row bearings are presumed to be symmetrical.

(4) Permissible maximum value of F_a/C_o depends on the bearing design.

(5) Values of X, Y and e for a load or contact angle other than shown in Table II-2 are obtained by linear interpolation.

(5) This standard is limited to bearings whose ring raceways have a cross sectional radius not larger than:

In deep groove and angular contact ball bearing inner rings:	52% of the ball diameter.
In deep groove and angular contact ball bearing outer rings:	53% of the ball diameter.
In self-aligning ball bearing inner rings:	53% of the ball diameter.

The basic load rating is not increased by the use of smaller groove radii, but reduced by the use of larger radii than those given above.

Appendix 1. A recommended value of the factor f based on current tests of ball bearings of good quality, hardened ball bearing steel is

f = 10 when kg and mm units are used
f = 7450 when pound and inch units are used.

III. METHOD OF EVALUATING DYNAMIC LOAD RATINGS FOR BALL BEARINGS HAVING CROSS SECTION RADII OF THE RING RACEWAYS 57% OF THE BALL DIAMETER

A. Definitions are as given in II A above.

B. Calculation of Basic Load Rating, Rating Life and Equivalent Load

(1) It is recognized that revisions of this recommendation may be required from time to time as the result of improvements or new developments.

(2) **Basic Load Rating:** The magnitude of the basic load rating C, for radial and angular contact ball bearings, is

$$C = f_c (i \cos \alpha)^{0.7} Z^{2/3} D^{1.8}$$

where i, α, Z, D and f_c are as defined in II B above.

Values of f_c are obtained by multiplying the value of f_c/f from the appropriate column of Table III-1 by a factor f, covered in Appendix 1 of Section II.

(3) **Rating Life:** The approximate magnitude of the rating life L, for ball bearings, is

$$L = (C/P)^3 \text{ million revolutions}$$

where P = the equivalent load.

(4) **Equivalent Load:** The magnitude of the equivalent load P, for radial and angular contact ball bearings of conventional types, under combined constant radial and constant thrust loads, is

$$P = XVF_r + YF_a$$

where X = a radial factor

V = a rotation factor = 1.0 for inner ring rotating in relation to load
= 1.2 for inner ring stationary in relation to load

Y = a thrust factor, F_r = the radial load, F_a = the thrust load.

Values of X and Y are given in Table III-2. The factor V, due to lack of sufficient experimental evidence, is used as a matter of precaution.

Table III-1

Factor $\frac{f_c}{f}$

$\frac{D \cos \alpha}{d_m}$ (1)	$\frac{f_c}{f}$ Radial and angular contact groove ball bearings (2)
0.05	0.296
0.06	0.311
0.07	0.324
0.08	0.335
0.09	0.344
0.10	0.352
0.12	0.364
0.14	0.373
0.16	0.378
0.18	0.380
0.20	0.380
0.22	0.378
0.24	0.373
0.26	0.368
0.28	0.362
0.30	0.355
0.32	0.347
0.34	0.337
0.36	0.327
0.38	0.317
0.40	0.306

Notes (1) and (2) under Table II-1 apply also to Table III-1.

Table III-2

Factors X, Y and e

Bearing Type		Single Row Bearings (1)		Double Row Bearings (3)				e
		$\frac{F_a}{VF_r} > e$		$\frac{F_a}{VF_r} \leqq e$		$\frac{F_a}{VF_r} > e$		
		X	Y	X	Y	X	Y	
Radial Contact Groove Ball Bearings	$\frac{F_a}{iZD^2}$ **Units** lb, in.							
	25		3.09				3.09	0.09
	50		2.77				2.77	0.12
	100		2.43				2.43	0.14
	150		2.23				2.23	0.15
	200	0.56	2.10	1	0	0.56	2.10	0.16
	300		1.92				1.92	0.18
	500		1.71				1.71	0.21
	750		1.56				1.56	0.23
	1000		1.44				1.44	0.24
Angular Contact Groove Ball Bearings with Contact Angle:	$\frac{F_a}{ZD^2}$ **Units** lb, in.	For this type use the X, Y and e values applicable to single row radial contact bearings						
5°	25				3.69		5.02	0.17
	50				3.30		4.49	0.19
	100				2.89		3.94	0.22
	150			1	2.66	0.78	3.63	0.24
	200				2.50		3.41	0.25
	300				2.29		3.12	0.27
	500				2.04		2.78	0.31
	750				1.86		2.53	0.34
	1000				1.72		2.35	0.36
10°	25		2.20		2.55		3.58	0.25
	50		2.09		2.41		3.39	0.26
	100		1.94		2.24		3.14	0.28
	150		1.84		2.13		2.99	0.29
	200	0.46	1.77	1	2.04	0.75	2.87	0.31
	300		1.66		1.92		2.69	0.33
	500		1.53		1.77		2.49	0.35
	750		1.44		1.66		2.33	0.38
	1000		1.36		1.57		2.21	0.40
15°	25		1.55		1.74		2.52	0.35
	50		1.51		1.70		2.46	0.36
	100		1.48		1.66		2.41	0.36
	150		1.42		1.59		2.31	0.38
	200	0.44	1.39	1	1.56	0.72	2.25	0.39
	300		1.34		1.50		2.17	0.41
	500		1.26		1.42		2.05	0.43
	750		1.20		1.35		1.96	0.45
	1000		1.16		1.30		1.88	0.47
20°		0.43	1.14	1	1.25	0.70	1.86	0.50
25°		0.41	0.95	1	1.00	0.67	1.55	0.62
30°		0.39	0.81	1	0.83	0.63	1.31	0.75
35°		0.37	0.69	1	0.69	0.60	1.12	0.91
40°		0.35	0.60	1	0.58	0.57	0.97	1.08

Notes: (1) For single row bearings, when $\frac{F_a}{VF_r} \leqq e$, use $X = 1$ and $Y = 0$.

Two similar single row angular contact ball bearings mounted "face-to-face" or "back-to-back" are considered as one double row angular contact bearing.

For two or more similar single row ball bearings mounted "in tandem", use the values of X, Y and e which apply to one single row ball bearing. When α is smaller than 20°, F_r and F_a are not the total loads but the loads per single row bearing.

(2) Maximum permissible thrust load depends on bearing geometry.

(3) Double row bearings are presumed to be symmetrical.

(4) Values of X, Y and e for a load or contact angle other than shown in Table III-2 are obtained by linear interpolation.

(5) This standard is limited to bearings whose ring raceways have a cross section radius of 57%.

EQUIVALENT LOAD under conditions of varying loads is given by the constant cubic mean load, or mean effective load F_m, which gives the same life as the variable loads. The various forms given below are alternate expressions for the mean cubic load F_m.

If the loads are constant for periods,

$$F_m = \sqrt[3]{\frac{\Sigma F^3 N}{L_n}} = \sqrt[3]{\frac{F_1^3 N_1 + F_2^3 N_2 + F_3^3 N_3 + \ldots}{L_n}}$$

where F_m = mean cubic load, lb
F = force acting, lb, for N revolutions
L_n = total revolutions for the mean cubic load F_m
F_1, F_2, F_3 = loads acting respectively for N_1, N_2, N_3 revolutions.

If the loads are variable,

$$F_m = \sqrt[3]{\frac{\int_0^{L_n} F^3\, dN}{L_n}}$$

where F = the load at any arbitrary number of revolutions
N = variable number of revolutions
L_n = life, in revolutions, for the mean cubic load F_m.

If the speed of rotation is constant, the load varying with time,

$$F_m = \sqrt[3]{\frac{\Sigma F^3 t}{T}} = \sqrt[3]{\frac{\int_0^{T} F^3\, dt}{T}}$$

where F = the force at any instant of time t
T = time for one cycle of the load variation.

If the load is constant and the speed varies, the average speed may be used, since fatigue occurs in bearings after a certain number of stress repetitions.

Dynamic effect is an additional quantity that has to be taken into account. Factors which SKF recommend be used to multiply the equivalent load based on steady loads vary from 1 to 3.5, depending upon the application.

BEARING SELECTION. A general word of caution is in order regarding bearing selection. While each bearing manufacturer may interpret its test data differently and use different bases of rating, it is necessary that a designer, in selecting bearings, be throughly familiar with the procedures as outlined in the particular catalog he is using. Individual variations occur, as interpretation of life of a group of bearings. [*New Departure* bases its ratings on the expected *average* life of a bearing of 3800 hours and uses a base speed of 1000 rpm. Conversion from the catalog rating of 3800 hours at 1000 rpm to another life (in hours) and another speed (rpm) is given by

$$\text{Desired life, in hours} = (3800\ \text{hr})\left(\frac{1000\ \text{rpm}}{N}\right)\left(\frac{\text{catalog rating, lb, at 1000 rpm}}{F}\right)^4$$

where N is in rpm and F is the actual load in lb.]

INSTALLATIONS OF ROLLING BEARINGS occur with many variations. The designer is usually confronted with the problem of selecting one of many possible variations, taking into account cost, ease of assembly, reliability, ease of disassembly, machining. No exact rules can be laid down as to the specific type of bearing to be used in a given application or to the type of assembly.

Several arrangements for securing the inner race to the shaft, where the shaft is to rotate with the inner race, are shown. Usually the bearing is press fitted on the shaft, with shaft machining dimensions given in the bearing catalogs for different applications.

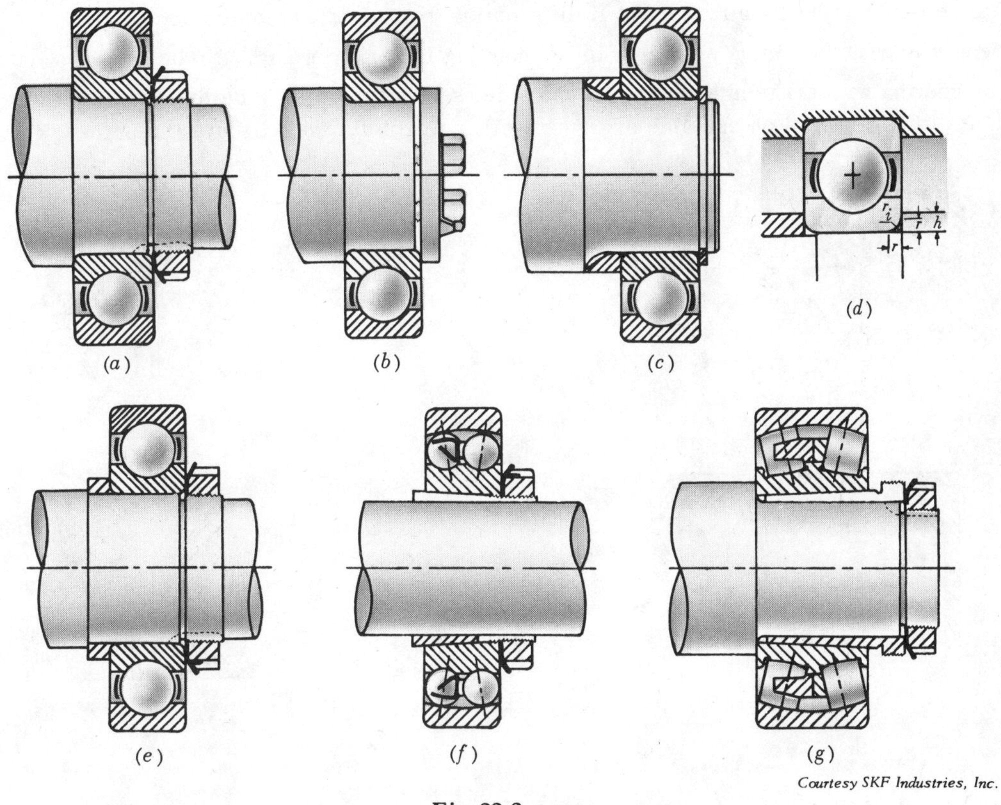

Courtesy SKF Industries, Inc.

Fig. 22-2

Fig. 22-2 above, furnished through the courtesy of SKF and reproduced with their permission, gives the following details:

(*a*) shows a lock nut and washer.

(*b*) shows a plate fastened with screws, a modification of (*a*).

(*c*) shows use of a snap ring and shoulder obtained with an auxiliary piece.

(*d*) shows details of fillets and good contact of the bearing with shoulders. See bearing catalogs for recommended machining dimensions.

(*e*) shows the use of a spacer ring to obtain the necessary shoulder for the bearing. The spacer is fitted with a loose fit on the shaft.

(*f*) shows the use of an adapter sleeve for use on long shafts (cold rolled with no machining) where it is impractical to apply bearings with an interference fit. Friction developed by the press fit is sufficient to prevent displacement of the sleeve axially on the shaft.

(*g*) shows a removable sleeve used in applications where the bearing must be applied with some interference fit, yet must be removed at intervals for inspection or adjustment of machine parts.

The standard bearing mounting provides for bearings to be held rigidly on the shaft by lock nuts and washers. See Fig. 22-3 below. One bearing is held in the housing and the other is free to move in the housing in an axial direction to provide for variations in dimensions and thermal expansion. The left bearing can take thrust in either direction. Figures 22-3 to 22-8 inclusive are furnished through the courtesy of *New Departure* and reproduced with their permission.

An alternate arrangement, where axial movement need not be restricted, is shown in Fig. 22-4 below. Lock nuts and washers are not necessary. The total movement for the bearings is from 0.015″ 0.020″. Thrust to the right is taken by the right bearing and thrust to the left is taken by the left bearing. Note that shims can be used with this arrangement if axial movement is to be restricted. Care should be taken with this arrangement if differential thermal expansion occurs.

An arrangement using a snap ring in the housing is shown in Fig. 22-5 below.

A bearing with a shield and seal on one side, shown in Fig. 22-6 below, is used where protection against dirt is required on one side and where oil is available, usually by splash feed, on the other.

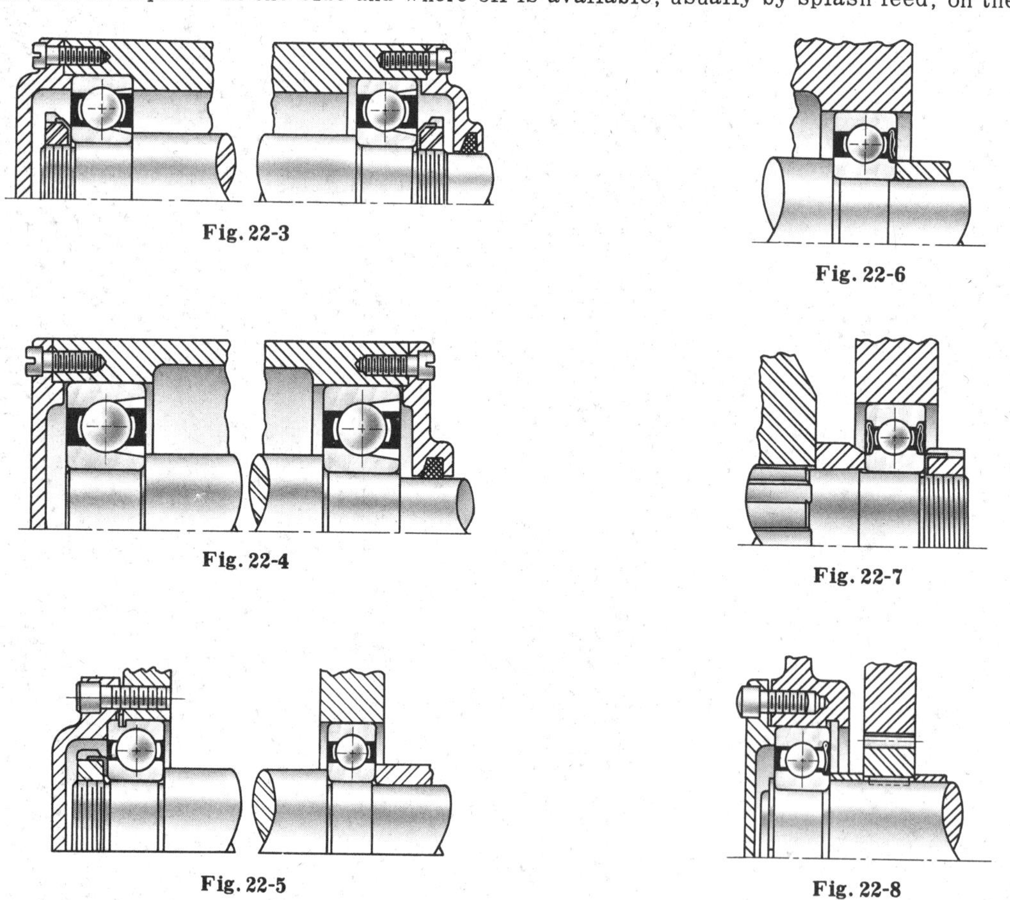

Fig. 22-3

Fig. 22-6

Fig. 22-4

Fig. 22-7

Fig. 22-5

Fig. 22-8

Courtesy New Departure

A bearing with a shield and seal on both sides, shown in Fig. 22-7 above, protects the bearing from contamination and grease leakage. The bearing is packed with grease by the manufacturer.

A bearing with a shield only, shown in Fig. 22-8 above, protects the bearing from dirt or metal particles that might come from within the machine, except for that fine enough to be carried in by the splash oil.

Artificial cooling is required in applications where the heat generated cannot be readily dissipated for reasonable temperatures of operation. A high bearing temperature (generally above 200°F, with most industrial applications running at 110°-180°F) would in general require special bearing design, or a shortened life of the bearing would result. A determination of heat generated and heat dissipation capacity should be made in critical designs.

SOLVED PROBLEMS

1. What is the approximate friction horsepower loss in a single radial ball bearing having a bore diameter of 2.1654″ and subjected to a radial load of 5000 lb? The shaft rotates at 600 rpm.

Solution:

$$\text{Friction torque } M_t = Ff(D/2) = (5000)(0.0015)(2.1654/2) = 8.1 \text{ in-lb}$$

$$\text{Friction hp loss} = M_t N/63{,}000 = (8.1)(600)/63{,}000 = 0.077 \text{ hp}$$

2. Determine the approximate friction torque M_t expected in a radial deep groove bearing under a radial load of 1960 lb. The bearing is series 302, with a bore of 0.5906″ – 0.5903″.

Solution:

$$\text{Friction torque } M_t = Ff(D/2) = (1960)(0.0015)(0.5906/2) = 0.868 \text{ in-lb}$$

3. Derive Stribeck's equation for the static capacity of a single row radial deep groove ball bearing, assuming rigid races and equally spaced balls. Also, determine the maximum load on a ball. (Express the result in terms of the diameter D of the balls and the number of balls, Z.)

Solution:

(*a*) The radial load C_o is balanced by the vertical components of the forces acting on the race through the balls in the lower half of the bearing:

$$C_o = F_1 + 2F_2 \cos\theta + 2F_3 \cos 2\theta + \ldots$$

(*b*) A second consideration to permit solution of the above is obtained from deflection relations. The radial deflection at load F_1 is δ_1, that at load F_2 is δ_2, etc., with

$$\delta_2 = \delta_1 \cos\theta, \quad \delta_3 = \delta_1 \cos 2\theta, \quad \text{etc.}$$

if the races are assumed to remain circular in shape.

(*c*) Also, the relation of deflections and loads is given by the following, which are verified from the Hertz stress equations:

$$\frac{F_1}{F_2} = \frac{\delta_1^{3/2}}{\delta_2^{3/2}}, \quad \frac{F_1}{F_3} = \frac{\delta_1^{3/2}}{\delta_3^{3/2}}, \quad \text{etc.}$$

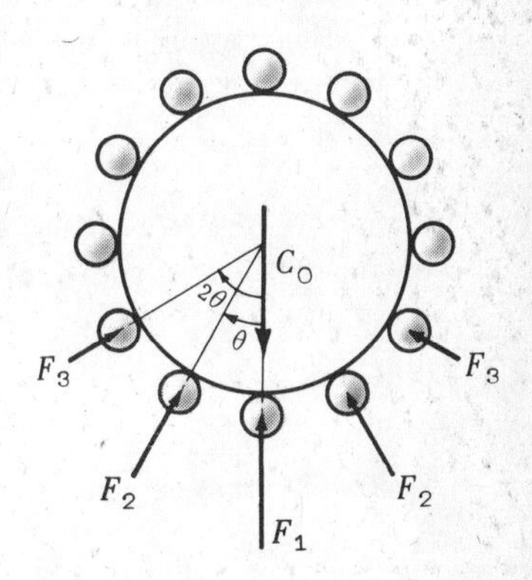

Fig. 22-9

(*d*) Substitution of (*b*) and (*c*) into (*a*) gives

$$C_o = F_1[1 + 2(\cos\theta)^{5/2} + 2(\cos 2\theta)^{5/2} + \ldots].$$

(*e*) The angle θ depends upon the number of balls Z: $\theta = 360°/Z$.

(*f*) Rewrite (*d*) as $C_o = F_1 M$, where $M = [1 + 2(\cos\theta)^{5/2} + 2(\cos 2\theta)^{5/2} + \ldots]$.

(*g*) Stribeck found that Z/M was practically a constant quantity regardless of the number of balls, the average value being about 4.37. He suggested using a value of 5 for practical conditions to account for internal clearance and out-of-round deformations that occured. Later experimental work confirmed his conclusion. Thus the maximum load on a ball can be expressed, for a radial bearing under radial loading, as

$$F_1 = \frac{C_o Z}{ZM} = \frac{C_o(5)}{Z}$$

(*h*) Stribeck found from experimental work that the load F_1 to produce a given permanent deformation between two balls of the same diameter could be given by

$$F_1 = KD^2$$

where K is a proportionality constant. Thus $KD^2 = 5C_o/Z$, or the static radial capacity of a bearing is

$$C_o = KZD^2/5$$

Hence the static capacity $C_o = KZD^2/5$, and the maximum load on a ball is $F_1 = 5C_o/Z$.

4. Using the constant $K = 8820$ in Stribeck's equation, compute the static capacity of a single row deep groove ball bearing series 208 with 9 balls having a diameter of 15/32 in. and compare with:

(a) SKF static rating for a deep groove single row bearing series 6208 having 9 balls of diameter 15/32 in.

(b) New Departure static rating for a deep groove bearing 3208 having 9 balls of diameter 15/32 in.

(c) Using the AFBMA rating, determine the static rating for a single row radial contact groove ball bearing having 9 balls of diameter 15/32 in.

Solution:

$$C_o = KZD^2/5 = (8820)(9)(15/32)^2/5 = 3490 \text{ lb}$$

(a) From SKF Catalog, the static rating of a 6208 bearing is 3520 lb.

(b) From New Departure Catalog, the quiet running limiting rating for a stationary 3208 bearing is given as 3350 lb. For the particular bearing chosen, for the same size balls and number of balls, the discrepancy is small and is due to a difference of interpretation and different constants used by the manufacturers.

(c) The AFBMA rating is determined from

$$C_o = f_o iZD^2 \cos\alpha = (1780)(1)(9)(15/32)^2(\cos 0^\circ) = 3520 \text{ lb}$$

where f_o is found in Table I-1.

It is of interest to note that if the bearing is not to operate at high speed after static loading, the loading may be increased to perhaps 4 times as much as computed above ($4 \times 3520 = 14{,}080$ lb) and the load to fracture is about 8 times as much as computed above ($8 \times 3520 = 28{,}160$ lb).

5. Using the AFBMA rating, determine the equivalent radial static load for a radial deep groove ball bearing subjected to a radial load $F_r = 3000$ lb and a thrust load $F_a = 1000$ lb. ($X_o = 0.6$ and $Y_o = 0.5$, Table I-2.)

Solution:

$$P_o = X_o F_r + Y_o F_a = (0.6)(3000) + (0.5)(1000) = 2300 \text{ lb}$$

But P_o must be equal to or greater than F_r; hence the equivalent radial load = 3000 lb.

6. Using the AFBMA rating, determine the equivalent radial static load for an angular contact ball bearing subjected to a radial load of 2000 lb and a thrust load of 3600 lb. ($X_o = 0.5$, $Y_o = 0.33$ for a contact angle = 30°, Table I-2.)

Solution:

$$P_o = X_o F_r + Y_o F_a = (0.5)(2000) + (0.33)(3600) = 2200 \text{ lb}$$

Since P_o must be equal to or greater than F_r, the equivalent radial load = 2200 lb.

7. Same as Problem 6, except that the thrust load $F_a = 1200$ lb.

Solution:

$$P_o = X_o F_r + Y_o F_a = (0.5)(2000) + (0.33)(1200) = 1400 \text{ lb}$$

which is less than F_r; therefore the equivalent radial load is 2000 lb.

8. Although bearing catalogs tabulate the basic static load rating for bearings, determine the AFBMA static rating for a single row deep groove bearing 6309 which has 8 balls of diameter 11/16 in.

Solution:

The basic static load rating $C_o = f_o iZD^2 \cos\alpha = (1780)(1)(8)(11/16)^2 \cos 0^\circ = 6730$ lb.

(The SKF catalog using the AFBMA standards lists $C_o = 6730$ lb for a 6309 bearing.)

9. An SKF self-aligning ball bearing No. 1310 has a specific dynamic capacity $C = 7510$ lb, (that is, a rating of 7510 lb such that 90% of a group of bearings will last 500 hours at 33.3 rpm). If the equivalent radial load actually applied to the bearing is $P = 10{,}000$ lb, determine:

(*a*) The life in millions of revolutions expected (such that 90% of a group of bearings of the same number will survive), the speed of rotation being 1800 rpm.

(*b*) The life in hours for 90% of the bearings.

(*c*) The average life in hours that can be expected.

Solution:

(*a*) Life in millions of revolutions $= (C/P)^3 = (7510/10{,}000)^3 = 0.423$ million revolutions.

Note that the speed does not enter into the above calculation.

(*b*) Life in hours $= \dfrac{423{,}000 \text{ rev}}{1800 \text{ rev/min}} \times \dfrac{1 \text{ hr}}{60 \text{ min}} = 3.92$ hr.

Thus the life expected for 90% of the bearings is 3.92 hr.

(*c*) The average life expectancy is 5 times as much, or 19.6 hr.

10. Same as Problem 9, except that the equivalent radial load P is 1000 lb.

Solution:

(*a*) Life in millions of revolutions $= (C/P)^3 = (7510/1000)^3 = 423$ million revolutions.

(*b*) Life in hours $= \dfrac{423 \times 10^6 \text{ rev}}{1800 \text{ rev/min}} \times \dfrac{1 \text{ hr}}{60 \text{ min}} = 3920$ hr.

(*c*) The average life expectancy is 5 times as much, or 19,600 hr.

11. A bearing has a specific dynamic radial capacity of 8800 lb. What equivalent radial load P can the bearing carry at 400 rpm if the desired life H is 5000 hours for 90% of the bearings?

Solution:

Desired life in revolutions $= (5000 \times 60)$ min $\times$ 400 rev/min $= 120 \times 10^6$ rev.

Life in millions of revolutions $= (C/P)^3$ or $120 = (8800/P)^3$, from which $P = 1780$ lb.

12. What specific dynamic capacity C is necessary for a desired life of $H = 10{,}000$ hours (for 90% of the bearings) for a speed of 650 rpm and radial load $P = 670$ lb?

Solution:

Desired life in revolutions $= (10{,}000 \times 60)$ min $\times$ 650 rev/min $= 390 \times 10^6$ rev.

Life in millions of revolutions $= (C/P)^3$ or $390 = (C/670)^3$, from which $C = 4900$ lb.

13. Select a deep groove ball bearing for the lower bearing of the vertical shaft, shown in Fig. 22-10, driven by a V-belt. It has been determined that the resultant force $(T_1 + T_2)$ acting on the pulley is 1200 lb. Base the selection on steady loading and a life of 9000 hours (for 90% of a group of bearings). The minimum shaft diameter, based on strength, at the lower bearing is 15/16 in. The shaft rotates at 300 rpm. An SKF bearing catalog will be used for the selection of the bearing in this problem.

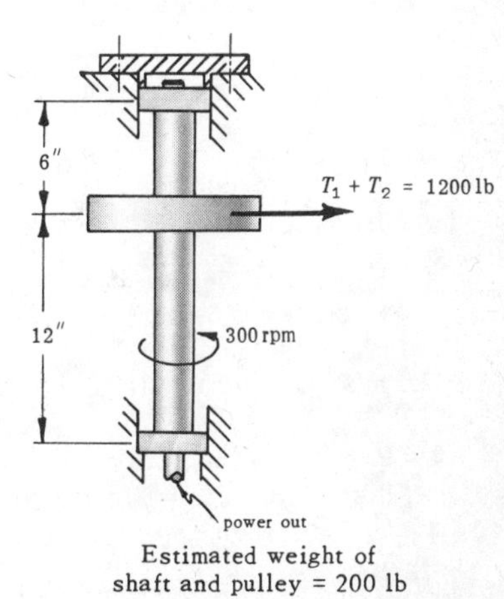

Estimated weight of shaft and pulley = 200 lb

Fig. 22-10

Solution:

(*a*) Even though the load is steady, SKF recommends a factor to take into account both the dynamic effect of belt vibration and the additional force necessary to maintain the proper tension in the belt. The factor recommended is 1.5 to 2.0 for a V-belt. Arbitrarily use 1.5.

(*b*) The steady radial load on the lower bearing is 400 lb, and with a shock factor of 1.5 we will use $F_r = 600$ lb.

(*c*) The thrust load in the vertical direction taken by the lower bearing is $F_a = 200$ lb. No dynamic factor will be applied to this load since the weight is constant.

(*d*) The equivalent radial load is

$$P = XVF_r + YF_a$$

where, for a single row, deep groove bearing:

X = a radial factor given below
V = a rotation factor = 1.0 for inner ring rotating in relation to load
= 1.2 for outer ring rotating in relation to load
Y = a thrust factor given below
e = a reference value given in the table below.

When F_a/VF_r is smaller than or equal to e, use $X = 1$ and $Y = 0$.

When F_a/VF_r is greater than e, use $X = 0.56$ and Y from the table below.

F_a/C_o	0.014	0.028	0.056	0.084	0.11	0.17	0.28	0.42	0.56
e	0.19	0.22	0.26	0.28	0.30	0.34	0.38	0.42	0.44
Y	2.30	1.99	1.71	1.55	1.45	1.31	1.15	1.04	1.00

C_o = basic static load rating (tabulated for convenience in the bearing catalog). The values for F_a/C_o, e and Y are as given in Table II-2 of the AFBMA standards, and are the same in the SKF catalog.

(*e*) Since the bearing is unknown at this point, a trial and error solution is indicated to obtain the necessary constant. Since the shaft size is known to be 15/16 in. from a strength consideration, let us find a single row bearing which has the proper bore and check the capacity. The following sizes are found:

Bearing	6005	6006	6205	6206	6305	6306	6405	6406
Bore (in.)	0.9843	1.1811	0.9843	1.1811	0.9843	1.1811	0.9843	1.1811

(*f*) Let us arbitrarily check a 6205 bearing. The values given for the bearing are: $C_o = 1560$ lb, $C = 2420$ lb. Then $F_a/C_o = 200/1560 = 0.128$ which (by interpolation) corresponds to $e = 0.31$ and $Y = 1.41$.

Since $\dfrac{F_a}{VF_r} = \dfrac{200}{(1)(600)} = 0.33 > e$, use $X = 0.56$ and $Y = 1.41$. Hence

$$P = XVF_r + YF_a = 0.56(1)(600) + 1.41(200) = 618 \text{ lb}$$

Life expectancy $L = (C/P)^3 = (2420/618)^3 = 60$ million revolutions.

Desired life in revolutions = $(9000 \times 60 \text{ min})(300 \text{ rev/min}) = 162 \times 10^6$ revolutions.

Thus a 6205 bearing does not have sufficient capacity in this application.

(*g*) Try a 6305 bearing, which has the bore desired. Then $C_o = 2390$ lb, $C = 3660$ lb; $F_a/C_o = 0.084$; and $e = 0.28$, $Y = 1.55$.

Since $\dfrac{F_a}{VF_r} = \dfrac{200}{(1)(600)} = 0.33 > e$, use $X = 0.56$ and $Y = 1.55$. Hence

$$P = XVF_r + YF_a = 0.56(1)(600) + 1.55(200) = 646 \text{ lb}$$

Life expectancy $L = (C/P)^3 = (3660/646)^3 = 182$ million revolutions, and the desired life is 162 million revolutions.

A 6305 bearing has a larger capacity than necessary, but with the bore limited to approximately 15/16 in. the stock 6305 bearing is closest to the requirements. The preferred shaft shoulder diameter is 1.220 in. for the 6305 bearing.

14. Select a ball bearing for the upper mounting of the arrangement shown with problem 13. Radial load $F_r = 800$ lb; desired life = 9000 hr at 300 rpm, or 162×10^6 revolutions. No thrust load is present, i.e. $F_a = 0$.

Solution:

(*a*) The required shaft size is determined by the minimum bearing bore or by the shaft strength requirement.

From the standpoint of the strength requirement, bending is zero at the upper bearing but there is a transverse load causing transverse shear stresses. We will select the minimum bearing bore which will be consistent with strength.

(*b*) The radial load F_r, taking into account the dynamic factor of 1.5, is 800(1.5) = 1200 lb.

(*c*) The necessary specific dynamic capacity C can be found from $L = (C/P)^3$, where $P = XVF_r + YF_a = (1)(1)(1200) + Y(0) = 1200$ lb. Then $162 = (C/1200)^3$ and $C = 6550$ lb.

(*d*) Examination of the bearing catalog gives the following bearings with the corresponding specific dynamic capacity, bore, and outside diameter.

Bearing	C	Bore	O.D.
6015	6830 lb	2.9528″	4.5276″
6211	7500 lb	2.1654″	3.9370″
6308	7040 lb	1.5748″	3.5433″
6406	7460 lb	1.1811″	3.5433″

(The values of C for the bearings above are greater than the desired value of $C = 6550$ lb, but are closest to the desired rating.)

(*e*) If the allowable shear stress in the shaft is taken arbitrarily as 12,000 psi, the size of shaft based on stress is found from

$$s_s = \frac{4V}{3A}, \qquad 12{,}000 = \frac{4(800)}{3(\frac{1}{4}\pi d^2)}, \qquad d = 0.34''$$

We find by comparing (*d*) and (*e*) that the bearing size dictates the size of shaft. If the smallest bore is desired, a 6406 bearing should be used. If the smallest O.D. is desired, either a 6308 or 6406 bearing can be used. (If the preferred shaft shoulder diameter is considered, the value for a 6308 bearing is 1.929″ and the value for a 6406 bearing is 1.535″.)

Thus the use of a 6406 bearing with a smaller shaft size or a 6308 bearing with a larger shaft size are possible. The final choice depends upon actual cost figures of machining and bearings, as well as rigidity and critical speed considerations.

15. One of the bearings that could be selected in the previous problem is an SKF 6406 which has Z = 7 balls of diameter $D = 21/32$ in. The bearing has a specific dynamic capacity $C = 7460$ lb, as listed in the SKF catalog. Determine (*a*) the AFBMA rating for basic static load rating C_o and (*b*) the basic rating C, with $f_o = 1780$ (Table I-1) and $f_c = 4340$ (found below).

Solution:

(*a*) $C_o = f_o iZD^2 \cos\alpha = 1780(1)(7)(21/32)^2 \cos 0^\circ = 5370$ lb (same as SKF rating).

(*b*) $C = f_c(i\cos\alpha)^{0.7} Z^{2/3} D^{1.8} = 4340(1\cos 0^\circ)^{0.7}(7)^{2/3}(21/32)^{1.8} = 7460$ lb (same as SKF rating).

The value of f_c is found as follows, using Table II-1 and Appendix 1.

$\dfrac{D}{d_m}\cos\alpha \approx \dfrac{(21/32)}{2.36}\cos 0^\circ \approx 0.278.$ The approximate relation is used since the pitch diameter d_m of the ball set is assumed to be the average of the inner and outer race diameters, in the absence of specific dimensions. The outer race diameter of a 6406 bearing is 3.5433″ and the bore is 1.1811″. The average pitch diameter d_m of the ball set is approximately $\frac{1}{2}(3.5433 + 1.1811)''$ or 2.36″.

From Table II-1, for $\dfrac{D}{d_m}\cos\alpha \approx 0.278$, $\dfrac{f_c}{f} = 0.583$. From Appendix 1, $f = 7450$. Hence $f_c = 4340$ lb.

Note that the catalog values of the basic rating should be taken from the manufacturer's catalog in actual selection of a bearing.

16. A radial load $F_1 = 1000$ lb acts for two hours on a rolling bearing and then reduces to $F_2 = 500$ lb for one hour. The cycle then repeats itself. The shaft rotates at 300 rpm. Determine the mean cubic load F_m which should be used in rating the bearing for a life of 12,000 hours.

Solution:

$$F_m = \sqrt[3]{\frac{F_1^3 N_1 + F_2^3 N_2}{L_n}} = \sqrt[3]{\frac{(1000)^3(8000\times 60\times 300) + (500)^3(4000\times 60\times 300)}{(12{,}000\times 60\times 300)}} = 893 \text{ lb}$$

where N_1 = revolutions for F_1, N_2 = revolutions for F_2, L_n = total revolutions.

17. A load varies continuously in magnitude in a sinusoidal manner. The direction remains fixed. For a total life of 20,000,000 revolutions at a speed of 400 rpm, determine the mean cubic load F_m if the maximum load is 1000 lb.

Solution:

Since the load variation is repetitive, the mean cubic load for one cycle will be the same as for every cycle. Therefore consider one cycle, or 1 revolution.

The load after any part of a revolution is given by $F = +500 - 500\cos 2\pi N$, where N is the fraction of a revolution (when $N = 0$, $F = 0$; when $N = 1/2$ rev, $F = +1000$; when $N = 1$ rev, $F = 0$).

$$F_m = \sqrt[3]{\frac{\int_0^{L_n} F^3\,dN}{L_n}} = \sqrt[3]{\frac{\int_0^1 (500 - 500\cos 2\pi N)^3\,dN}{1}}$$

$$= \sqrt[3]{(500)^3\left[N - \frac{3\sin 2\pi N}{2\pi} + \frac{3}{2\pi}\left(\pi N + \frac{\sin 4\pi N}{4}\right) - \frac{\sin 2\pi N}{6\pi}(\cos^2 2\pi N + 2)\right]_0^1}$$

$$= \sqrt[3]{(500)^3(2.5)} = 679\text{ lb}$$

Bearing catalogs state that for the case where the load varies as a sine curve, the cubic mean load is obtained by the approximate formula of $F_m = 0.68\,F_{max}$, which agrees with the above calculation.

18. A shaft rotating at constant speed has variable load applied to it. The radial load on a bearing is $F_1 = 500$ lb for $t_1 = 1$ second, $F_2 = 300$ lb for $t_2 = 2$ seconds, $F_3 = 100$ lb for $t_3 = 3$ seconds. The load variation then repeats itself. What is the equivalent load F_m?

Solution:

$$F_m = \sqrt[3]{\frac{\Sigma F^3 t}{T}} = \sqrt[3]{\frac{F_1^3 t_1 + F_2^3 t_2 + F_3^3 t_3}{T}} = \sqrt[3]{\frac{(500)^3(1) + (300)^3(2) + (100)^3(3)}{6}} = 312\text{ lb}$$

Note. The equation $F_m = \sqrt[3]{\frac{\Sigma F^3 N}{L_n}} = \sqrt[3]{\frac{F_1^3 N_1 + F_2^3 N_2 + F_3^3 N_3}{L_n}}$ could also be used here with the same final result. The revolutions for loads F_1, F_2 and F_3, for H hours of operation, are respectively $N_1 = \frac{1}{6}(60H)(\text{rpm})$, $N_2 = \frac{2}{6}(60H)(\text{rpm})$, $N_3 = \frac{3}{6}(60H)(\text{rpm})$; and the total revolutions $L_n = (60H)(\text{rpm})$. Substituting the values in the above equation, we obtain $F_m = 312$ lb.

19. The shaft shown in Fig. 22-11 below has mounted on it a spur gear G and a pulley P. Power is supplied to the pulley by means of a flat belt; power is taken from the shaft through the gear. The shaft is supported by two deep groove bearings. The following information has been established:

Horsepower = 10 (steady load conditions)
Speed of shaft = 900 rpm
Shaft to be machined from hot rolled AISI 1035
Diameter of the pulley = 10.0″
Pitch diameter of the gear = 10.0″
Weight of the pulley is approximately 30 lb
Weight of the gear is approximately 30 lb
Ratio of belt tensions $T_1/T_2 = 2.5$
Gear pressure angle = 20°
The pulley and gear are assembled with light press fits and keyed to the shaft.

The belt forces are perpendicular to the paper with the tight side being T_1 and the slack side being T_2. The tangential force on the gear is F_t and the separating force is F_r. F_t is perpendicular to the paper.

The design of the shaft for strength, critical speed, and rigidity is discussed in the chapters on variable stresses, shaft design, and deflections. The selection of proper single row, deep groove ball bearings is to be made now.

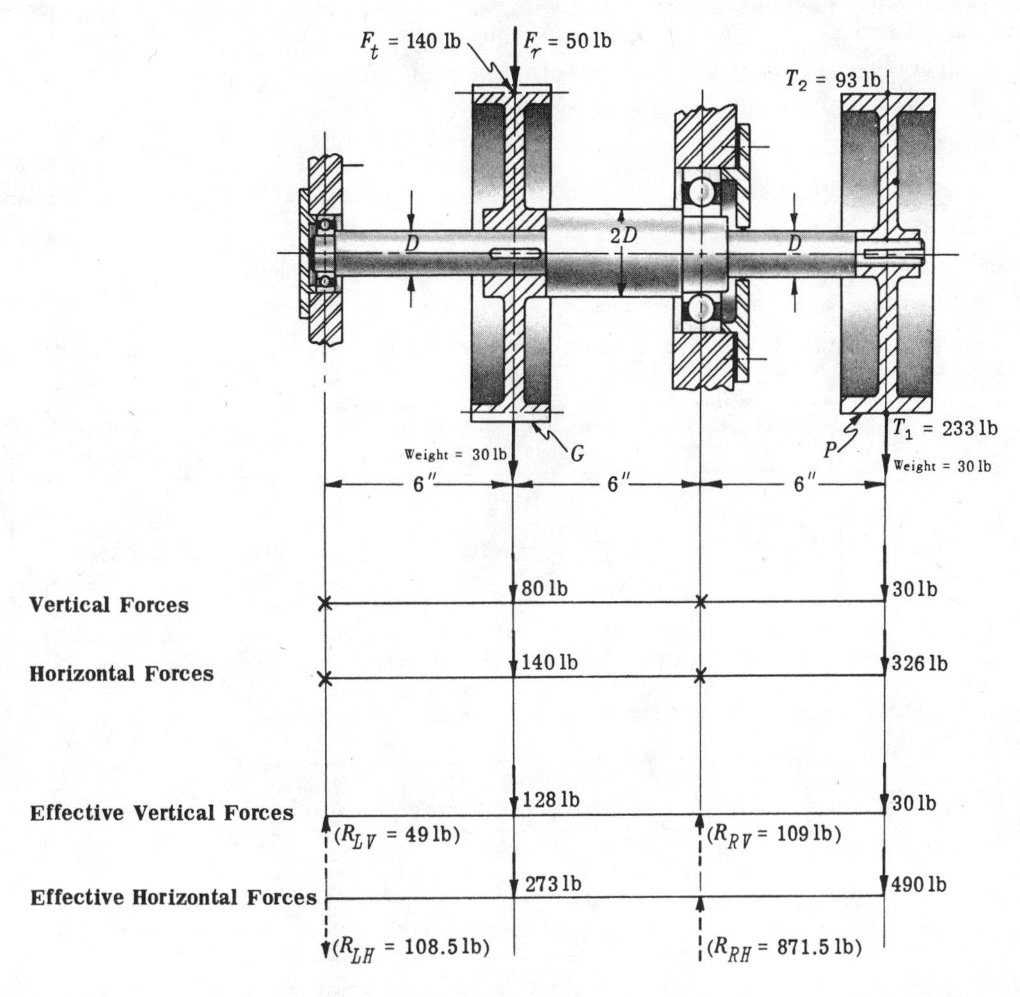

Fig. 22-11

Solution:

Preliminary information that has to be specified is the application and particulars of operation. A bearing suitable for, say, 500 hours need be much smaller than one, say, for 50,000 hours of operation. SKF recommends a life of 20,000 to 30,000 hours for machines in general in the mechanical industries, where machines are fully utilized for 8-hour service. Let us assume that our application is of such a type, with a desired life of 25,000 hours.

The dynamic effect in gear drives is due to two dynamic effects:

(*1*) the vibration introduced by inaccuracies in the gear tooth form, f_k

(*2*) the dynamic effect of the driven machine, f_d.

The gear force is found from $$F_{eff} = F f_k f_d$$

where F is the theoretical load calculated from the torque and geometry. Values of f_k recommended by SKF range from 1.0 to 1.3, and values of f_d recommended by SKF range from 1.0 to 3.0. Let us arbitrarily use $f_k = 1.3$ and $f_d = 1.5$. Thus, $F_{eff} = F(1.3)(1.5) = 1.95F$.

For V-belt drives, a factor f_k to take care of both the dynamic effect of belt vibration and the additional force necessary to maintain the proper tension in the belt varies from 1.5 to 2. Let us use $f_k = 1.5$ for the belt. Thus the effective belt force is $1.5F$.

The forces to be used in the calculations are:

Effective tangential force on the gear	=	1.95 (140)	=	273 lb.
Effective radial force on the gear	=	1.95 (50)	=	98 lb.
Effective belt force T_1	=	1.5 (233)	=	350 lb.
Effective belt force T_2	=	1.5 (93)	=	140 lb.

The effective sum of the belt tensions, $T_1 + T_2$, with the belt strands horizontal, is $350 + 140 = 490$ lb. Note that the dynamic effects are not considered applied to the weight of the pulley or gear.

The reactions for the effective forces are shown on the figure in dashed lines.

Resultant radial load on the left bearing is $R_L = \sqrt{(49)^2 + (108.5)^2} = 119$ lb.

Resultant radial load on the right bearing is $R_R = \sqrt{(109)^2 + (871.5)^2} = 879$ lb.

Revolutions L_n required for 90% of the bearings $= (25{,}000)(60)(900) = 1350 \times 10^6$ revolutions.

Specific dynamic capacity C required for each bearing is:

Left bearing: $L = (C/P)^3$ where $P = R_L$. Then $1350 = (C/119)^3$ or $C = 1300$ lb.

Right bearing: $L = (C/P)^3$ where $P = R_R$. Then $1350 = (C/879)^3$ or $C = 9650$ lb.

Investigation of the SKF bearing catalog reveals the following minimum sizes of single row deep groove bearings which have a basic dynamic capacity closest to $C = 1300$ lb:

Bearing	Basic Dynamic Capacity	Preferred Shaft Shoulder Diameter	Bore	Outside Diameter
6907	1690 lb	1.578″	1.3780″	2.1654″
6004	1620 lb	0.890″	0.7874″	1.6535″
6202	1320 lb	0.703″	0.6693″	1.5748″
6300	1400 lb	0.563″	0.3937″	1.3780″

Since the diameter D of the shaft, based on deflections, is 1.288″, the preferred shoulder diameter can be used as a basis of selection, the 6907 bearing requiring a shaft shoulder diameter which is too large and the 6004 bearing requiring one which is too small. Further investigation of the catalog shows that the preferred shoulder diameter coming closest to 1.288″ in various bearings having greater load capacities than required are:

Bearing	Preferred Shaft Shoulder Diameter	Outside Diameter
6006	1.346″	2.1654″
6206	1.406″	2.4409″
6305	1.469″	2.4409″
6405	1.339″	3.1496″

Considering the economics and size requirements, it appears that a 6006 bearing would be best for the application.

A similar analysis for the right bearing, with a shaft diameter of $2D = 2.576''$, determined from a rigidity analysis, and a minimum specific dynamic capacity requirement of 9650 lb, gives the following minimum sizes in the various series of single row deep groove bearings, based upon load capacity only:

Bearing	Basic Dynamic Capacity	Preferred Shaft Shoulder Diameter	Bore	Outside Diameter
6018	11,500 lb	3.898″	3.5433″	5.5118″
6216	10,000 lb	3.504″	3.1496″	5.5118″
6310	10,700 lb	2.362″	1.9865″	4.3307″
6408	11,000 lb	1.969″	1.5478″	4.3307″

Examination of the catalog gives the minimum size bearing, shown in the adjacent table, coming closest to the required shaft shoulder diameter of $2D = 2.576''$ (and having a specific dynamic capacity larger than 9650 lb. From an economic and size requirement, the 6311 bearing is suitable.

Bearing	Preferred Shaft Shoulder Diameter	Outside Diameter
6311	*2.559″	4.7244″
6411	2.638″	5.039″

*Slightly smaller than 2.576″, but satisfactory.

The diameters as calculated for the different considerations are:

	Diameter D	Diameter $2D$
Strength: Soderberg equation (design factor 1.5)	$1\frac{1}{8}''$	$2\frac{1}{4}''$
ASME shafting code	1.01″	2.02″
Critical Speed (not considering transverse shear deflection)	0.597″	1.194″
Maximum slope of 1° at either bearing	0.470″	0.940″
Maximum deflection of 0.001″ at the gear	1.288″	2.576″

SUPPLEMENTARY PROBLEMS

20. Determine the approximate friction torque expected in a single row deep groove ball bearing under a radial load of 6000 lb. The bore of the bearing is 2.1654″.

Ans. With a coefficient of friction taken as 0.0015, the friction torque is 9.75 in-lb.

21. Using the AFBMA, determine the equivalent radial static load P_o for a radial contact groove bearing subjected to a radial load of $F_r = 2000$ lb and an axial load of $F_a = 2000$ lb.

Ans. $P_o = 2200$ lb (with $X_o = 0.6$ and $Y_o = 0.5$)

22. Same as Problem 21, except that $F_r = 2000$ lb and $F_a = 500$ lb. *Ans.* $P_o = 2000$ lb

23. Determine the AFBMA basic static load rating of a single row, deep groove ball bearing having 10 balls of 5/8 in. diameter. *Ans.* $C_o = 6950$ lb

24. A single row, deep groove ball bearing has a specific dynamic capacity of 10,400 lb (for 1,000,000 revolutions or 500 hours at 33.3 rpm, that 90% of a group of bearings will complete or exceed). (*a*) If the speed of rotation is 1800 rpm and the actual radial load applied to the bearing is 2000 lb, what is the life in revolutions? (*b*) How many hours of operation can be expected for the above? (*c*) What is the average life that can be expected? *Ans.* (*a*) 141×10^6 rev, (*b*) 1310 hr, (*c*) 6550 hr

25. A bearing has a specific dynamic radial capacity of $C = 5500$ lb. What radial load can the bearing carry at 1200 rpm if the desired life is 2000 hours (for 90% of a group of bearings)? *Ans.* 1050 lb

26. A radial load of 2000 lb acts for 5 revolutions and reduces to 1000 lb for 10 revolutions. The load variation then repeats itself. What is the mean cubic load? *Ans.* 1495 lb

27. Determine the 6200 series bearing which will be suitable for a radial load of 400 lb with operation at 1200 rpm for 2000 hours. Loading is steady. Basic dynamic capacities C of various 200 series bearings are:

Bearing	6200	6201	6202	6203	6204
C, lb	805	1180	1320	1650	2210

Ans. $C = 2100$ lb; 6204 bearing is suitable.

28. A 6203 single row, deep groove bearing has a basic static load rating of $C_o = 1000$ lb and a basic dynamic capacity of $C = 1650$ lb. What is the life expectancy (that 90% of the bearings will reach or exceed) for a radial load of $F_r = 300$ lb and a thrust load of $F_a = 280$ lb? The outer ring is stationary.

Ans. $F_a/C_o = 280/1000 = 0.28$, $e = 0.38$, $Y = 1.15$, and the equivalent thrust load is $P = 490$ lb. The life expectancy is 38.2×10^6 revolutions.

29. Same as Problem 28, except that $F_a = 56$ lb.

Ans. $F_a/C_o = 56/1000 = 0.056$, $e = 0.26$, $F_a/VF_r = 56/(1)(300) = 0.187$, $X = 1$ and $Y = 0$, and the equivalent radial load is 300 lb. The life expectancy is 166×10^6 revolutions.

30. A certain ball bearing has dimensions to be taken as shown in Fig. 22-12. If the outer race rotates at 1000 rpm and the inner race is held stationary, what will be the rpm of the cage (spacer)? Assume no slip between the balls and races. *Ans.* 612 rpm

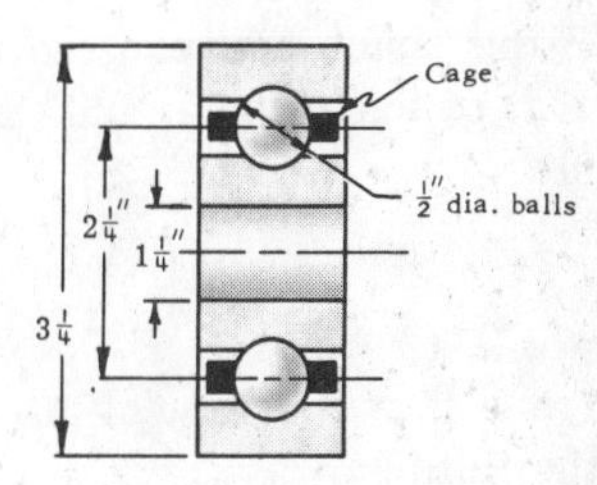

Fig. 22-12

Chapter 23

Lubrication and Bearing Design

LUBRICATION involves the use of a lubricant between the rubbing surfaces of certain machine elements in order to prevent or reduce the actual surface contact, which results in less wear and a lower coefficient of friction. Oils and greases are the most common lubricants, although any substance having the required viscosity properties may be used. The lubricant is usually a liquid. However, some solids, such as graphite, soapstone and other greasy nonabrasive solids, may be used. Even gases, under some circumstances, make good lubricants.

VISCOSITY is one very important property of a lubricant. The fundamental meaning of viscosity may be illustrated by considering a flat plate moving under a force P parallel to a stationary plate, the two plates being separated by a thin film of a fluid lubricant of thickness h, as shown in Fig. 23-1 below.

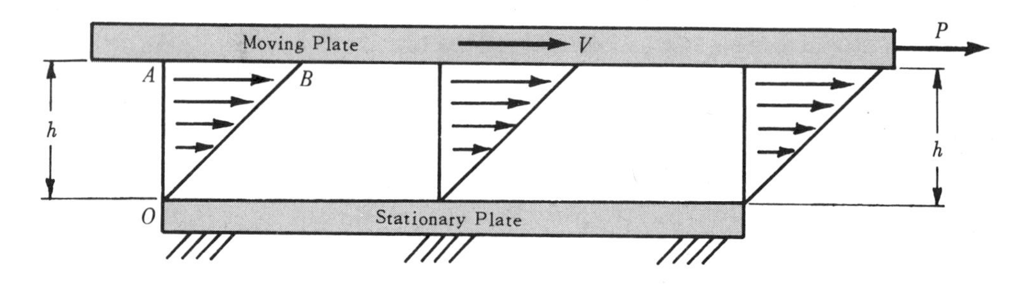

Fig. 23-1

The particles of the lubricant adhere strongly to the moving and stationary plates. Motion is accompanied by a linear slip or shear between the particles throughout the entire height of the film thickness.

If A is the area of the plate in contact with the fluid, the unit shearing stress s_s is

$$s_s = P/A$$

Newton determined that the magnitude of this shearing stress varies directly with the velocity V of the moving plate and inversely with the film thickness h. It is assumed that the fluid completely fills the space between the two surfaces, that the velocity of the fluid at each surface is the same as that of the surface, and that any flow of the fluid perpendicular to the velocity of the plate is negligible.

$$\frac{P}{A} \propto \frac{V}{h}, \qquad \frac{P}{A} = Z\frac{V}{h}$$

where Z is a constant of proportionality and is numerically equal to what is defined as the viscosity of the fluid.

$$Z = \frac{P/A}{V/h} = \frac{\text{shearing stress}}{\text{rate of shearing strain}}$$

If a force of one dyne is required to maintain a plate at a velocity of one centimeter per second, the plate having a constant area of one square centimeter and being separated from the stationary plate by a fluid film thickness of one centimeter, the fluid would have an absolute viscosity of one **poise**. Then 1 poise = 1 dyne-sec/cm². The viscosities of most lubricating fluids are less than a poise, so it is common practice to report absolute viscosity in terms of the **centipoise** which is one hundredth of a poise.

When absolute viscosity is expressed in the English System, the units are lb-sec/in² and unit viscosity is the **reyn** and is represented by

$$\mu\ (\text{reyns}) \;=\; \frac{Z\ (\text{centipoises})}{6.9\times 10^{6}}$$

Two other ways of reporting viscosity which are commonly employed in lubrication work are Saybolt Universal viscosity and Kinematic viscosity, as defined by the following equations,

$$Z \;=\; (0.22\tau - \frac{180}{\tau})\ (\text{centipoises})$$

$$\text{Kinematic Viscosity} \;=\; \frac{Z}{\rho}\ (\text{centistokes})$$

where Z = absolute viscosity, centipoises
τ = Saybolt Universal viscosity, seconds
ρ = density of the lubricant, grams per cm³.

For oils, an average value of $\rho = 0.9$ is usually satisfactory for design calculations. For a more accurate evaluation of ρ at any fahrenheit temperature t, use, for petroleum oils,

$$\rho \;=\; \rho_{60^\circ} - 0.000365(t - 60^\circ)$$

Also, the viscosity of crankcase oils is reported by an SAE viscosity number, related to Saybolt Universal as listed below.

SAE viscosity number	Saybolt viscosity range, sec, at 130°F	SAE viscosity number	Saybolt viscosity range, sec, at 210°F
10	90-120	40	80
20	120-185	50	80-105
30	185-255	60	105-125
40	255	70	125-150

When the stationary plate is parallel to the moving plate as shown in Fig.23-1 above, the velocities of the various laminae of fluid are proportional to their distances from the stationary plate, and the area of the velocity gradient triangle *OAB* is proportional to the volume of fluid per unit time passing a section having unit width. In this case the moving plate will not support a vertical load. If the stationary plate is inclined so that the film thickness varies from h_1 where the oil enters to h_2 where it leaves, the velocity gradient cannot be the same at both positions. The velocity curve is concave at the entrance and convex at the exit as shown in Fig.23-2. The figures thus formed by the velocity curves in the converging film are not triangular but do have equal areas

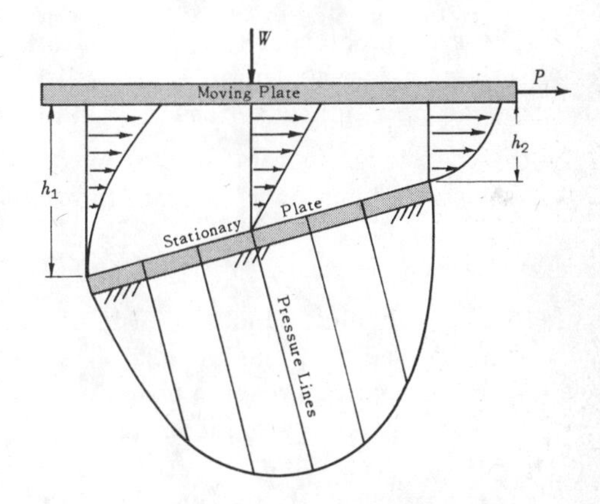

Fig. 23-2

if no end leakage is assumed. The moving plate will now support a load W due to the velocity-pressure relations, which cause a pressure buildup in the oil film from zero to a maximum and back to zero as shown.

JOURNAL BEARINGS make use of the basic theory of the converging film in order to support loads on a film of lubricant. Fig.23-3 below shows the end view of a journal bearing for the three positions of "rest", "start", and "run". Note that in the "rest" and "start" positions

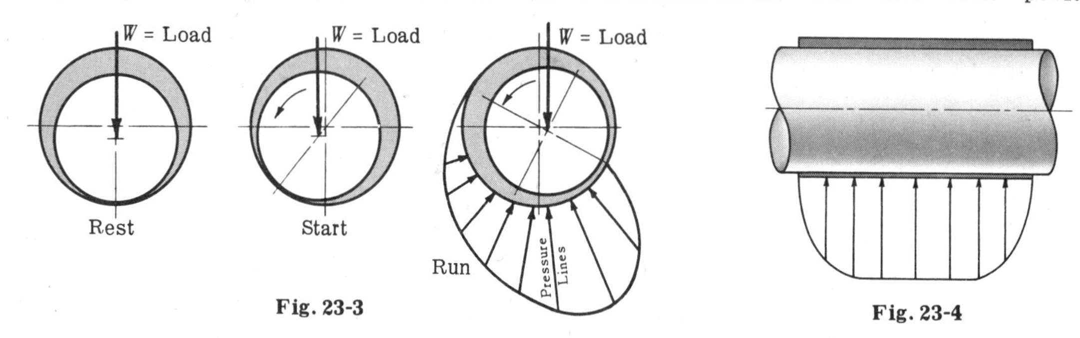

Fig. 23-3

Fig. 23-4

there is contact between the journal (shaft) and the bearing (outer member). However, if the required conditions, as explained later, for perfect or thick-film lubrication are met, the shaft will be separated from the bearing by a film of lubricant as indicated in the "run" position, and the load will be supported by the film pressure. The terms thin-film or imperfect lubrication apply to the situation where bearing design and selection of lubricant have not met all the requirements for thick-film or perfect lubrication, and contact between journal and bearing is not completly prevented. Due to leakage of the lubricant from the ends of the bearing, there is a distribution of pressure in the axial direction as shown in Fig.23-4 above. The load carrying capacity of a journal bearing with perfect lubrication is a function of many variables, but essentially it involves the selection of the proper lubricant to provide perfect lubrication for specified operating conditions, and at the same time to provide for the proper heat balance between the heat generated within the bearing and the heat dissipated in order that the bearing will not exceed a safe specified operating temperature.

HEAT GENERATED, H_g, within a journal bearing is a function of the journal coefficient of friction f,

$$H_g = fW \frac{\pi DN}{12} \text{ ft-lb/min}$$

where H_g = heat generated, ft-lb/min
f = journal coefficient of friction
D = journal diameter, in.
N = journal speed, rpm
W = total radial bearing load, lb.

The main problem at this point is to be able to determine as closely as possible the value of the coefficient of journal friction. It is difficult to obtain a precise value for f, since it varies widely with operating conditions. The discussion in this chapter will be limited to full (360°) journal bearings.

Various investigators, employing dimensional analysis, have shown that the journal coefficient of friction is a function of at least three dimensionless parameters,

$$ZN/p, \qquad D/C, \qquad \text{and} \qquad L/D$$

where Z = absolute viscosity of lubricant at its operating temperature, centipoise
N = speed of journal, rpm; N' = speed of journal, rps (for later use)
p = bearing pressure based on projected area, W/LD psi
W = radial bearing load, lb
D = journal diameter, in.
C = diametral clearance between journal and bearing, in.
L = length of bearing, in.

The relationship between the coefficient of friction and the parameter ZN/p, called the bearing modulus, is of particular interest. The curve of Fig.23-5 is typical, but the slope and intercept of the straight line portion in the thick-film region depend upon variables such as the clearance ratio C/D, and the L/D ratio. Experimental data on small journal bearings by McKee established the following approximate equation for the coefficient of friction,

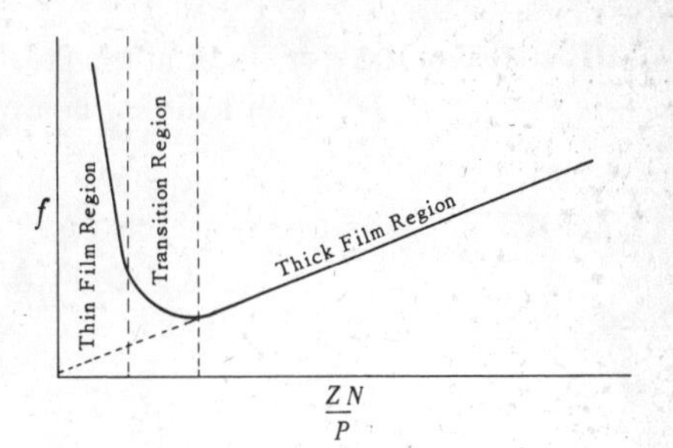

Fig. 23-5

$$f = \frac{473}{10^{10}}\left(\frac{ZN}{p}\right)\frac{D}{C} + k$$

This equation, which is that of the straight line portion of the curve in the thick-film region, may be used for estimating the coefficient of friction.

Experimental data indicate that the value of k may be taken as 0.002 for L/D ratios from 0.75 to 2.8. Fig.23-6 shows how k varies, in general, with the L/D ratio. A practical average value for D/C is 1000, and practical values of L/D range from 1 to 2 when space requirements permit using a long bearing. Practical operating values of ZN/p have been determined for a number of typical applications as listed below. The operating value of ZN/p must be sufficiently large to avoid entering the transition or thin-film regions.

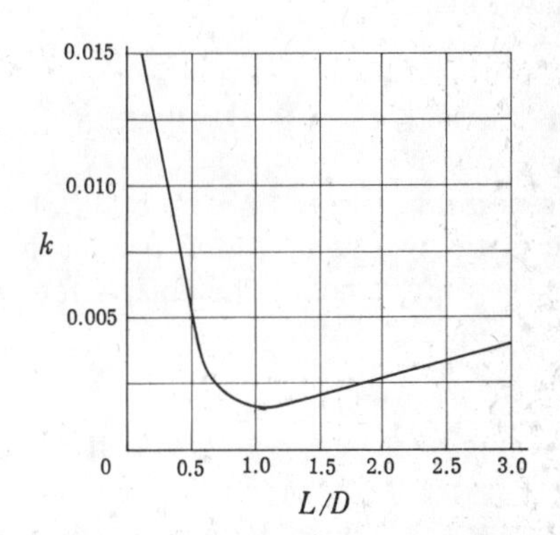

Fig. 23-6

TYPICAL JOURNAL BEARING PRACTICE

Equipment	Bearing	Max Pressure p	Lubricant Z	Lubricant ZN/p
Automobile and Aircraft engines	Main	700-1700	7	15
	Crankpin	1400-3400	8	10
	Wrist pin	2000-5000	8	
Gas and Oil Engines	Main	500-1200	20	20
	Crankpin	1000-1800	40	10
	Wrist pin	1200-2000	65	
Marine Engines	Main	500	30	20
	Crankpin	600	40	15
	Wrist pin	1500	50	
Stationary Steam Engines	Main	200-400	15-60	20
	Crankpin	600-1500	30-80	6
	Wrist pin	1800	25-60	
Reciprocating pumps and compressors	Main	250	30	30
	Crankpin	600	50	20
	Wrist pin	1000	80	
Steam turbines	Main	100-300	2-16	100
Rotary motors and pumps	Shaft	100-200	25	200

OTHER METHODS for determining the coefficient of journal friction are based on Petroff's equation or on hydrodynamic theory.

PETROFF'S EQUATION, which was developed back in 1883, gives an expression for the coefficient of journal friction based on a journal concentric with the bearing (no radial load) and neglects end leakage.

$$f = \frac{\pi^2}{30}\left(\frac{\mu N}{p}\right)\frac{D}{C} = 2\pi^2\left(\frac{\mu N'}{p}\right)\frac{D}{C}$$

Since this equation was derived for an unloaded bearing, it is only an approximation for lightly loaded bearings.

THE SOMMERFELD NUMBER, S, is another dimensionless parameter used extensively in lubrication analysis. Based on hydrodynamic theory, it can be shown that the Sommerfeld number is a function of **attitude** only, as defined below. It may then be plotted against the quantity $f(D/C)$ which is also a function of **attitude** only, and the coefficient of journal friction may be determined. The Sommerfeld number is

$$S = \frac{\mu N'}{p}\left(\frac{D}{C}\right)^2$$

One of the main factors that Petroff's equation fails to take into account is the eccentricity of the bearing when under load. The Sommerfeld number when plotted against $f(D/C)$ in accordance with hydrodynamic theory takes this eccentricity into account. The center of the journal when under load is not concentric with the bearing, but moves approximately along a semicircular arc of diameter $C/2$. This results in the establishment of a **minimum film thickness**, h_o, as shown in Fig. 23-7 (shown greatly exaggerated). The distance between the bearing center and the shaft center is called the **eccentricity** and is denoted by e. The ratio of this eccentricity to the radial clearance is called the **attitude** or **eccentricity ratio**.

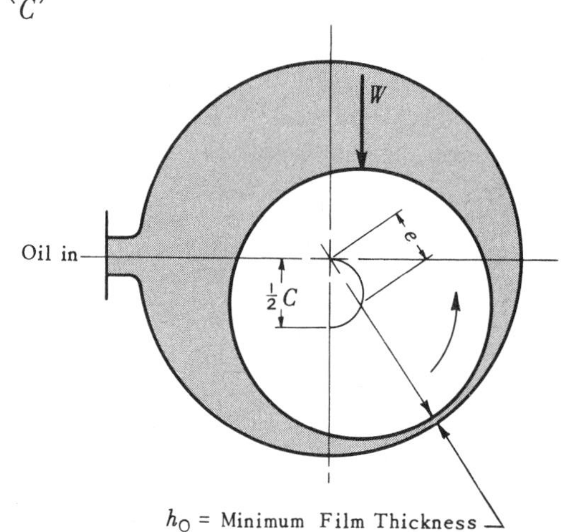

Fig. 23-7

$$\text{Attitude } \epsilon = \frac{2e}{C} = 1 - \frac{2h_o}{C}$$

It should be noted that both the Petroff equation and early plots of $f(D/C)$ versus the Sommerfeld number were based on ideal bearings (no end leakage). Several design methods have proposed the use of end leakage and eccentricity correction factors in conjunction with these equations. In the past most of these methods have been rather inaccurate and not entirely satisfactory.

DESIGN CURVES corrected for end leakage and for various L/D ratios in which performance variables are plotted versus the Sommerfeld number have been prepared by A. A. Raimondi and John Boyd of the Westinghouse Research Laboratories. (ASLE Transactions Volume 1, No. 1, April 1958). Their latest curves were developed on a completly rational basis and the results were obtained by the use of computers. These curves supersede previous curves published by the same authors in 1951. Their previous curves required correction factors for end leakage. The use of these latest curves eliminates completely the need for applying end leakage factors and thus greatly simplifies the task of calculating bearing performance. A portion of these charts arbitrarily chosen for a full journal bearing (360°) having an L/D ratio of one have been approximately reproduced to demonstrate their use. These curves are also based on the possibility that rupture of the film may occur.

The reader should refer to the original article for partial bearings and other L/D ratios, as well as design of a bearing for optimum performance. The original article also covers the case of submerged bearings operating under pressure where film rupture is not likely to occur. Note use of a linear plot in the corner block of the following curves.

COEFFICIENT OF FRICTION may be determined from Fig. 23-8 below, where the coefficient of friction variable $f(D/C)$ is plotted against the Sommerfeld number.

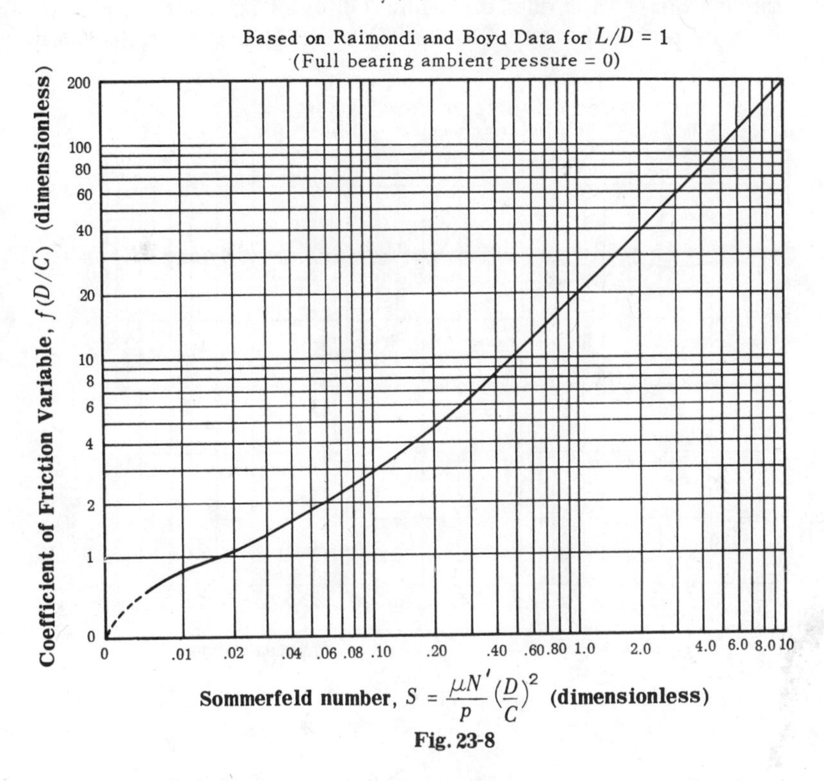

Fig. 23-8

MINIMUM FILM THICKNESS may be determined from Fig. 23-9 below, where the minimum film thickness variable $2h_o/C$ is plotted against the Sommerfeld number.

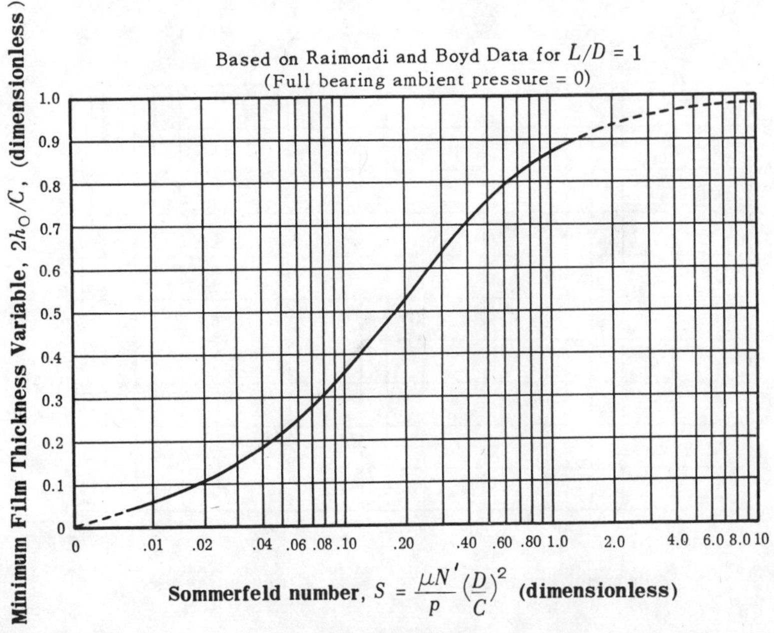

Fig. 23-9

The permissible minimum film thickness depends mainly upon the size and surface finish of the bearing; the rougher the surface, the thicker the film required. For ordinary babbitt lined bearings the film thickness should not be less than 0.00075 in. On larger power machinery the minimum film thickness may be limited to 0.001 to 0.005 in. One rule of thumb is to limit the minimum film thickness to $0.00025D$.

OIL FLOW, Q in^3/sec, through the bearing due to pumping action of the shaft may be determined from Fig. 23-10 below, where the flow variable $4Q/DCN'L$ is plotted against the Sommerfeld number.

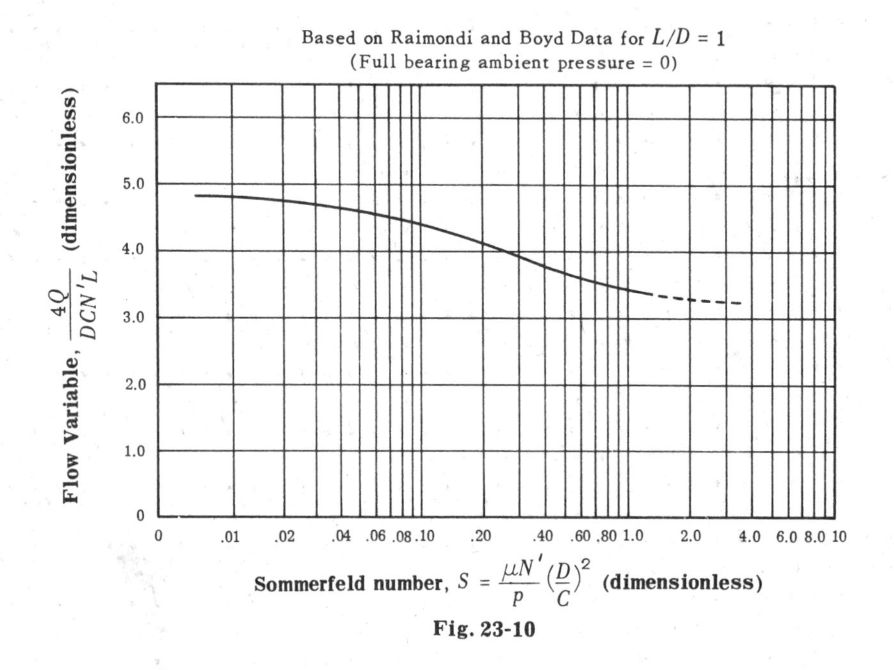

Fig. 23-10

END LEAKAGE, Q_s in^3/sec, from both ends of the bearing may be determined from Fig. 23-11 below, where the Q_s/Q ratio is plotted against the Sommerfeld number. Q_s is the amount of lubricant that must be supplied to a bearing operating under atmospheric pressure to compensate for the loss due to end leakage.

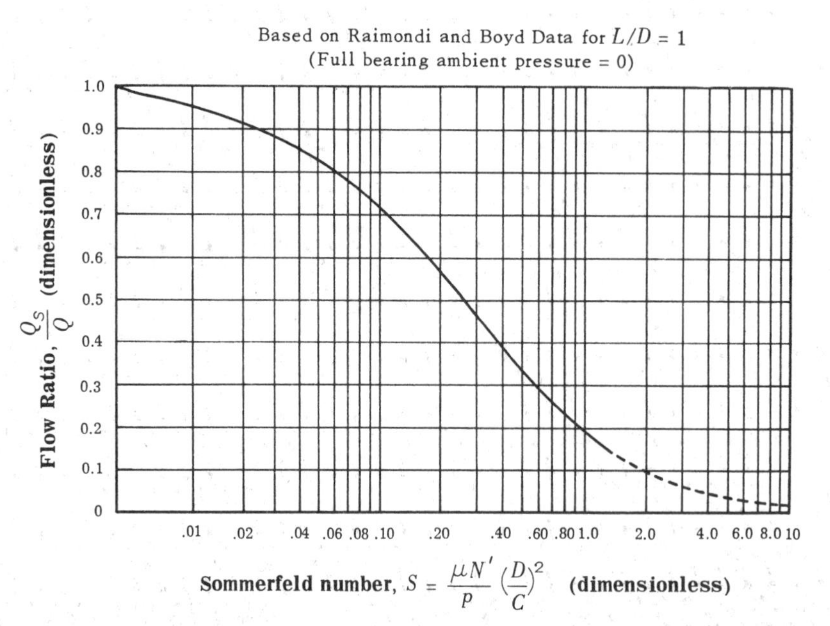

Fig. 23-11

TEMPERATURE RISE of the lubricant as it passes through the bearing may be determined from Fig. 23-12 below, where the temperature rise variable $J\gamma c\,\Delta T/p$ is plotted against the Sommerfeld number. It is assumed that all of the heat generated by friction is effective in raising the temperature of the lubricant as it flows through the bearing.

J = mechanical equivalent of heat = 9336 in-lb/Btu

γ = weight per unit volume of lubricant, lb/in^3 (0.03 for oil)

c = specific heat of lubricant, Btu/lb-°F (0.4 for oil)

ΔT = temperature rise of the lubricant as it passes through the bearing, °F. It may be considered as the temperature rise of the film between the leading and trailing edges of the wedge.

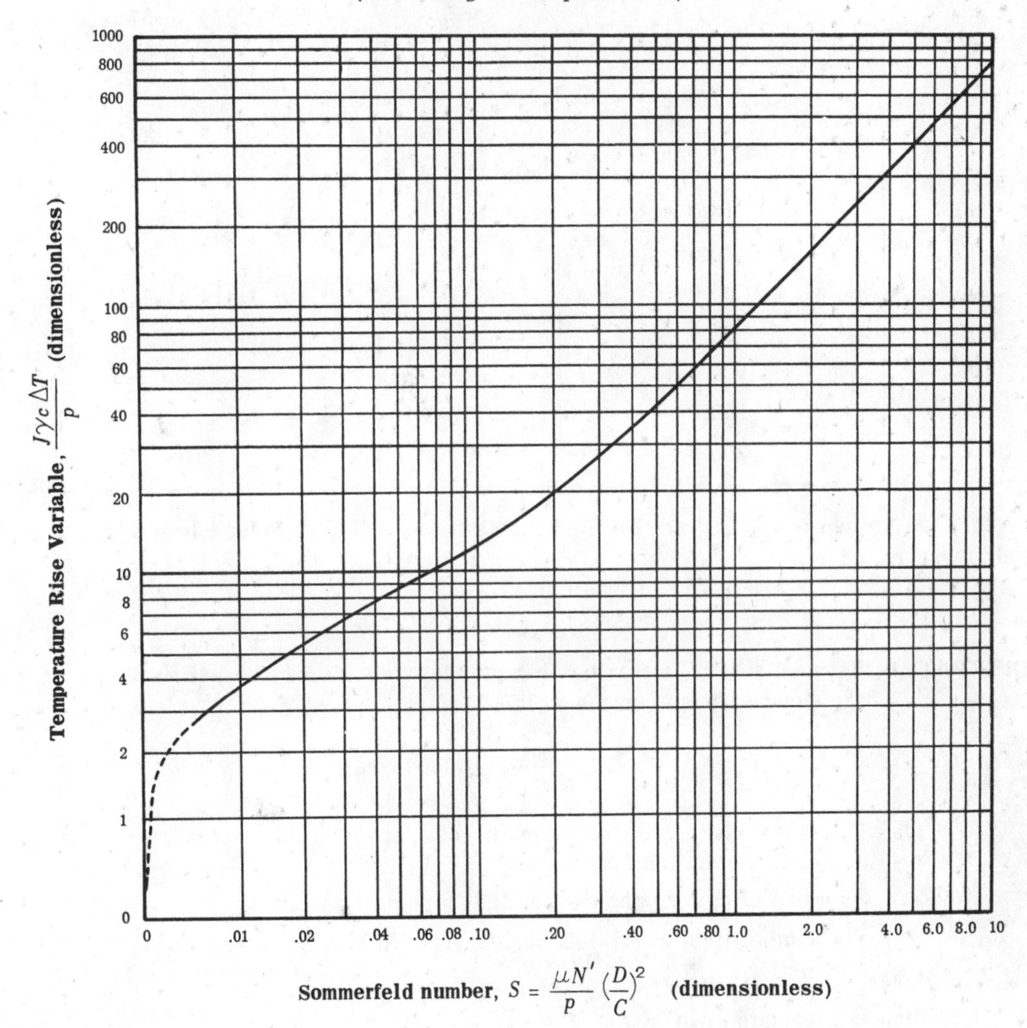

Fig. 23-12

COMPARISON OF THE RAIMONDI-BOYD data with **McKee** data, and with **Petroff's** equation when plotting $f(D/C)$ against the **Sommerfeld** number for a 360° journal bearing having an L/D ratio of one is shown in the following table.

$f(D/C)$ for a 360° journal bearing, $L/D = 1$

Sommerfeld number S	Raimondi-Boyd data for ambient pressure = 0	Petroff's equation	McKee equation assuming D/C = 1000 and using $f = 0.002 + \frac{473}{10^{10}}(\frac{ZN}{p})(1000)$
.01	0.8	0.197	2.196
.02	1.1	0.395	2.39
.04	1.6	0.789	2.79
.06	2.1	1.17	3.12
.08	2.4	1.58	3.57
.10	2.8	1.97	3.96
.20	4.6	3.95	5.92
.40	8.4	7.89	9.84
.60	12.0	11.7	13.8
.80	16.0	15.8	17.7
1.00	20.0	19.7	21.6
2.00	40.0	39.5	41.2
4.00	80.0	78.9	80.
6.00	120.0	117.	119.
8.00	160.0	158.	159.
10.00	200.0	197.	198.

Note that the values for $f(D/C)$ are in close agreement for lightly loaded bearings, i.e. for high Sommerfeld numbers.

HEAT DISSIPATED, H_d, from a 360° journal bearing by heat transfer may be estimated by the following equation based on the work of Lasche,

$$H_d = \frac{(\Delta T + 33)^2}{K}(LD) \text{ ft-lb/min}$$

where $\Delta T = (T_B - T_A)$ = the difference between the bearing surface temperature T_B and the temperature T_A of the surrounding air, °F

K = 31 for bearing of heavy construction that is well ventilated

K = 55 for bearing of light or medium construction in still air

L = length of journal, inches

D = diameter of journal, inches.

The relationship for the operating temperature T_O of the oil, the air temperature T_A and the bearing temperature T_B may be approximated by

$$\Delta T = (T_B - T_A) = \tfrac{1}{2}(T_O - T_A)$$

Average absolute viscosities for typical SAE number oils are plotted vs temperature in Fig. 23-13 below.

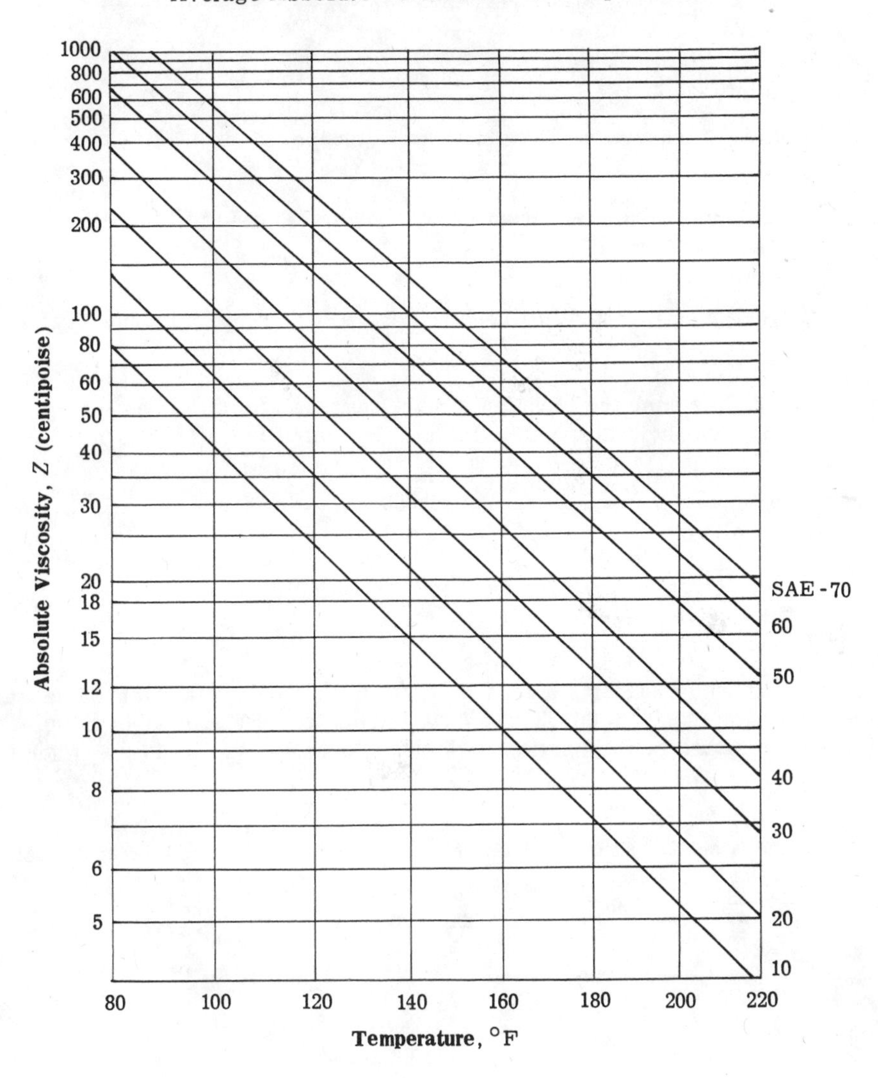

Fig. 23-13

SOLVED PROBLEMS

1. A 3 in. long full journal bearing of diameter 3 in. supports a load of 2700 lb on a journal turning at 1800 rpm. Assuming a D/C ratio of 1000, and an oil having viscosity 10 centipoise at the operating temperature, determine the coefficient of friction by using (*a*) the McKee equation, (*b*) the Raimondi and Boyd curve of Fig.23-8. (Note: $L/D = 1$.)

Solution:

(*a*) Using the McKee equation, $f = 0.002 + \frac{473}{10^{10}}(\frac{ZN}{p})\frac{D}{C} = 0.002 + \frac{473}{10^{10}}\left(\frac{(10)(1800)}{300}\right)(1000) = 0.00484$

(*b*) To use the Raimondi and Boyd curve of Fig.23-8, first calculate the Sommerfeld number S.

$$S = \frac{\mu N'}{p}\left(\frac{D}{C}\right)^2 = 0.145$$

where $\mu = \dfrac{10}{6.9 \times 10^6}$ reyns, $N' = \dfrac{1800}{60} = 30$ rps, and $p = \dfrac{W}{LD} = \dfrac{2700}{3(3)} = 300$ psi.

From Fig.23-8, $S = 0.145$ gives $f(D/C) = 3.7$; then $f(1000) = 3.7$ or $f = 0.0037$.

2. Referring to Problem 1, determine the amount of heat generated using the coefficient of friction as calculated by the McKee equation.

Solution:

$$H_g = fW\frac{\pi DN}{12} = (0.00484)(2700)\frac{\pi(3)(1800)}{12} = 18{,}500 \text{ ft-lb/min}$$

3. For Problems 1 and 2, determine the probable surface temperature of the bearing, using the Lasche equation and assuming that the heat generated is all dissipated in still air at 70° F.

Solution:

Setting the heat dissipated H_d equal to the heat generated H_g, we have

$$H_d = \frac{(\Delta T + 33)^2}{55}LD = H_g, \qquad \frac{(\Delta T + 33)^2}{55}(3)(3) = 18{,}500, \qquad \Delta T = 305^\circ \text{F}$$

Then $T_B = \Delta T + T_A = 305 + 70 = 375^\circ$F (too high).

4. A journal bearing 3 in. long supports a load of 1645 lb on a 2 in. diameter journal turning at 750 rpm. The diametral clearance is 0.00273 in. What should be the viscosity of the oil in centipoise if the operating temperature of the bearing surface is to be limited to 170° F when in still air at 70° F?

Solution:

Use the McKee and Lasche equations and assume the heat generated equals the heat dissipated.

$$f = 0.002 + \frac{473}{10^{10}}\left(\frac{ZN}{p}\right)\left(\frac{D}{C}\right) = 0.002 + \frac{473}{10^{10}}\left(\frac{750Z}{274}\right)\left(\frac{2}{0.00273}\right) = 0.002 + 0.000095Z$$

$$H_g = fW\frac{\pi DN}{12} = (0.002 + 0.000095Z)(1645)\frac{\pi(2)(750)}{12} = 1290 + 61.3Z$$

$$H_d = \frac{(\Delta T + 33)^2}{55}LD = \frac{(170 - 70 + 33)^2}{55}(3)(2) = 1930 \text{ ft-lb/min}$$

Then assuming $H_g = H_d$, we have $(1290 + 61.3Z) = 1930$ or $Z = 10.45$ centipoise.

5. A journal bearing 6 in. in diameter and 9 in. long is supporting a load of 2000 lb at 1200 rpm. If the radial clearance is 0.003 in. and the bearing wastes 2 hp (66,000 ft-lb/min) in friction, what is the oil viscosity at the operating temperature?

Solution: Based on the McKee equation.

$$66{,}000 = fW\frac{\pi DN}{12} = \left[0.002 + \frac{473}{10^{10}}\left(\frac{1200Z}{2000/54}\right)\left(\frac{6}{0.006}\right)\right](2000)\frac{\pi(6)(1200)}{12} \quad \text{or} \quad Z = 10.1 \text{ centipoise}$$

6. A full journal bearing of 4 in. diameter by 6 in. long supports a radial load of 1200 lb. The speed of the shaft is 500 rpm. The room temperature is 90° F and the surface of the bearing is to be limited to 145° F. Select a suitable oil to satisfy the above requirements, if the bearing is well ventilated and no artificial cooling is to be used. Assume $D/C = 1000$.

Solution:

Equate heat generated to heat dissipated, using the McKee and Lasche equations.

$$H_g = fW\frac{\pi DN}{12} = \left[0.002 + \frac{473}{10^{10}}(\frac{500Z}{1200/24})(1000)\right](1200)\frac{\pi(4)(500)}{12}$$

$$H_d = \frac{(\Delta T + 33)^2}{31}LD = \frac{(\Delta T + 33)^2}{31}(24)$$

$\Delta T = T_B - T_A = 145-90 = 55$. Also, $\Delta T = \frac{1}{2}(T_O - T_A)$ or $55 = \frac{1}{2}(T_O - 90)$, and $T_O = 200$.

Now equate $H_g = H_d$ and obtain Z = 16 centipoise at 200°F. This corresponds to an oil having an SAE number between 50 and 60, using Fig.23-13.

7. A tentative design for a full journal bearing calls for a diameter of 3 in. and a length of 5 in. to support a load of 4500 lb. The shaft is to operate at 1000 rpm. It is desired to operate at a bearing surface temperature not to exceed 170°F in a room temperature of 100°F. The oil used has a viscosity of 9.8 centipoise at 240°F. Determine the amount of artificial cooling required, by means of an external oil cooler, if it is expected that the bearing dissipate heat in accordance with $H_d = (\Delta T + 33)^2(15/55)$.

Solution:

$$f = 0.002 + \frac{473}{10^{10}}(\frac{ZN}{p})(\frac{D}{C}) = 0.002 + \frac{473}{10^{10}}(\frac{9.8 \times 1000}{4500/15})(1000) = 0.00355$$

$$H_g = fW\frac{\pi DN}{12} = (0.00355)(4500)\frac{\pi(3)(1000)}{12} = 12{,}550 \text{ ft-lb/min}$$

$$H_d = (170-100+33)^2(15/55) = 2890 \text{ ft-lb/min}$$

Amount of artificial cooling needed = 12,550−2890 = 9660 ft-lb/min

8. A shaft running at 900 rpm is supported by bearings 2 in. in diameter by 3 in. in length. The bearing surface temperature is 180°F while the room temperature is 90°F. The oil used has a viscosity of 12.8 centipoise at the operating temperature of 270°F, the diametral clearance is 0.002 in., and each medium bearing in still air is to operate without artificial cooling. Determine the permissible load W per bearing and the power loss per bearing.

Solution:

$$T_B - T_A = \tfrac{1}{2}(T_O - T_A), \qquad T_B - 90^\circ = \tfrac{1}{2}(270-90), \qquad T_B = 180^\circ\text{F}$$

$$H_g = fW\frac{\pi DN}{12} = \left[0.002 + \frac{473}{10^{10}}(\frac{12.8 \times 900}{W/6})(\frac{2}{0.002})\right]W\frac{\pi(2)(900)}{12}$$

$$H_d = \frac{(\Delta T + 33)^2}{55}LD = \frac{(90+33)^2}{55}(3)(2)$$

Equate $H_g = H_d$ to obtain W = 117 lb. Substitute W = 117 lb into the equation for H_g to get H_g = 1650 ft-lb/min. Hence the power loss = 1650/33,000 = 0.05 hp.

9. A gear is so mounted on a shaft that the total radial load on one bearing is 3000 lb and the total radial load on the other supporting bearing is 4000 lb. Each bearing is 6 in. long. The bearings are machined to 3.502/3.500 and the journals are machined to 3.497/3.495. The viscosity of the oil at various temperatures is given in the table.

Temperature, °F	200	220	240	260	280
SUV, sec	300	175	105	76	60
Kinematic Viscosity, centistokes	65	38	22	14	10

Which bearing will run hotter? What combination of journal and bearing diameters will produce highest operating temperature? Also determine the probable bearing surface temperature of the hotter bearing, using the McKee equation for estimating the coefficient of friction. Assume specific gravity of oil is 0.9 at its operating temperature. The shaft operates at 500 rpm.

Solution:

The heavier loaded bearing with its minimum clearance will run hotter.

Minimum clearance = 3.500 − 3.497 = 0.003″. p = 4000/(6 × 3.5) = 190 psi.

$$f = 0.002 + \frac{473}{10^{10}}\left(\frac{ZN}{p}\right)\left(\frac{D}{C}\right) = 0.002 + \frac{473}{10^{10}}\left(\frac{500Z}{190}\right)\left(\frac{3.5}{0.003}\right) = 0.002 + \frac{145Z}{10^6}$$

Assuming that all the heat generated leaves the bearing by heat transfer and that the bearing is in still air,

$$fW\frac{\pi DN}{12} = \frac{(\Delta T + 33)^2}{55}DL$$

$$\left(0.002 + \frac{145Z}{10^6}\right)(4000)\frac{\pi(3.5)(500)}{12} = \frac{(T_B - 70 + 33)^2}{55}(6)(3.5)$$

$$3660 + 265Z = (T_B - 37)^2(21/55)$$

The last equation may be balanced by trial and error.

Try: temperature of oil, T_O = 270°F. Now kinematic viscosity = 12 centistokes, Z = 12(0.9) = 10.8 centipoise, and temperature of bearing surface $T_B = \frac{1}{2}(270° - 70) + 70$ = 170°F. Then

$$3660 + 265(10.8) = 6520 \quad \text{and} \quad (170 - 37)^2(21/55) = 6750$$

a close enough balance. This indicates that the bearing surface temperature will be about 170°F.

10. A 3 in. diameter full journal bearing supports a radial load of 800 lb. The bearing is 3 in. long and the shaft operates at 400 rpm. Assume a permissible minimum film thickness of 0.00075 in. and a class 3 fit for the bearing bore. Using Raimondi and Boyd curves, determine (*a*) the viscosity μ of a suitable oil, (*b*) the coefficient of friction f, (*c*) the heat generated H_g, (*d*) the amount of oil Q pumped through the bearing, (*e*) the amount of end leakage Q_s (the amount of oil to be supplied to the bearing), (*f*) the temperature rise of the oil flowing through the bearing.

Solution:

(*a*) For a class 3 fit, the maximum clearance is 0.004 in.

The value of the Sommerfeld number S can be determined from Fig.23-9 by entering with the value $2h_o/C$ = 2(0.00075)/0.004 = 0.375 which corresponds to S = 0.105.

Then $S = 0.105 = \frac{\mu N'}{p}\left(\frac{D}{C}\right)^2 = \frac{\mu(400/60)}{800/(3\times 3)}\left(\frac{3.000}{0.004}\right)^2$ from which $\mu = 2.49 \times 10^{-6}$ reyns.

(*b*) From Fig.23-8, S = 0.105 gives $f(D/C)$ = 3.0. Then $f(3/0.004)$ = 3.0 and f = 0.004.

(*c*) $H_g = fW\pi DN/12$ = (0.004)(800)(π)(3)(400)/12 = 1005 ft-lb/min

(*d*) From Fig.23-10, S = 0.105 gives $\frac{4Q}{DCN'L}$ = 4.4. Then $\frac{4Q}{(3)(0.004)(400/60)(3)}$ = 4.4 and Q = 0.264 in³/sec.

(*e*) From Fig.23-11, S = 0.105 gives Q_s/Q = 0.7. Then Q_s = (0.7)(0.264) = 0.185 in³/sec.

(*f*) From Fig.23-12, S = 0.105 corresponds to $\frac{J\gamma c\,\Delta T}{p}$ = 13.5, where J = 9336 in-lb/Btu, γ = 0.03 lb/in³, c = 0.4 Btu/lb-°F (assumed), and p = 800/9 psi. Then ΔT = 10.7°F is the temperature rise in the oil *film* between the leading and trailing edges of the wedge.

SUPPLEMENTARY PROBLEMS

11. A 4 inch diameter shaft operating at 2000 rpm is supported by means of a 6 inch long full journal bearing which is subjected to a radial load of 9600 lb. Operating temperature of the oil is to be limited to 175°F and the surrounding air temperature is 100°F. Assume $ZN/p = 200$, and use the McKee and Lasche equations. Determine the coefficient of friction, bearing pressure, heat generated, heat dissipated, oil to use. Is artificial cooling required? *Ans.* 0.01146, 400 psi, 231,000 ft-lb/min, 1725 ft-lb/min, SAE 70. Yes.

12. A 2 inch medium weight full journal bearing has a length of 4 in. and supports a load of 600 lb when the shaft rotates at 800 rpm. Assuming a temperature difference of 70°F between the operating temperature of the bearing surface and the surrounding still air, which coefficient of friction 0.00432, 0.00615, 0.00715, 0.00816, or 0.00256 will be required in order to eliminate the need for artificial cooling? Use the McKee and Lasche equations. *Ans.* $f = 0.00615$

13. A $2\frac{7}{16}$ in. journal bearing, 4 in. long, supports a load of 500 lb at 600 rpm. If the room temperature is 75°F, what viscosity oil should be used to limit the bearing surface temperature to 140°F? Use the McKee and Lasche equations. *Ans.* $Z = 12.45$ centipoise

14. A 1200 lb rotor is supported midway between two journal bearings on a 2 in. shaft which rotates at 800 rpm. An oil has been selected which has a viscosity of 7.2 centipoise at an operating temperature of 230°F. What must be the length of the bearing, if it is necessary to operate in an atmosphere of 90°F without artificial cooling? Use the McKee and Lasche equations. *Ans.* $L = 3.2$ in.

15. A 600 lb load is supported by a journal bearing 3 in. long on a 2.5 in. shaft. The bearing has clearance 0.002 in. and is lubricated with an oil of viscosity 20.7 centipoise at its operating temperature. Determine the maximum speed of rotation if the bearing is capable of dissipating 3500 ft-lb/min by means of heat transfer. Use the McKee equation. *Ans.* 700 rpm

16. A journal bearing 6 in. in diameter and 9 in. long carries a radial load of 2000 lb at 1200 rpm. The diametral clearance is 0.003 in. If 2 hp is being wasted in friction, what is the viscosity of the oil being used in centipoise at the operating temperature? Use the McKee equation. *Ans.* $Z = 10.1$ centipoise

17. A full journal bearing is 3.5 in. diameter by 6 in. long and has a radial load of 300 psi of projected area. The shaft speed is 500 rpm and a class 2 fit is used. The surrounding air temperature is 70°F and the oil used has viscosity 9.9 centipoise at its operating temperature. Determine the probable temperature of the bearing surface, assuming all of the heat generated is dissipated by heat transfer according to $H_d = \frac{(T_B - T_A + 33)^2}{55} \times LD$. Use the McKee and Lasche equations. *Ans.* $T_B = 180°F$

18. A 3 in. diameter journal bearing, 5 in. long, has a minimum diametral clearance of 0.003 in. and supports a load of 4000 lb. The journal rotates at 500 rpm. The oil used has the following viscosity-temperature characteristics:

Temperature, °F	240	260	280
Viscosity, centipoise	19.8	13.0	9.0

Using the McKee equation, determine the approximate oil temperature, assuming a room temperature of 80°F and assuming that all the heat generated is dissipated by heat transfer in accordance with $H_d = (\Delta T + 33)^2 (15/55)$. *Ans.* $T_O = 270°F$

19. A water lubricated 4 in. diameter by 4 in. long full bearing supports a load of 300 lb. The shaft rotates at 1000 rpm. The diametral clearance is 0.004 in. and the water has viscosity 4.35×10^{-8} reyns. Assume $c = 1.0$ Btu/lb-°F and $\gamma = 0.035$ lb/in³. Using Raimondi and Boyd curves, determine the coefficient of friction, the minimum film thickness, the flow of lubricant into bearing, the end leakage of lubricant, the temperature rise of oil, and the power loss due to friction.
Ans. $f = 0.0016$, $h_o = 0.00034$ in., $Q = 4.4$ in³/sec, $Q_s = 3.83$ in³/sec, $\Delta T = 1.38°F$, 0.015 hp

20. A full journal bearing, 8 in. diameter by 8 in. long, supports a radial load of 10,000 lb. The journal rotates at 1200 rpm and the D/C ratio is 1000. The viscosity of the oil at its operating temperature (180°F) is 2.5×10^{-6} reyns. Using Raimondi and Boyd curves, determine the minimum film thickness, the heat generated in the bearing, the natural heat loss from the bearing assuming $H_d = \frac{(\Delta T + 33)^2}{31}$(projected area), the amount of oil leaking out of both ends, and the heat removed from the bearing due to end leakage.
Ans. $h_o = 0.0026$ in., $H_g = 1.76 \times 10^6$ ft-lb/min, $H_d = 16{,}000$ ft-lb/min, $Q_s = 4.38$ in³/sec, 1.025 Btu/min

Chapter 24

Belt Drives

FLAT BELTS AND V-BELTS may be employed to transmit power from one shaft to another where it is not necessary to maintain an exact speed ratio between the two shafts. Power losses due to slip and creep amount to from 3 to 5 percent for most belt drives. In the following discussion it will be assumed that the shafts are parallel. However, both flat and V-belts may be used between non-parallel shafts to meet special requirements. In this case, in order for the belt to stay on the pulleys, it must approach each pulley in a central plane perpendicular to the pulley's axis of rotation.

BELT DESIGN INVOLVES either the proper belt selection to transmit a required power or the determination of the power that may be transmitted by a given flat belt or by one V-belt. In the first case the width of the belt is unknown, while in the second case the width is known. The belt thickness is assumed for both cases.

The power transmitted by a belt drive is a function of the belt tensions and belt speed.

$$\text{Power} = \frac{(T_1 - T_2)v}{550} \quad \text{in horsepower}$$

where T_1 = belt tension in tight side, lb
T_2 = belt tension in loose side, lb
v = belt speed, ft/sec.

The following formula for determining the stress, s_2 psi, for flat belts applies when the thickness of the belt is given but the width is unknown.

$$\frac{s_1 - w'v^2/g}{s_2 - w'v^2/g} = e^{f\alpha}$$

where s_1 = maximum allowable stress, psi
s_2 = stress in slack side of belt, psi
w' = weight of 1 ft of belt 1 in^2 in cross section
v = belt velocity, ft/sec
g = acceleration due to gravity, 32.2 ft/sec^2
f = coefficient of friction between belt and pulley
α = angle of wrap of belt on pulley, radians.

The required cross section area of the belt for the case of the width unknown may be determined by

$$\frac{T_1 - T_2}{s_1 - s_2} = \text{required cross section area}$$

The required belt width b is therefore b = area/thickness. The value of $(T_1 - T_2)$ may be determined from the horsepower requirement, hp = $(T_1 - T_2)v/550$.

The maximum tension in the tight side of the belt depends on the allowable stress of the belt material. Leather and cotton duck impregnated with rubber built up in plies are generally used. The allowable tensile stress for leather belting is usually 300 to 500 psi, and the allowable stress for rubber belting will run from 150 to 250 psi, depending on the quality of the material. Leather belting can be obtained in single ply thickness of 1/8 in., 5/32 in., and 3/16 in. Double and triple ply belts are also available in multiples of these increments. The specific weight of leather is about 0.035 lb/in^3. Rubber belting can be obtained in ply thicknesses of 3/64 to 5/64 in. and has a specific weight of about 0.045 lb/in^3.

The following formula for determining the value of T_2 for both flat and V-belts applies when the width and thickness of the belt are known.

$$\frac{T_1 - wv^2/g}{T_2 - wv^2/g} = e^{f\alpha/\sin\frac{1}{2}\theta}$$

where w = the weight of 1 ft of belt; v = belt velocity, ft/sec; g = acceleration due to gravity, 32.2 ft/sec^2; f = coefficient of friction between belt and pulley; α = angle of wrap, radians; θ = groove angle for the V-belt (θ is 180° for a flat belt).

The quantity wv^2/g is due to centrifugal force, which tends to cause the belt to leave the pulley and reduces the power that may be transmitted.

THE LOAD CARRYING CAPACITY of a pair of pulleys is determined by the one which has the smaller $e^{f\alpha/\sin\frac{1}{2}\theta}$. It is for this reason that a V-belt may be used with one grooved pulley and one flat pulley, saving the expense of unnecessary machining.

Excessive flexing of a belt will result in a shortened life. A minimum ratio of the diameter of a pulley to the thickness of the belt is about 30 for reasonable life.

SELECTION OF BELTS can be made on the basis of application of the appropriate equations or by use of tables supplied by the American Leather Belting Association for leather belts and by use of catalogs supplied by the various V-belt manufacturers. In this book, the application of the equations will be used, although the recommendations of the A.L.B.A. or V-belt manufacturers will generally give safer designs incorporating suitable application factors.

ANGLES OF WRAP. The angles of wrap for an **open belt** may be determined by:

$$\sin\beta = \frac{R-r}{C}$$

$$\alpha_1 = 180° - 2\beta = 180° - 2\sin^{-1}\frac{R-r}{C}, \qquad \alpha_2 = 180° + 2\beta = 180° + 2\sin^{-1}\frac{R-r}{C}$$

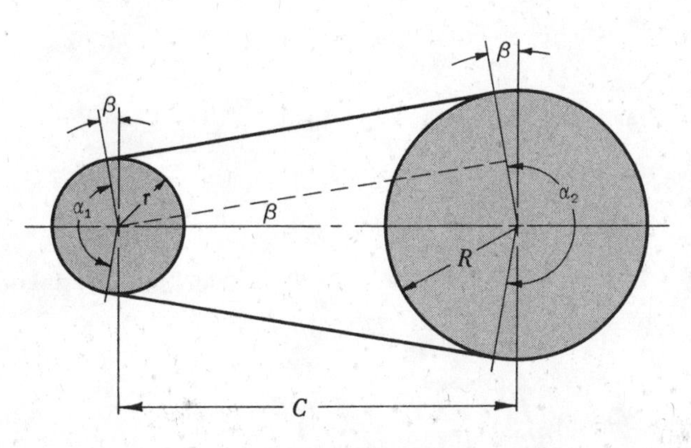

Fig. 24-1

The angles of wrap for a **crossed belt** drive may be determined by:

$$\sin\beta = \frac{R+r}{C}$$

$$\alpha_1 = \alpha_2 = 180^\circ + 2\beta$$

$$= 180^\circ + 2\sin^{-1}\frac{R+r}{C}$$

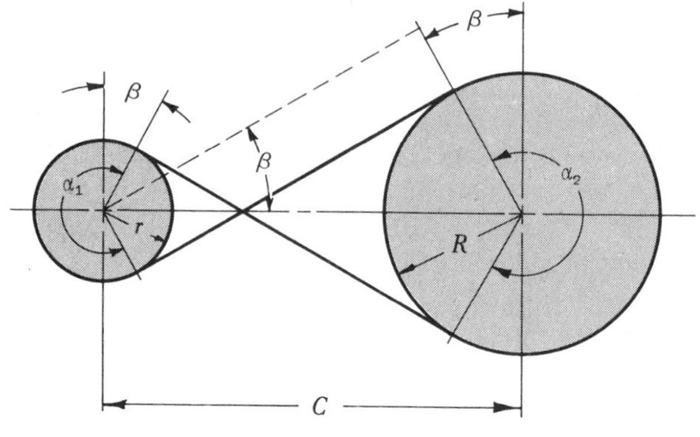

Fig. 24-2

SOLVED PROBLEMS

1. Derive $\dfrac{T_1 - wv^2/g}{T_2 - wv^2/g} = e^{f\alpha}$ for a flat belt.

Solution:

(a) Consider a differential element of belt. The forces acting on the differential element are (1) tensions T and $(T+dT)$, (2) centrifugal force $(wv^2/g)\,d\phi$, (3) normal force dN, (4) frictional force $f\,dN$.

Note that there is no bending moment and no shear force acting on the belt. The belt is a flexible member and cannot sustain shear and bending of any appreciable magnitude compared to the other forces.

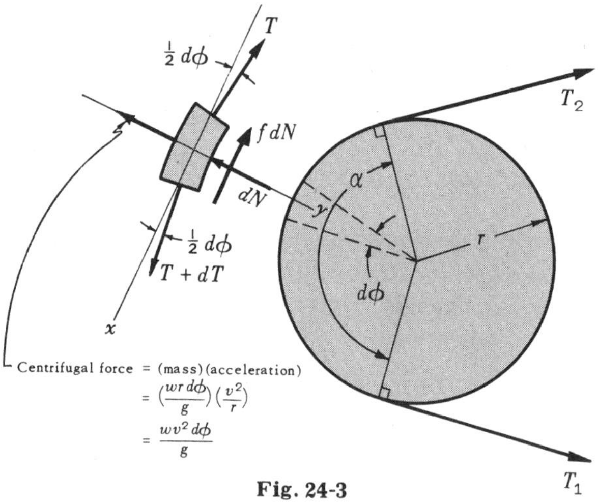

Centrifugal force = (mass)(acceleration) $= \left(\frac{wr\,d\phi}{g}\right)\left(\frac{v^2}{r}\right) = \frac{wv^2\,d\phi}{g}$

Fig. 24-3

(b) Setting up an arbitrary x and y direction for the element of belt and considering the element in equilibrium since the inertia force is included,

$$\Sigma F_x = 0 \quad \text{or} \quad (T+dT)\cos\tfrac{1}{2}d\phi - f\,dN - T\cos\tfrac{1}{2}d\phi = 0$$

$$\Sigma F_y = 0 \quad \text{or} \quad (T+dT)\sin\tfrac{1}{2}d\phi + T\sin\tfrac{1}{2}d\phi - (wv^2/g)\,d\phi - dN = 0$$

(c) Since $\cos\frac{1}{2}d\phi = 1$ and $\sin\frac{1}{2}d\phi = \frac{1}{2}d\phi$ in the limit,

$$1)\quad (T+dT)(1) - f\,dN - T = 0 \quad \text{or} \quad dN = dT/f$$

$$2)\quad (T+dT)(\tfrac{1}{2}d\phi) + T(\tfrac{1}{2}d\phi) - dN - (wv^2/g)\,d\phi = 0$$

Substituting $dN = dT/f$ from (1) into (2), and dropping out differentials of the second order,

$$T\,d\phi - dT/f - (wv^2/g)\,d\phi = 0$$

(d) Then $\dfrac{dT}{T - wv^2/g} = f\,d\phi$, $\displaystyle\int_{T_2}^{T_1}\frac{dT}{T - wv^2/g} = \int_0^\alpha f\,d\phi$, and finally $\dfrac{T_1 - wv^2/g}{T_2 - wv^2/g} = e^{f\alpha}$.

(See Page 291 for proper units.)

2. Modify the equation in Prob. 1 to take care of a V-belt.

Solution:

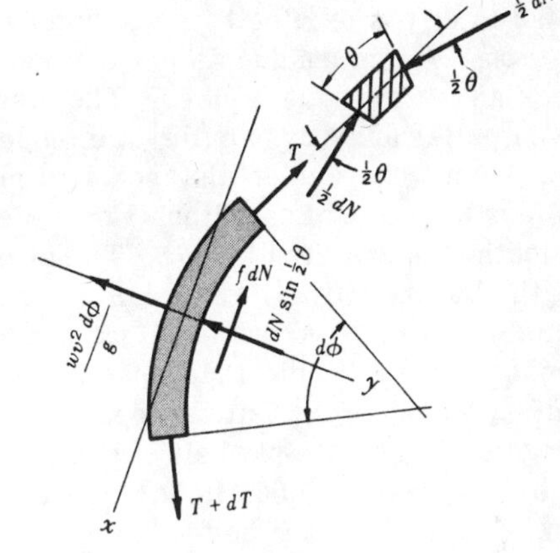

Fig. 24-4

(a) Comparing Fig. 24-4 with Fig. 24-3, the forces which can be shown as in the flat belt are: T, $T+dT$, $(wv^2/g)\,d\phi$. The difference occurs in the normal and frictional forces. The normal forces on the sides of the V-belt are assumed equal on both sides: $\frac{1}{2}dN$. The resultant normal force in the x-y plane is $dN \sin \frac{1}{2}\theta$, where θ is the V-belt angle. Note that the sum of the frictional forces is not dependent on the angle θ, but is $2[f(\frac{1}{2}dN)] = f\,dN$.

(b) $\Sigma F_x = 0$ or

$$(T+dT)\cos\tfrac{1}{2}d\phi - f\,dN - T\cos\tfrac{1}{2}d\phi = 0$$

$\Sigma F_y = 0$ or

$$(T+dT)\sin\tfrac{1}{2}d\phi + T\sin\tfrac{1}{2}d\phi - dN\sin\tfrac{1}{2}\theta - (wv^2/g)\,d\phi = 0$$

(c) Since $\cos\frac{1}{2}d\phi = 1$ and $\sin\frac{1}{2}d\phi = \frac{1}{2}d\phi$ in the limit,

1) $(T+dT) - f\,dN - T = 0$ or $dN = dT/f$

2) $(T+dT)(\frac{1}{2}d\phi) + T(\frac{1}{2}d\phi) - dN\sin\frac{1}{2}\theta - (wv^2/g)d\phi = 0$

Substituting $dN = dT/f$ into (2) and dropping out differentials of the second order,

$$T\,d\phi - (dT/f)\sin\tfrac{1}{2}\theta - (wv^2/g)\,d\phi = 0$$

(d) Then $\dfrac{dT}{T - wv^2/g} = \dfrac{f}{\sin\frac{1}{2}\theta}\,d\phi$, $\displaystyle\int_{T_2}^{T_1}\frac{dT}{T - wv^2/g} = \int_0^{\alpha}\frac{f}{\sin\frac{1}{2}\theta}\,d\phi$, and finally $\dfrac{T_1 - wv^2/g}{T_2 - wv^2/g} = e^{f\alpha/\sin\frac{1}{2}\theta}$

Note that if θ is taken as 180° for a flat belt, this equation reduces to that derived in Problem 1.

3. A shaft transmits maximum power from a pulley to a flexible coupling. The shaft rotates at 900 rpm, the pulley is 16 in. in diameter, the belt strands are horizontal, and the leather belt is 2 in. wide and $\frac{1}{4}$ in. thick. Maximum stress in the belt is 300 psi, and the coefficient of friction is 0.3. If the shaft is to be checked for strength at section A-A, what bending moment and what torque should be used? Leather weighs 0.035 lb/in³.

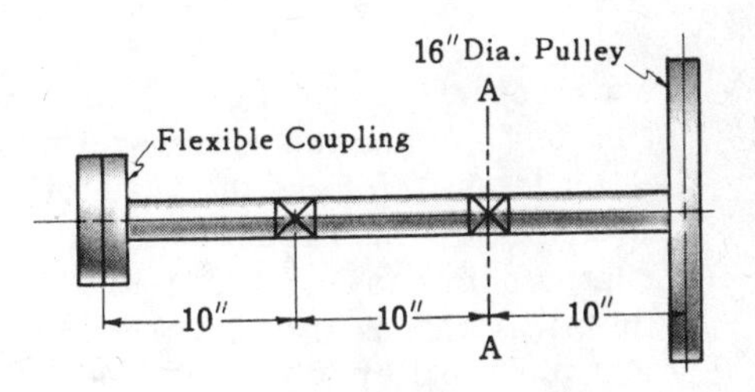

Fig. 24-5

Solution:

(a) $\dfrac{T_1 - wv^2/g}{T_2 - wv^2/g} = e^{f\alpha}$, $\dfrac{150 - 25.7}{T_2 - 25.7} = e^{0.3\pi}$, $T_2 = 74.3$ lb

where $w = (12)(2)(\frac{1}{4})(0.035) = 0.210$ lb/ft, $g = 32.2$ ft/sec², $\alpha = \pi$ radians

$v = \pi DN = \pi(16/12\text{ ft})(900/60\text{ rps}) = 62.8$ ft/sec, $T_1 = (300\text{ lb/in}^2)(2\times\frac{1}{4}\text{ in}^2) = 150$ lb

(b) Bending moment at section A-A is

$$(T_1 + T_2)(10) = (150 + 74.3)(10) = 2243 \text{ in-lb}$$

(c) Torque at section A-A is

$$(T_1 - T_2)(R) = (150 - 74.3)(8) = 606 \text{ in-lb}$$

4. A fan is driven by a belt from a motor which runs at 880 rpm. A medium double ply leather belt 5/16 in. thick and 10 in. wide is used. The diameters of the motor pulley and driven pulley are respectively 14 in. and 54 in. The center distance is 54 in., and both pulleys are made of cast iron. Coefficient of friction of leather on cast iron is 0.35. The allowable stress for the belt is 350 psi, which allows for the factor of safety and also for the fact that a double ply belt does not have double the capacity of a single ply belt. (A double ply belt has approximately 85% the capacity of a single ply belt of the same thickness.) The belt weighs 0.035 lb/in³. What is the horsepower capacity of the belt?

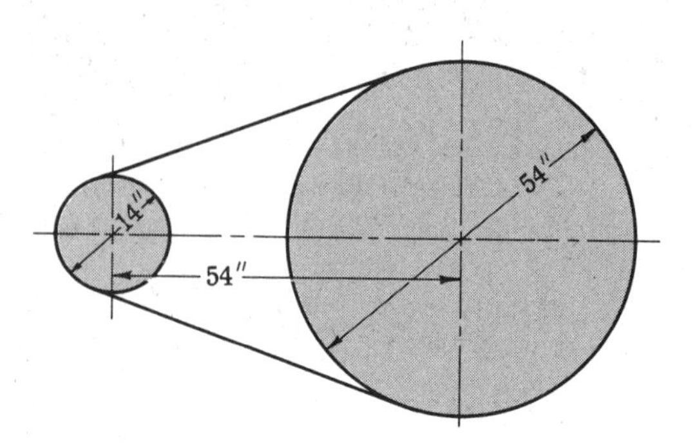

Fig. 24-6

Solution:

Angles of wrap of smaller and larger pulleys are respectively

$$\alpha_1 = 180^\circ - 2\sin^{-1}(R-r)/C = 180^\circ - 2\sin^{-1}(27-7)/54 = 136.6^\circ$$

$$\alpha_2 = 180^\circ + 2\sin^{-1}(R-r)/C = 223.4^\circ$$

The pulley which governs the design is the one with the smaller $e^{f\alpha}$. Here the smaller pulley governs, i.e. the smaller pulley is transmitting its maximum power with the belt on the point of slip while the larger pulley is not developing its maximum capacity. Then

$$\frac{T_1 - wv^2/g}{T_2 - wv^2/g} = e^{f\alpha_1}, \qquad \frac{1094 - 117}{T_2 - 117} = e^{0.35\,(136.6\pi/180)} = 2.30, \qquad T_2 = 542 \text{ lb}$$

where $w = 12(10)(5/16)(0.035) = 1.31$ lb/ft, $\quad g = 32.2$ ft/sec²,

$v = \pi DN = \pi(14/12 \text{ ft})(880/60 \text{ rps}) = 53.7$ ft/sec, $\quad T_1 = (350 \text{ lb/in}^2)(\frac{5}{16}\times 10 \text{ in}^2) = 1094$ lb.

$$\text{Horsepower capacity} = \frac{(T_1 - T_2)v}{550} = \frac{(1094-542)(53.7)}{550} = 53.9 \text{ hp.}$$

5. A compressor is driven by a 900 rpm motor by means of a $\frac{3}{8}''$ by 10'' flat belt. The motor pulley is 12'' in diameter and the compressor pulley is 60'' in diameter. The shaft center distance is 60'' and an idler is used to make the angle of wrap on the smaller pulley 220° and on the larger pulley 270°. The coefficient of friction between the belt and the small pulley is 0.3, and between the belt and the large pulley is 0.25. The maximum allowable belt stress is 300 psi and the belt weighs 0.035 lb/in³. (*a*) What is the horsepower capacity of this drive? (*b*) Would changing the small pulley to a multiple V-pulley (groove angle $\theta = 34^\circ$ and coefficient of friction 0.25) using the same compressor pulley, and eliminating the idler pulley, provide a more effective drive with greater horsepower capacity? Assume that the pitch diameter of the V-belt and the pitch diameter of the large pulley remain the same as for the flat belt arrangement: 12'' and 60''. Assume also that the total of the maximum force in each belt is the same as for the flat belt (i.e. T is constant) and that the centrifugal effect of all the belts is the same as for the flat belt.

Solution:

(*a*) For small pulley, $e^{f\alpha} = e^{0.3(220\pi/180)} = 3.16$; for large pulley, $e^{f\alpha} = e^{0.25(270\pi/180)} = 3.26$. Hence the small pulley governs. Then

$$\frac{T_1 - wv^2/g}{T_2 - wv^2/g} = e^{f\alpha}, \qquad \frac{1125 - 108}{T_2 - 108} = 3.16, \qquad T_2 = 430 \text{ lb}$$

where $T_1 = (300)(10)(3/8) = 1125$ lb, $w = 12(10)(3/8)(0.035) = 1.57$ lb/ft, $v = \pi(1)(15) = 47.1$ fps.

$$\text{Horsepower capacity} = \frac{(T_1 - T_2)v}{550} = \frac{(1125 - 430)(47.1)}{550} = 59.6 \text{ hp}$$

(b) For an open belt arrangement with no idler: angle of wrap on smaller pulley = $180^\circ - 2\sin^{-1}(30-6)/60 = 132.8^\circ$, on larger pulley = 227.2°. Now

for small pulley (V-belt in the groove), $e^{f\alpha/\sin\frac{1}{2}\theta} = e^{0.25(132.8\pi/180)/\sin 17^\circ} = 7.27$

for large pulley (V-belt on a flat pulley), $e^{f\alpha} = e^{0.25(227.2\pi/180)} = 2.69$.

Thus, although the capacity of the small pulley is increased, the larger pulley is now the criterion with $e^{f\alpha} = 2.69$. Using $\dfrac{1125-108}{T_2-108} = 2.69$ or $T_2 = 486$ lb, the new (decreased) horsepower capacity = $\dfrac{(1125-486)(47.1)}{550} = 54.8$ hp.

6. A crossed belt drive is to transmit 10 hp at 1000 rpm of the smaller pulley. The smaller pulley has diameter 10", the velocity ratio is 2, and the center distance is 50". It is desired to use a flat belt $\frac{1}{4}$" thick with an expected coefficient of friction 0.3. If the maximum allowable stress in the belt is 250 psi, determine the necessary leather belt width b. The leather weighs 0.035 lb/in³.

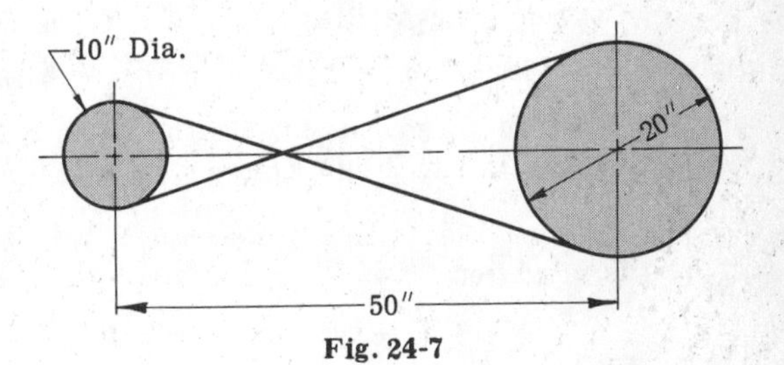

Fig. 24-7

Solution:

Both pulleys have the same angle of wrap α and the same horsepower capacity.

$$\alpha = 180 + 2\sin^{-1}(R+r)/C = 180 + 2\sin^{-1}(10+5)/50 = 214.8^\circ$$

$$\frac{s_1 - w'v^2/g}{s_2 - w'v^2/g} = e^{f\alpha}, \qquad \frac{250-24.8}{s_2-24.8} = e^{0.3(214.8\pi/180)}, \qquad s_2 = 97.8 \text{ psi}$$

where $w' = 12(0.035) = 0.42$ lb/ft-in², $v = \pi(10/12)(1000/60) = 43.6$ ft/sec.

Using $(T_1 - T_2) = \dfrac{(\text{hp})(550)}{v} = \dfrac{(10)(550)}{43.6} = 126$ lb, $A = \dfrac{T_1-T_2}{s_1-s_2} = \dfrac{126}{250-97.8} = 0.83$ in² and the belt width $b = (0.83\text{ in}^2)/(\frac{1}{4}\text{ in.}) = 3.32$ in. Use $3\frac{1}{2}$ in. belt width.

7. A V-belt drive is to transmit 25 hp from a 10 inch pitch diameter sheave operating at 1800 rpm to a 36 inch diameter flat pulley. The center distance between the input and output shafts is 40". The groove angle $\theta = 40^\circ$, and the coefficient of friction for the belt and sheave is 0.2, and the coefficient of friction between the belt and flat pulley is 0.2. The cross section of the belt is $b_2 = 1.5$" wide at the top and $b_1 = 0.75$" wide at the bottom by $d = 1.0$" deep. Each belt weighs 0.04 lb/in³ and the allowable tension per belt is 200 lb. How many belts are required? (Note: analyze for one belt first.)

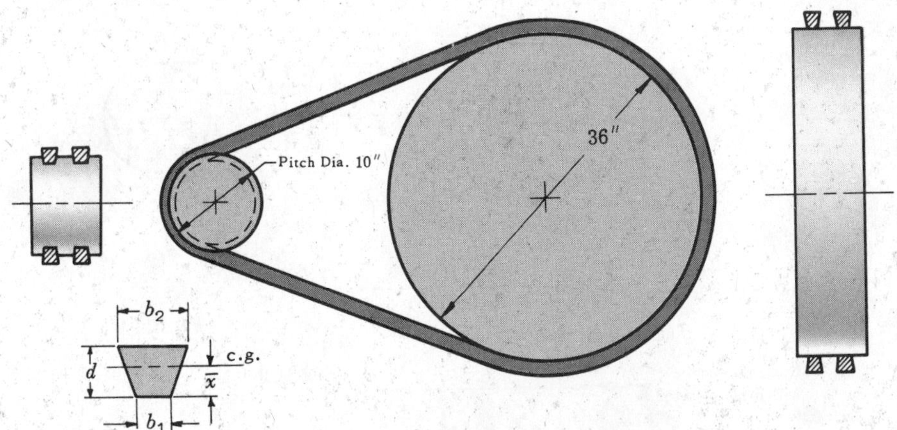

Fig. 24-8

Solution:

While the thickness of a flat belt is ordinarily negligible with respect to the diameter of a pulley, the thickness of a V-belt may not be negligible. Determine the pitch diameter of the V-belt on the flat pulley by assuming that the pitch diameter is measured to the centroid of the belt section.

Distance from base to C.G. is $\bar{x} = \dfrac{d(b_1+2b_2)}{3(b_1+b_2)} = \dfrac{1(0.75+2\times1.5)}{3(0.75+1.5)} = 0.56$ in.

Pitch diameter of larger pulley = 36 + 2(0.56) = 37.1'', or pitch radius = 18.6''.

For small pulley, $\alpha = 180^\circ - 2\sin^{-1}(18.6-5)/40 = 140.4^\circ$. For large pulley, $\alpha = 219.6^\circ$.

Compare the capacities, $e^{f\alpha/\sin\frac{1}{2}\theta}$, of the two pulleys:

Small, $e^{0.2(140.4\pi/180)/\sin 20^\circ} = 4.18$. Large, $e^{0.2(219.6\pi/180)/\sin 90^\circ} = 2.15$.

The larger pulley governs the design. (Note that the angle of the V-belt is slightly larger than 40°, but the belt will wedge into the 40° groove.)

The area of one belt = $\frac{1}{2}(b_1+b_2)(d) = \frac{1}{2}(0.75+1.5)(1) = 1.125\text{ in}^2$, and the tension on the slack side of a belt is found from

$$\frac{T_1 - wv^2/g}{T_2 - wv^2/g} = e^{f\alpha/\sin\frac{1}{2}\theta}, \qquad \frac{200-103.5}{T_2-103.5} = 2.15, \qquad T_2 = 148\text{ lb}$$

where $w = 12(1.125)(0.04) = 0.54$ lb/ft, $v = \pi(10/12)(1800/60) = 78.5$ fps.

Horsepower per belt = $(T_1 - T_2)v/550$ = (200 − 148)(78.5)/550 = 7.43 hp/belt.

Number of belts required = (25 hp)/(7.43 hp/belt) = 3.37. Use 4 belts.

8. A 9'' pulley is keyed to a shaft, and the center plane of the pulley overhangs the nearer bearing by 10'', as shown in Fig. 24-9 below. An open belt arrangement is used. The pulley is driven by an 1800 rpm motor through a flat belt with a 1 to 1 velocity ratio of the pulleys. The belt is $\frac{3}{8}$'' by 6'', and weighs 0.035 lb/in³. The coefficient of friction between the belt and pulleys is 0.3. The belt is run at its maximum capacity with a maximum belt stress of 300 psi.

It is decided that the horsepower capacity is to be doubled; and, of the several possibilities, this problem will concern itself with the effect of increasing the belt width. Assume that the belt width is to be increased, with all other conditions remaining the same. (*a*) How much should the belt width be increased to double the horsepower capacity? (*b*) Assuming that the center plane of the pulley remains at the same distance from the nearer bearing (that is, 10''), by how many pounds are the bearing forces increased? The distance between bearings is 18''. Assume that power is taken from the shaft through a flexible coupling.

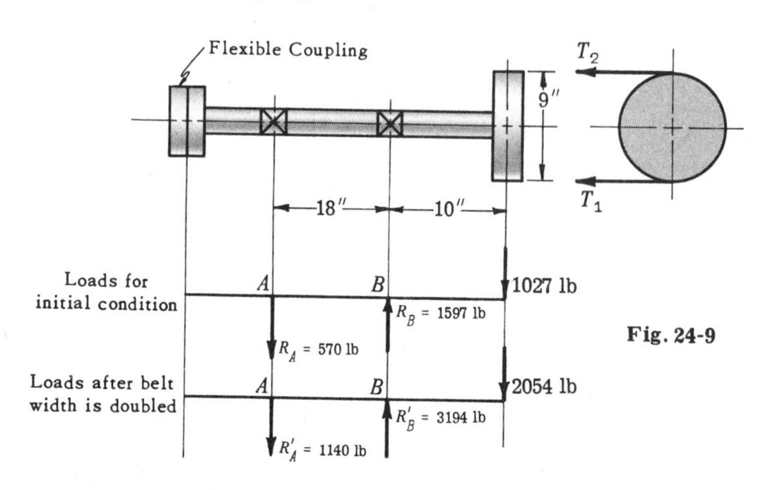

Fig. 24-9

Solution:

(*a*) If the width of the belt is doubled, the horsepower capacity is also doubled.

(*b*) If the belt is transmitting its maximum capacity, the tension T_1 on the tight side = 300(6)(3/8) = 675 lb. To find T_2 for the initial condition (both pulleys have the same capacity):

$$\frac{T_1 - wv^2/g}{T_2 - wv^2/g} = e^{fa}, \qquad \frac{675 - 146.5}{T_2 - 146.5} = e^{0.3\pi}, \qquad T_2 = 352 \text{ lb}$$

where $w = 12(6)(3/8)(0.035) = 0.94$ lb/ft, $v = \pi(9/12)(1800/60) = 70.6$ ft/sec.

Resultant force at pulley causing bearing reactions = $T_1 + T_2$ = 675 + 352 = 1027 lb.

The bearing reaction at B is found by taking moments about A. The bearing reaction at A is found by summing forces.

$$1027(28) - R_B(18) = 0, \quad R_B = 1597 \text{ lb} \qquad \text{and} \qquad R_A + 1027 - 1597 = 0, \quad R_A = 570 \text{ lb}$$

If the power is doubled, the bearing reactions are doubled, i.e. R'_A = 1140 lb and R'_B = 3194 lb. Thus the increases in the bearing forces are 570 lb for the left bearing at A and 1597 lb for the right bearing at B.

9. A pivoted motor drive has several advantages over a fixed center drive. One of the advantages is that the stretch in the belt is automatically taken care of by the effect of the weight of the motor. Another advantage claimed is the reduction in bearing loads for operation at partial loads, depending on the proportions used. If the power transmitted from the motor to the pulley A is 25% of *full load capacity*, what are the bearing loads at C and D, expressed as a percentage of full load bearing loads? Neglect the weight of the armature.

	Pulley A	**Pulley B**
Diameter	6"	6"
Coefficient of friction	0.4	0.5
Angle of wrap	180°	180°

The belt has speed 3000 ft/min, is 4" wide by $\frac{1}{8}$" thick, and weighs 0.04 lb/in³. The motor weighs 150 lb.

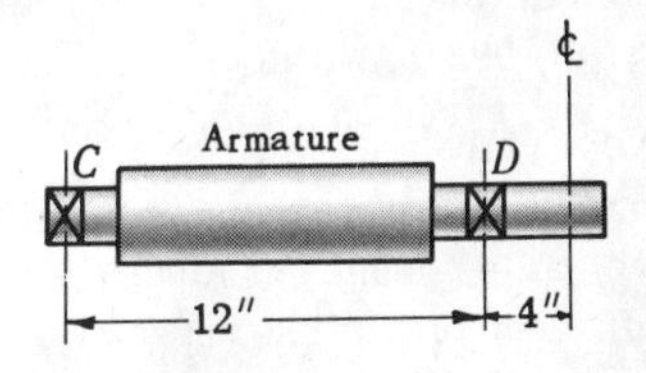

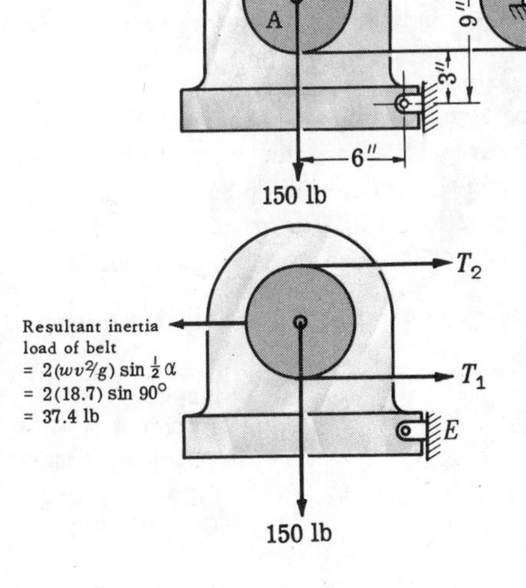

Fig. 24-10

Solution:

(*a*) The first step is to analyze for *full load* capacity. Isolate the motor and pulley as shown. Taking moments about the center of the pin E,

$$-150(6) + T_1(3) + T_2(9) - 37.4(6) = 0$$

or $\quad$ (*1*) $\quad T_1 + 3T_2 = 374.8$

Since maximum capacity means that the belt is on the point of slip, or maximum friction is being utilized on the motor pulley (with e^{fa} for the motor pulley being less than e^{fa} for the driven pulley),

$$\frac{T_1 - wv^2/g}{T_2 - wv^2/g} = e^{fa}, \qquad \frac{T_1 - 18.7}{T_2 - 18.7} = e^{0.4\pi}$$

or $\quad$ (*2*) $\quad T_1 - 3.51T_2 = -47$

where $w = 12(4)(1/8)(0.04) = 0.24$ lb/ft
$v = 3000/60 = 50$ ft/sec.

The simultaneous solution of (*1*) and (*2*) is T_1 = 180.4 lb, T_2 = 64.8 lb; and $T_1 + T_2$ = 245.2 lb.

(*b*) At quarter load, designate the forces on the belt as T_1' and T_2'. Taking moments about E,

$$(3) \quad -150(6) + T_1'(3) + T_2'(9) - 37.4(6) = 0$$

and recognizing that at quarter load $(T_1' - T_2') = \frac{1}{4}(T_1 - T_2)$,

$$(4) \quad T_1' - T_2' = \tfrac{1}{4}(180.4 - 64.8) = 28.9$$

Solving equations (*3*) and (*4*) simultaneously, $T_1' = 115.4$ lb and $T_2' = 86.5$ lb.

Note that $\dfrac{T_1 - wv^2/g}{T_2 - wv^2/g} = e^{f\alpha}$ does not apply at quarter load since maximum power is not being transmitted, i.e. the belt is not on the point of slip.

(*c*) The bearing loads at quarter capacity, as a percentage of those at full capacity, are

$$\frac{T_1' + T_2' - 2wv^2/g}{T_1 + T_2 - 2wv^2/g} = \frac{201.9 - 37.4}{245.2 - 37.4} = 0.79 = 79\%$$

SUPPLEMENTARY PROBLEMS

10. A workman raises a load with the aid of a winch, as shown in Fig.24-11, having an ungrooved cast iron drum. He takes 4 turns of the one inch rope about the drum and exerts a pull of 75 lb on one end of the rope. The drum is 10 in. in diameter and rotates at 25 rpm. The rope weighs 0.20 lb/ft, and the coefficient of friction is 0.10. (*a*) What load can be raised by this combination? (*b*) How much power is required?
Ans. (*a*) 992 lb, with centrifugal effect negligible. (*b*) 1.85 hp, based on a torque of (922 – 75)(5.5) = 466 in-lb.

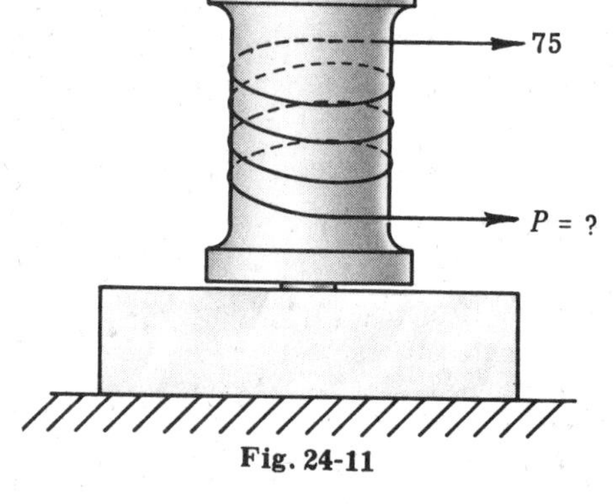

Fig. 24-11

11. A leather belt is to transmit 30 hp from a 10 in. fibre-covered driver pulley running at 1200 rpm to a 24 in. steel pulley. The coefficient of friction between the steel pulley and belt is 0.30 and that between the driver and belt is 0.40. The distance between shafts is 72 in. Assume that the maximum allowable working stress in the belt is 250 psi and that the belt weighs 0.035 lb/in³. Which of the following belts would be more suitable, a belt $\frac{5}{16}''$ thick or a belt $\frac{1}{2}''$ thick? Calculate the required width of belt.
Ans. A $\frac{5}{16}''$ belt would be preferable for a greater belt life ($\frac{d}{t} = \frac{10}{5/16} = 32$) than a $\frac{1}{2}''$ belt ($\frac{d}{t} = \frac{10}{1/2} = 20$). The belt width for a $\frac{5}{16}''$ belt is 7.45'' (use $7\frac{1}{2}''$).

12. A V-belt operates on two sheaves having pitch diameters of 10'' and 32'', respectively. The groove angle of the sheaves is 36° and the contact angle of the small sheave is 140°. The maximum allowable belt load is 200 lb and a V-belt weighs 0.35 lb/ft. The smaller sheave rotates at 1150 rpm, and 35 hp is to be transmitted. For a coefficient of friction of 0.2, how many V-belts should be used, assuming each one takes its proportional part of the load. *Ans.* 2.88 belts; use 3 belts.

13. An electric motor drives a compressor through V-belts. The following data are known:

	Motor Pulley	Compressor Pulley
Pitch diameter	9''	48''
Angle of contact	2 radians	4.28 radians
Coefficient of friction	0.3	0.3
Groove angle	34°	flat pulley
Power transmitted	25 hp	
Speed	1800 rpm	

Each belt weighs 0.20 lb/ft and the maximum permissible force is 100 lb per belt. Determine (*a*) $f\alpha/(\sin\frac{1}{2}\theta)$ for motor pulley and for compressor pulley, (*b*) wv^2/g for one belt, (*c*) the tension on the slack side of the belt, (*d*) the horsepower per belt, (*e*) the number of belts required.
Ans. (*a*) 2.06 for motor pulley, 1.284 for compressor pulley; compressor pulley governs design.
(*b*) 31.0 lb. (*c*) 50.2 lb. (*d*) 6.4 hp/belt. (*e*) 3.91; use 4.

14. An electric motor is to drive an exhaust fan. A flat leather belt is to be used. The following data are known:

	Motor Pulley	Fan Pulley
Diameter	12"	48"
Contact angle	2.5 radians	3.78 radians
Coefficient of friction	0.3	0.25
Speed	900 rpm	
Power transmitted	30 hp	

The belt is $\frac{1}{4}$" thick, the maximum permissible stress is 300 psi, and the weight is 0.035 lb/in^3. (*a*) Which pulley governs the design? (*b*) What width should be used?

Ans. (*a*) $f\alpha$ for smaller pulley = 0.75, $f\alpha$ for larger pulley = 0.945; smaller pulley governs.
(*b*) 9.78"; use 10".

15. An electric motor drives a compressor by means of a flat leather belt. The following data are known:

	Motor Pulley	Compressor Pulley
Diameter	10"	60"
Angle of wrap	4 radians	3.5 radians
Coefficient of friction	0.25	0.3
Speed	1200 rpm	

(Note that an idler pulley is used.) The belt is $\frac{1}{4}$" by 8" in cross section and weighs 0.035 lb/in^3. If the maximum allowable belt tension is 600 lb, determine the horsepower capacity. *Ans.* 31.9 hp

16. An open belt drive delivers 20 hp when the motor pulley which is 12" in diameter turns at 1750 rpm. The belt is $\frac{3}{8}$" by 6" and weighs 0.035 lb/in^3. The driven pulley, which is 48" in diameter, has an angle of contact of 200°. What is the maximum stress in the belt assuming a coefficient of friction 0.3 for both pulleys?
Ans. 203 psi

17. A V-belt drive transmits 15 hp at 900 rpm of the smaller sheave. The sheave pitch diameters are 6.8" and 13.6". The center distance is 30". If the maximum permissible working *force* per belt is 126 lb, determine the number of belts required if the coefficient of friction is 0.15 and the groove angle of the sheaves is 34°. The belt weighs 0.13 lb/ft. *Ans.* 3.23; use 4 belts.

18. A 53" diameter steel flywheel is to be connected to a 16" diameter rubber faced motor pulley by means of a double ply leather belt which has a thickness of $\frac{5}{16}$". The center distance is 10 ft. The coefficient of friction for leather on steel is 0.20 and for leather on rubber is 0.40. The leather has an allowable stress of 400 psi, and the joint efficiency is 80%. Leather weighs 0.035 lb/in^3. If 60 hp is transmitted with a belt speed of 4800 ft/min, determine
(*a*) the maximum permissible working stress,
(*b*) $e^{f\alpha}$ for the pulley which governs the design,
(*c*) the necessary belt width.

Standard widths of belt vary by:
1/8" increments from $\frac{1}{2}$" to 1"
1/4" increments from 1" to 4"
$\frac{1}{2}$" increments from 4" to 7"
1" increments from 7" to 12"

Ans. (*a*) 320 psi, (*b*) 1.99, (*c*) 11.2", use 12"

19. Design the flat belt drive, given the following information. A transmission shaft rotating at 500 rpm drives a milling machine which requires 5 hp at 750 rpm. A 12" diameter cast iron pulley is located on the transmission shaft. A preliminary design proposes using a belt $\frac{3}{16}$" thick which weighs 0.035 lb/in^3. The allowable stress is 300 psi, the two pulleys rotate in opposite directions, the center distance of the shafts is 30", and the coefficient of friction is 0.30 for both pulleys. Determine (*a*) the diameter of the smaller pulley, (*b*) the stress on the slack side, (*c*) the required area of the belt, (*d*) the necessary width.

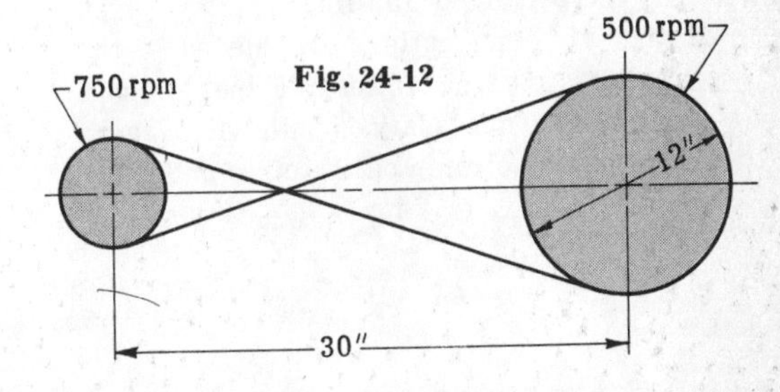

Fig. 24-12

Ans. (*a*) 8", (*b*) 101 psi, (*c*) 0.527 in^2, (*d*) 2.82", use 3"

20. Determine the percentage increase in horsepower capacity made possible in changing over from a flat belt to a V-belt drive. The diameter of the flat pulley is the same as the pitch diameter of the grooved pulley. The pulley rotates at the same speed as the grooved pulley. The coefficient of friction for the flat belt and the V-belt is the same, 0.3. The V-belt pulley groove angle θ is 60°. The belts are of the same material and have the same cross section area. In each case the angle of wrap is 150°.

Ans. 45%. (Ratio of power capacity of V-belt to that of flat belt is 1.45.)

21. (*a*) Determine the number of V-belts required to transmit 40 hp under the following conditions:

	Small Sheave	Large Sheave
Speed	1120 rpm	280 rpm
Pitch diameter	9"	36"
Groove angle	34°	34°

Maximum working load per belt = 126 lb, coefficient of friction = 0.15, center distance of sheaves = 35", weight of belt = 0.20 lb/ft.

(*b*) To save expense, it is proposed that the large sheave be made without grooves and that the V-belts run on the surface of the ungrooved pulley. Assuming that the length of the belt will not change (and also that the angles of wrap will not change), what is the horsepower capacity?

Ans. (*a*) 6.3, use 7. (*b*) For 7 belts, 28.7 hp.

22. A pivoted motor drive is shown schematically in Fig. 24-13. The two pulleys are of the same size, 12" in diameter, and the belt strands are horizontal. The driving motor runs at 800 rpm, the belt is $\frac{1}{4}$" thick and 9" wide, the motor weighs 600 lb, the coefficient of friction is 0.2, and the belt weighs 0.035 lb/in^3. Determine:

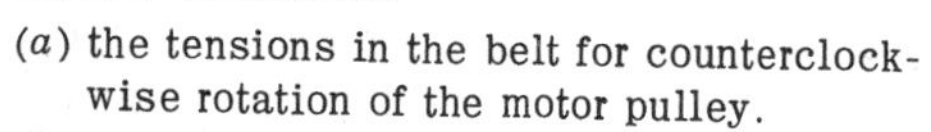

(*a*) the tensions in the belt for counterclockwise rotation of the motor pulley.

(*b*) the horsepower capacity for counterclockwise rotation of the motor pulley.

(*c*) the maximum stress in the belt for counterclockwise rotation of the motor pulley.

(*d*) the tensions in the belt for clockwise direction of rotation of the motor pulley.

(*e*) the horsepower capacity for clockwise rotation of the motor pulley.

(*f*) the maximum stress in the belt for clockwise rotation of the motor pulley.

Ans. (*a*) 413 lb, 244 lb (*b*) 12.8 hp (*c*) 184 psi (*d*) 468 lb, 368 lb (*e*) 7.6 hp (*f*) 208 psi

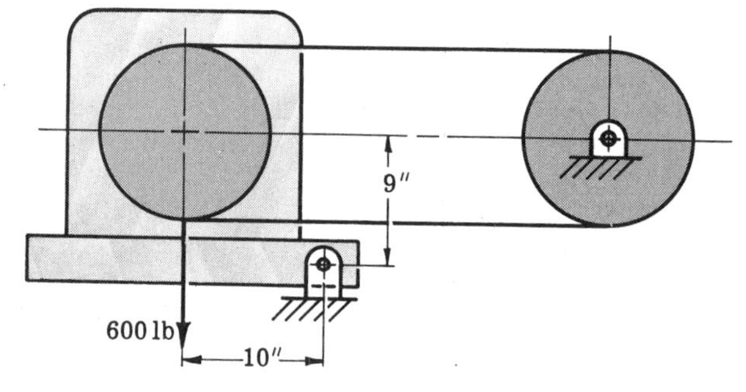

Fig. 24-13

23. Several pulleys are driven by the same belt, as shown in Fig. 24-14. Pulley 1 drives the belt; pulleys 2, 3, and 4 take power from the belt. Assume for all pulleys the same value of friction coefficient between belt and pulley. The belt is not to slip on pulley 1 even though all other pulleys are loaded to the point of slippage. Determine the minimum angle of wrap necessary on pulley 1, in terms of the angles of wrap on the other pulleys.

Ans. $\alpha_1 = \alpha_2 + \alpha_3 + \alpha_4$

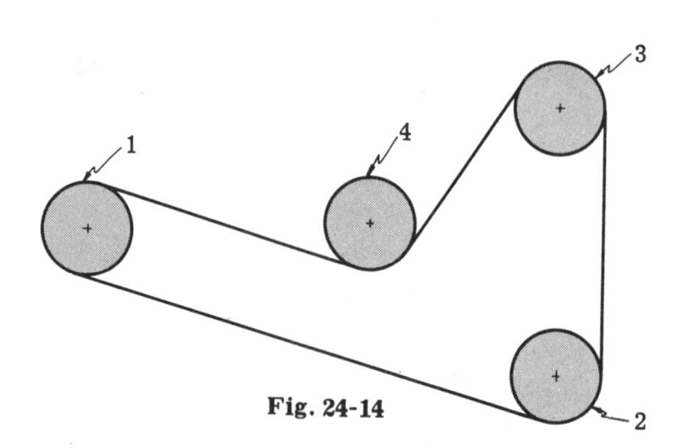

Fig. 24-14

Chapter 25

Welding

INTRODUCTION. There are many phases of welding which are important and rightly deserve a place in machine design considerations. For the designer, the immediate problem is the determination of the size of weld necessary for a given part, and this dictates a stress analysis where parts are subject to load, either static or fluctuating. The procedures as recommended by the American Welding Society (AWS) with modifications as recommended by The Lincoln Electric Company, will be used.

A designer is required to use the design stresses and procedures as specified by the various codes for structures, bridges, and pressure vessels where procedures are conservative. A machine designer, on the other hand, has greater freedom in designing machines, in general. The viewpoint in this chapter is one to permit freedom and flexibility in design.

TYPES OF WELDED JOINTS.

(1) Butt welds. See Fig.25-1.

According to the Lincoln Electric Co., a butt weld, when properly made, has equal or better strength than the plate and there is no need for calculating the stress in the weld or attempting to determine its size. It is necessary to match the electrode strength to plate strength when welding alloy steels.

Several of the codes suggest reducing the strength by some factor, the efficiency of the joint. Where the strength is to be reduced, the equation for the allowable force on a butt weld is given by

$$F_{all} = s_t tLe$$

where

F_{all} = allowable force, lb
s_t = allowable stress for the weld, psi
t = thickness of plate, inches
L = length of the weld, inches
e = efficiency.

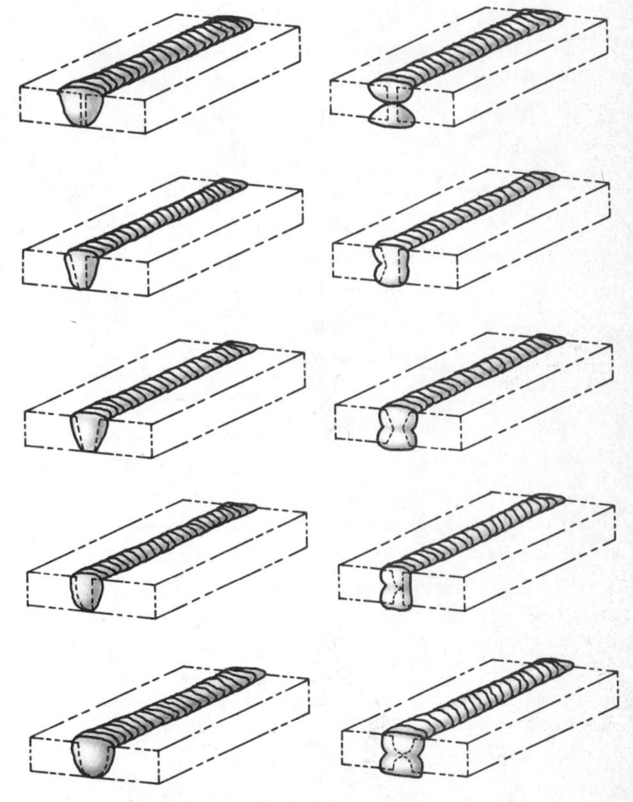

Fig.25-1 Butt Welds

(2) Fillet welds.

Fillet welds are classified according to the direction of the load: (*a*) parallel load, (*b*) transverse load. See Fig.25-2 below.

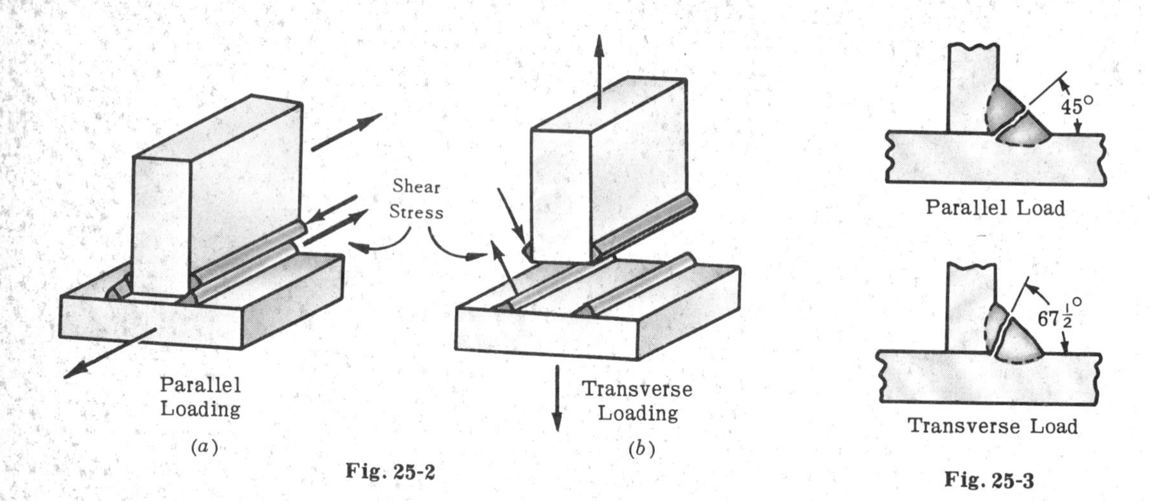

Fig. 25-2

Fig. 25-3

The plane of maximum shear stress in the conventional 45° fillet weld is the 45° throat when subjected to a parallel load and the $67\frac{1}{2}°$ throat when subjected to a transverse load, as shown in Fig.25-3 above. This results in greater strength for a transverse load.

Leg size is the basis of specifying a weld in the United States (throat is used in Europe). The size of a fillet weld is specified by the leg length of the largest inscribed isosceles right triangle or the leg lengths of the largest inscribed right triangle.

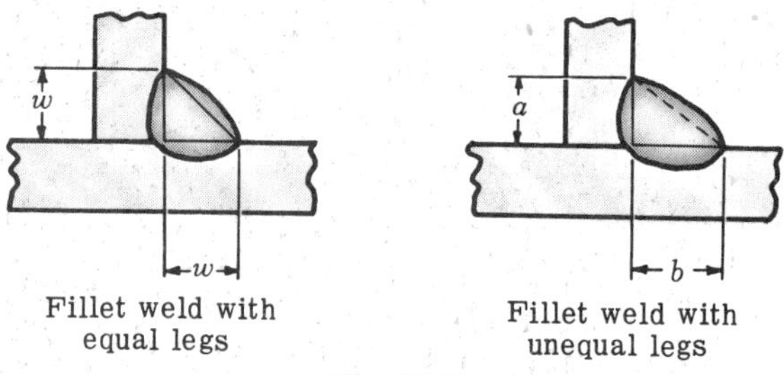

Fillet weld with equal legs

Fillet weld with unequal legs

Fig. 25-4

The leg length of a fillet weld with equal legs is given by w and the leg lengths of a fillet weld with unequal legs are given by a and b, as shown in Fig.25-4.

The throat dimension t for a fillet weld having equal legs is obtained by multiplying the size of the fillet weld (the leg length) by 0.707, i.e. $t = 0.707w$. See Fig.25-5.

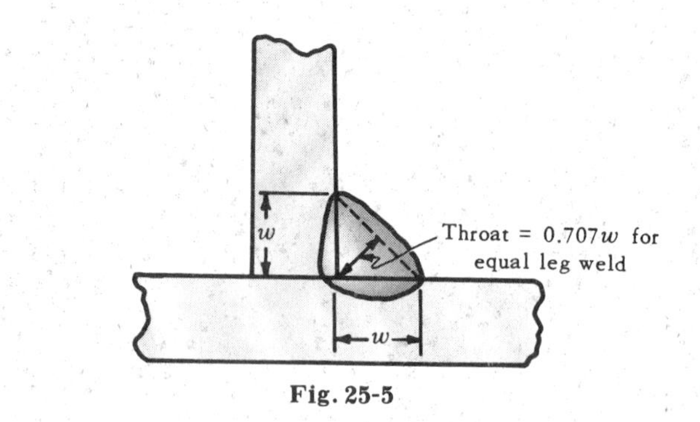

Fig. 25-5

The actual throat t_a obtained with automatic welding is larger than the theoretical throat t (See Fig.25-6). For a penetration of p, the leg length is $(w + p)$, and the throat dimension is $0.707(w + p)$. AWS does not allow for the extra strength due to penetration, although the effect can be taken into account if desired.

Stress in a fillet weld shall be considered as shear stress on the throat for any direction of applied load.

The allowable parallel load per inch of weld in a statically loaded fillet weld is

$$F_{all} = s_{all}A = 13{,}600(0.707w) = 9600w$$

where s_{all} = allowable shear stress = 13,600 psi, according to AWS Code.

A = throat area of 1" of weld at 45°, which is $0.707w$

w = leg size, inches.

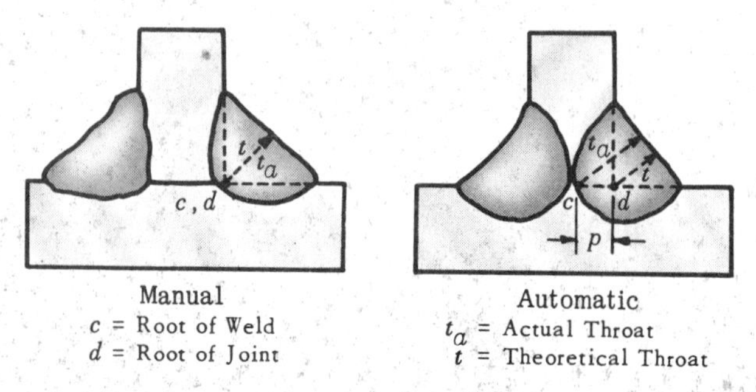

Manual
c = Root of Weld
d = Root of Joint

Automatic
t_a = Actual Throat
t = Theoretical Throat

Fig. 25-6

The allowable transverse load per inch of weld in a statically loaded fillet weld is

$$F_{all} = s_{all}A = 13{,}600(0.765w)/\cos 22\tfrac{1}{2}^\circ = 11{,}300w$$

where s_{all} = allowable stress = 13,600 psi, the same as for a parallel loaded fillet weld
A = throat area of 1'' of weld at $67\frac{1}{2}^\circ$, which is $0.765w$.

According to AWS, if part of the load is applied parallel and part transverse, the allowable parallel load must be used. Where bending or torsion is encountered, the procedure of analyzing the weld is to treat it as a line with no cross sectional area. It can be shown that the property, such as section modulus, of any thin area is equal to the property of the section when treated as a line multiplied by its thickness, with negligible error.

Consider bending: $$s = \frac{M}{Z}$$

where M = bending moment, in-lb; Z = section modulus, in^3; s = stress, psi.

If the section modulus Z_w of a weld, treated as a line, is determined, the units are in^2. $(Z_w)(w)$ gives the section modulus of the weld, where w is the leg size of the weld. Thus

$$s = \frac{M}{(Z_w)(w)} \quad \text{or} \quad sw = \frac{M}{Z_w}$$

The product of s and w gives units of lb/in and is represented by the symbol f. Thus

$$f = \frac{M}{Z_w}$$

where f is the load per inch, M (in-lb) is the bending moment, and Z_w (in^2) is the section modulus of the weld treated as a line. The above procedure permits finding the size of weld directly.

The corresponding section modulus in bending, Z_w, and polar moment of inertia in torsion, J_w, of 13 typical welded connections with the weld treated as a line are shown in Fig.25-7 below. Section moduli from these formulas are for maximum force at the top as well as the bottom portions of the welded connections. For the unsymmetrical connections shown, maximum bending force is at the bottom.

If there is more than one force applied to the weld, these are found and combined. All forces which are combined must occur at the same point in the welded joint.

The section modulus and polar moment of inertia are used in the standard design formulas, as listed. For secondary welds, the weld is not treated as a line, but standard design formulas are used to find the force per inch of weld on the weld. The symbols used are:

b = width of connection, in.
d = depth of connection, in.
A = area of flange material held by welds in shear, in^2
I = moment of inertia of entire section, in^4
C = distance to outer fiber, in.
t = thickness of plate, in.
J = polar moment of inertia of section, in^4
P = tensile or compressive load, lb
N_x = distance of x axis to face, in.
N_y = distance of y axis to face, in.
V = vertical shear load, lb
M = bending moment, in-lb
T = twisting moment, in-lb
L_w = length of weld, in.
Z_w = section modulus of weld, in^2
J_w = polar moment of inertia of weld, in^3
s = stress in standard design formula, psi
f = force per inch in standard design formula when weld is treated as a line, lb/in
n = number of welds.

Properties of Weld Treated as a Line		
Outline of Welded Joint b = width d = depth	**Bending** (about horizontal axis X-X)	**Twisting**
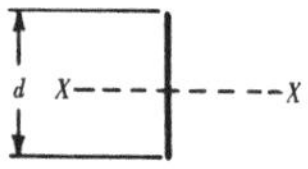	$Z_w = \frac{d^2}{6}$	$J_w = \frac{d^3}{12}$
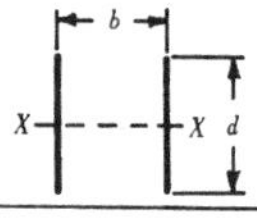	$Z_w = \frac{d^2}{3}$	$J_w = \frac{d(3b^2+d^2)}{6}$
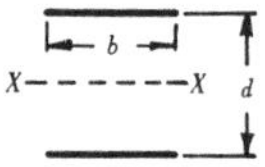	$Z_w = bd$	$J_w = \frac{b^3+3bd^2}{6}$
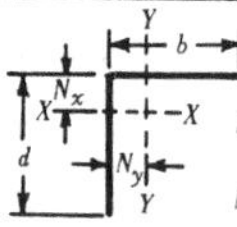 $N_y = \frac{b^2}{2(b+d)}$ $N_x = \frac{d^2}{2(b+d)}$	$Z_w = \frac{4bd+d^2}{6}$ top $= \frac{d^2(4bd+d)}{6(2b+d)}$ bottom	$J_w = \frac{(b+d)^4 - 6b^2d^2}{12(b+d)}$
$N_y = \frac{b^2}{2b+d}$ 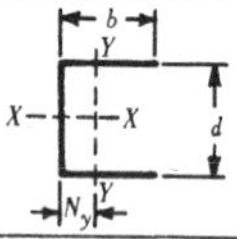	$Z_w = bd + \frac{d^2}{6}$	$J_w = \frac{(2b+d)^3}{12} - \frac{b^2(b+d)^2}{(2b+d)}$
$N_x = \frac{d^2}{b+2d}$ 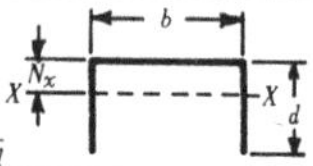	$Z_w = \frac{2bd+d^2}{3}$ top $= \frac{d^2(2b+d)}{3(b+d)}$ bottom	$J_w = \frac{(b+2d)^3}{12} - \frac{d^2(b+d)^2}{(b+2d)}$
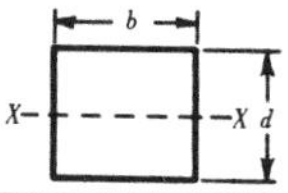	$Z_w = bd + \frac{d^2}{3}$	$J_w = \frac{(b+d)^3}{6}$
$N_y = \frac{d^2}{b+2d}$ 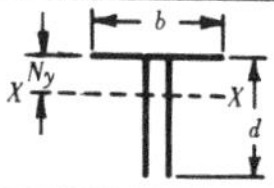	$Z_w = \frac{2bd+d^2}{3}$ top $= \frac{d^2(2b+d)}{3(b+d)}$ bottom	$J_w = \frac{(b+2d)^3}{12} - \frac{d^2(b+d)^2}{(b+2d)}$
$N_y = \frac{d^2}{2(b+d)}$ 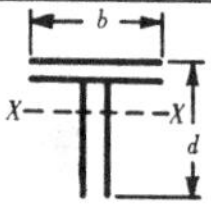	$Z_w = \frac{4bd+d^2}{3}$ top $= \frac{4bd^2+d^3}{6b+3d}$ bottom	$J_w = \frac{d^3(4b+d)}{6(b+d)} + \frac{b^3}{6}$
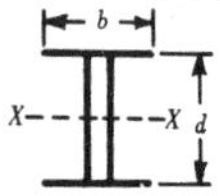	$Z_w = bd + \frac{d^2}{3}$	$J_w = \frac{b^3+3bd^2+d^3}{6}$
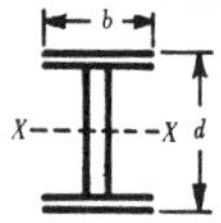	$Z_w = 2bd + \frac{d^2}{3}$	$J_w = \frac{2b^3+6bd^2+d^3}{6}$
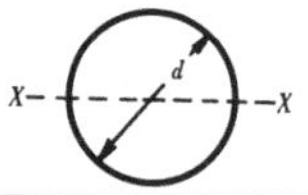	$Z_w = \frac{\pi d^2}{4}$	$J_w = \frac{\pi d^3}{4}$
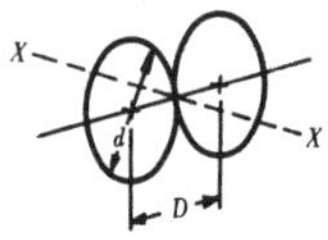	$Z_w = \frac{\pi d^2}{2} + \pi D^2$	

Courtesy The Lincoln Electric Co.

Fig. 25-7 (a)

Type of Loading		Standard Design Formula Stress lb/in^2	Treating the Weld as a Line Force lb/in
	Primary Welds transmit entire load		
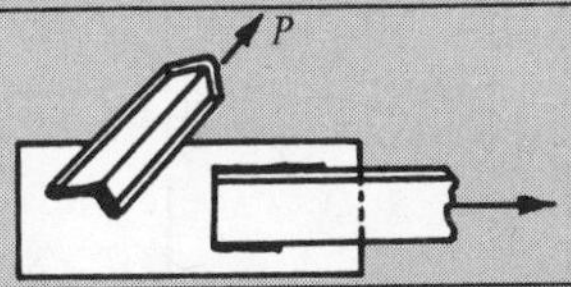	**tension or compression**	$s = \frac{P}{A}$	$f = \frac{P}{L_w}$
	**vertical shear**	$s = \frac{V}{A}$	$f = \frac{V}{L_w}$
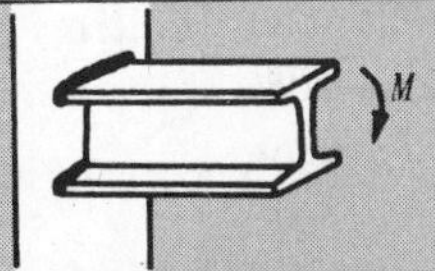	**bending**	$s = \frac{M}{Z}$	$f = \frac{M}{Z_w}$
	**twisting**	$s = \frac{TC}{J}$	$f = \frac{TC}{J_w}$
	Secondary Welds hold section together — low stress		
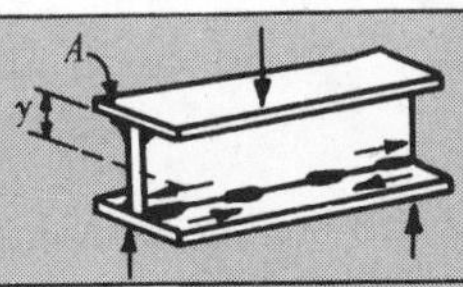	**horizontal shear**	$s = \frac{VAy}{It}$	$f = \frac{VAy}{In}$
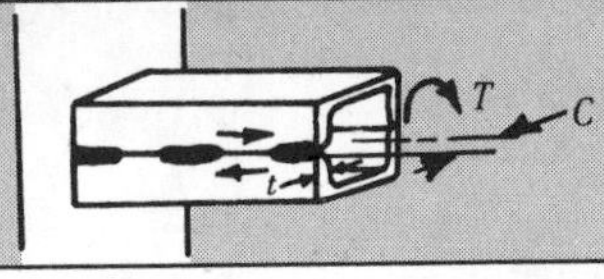	**torsional horizontal shear**	$s = \frac{TC}{J}$	$f = \frac{TCt}{J}$

Courtesy The Lincoln Electric Co.

Fig. 25-7 (b)

If intermittent welds are to be used, determine the ratio R of the calculated leg size for contionous welding and the actual leg size to be used with intermittent welding:

$$R = \frac{\text{calculated leg size, continuous weld}}{\text{actual leg size to be used, intermittent weld}}$$

The length of intermittent welds and distance between centers is given as a function of R. A representation such as 3–4 means a weld 3'' long with a distance of 4'' between the centers of two consecutive welds.

R (percent of continuous weld)	Length of intermittent welds and distance between centers		
75%		3–4	
66			4–6
60		3–5	
57			4–7
50	2–4	3–6	4–8
44			4–9
43		3–7	
40	2–5		4–10
37		3–8	
33	2–6	3–9	4–12
30		3–10	
25	2–8	3–12	
20	2–10		
16	2–12		

The following values of **fatigue strength** (lb per inch of fillet welds) are a guide to design of fillet welds under varying load. The values are based on a more conservative limiting value of 8780 lb per inch of fillet weld as used in bridge design as recommended by AWS.

(*1*) Allowable fatigue strength for fillet welds for 2,000,000 cycles = $\frac{5090}{1-\frac{1}{2}K}$ lb/in (if the value computed is greater than 8780 lb/in, use 8780 lb/in).

(*2*) Allowable fatigue strength for fillet welds for 600,000 cycles = $\frac{7070}{1-\frac{1}{2}K}$ lb/in (if the value computed is greater than 8780 lb/in, use 8780 lb/in).

(*3*) Allowable fatigue strength for fillet welds for 100,000 cycles = $\frac{8484}{1-\frac{1}{2}K}$ lb/in (if the value computed is greater than 8780 lb/in, use 8780 lb/in).

(For other types of welds, refer to the AWS Bridge Code, Section 208, Design for Repeated Stress.)

In the above, $K = \frac{\text{minimum load}}{\text{maximum load}} = \frac{\text{minimum stress}}{\text{maximum stress}}$. $K = +1$ for steady stress, $K = 0$ if load is released (varies in one direction), $K = -1$ if load is completely reversed.

Any abrupt change in section along the path of stress flow will reduce the fatigue strength. It is not so much a matter of welding reducing the fatigue strength as it is the effect of the shape or geometry.

The fatigue strength related to the number of cycles can be expressed by the empirical formula

$$F_A = F_B\left(\frac{N_B}{N_A}\right)^c$$

where F_A = the fatigue strength for N_A cycles
F_B = the fatigue strength for N_B cycles
c = the constant which varies slightly with the specimen. 0.13 has been used for butt welds and 0.18 for plates in axial loading, tension and/or compression.

Rule of thumb for welds which are not calculated: For a full strength weld for both parallel and transverse loading, the leg size of the weld should be 3/4 the thickness of the plate the full length of the plate, and the plate should be welded on both sides. For design where rigidity is the criterion, use a leg size of the weld equal to 3/8 the thickness of the plate.

SOLVED PROBLEMS

1. Show that the plane of maximum shear occurs at 45° for a parallel load on a fillet weld of equal legs, as shown in Fig. 25-8; neglect bending. Determine the allowable force F_{all} per inch of weld if the allowable shear stress is 13,600 psi according to AWS.

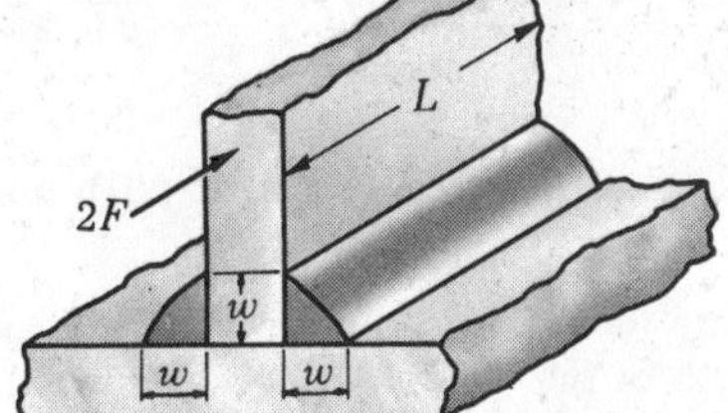

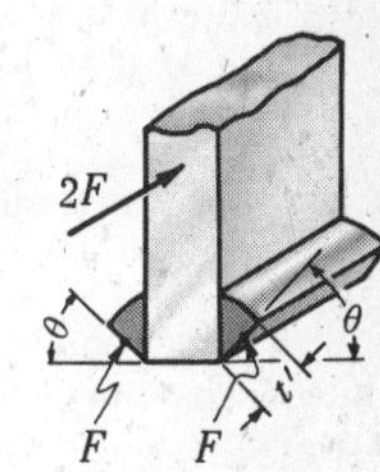

Fig. 25-8

Solution:

(*a*) Consider the free body with the two welds cut symmetrically with the vertical.

(*b*) Designate the dimension of the throat of the arbitrary section as t'. The area of a weld of the isolated portion is $A = t'L$, where $t' = w/(\sin\theta + \cos\theta)$.

(*c*) The shear stress is $s_s = \dfrac{F}{A} = \dfrac{F}{t'L} = \dfrac{F(\sin\theta + \cos\theta)}{wL}$.

(*d*) Differentiate s_s with respect to θ, and set the derivative equal to zero for maximum:

$$\frac{ds_s}{d\theta} = \frac{F}{wL}(\cos\theta - \sin\theta) = 0$$

which is satisfied when $\cos\theta = \sin\theta$, or $\theta = 45^\circ$.

(*e*) Substituting $\theta = 45^\circ$ into (*c*), $s_{s(max)} = \dfrac{\sqrt{2}F}{wL} = \dfrac{F}{tL}$ where t is the throat at 45°.

(*f*) The allowable load per inch of weld is $F_{all} = s_{s(all)}wL/\sqrt{2} = 13{,}600w(1)/\sqrt{2} = 9600w$, where w is the leg size.

2. Show that the plane of maximum shear force occurs at $67\frac{1}{2}^\circ$ for a transverse load on a fillet weld of equal legs. Neglect bending. Determine the allowable force per inch of weld if the allowable shear stress is 13,600 psi according to the AWS.

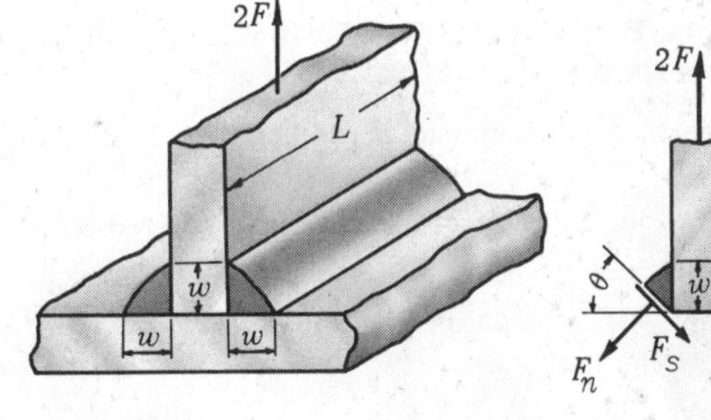

Fig. 25-9

Solution:

(*a*) The free body is shown in Fig. 25-9. Assume the two welds share the load equally. The shear force is F_s and the normal force is F_n. Summing the vertical components,

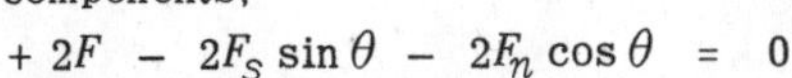

$$+2F - 2F_s\sin\theta - 2F_n\cos\theta = 0$$

(*b*) Assuming that the resultant of F_s and F_n is vertical, then the horizontal components are equal and opposite: $F_s\cos\theta = F_n\sin\theta$. Substituting $F_n = (F_s\cos\theta)/(\sin\theta)$ into (*a*),

$$+2F - 2F_s\sin\theta - \frac{2F_s\cos\theta}{\sin\theta}(\cos\theta) = 0 \quad \text{or} \quad F_s = F\sin\theta$$

(*c*) The throat dimension for the section taken is $t' = w/(\cos\theta + \sin\theta)$.

(*d*) The shear stress is $s_s = \dfrac{F_s}{A} = \dfrac{F_s}{t'L} = \dfrac{(F\sin\theta)(\cos\theta + \sin\theta)}{wL}$.

(*e*) For maximum s_s, find angle θ which defines the maximum shear by setting $ds_s/d\theta = 0$.

$$\frac{ds_s}{d\theta} = \frac{F}{wL}[(\sin\theta)(-\sin\theta + \cos\theta) + (\cos\theta + \sin\theta)(\cos\theta)] = 0$$

Using the substitutions $\cos^2\theta - \sin^2\theta = \cos 2\theta$ and $\sin\theta\cos\theta = \frac{1}{2}\sin 2\theta$, this gives $\sin 2\theta = -\cos 2\theta$, $\tan 2\theta = -1$, $2\theta = 135^\circ$, and $\theta = 67\frac{1}{2}^\circ$.

(*f*) Maximum stress is found by substitution of $\theta = 67\frac{1}{2}^\circ$ into (*d*):

$$s_{s\,(\max)} = \frac{(F \sin 67\tfrac{1}{2}^\circ)(\cos 67\tfrac{1}{2}^\circ + \sin 67\tfrac{1}{2}^\circ)}{wL} = \frac{1.21F}{wL} = \frac{0.924F}{tL} \quad \text{where } t \text{ is the throat at } 67\tfrac{1}{2}^\circ$$

(g) Allowable force per inch of weld is $F = \dfrac{s_{s\,(\text{all})}wL}{1.21} = \dfrac{13{,}600w(1)}{1.21} = 11{,}300w$, where w is the leg size.

3. How is the loading distributed in welds with parallel loading if the welds are relatively long?

Solution:

If the welds are long, the loading is not distributed uniformly. The maximum loading per inch of weld depends on the length of the weld. Values of allowable load per inch of weld should be reduced to about 90% that for short welds.

4. Treating the weld as a line, determine the section modulus Z_w in bending of a weld d inches high. Refer to Fig. 25-10.

Solution:

Moment of inertia $I = \displaystyle\int_{-\frac{1}{2}d}^{+\frac{1}{2}d} y^2\,dy = \frac{d^3}{12}$, and $Z_w = \dfrac{I}{d/2} = \dfrac{d^2}{6}$.

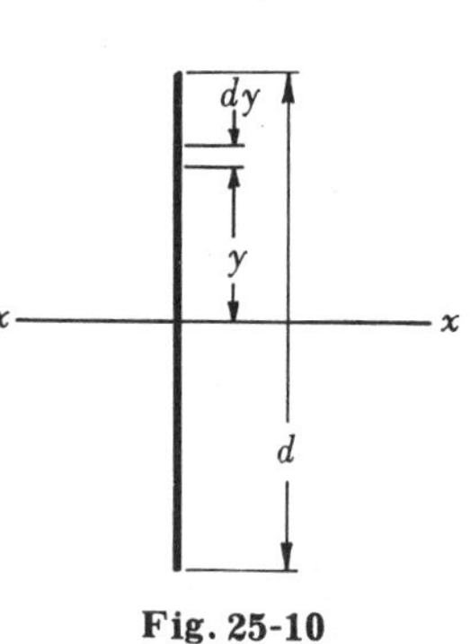

Fig. 25-10

5. Treating the weld as a line, determine the moment of inertia J_w about the center.

Solution:

Referring to Fig. 25-10, $J_w = \displaystyle\int_{-\frac{1}{2}d}^{+\frac{1}{2}d} y^2\,dy = \frac{d^3}{12}$.

6. Treating the weld as a line, determine the section modulus Z_w about the x-x axis. Refer to Fig. 25-11.

Solution:

From Prob. 4, the moment of inertia of the vertical lines about the x-x axis is $I_1 = 2(d^3/12) = d^3/6$.

The moment of inertia of the horizontal lines is $I_2 = 2[b(d/2)^2] = bd^2/2$.

The total moment of inertia about the x-x axis is $I = I_1 + I_2 = (d^3/6) + (bd^2/2)$.

The section modulus $Z_w = \dfrac{I}{c} = \dfrac{(d^3/6) + (bd^2/2)}{d/2} = \dfrac{d^2}{3} + bd$.

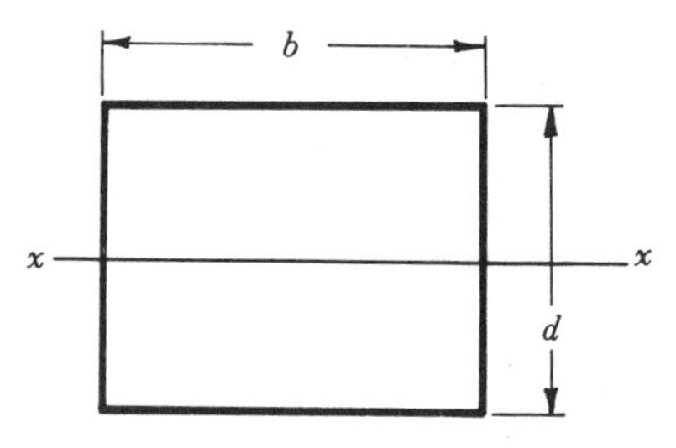

Fig. 25-11

7. Treating the weld as a line, determine the moment of inertia J_w about the center of gravity. Refer to Fig. 25-12.

Solution:

Consider each line separately, determine the effect of each, and add the parts.

Consider the top line, with a differential element dx. The integral of the product of the length of the element and the square of the variable distance to the center of gravity is

$$J_{w_1} = \int r^2\,dx = 2\int_0^{\frac{1}{2}b} [(d/2)^2 + x^2]\,dx$$

$$= 2(\tfrac{d}{2})^2(\tfrac{b}{2}) + \tfrac{2}{3}(\tfrac{b}{2})^3 = \frac{d^2b}{4} + \frac{b^3}{12}$$

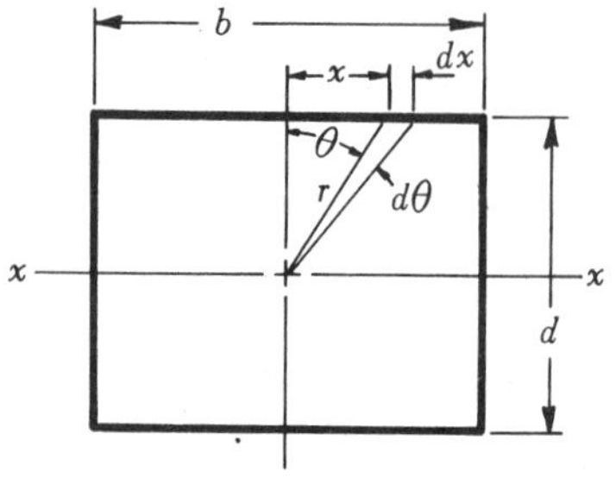

Fig. 25-12

The contribution by the bottom line is the same: $J_{w_2} = \dfrac{d^2b}{4} + \dfrac{b^3}{12}$.

By analogy, the polar moment of inertia of each vertical line is $J_{w_3} = J_{w_4} = \dfrac{db^2}{4} + \dfrac{d^3}{12}$.

The total polar moment of inertia $J_w = J_{w_1} + J_{w_2} + J_{w_3} + J_{w_4} = \dfrac{b^3 + 3b^2d + 3bd^2 + d^3}{6} = \dfrac{(b+d)^3}{6}$.

8. Determine the required fillet weld size for the bracket shown in Fig. 25-13 below.

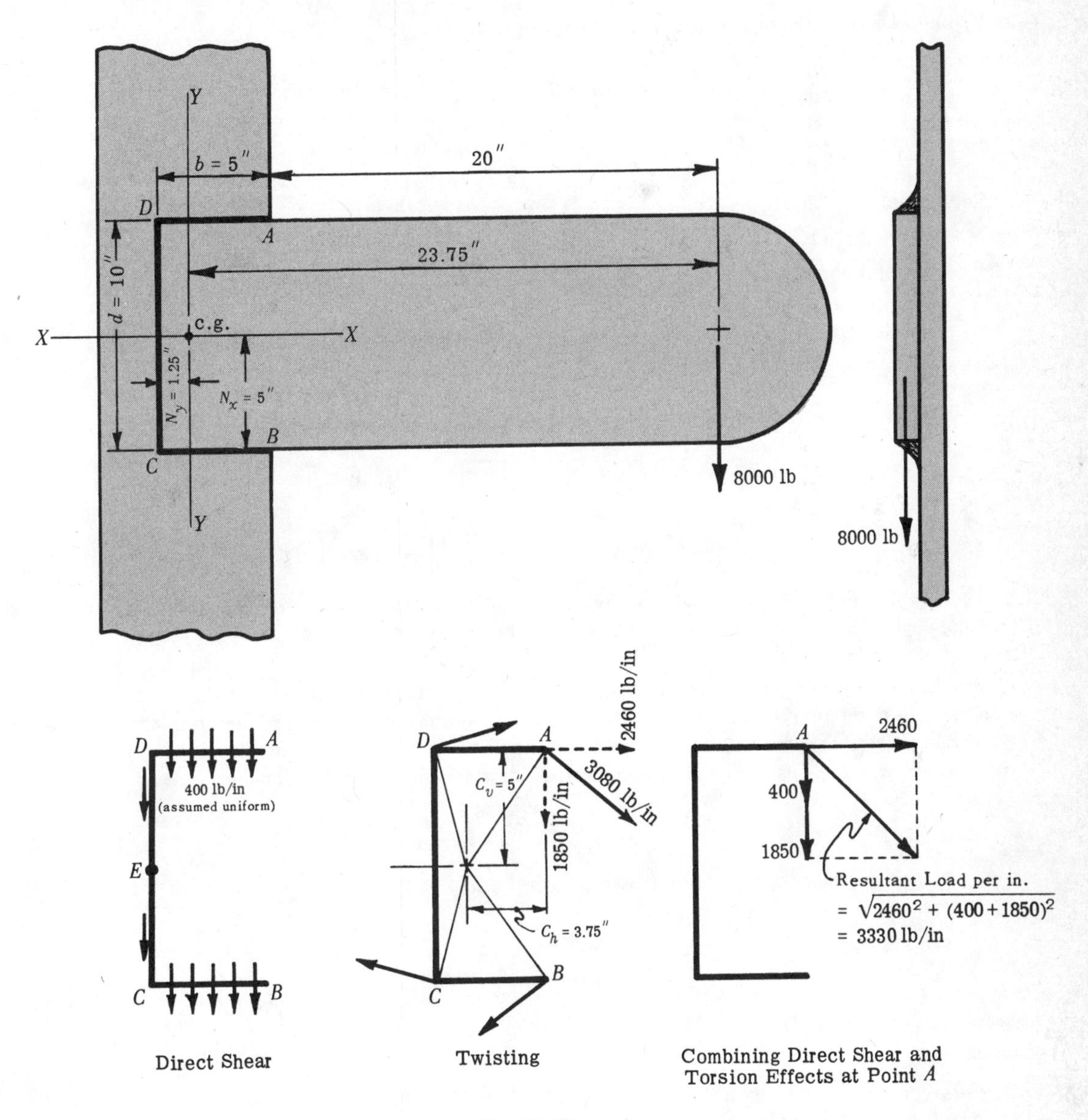

Fig. 25-13

Solution:

(a) Determine the center of gravity of the weld, treating the weld as a line with no thickness. See Fig. 25-7(a).

By symmetry, $N_x = 5''$. $N_y = \dfrac{b^2}{2b+d} = \dfrac{5^2}{2(5)+10} = 1.25''$.

(b) Replace the original 8000 lb force by a force of 8000 lb at the c.g. and a couple = 8000(23.75) = 190,000 in-lb (causing twisting).

(c) The vertical force of 8000 lb is assumed uniformly distributed over the weld and causes a loading of (8000)/(5+10+5) = 400 lb per inch of weld.

(*d*) Now determine the effect of the twisting couple. The polar moment of inertia of the weld, treating it as a line, is

$$J_w = \frac{(2b+d)^3}{12} - \frac{b^2(b+d)^2}{2b+d} = \frac{(10+10)^3}{12} - \frac{5^2(5+10)^2}{2(5)+10} = 385.4 \text{ in}^3$$

(*e*) At points A and B, the maximum loading f from twisting is

$$f = \frac{TC}{J_w} = \frac{(190{,}000)\sqrt{5^2+3.75^2}}{385.4} = 3080 \text{ lb/in}$$

where C = distance from center of gravity to point being analyzed.

The vertical component $f_v = \dfrac{3.75}{\sqrt{5^2+3.75^2}}(3080) = 1850$ lb/in.

The horizontal component $f_h = \dfrac{5}{\sqrt{5^2+3.75^2}}(3080) = 2460$ lb/in.

Note that f_v and f_h can be obtained directly by using the horizontal and vertical distances $C_h = 3.75''$ and $C_v = 5''$ in $f = TC/J_w$.

(*f*) Combining the horizontal and vertical components at point A, the loading per inch is

$$F = \sqrt{(2460)^2 + (400+1850)^2} = 3330 \text{ lb/in}$$

(*g*) For steady loads, the weld size is $w = \dfrac{f_{\text{actual}}}{f_{\text{allowable}}} = \dfrac{3330}{9600} = 0.347''$. Use a $\frac{3}{8}''$ weld.

Note that the allowable loading is 9600 lb per inch of weld, the allowable loading for parallel loading being used where there is a combination of transverse and parallel loading.

(*h*) An alternate analysis, which is justifiable on the basis of the distribution of the transverse shear force as used in beam analysis, is to consider the top and bottom welds as carrying no transverse shear force. The maximum transverse shear stress in a rectangular section is $3V/2A$ at the neutral axis. Thus the direct shear at point A is zero and at point E the maximum shearing force per inch is

$$f_s = \frac{3}{2}\left(\frac{V}{L_w}\right) = \frac{3}{2}\left(\frac{8000}{10}\right) = 1200 \text{ lb/in}$$

At point A the resultant force per inch of weld, due to torsion alone, is 3080 lb/in, as determined in (*e*) above.

The size of weld is critical at point A (and point B) and is

$$w = \frac{f_{\text{actual}}}{f_{\text{allowable}}} = \frac{3080}{9600} = 0.321''. \text{ Use a } \frac{5}{16}'' \text{ or } \frac{3}{8}'' \text{ weld.}$$

9. A circular bar is welded to a steel plate. The bar diameter $d = 2$ in. Determine the size of weld required.

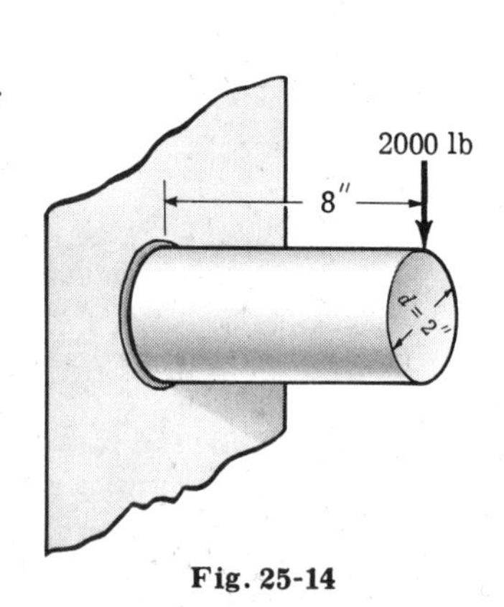

Fig. 25-14

Solution:

Bending moment = 2000(8) = 16,000 in-lb. Shearing force = 2000 lb.

Section modulus of weld treated as a line is [see Fig. 25-7(*a*)]

$$Z_w = \tfrac{1}{4}\pi d^2 = \tfrac{1}{4}\pi(2)^2 = 3.14 \text{ in}^2$$

Force per inch of weld, at top and bottom, is

$$f_B = M/Z_w = 16{,}000/3.14 = 5100 \text{ lb/in}$$

Vertical shear, assuming uniform distribution of the shear force, is

$$f_s = V/L_w = 2000/2\pi = 318 \text{ lb/in}$$

Resultant load $f = \sqrt{5100^2 + 318^2} = 5110$ lb/in.

Size of weld $w = \dfrac{f_{\text{actual}}}{f_{\text{allowable}}} = \dfrac{5110}{9600} = 0.53''$. A $\frac{1}{2}''$ weld should be satisfactory.

10. A plate girder is fabricated by welding. What size of fillet welds to join the flanges to the web is required for a transverse load (shear force) of 150,000 lb applied at the section under consideration? Refer to Fig. 25-15.

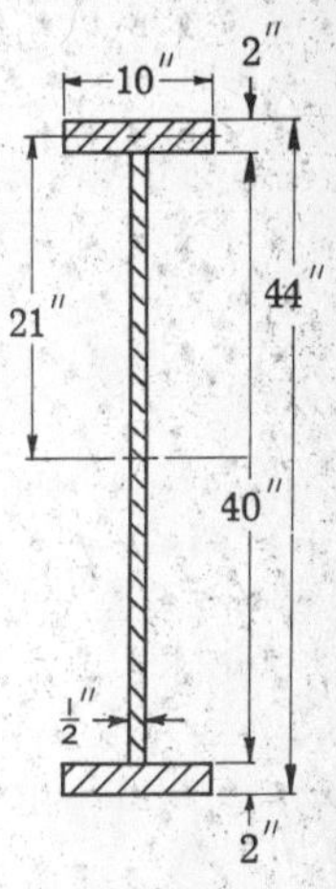

Fig. 25-15

Solution:

The weld required at the junction of the web and flange is considered as a secondary weld, inasmuch as it is required to hold the parts together. The deflection of the beam is not affected significantly even if the weld is omitted.

The loading per inch of weld at the junction of the web and flange is

$$f = \frac{VAY}{In} = \frac{(150{,}000)(20)(21)}{(20{,}020)(2)} = 1575 \text{ lb/in}$$

where V = shear force = 150,000 lb
A = area of section above the weld = 10(2) = 20 in^2
Y = distance to the center of gravity of the area above the weld (= 21 in.)
I = moment of inertia of the whole section about c.g. axis of I-beam (= 20,020 in^4)
n = number of welds (= 2).

The weld leg size w = 1575/9600 = 0.164″ (leg size of continuous weld).

Even though there may be little or no stress on some welds, for practical reasons it is best not to put too small a weld on a thick plate. The adjacent table, given by American Welding Society, can be used as a guide. Thus the minimum weld size as calculated is 0.164″ for a continuous weld. However, by the adjacent table, the minimum weld is $\frac{3}{8}$″ for a 2″ plate. Note that the leg size of the fillet weld need not exceed the thickness of the thinner plate.

Thickness of thicker plate	Minimum weld size
up to $\frac{1}{2}$″	3/16 in.
over $\frac{1}{2}$″ up to $\frac{3}{4}$″	1/4 in.
over $\frac{3}{4}$″ up to $1\frac{1}{4}$″	5/16 in.
over $1\frac{1}{4}$″ up to 2″	3/8 in.
over 2″ up to 6″	1/2 in.
over 6″	5/8 in.

Because of the greater strength of the $\frac{3}{8}$″ weld, intermittent welds can be used. Lincoln Electric Co. recommends, also, that the size of the fillet weld used for design calculations or determination of length must not exceed $\frac{2}{3}$ of the web thickness, or $\frac{2}{3}(\frac{1}{2})$ = 0.333″. This recommendation is based on limiting the shear stress in the thinner plate to 13,000 psi (as given by the AWS Bridge Code). Thus, even though a $\frac{3}{8}$″ weld is to be used, the calculations will be based on a weld 0.333″.

$$R = \frac{\text{size of continuous weld needed}}{\text{size of intermittent weld used}} = \frac{0.164}{0.333} = 49\%$$

From the table for percent of continuous weld, using the value for 50%, the length of intermittent weld and spacing can be 2-4, 3-6, or 4-8.

A final recommendation, then, for the weld is a $\frac{3}{8}$″ weld (leg size), two inches long, on 4 inch centers.

11. A rectangular beam is to be welded to a plate. The maximum load of 3000 lb is applied repetitiously. Determine the size of weld required for 10,000,000 cycles. Assume the shear load is distributed uniformly over the entire weld. Refer to Fig. 25-16 below.

Solution:

Consider the horizontal welds where the bending stress is maximum (the top and bottom welds are stressed the same).

The bending moment varies from a maximum of 3000(6) = 18,000 in-lb in one direction to a maximum of 3000(6) = 18,000 in-lb in the opposite direction. The shear force varies from 3000 lb up to 3000 lb down.

The section modulus of the weld is $Z_w = bd + d^2/3 = (2)(3) + 3^2/3 = 9 \text{ in}^2$

The load in lb/in due to bending is $f = M/Z_w = 18{,}000/9 = 2000$ lb/in

$$\text{Average shear force} = \frac{V}{L_w} = \frac{3000}{2+3+2+3} = 300 \text{ lb/in}$$

$$\text{Maximum force/in} = \sqrt{2000^2 + 300^2} = 2020 \text{ lb/in.}$$

The maximum force varies from 2020 lb/in in one direction to 2020 lb/in in the opposite direction. This is true for both top and bottom welds.

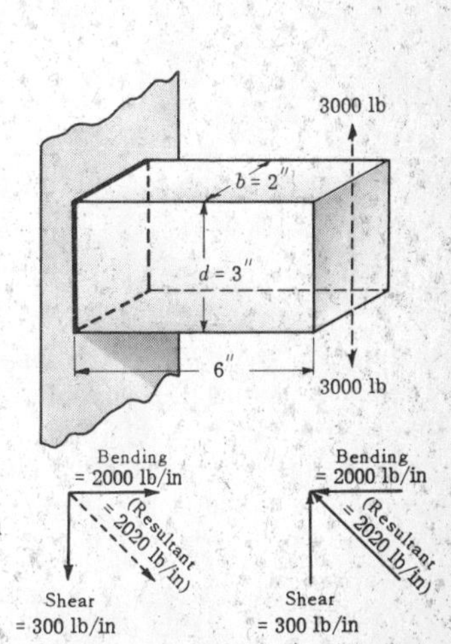

Fig. 25-16

The allowable force/in for 2,000,000 cycles is

$$f_{2{,}000{,}000} = \frac{5090}{1-\frac{1}{2}K} = \frac{5090}{1-\frac{1}{2}(-1)} = 3390 \text{ lb/in}$$

where $K = \frac{\text{minimum stress}}{\text{maximum stress}} = -1$ since the load is completely reversed.

The allowable force per inch of weld for 10,000,000 cycles is

$$f_{10,000,000} = (3390)\left(\frac{2,000,000}{10,000,000}\right)^{0.13} = 2750 \text{ lb/in}$$

The weld size $w = 2020/2750 = 0.734''$. Use $w = \frac{3}{4}''$.

12. Determine the load capacity of the single plug weld shown in Fig. 25-17. Use an allowable shear capacity of 13,600 psi. The load is steady.

Solution:

Shear area $= \frac{1}{4}\pi D^2 = \frac{1}{4}\pi(\frac{3}{4})^2 = 0.441 \text{ in}^2$.

Allowable force $F = (13,600)(0.441) = 6000$ lb.

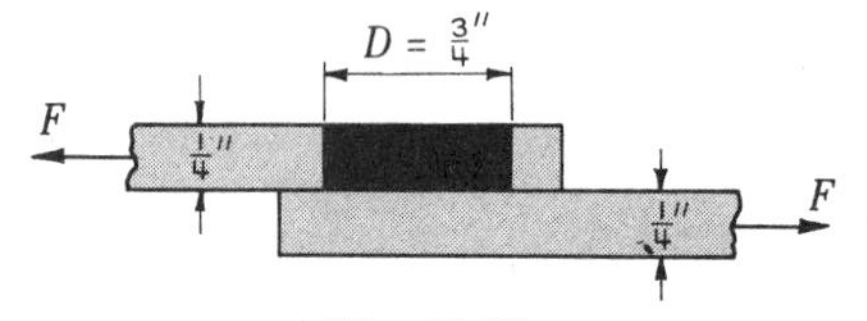

Fig. 25-17

SUPPLEMENTARY PROBLEMS

13. A $1'' \times \frac{1}{2}''$ bar is welded to a 4 in. diameter cylinder. Determine the size of a 45° fillet weld. Assume transverse shear is uniformly distributed in the weld. Use an allowable load of 9600 lb per inch of weld.
Ans. For a bending moment of 1800 in-lb, a section modulus of weld $Z_w = bd + d^2/3 = \frac{1}{2}(1) + 1^2/3 = 0.83 \text{ in}^2$, and a resultant load per inch of weld $= \sqrt{2160^2 + 50^2} = 2160$ lb, the size of weld $= 2160/9600 = 0.225''$; use $\frac{1}{4}''$. Since the load is essentially transverse to the weld, a smaller weld could be used, based on an allowable load of 11,300 lb per inch of weld. However, a final size of $w = \frac{1}{4}''$ is satisfactory.

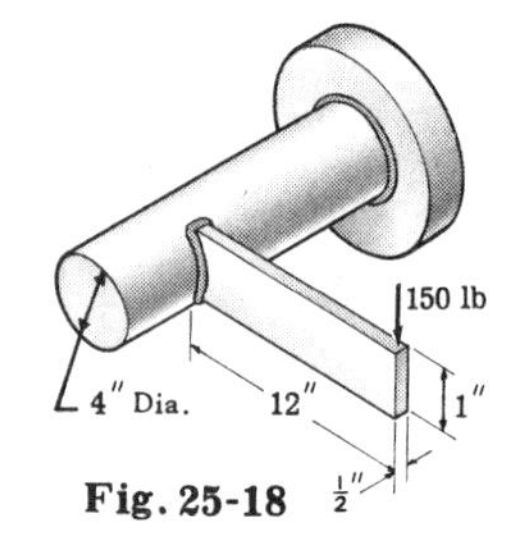

Fig. 25-18

14. Determine the size of fillet weld required for the flat plate loaded as shown in Fig. 25-19 below.
Ans. $w = 0.368''$, use $w = \frac{3}{8}''$ for an allowable load of 9600 lb/in.

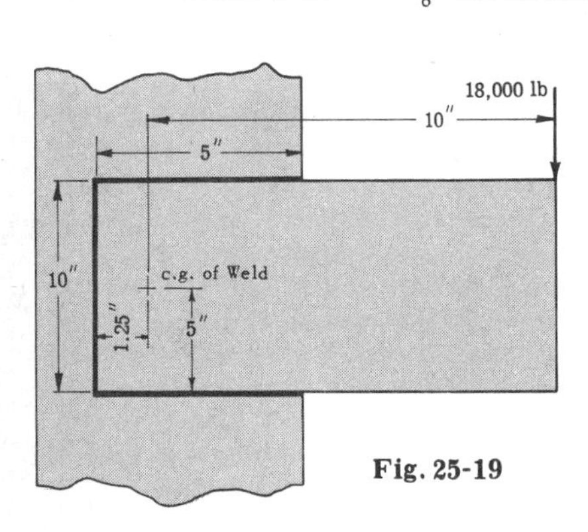

Fig. 25-19

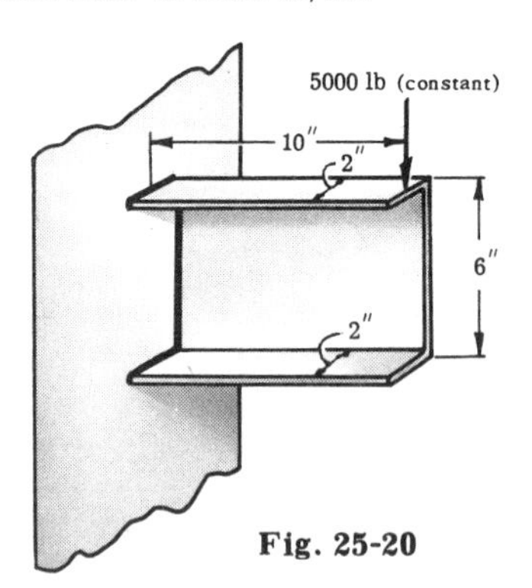

Fig. 25-20

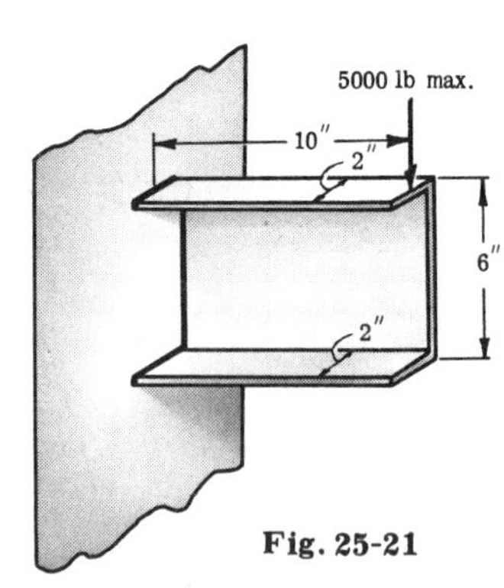

Fig. 25-21

15. A channel is welded to a support. For a steady load of 5000 lb, determine the size of weld required. Assume that the vertical load is uniformly distributed on the weld. Refer to Fig. 25-20 above.
Ans. $Z_w = 18 \text{ in}^2$, 2780 lb/in due to bending, 500 lb/in due to shear, resultant 2830 lb/in, and $w = 0.294''$ for allowable load of 9600 lb per inch of weld; use $w = \frac{5}{16}''$.

16. A channel is welded to a support as shown in Fig. 25-21 above. The load is applied in a varying fashion from zero to a maximum of 5000 lb. Assume the vertical load is uniformly distributed on the weld. Determine (*a*) the maximum resultant load on the weld, (*b*) the minimum load on the weld, (*c*) the allowable load per inch on the weld for 2,000,000 cycles, and (*d*) the size of weld.
Ans. (*a*) 2830 lb per inch (same as Prob. 15). (*b*) Zero. (*c*) For $K = 0$, allowable load per inch of weld is 5090 lb/in. (*d*) $w = 0.556''$; use $w = \frac{5}{8}''$.

17. A calculated necessary weld size is $0.180''$. A $\frac{3}{8}''$ fillet weld is to be used intermittently. Determine the spacing. *Ans.* Use a $\frac{3}{8}''$ weld, 3 in. long, with 6 in. spacing.

18. A plug weld used in a plate 1 in. thick has a diameter of $1\frac{1}{2}$ in. What is the design load for an allowable shear stress of 13,600 psi? *Ans.* 24,000 lb

Chapter 26

Flywheels

FLYWHEELS. A flywheel and a governor are devices to control speed variation in an engine, the difference being that a flywheel redistributes energy within a cycle to control speed, while a governor controls the amount of fuel to an engine to match the load requirements to maintain a specified speed. If we picture a governor operating in a fixed position, the function of the flywheel is then isolated in its function of limiting the speed variation.

If the load output requirements are constant and the power input is constant, no flywheel is needed. If the power input is variable, with the load output requirements constant, a flywheel can be used to advantage to smoothen out the operation; if the power input is constant and the load output requirements are variable, again a flywheel can be used to advantage to smoothen out the operation.

Examples of machines that use flywheels effectively are punch presses and internal combustion engines. In punch presses the rate of energy input can be thought of as constant and the output variable; in internal combustion engines the rate of energy input is variable and the rate of load output may be constant or variable.

RIM FLYWHEEL. The weight of the rim of a rimmed flywheel can be determined by any one of the following equivalent forms:

$$W_r = \frac{KgE}{V^2\delta} = \frac{2KgE}{V_1^2 - V_2^2} = \frac{2KgE}{r^2(\omega_1^2 - \omega_2^2)}$$

where W_r = weight of rim alone, lb

K = empirical number to account for the effect of the hub, spokes, shaft, etc., which unless otherwise specified can be taken as 0.90

g = 32.2 ft/sec^2

E = energy to be given up by the flywheel, or energy to be stored in the flywheel. This can also be considered as the maximum variation of energy from the mean energy requirements, ft-lb.

V_1 = maximum speed of a point on mean radius r of rim, ft/sec

V_2 = minimum speed of a point on mean radius r of rim, ft/sec

$V = \frac{1}{2}(V_1 + V_2)$ = mean speed of a point on mean radius of rim, ft/sec

δ = coefficient of speed fluctuation = $(V_1 - V_2)/V = (\omega_1 - \omega_2)/\omega$

ω_1 = maximum angular velocity of the flywheel, rad/sec

ω_2 = minimum angular velocity of the flywheel, rad/sec

$\omega = \frac{1}{2}(\omega_1 + \omega_2)$ = mean angular velocity of the flywheel, rad/sec.

SOLID DISK FLYWHEEL.

$$W = \frac{2gE}{V_m^2\delta} = \frac{4gE}{V_{1_o}^2 - V_{2_o}^2} = \frac{4gE}{r_o^2(\omega_1^2 - \omega_2^2)}$$

where W = weight of the disk flywheel, lb
g = 32.2 ft/sec^2
E = energy to be supplied by the flywheel, ft-lb
V_m = mean velocity of a point on the outside radius of the disk
δ = coefficient of speed fluctuation = $(V_{1_o} - V_{2_o})/V_m = (\omega_1 - \omega_2)/\omega$
V_{1_o} = maximum velocity of a point on outside radius of disk flywheel, ft/sec
V_{2_o} = minimum velocity of a point on outside radius of disk flywheel, ft/sec
r_o = outside radius of plate flywheel
ω_1 = maximum angular velocity of disk flywheel, rad/sec
ω_2 = minimum angular velocity of disk flywheel, rad/sec
ω = mean angular velocity of flywheel, rad/sec.

SOLVED PROBLEMS

1. Derive the equation for the necessary weight of the rim of a rimmed flywheel: $W_r = \dfrac{KgE}{V^2\delta}$.

Solution:

The kinetic energy E in ft-lb given up by a flywheel is

$$E = \tfrac{1}{2}I_O(\omega_1^2 - \omega_2^2) = \frac{I_O}{2r^2}(r^2\omega_1^2 - r^2\omega_2^2)$$

where I_O = moment of inertia of the flywheel and shaft on which flywheel is mounted, lb-ft-sec^2
ω_1, ω_2 = respectively the maximum and minimum angular velocity of flywheel, rad/sec
r = any arbitrary radius. If r is taken specifically as the **mean** radius of the flywheel rim, then the equation can be written

$$E = \frac{I_O}{2r^2}(V_1^2 - V_2^2) = \frac{I_O}{2r^2}(V_1 + V_2)(V_1 - V_2) = \frac{I_O}{2r^2}(2V)(\delta V) = \frac{I_O}{r^2}V^2\delta$$

where V_1, V_2 = respectively the maximum and minimum velocity of a point on the mean radius of the rim
V = mean velocity of a point on the mean radius = $\tfrac{1}{2}(V_1 + V_2)$.
δ = coefficient of speed fluctuation = $(V_1 - V_2)/V$.

Consider that the moment of inertia of the flywheel is made up of two parts:

$$I_O = \frac{W_r k_r^2}{g} + \frac{W_s k_s^2}{g} \qquad (1)$$

where W_r = weight of rim, lb
k_r = radius of gyration of rim, ft
W_s = weight of hub, spokes, shaft and other masses rotating with the shaft, lb
k_s = radius of gyration of hub, spokes, shaft and other masses rotating with the shaft, ft
g = 32.2 ft/sec^2.

If the rim thickness is small compared to the mean radius of the rim, k_r is almost equal to the mean radius r: $k \approx r$. Dividing equation (1) by r^2 and setting $k_r^2 = r^2$, we obtain

$$\frac{I_O}{r^2} = \frac{W_r}{g} + \frac{W_s k_s^2}{gr^2}$$

which when substituted into $E = (I_O/r^2)V^2\delta$ gives

$$E = \left(\frac{W_r}{g} + \frac{W_s k_s^2}{gr^2}\right)V^2\delta \qquad \text{or} \qquad \frac{W_r}{g} = \frac{E}{V^2\delta} - \frac{W_s k_s^2}{gr^2}$$

Rewriting and then setting $K = 1 - \dfrac{W_s k_s^2 V^2\delta}{gr^2 E}$,

$$W_r = \frac{gE}{V^2\delta}\left(1 - \frac{W_s k_s^2}{gr^2}\cdot\frac{V^2\delta}{E}\right) = \frac{KgE}{V^2\delta}$$

The value of K is generally around 0.90, and unless otherwise specified may be taken as 0.90. In other words, the effect of the hubs, spokes, and shaft is to contribute about 10% of the required moment of inertia.

In general, the total weight of the flywheel can be taken as about $1.15\,W_r$ in preliminary analysis before final dimensions are established.

2. A cast iron flywheel rim has mean radius 24", thickness 6", and width 8". Compare the exact moment of inertia with the approximate value of Wr^2/g, where r is the mean radius. The weight density of cast iron is 0.255 lb/in³.

Solution:

(*a*) The exact moment of inertia of the rim, considering the difference of the moment of inertia of two cylinders, is

$$I = \frac{1}{2}\cdot\frac{W_o}{g}r_o^2 - \frac{1}{2}\cdot\frac{W_i}{g}r_i^2 = \frac{1}{2}\left(\frac{4670\,(2.25)^2}{32.2}\right) - \frac{1}{2}\left(\frac{2825\,(1.75)^2}{32.2}\right) = 233 \text{ lb-ft-sec}^2$$

where W_o = weight of cylinder with radius $r_o = \pi r_o^2 b\rho = \pi(27)^2(8)(0.255) = 4670$ lb
W_i = weight of cylinder with radius $r_i = \pi r_i^2 b\rho = \pi(21)^2(8)(0.255) = 2825$ lb
r_o = outside radius = 27" = 2.25', r_i = inside radius = 21" = 1.75'
b = width of rim = 8", ρ = weight density = 0.255 lb/in³.

(*b*) The approximate moment of inertia, considering the rim as a thin ring, is

$$I_{approx} = \frac{W}{g}r^2 = \frac{1845}{32.2}(2)^2 = 229 \text{ lb-ft-sec}^2$$

$$\text{The percent error} = \frac{233-229}{233}(100) = 1.7\%.$$

3. Derive the equation for the required weight of a circular plate used as a flywheel: $W = \dfrac{4gE}{r_o^2(\omega_1^2 - \omega_2^2)}$.

Solution:

The kinetic energy E in ft-lb given up by a flywheel is

$$E = \tfrac{1}{2}I(\omega_1^2 - \omega_2^2)$$

where I = moment of inertia of plate flywheel, lb-ft-sec²
ω_1 = maximum angular velocity of flywheel, rad/sec
ω_2 = minimum angular velocity of flywheel, rad/sec.

The moment of inertia of a flat plate flywheel of weight W and outside radius r_o is $I = \frac{1}{2}(W/g)r_o^2$. Then

$$E = \frac{1}{2}\left(\frac{1}{2}\frac{W}{g}r_o^2\right)(\omega_1^2 - \omega_2^2) \quad \text{or} \quad W = \frac{4gE}{r_o^2(\omega_1^2 - \omega_2^2)}$$

4. A flywheel for a punch press must be capable of furnishing 2000 ft-lb of energy during the $\frac{1}{4}$ revolution while the hole is being punched. The maximum speed of the flywheel is 200 rpm and the speed decreases 10% during the cutting stroke. The mean radius of the rim is 36 in. (*a*) Calculate the approximate weight of the flywheel rim assuming that it contributes 90% of the energy requirements ($K = 0.90$). (*b*) Determine the approximate total weight of the flywheel assuming that the weight of the flywheel is 1.15 times that of the rim. (*c*) What is the coefficient of speed fluctuation?

Solution:

(*a*) $$W_r = \frac{2KgE}{r^2(\omega_1^2 - \omega_2^2)} = \frac{2(0.90)(32.2)(2000)}{(36/12)^2[(2\pi\times 200/60)^2 - (2\pi\times 180/60)^2]} = 155 \text{ lb}$$

(*b*) Approximate total weight = 1.15(155) = 178 lb.

(*c*) Coefficient of speed fluctuation $\delta = \dfrac{\omega_1 - \omega_2}{\omega} = \dfrac{200-180}{1.90} = 0.105.$

5. A two cylinder engine with cranks at right angles develops 100 hp at mean speed 400 rpm. The coefficient of speed fluctuation is to be no greater than 0.03. The mean diameter of the flywheel is 4 ft. The maximum variation of energy per revolution is found to be 20% of the mean energy, as found from a dynamic analysis of the actual forces in the engine. If the arms and hub contribute 5% of the flywheel effect ($K = 0.95$), determine the necessary dimensions of a square rim section of cast iron which weighs 0.250 lb/in³.

Solution:

$$\text{Energy output per cycle, } M_t\theta = \left[\frac{100\,(63{,}000)}{400\times 12}\text{ lb-ft}\right]\left[2\pi \text{ rad}\right] = 8230 \text{ ft-lb}$$

Maximum variation of energy per cycle, $E = 0.20(8230) = 1650$ ft-lb

Mean velocity $V = r\omega = 2[2\pi(400/60)] = 83.8$ ft/sec

$$\text{Weight of rim, } W_r = \frac{KgE}{V^2\delta} = \pi D_m t b \rho$$

$$\frac{0.95(32.2)(1650)}{(83.8)^2(0.03)} = \pi(48)tb(0.250)$$

where D_m = mean diameter, in.; t = rim thickness, in.; b = rim width, in.; ρ = weight density, lb/in^3. Solving, $t = b = 2.47''$; use $2\frac{1}{2}''$.

SUPPLEMENTARY PROBLEMS

6. A gas engine develops 80 indicated horsepower at 1800 rpm mean speed. The maximum variation of energy per revolution is 27% of the mean energy, and the allowable coefficient of speed fluctuation is 0.02. Assume that the rim provides 95% of the needed flywheel effect ($K = 0.95$). The mean velocity of the flywheel rim is limited to 8460 ft/min. Determine the mean diameter and the weight of rim required. *Ans.* 18 in., 30.7 lb

7. A gas engine develops 80 indicated horsepower at 1800 rpm mean speed. If the maximum variation of energy per revolution is 27% of the mean energy, and if the allowable coefficient of speed fluctuation is 0.02, determine the necessary weight of flywheel. Assume all the flywheel effect comes from the flywheel. The flywheel is to be a plate of outside diameter 18 in. mounted on the shaft. *Ans.* Weight of plate = 64.6 lb

8. A crusher drive-shaft rotates at maximum speed of 60 rpm and requires an average power input of 10 hp. If the maximum energy variation per cycle is equal to the mean energy of the cycle and if the speed must not drop more than 10% during the crushing operation, determine the required weight of a flywheel rim with a mean diameter of 80 in. The crushing operation occurs in each revolution of the drive-shaft. Assume $K = 0.95$. *Ans.* 4040 lb

9. A cast iron flywheel rotating at 40 rpm maximum is to furnish 75,000 ft-lb of energy to a punch during $\frac{1}{4}$ revolution with a 10% reduction in speed. The maximum velocity at the mean radius of the rim is not to exceed 3000 ft/min. What cross section area of the rim is necessary if 95% of the flywheel effect is produced by the flywheel? Cast iron weighs 0.255 lb/in^3. *Ans.* 41.8 in^2

10. A single cylinder double acting engine delivers 250 hp at 100 rpm mean speed. The maximum variation of energy per revolution is 10% of the mean energy, and the speed variation is limited to 2% either way from the mean speed. The mean diameter of the rim is 8 ft. Assuming that the hub, spokes, and shaft contribute 5% of the flywheel effect ($K = 0.95$) and that cast iron weighs 0.255 lb/in^3, determine (*a*) the coefficient of speed fluctuation, (*b*) the weight of rim, (*c*) the cross section area of the rim. *Ans.* 0.04, 3600 lb, 46.8 in^2

STRESSES IN FLYWHEELS. The stress in what is called a free rotating ring is a very simple quick approximation for the stresses in the thin rim of a rotating flywheel. The effect of the spokes is neglected and only the stress due to inertia loading is considered.

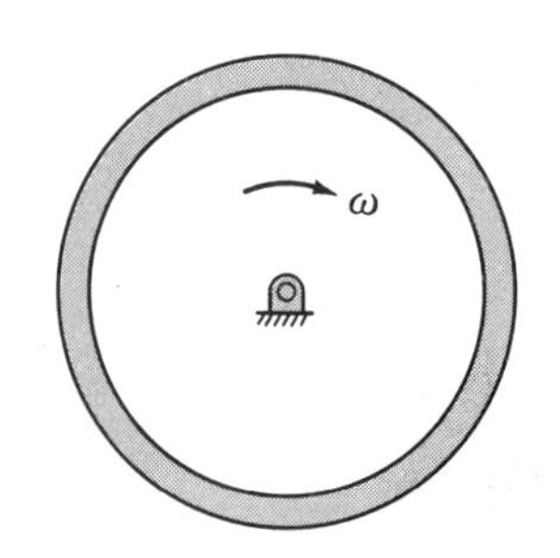

(*a*) Consider half a ring isolated as shown in Fig. 26-1. The differential mass dM is

$$dM = \frac{r(d\theta)tb\rho}{g}$$

where r = mean radius, in.
$d\theta$ = differential angle subtended by the differential mass, radians
t = thickness of rim, in.; b = width of rim, in.
ρ = weight density, lb/in^3; g = 386 in/sec^2.

(*b*) The differential inertia load f = (mass)(acceleration) = $\left(\frac{r(d\theta)tb\rho}{g}\right)(r\omega^2)$, where ω = angular velocity in rad/sec.

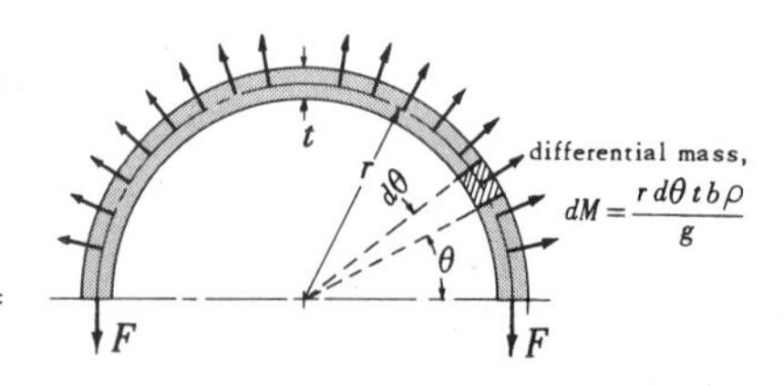

Fig. 26-1

(c) The vertical component of the differential inertia load is $df_V = \left[\frac{r(d\theta)tb\rho}{g}(r\omega^2)\right]\sin\theta$. Note that horizontal components balance.

(d) The vertical component of the inertia load is balanced by the tensile forces at the cut sections:

$$2F = \int_0^{\pi} \frac{r(d\theta)tb\rho}{g}(r\omega^2)\sin\theta = \frac{r^2tb\rho\omega^2}{g}\Big[-\cos\theta\Big]_0^{\pi} = \frac{r^2tb\rho\omega^2}{g}(2)$$

(e) Assuming that the tensile stress s_t (psi) is uniformly distributed across a section, then

$$2F = 2(s_t tb) = \frac{r^2tb\rho\omega^2}{g}(2)$$

or

$$s_t = \frac{r^2\rho\omega^2}{g} = \frac{\rho v^2}{g}$$

where $v = r\omega$ is the velocity (in/sec) at the mean radius.

SOLVED PROBLEM

11. Determine the maximum permissible velocity v in a cast iron thin rim of a flywheel if the maximum allowable tensile stress s_t in cast iron is 4000 psi. Cast iron weighs 0.255 lb/in^3.

Solution:

$$s_t = \frac{\rho v^2}{g}, \qquad 4000 = \frac{0.255\,v^2}{386}, \qquad v = 2460 \text{ in/sec} = 205 \text{ ft/sec}$$

Note that bending in the rim has been neglected.

SUPPLEMENTARY PROBLEMS

12. Determine the maximum permissible velocity in a steel thin rim of a flywheel if steel weighs 0.283 lb/in^3 and the allowable stress is 20,000 psi. *Ans.* 435 ft/sec

13. Considering the cast iron rim of a flywheel as a thin ring and considering the thin rim as a free rotating ring, determine the maximum tensile stress due to rotation. The rim has width 6 in., thickness 4 in., and mean diameter 30 in. The flywheel is rotating at 2000 rpm. Cast iron weighs 450 lb/ft^3. *Ans.* 6660 psi

THE MAXIMUM TENSILE STRESS in a thin rotating rim of a flywheel where bending as well as the normal stress due to inertia is considered, is a bit more complicated. An equation developed from those derived by Timoshenko on a rational basis, taking into account the axial force in the **spokes**, bending, and normal stress, obtained on the basis of treating the rim as a thin ring and neglecting the curvature in the rim is, from $\frac{P}{A} \pm \frac{Mc}{I}$, using the sign which gives the larger value,

$$s_t = \frac{qv^2}{btg}\left[1 - \frac{\cos\phi}{3C\sin\alpha} \pm \frac{2r}{Ct}\left(\frac{1}{\alpha} - \frac{\cos\phi}{\sin\alpha}\right)\right]$$

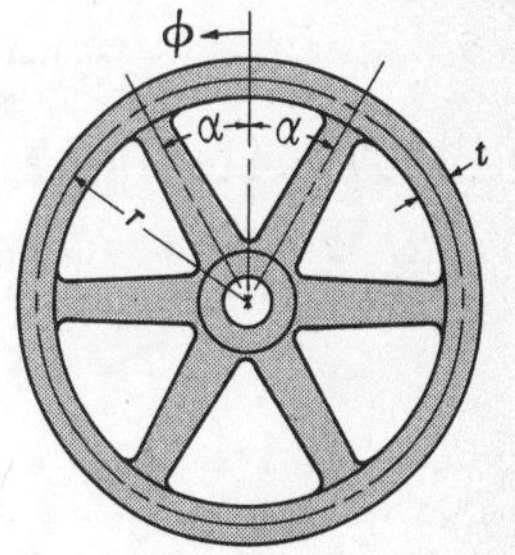

where s_t = tensile stress, psi
q = weight of rim per inch of length = $bt\rho$, lb/in
v = velocity at the mean radius, in/sec
b = width of rim, in.; t = thickness of rim, in.; g = 386 in/sec^2
ϕ = angle from centerline between spokes to the section where the stress is being found
2α = angle between spokes
r = mean radius of rim, in.
C = a constant depending on the cross section area of the rim, area of a spoke, proportions of the rim, and angle between spokes. C is given by

$$C = \frac{12r^2}{t^2}\left[\frac{1}{2\sin^2\alpha}\left(\frac{\sin 2\alpha}{4} + \frac{\alpha}{2}\right) - \frac{1}{2\alpha}\right] + \frac{1}{2\sin^2\alpha}\left(\frac{\sin 2\alpha}{4} + \frac{\alpha}{2}\right) + \frac{A}{A_1}$$

where A = area of cross section of the rim = bt
A_1 = area of cross section of a spoke.

Fig. 26-2

The numerical values for C for different numbers of spokes, to simplify the arithmetic, are:

$$\text{4 spokes } (2\alpha = 90^\circ): \quad C = \frac{12r^2}{t^2}(0.00608) + 0.643 + \frac{A}{A_1}$$

$$\text{6 spokes } (2\alpha = 60^\circ): \quad C = \frac{12r^2}{t^2}(0.00169) + 0.957 + \frac{A}{A_1}$$

$$\text{8 spokes } (2\alpha = 45^\circ): \quad C = \frac{12r^2}{t^2}(0.00076) + 1.274 + \frac{A}{A_1}$$

The axial force F in each spoke is $F = \dfrac{2qv^2}{3gC}$ lb.

SOLVED PROBLEM

14. (*a*) Determine the maximum tensile stress in the thin rim of a steel flywheel rotating at 600 rpm (20π rad/sec). The mean radius of the rim is 60″ (r = 60″). The flywheel rim is 8″ thick (t = 8″) and 12″ wide (b = 12″). The area of a cross section of the rim is $A = bt = 96\text{ in}^2$. Each of the six spokes is constant in cross section with a cross section area $A_1 = 16\text{ in}^2$. (Find the maximum tensile stress in the rim at two sections, $\phi = 30^\circ$ and $\phi = 0^\circ$.)

(*b*) Compare the stress determined with that of a free rotating ring.

(*c*) Calculate the axial stress in each spoke.

Solution:

(*a*) For 6 spokes, $C = \dfrac{12r^2}{t^2}(0.00169) + 0.957 + \dfrac{A}{A_1} = \dfrac{12(60)^2}{8^2}(0.00169) + 0.957 + \dfrac{96}{16} = 8.10.$

At the section of the rim where the spoke is located, $\phi = 30^\circ$. The stress at this section is

$$s_t = \frac{qv^2}{btg}\left[1 - \frac{\cos\phi}{3C\sin\alpha} \pm \frac{2r}{Ct}\left(\frac{1}{\alpha} - \frac{\cos\phi}{\sin\alpha}\right)\right]$$

$$= \frac{27.2(3770)^2}{12(8)(386)}\left[1 - \frac{\cos 30^\circ}{3(8.10)\sin 30^\circ} \pm \frac{2(60)}{8.10(8)}\left(\frac{1}{\pi/6} - \frac{\cos 30^\circ}{\sin 30^\circ}\right)\right]$$

$$= 10{,}400\,[1 - 0.0714 \pm 1.85(1.91 - 1.74)]$$

$$= 12{,}900 \text{ psi, using the + sign for the maximum}$$

where $q = bt\rho = 12(8)(0.283) = 27.2$ lb/in, $v = r\omega = 3770$ in/sec, $2\alpha = 60^\circ$ for 6 spokes.

At the section of the rim midway between spokes, $\phi = 0^\circ$. The stress at this section is

$$s_t = \frac{27.2(3770)^2}{12(8)(386)}\left[1 - \frac{1}{3(8.10)\sin 30^\circ} \pm \frac{2(60)}{8.10(8)}\left(\frac{1}{\pi/6} - \frac{1}{\sin 30^\circ}\right)\right]$$

$$= 10{,}400\,[1 - 0.0824 \pm 1.85(1.91 - 2)]$$

$$= 11{,}300 \text{ psi, using the } - \text{ sign for the maximum.}$$

The maximum tensile stress in the rim occurs at the section where the spoke is located and is 12,900 psi.

(*b*) The stress in a free rotating ring $= \dfrac{\rho v^2}{g} = \dfrac{0.283(3770)^2}{386} = 10{,}400$ psi.

The maximum stress taking into account bending is 12,900 psi, an increase of $\dfrac{12{,}900 - 10{,}400}{10{,}400}(100) =$ 24% from that obtained with a very simple case of a free rotating ring for the particular given data.

(*c*) The axial force in each spoke is $F = \dfrac{2qv^2}{3gC} = \dfrac{2(27.2)(3770)^2}{3(386)(8.10)} = 82{,}500$ lb.

The stress in each spoke $= F/A_1 = 82{,}500/16 = 5160$ psi.

SUPPLEMENTARY PROBLEMS

15. Given the same data as for Problem 14 except that cast iron is to be used instead of steel, determine the maximum stress in the rim. Cast iron weighs 0.255 lb/in^3. *Ans.* 11,700 psi

16. A cast iron flywheel rim is 4″ thick by 8″ wide and has mean radius 36″. The maximum tensile stress in the rim is to be limited to 8000 psi. The cross section area of each of 4 spokes is set at 10 in^2. Cast iron weighs 0.255 lb/in^3.

(*a*) Determine the maximum velocity at the mean radius without exceeding the maximum permissible stress for the following:

(*1*) Assuming the rim is to be treated as a free rotating ring.

(*2*) Analyzing for the section of the rim at the spoke ($\phi = 45^\circ$).

(*3*) Analyzing for the section of the rim midway between spokes ($\phi = 0^\circ$).

(*b*) Determine the maximum stress in a spoke for the maximum velocity determined.

Ans. (*a*) 3480 in/sec, 2870 in/sec, 3150 in/sec. Maximum velocity without exceeding 8000 psi is 2870 in/sec, as dictated by the most stressed section occurring in the rim where the spoke is located.

(*b*) 1190 psi (for v = 2870 in/sec)

APPROXIMATE STRESSES IN FLYWHEEL RIMS of ordinary construction are given by the Lanza equation:

$$s = V^2\left(0.075 + \frac{0.25d}{tn^2}\right)$$

where s = tensile stress, psi
d = mean diameter of rim, inches
t = thickness of rim, inches
V = velocity of the mean radius, ft/sec
n = number of spokes

where the effects of inertia loading and bending are accounted for by the two terms, with approximately 3/4 of the stress being due to the tensile stress in the rim due to the inertia loading and 1/4 of the stress being due to the bending of the rim considered as a beam fixed at the ends (at the spokes) and loaded between spokes by the inertia load.

SOLVED PROBLEMS

17. Assuming the maximum stress in a flywheel rim can be approximated, as suggested by Lanza, by adding 3/4 of the stress computed by considering the rim as a free rotating ring and 1/4 of the stress computed by considering the rim as a straight beam of length equal to the arc between arms, fixed at both ends, and loaded uniformly with inertia forces, derive the equation for the maximum stress s. Take the weight density as 0.270 lb/in^3.

Solution:

(*a*) The stress s_1 (psi) in a free rotating ring is

$$s_1 = \frac{\rho v^2}{g} = \frac{0.270(12V)^2}{386} = 0.10V^2$$

where v = velocity in in/sec, V = velocity in ft/sec, g = 386 in/sec^2.

(*b*) Consider next the bending stress s_2 in the rim treated as a straight beam fixed at both ends, the length being the arc distance between spokes.

$$s_2 = \frac{Mc}{I} = \frac{6M}{bt^2} \quad \text{for a rectangular section beam}$$

The bending moment M at the ends of a beam rigidly held at both ends and uniformly loaded is

$$M = \frac{1}{12}WL = \frac{1}{12}\left[\frac{\pi d b t \rho}{ng}\left(\tfrac{1}{2}d\omega^2\right)\right]\frac{\pi d}{n} = \frac{0.000287\,d^3 b t \omega^2}{n^2}$$

where W = inertia load = (mass)(acceleration) = $\dfrac{(\pi d)(bt)\rho}{ng}\left(\tfrac{1}{2}d\omega^2\right)$, lb

d = mean diameter of rim, in.; b = width, in.; t = thickness, in.

ω = angular velocity, rad/sec; n = number of spokes; $L = \pi d/n$, in.

Substitute this value of M into the equation for s_2 and obtain

$$s_2 = \frac{6M}{bt^2} = \frac{0.00172d^3\omega^2}{tn^2} = \frac{0.990dV^2}{tn^2}$$

where $d\omega = 24V$, since $v = 12V = \frac{1}{2}d\omega$.

(c) Then $s = 0.75s_1 + 0.25s_2 = 0.75(0.10V^2) + 0.25(\frac{0.990dV^2}{tn^2})$

$$= V^2(0.075 + \frac{0.25d}{tn^2}),$$ the Lanza equation.

18. Use the Lanza equation to determine the maximum tensile stress in the thin rim of a cast iron flywheel rotating at 600 rpm. The rim has mean radius 60″, thickness 8″ and width 12″. Six spokes are used. Note that the data is the same as for Problem 15 above.

Solution:

$$V = r\omega = \left(\frac{60}{12}\text{ ft}\right)\left(\frac{2\pi(600)}{60}\text{ rad/sec}\right) = 314 \text{ ft/sec (high for cast iron).}$$

$$s = V^2\left(0.075 + \frac{0.25d}{tn^2}\right) = (314)^2\left(0.075 + \frac{0.25(120)}{8(6)^2}\right) = 17{,}600 \text{ psi}$$

Comparison of the approximate result above with the stress of 11,700 psi using the rationally derived equation in Problem 15 of the preceding section shows that the approximate equation gives a greater value of stress and is on the conservative side.

Note also that for the procedure used, the maximum stress could be reduced considerably by increasing the number of spokes.

STRESSES IN ROTATING DISKS OF UNIFORM WIDTH, as might occur in solid plates used as flywheels, are given by the following equations:

Disks with holes:

Radial stress for any radius r:

$$s_r = \frac{\rho v^2}{g}\left(\frac{\mu+3}{8}\right)\left[1 + \left(\frac{r_i}{r_o}\right)^2 - \left(\frac{r}{b}\right)^2 - \left(\frac{r_i}{r}\right)^2\right]$$

Tangential stress for any radius r:

$$s_t = \frac{\rho v^2}{g}\left(\frac{\mu+3}{8}\right)\left[1 + \left(\frac{r_i}{r_o}\right)^2 - \left(\frac{3\mu+1}{\mu+3}\right)\left(\frac{r}{r_o}\right)^2 + \left(\frac{r_i}{r}\right)^2\right]$$

The maximum radial stress occuring at $r = \sqrt{r_i r_o}$ is

$$s_{r\,max} = \frac{\rho v^2}{g}\left(\frac{\mu+3}{8}\right)\left(1 - \frac{r_i}{r_o}\right)^2$$

The maximum tangential stress occuring at $r = r_i$ is

$$s_{t\,max} = \frac{\rho v^2}{g}\left(\frac{\mu+3}{4}\right)\left[1 + \frac{1-\mu}{\mu+3}\left(\frac{r_i}{r_o}\right)^2\right]$$

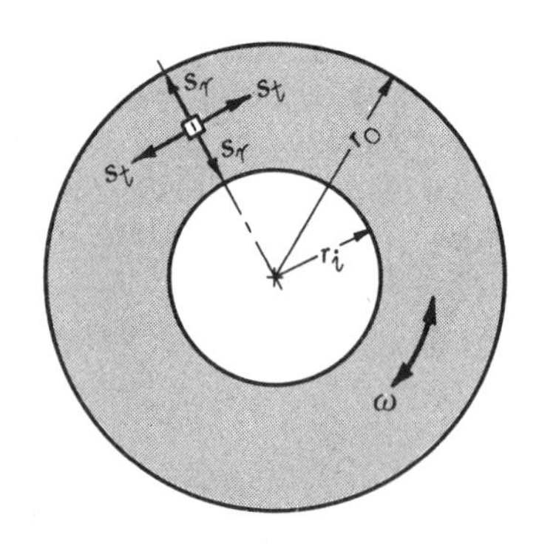

Fig. 26-3

where $s_{r\,max}$ = maximum radial stress, psi
$s_{t\,max}$ = maximum tangential stress, psi
ρ = weight density, lb/in³
g = 386 in/sec²
μ = Poisson's ratio (0.30 for steel, 0.27 for cast iron)
v = $r_o\omega$, peripheral velocity, in/sec
r_i = inside radius of plate, in.
r_o = outside radius of plate, in.
r = variable radius, in.

Solid disks:

The general equations for radial and tangential stresses in solid rotating disks are a bit different from those for disks with holes.

Radial stress for any radius r:

$$s_r = \frac{\rho v^2}{g}\left(\frac{\mu+3}{8}\right)\left[1 - \left(\frac{r}{r_o}\right)^2\right]$$

Tangential stress for any radius r:

$$s_t = \frac{\rho v^2}{g}\left(\frac{\mu+3}{8}\right)\left[1 - \frac{3\mu+1}{\mu+3}\left(\frac{r}{r_o}\right)^2\right]$$

The maximum radial stress and maximum tangential stress are equal and both occur at $r = 0$:

$$s_{r\,max} = s_{t\,max} = \frac{\rho v^2}{g}\left(\frac{\mu+3}{8}\right)$$

SOLVED PROBLEMS

19. Determine the maximum radial stress and the maximum tangential stress in a steel plate (Poisson's ratio $\mu = 0.3$) rotating at 3000 rpm. The radius of the hole in the plate is $r_i = 4''$ and the outside radius of the plate is $r_o = 12''$. Where do the maximum stresses occur? Steel weighs 0.280 lb/in^3.

Solution:

(a) The maximum radial stress is, for $v = r_o\omega = 12(2\pi \times 3000/60) = 3770$ in/sec,

$$s_{r\,max} = \frac{\rho v^2}{g}\left(\frac{\mu+3}{8}\right)\left(1 - \frac{r_i}{r_o}\right)^2 = \frac{0.280\,(3770)^2}{386}\left(\frac{0.3+3}{8}\right)\left(1 - \frac{4}{12}\right)^2 = 1890 \text{ psi}$$

This stress is located at $r = \sqrt{r_i r_o} = \sqrt{4(12)} = 6.93$ in.

(b) The maximum tangential stress is

$$s_{t\,max} = \frac{\rho v^2}{g}\left(\frac{\mu+3}{4}\right)\left[1 + \frac{1-\mu}{\mu+3}\left(\frac{r_i}{r_o}\right)^2\right]$$

$$= \frac{0.280\,(3770)^2}{386}\left(\frac{0.3+3}{4}\right)\left[1 + \frac{1-0.3}{0.3+3}\left(\frac{4}{12}\right)^2\right] = 8700 \text{ psi}$$

This stress occurs at $r = r_i = 4$ in.

20. A solid steel rotor 3 ft long and 12 in. in diameter rotates at 3000 rpm. What are the maximum radial and tangential stresses and where do they occur? Steel weighs 0.280 lb/in^3, and Poisson's ratio $\mu = 0.3$.

Solution:

Here $v = r_o\omega = 6(2\pi \times 3000/60) = 1884$ in/sec.

$$s_{r\,max} = s_{t\,max} = \frac{\rho v^2}{g}\left(\frac{\mu+3}{8}\right) = \frac{0.280\,(1884)^2}{386}\left(\frac{0.3+3}{8}\right) = 1060 \text{ psi}$$

The maximum stresses occur at the center of the rotor.

SUPPLEMENTARY PROBLEM

21. A steel forging has a diameter of 24″ and rotates at 600 rpm. The center of the forging is defective and it is proposed to bore out the center to a diameter of 8″. Determine the maximum stresses for the solid and hollow forgings. Steel weighs 0.280 lb/in^3. Poisson's ratio is 0.3.

Ans. Solid forging: $s_{r\,max} = 17{,}000$ psi, $s_{t\,max} = 17{,}000$ psi
Hollow forging: $s_{r\,max} = 7560$ psi, $s_{t\,max} = 34{,}900$ psi
Note that the bored forging has a higher tangential stress.

Chapter 27

Projects

The following projects are suggested for practice in applying the principles of the preceding chapters in more comprehensive situations. These projects involve, in varying degrees, combinations of analysis, synthesis, ingenuity, proportioning of parts, use of codes, drawing and sketching, selection of materials, safety considerations, economic factors, life expectancy, and other related ideas.

1. Design of a Hand Screw Press – one ton capacity

A one ton capacity hand screw press for general usage is to be designed. Preliminary specifications have been established as shown in Fig. 27-1. While a complete design would require the making of the detailed drawings, this project will involve only the analysis of the various parts together with an assembly layout drawing on $18'' \times 24''$ paper. A scale sketch of each proposed part as necessary for analysis purposes is to accompany the calculations. Sufficient information should be shown on the scale sketches to permit a draftsman to make detail drawings.

The layout drawing is to show two views: the one shown in the figure and a side view.

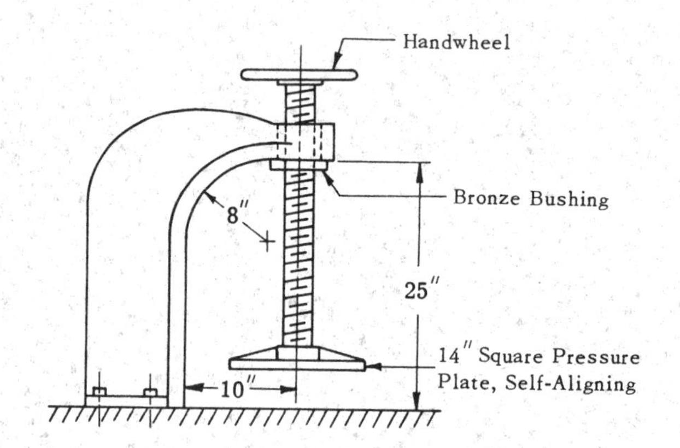

Fig. 27-1

Suggested Materials

1. Frame - Cast Iron
2. Pressure Plate - Cast Iron
3. Screw - SAE 1025 Steel
4. Bushing - Mn. Bronze
5. Bolts - Steel

The following questions indicate some of the factors to be considered in the design.

A. Design of Screw

(*1*) What type of thread should be used? Acme thread? Square thread? American Standard or Unified National coarse or fine thread?

(*2*) May this screw be treated as a short compression member? A column?

(*3*) If a column, what is the unsupported length? What is the end conditions constant?

(*4*) Is there an axial load? A bending load? A torsional load? An eccentric load? Any other load?

(*5*) Is the type of loading the same on either side of the nut?

(*6*) What combination of loading will cause the maximum stress and at what point (or points) will it occur?

(*7*) What should be the efficiency of the screw? Is overhauling desirable?

(*8*) What provisions, if any, should be made for lubrication?

(*9*) What factor of safety is required? On what physical properties of the materials should it be based? Ultimate strength? Endurance limit? Yield point? What is the danger of overload? To press? To operators?

Should design be based on rigidity or strength? Design for steady or variable loading? Shock? Stress concentration?

(10) What is the probable range of the coefficient of friction for the screw and nut? For the collar? What effect does this have on the loading? Is the design safe if the maximum probable coefficient of friction is used? What effect does the choice of materials have on the values of the coefficients to be used? How is the thrust to be transferred from the screw to the pressure plate? What effect does this have on the torque required?

(11) What size handwheel is required?

B. Design of Bushing

(1) What should be the length of the nut? What effect does increasing the length to diameter ratio have on load distribution on threads?

(2) Should it be integral with the frame? If not, how should it be attached?

(3) How is the thrust to be transferred from screw to frame?

(4) Should bushing or frame fail first due to overload?

(5) What is the stress distribution in bushing? What thickness wall should be used?

C. Design of Pressure Plate

(1) What is the pressure distribution on plate?

(2) Is resultant load eccentric?

(3) What is the stress in plate? Are approximations needed?

(4) How is screw to be attached to plate and still allow self-alignment?

D. Design of Frame

(1) What are the loads in the vertical section? In the curved section? In the horizontal section?

(2) As a first approximation, assume a rectangular section in which the width is equal to five-eighths of the depth.

(3) Modify this section to form a T-section and check. Make any changes indicated.

(4) What should be the width of the T-section? Is there a minimum set by other parts such as the hub around the bushing? The width of base required for foundation bolts?

(5) May the curved section be analyzed as for a straight beam?

(6) Is rigidity of the frame important?

E. Design of Foundation Bolts

(1) What loads must the bolts resist?

(2) What is the distribution of loads among the bolts?

(3) Should all bolts be the same size? Why?

(4) What allowances should be made for wrench clearances?

(5) What size bolts should be used?

2. Valve Stem Analysis

A cam of circular profile works against a $3''$ diameter flat faced follower as shown in Fig. 27-2 below. The analysis is to be made for 90° of counterclockwise rotation of the cam.

For the position shown, the spring force is 70 lb and the force P is 100 lb. As the follower is raised the spring force increases linearly to 120 lb and the applied force P decreases linearly to 40 lb.

The weight of the follower is to be determined. The follower is made of steel, 0.28 lb/in^3. The weight of the spring may be assumed to be approximately 0.6 lb.

The cam rotates at a uniform speed of 1800 rpm counterclockwise. Coefficient of sliding friction is 0.25.

Find:

(*a*) The maximum stress in the valve stem for the position shown.

(*b*) The maximum stress in the valve stem during 90° counterclockwise rotation of the cam. (Analyze for 0°, 30°, 60°, 90°. Plot results. Analyze for any other position, as necessary.) Assume that the equivalent mass of the spring in the inertia analysis is 1/3 the mass of the spring.

(*c*) The maximum contact stress between the cam and follower during the 90° of rotation.

(*d*) Design a spring for the given specifications. A maximum design stress for the spring is limited to 75,000 psi, shear.

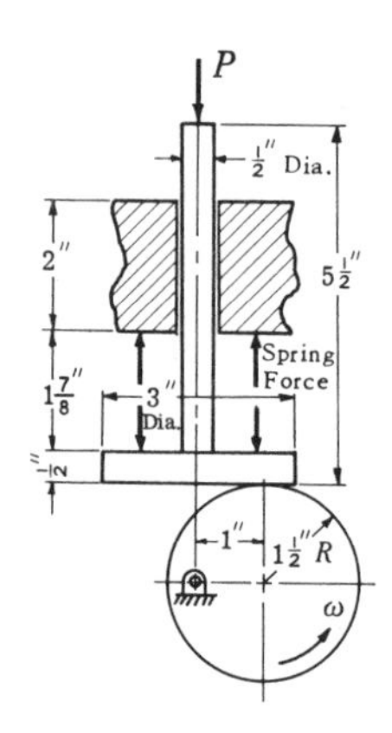

Fig. 27-2

3. Single Stage Speed Reducer

A single stage right-angle speed reducer is to be designed as compact as possible for application with a bread mixing machine. Five horsepower is to be transmitted at 1150 rpm of the high speed shaft with a velocity reduction of 3 to 1. Power is to be applied through a V-belt drive and taken from the output shaft through a flexible coupling. The velocity ratio of the pulleys is 1 to 1.

Base the selection of the bearings on satisfactory operation for two years, with 10 hours per day, 6 days a week operation. Limit the pitch diameter of the pulleys to 6" minimum.

Since the machine is to operate in a dusty atmosphere, proper sealing is extremely important.

An itemized two view assembly drawing with a bill of materials is required.

4. Speed Reducer

The planetary spur gear speed reducer shown in Fig. 27-3 below has 4 hp supplied to the input shaft through a flexible coupling. The input shaft rotates at 1200 rpm. Power is transmitted with no shock under 24 hours/day service.

There are three planet gears, equally spaced. The internal gear is held stationary.

The gears are to be made from SAE 1030 steel.

(*a*) Determine the size of shafts for the transmission of the power. Power is taken from the shaft by a coupling.

(*b*) Determine the smallest diameter gears which can be used if the velocity ratio is 8:1. No fewer than 15 teeth are to be used on any gear. Use 20° stub teeth. Check dynamic and wear loads.

(*c*) Determine the face width of the gears.

(*d*) Determine the size of the pin in the arm on which a planet gear rotates. The pin is SAE 1030.

(*e*) Determine the bearing loads. The bearings on each shaft are 6 inches apart.

(*f*) Describe the transfer of the torque in the unit. How much torque must be applied to the base? Does this torque depend on the direction of rotation of the input shaft?

(*g*) Specify the size of bolts to be used in the base.

(*h*) Determine the size of key to be used with the gear on the input shaft. Key is to be made from SAE 1020.

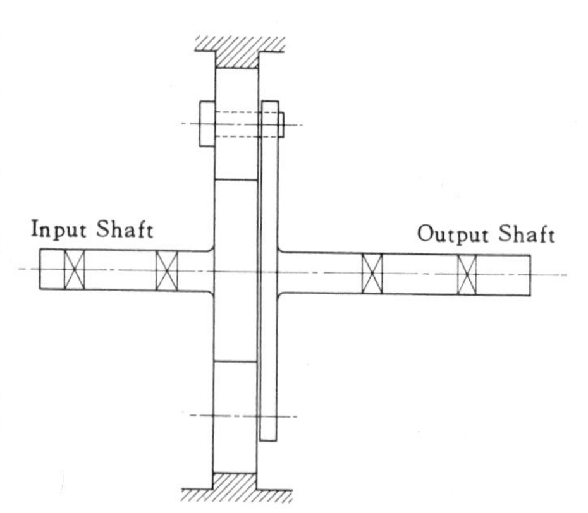

Fig. 27-3

5. "Turbo-prop" Speed Reducer

An 800 hp turbine-propeller aircraft engine rotates at 13,500 rpm and the propeller is to be geared down to 900 rpm. 600 hp is transmitted to the propeller, the rest being used in the jet thrust. Design requirements for aircraft and aircraft accessories are prescribed in detail by the NACA to account for wind gusts, gyroscopic forces, maneuvering, and landing. This project will be simplified by assuming essentially steady loading conditions. One of the tests that the reducer must pass is a 1000 hour bench test. While the manner of loading during the bench test is involved, exacting, and rigorous, again a simplification will be made that the engine will be subjected to 200% loading for 250 hours and 100% loading for 750 hours.

Minimum weight is an essential requirement.

The reduction from 13,500 rpm to 900 rpm is too much for a single stage reduction. The proposal is made that a single stage reduction be used in conjunction with a planetary gear arrangement, as shown in Fig. 27-4.

The diameter of gear 2 may be taken as 6". The diameter of gear 7 is to be three times that of gear 8.

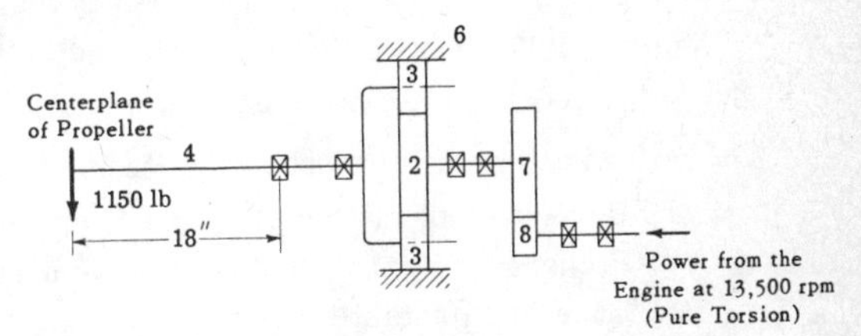

Fig. 27-4

A sectional layout of the parts, to scale, is to be made, including bearing assemblies.

The housing for the reducer is a project in itself. Do not take time to analyze the housing. Design the gears and shafts and select bearings and proportion the housing to suit the gears, shafts, and bearings for the layout.

The number of planet gears to be used affects the proportions. Arbitrarily, use three planet gears.

Further considerations:

1. Materials: Use high strength steel or alloys.
2. For assembly of the gears, two conditions must be met:

   (*a*) $N_2 + N_6$ = even number (*b*) $(N_2 + N_6)/n$ = integer

   where N_2 = number of teeth on gear 2, N_6 = number of teeth on gear 6, n = number of equally spaced planet gears.
3. Use velocity of engagement of gear teeth, not absolute velocity, in finding gear dynamic loads.
4. Use mean cubic loads for bearing, shaft, and gear loads.
5. Minimum margin of safety for the gears should be 0.2.
6. Consider possibility of hollow shafting.
7. Note that gear tooth loads on the planet are completely reversed.
8. The airplane has a design speed of 300 mph. The efficiency of the propeller may be taken as 85%. Neglect friction loss in the reducer.

6. Air Cylinder

An air cylinder is to be designed for operation at 80 psi. The maximum air pressure available in the plant where the cylinder is to be used is 150 psi. Thus the size of cylinder is to be based on a pressure of 80 psi, but the stress analysis will be based on 150 psi.

The applied force required during the "out" stroke of the piston is 1200 lb. Although the frictional resistance in a well designed cylinder is approximately 5% of the theoretical force of the cylinder, it is advisable that the cylinder size be determined which is capable of exerting approximately $1\frac{1}{2}$ times the force which is considered sufficient for the job. Thus, the size of the cylinder will be based on a pressure of 80 psi and a total required force of $(1\frac{1}{2})(1200) = 1800$ lb.

The required force on the "in" stroke of the piston is 150 lb, which, on the basis of the $1\frac{1}{2}$ factor given above, requires a force 225 lb in design of the cylinder on the return or "in" stroke.

The stroke of the cylinder is to be 60 inches.

The cylinder is to be double acting and is to be cushioned 1'' at both ends. Needle valves are to be used to control the flow of air from the cushioning area. Provision is to be made to allow a fast start of the piston.

The materials to be used for the various parts are:

Piston rod	SAE 1020
Cylinder	Seamless steel tubing
Cylinder heads	Good grade of cast iron
Piston	Good grade of cast iron or SAE 1020

The cylinder is to be mounted, by appropriate lugs, on a surface parallel to the piston rod. Four mounting bolts are to be used. To minimize the stress in the mounting bolts and to maintain alignment, thrust blocks may be located at the inner edges of the mounting surfaces.

The piston rod end is to be designed for a pin connection.

The following points are some of the items to be considered in the design:

(1) Prevention of rusting of cylinder bore from the condensed moisture from the compressed air.
(2) Proper glands and packing to prevent air leakage.
(3) Ease in adjustability of the packings.
(4) Use of fine threads versus coarse threads.

Required: 1. A complete set of calculations.
2. Sketches of all parts.
3. A sectional view, with parts itemized, on an 18'' × 24'' drawing size sheet.

7. Bearing Puller

Various methods are available for removing machine members which are fitted with interference. One method is the use of an arbor press, another method is the use of a vise and drift, and still another method is the use of a puller (known as a wheel puller).

For this project, it is desired to design a puller for a specific application: the removal of ball bearings assembled with interference between the inner race and shaft.

The puller is to be adjustable so that it may be used with single row radial types of bearings having outside diameters ranging from 3.1496'' to 5.1181''. The bore diameters range from 1.5748'' to 2.1654''.

The maximum interference between the shaft and inner bore of the largest bearing encountered in the large size bearings is 0.0015'' for the tightest fit used. For this fit, the maximum radial pressure between the inner race and shaft is approximately 3000 psi.

The bearing puller is to operate by pressing against the inner race so as not to damage the bearing.

The maximum bearing width is 1.30''. The centerline of the bearing is at a maximum distance of 8'' from the end of the shaft .

Required: 1. An assembly drawing on an 18'' × 24'' sheet of drawing paper.
2. A complete set of calculations.
3. Sketches of each part.

8. Geneva Index

A belt conveyor is moved intermittently by means of a geneva mechanism, Fig. 27-5 below. The conveyor is driven by a sprocket mounted on the same shaft as the geneva wheel. For this particular application the design data are:

Angular velocity of driving crank = 12 rpm (constant)
Driving crank radius = 6 inches
Distance between pivots = $6\sqrt{2}$ inches
Sprocket diameter = 7.6 inches
Conveyor belt and load = 2500 lb
Friction drag of belt = 170 lb (constant)
Roller and wheel width = $\frac{3}{4}''$
Roller diameter = $\frac{3}{4}''$

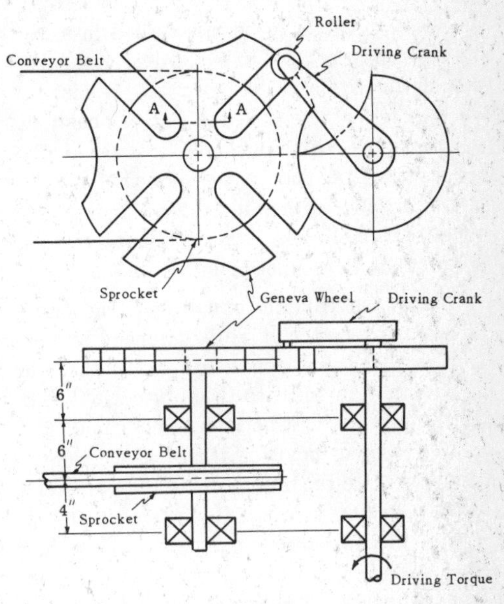

Fig. 27-5

1. To determine if this design is satisfactory an analysis of the accelerations, forces, and stresses is required. The following are to be determined:
   (*a*) Maximum angular acceleration of the geneva wheel
   (*b*) Maximum roller force
   (*c*) Maximum torque on driven shaft
   (*d*) Maximum roller contact stresses for given roller
   (*e*) Maximum stress at Section A-A
   (*f*) The shaft diameter for the driving shaft
   (*g*) The shaft diameter for the driven shaft
   (*h*) For the $\frac{3}{4}''$ steel roller, determine the brinell hardness required for the roller.
   (*i*) A satisfactory roller diameter if the roller width is reduced to $\frac{1}{2}$ inch and the contact stress is limited to 100,000 psi.
2. The total equivalent mass polar moment of inertia of the rotating parts (referred to the axis of the sprocket wheel) is 112 lb-in-sec^2. Taking this into account determine the same information required in part 1.
3. The conveyor belt rests on 200 rollers each 2 in. in diameter with a polar moment of inertia of .02 lb-in-sec^2, the polar moment of inertia of each of the two sprocket wheels (one at each end of the conveyor belt) is 7 lb-in-sec^2, and the polar moment of inertia of the geneva wheel is 3 lb-in-sec^2. For this case determine an equivalent mass polar moment of inertia referred to the sprocket axis. Solve for the information requested in part 1.

9. Automatic Control

A sequence of operations in an electrically controlled machining operation is to be initiated by an operator pressing a pushbutton. The following events are to occur:

(*1*) Pressing a pushbutton actuates an oil pump motor and a four way electric solenoid valve controlling a hydraulic cylinder, providing that a work piece is not in position. A green light goes off and a red light goes on to inform the operator that the machine is loaded.

(*2*) The piston rod moves to its extreme outward position, locating the work piece in position. The piston rod is retracted automatically to its initial position.

(*3*) The four way solenoid valve of a hydraulic clamp is actuated to hold the work piece in position.

(*4*) When the hydraulic clamp is applied, a hole is drilled, the drill retracts, and the hydraulic clamp is released.

(*5*) The four way solenoid valve controlling a second hydraulic cylinder is actuated to push the work piece to its next position, the travel being perpendicular to the cylinder feeding the machine.

(*6*) When the piston rod reaches its limit of travel, the piston rod is caused to return to its initial position, lighting a green light for the operator's benefit to inform him that the cycle can be repeated. The red light goes off.

Providing all necessary interlocks and safeties and providing for manual operation in case of a jam, design a control circuit to perform the required operations. 220 V three phase power supply is available.

10. Water Level Automatic Control

Water level is to be maintained in a $10'' \times 10''$ vertical tank as shown in Fig. 27-6. Water is flowing through an orifice in the bottom of the tank at a rate of $CA_O\sqrt{2gh}$, where C is the orifice constant, A_O is the area of the orifice, and h is the water level height. The values of C and A_O are such that the flow rate is $\sqrt{h}$ in^3/sec, with h in inches. A float having a cross sectional area A in^2 is connected to a regulating valve V, as shown.

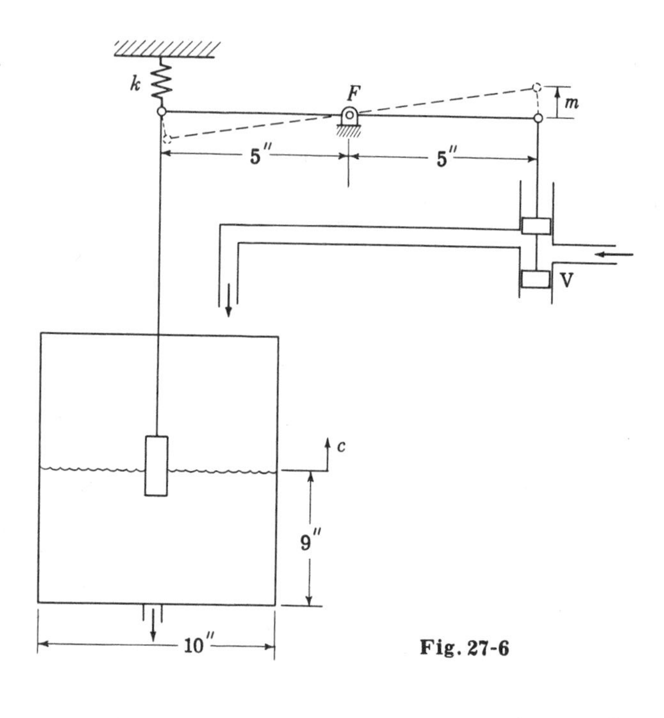

Fig. 27-6

Under equilibrium conditions, the fluid force tending to close the valve is balanced by the spring force. Equilibrium conditions exist when the flow into the tank is equal to the flow out of the orifice, and the lever is in a horizontal position. For a deviation in lever position, there is a change in the hydraulic force tending to close the valve of $10m$ lb where m is the vertical displacement of the valve disk in inches. The change of rate of flow from equilibrium of the water through the valve is given by $100m$ in^3/sec. The change in water level, or deviation, is denoted by c. The moment of inertia of the lever assembly, including the float, float rod, and valve referred to the fulcrum of the lever may be taken as 0.05 lb-in-sec^2.

Determine the best choice of the float area A and the spring constant k, when the area of the float is limited to a range of 0.1 to 1.0 in^2 and the spring constant k is limited to a range of 1.0 to 100 lb/in. Also, determine whether damping is necessary for stability.

11. Tank Design

The purpose of this project is to acquaint the student with the general procedure of design under the ASME Code.

Problem: It is required to store approximately 10,000 gallons of liquid propane for use as a gaseous fuel. Propane has a vapor pressure of 120 psi at 70°F and 210 psi at 105°F. The storage tank is to be designed for a working pressure of 250 psi in accordance with the ASME Code for unfired pressure vessels.

12. Bar Cutter

A portable, dependable, light weight, hand operated device is required to cut $\frac{1}{2}$ inch low carbon steel bars. It is desirable to have the minimum of distortion at the cut surfaces. The unit should be compact and easily carried. The unit is to be hydraulic.

Reference: U.S. Patents 2236833 and 2384130.

Required: (*1*) A complete set of calculations together with sketches of each part.
(*2*) An assembly drawing with at least 2 views, on an $18'' \times 24''$ sheet.

13. Book Alternator

Books come from the binding operations, pass through a wrapping machine, and proceed to the packing section.

Before the books can be properly packed for shipment, it is necessary that every other book be rotated through 180 degrees. Fig. 27-7 shows the books before and after rotation.

60 books a minute is the rate of production.

Design a device to rotate every other book. Sufficient design should be shown to permit management to decide if the idea is worthy of consideration and subsequent detailed design and construction.

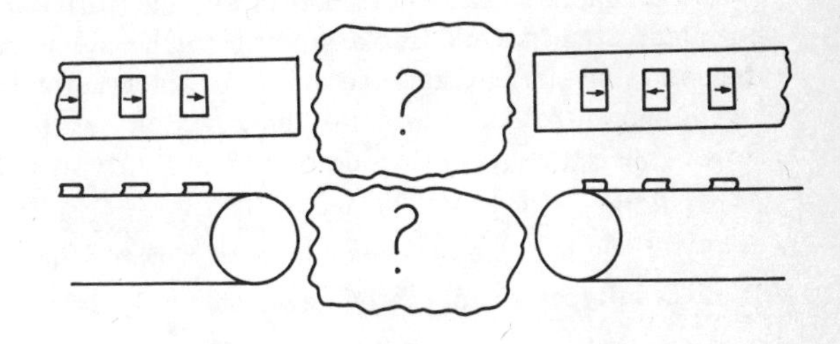

Fig. 27-7

Consider that sufficient space is available to provide for the necessary arrangement.

Spaces between books = $1\frac{1}{2}$ times book length.

14. One Man Passenger Elevator

Purpose:

The purpose of this project is to create a preliminary design and to make recommendations for the installation of a one man passenger elevator which has been requested by a customer. This preliminary design will be concerned only with the functional and engineering aspects of the installations.

Problem:

A residence has a conventional stairway from the first floor to the second floor, but no provision is provided for going from the first floor to the basement except by ladder or outside entrance. It is proposed to install a one man passenger elevator to operate between the first floor and basement. Fig. 27-8 shows the permissible head room and clearances provided. Note that it is necessary to enter the elevator from the right on the first floor and leave from the left in the basement.

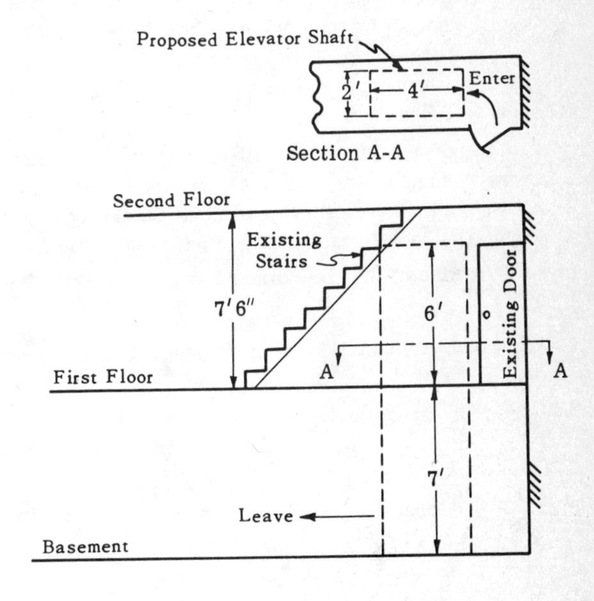

Fig. 27-8

Preliminary Design Requirements:

(*1*) Since this is a preliminary study, several alternate arrangements for the proposed installation should be investigated.

(*2*) After having decided upon a feasible arrangement, prepare a preliminary scale drawing showing the necessary elevation, plan, and auxiliary views.

(*3*) Prepare a preliminary estimate covering the cost of equipment and installation.

(*4*) Write a letter of transmittal to the customer in the form of an engineering proposal.

15. Grass Mower

A manufacturer has decided to build and sell lawn mowers. With the recent number of serious accidents, he is interested in marketing a product that is safer than any mower now available. In fact the sales appeal of safeness is so strong that large quantities of a mower could be sold on safeness alone. A survey of the present mowers shows that there are only three basic types:

(*1*) Conventional reel

(*2*) Rotary

(*3*) Sickle bar (the type used on farm mowers and mowers that cut along the highway).

All of these types are dangerous even though guards are placed on them for protection.

As a design engineer for the company, you are given the following job: Design a machine that will remove all grass to a proper level and will be safer than conventional types.

16. Barrel Hoist

A manufacturing company has the following problem:

Small parts are a large portion of this business and several operations are required on each part. The nature of the operations required on different orders is such that it is not practical to handle these parts on a production line. As a result, parts are shipped from one department to another in steel drums. Even though these drums are normally not filled over three-quarters full, some drums weigh as much as 500 pounds. These drums are transferred between departments by motorized cart and are set within 6 ft of the hopper for the machine that is to perform the next operation. The operator of the machine must dump the contents of the drum into the hopper beside his machine. The top edge of the hopper is 5 ft from the floor.

Design a device that will enable each operator to fill his hopper when necessary. State clearly any necessary assumptions and design with the following in mind: safety, original cost, ease of operation, power requirements, space requirements, versatility.

The size of the steel drums is shown in Fig. 27-9.

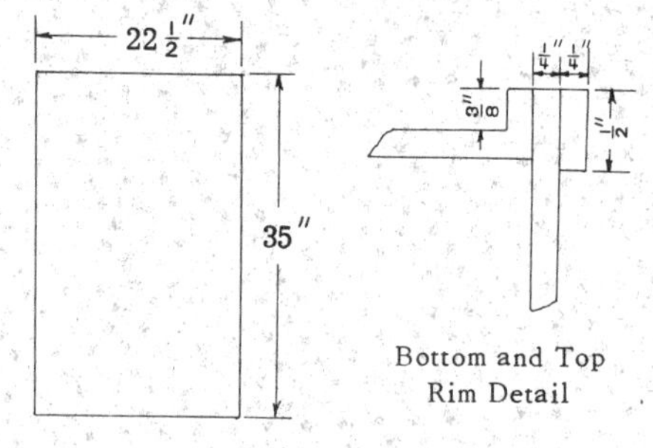

Fig. 27-9

17. Globe Valve Design

A 1" Globe Valve is to be designed for use with salt water at 200° F. The following specifications are to be met:

(*a*) Valve to be suitable for 400 psi operating pressure.

(*b*) Monel metal to be used, except for handwheel, which is to be malleable iron. (A satisfactory substitute metal for monel may be used.)

(*c*) Non-metallic valve seat disc to be used.

(*d*) Proper seals to be used to insure no leakage.

(*e*) Ample flow areas to be provided.

(*f*) Minimum thickness of monel castings to be 1/8".

(*g*) "Non-rotating" valve seat disc to be used.

(*h*) A non-rising valve stem is a necessary feature of the design.

(*i*) Valve stem to be 45° with the axis of the pipe.

Required: (*1*) An itemized section assembly drawing, together with a bill of materials. Overall dimensions only are to be shown.

(*2*) A complete detail drawing of the valve stem, showing all necessary dimensions and machined surfaces.

18. Statistical Fits

Statistical quality control makes use of the natural laws of the statistical distribution of dimensions which exists when parts are machined and assembled. The spread of dimensions resulting from a machining process closely follows the frequency distribution pattern of the standard normal statistical or probability curve. The natural spread of a machining process is usually taken as $\pm 3\sigma$ since 99.73% of the area under the normal curve falls within these boundaries. Each machine has its own natural spread which may be determined by measuring a large number of parts and preparing a frequency histogram, or the standard deviation σ may be calculated as

$$\sigma = \sqrt{\frac{\sum (x-\bar{x})^2}{n}}$$

where n = total number of parts measured
x = dimension of individual parts
$\bar{x} = \frac{\sum x}{n}$

The standard deviation, σ, as determined from the above, is then multiplied by six to give the natural spread of the process based on $\pm 3\sigma$ spread.

When applying the above to the fitting of mating parts such as a shaft and bearing, the standard deviation for the two processes σ_s and σ_b are related to the standard difference deviation, σ_d, by

$$\sigma_d = \sqrt{\sigma_s^2 + \sigma_b^2}$$

where σ_s = standard deviation of shaft producing process
σ_b = standard deviation of bearing boring process
σ_d = standard deviation of the shaft and bearing dimension differences

If all the processes are kept centered with respect to a mean dimension, we may then expect that 99.73% of all the mating parts will have fits ranging from $-3\sigma_d$ to $+3\sigma_d$.

The experiment called for in this project is intended to demonstrate the application of statistical quality control to the assembly of mating parts, if we pretend that the number of spots which show for each throw of the dice corresponds to the measurement of a dimension. The experiment will show that statistically the range of clearances is considerably less than might be predicted by assuming the worst possible combination of fits.

Dimensioning of machine parts should take advantage of the random statistical distribution which occurs in practice. Consider a shaft dimensioned as $3.00105^{+.00075}_{-.00075}$, or $\frac{3.0018}{3.0003}$ and a bearing dimensioned as $3.0021^{+.0015}_{-.0015}$, or $\frac{3.0036}{3.0006}$. The dimensions shown have been selected in such a way so as to correspond to numbers as might be obtained in throwing dice, three dice for the shaft and 6 dice for the bearing. The analogy can be considered as follows: If three dice are thrown, the maximum sum of the spots is 18 and the minimum sum is 3. Then the range of the sum of the spots corresponds to the range in dimensions in tenths of a thousand. (3 to 18 ≡ 0.0003" to .0018".) Or, if the analogy is considered further, a throw of 3 points on the dice would correspond to a shaft size of 3.0003 and a throw of 18 points would correspond to a shaft size of 3.0018. Since measurement of actual shafts would involve a necessary variation or error, we can think of the numbers on the dice as corresponding to actual shaft dimensions as might be found by measurement in the shop.

In a similar fashion, the hole dimensions correspond to the values as might be found from throwing 6 dice, with a minimum point value of 6 (or minimum hole of 3.0006) and a maximum value of 36 (or maximum hole of 3.0036).

A. Determine each of the following:

(*1*) The mean value of shaft diameter.
(*2*) The mean value of hole diameter.
(*3*) The maximum possible clearance.
(*4*) The maximum possible interference.
(*5*) Assuming that the natural spread of the machining operations corresponds to the tolerance, find the 6σ spread of the shaft.
(*6*) Assuming that the natural spread of the machining operations corresponds to the tolerance, find the 6σ spread of the hole.
(*7*) Find the 6σ deviations of the assemblies.
(*8*) Find the mean deviation.
(*9*) Determine the maximum clearance expected for 99.73% of the parts and the minimum clearance expected for 99.73% of the parts.

B. Using nine dice, determine and record the interference or clearance obtained by throwing 6 dice to correspond to a hole dimension and 3 dice to correspond to a shaft dimension. Since a large enough sample is necessary, perform the operation 100 times. Plot the following:

(*1*) A frequency distribution curve or histogram of the shaft dimensions.

(*2*) A frequency distribution curve or histogram of the hole dimensions.

(*3*) A frequency distribution curve or histogram of the differences of hole and shaft dimensions.

(*4*) Calculate the mean value $\overline{x}$ of the clearances, $\overline{x} = \frac{\sum x}{n}$
where x = a measured clearance, n = total number of measurements.

(*5*) Calculate the standard deviation, $\sigma = \sqrt{\frac{\sum (x - \overline{x})^2}{n}}$.

C. Summarize your findings.

19. Card Feeder

Cards of different colors are received in stacks of 2000. The cards measure 5″×3″×0.006″. The cards are to be fed into a machine which, by photoelectric means, will sort the cards into separate stacks of the same color. The rate of feed is to be no less than 1000 per minute.

Two problems exist:

(*1*) The means by which the cards are to be fed singly into the machine.

(*2*) The means by which cards which have been identified as to color are to be separated into separate stacks.

Solutions involving sketches of proposed designs for either or both problems are desired.

20. Runaway Truck Project

Occasionally trucks have brake failures on level roads or on steep inclines. You, as a designer, are asked to submit a bid for an emergency means of bringing a runaway truck to rest. The design is to be made for a semi-trailer truck loaded to its capacity.

The requirements of this project are as follows:

(*1*) Investigate the means by which a runaway truck may be brought to rest and investigate the feasibility of the idea.

(*2*) Specify the requirements of a satisfactory design, as capacity, manner of operation, safety features, cost, and other pertinent specifications.

(*3*) Propose as many methods as possible.

(*4*) Select what you feel to be the best method and make a design layout drawing, to scale. Make such views and/or sections as are necessary for clarity or description of the design. Dimensions need not be shown on the drawing. All necessary calculations for sizing of parts must accompany the layout.

(*5*) Estimate the cost per unit. If the design is used, it is estimated that 10,000 units will be made.

(*6*) Submit a report to management with the proposed design, briefly summarizing advantages, disadvantages, salient features of the design, cost, and your recommendation as to the desirability of pursuing the project further.

21. Automatic Control Preform Press

A description of the mechanical operation of an automatic preform press is given on pages 10 and 11 of *Design News*, Volume 16, No.2. The operation is summarized as follows:

(*1*) A sliding block with an appropriate cavity to measure the proper volume of phenol resin transports the powder to a die chamber and ejects a completed preformed disk. A pneumatic cylinder operates the sliding block.

(*2*) The die chamber is formed by the retraction of the lower ram. After dropping the powder into the chamber, the sliding block immediately moves back to its initial position beneath the hopper.

(*3*) The upper ram then moves down, compressing the powder into shape at approximately 6000 psi. The upper ram dwells for several seconds under load after which it rises.

(*4*) The lower ram then elevates the completed preform to the table top and stays in position until the sliding block moves forward on its next cycle.

(*5*) When the sliding block moves forward, its leading edge pushes the completed preform over the edge of the table to a conveyor belt. The lower ram then descends to form the cavity for the preform powder.

The entire action is controlled by limit switches which energize the hydraulic and pneumatic circuits through solenoid valves. The timer is adjustable to allow for a variable dwell of the upper ram. The lower ram has an adjustable stroke which is varied by an adjustment screw.

Providing for all necessary interlocks and safeties, design a control circuit to perform the required operations. The air cylinder uses plant air pressure, 90 psi. A separate electric motor and pump are required for the hydraulic cylinders.

Manual operation should be provided for in case of a jam.

220 V three phase power supply is available.

22. Automatic Auto-Throttle Control

Since the construction of super-highways has been extensive and will increase in the future, longer continuous auto trips are being made.

The use of the present foot accelerator causes considerable fatigue to many drivers during long trips. A manufacturer of auto specialty parts has asked you as a member of its design staff to investigate the feasibility of installing a manually set, automatically released throttle to alleviate fatigue caused by use of the foot actuated accelerator.

Submit a report of your feasibility study including the following items:

(*1*) Make a preliminary sketch of a practical design which might be used. Safety features must be incorporated in the design.

(*2*) Prepare a rough estimate of the manufacturing cost to produce your design at a rate of 10,000 units per month.

(*3*) Prepare a preliminary customer's manual giving a step-by-step procedure for installing your unit on a specific make of car.

The following projects (23 through 36) were used at Purdue University in an experimental design course by P.G. Reynolds of the E.I. duPont de Nemours and Company, Inc.

23. Catalyst Injection System

A continuous process for making a plastic requires injection of a catalyst into a pipe line at a uniform rate of 10 cm^3 per hour against an operating pressure of 10,000 psi. This requires the time of one operator on a continuous basis to do the work by essentially a hand technique, so the operating superintendent has requested you to design a system to do this job automatically. Normally a run lasts for about 30 days before the unit is shut down for a catalyst change.

Changes must be justified on a saving basis. Operation costs are $6000 per year per man and continuous operation requires 4 men per week on the basis of a 40 hour work week. A return of about 20% is expected on the investment because of the risk of early obsolescence. The return on investment should be based on a depreciation of 6% and a tax rate of 52% on the profits.

Note: The information in the above paragraph can be used for problems 23 through 36 where labor savings apply.

24. Safety Device on Powder Belt

A belt 6'' wide is conveying black powder between two buildings 25 ft apart. The second building is a storage unit holding 4000 lb of powder which may explode if there is a spark. It is necessary to design a mechanism which will cut the belt, shower the area with water and seal the hole in the baricade if fire becomes visible on the belt.

The operating people indicate that about $25,000 is the maximum which can be spent on this type of device. Otherwise, an intermittent conveyor system can be justified.

25. Bite-Wing X-Ray Assembly Machine

Develop the design of a machine to assemble bite-wing dental X-ray films at a rate of thirty a minute. The machine should cut the film from a roll, wrap it with the covering materials, inspect it and collect the finished products in boxes of 100.

This machine would do the work of 10 people using hand methods and must be justified on that basis. Determine the return on the investment on the machine.

(The student should obtain samples of bite-wing X-ray film to see what is involved in this operation.)

26. Bag Packing Machine

Dynamite with the general characteristics of brown sugar is packed into 12 lb bags by hand. In order to handle 40,000 lb/shift of the material, a five man operating group is required plus a one man trucker to bring material and take away the packaged material. Two operators scrape up the material, put it into a bag and weigh it at the rate of 5 bags per minute for each operator. Two additional men then fold the bags shut and tape the tops closed. A final man takes the bags, puts them into a box, and tapes it closed.

We have been asked to design a machine to do this work with one operator plus the trucker. Please provide the optimum unit to do this job in terms of reliability and cost.

Also investigate what is the most economical solution to the problem: complete mechanization or a combination of part mechanization and the rest hand labor.

27. 22 Cartridge Assembly Machine

A munitions manufacturer decided that it would be necessary to modernize their production facilities for producing 22 caliber cartridges. About 20,000,000 cartridges per year are manufactured, of which about 50% are long rifles and 25% each are longs and shorts.

You, as the engineers, have been requested to develop preliminary designs for a machine to assemble the cartridges from the components and collect them in groups of fifty for boxing. The machine should have a capacity 50% greater than the annual requirements to take care of seasonal swings. It has been estimated that $350,000 could be invested in the machine if it did not require more than 3 operators per shift. Shells, bullets, powder and primers will be supplied as components to the machine.

28. Automatic Tire Mounting Machine

Automobiles are being assembled at the rate of 40 per hour on an assembly line. This requires, by hand techniques, a crew of about 12 men for the tire installation on wheels. Design a machine for assembling tires on the wheels semi-automatically, requiring no more than two operators. Can the cost of the machine be justified by the savings?

29. Tube Fitting Tester

Hydraulic operation of equipment and servo controls requires the use of a large number of hydraulic fittings. In the field these fittings often leak and cause trouble even though tightened. We have been asked to work out some sort of testing machine which will take the many types of hydraulic fittings and test them to determine which would be most suitable for field installation.

It has been decided that a maximum of $25,000 would be spent for the construction of such a unit.

30. Refrigeration Unit

A plant has a refrigeration load of 750 tons/day in the summer met by evaporation of ammonia at a pressure of 25 psig. It has been the practice to use this vapor in a process, but the operation is changed so this can no longer be done. During the summer, as a result of the decreased heating load, there is a large surplus of 15 psig steam available for process use. Determine the most suitable system to handle this refrigeration load in terms of operating economy and develop the design and control system. Determine the cost.

31. Circulating Pump

An ammonia synthesis unit is being designed to produce ammonia at a pressure of 6000 psi. This requires a circulating unit to process about 200 ft^3/min of gas of approximately 75% N_2 & 25% H_2 at operating conditions. The pressure drop is 450 psi across the pumping unit. You have been asked to evaluate possibilities and propose a design which will cost less than $75,000 and result in the minimum operating and maintenance cost.

32. Wire Spooling Machine

At the present time a plant is operating wire spooling equipment with 3 operators per shift around the clock to supply wire wound on spools. The wire is double 22 gage copper with a .020" thick plastic coating. The spools vary in length from 50 ft to 350 ft in 50 ft intervals. 40% of the spools are 100 ft in length; 30%, 150 ft in length; 10%, 50 ft in length; and the remainder 5% each. We have been asked to design a machine which will produce 22 spools/min and convey them to another production machine and to operate with one man. This machine would normally need to operate only one shift. We are to work up the design of a machine which will do the work and can be justified on a monetary basis.

33. Operator Protection

A man is operating a press which has to produce 20-25 pieces a minute. The operator has to put in the fresh piece and remove the finished piece. Work out controls and protection systems which will eliminate any chance of the operator or his assistant getting hurt. Inadequate safety control has handicapped the machine to the point where we can only obtain 75% of its capacity. Can we justify the installment of the safety equipment?

34. Paint Remover

A new paint product is to be marketed which has outstanding life if applied over bare wood. To sell this broadly requires a device or technique which will rapidly remove old paint. This device must work at least 10 times as fast as any presently available device and must be able to sell for no more than $50. Provide a solution to this requirement.

35. Box Lining Device

We are confronted with the problem of lining boxes, at the rate of 6 per minute, with wax paper. The boxes at present vary from 12" to 18" width by 1" variations and from 16" to 24" in length by 1" increments. It requires three operators per shift to line boxes at this rate by hand techniques. The lining when folded into the boxes must provide a complete waterproof pocket and the edges must extend 3" beyond the edge of the box. Develop a machine to do this operation efficiently and determine whether it can be justified.

36. 100,000 RPM Motor

We have need for a prime mover to provide an output of a minimum of $\frac{1}{2}$ hp at 100,000 rpm. It is possible to spend up to $10,000 to fabricate a unit to meet this requirement. If possible, a $1\frac{1}{2}$ hp motor would be desirable for general use and it could be used by the hundreds if it could be manufactured for as low as $1000 each. What could be provided?

Index